Check for abbreviations that should be spelled out (443–445)
Use adverb form to modify verbs and other modifiers (383–385)
Check agreement of subject and verb, pronoun and antecedent (362, 373)
Check for omission or misuse of apostrophe (458–460)
Rewrite the sentence to make it clearer or more natural (312–320)
Check for words that should be capitalized (461–463)
Strengthen sequence of ideas; show relevance of detail (38, 323–329)
Use semicolon or period between independent clauses (413–414)
Check for awkward, inaccurate, inappropriate wording (281–284, 289–298)
Define or explain general and technical terms (107 ff.)
Develop your point more fully—support, explain, illustrate (332–333)
Check dictionary for syllabication of the word (442–443)
Rewrite the sentence to indicate what the modifier modifies (386–387)
Check for unemphatic, anticlimactic diction or organization (308–310)
Put items joined by "and," "but," "or" in same grammatical category (399–401)
Do not punctuate as a sentence—lacks an independent clause (408–411)
Check standing of debatable usage in glossary (466 ff.)
Check for unsatisfactory forms or constructions (345 ff.)
Check for unidiomatic, un-English expression (274–275)
Expression is too informal or colloquial for its context (282–283)
Check for faulty or unnecessary capitalization (461–463)
Examine for logical weaknesses (125 ff.)
Shift modifier into more appropriate position or rewrite sentence (386–387)
Change nonstandard to standard form (282)
Check for omission or misuse of punctuation (405 ff.)
Use right form of the pronoun (379–382)
Break into paragraphs that reflect organization (323 ff.)
Avoid confusing or unnecessary paragraph break (323 ff.)
Check reference of pronouns (373–378)
Avoid unnecessary or awkward repetition (317–318)
Check for shift in time or use of pronouns, shift to passive (395–401)
Expression is too slangy for its context (283–284)
Check for spelling errors (455 ff.)
Check faulty predication, incomplete or mixed construction (388–391)
Check for inadequate or inappropriate subordination (304, 315–316)
Use appropriate tense of verb (369–370, 396–397)
Strengthen transition from point to point (38–44, 328)
Use right form of verb (370–372)
Remove deadwood (294–295, 312–313)
Correct obvious error
Correct obvious omission
Use punctuation mark indicated (see reference chart, 405)

WORDS AND IDEAS

A Handbook for College Writing
Fifth Edition

Hans P. Guth
San Jose State University

Wadsworth Publishing Company
Belmont, California
A Division of Wadsworth, Inc.

English Editor: Kevin Howat
Production Editor: Mary Arbogast
Designer: Cynthia Bassett
Copy Editor: Gary Mcdonald

Printed in the United States of America
1 2 3 4 5 6 7 8 9 10—84 83 82 81 80

Library of Congress Cataloging in Publication Data

Guth, Hans Paul, 1926–
    Words and ideas.

    Includes index.
    1. English language—Rhetoric. 2. English
language—Grammar—1950–   I. Title.
PE1408.G936 1980   808'.042   79-21350
ISBN 0-534-00815-1

ACKNOWLEDGMENTS

I am indebted to the following for permission to reprint copyrighted material:

Cyrilly Abels for a passage from Warren Hinckle, "The Adman Who Hated Advertising" from *If You Have a Lemon, Make Lemonade.* Copyright © 1974 by Warren Hinckle III, reprinted by permission of Cyrilly Abels, Literary Agent.

American Heritage Publishing Co., Inc. for a passage from Enrique Hank Lopez, "Back to Bachimba." Copyright © 1967, American Heritage Publishing Co., Inc. Reprinted by permission from *Horizon* (Winter, 1967).

The American Scholar for passages from articles by Joseph Wood Krutch, Donald J. Lloyd, and Philip M. Wagner.

Appleton-Century-Crofts, Inc. for a passage from *A History of the English Language,* Second Edition, by Albert C. Baugh. Copyright © 1957, Appleton-Century-Crofts, Inc.

Isaac Asimov for a passage from his article "Nuclear Fusion," in *Parade,* February 18, 1979.

The Atlantic Monthly for passages from articles by Saul Bellow, Paul Brooks, John K. Galbraith, Oscar Handlin, Alfred Kazin, Walter Lippmann, T. S. Matthews, and Joseph Wechsberg.

Paul Bacon for the photograph of the jacket of *American Caesar* by William Manchester. Published by Little Brown and Company and used by permission of the designer, Paul Bacon.

Beacon Press for a passage from *Notes of a Native Son* by James Baldwin, reprinted by permission of the Beacon Press. © 1955 by James Baldwin.

Caroline Bird for a passage from "The Job Market" by Caroline Bird which appeared in the August 27, 1973 issue of *New York.*

Harry M. Caudill for a passage from "There Is No Land to Spare" in *Farming and Mining* by Harry M. Caudill. Copyright © 1973 by the Atlantic Monthly Company, Boston, Massachusetts.

Preface

TO THE TEACHER

The aim of *Words and Ideas* is to provide a productive approach to composition that works with today's students. The book provides a textbook for a course that

- gets students to take their writing seriously;

- shows them how structures and forms become meaningful when they are used for a purpose;

- leads them to present their own experiences and opinions effectively and responsibly;

- stresses substance and structure in student writing, as well as style;

- does not substitute irony at the students' expense for the teaching of literacy;

- makes use of sentence writing and paragraph work as preparation for major assignments.

Words and Ideas was one of the first books to move from the academic rhetoric of parts toward the current teaching emphasis on the process of composition. Over the years, course patterns around the country have changed widely to reflect the assumptions of a process approach: To do writing that is worth reading, students must learn to anchor their writing to their own observation and experience. They must learn how to shape materials and give them focus and coherence. They must learn how to involve the reader, and how to satisfy the reader's expectations.

A special effort has been made in the current edition to reflect changing patterns of awareness concerning sex roles and sexism in language and education.

ORGANIZATION OF THE BOOK

Words and Ideas is a rhetoric-handbook that is divided into three parts.

Part One: A Writing Program The Writing Program takes up, in turn, different kinds of writing. It thus keeps before the student the two central questions in the process of composition: "What am I trying to do?" and "How am I going to go about it?" The assignments in the Writing Program move naturally from emphasis on *substance* to emphasis on *structure* and from there to emphasis on *style*. The sequence begins with a preview of the whole theme. Early chapters (Observation, Personal Experience) stress perception, observation, experience—what gives writing substance. The middle chapters (Opinion, Definition, Argument) shift the emphasis to how the writer clarifies and shapes the material. They involve the student in the kind of thinking that channels observation and interprets experience—the kind of thinking that gives writing structure. Later chapters (Persuasion, Tone and Style) direct the writer's attention to the audience. They examine the effect of writing on the reader; they explore the strategies for dealing with the reader's needs and expectations. The final chapters of the Writing Program deal with kinds of writing that interpret and evaluate the student's *reading* (The Research Paper, Writing About Literature).

Part Two: The Writer's Tools   The three chapters in this section develop the student's competence and confidence in dealing with words, sentences, and paragraphs. They acquaint the student with a writer's technical resources; they provide the finger exercises and practice runs that can help make the student's writing less labored. Teachers may use these materials in a number of different ways: by way of *preview* early in the course; *concurrently* with the Writing Program for study and practice; or *selectively*, to deal with needs demonstrated in the students' current writing.

Part Three: A Reference Handbook   The handbook provides help with basic problems of usage and mechanics. The focus is on basic requirements of literacy. This section of the book has a double aim: to give the student fair warning of the standards of conservative readers, while at the same time avoiding minor and debatable points.

For students who need more help with the basics, a supplementary workbook *(Wadsworth English Workbook)* provides instructions and exercises clearly focused on essentials.

THE CURRENT EDITION

The new fifth edition has been carefully revised in the light of classroom experience and in response to changing interests of teachers and students. The following are special features of the new edition:

• streamlined presentation for more effective classroom teaching;

• strengthened exercise materials aimed at promoting student participation;

- simpler and more up-to-date examples for many key concepts;

- much new professional and student writing dealing with current concerns;

- more extended sentence work, in response to current interest in sentence rhetoric and sentence style;

- new diagnostic tests for usage and mechanics.

In preparing this fifth edition, I have profited greatly from listening to other teachers of composition. Among the people who have assisted me and boosted my morale, I want to thank especially Wayne Harsch of University of California, Davis; LaVerne Gonzalez of Purdue University; Frank Cunningham of University of South Dakota; and Charles Saunders of University of Illinois. I am especially grateful to Thomas Barton of Washington State University, Elizabeth Penfield of University of New Orleans, and Peter Dingus at University of Houston for allowing me to meet and exchange ideas with their teaching staffs. I am indebted for criticism and advice to John Bruce Cantrell, University of South Carolina; Fay Chandler, Pasadena City College; Robert Cosgrove, Texas Tech University; Francis Fennell, Loyola University of Chicago; and Robert Noreen, California State University, Northridge; and to Stella Bruton, West Chester State College; Julie Carson, University of Minnesota, Minneapolis; Lisa Ede, State University of New York, Brockport; Jim Forester, Ohio State University; Joan Grumman, Santa Barbara City College; Ann Imbrie, University of North Carolina; Steve Robins; and Larry Tjernell, Foothill College. I have learned much from the dedicated people who teach composition at San Jose State University, and from the students I have taught there.

H. Guth

Contents

INTRODUCTION   1

Kinds of Writing
The Standards of Good Writing
A Program for Writing
Preview Exercise
First Themes

PART ONE   A WRITING PROGRAM   7

Chapter One   Preview: The Whole Theme   8

1.   Gathering Material   9
Exercises

2.   Bringing Things into Focus   12
Limiting the Subject
Choosing a Key Question
Stating a Thesis
Supporting Your Thesis
Exercises

3.   Getting Organized   19
Process
Classification
Comparison and Contrast
Exercises

4.   Beginnings and Endings   29
Titles
Introductions
Conclusions
Exercises

5.   Coherence and Transition   38
Synonyms and Recurrent Terms
Patterns of Expectation
Transitions
Outlines

Review Exercises   44
Theme Topics   47

Chapter Two   Observation   50

1.   The Uses of Description   51
Exercises

2. The Need for Detail 53
 General and Specific
 Sensory Detail
 Relevant Detail
 Exercises

3. Finding the Right Word 58
 Specific Words
 Concrete Words
 Figurative Language
 Exercises

4. Organizing the Descriptive Theme 62
 Tracing the Pattern
 The Key Idea
 Then and Now
 The "Detail-First" Paper

 Review Exercise 65
 Theme Topics 67

Chapter Three   Personal Experience 68

1. The Uses of Autobiography 69
 Exercise

2. Words and Experience 71
 Involving the Reader
 Being Yourself
 Exercises

3. Organizing the Autobiographical Theme 77
 The Incident with a Point
 The Study in Contrasts
 The Unifying Theme
 The Process of Growing Up
 Exercises

 Theme Topics 82

Chapter Four   Opinion 84

1. A Matter of Opinion 85
 Exercises

2. Opinions Worth Writing Down 86
 Fact and Inference
 Identifying an Issue
 Forming an Opinion
 Changing Your Mind
 Exercises

3. The Opinions of Others 95
 Cross-Examining Your Witnesses

Questioning Conventional Views
Staying Clear of Verbal Traps
Exercises

4. Organizing the Essay of Opinion   99
Defending a Thesis
The "Yes, But" Paper
The Change of Mind

Review Exercise   102
Theme Topics   105

Chapter Five   Definition   106

1. The Need for Definition   107
Relative Words
Vague Words
Ambiguous Words
Overlapping Terms
Specialized Terms
Exercises

2. Getting Down to Cases   110
Exercises

3. Formulating and Supporting Definitions   114
Dictionary Definitions
Formal Definitions
Aids to Definition
Exercises

4. Writing an Extended Definition   119
The History of a Term
Providing the Key
Finding the Common Denominator
Drawing the Line

Review Exercise   122
Theme Topics   123

Chapter Six   Argument   124

1. Writing and Thinking   125
Exercise

2. How We Generalize   126
The Uses of Induction
Effective Generalizations
Hasty Generalization
Exercises

3. Thinking the Matter Through   133
Valid Deductions
Checking Your Premises

Interpreting Statistics
Avoiding Common Fallacies
Exercises

4. Structuring an Argument 142
The Inductive Paper
The Pro-and-Con Paper
Analyzing Cause and Effect
Analyzing Alternatives
Exercises

Theme Topics 148

Chapter Seven   Persuasion 150

1. You and Your Reader 151
Exercise

2. The Tools of Persuasion 153
Taking a Stand
Dramatizing the Issue
Appealing to Emotions
Aids to Persuasion
The Limits of Persuasion
Exercises

3. The Language of Persuasion 159
Denotation and Connotation
The Power of Words
Statement and Implication
Exercises

4. The Strategies of Persuasion 167
The Common Cause
Persuading by Degrees
The Cause Célèbre
Refuting Objections

Review Exercises 170
Theme Topics 172

Chapter Eight   Tone and Style 174

1. The Personal Voice 175
Exercise

2. Setting the Right Tone 177
Formal Writing
Informal Writing
Exercises

3. The Elements of Style 183
The Right Word
The Graphic Image

Appropriate Emphasis
A Fresh Point of View
Exercises

4.   Writing with the Lighter Touch   189
The Uses of Humor
Irony and Sarcasm
Satire
Parody
Exercises

Theme Topics   194

Chapter Nine   The Research Paper   196

1.   Getting Started   197

2.   Going to the Sources   198
General Reference Works
Specialized Reference Works
Library Catalogs
Bibliography Cards
Evaluating Your Sources
Exercises

3.   From Notes to the First Draft   208
Taking Notes
Using Your Notes
Organizing Your Notes
Revising the First Draft
Exercises

4.   Footnotes and Bibliographies   217
Footnotes
First References
Later References
Abbreviations
Final Bibliography
Exercises

Review Exercise: Sample Research Paper   228

Chapter Ten   Writing About Literature   248

1.   The Responsive Reader   249
Exercise

2.   Kinds of Critical Prose   251
Explication
Studying a Character
The Central Symbol
Tracing the Theme
Defining a Critical Term
Exercises

3. Organizing the Critical Essay   259
    Focusing on a Major Issue
    Following Logical Order
    Comparison and Contrast

    Theme Topics   263

PART TWO   THE WRITER'S TOOLS   267

Chapter Eleven   Words   268

D 1   College Dictionaries   269
    D 1a   Synonyms and Antonyms
    D 1b   Denotation and Connotation
    D 1c   Context
    D 1d   Grammatical Labels
    D 1e   Idiom
    Exercises

D 2   Word History   277
    D 2a   Latin and Greek
    D 2b   Borrowings from Other Sources
    Exercises

D 3   Varieties of Usage   281
    D 3a   Nonstandard Words
    D 3b   Informal Words
    D 3c   Slang
    Exercises

D 4   Words in Limited Use   285
    D 4a   Regional Labels
    D 4b   Obsolete and Archaic
    D 4c   Neologisms
    D 4d   Subject Labels
    Exercises

D 5   Expressive Language   289
    D 5a   Accurate Words
    D 5b   Specific Words
    D 5c   Figurative Words
    D 5d   Fresh Words
    Exercises

D 6   Directness   294
    D 6a   Redundancy
    D 6b   Euphemisms
    D 6c   Jargon
    D 6d   Flowery Diction
    Exercises

Chapter Twelve   Sentences   300

S 1   Sentence Building   301
    S 1a   Effective Predication
    S 1b   Effective Coordination
    S 1c   Effective Subordination
    S 1d   Effective Modifiers
    Exercises

S 2   Sentence Variety   307
    S 2a   Sentence Length
    S 2b   Varied Word Order
    Exercises

S 3   Awkward Construction   312
    S 3a   Deadwood
    S 3b   Awkward Passive
    S 3c   Impersonal Constructions
    S 3d   Excessive Subordination
    S 3e   Awkward Modifiers
    Exercises

S 4   Repetition   317
    S 4a   Awkward Repetition
    S 4b   Emphatic Repetition
    S 4c   Parallel Structure
    Exercises

Chapter Thirteen   Paragraphs   322

O 1   The Well-Made Paragraph   323
    O 1a   The Topic Sentence
    O 1b   Relevant Detail
    O 1c   Transition
    O 1d   Recurrent Terms
    Exercises

O 2   Organizing the Paragraph   322
    O 2a   The All-Purpose Paragraph
    O 2b   Paragraphs with a Special Purpose
    O 2c   Paragraphs with a Special Strategy
    Exercises

PART THREE   A REFERENCE HANDBOOK   343

Chapter Fourteen   Grammar and Usage   344

G 1   A Bird's-Eye View of Grammar   346
    G 1a   Grammatical Devices
    G 1b   Basic Sentence Elements
    G 1c   Modifiers
    G 1d   Joining Clauses

G 1e   Appositives and Verbals
Exercises

G 2   Grammar Usage   359
    G 2a   Standard and Nonstandard
    G 2b   Formal and Informal

Diagnostic Test   361
G 3   Agreement   362
    G 3a   Irregular Plurals
    G 3b   Confusing Singulars and Plurals
    G 3c   Compound Subjects
    G 3d   Blind Agreement
    G 3e   Agreement After *There* and *It*
    G 3f   Agreement After *Who, Which,* and *That*
    G 3g   Logical Agreement
Exercises

G 4   Verb Forms   369
    G 4a   Irregular Verbs
    G 4b   *Lie, Sit,* and *Rise*

G 5   Pronoun Reference   373
    G 5a   Ambiguous Reference
    G 5b   Reference to Modifiers
    G 5c   Vague *This* and *Which*
    G 5d   Implied Antecedents
    G 5e   Indefinite Antecedents
Exercises

G 6   Pronoun Case   379
    G 6a   Subject and Object Forms
    G 6b   *Who* and *Whom*
Exercises

G 7   Modifiers   383
    G 7a   Adjectives and Adverbs
    G 7b   Misplaced Modifiers
Exercises

G 8   Confused Sentences   388
    G 8a   Omission and Duplication
    G 8b   Mixed Construction
    G 8c   Faulty Predication
    G 8d   Faulty Equation
    G 8e   Faulty Appositives
Exercises

G 9   Incomplete Constructions   392
    G 9a   Incomplete Comparison
    G 9b   Contraction of Coordinate Elements
Exercises

G 10   Consistency   395
    G 10a   Shifts in Tense
    G 10b   Shifts in Reference

G 10c   Shifts to the Passive
G 10d   Faulty Parallelism
Exercises

Chapter Fifteen   Punctuation   404

Diagnostic Test   406
P 1   End Punctuation   407
          P 1a   Sentences and Fragments
          P 1b   Exclamations and Questions
          Exercises

P 2   Linking Punctuation   413
          P 2a   Comma Splice
          P 2b   Coordinating Connectives
          P 2c   Adverbial Connectives
          P 2d   Subordinating Connectives
          Exercises

P 3   Punctuating Modifiers   421
          P 3a   Unnecessary Commas
          P 3b   Restrictive and Nonrestrictive
          P 3c   Sentence Modifiers
          Exercises

P 4   Coordination   425
          P 4a   Series
          P 4b   Coordinate Adjectives
          P 4c   Dates and Addresses
          P 4d   Repetition and Contrast
          Exercises

P 5   Parenthetic Elements   429
          P 5a   Dashes
          P 5b   Parentheses
          P 5c   Commas for Parenthetic Elements
          Exercise

P 6   Quotation   433
          P 6a   Direct Quotation
          P 6b   Terminal Marks in Quotations
          P 6c   Insertions and Omissions
          P 6d   Indirect Quotation
          P 6e   Words Set Off from Context
          Exercises

Chapter Sixteen   Mechanics and Spelling   440

M 1   Manuscript Mechanics   441
          M 1a   Penmanship and Typing
          M 1b   Titles of Themes
          M 1c   Spacing and Syllabication
          M 1d   Italics

M 2   Abbreviations and Numbers   443
          M 2a   Abbreviations

M 2b   Numbers
Exercise

SP 1   Spelling Problems   445
         Diagnostic Test   447
         SP 1a   Spelling and Pronunciation
         SP 1b   Variant Forms
         SP 1c   Confusing Pairs
         Exercises

SP 2   Spelling Rules   452
         SP 2a   *I* Before *E*
         SP 2b   Doubled Consonant
         SP 2c   *Y* as a Vowel
         SP 2d   Final *E*
         Exercises

SP 3   Words Often Misspelled   455
         Exercise

SP 4   The Apostrophe   458
         SP 4a   Contractions
         SP 4b   Possessives
         SP 4c   Plurals of Letters and Symbols
         Exercises

SP 5   Capitals   461
         SP 5a   Proper Names
         SP 5b   Titles of Publications
         Exercise

SP 6   The Hyphen   463
         SP 6a   Compound Words
         SP 6b   Prefixes
         SP 6c   Group Modifiers
         Exercise

Chapter Seventeen   Glossary of Usage   466

Chapter Eighteen   Practical Prose Forms   478

X 1   Summaries   479
         Exercises

X 2   Letters   482
         X 2a   Format and Style
         X 2b   The Request
         X 2c   The Letter of Application
         X 2d   The Follow-Up Letter
         X 2e   The Letter of Refusal
         Exercises

X 3   The Essay Examination   497
         Exercises

INDEX   501

Introduction

Why learn to write? Contrary to what some people predicted five or ten years ago, production and consumption of the written word around the world are at an all-time high. Paperwork of all kinds plays an ever-growing role in all of our lives. There are few simple jobs or activities left that do not require forms to fill in or reports to file. Hundreds of major fields of interest produce a constant stream of newsletters, magazines, and books. One of the most basic tools of education, business, industry, and politics is the written word.

This is a book about writing. It is designed to help you mobilize your resources as a writer. It will show you how writers shape and structure their materials. It will show how you can make your writing serve your purpose. Throughout this book, discussion and examples stay close to how writers actually work and the kinds of writing they actually do.

KINDS OF WRITING

The aim of this book is to help you write **expository prose**—ordinary nonfiction prose, conveying facts, opinions, ideas. Expository prose serves us in many different situations. It does much of the world's work. We find it in instructions, letters of application, business memos, and technical reports. It also provides the language of politics and social change. We find it in campaign literature, articles about inflation, newspaper editorials, and letters to the editor. Finally, it serves us for self-expression. We use it to explain to ourselves and to others what we think, how we feel, who we are. We find it in personal letters, in diaries and memoirs, in statements of personal belief.

Successful writers learn by doing. They start by taking on fairly simple tasks. By trial and error, they learn how to do things right. As they go on to more challenging assignments, they put to work what they learned earlier. The basic method of this book is to have you work at a series of tasks that gradually become more challenging. You will study different kinds of writing situations and do different kinds of writing.

The kinds of writing you will practice include some or all of the following:

Description   A good writer is first of all a good observer. Descriptive writing teaches us to do justice to what is *there*. It teaches us to use our own eyes and ears. It teaches us how to make our writing real by drawing on authentic firsthand observation.

Autobiography   Autobiography takes stock of the writer's personal experience. It tells the story of events that have special meaning for the writer. Good autobiographical writing is not just a candid record of events as they happen. It helps us understand what has happened.

Informed Opinion   In much of the writing we do, we want to let others know what we think. But we do not merely want to state our opinion. We want others to respect it and to take it in. We have to learn to bring a subject into focus for the reader who wants to know: "What is the point?" We have to learn to support our opinions for the reader who asks: "What makes you think so?"

Definition   In much writing about ideas and issues, important words and key terms play a central role: *equal opportunity*, *poverty line*, *conservation*. Often such a key term itself becomes the central issue. To make people understand, or to make them see our side, we have to define our terms. We have to explain the meaning of important words.

Argument   In structured argument, we take the reader along as we think the matter through. Argument takes the reader from known facts or shared assumptions step by step to logical conclusions. When opinions clash, we sooner or later have to face the question: "How did you reach this conclusion? How does this follow?"

Persuasion   When constructing an argument, we may concentrate on getting things straight in our own minds. We clarify the issue to our own satisfaction. Then, if we present the argument well, it will in turn make things clear and convincing for the reader. But often our need or desire to take the reader along becomes very strong. In writing an advertisement, a campaign pamphlet, or a personal plea for support, the overriding purpose is to change the reader's mind or to change the reader's ways. We then need effective strategies for swaying the reluctant reader.

Research   Research checks out facts and interprets them for the reader. We try to stay close to the facts and keep out guesswork and personal likes or dislikes. Scholarly research draws on previously published sources. It sifts evidence and hunts down missing links. In a research report or a scholarly article, we expect conclusions carefully worked out and solidly supported.

THE STANDARDS OF GOOD WRITING

What makes one piece of writing better than another? Here are some basic principles that apply to most of the writing you will encounter:

- *Good writing is authentic.* Rely on your own firsthand observation, your own study of the evidence. Do not merely repeat secondhand ideas. Find your own answers to the questions at hand.

- *Good writing is coherent.* It hangs together. Take up one major point at a time, so that your readers can get their bearings. Move on in such a way that your readers can follow. Make them see the connections. Make them feel they are moving ahead according to an overall plan.

- *Good writing is effective.* Show that you are aware of your audience. Fill in the explanations or the information you think your readers need. Answer the objections they are likely to raise. Come on strong when it's time to make them say: "Yes, you are right!"

- *Good writing is well written.* Show that you care about language, about words. Take time to find the right word. Take time to straighten out an awkward sentence. Develop your ear for a word's overtones and associations. Make your reader want to write in the margin: "Well put!" "Well said!"

A PROGRAM FOR WRITING

The first part of this book, "A Writing Program," is set up to help you develop your skill and confidence as a writer. Each chapter deals with a particular kind of writing assignment. It describes the kind of writing involved, gives you advice on how to work up and structure material, provides models and topics. Each chapter serves a double function: It helps you deal with the particular problems of a kind of writing—description, autobiography, definition, persuasion. At the same time, it shows you what a particular kind of assignment can teach you about writing in general.

The second part of this book, "The Writer's Tools," shifts attention from the larger questions of structure and strategy to more specific questions of style. It makes you take a look at words, sentences, and paragraphs—and at how an effective writer makes these building blocks serve the larger purposes.

The third part of this book, "A Reference Handbook," serves as a guide to revision. This part of the book summarizes the standards of written English. It stresses *positive features* that make prose clear and effective. In recent years, the teaching of English in school and college has moved away from an overemphasis on mechanical correctness. The purpose of good writing is not to avoid errors but to communicate effectively with the reader. The handbook stresses the relationship between outward form and the *substance* of what is said.

Remember: Composition is not the kind of subject that can be learned once and for all. Proficiency in writing comes from practice. It comes from tackling different kinds of writing assignments and from exploring the problems they present. A competent writer has written a great deal and has learned from the experience.

PREVIEW EXERCISE

Study the following writing samples carefully. What kind of writing does each represent? Answer the following questions about each:

A. What is the main idea or key point of the passage? State it in your own words.

B. What do you think was the main purpose of the author in writing the passage? (Do you and your classmates agree?)

C. What kind of person do you think the author was? What clues can you point to in the passage?

D. What kind of person would be an ideal reader for this passage? How would that person react?

1. Three-fourths of the world's people receive very little attention from American reporters. They are the peasants, the three billion people who are still traditional subsistence cultivators of the land. There should be no doubt that these people are worth our attention: all the major contemporary revolutions—in Mexico, Russia, Cuba, Angola—have involved peasant societies. In almost every case the revolution was preceded by cultural breakdown out in the villages, because the old peasant ways and views of life no longer worked. The 450 or so American foreign correspondents only rarely report on these billions, because the

peasants live in the world's two million villages, while the governments, wealth, and power—as well as telephones, cable offices, files and typewriters—are in the cities.—Richard Critchfield, *Columbia Journalism Review*

2. Ever since Cinderella's father remarried, stepmothers have had a bad name. They have been portrayed as cruel, selfish, vain, competitive and even abusive. They've been accused of giving preferential treatment to their own children, and attempting to monopolize the affections of the men they married—their stepchildren's father. The children resent them. The children's mothers don't even dignify them with recognition; and the fathers—the very men who seemed so eager to marry them—often don't trust them to spend five minutes with the children without messing things up. It's not easy being a stepmother. Yet, given the circumstances of modern life, it's an increasingly common job.—Phyllis Rachel, "The Stepmother Trap," *McCall's*

3. The headmistress had been in India, I suppose, fifteen years or so, but she still smiled at her helpless inability to cope with Indian names. Her rimless halfglasses glittered, and the precarious bun on the top of her head trembled as she shook her head. "Oh, my dears, those are much too hard for me. Suppose we give you pretty English names. Wouldn't that be more jolly? Let's see, no—Pamela for you, I think." She shrugged in a baffled way at my sister. "That's as close as I can get. And for you," she said to me, "how about Cynthia? Isn't that nice?" My sister was always less easily intimidated than I was, and while she kept a stubborn silence, I said, "Thank you," in a very tiny voice.—Santha Rama Rau, *Gifts of Passage*

4. Until as recently as a decade ago, the word *regulation* was applied almost exclusively to the government's attempt to control prices and licensing in such fields as transportation, electrical and gas utilities, communications, and oil. Today such agencies as the Civil Aeronautics Board, the Interstate Commerce Commission, and the Federal Communications Commission have this role. But the 1970s witnessed the growth of a new form of regulation that involves health, safety, and environmental protection. In less than 10 years Congress has created a federal bureaucracy employing 80,000 people, with the mission of protecting consumers or workers from harm. These new agencies act as agents for the public (including workers), which has no way of bargaining with business over product safety, pollution, or workplace hazards. We owe to these various organizations better air, less muck in our waterways, and fewer fatal mining accidents, among other achievements. Yet there are problems with this new "social" regulation. Thousands of highly detailed standards proved both confusing and costly. Automobile safety requirements have had no demonstrable effect on the highway death toll. A new program to make public transportation available to the handicapped costs more than providing them limousine service. The cost of social regulation has grown to vast proportions because society is billed for it indirectly.

5. The word *ethnic* has come to have many different meanings during the years of the revival. It is not that the word means nothing, but rather it means whatever the user wants it to mean. Sometimes it stands for "minority" and refers primarily to black, brown, native American, and Asian American, as in "ethnic studies" programs at universities. Other times it is a code word for Catholics, as in "the white ethnic backlash" or "white ethnic opposition to the candidate because of his Baptist religion." When the national news magazines or journals of opinion

speak of ethnics, they mean Catholics, as when the *Nation* announced Daniel P. Moynihan as "ethnic." When I use the word, I normally refer simply to the variety of American subcultures whether that variety be based on race, religion, nationality, language, or even region.—Andrew M. Greeley, "After Ellis Island," *Harper's*

FIRST THEMES

1. The traditional American "work ethic" encouraged people to do their work with a sense of pride and satisfaction. In recent years, well-known authors have claimed that many Americans are dissatisfied with their work or frustrated by it. Many Americans, we are told, hate their jobs. To judge from what you have seen of the world of work, how true are these charges? Draw on your own observation or experience.

2. A few years ago, observers of the American scene started to talk about the "nostalgia wave." They saw a return to the old-fashioned in dress, home furnishings, and popular entertainment. In recent years, have you seen such a return to old ways or old ideas in an area of our lives where it is not just a matter of superficial fashion? Describe the change, using detailed examples. Or, do you know an area of our lives where there has been a major change toward the different and new? Describe the change with detailed examples.

3. Is prejudice on the decline? Are the barriers of prejudice gradually breaking down in our society? Or are prejudice and discrimination merely taking new forms, with people being kept out in new ways? Answer the question on the basis of your experience and observation. Focus on one group of people who have been or still are the target of discrimination.

4. Among books that a whole generation of students have chosen for "unrequired reading" are Salinger's *Catcher in the Rye* and Heller's *Catch-22*. Have you recently read a book that could be called a current campus favorite? Write a book review explaining to someone over thirty what the book has to offer to young people.

5. Television has been called "a cruel caricature, aimed well below the lowest common denominator of American life." How true is this charge? Limit yourself to one area of American life that you know well. Examine the way it is reflected on commercial television.

Part One
A Writing Program

1   Preview: The Whole Theme

2   Observation

3   Personal Experience

4   Opinion

5   Definition

6   Argument

7   Persuasion

8   Tone and Style

9   The Research Paper

10   Writing About Literature

Preview:
The Whole Theme

CHAPTER ONE

1. **Gathering Material**

2. **Bringing Things into Focus**
   Limiting the Subject
   Choosing a Key Question
   Stating a Thesis
   Supporting Your Thesis

3. **Getting Organized**
   Process
   Classification
   Comparison and Contrast

4. **Beginnings and Endings**
   Titles
   Introductions
   Conclusions

5. **Coherence and Transition**
   Synonyms and Recurrent Terms
   Patterns of Expectation
   Transitions
   Outlines

There is excitement in the very act of composition. Some of you know this at first hand—a deep satisfaction when the thing begins to take shape.

CATHERINE DRINKER BOWEN

What does it take to put a paper together?

When you write an expository theme, you move through five closely related stages:

(1) *You explore your subject.* You gather material; you mobilize your resources.

(2) *You bring your subject into focus.* You zero in on a key question or a major point. You limit yourself to what you can handle in detail.

(3) *You organize your material.* You sort things out and put them in order. You work out some overall strategy that suits your material and that fits your purpose.

(4) *You write your first draft.* You try to make sure that your ideas come through clearly, that they catch and hold the attention of your reader.

(5) *You revise your paper as necessary.* You fill in missing links, or reshuffle parts that seem out of order. You proofread your final draft for spelling and punctuation and the like.

1.   GATHERING MATERIAL

Take time to *work up* your subject. When you start discussing a topic, the first and most basic question in your reader's mind is: "What do you know about it?" Take time for *pre*writing—work up a rich fund of materials to draw on when you put the actual paper together.

Suppose you are going to write a paper about welfare, or about the "welfare problem." Your first question should be: "What do I know?" What do you know that could serve as food for thought on this topic? Explore avenues like the following:

(1) "Where has welfare or the welfare problem touched my own experience?" Here are some ways welfare might have touched the lives of your family, friends, acquaintances:

- Elderly relatives were concerned about the passage of Medicare legislation. What were they worried about? What did they say?
- A neighbor is always complaining about people on welfare who are driving a sports car or spending their days on the beach.
- A friend told you about his problems in trying to collect unemployment insurance.
- A friend of the family lost his job and tried to stay "off welfare."

Do these different situations have anything in common? What did you learn from them about how welfare works? Would you go back to any of these people to learn more?

(2) "What role does welfare play in current news and in current controversy?" When is the last time you read a newspaper report about investigations of alleged welfare chiseling? When is the last time you listened to a political candidate who seemed to be running against the people on the welfare rolls? When is the last time you heard someone advance some tangible ideas on how to deal with poverty? What groups and individuals in our society seem to care?

(3) "What reading have I done that would provide some background for current discussion of welfare and of poverty?" In a book like Charles Dickens' *Hard Times*, we see impoverished workers put in long hours in the sweatshops of the nineteenth century. We see their children grow prematurely old, working for pennies. In John Steinbeck's *Grapes of Wrath*, we see the small farmers uprooted by an economy out of control, people willing to work but with no place to go. Books such as these vividly recreate the *conditions* that led to much of the welfare legislation with which we are familiar: minimum wage laws, child labor laws, unemployment insurance, social security.

The kind and extent of your preliminary exploration will vary for different assignments. Usually you will be able to draw on one or more of the following sources of material:

- Current *observation*—close firsthand study of scenes, people, objects, events.

- Past *experience*—the memory bank of everything you have experienced and read.

- Informed *opinion*—the views of others who have studied the same subject.

- Organized *research*—the systematic sifting of evidence from records, documents, and other printed sources.

EXERCISES

A. In the following pair, the first passage is the kind of very general statement anyone could make on the basis of hearsay. The second passage is packed with specific details that tell us, "I was there." Study the author's use of striking detail. Then write a similar passage for one of the five general statements listed at the end.

GENERAL: American vaudeville at the height of its popularity was a colorful institution.

SPECIFIC: An endless, incongruous swarm crawled over the countryside dragging performing lions, bears, tigers, leopards, boxing kangaroos, horses, ponies, mules, dogs, cats, rats, seals and monkeys in their wake. Others rode bicycles, did acrobatic and contortion tricks, walked wires, exhibited sharpshooting skills, played violins, trombones, cornets, pianos, concertinas, xylophones, harmonicas and any other known instrument. There were hypnotists, iron-jawed ladies, one-legged dancers, one-armed cornetists, mind readers, female impersonators, male impersonators, Irish comedians, Jewish comedians, blackface, German, Swedish, Italian, and rube comedians, dramatic actors, Hindu conjurers, ventriloquists, bag punchers, singers and dancers of every description, clay modelers, and educated geese: all traveling from hamlet to town to city presenting their shows. Vaudeville asked only that you own an animal or an instrument, or have a minimum of talent or a maximum of nerve. With these dubious assets, vaudeville offered fame and riches. (Fred Allen)

1. Today's college brings together many different kinds of people.
2. A real circus is a colorful spectacle.
3. A good zoo is a living reminder of the rich variety of life on our planet.
4. A modern amusement park has every kind of gadget and life-sized mechanical toy.
5. Television presents a constant stream of commercials promising to make our lives brighter and more glamorous.

B. Assume you have become interested in how our society treats *the handicapped*. Bring together from your own experience and observation everything you can remember about people who were handicapped. Keep writing—just get down on paper any details and incidents as they come to mind. (Leave any sorting out for some future time when you might want to draw on this preliminary collection of material.)

C. Assume you have been asked to write about a *vanishing institution*: the farm horse, street cars, the passenger train, the corner grocery, the railroad station, or the like. Write down all you can remember about your experiences with it. Start from your earliest childhood memories. Write as fast and as much as you can.

2.   BRINGING THINGS INTO FOCUS

A writer has to learn how to bring a big sprawling subject under control. In practice, we do not write about birds in general, or about welfare as a large, umbrella topic. We write because some part of our general subject is not well known, and we want to fill the gap. We write because an issue has come up, and we want to take a stand. We write because a question has come up, and we want to answer it.

Our reader wants to know: "What are you trying to accomplish? What are you trying to say?" This kind of question helps us bring a paper into **focus.** It helps us pull things together. The more clearly focused a paper, the better the chance that our point will sink in, or that our information will be put to use. To bring your subject into focus,

- narrow down the *area* to be covered;
- close in on one limited *question* to be answered;
- use your paper to support *one central point*.

Limiting the Subject

Limit the area to be covered. No one could write a paper on "Education in America." You might limit this field according to *kind:* academic, physical, religious. You might limit it according to *area:* a state, a town, the nation's capital, Indian reservations in Arizona. You might want to study a particular *level:* grade school, high school, college. You might limit discussion to a certain *type of student:* gifted, retarded, emotionally disturbed. A manageable topic might look like this:

Space-age science at Washington High
"Released time" and the Winchester Public Schools: No time for God

Talking typewriters for the retarded
Home economics for boys
Stagnant schools and the migrant child
How to succeed in a military academy

Each large subject can be split up into several medium-sized subjects. Each of these in turn will yield many limited subjects narrow enough to serve as topics for short papers:

GENERAL AREA: Conflict Between the Generations

INTERMEDIATE: Conflict over Drugs
                 Different Attitudes Toward Sex
                 Different Definitions of Success
                 Different Attitudes Toward Progress
                 Changing Views of Marriage
                 What Happened to Patriotism
                 Youth and the Military
                 Religion Old and New

SUCCESS TOPIC FURTHER BROKEN DOWN:

                 What Young People Look for in a Job
                 Competition vs. "Working with People"
                 The Good Things That Money Can't Buy
                 Making Do vs. Compulsory Consumption
                 Staying Close to the Earth

What would you include in a list of limited topics for one of the *other* medium-sized subjects in the above list?

Choosing a Key Question

Formulate a key question that your paper will answer. The more *specific* the key question you choose, the more likely your paper is to have a clear focus. "How do crime comics shape their readers' attitudes?" is a very *general* question. Crime comics could affect the reader's attitude toward many things: police work, violence, minority groups, criminals, courts. Try to point your question at a more limited issue. Choose a question like the following:

1. Is it true that crime comics equate ugliness with depravity, thus encouraging the reader to judge by appearances?
2. Is it true that heroes look white, Anglo-Saxon, and Protestant, while villains look Latin, for instance, or Oriental?

3. Is it true that in the crime comics people are either all good or all bad?
4. Do crime comics reveal the political sympathies of their authors?

A *pointed* question is more likely to produce a focused paper than a question that is merely exploratory. Avoid questions like "What are some of the causes of adolescent crime?" The "What-are-some" kind of question often leads to a paper in which many different things are mentioned but few of them studied in detail. Substitute a "What-is-the-most" or "What-is-the-best" kind of question:

- What is the most serious obstacle to communication between teenagers and their parents?
- What are three key features shared by successful television comedians?
- What is the best source of alternative energy?

Stating a Thesis

State one major point and drive it home. We scatter and lose the attention of an audience by saying a little something about many different points. We make an impact by concentrating on one major point and supporting it as fully as we can. For example, the writer of a travel article could get our attention by claiming that people in Eastern Europe are fascinated by everything American. The rest of the article could then provide many striking examples. We call the central idea that the rest of a paper supports the **thesis**. The thesis is the writer's central assertion, generalization, or claim. The thesis satisfies the reader who wants to know: "What is the point?"

Writing that first states a thesis and then supports it has many uses. We use it, for instance, when we

- defend a *generalization* in an essay exam;
- call for *action* in a letter to the editor;
- make good a *promoter's* claim in an advertising brochure;
- establish someone's aptitude for a job, in a letter of *recommendation;*
- defend a political candidate against a rival's *charge.*

Remember:

(1) *Make sure your thesis pulls together your previous observations or impressions.* Writing about the heroine of an Ibsen play, you may

wish to say that she was gifted but bored, angry and cruel, hungry for excitement but at the same time afraid of scandal. Formulating a thesis, you try to make these various points add up to a coherent overall view. Your thesis might be one of the following:

THESIS: The heroine expected too much of people and as a result was invariably disappointed.

THESIS: This woman was a born rebel because she was unable to accept the limitations of her environment.

(2) *Make sure your thesis is a clear statement of a limited point.* Whenever possible, state your thesis in a *single* sentence:

TOPIC: Urban Redevelopment

THESIS: Redeveloped neighborhoods lack the varied life of the grown neighborhoods they replace.

TOPIC: Life in Suburbia

THESIS: Living in the suburbs does not prevent people from developing a sense of community.

Supporting Your Thesis

Fill in the material that will support your thesis. When you state a thesis, you commit yourself. You take a stand. When you support your thesis, you follow through. You deliver the goods.

In the following excerpt, from Gordon Parks' *A Choice of Weapons*, the first sentence serves as a thesis; and each of the three paragraphs of the excerpt takes up one incident that bears out the point made by the thesis:

THESIS   *When I was eleven, I became possessed of an exaggerated fear of death.* It started one quiet summer afternoon with an explosion in the

First incident   alley behind our house. I jumped from under a shade tree and tailed Poppa toward the scene. Black smoke billowed skyward, a large hole gaped in the wall of our barn. . . .

Second incident   Then once, with two friends, I had swum along the bottom of the muddy Marmaton River, trying to locate the body of a Negro man. We had been promised fifty cents apiece by the same white policeman who had shot him while he was in the water trying to escape arrest. . . .

Third incident   One night at the Empress Theater, I sat alone in the peanut gallery watching a motion picture, *The Phantom of the Opera*. When the curious heroine, against Lon Chaney's warning, snatched away his mask, and the skull of death filled the screen, I screamed out loud. . . .

A good thesis sentence serves as a *program* for the paper as a whole. It helps you decide what to include and what to keep out. It helps you decide what is **relevant**. Suppose your thesis reads as follows:

THESIS   Nineteenth-century American fiction often lacks strong female characters.

The reader is likely to say: "Let's take a look—maybe you are right." You then provide striking familiar examples:

First example   In Mark Twain's *Huck Finn*, the aunt is left behind, and the story revolves around the boy, his father, and Jim, the runaway slave. . . .

Second example   In Melville's *Moby Dick*, we follow Ishmael and the all-male crew of the whaling ship in pursuit of the White Whale. . . .

Third example   In Cooper's Leatherstocking novels, we move in a frontier world of hunters and scouts and braves. . . .

EXERCISES

A. Suppose you wanted to write a paper relevant to a general topic of current concern. How much narrowing would you have to do before you reach the level where people can see actual effects on their own lives? Or where they could get their own hands dirty trying to do something about the problem? Note how the following general topics have been scaled down:

VERY GENERAL: How Technology Runs Our Lives

LESS GENERAL: The Spread of Automation
                  The Motorized Society
                  The Proliferation of Gadgets

SPECIFIC: The Automated Assembly Line
                  Your Checking Account and the Computer
                  How Appliances Put the Customer to Work

VERY GENERAL: Improving the Quality of Life

LESS GENERAL: Cleaning Up the Environment
                  Solving Chronic Unemployment
                  Transportation Fit for Human Beings

SPECIFIC: Bottles vs. Cans: A Problem in Ecology
                  Plastics That Decompose
                  The Psychology of Litterbugs

Provide a similar set of intermediate and specific topics for two of the following general subjects:

The Plight of the City
The Future of Marriage
Educational Opportunities for Minorities
Jobs for the Class of 2001
Freedom of the Press
Protecting the Consumer

B. Prepare five pointed questions for an *interview* with one of the following: a college president, a police chief, a black minister, a White House aide, a diplomat from a country currently in the news. Formulate questions *limited* enough to steer the interview away from vague generalities. The class as a whole may want to choose the two or three sets of questions most likely to produce significant, detailed responses.

C. Study the following example of a thesis-and-support paper. How, and how well, did the student who wrote it support her thesis? How relevant is the material she provides?

Success Is (Is Not) Having a Good Job

THESIS

Parents view success in terms of security and a good job, but today's youth value people more than things. Parents want and expect their children to succeed. Parents believe in what the future should be, while the young look at the present and do not think that far ahead in their lives.

SUPPORT
(First
example)

A girl from a family I know is in a situation that illustrates this point. Her parents want her to marry a boy who has a good job and makes good money. She is twenty-two and going to school at the moment. She has known a boy for about a year now, and she wants to marry him. But he is an auto mechanic. When she first started dating him, her parents objected because he was not good enough for her. They kept telling her how she wouldn't be able to have all the things she was used to in life. They told her she wouldn't be able to go to fancy places to eat or have a nice car to sit in. She handled the situation by just disregarding what her parents told her.

She didn't care what the boy's background was, or if he had a good job. Her parents tried unsuccessfully to influence her feelings about him. They were pointing out his bad qualities. They told her he was poor and lazy (because he didn't finish college). His hair was too long. She went through many arguments with her parents. Finally she gave up trying to defend her ideals. It is difficult for her to talk to her parents about anything, because they always bring up the subject of her friend. She gets frustrated because her parents are always mimicking him.

(Second
example)

My own situation fits into this general picture. My parents think that I should study hard and get a good job. They are constantly reminding me. As far back as grammar school, they were pouring all this into my head. When I used to get allowances on Sundays, they would always say, "Study hard so you'll get a good job in the future."

My parents emphasized education so much that it was coming out of our ears. All the children had to complete four years of college. There was no chance of anyone dropping out. I remember one semester in junior college, I was carrying twelve units. My father asked me how many units I was carrying. When I told him, he really got upset. He began to make a big thing out of it. He kept asking why I was carrying so few units. I tried to explain to him that at the beginning twelve units was an average load, but he didn't agree. I finally gave up. I let him continue lecturing me, but my mind had stopped listening.

When the next semester came, he again asked me how many units I was carrying. I was reliving in my mind what we had gone through the semester before in those two weeks. When I answered his question, he called the school to check up on me. My mind was going through the stages of losing respect for him for not trusting me. I was at the point where I was losing total interest in education. Today I can no longer and do not wish to discuss school with my parents.

(Third example)   My girlfriend has a problem with her parents regarding marriage. She is the eldest child in the family. Her mother and father want her to marry someone who is in a profession—a doctor, or a pharmacist. She was about to get married a year ago to a premedical student, but something happened. Her mother told her she had made a mistake in not marrying the boy. Her mother even told her to try and get back together with him. He was a medical student and would be able to give her security. She is now in this constant battle with her mother about getting married.

There is indeed a generation gap between the young and their parents on the topic of success.

D. Of the thesis sentences presented in the following brief passages, select the three that come closest to your own views. For each one, jot down briefly what *supporting material* you could supply from your own experience and reading to back up the point made.

1. *Students profit as much (or more) from a summer of work, travel, or reading as from additional course work in summer sessions.* Though such experiences are less systematic than academic learning, they are educational in the sense that they broaden the student's perspective.
2. *The public schools do not fully practice the constitutional principle of separation of church and state.* Students, whether of Christian, Jewish, or agnostic parents, participate in Christmas plays and Easter pageants, and sing religious songs.
3. *Teenage fads and fashions have increasing influence on the adult world.* Teenage styles set the pace for much advertising and strongly influence adult fashions and even hairstyles.
4. *The population of the typical big city is declining in income and social status.* The unskilled and the less educated remain, while the middle class moves out to the suburbs to find living space and better schools for the children.
5. *Fear of violence restricts the activities of many Americans.* People stay away from public parks; older people are afraid to venture out into the streets.
6. *Minority groups are becoming proud of their separate heritage.* Americans who used to feel like second-class citizens are asserting their separate identity.

3. GETTING ORGANIZED

When we present material in a paper, we have to make sure that our readers can find their way. We organize the material in some overall pattern that will make sense. An effective plan of organization keeps the reader from asking: "Where are we going? Where is this paper headed? What are you trying to do?" Three familiar kinds of themes illustrate patterns of organization that help us give shape and direction to a piece of writing.

Process

Present essential steps in the right order. Describing the process of paper making, we trace the necessary steps that turn wood chips first into pulp, then into a paper web, and finally into sheets of paper. Describing the process of radio transmitting, we follow the newscaster's voice through microphone and transmitter to the receiving set and the listener's ear.

What we learn from the **process theme** has many applications. We apply it when we

- explain a *scientific* process:
  How energy of motion converts into electricity
  How sediments build up on the ocean floor
  How a translation machine scans a sentence

- give *directions:*
  How to plant a lawn
  How to make wine from your own grapes
  How to make pottery

- trace a *historical* chain of events:
  How nomads became villagers
  How the railroad transformed rural America

The following instructions will help you write better process themes:

(1) *Pay attention to detail.* No one can make a machine work, or produce an enameled vase, who does not have a concern for the *little* things that add up to the whole. Take in details like those in the following paragraph. Note that they follow **chronological** order— step by step as they happen in time:

A black and white garden spider dropped down from one of the higher branches of the tree. He picked a flimsy, forked twig, covered with large drops of water from the rain, and swung in on it like a toy glider coming in for a landing. As he caught hold of it, it sagged under his weight, and several large water drops slid off to the ground below. The spider sat on the twig until it ceased vibrating. Then he carefully moved to the end of one of the forks. He first walked rather fast, but halfway down the twig fork he slipped and turned upside down. He tried to right himself but failed, so he moved along the twig upside down, fighting both the vibrations of the twig and the large water drops. When the spider reached the end of the twig fork, he carefully fastened a silver thread to the end of the fork. Then he slowly righted himself on the twig. He proceeded to crouch in a peculiar position, somewhat like a sprinter set in his starting blocks. With a mighty leap, he jumped toward another twig fork, but he missed it. He swung down below the twig and hung by his silver thread until the vibrations and his swinging stopped. He climbed up the thread and repeated the maneuver, and again he failed. The third time he jumped, he caught the other twig and proceeded to fasten his silver thread to it. Running back between the two forks the spider began to build his web.

(2) *Concentrate on what is essential.* At a given stage of the process, ask yourself: "What is needed to make the work proceed? What, if left out, would prevent my reader from producing the desired result?" Note the grimly businesslike fashion in which the author of the following passage makes us see "how it works":

The sergeant turned to the captain, saluted and placed himself immediately behind that officer, who in turn moved apart one pace. These movements left the condemned man and the sergeant standing on the two ends of the same plank, which spanned three of the crossties of the bridge. The end upon which the civilian stood almost, but not quite, reached a fourth. This plank had been held in place by the weight of the captain; it was now held by that of the sergeant. At a signal from the former the latter would step aside, the plank would tilt and the condemned man go down between two ties.—Ambrose Bierce, "An Occurrence at Owl Creek Bridge"

(3) *Relate the new and technical to what is familiar.* How is the process you describe similar to something the reader already knows? The following short process theme uses extended **analogy** to make us understand the process of vision:

How We See

The eye operates like a simple box camera. Such a camera has four essential parts: a shutter, a lens, a chamber or box, and a sensitized plate or film. The shutter's job is to allow light to pass through the lens. The lens is a circular piece of glass with curved faces to concentrate the light upon the plate or film. After being concentrated by the lens, a beam of light must pass through the chamber to reach the sensitized plate. The sensitized plate or film then receives an impression of the projected image.

The four corresponding parts of the eye are the iris, the lens, the vitreous body, and the retina. The iris is a muscular diaphragm which can close or dilate to regulate the passage of light to the lens. The lens is composed of a semi-solid, crystalline substance. Like the lens of the camera, the lens of the eye serves to concentrate and focus light. The vitreous body is a large area between the lens and the retina. It is void of any material save a transparent liquid. The retina, through its rods and cones, receives an impression of the projected image.

In the camera, a beam of light passing through the shutter strikes the lens. It is then focused and projected through the chamber to the rear wall of the camera. There, a sensitized plate or film registers an impression of the image carried by the beam of light. In the eye, a beam of light passing through the iris hits the lens. The lens focuses the beam and projects it through the vitreous body to the rear wall of the eye. There, the retina receives an impression of the image carried on this beam of light. From the retina, a stimulus is then flashed to the brain through the optic nerve.

(4) *Break up the whole sequence into major divisions, or emphasize the most significant steps.* An "and-then" sequence becomes confusing, because it gives equal emphasis to many parts, events, or operations. Suppose your paper follows the assembly line in an automobile factory: The basic parts of the body are welded together; the doors are hung; the body shells are dipped into a chemical solution; they are spray-painted; they are dried in ovens; electrical wiring is laid; door locks and other mechanisms are installed; glass is installed; interior lining is installed; and so on. Try to break up the body's progress into three major stages:

I. Building the body shell
II. Painting the body
III. Outfitting the painted shell

Could you set up three or four major stages for one or more of the following?

Repainting the House
Setting up Camp
Courting—the Old-Fashioned Way
Putting in a Lawn
Putting in a Concrete (Sidewalk) (Driveway) (Wall)

Classification

Sort out your material into plausible categories. When we classify things, we group them together on the basis of what they have in common. No two people are exactly alike. Yet we constantly sort them out according to features they share: extrovert and introvert; single, married, and divorced; joiners and loners; upper class, upper middle class, lower middle class, lower class.

Classification is the most common way of organizing the material for a piece of writing. Here is a collection of material for a paper about a person:

SUBJECT: Last semester's psychology teacher
 (1) Had a loud, clear voice
 (2) Told some interesting stories about students helped by psychology
 (3) Came to class late several times
 (4) Explained difficult words
 (5) Wasn't sarcastic toward students
 (6) Wore colorful neckties
 (7) Walked with a limp
 (8) Had been an exchange teacher in France
 (9) Outlined subject clearly
 (10) Spaced assignments well
 (11) Talked over test I did poorly on
 (12) Served in the Army Signal Corps

What goes with what? Here are four possible categories:

 I. *Teaching methods:* (2) relevant anecdotes, (4) explanation of terms, (9) clear outline, (10) spacing of assignments, and perhaps (1) effective speech habits
 II. *Attitude toward students:* (5) absence of sarcasm, (11) assistance after class
 III. *Personal traits:* (6) sporty clothes, (7) limp, (3) lack of punctuality
 IV. *Background:* (8) teaching experience abroad, (12) service in Signal Corps

A student concerned about success in school may conclude that categories I, II, and IV are most significant. A second look at III might suggest an effective strategy for the paper as a whole: an unpromising first impression, belied by the teacher's effectiveness. The outline of the finished paper might look like this:

 I. Unpromising external characteristics
 II. Effectiveness as a teacher
   A. Interesting background
   B. Effective presentation of subject
   C. Positive attitude toward students
 III. Lesson learned

Here are some other subjects with material sorted out into major categories:

SUBJECT: Types of comic strips
 I. Righteous crime fighters (Dick Tracy, Superman, Wonder Woman)

II. Comic stereotypes (Dennis the Menace, Blondie, Bugs Bunny)
III. Social satire (L'il Abner, Doonesbury)
IV. Amusing human foibles (Peanuts, Pogo)

SUBJECT: Types of high school teachers
   I. The *authoritarian* personality (strict discipline, one-way teaching, heavy assignments, severe grading)
  II. The *average* teacher (reliance on the textbook, moderate assignments, "don't-rock-the-boat" attitude)
 III. The students' *friend* (chummy attitude, many bull sessions, unusual projects, fraternizing outside of school)

Remember:

(1) *Make sure your categories serve your purpose.* Let the subject of your paper help you determine appropriate categories. Writing about campus social life, you might divide students into Greeks, Co-op dwellers, and Independents. Writing about courses for vocational students, you might divide them into nursing majors, engineering majors, police majors, and so on.

(2) *Avoid a confusing mixture of criteria.* It does not make sense to divide students into graduates of local high schools, disadvantaged students, and Catholics. It *does* make sense to sort them out according to geographical origin (local, rest of the state, out of state, foreign), *or* according to belief (Catholics, Protestants, Jews, agnostics), *or* according to social and economic background.

Comparison and Contrast

Show connections between things normally considered separately. The need for comparison and contrast often arises when we are faced with a choice. We often compare and contrast to justify a preference. To justify our preference for a lackluster incumbent over a more dynamic challenger, we may compare their records on a number of crucial points. More basically, comparison and contrast helps us *notice* things we previously took for granted. We learn to identify a style of architecture by noting the features it shares with other styles and those features that set it apart. We are more vividly aware of the American way of doing things after we spend a year in Mexico or in France.

For fruitful comparison and contrast, the author must *line up* the material so that one thing throws light upon the other. Here are the two basic ways of organizing the comparison-and-contrast paper:

(1) *The author discusses two things together—feature by feature, point by point.* A **point-by-point comparison** takes up one feature of, say, the Volkswagen, and then immediately asks: "Now what does this look like for the Ford?" A typical outline would look like this:

    I. Economy
       A. Initial cost (data for both cars)
       B. Cost of operation (data for both cars)
       C. Resale value (data for both cars)
    II. Comfort and convenience
       A. Space for passengers and luggage (data for both cars)
       B. Maneuverability (data for both cars)
    III. Performance
       A. Acceleration and speed (data for both cars)
       B. Durability (data for both cars)

(2) *The author discusses two things separately but takes up the same points in the same order.* Such a **parallel-order comparison** gives a coherent picture of each of the two things being compared. At the same time it helps the reader see the connections between the two. In the following portrait of two types of baseball fans, the same three points are taken up both times in the identical order: I. absorption in the game; II. attitude toward fellow fans; III. interest in the players.

THESIS	The true baseball fan is found in the bleachers, not in the grandstand.
Point 1	The fans in the bleachers *forget everything except the game.* When they get excited . . .
Point 2	They are apt to *turn to a total stranger,* tap him on the shoulder, and say, "Ain't that Aaron the berries!" . . .
Point 3	Though their seats may be far from the diamond and they cannot see the batters' faces, they *recognize each one* of them as they come up. . . .
Transition	The fans in the grandstand look at the game differently. . . .
Point 1	They never quite *give themselves up to the game.* They never cut loose with a wild yell. . . .
Point 2	If they are sitting among people who are strangers, they *treat them like strangers.* . . .
Point 3	They have to refer to a scorecard to get the *names of the players.* . . .

EXERCISES

Process

    A. In the following excerpt from a magazine article, the author describes what happened near "a small but growing city like many others around the country" after a planning commission was asked to approve a housing development on ten wooded acres just south of the city. The author vividly describes the process that turns a rural countryside into a modern suburb. He shows us several major stages, stressing how one thing leads to another. *Outline and explain* the major stages in your own words.

The three commissioners voted to approve the development. A few months after that, the city council, on the recommendation of the planning commission, agreed to annex the property to the city, thus guaranteeing that the subdivision would be provided with sewer, water, and electrical lines and police and fire protection. Then, because of a state law that forbade "islands" of noncity land within city limits, most of the property of owners who had fought against the development was automatically annexed to the city. Next came a flock of other developers, now assured of city services, knocking on the doors of once-irate residents, offering as much as $8,000 for an acre of land that—only months before—was worth $1,000 at best. The tax assessors came, too: Not only would tax rates be higher—to pay for the added services the city was obliged to provide all of its residents—but the assessed value of the property would have to be adjusted to reflect the change in market value. Almost overnight, property taxes jumped wildly. One by one the residents, many of whom had owned their ten or twenty or thirty acres of green and wooded hillsides for a generation or more, sold. Those who didn't soon began receiving notices from the city asking for permission to cross their land with sewer or water lines to the new developments. If permission was refused, the city began "condemnation" proceedings to acquire an easement on, or title to, the land it needed. Legal fees soon became another major cost of owning the land. Meanwhile, earthmoving machines were leveling hillsides, bulldozers were uprooting trees, huge dump trucks were unloading their tons of gravel, steamrollers were packing the new asphalt streets and four-lane thoroughfares were being laid over old country roads in anticipation of the traffic.—Peter Meyer, "Land Rush," *Harper's*

B. Identify the ten or twelve *essential steps* in a complicated process that is well known to you from firsthand observation or experience. Try to group the various steps into several major stages. Use the following outline form to report your findings.

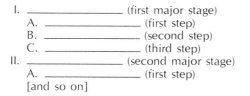

    I. _____ (first major stage)
       A. _____ (first step)
       B. _____ (second step)
       C. _____ (third step)
   II. _____ (second major stage)
       A. _____ (first step)
    [and so on]

C. Assume you are giving your reader instructions for a complicated task. Write a paragraph describing *in full detail* one essential step. Try to include everything that the reader would have to know and do to produce the right results.

D. In one sentence each, explain the six most essential *technical terms* that you would need in tracing one of the following processes: generating electricity, pollination, the life cycle of a butterfly, transmission of a visual image by television, the making of sugar, preparing a French (Spanish, Italian, Arabic, Mexican, Chinese) dish.

Classification

E. Study the following example of a brief *classification paper*. Prepare an outline showing the three or four major categories that were set up by the author. Include subcategories where appropriate.

A Life of Crime

"Lawlessness" and the "breakdown of law and order" have long been clichés of conservative political oratory. Candidates to the right of the political spectrum have often run against "crime in the streets." Today, many Americans find that reality has caught up with rhetoric. Crime is everywhere becoming a familiar facet of everyday life.

According to police statistics, professional crime is steadily increasing. Burglaries are now an everyday occurrence in what used to be "nice quiet neighborhoods." In spite of television cameras and other safety precautions, bank holdups have tripled in number during the last ten years in many parts of the country. Increasingly, major robberies are planned commando-style and executed with military precision and ruthlessness.

Just as disturbing is the steady growth in personal moral laxity on the part of ordinary people: petty pilfering, routine stealing, "ripping off" the employer or the customer. Dresses put on the clothesline to dry disappear. Watches and wallets disappear from high school locker rooms. Recently a principal was caught stealing petty change from vending machines.

In many areas of our lives, we see a steady increase of personal aggressiveness and vindictiveness. Students threaten and bully teachers. Customers settle an argument with the bartender by firebombing the establishment. People taken to court vow to "get" witnesses who testify against them.

We see the same trend toward more lawlessness on the political scene, where it is projected onto a larger screen. Newspaper readers and television viewers have become accustomed to assassinations, bombings, and reprisals as part of the daily news. For many years, terrorism has been a major unsolved political problem in places like Northern Ireland, Italy, or the Near East. People are not allowed on airplanes until they have been searched for deadly weapons. High government officials drive to work surrounded by bodyguards.

As the result of these and similar trends, many ordinary citizens are losing faith in traditional law enforcement. People are ready to join vigilante groups and to "take the law in their own hands." Can you blame them?

F. The following "interest inventory" was adapted from a student paper. How would you *classify* the items in order to present them in a plausible sequence? Prepare a brief outline showing how you have sorted them out.

1. contact sports
2. coffee dates
3. religious retreats
4. taking a friend to the movies
5. work for worldwide disarmament
6. long hikes
7. beach barbecues
8. vacation trips
9. fellowship meetings
10. swimming
11. social work
12. student government

G. A student paper listed the following points as guidelines for parents. How would you sort these points out into *major categories*? Prepare an outline reflecting what you would consider the most plausible classification.

1. Parents should avoid swearing or vulgarity.
2. Parents should not contradict each other in the presence of their children.
3. Parents should provide encouragement when children do something constructive.
4. Punishment should be impartial when there are several children.
5. Parents should not shower their children with gifts.
6. One parent should not overrule the other in matters of discipline.

7. Parents should show affection, whether by a pat on the back or a good word.
8. Parents should respect children as individuals, letting them develop their own likes and dislikes.
9. Parents should not be overprotective.
10. Children should be allowed to learn from their own mistakes.
11. Parents should refrain from quarreling in the presence of their children.
12. Parents should teach good manners by example.
13. Parents should allow their children to choose their own friends.
14. Parents should not give vent to their frustrations or irritations by punishing their children.
15. Parents should not take notice of a child only when it does something wrong.

H. What is your favorite reading matter? Have you ever sorted it out into recurrent types? Choose one of the following: science fiction, detective novels, Western novels, historical novels, nineteenth-century British fiction, current American short stories, biographies, autobiographies, books on travel or exploration. Sort the books you have read in this major category out into a few major types. For each, write a short paragraph indicating the major features that examples of the type have in common.

Comparison and Contrast

I. Study the following excerpt from a magazine article about nuclear energy. Summarize briefly the comparison and contrast that occurs early in this excerpt. Then find and outline the *point-by-point comparison* that the author uses later.

The simplest way of getting energy out of hydrogen is to combine it with oxygen—to let it burn and deliver heat. Such a process, however, involves merely the outermost fringe of the hydrogen atom and delivers only a tiny fraction of the energy store available at its compact "nucleus."

Something other than hydrogen-burning—something much more dramatic—takes place at the center of the sun. Under enormous gravitational pressures, the substance at the sun's core is squeezed together, raising the temperature there to a colossal 15 million degrees Centigrade (24 million degrees Fahrenheit).

At such pressures and temperatures, the very atoms of matter smash to pieces. Their outer shells break away and expose the tiny nuclei at the center, which then drive into each other at thousands of miles per second and sometimes stick. When hydrogen nuclei stick together to form the slightly larger nuclei of helium atoms, the process is called "hydrogen fusion."

Every second, 650 million tons of hydrogen are fusing into 645.4 million tons of helium at the sun's center. This process produces energy. Each missing 4.6 million tons per second represents the energy that pours out of the sun in all directions. A very small fraction is intercepted by the earth, and on that energy all life is supported.

Can we somehow take advantage of this process on earth? The trouble is we can't duplicate the conditions at the center of the sun in the proper way. . . . We want *controlled* fusion—the kind that produces energy a little bit at a time in usable, nondestructive quantities.

We still haven't reached controlled fusion. Still, at the rate we are going now, it seems that sometime before the mid-1980s, one or the other method will work. We have atomic power now in the form of uranium fission, but hydrogen fusion would be much better.

Fission uses uranium and plutonium as fuel—rare metals that are hard to get and handle. Fusion uses hydrogen, easy to obtain and handle.

Fission must work with large quantities of uranium or plutonium, so runaway reactions can take place by accident and cause damage. Fusion works with tiny quantities of hydrogen at any one time, so even runaway fusions would produce only a small pop.

Fission produces radioactive ash, which can be extremely dangerous and may not be disposed of safely. Fusion produces helium, which is completely safe, plus neutrons and tritium, which can be used up as fast as they are produced.

Finally, fission only produces a tenth as much energy as fusion, weight for weight.—Isaac Asimov, "Nuclear Fusion," *Parade*

J. Of the following topics, choose the one that seems most promising for fruitful comparison and contrast. Write *two* rough outlines—one for a point-by-point comparison, the other for a parallel-order comparison. Choose one: your high school campus and your present college campus, two successful television comedians with different styles, old-style and "adult" Western movies, a student hangout and an expensive restaurant.

K. Write a rough outline for a comparison and contrast of *two major characters* from imaginative literature. Choose the central figures of two Shakespeare plays, two nineteenth-century British novels, or two modern American novels. Make it *either* a point-by-point or a parallel-order comparison, and be prepared to defend your choice.

L. Write a rough outline for a comparison and contrast of *two sets of attitudes*, or two distinct positions, on some major aspect of education: discipline in high school, sex education, supervision of the private lives of college students. Use either a point-by-point or a parallel-order comparison and be prepared to defend your choice.

4.   BEGINNINGS AND ENDINGS

As a paper begins to take shape, we increasingly think of the audience. How can we attract and hold the readers' attention? How can we make clear to them what we are trying to do? How can we leave them with a strong final impression?

Titles

Use your title to attract the reader. A good title is specific enough to stake out a limited area. It is honest enough to prevent later dis-

THE LURE OF TITLES

What kind of book does the title make you expect? Would you want to read it? Why, or why not?

appointment. Do not promise more than you can deliver. A good title is striking enough to compete with other claims on the reader's time. It often has a dramatic or humorous touch:

At Last Lincoln Found a General
The Crime of Punishment
Second Things First
God Helps Those That Help Each Other

Introductions

Use your introduction to attract the reader but also to do important groundwork for the paper. An effective introduction creates interest; it hooks the reader into the essay or story. It sketches out the territory to be covered, often by narrowing down a more general subject. It sets the tone for the rest of the essay. Above all, it *heads straight for the central idea* to be developed in the rest of the paper.

You will seldom write a paper requiring more than *one short introductory paragraph*. Here are some typical examples:

(1) The writer may attract the reader's attention by relating his subject to a *topical event* or *current trend*:

The Doom Boom

Until a few years ago sex was a taboo topic; now death is being freed of its taboos, at least as a subject for frank talk. In a sense, death has come into fashion. In polite society the act of dying no longer need be hinted at as "passing away." As opportunists discover that the hearse is a good bandwagon to jump on, the subject may even become overexploited. But the abuses that occur are far outweighed by the benefits. . . .—*Life*

(2) The writer may make the reader take a *new look at a familiar situation*:

The Life of Stress

A lot of sympathy is being wasted on executives for leading lives so full of stress and strain that it impairs their health. Actually, their subordinates suffer more from high blood pressure and artery disease. These surprising findings . . .—*Time*

(3) The writer may approach a general subject *from a personal angle*, showing his personal interest in or qualifications for the subject:

It Takes Four to Start a War

A few months ago a freak thunderstorm hit the city and sent a lightning bolt crashing to the ground a few blocks from my apartment. The sound jolted me in terror from my sleep. My body responded with a dose of adrenalin and sweat and a galloping heart. I crossed my fingers because I was sure it was nuclear war. I am not often conscious of this fear, but I suspect my subconscious dwells on it, for I am of that generation that was herded into the halls of elementary schools to lean against ceramic tile walls and tuck our heads between our knees. . . .

(4) The writer may use a *dramatic case* to lead us into a discussion of a more general problem or situation:

No Exit

Neal is twenty and has been on heroin since that day he remembers so well, his fifteenth birthday, when someone on his block took him to the Embassy Hotel in Manhattan and invited him to buy a fix. "Henry, my friend, was always fooling around with the goof balls, and now he had found something even better. I tried it and liked it." Of all the drug problems afflicting the world, heroin is the most deadly and the one that most seriously affects American young people. . . .

(5) *An initial quotation* may serve as the keynote for the rest of the paper:

Who Is Hamlet?

"It is a commonplace that the character of Hamlet holds up the mirror to his critics."[1] Shakespeare's Hamlet has been aptly described as the sphinx of the Western world, with each critic giving his own subjective answer to the riddle it proposes. . . .

(6) *Striking facts or statistics* may dramatize the issue to be discussed:

Monolingualism Is Obsolete

Last year, only one out of ten American high school graduates had studied a foreign language. In spite of the publicity recently given to the teaching of foreign languages in primary and secondary schools . . .

(7) A *striking contrast* may heighten the point to be made:

American Children Are Spoiled

Not too many decades ago, young children were early taught the difference between what they were, and were not, allowed to do. Today, many American parents treat their children as if they could do no wrong. The most obvious manifestation of this change . . .

(8) A *provocative statement* may challenge a familiar belief or ideal:

Freedom Is Impossible

Freedom in society is impossible. When the desires of two people do not agree, both cannot be satisfied. Who is going to be free to realize his or her desire—the person who wants to walk down the street shouting and singing, or a neighbor who seeks peace and quiet? Those who want to build a new highway, or those who want to retain the unspoiled natural beauty of the land? . . .

(9) An *amusing anecdote* may convey an important idea:

Medical Journalism—With and Without Upbeat

As a veteran writer of medical and psychological articles for the mass-circulation "slicks," I have a fellow feeling for the violinist who rebelled after having been with an orchestra for thirty years. One day, so the story goes, he sat with his hands folded during rehearsal, and when the conductor rapped on the podium with his baton and demanded furiously, "Why aren't you playing?" replied, with a melancholy sigh, "Because I don't like music." Sometimes I feel like sitting at my typewriter with my hands folded. I don't like popularization. It has gone too far. The little learning—with illustrations—which the magazines have been pouring into a thirsty public has become a dangerous thing. . . .—Edith M. Stern, *Saturday Review*

Some common ways of introducing a theme are usually *ineffective*:

- A *repetition*, often verbatim, *of the assignment*.

- A *colorless summarizing statement*: "There are many qualities that the average college graduate looks for in a job. Most of them probably consider the following most important. . . ."

- An *unsupported claim to interest*: "Migratory birds are a fascinating subject. Ever since I was a little child I have been interested in the migration of birds. Studying them has proved a wonderful hobby. . . ."

- *Complaints or apologies*: "I find it hard to discuss prejudice in a paper of 500 words. Prejudice is a vast subject. . . ."

Conclusions

Use your conclusion to tie together different parts of your paper and reinforce its central message. Avoid conclusions that are merely lame restatements of points already clear. Try making your conclusion fulfill an expectation created earlier in your paper. For instance, make it give a direct answer to a question asked in your title or introduction. Or tie it in with a key incident treated early in your paper.

Here are some examples of effective conclusions:

(1) A *final anecdote* that reinforces the central idea:

. . . Only once did I ever hear of an official football speech which met with my entire approval. It was made by a Harvard captain. His team had lost to Yale but by a smaller score than was expected. It had been a fast and interesting game. At the dinner when the team broke training the captain said, "We lost to Yale but I think we had a satisfactory season. We have had fun out of football and it seems to me that ought to be the very best reason for playing the game."

A shocked silence followed his remarks. He was never invited to come to Cambridge to assist in the coaching of any future Harvard eleven. His heresy was profound. He had practically intimated that being defeated was less than tragic.—Heywood Broun, "A Study in Sportsmanship," *Harper's*

(2) A strong *final quotation*:

. . . The drug epidemic seems to be the shadow of an end-of-century plague. It is part of a larger set of social problems that medical advances have done little to solve. As Horace Sutton has said, "Way ahead materially, we have done poorly in combating social diseases. It is a branch of medical science in which no Nobel Prizes are given."

(3) A *forecast or warning* based on facts developed in the paper:

. . . In education we have not yet acquired that kind of will. But we need to acquire it, and we have no time to lose. We must acquire it in this decade. For if, in the crucial years which are coming, our people remain as unprepared as they are for their responsibilities and their mission, they may not be equal to the challenge, and if they do not succeed, they may never have a second chance to try.—Walter Lippmann, "The Shortage in Education," *Atlantic*

(4) A suggestion for *remedial action*:

. . . If the leading citizens in a community would make it a point to visit their state prison, talk with the warden, then return to their communities with a better understanding of actual down-to-earth prison problems, they would have taken one of the most important and most effective steps toward a solution of our crime problem.—Erle Stanley Gardner, "Parole and the Prisons—An Opportunity Wasted," *Atlantic*

(5) A *return from the specific to the general*, relating the findings of the paper to a general trend:

> . . . Inge's family plays constitute a kind of aesthetic isolationism upon which the world of outside—the world of moral choice, decision, and social pressures—never impinges. Although he has endowed the commonplace with some depth, it is not enough to engage serious attention. William Inge is yet another example of Broadway's reluctance or inability to deal intelligently with the American world at large.—Robert Brustein, "The Men-Taming Women of William Inge," *Harper's*

Here are some examples of *ineffective* conclusions:

- The *platitude*: "This problem deserves the serious attention of every right-thinking American."

- The *silver lining*: "When things look their grimmest, a turn for the better is usually not far away."

- The *panacea*: "The restoration of proper discipline in the nation's schools will make juvenile delinquency a thing of the past."

- The *conclusion raising problems* that weaken or distract from the point of the paper: "Of course, a small car has obvious disadvantages for a family with numerous children or for the traveler in need of luggage space."

EXERCISES

A. Study the following *book titles* and rank the three best titles in order of their effectiveness. Explain what makes them effective. What kind of a book does each make you expect?

1. *George Washington, Man and Monument*
2. *Freedom in the Modern World*
3. *The City in History*
4. *The American Way of War*
5. *The Inner City Mother Goose*
6. *Number: The Language of Science*
7. *Lost Worlds of Africa*
8. *The Feminine Mystique*
9. *The Naked Ape*
10. *The Second Sex*

B. Look through recent issues of general-circulation *magazines* to find five articles whose titles you consider exceptionally effective. Defend your choices.

C. Describe the approach chosen in each of the following introductions. Evaluate the effectiveness of both *introduction and title*. Do they make the reader want to go on reading? Do they seem to lead clearly and directly into a specific subject? What kind of paper or article would you expect in each case?

1.   **Prison Reform: A Must**

By now, just about all of us are aware of the requests and demands by numerous organizations and groups, as well as individuals, for prison reform. Many people are somewhat skeptical of this trend as just being part of the movement to change nearly all of society. I was already convinced that prison wasn't a whole lot of fun, but also felt that the testimony of cons and ex-cons was biased, if not altogether lies. Being somewhat of an optimist, I felt that the whole world wasn't bad. But after doing only a minimal amount of research into the subject, I have decided that much of what is heard is true and there is a real need for such a reform of the prison system.

2.   **Spoiling the View**

The boy, who was about seven years old, wrinkled his face in revulsion as he entered the subway car. The walls were thick with graffiti and advertisements hung in shreds. "This is a dump train," he said loudly, glaring angrily at the other passengers. "Mama, why are we riding in a dump train?"
Vandalism in New York has leveled off in recent years, but the level is high and visible. . . .

3.   **From Ghetto to University**

In the long and eventful history of the Jewish people, the year 1881 is a year to remember for it marks a turning point both in the story of American Judaism and in the odyssey of the Jewish people as a whole. That was the year that the Russian government began to enforce a new policy aimed at its Jewish population, at that time the largest Jewish community in the world. . . .—Sarah Schmidt, *American Educator*

4.   **The Demise of Education**

America is in headlong retreat from its commitment to education. Political confusion and economic uncertainty have shaken the people's faith in education as the key to financial and social success. This retreat ought to be the most pertinent issue in any examination of the country's condition. At stake is nothing less than the survival of American democracy. . . .—Fred M. Hechinger, *Saturday Review*

5.   **"I Didn't Bring Anyone Here, and I Can't Send Anybody Home"**

When I recently went back to the great yellow prison at San Quentin, it was, in a sense, to make good on a debt incurred twenty years ago. I'd started my career as a prison teacher with a good liberal's prejudice in favor of prisoners and against their guards. When I left, about five years later, I wasn't so sure of myself, for I'd met more than one prisoner who fully deserved to be locked up and more than one guard who turned out to be a decent human being.

The debt I'm talking about, then, was an obligation to report as truly as I could about the prison guard—or, as he's officially known in California, the correctional officer. . . .—Kenneth Lamott, *Saturday Review*

6.   **More Catholic Than the Pope**

While standing in the lobby of the administration building of a moderately sized Catholic college, I saw a recruitment poster for an order of nuns that said, in those light, slanty letters that are supposed to indicate modern spirituality: Are you looking for an alternative life-style?—Mary Gordon, *Harper's*

D. Examine the introduction or "lead" in three current articles from different general-interest magazines. Write a well-developed paragraph about each one. Describe the approach followed and evaluate its effectiveness.

E. Describe the function and estimate the probable effectiveness of the following conclusions:

1. (A paper describing the game of badminton)
   . . . Badminton can be very exciting. If you are ever looking for a good time I suggest that you try this game. I know from experience that it can really be a lot of fun.

2. (A paper trying to demonstrate the futility of censoring comic books)
   . . . the parents can do most to counteract the comic-book habit. If they read to their children from good books, if they teach their children to treat good books as treasured possessions, if they make it a habit to talk about good books in the home, the positive attraction of good literature may prove more effective than censorship possibly can.

3. (A paper discussing several examples of "tolerance")
   . . . We thus conclude that by "tolerance" we mean allowing beliefs and actions of which we do not wholly approve. Since many of us approve wholeheartedly of only very few things, life without tolerance would be truly intolerable.

4. (A paper on race prejudice)
   . . . What can the individual do to combat racial prejudice? This question is very hard to answer, because nobody can predict the future.

5. (A paper on the democratic process)
   . . . The benefits society derives from the democratic process are often unspectacular, and slow in coming. Its weaknesses and disadvantages are often glaringly evident. By its very nature, democracy, in order to survive, must give its enemies the right to be heard and to pursue their goals. As Chesterton has said, "The world will never be safe for democracy—it is a dangerous trade."

6. (A paper on prison reform)

   . . . in spite of all the studies and reports done by numerous commissions and panels, the U.S. lags behind other countries in the implementation of penal reform. What are we waiting for? New methods in use around the world have proven their value, and yet we drag our feet. We are made to wonder if our government is capable of dealing with more than one or two of the popular issues that are splashed over the headlines in each election year.

5. COHERENCE AND TRANSITION

A paper has **coherence** when it takes the reader along. An effective writer knows how to make the reader follow from point to point. Good writing has a pied-piper effect; it is accompanied in the reader's mind by a running commentary somewhat like the following: "This I have to hear"; "Now I can see where you are headed"; "I hope you can make this stick"; "That's what I *thought* you were leading up to"; "Yes, I see."

Synonyms and Recurrent Terms

Use key terms and their synonyms to focus the reader's attention. In a paper on academic freedom, terms and phrases like "freedom," "liberty," "independent thought," "free inquiry," "responsible choice," "absence of interference," and "self-government" show that the writer is never straying far from the central issue. The echo effect of such synonyms reassures readers that they are not expected to take unexplained sudden jumps.

In the following excerpt, find all the words and phrases that in one way or another echo the idea of *work*:

What elements of the national character are attributable to this long-time agrarian environment? First and foremost is the habit of work. For the colonial farmer ceaseless striving constituted the price of survival. . . .

The tradition of toil so begun found new sustenance as settlers opened up the boundless stretches of the interior. "In the free States," wrote Harriet Martineau in 1837, "labour is more really and heartily honoured. . . ."

One source of Northern antagonism to the system of human bondage was the fear that it was jeopardizing this basic tenet of the American creed. "Wherever labor is mainly performed by slaves," Daniel Webster told the United States Senate, "it is regarded as . . ."

Probably no legacy from our farmer forebears has entered more deeply into the national psychology. If an American has no purposeful work on hand . . .

This worship of work has made it difficult for Americans to learn how to play. As Poor Richard saw it, "Leisure is . . ."

The first mitigations of the daily grind took the form of hunting, fishing, barnraisings and logrollings—activities that had no social stigma because they contributed to the basic needs of living. . . .

The importance attached to useful work had the further effect of helping to make "this new man" indifferent to aesthetic considerations. . . .—Arthur M. Schlesinger, *Paths to the Present*

Patterns of Expectation

Use a consistent overall pattern to guide the reader's expectations. If a writer sets up a clear-cut overall pattern, the reader is ready for the next step before it comes. Here are some familiar patterns that can help guide the expectations of a reader:

Enumeration Lining major points up in a numerical sequence makes for a formal, systematic presentation. In the following discussion of language, the key points gain force from marching across the page in a 1-2-3 order:

There are *five simple facts* about language in general which we must grasp before we can understand a specific language or pass judgment on a particular usage. . . .

In the first place, language is basically speech. . . .

In the second place, language is personal. . . .

The third fact about language is that it changes. . . .

The fourth great fact about language . . . is that its users are, in one way or another, isolated. . . .

The fifth great fact about language is that it is a historical growth of a specific kind. . . .—Donald J. Lloyd, "Snobs, Slobs, and the English Language," *The American Scholar*

Order of Importance Suppose an author is examining the causes of war. She takes up *minor* contributing causes first, as if to get them out of the way. She gradually moves on to major ones. The reader will be ready for a final central or crucial cause coming as the **climax** of the article or the book.

From Problem to Solution Can you see the logical pattern that helps move forward the following student paper?

PROBLEM   In any family, there is a network of antagonistic desires. A young
                     girl might want to practice her violin, while her brother insists that
                     the noise interferes with his studying. . . .
SOLUTION   These situations must be solved or managed. If one parent dic-
First   tates without consideration of the others, the family will be run in
alternative   an authoritarian manner. Women used to bend to the wishes of an
                     authoritarian husband. . . .
Second   If no authority figure guides and directs these daily decisions,
alternative   the individuals in the family must create some method of living to-
                     gether. . . .

Study of Alternatives   Systematic study of *different* possible choices
or different possible causes accounts for the purposeful forward
movement of much successful professional writing. Look at the following example:

THESIS   The diversity of higher education in the United States is
                     unprecedented. . . .
First problem is   Consider the *question of size.* The small campus offers . . .
taken up; one
alternative is
considered
Second alternative   Others feel hemmed in by these very qualities. They wel-
is considered   come the *comparative anonymity and impersonality* of the big
                     university. . . .
Second problem   Another familiar question is whether the student should
is taken up; first   go to a *college next door, in the next city, or a thousand miles
alternative is   away.* By living at home . . .
considered
Second alternative   Balanced against this, there are considerable advantages
is considered   to a youngster in *seeing and living in an unfamiliar region* of
                     the country. . . .
Alternatives are   But this question too must be decided in terms of the in-
weighed   dividual. . . .
Third problem is   *Coeducation* poses still another problem. Those who favor
taken up; first   it argue . . .
alternative is
considered
Second alternative   Others believe that *young men and women* will work
is considered   better if . . .
Alternatives are   There is no pat answer. It might be healthy for one young-
weighed   ster . . .
Fourth problem   The so-called *"prestige" colleges and universities* present
is taken up   a special problem. . . .—John W. Gardner, "How to Choose a
                     College, if Any," *Harper's*

Transitions

Use transitional phrases to help the reader move smoothly from one point to the next. In a well-written paper, the reader can see how the writer moves from point to point. But the connection is seldom as obvious as the writer thinks. Transitional phrases are directional signals that help the reader move along without stumbling.

Here are common transitional phrases:

ADDITION:	too, also, furthermore, similarly, moreover
ILLUSTRATION:	for example, for instance
PARAPHRASE OR SUMMARY:	that is, in other words, in short, to conclude, to sum up
LOGICAL CONCLUSION:	so, therefore, thus, accordingly, consequently, as a result, hence
CONTRAST OR OBJECTION:	but, however, nevertheless, on the other hand, conversely, on the contrary
CONCESSION:	granted that . . . , no doubt, to be sure, it is true that . . .
REITERATION:	indeed, in fact

Point out all transitional expressions in the following passage. In your own words, what kind of signal does each give the reader?

It is seldom hard to construct conspiracy theories of history in retrospect. Distinguished Southern historians, for example, worked diligently for many years to demonstrate that President Lincoln had deliberately tricked the South into the Civil War, that after the innocent Confederates fired on Fort Sumter, Lincoln rubbed his hands with glee and used the incident to justify mobilizing Union troops. Similarly, Franklin D. Roosevelt was attacked in immense detail by as distinguished an American historian as Charles A. Beard for instigating the Japanese assault on Pearl Harbor. Although these studies had a lunatic logic, they suffer from one overwhelming liability: They are not true. Lincoln did not want war. Roosevelt did—but with the Nazis, not the Japanese. In fact, if Hitler had not gone completely off his rails and declared war on the United States, we might well have gone roaring off into the Pacific in 1942 and left Europe to its fate.—John P. Roche, "The Pentagon Papers and Historical Hindsight," *The New Leader*

Outlines

Use outlines to help you work out and strengthen the organization of a piece of writing. Outlines help you visualize the structure of a paper; they help you confront and solve problems of organization.

The more clearly you have outlined a paper in your own mind, the better your reader will be able to follow.

(1) *Construct a working outline by jotting down major points in a tentative order.* To be useful as a help in *writing* a paper, an outline should be informal and flexible. **A working outline** resembles an architect's preliminary sketches rather than the finished blueprint. When jotting down a working outline, the writer is in effect saying: "Let's see what it would look like on paper."

Suppose a writer wants to discuss an important common element in books that have enjoyed a tremendous vogue with adolescents. He might first jot down titles as they come to mind:

> *The Pigman*
> *Catcher in the Rye*
> *Catch-22*
> *The Prophet*
> *Steppenwolf*
> *Lord of the Flies*

To arrange these titles in a plausible order, he might decide to start with a *classic* example: *Catcher in the Rye*, the book about a "turned-off" adolescent that at one time *everyone* had read. He would then discuss outstanding *recent* examples, taking them up roughly in the order in which they became popular. Finally, he would discuss in detail a *personal* example—a book that meant a great deal to him as an adolescent. His working outline might look like this:

> Classic example: *Catcher in the Rye*
> Recent examples:
>   *Lord of the Flies*
>   *Steppenwolf*
>   *Catch-22*
>   *The Pigman*
> My own favorite: *Slaughterhouse Five*

(2) *Use the final outline as a final check on organization and as a guide to the reader.* Your instructor may require you to submit a final outline with any paper that presents a substantial argument or a substantial body of material. Two major forms are common:

• The **topic outline** is most useful for quick reference. It presents, in logical order, the topics and subtopics that a paper covers. Like other outlines, it often starts with a thesis sentence summarizing the central idea of the paper. Here is an example:

```
                  To Join or Not to Join

THESIS: For today's realistic, cost-conscious college
        student, joining a fraternity or sorority
        makes sense.

   I. Academic benefits
      A. Inside information about teachers and classes
      B. Help with assignments

  II. Social benefits
      A. Informal social life
      B. Organized activities
      D. Inside track in campus politics

 III. Economic benefits
      A. Current living arrangements
      B. Future business contacts
```

• In a **sentence outline**, we sum up, in one complete sentence each, what we have to say on each topic and subtopic. The sentence outline thus forces us to think through our material more thoroughly than the topic outline, which merely indicates the ground to be covered. A sentence outline might look like this:

Main Street Isn't Pennsylvania Avenue

THESIS: A successful business career alone does not qualify an executive for government work.
 I. Prominent business executives have often occupied high positions in the federal government.
 II. Executives often have qualifications that government officials tend to lack.
    A. They are in close contact with the general public.
    B. They have thorough training in organizational problems.
       1. They are trained in administrative efficiency.
       2. They are cost-conscious.

III. But business executives often lack preparation for other aspects of government work.
    A. They tend to lack the experience necessary for dealing with people from foreign cultures.
        1. They may alienate foreign diplomats.
        2. They tend to ignore public opinion abroad.
    B. They have had little experience with the delays inherent in democratic processes.
IV. The personal qualifications of the individual executive are more important than a business background.

Check your finished outlines against the following suggestions:

(1) *Avoid single subdivisions.* If there is a subdivision *A*, there should be a subdivision *B*. If there is a section numbered *1*, there should be a section numbered *2*. If a section covers only one major point or one major step, leave it undivided.

(2) *Avoid a long sequence of parallel elements,* such as *I–X, A–F,* or *1–8.* Try to split the sequence into two or three major groups.

(3) *Use parallel grammatical structure* for headings of the same rank in order to emphasize their logical relation. For instance, if *A 1* reads "To revive the student's interest," *A 2* and *A 3* should also be worded as infinitives: "To promote the student's participation"; "To develop the student's independent judgment."

(4) *In a topic outline, make each topic specific and informative.* In a sentence outline, make each subdivision a complete sentence. Make each sentence sum up an idea rather than merely indicate a topic.

REVIEW EXERCISES

A. Point out all words that repeat or echo the ideas of fear and threat in the following passage:

What happened on the way to women's equality? What happened is a repetition of 1776, a rerun of the Fourteenth and Fifteenth Amendments and of the battles that defeated women's suffrage until 1920. The enemy is fear, and many of the fears are not irrational. Blue-collar and white-collar men, whose job security is already precarious, fear increasing competition from women for the same jobs. Other men, whose sense of identity has been heavily buffeted by a changing world, are threatened with loss of the faith that whatever may be their status among men, at least they are "better" than women. Women who are dependent upon men and cannot compete on equal terms fear that equality will force them into independence. Still other women and men fear equality as simply another unknown in a world already strewn with hidden pitfalls.—Shirley M. Hufstedler, *Women and the Law*

B. Read the following passage from Henry Steele Commager's *The American Mind*. Study it as an example of a passage clearly focused on a central topic, and supporting a clearly stated thesis. Answer the questions that follow it.

The temptation to experiment was deeply ingrained in the American character and fortified by American experience. America itself had been the greatest of experiments, one renewed by each generation of pioneers, and where every community was a gamble and an opportunity; the American was a gambler and an opportunist. He had few local attachments, pulled up stakes without compunction, and settled easily into new communities; where few regions or professions were overcrowded and every newcomer added to the wealth and the drawing power, he was sure of a welcome.

He was always ready to do old things in new ways, or for that matter, to do things which had not been done before. Except in law, tradition and precedent discouraged him, and the novel was a challenge. Pioneering had put a premium upon ingenuity and handiness, and where each man turned readily to farming, building, and trading, it seemed natural that he should turn with equal readiness to preaching, lawing, or doctoring, or combine these with other trades and professions.

The distrust of the expert, rationalized into a democratic axiom during the Jacksonian era, was deeply ingrained in the American character and persisted long after its original justification had passed. With opportunism went inventiveness, which was similarly invited by circumstances. Americans, who recorded at the Patent Office in Washington more inventions than were recorded in all the Old World nations together, likewise found more new roads to Heaven than had ever before been imagined, while their schools multiplied the seven liberal arts tenfold. Denominationalism and the inflated curriculum were not so much monuments to theological or secular learning as to the passion for experiment and inventiveness, and to an amiable tolerance.

1. How many words can you find in this passage that all echo or repeat the idea of "experiment"? Find all the synonyms or near-synonyms of this central term.
2. How many major instances of applications of the major thesis can you identify? Describe in your own words four or five *major kinds* of experiment that this passage maps out.
3. Select *one* of the major kinds of experiment mentioned here. Write a paragraph in which you fill in specific examples from your own reading or observation. Use a variety of transitional expressions. (Underline them in your finished paragraph.)

C. In each of the following pairs of sentences, a transitional word or phrase has been left out. Fill in a transition that will help the reader move smoothly from the first sentence to the second.

1. There are many special schools that should be considered by the young person who is not going on to college. The student who wishes to be an X-ray technician or a practical nurse, _____, will find many schools that offer the necessary training.
2. Apprenticeship systems are still operating in every industry and offer wide opportunities for ambitious youngsters. They must be warned, _____, that in some of the older crafts entry is jealously guarded.
3. The home environment is the largest single factor determining the grade school youngster's "scholastic aptitude." _____, how well children learn in school depends on what they have learned at home.
4. Rennie was lazy, self-indulgent, spoiled. _____, he did remarkably well in his favorite subjects.
5. The basic promise that American society has always held out to its citizens is equality of opportunity. The typical substandard big-city school, _____, is profoundly un-American.
6. Black athletes are not as pampered as some white sports fans seem to think. _____ the outstanding black athlete enjoys many privileges, but when a black and a white player are equally well qualified, coaches are likely to give preference to the latter.
7. The European system of education very early separates youngsters permanently on the basis of ability. The American system, _____, is designed to make possible numerous second chances.
8. In many Latin American countries, more young people study to be lawyers than are needed in their country. _____, in many underdeveloped countries more young people study to be engineers than a preindustrial society could support.
9. A highly specialized skill limits a person's job opportunities. It _____ makes the specialist a potential victim of technological unemployment.
10. Our leaders are fond of the phrase "the free world." In actual fact, _____ _____, societies that foster political freedom are the exception rather than the rule.

D. Prepare a rough outline of the following student paper. Is it hard to outline, or easy? How would you describe the overall pattern of the paper? What has the writer done to help the reader follow?

No More Favors, Please

Many times in a conversation I have heard it said that "a boss's son has it made." I doubt whether a person who makes that statement has ever worked for his father. At any rate, during the four years that I worked for my father's water softener firm, I was not treated nearly as well as were the other employees.

With them my father was generous and tolerant. They received good wages for their standard forty-hour week. And if Jerry or Fred helped to sell a new water softener to one of our customers, he was awarded a twenty-dollar commission. Whenever Jerry asked for a little time off to go fishing, my father promptly granted his request. And once Fred got two days off to take a trip to Chicago, and Dad didn't even dock his pay. If Jack and Kenny botched an installation job, my father would reprove them in a kindly tone and explain how they could have avoided the mistake. Once Kenny failed to tighten a packing nut on a valve, and the water leaked all over the customer's floor. Father sent over a man to clean up the mess and just told Kenny to be more careful next time. On another occasion Jack and Kenny dropped a softener down a customer's stairs, ruining the softener and damaging several steps. When they reported the incident to him with worried and anxious looks, Father calmed their fears and told them his insurance would cover the loss. If one of his men became involved in a dispute with a customer over a repair bill, it was his employee, and not the customer, who was always right.

But where I was concerned, my father was a closefisted and harsh employer. My weekly paycheck was an unvarying fifty dollars, whether I worked forty hours or fifty-five, and the occasional salary raises the other employees enjoyed were never extended to me. I rarely received a commission on the sales I made; my father would either say that he couldn't afford to pay me any extra just then, or else that I wasn't really entitled to the money. If I wanted to take part in some school activity or go on a beach party with some friends, my father would not only refuse to give me time off, but he would often find extra jobs that would force me to work overtime. My mistakes called forth only anger from my father, never understanding. If anything went wrong with one of the company trucks while I was driving, he always assumed I had been driving like my "hot rod friends." If a customer complained about my service or her bill, my father bawled me out for giving him and his business a bad name. Once when I forgot to reduce the water pressure in the backwash machine and caused about twenty dollars worth of mineral to be washed down the drain, he spent half an afternoon sarcastically analyzing my mistake and showing me, in minute detail, how my carelessness had "cut into the profits for the year." Insurance never covered *my* accidents; their cost was deducted from my salary, "to teach me to be more careful."

I don't know whether my father was so harsh with me because he didn't want to appear to be favoring me; but I do know that his constant criticism convinced me that the role of boss's son is a role I don't want to play for a lifetime.

THEME TOPICS 1

Thesis and Support

1. Write a paper in which you support as fully as you can *one limited statement* about one of the following areas:

   - toys as a reflection of American society

   - the role of women in current American movies

   - images of childhood in American advertising

   - the image of the Indian in American westerns

   - the treatment of conflict or violence in science fiction

   - guidance from teachers and counselors concerning jobs for girls

   - teachers' attitudes toward children from bilingual backgrounds

Process

2. Assume that your reader is a high school graduate with little detailed knowledge of science or engineering. Describe the *process* underlying one of the following: the operation of a television set, jet engine, or computer; the life cycle of a butterfly or frog; the manufacture of paper, sugar, or other product that goes through numerous stages in the production process.

3. Write *instructions* that will help your readers perform a difficult task well. Choose one requiring a skill that you have acquired but that is not generally shared. Preferably the task to be performed should require loving care: the preparation of an unusual and difficult dish; the grafting of a bush or tree; the grooming of a horse.

Classification

4. Write a paper in which you divide a *group of people* into three or four major categories. For instance, you might classify children as leaders, followers, and loners; or teachers as authoritarian, chummy, and withdrawn. Make sure to establish categories that reflect your own experience and that you can fill in with graphic detail.

5. Have you found that one of the following labels covers *different things*? Classify them, setting up several major categories and describing them as fully as you can. Choose one of the following:

- crime comics
- war movies
- commercials
- college courses
- comedians
- radicals
- fads

Comparison and Contrast

6. Compare and contrast two fairly complicated pieces of *equipment or machinery* designed for basically the same job. For instance, compare and contrast an ordinary car motor with a diesel or jet engine. Or compare and contrast two related forms of *music or dance*: the polka and the waltz, dixieland and progressive jazz, gospel and blues.

7. Compare and contrast one of the following: current men's fashions and women's fashions, old and new ways of dealing with children, behavior of boys (or girls) among themselves and in a mixed group.

8. Compare and contrast an old-fashioned city neighborhood with a Manhattanized modern city. Or compare and contrast traditional campus architecture with very modern or recent campus buildings.

Observation

CHAPTER TWO

1. **The Uses of Description**

2. **The Need for Detail**
    General and Specific
    Sensory Detail
    Relevant Detail

3. **Finding the Right Word**
    Specific Words
    Concrete Words
    Figurative Language

4. **Organizing the Descriptive Theme**
    Tracing the Pattern
    The Key Idea
    Then and Now
    The "Detail-First" Paper

1.   THE USES OF DESCRIPTION

A good writer is first of all an alert observer. Good writers have an eye for scenes, people, and events. They notice things. An ordinary tourist in the Southwest may see only a vaguely Spanish-looking building. A good observer sees the whitewashed plaster walls; the roofs of curved red tile; the palm trees in the courtyard, clipped like poodles.

Description is the record of firsthand observation. As descriptive writers, we put into words what we have seen, heard, and felt. Description can teach us to keep our writing honest by making us stay close to what we have observed. When readers get wary of just words, we can turn to them to say: "This is real. This is what was there."

Here are three major uses of effective description:

(1) *Imaginative description makes us aware of the world in which we live.* It makes us respond to the objects and scenes around us. The following piece of imaginative description helps us share in the sights and sounds of the natural world. In your own words, what does the writer make you see? What does he make you feel?

I climbed up the gully slowly, for the icy air hurt in my lungs, and all the while over my head a hawk made his sound. . . . Almost I could make out the notching of his outer primaries as he wheeled in slow spread-winged arcs above me, peering and crying. The red-tails are always leisurely, even at their killing. Sometimes—once or twice in a season—we surprise one of those slaty hawks called Cooper's in the thick pine woods on the mountain, and always they flash from sight almost before we know what they are, and there is only the harsh staccato of their cac-cac-cac! receding in the far distance. But the red-tails, seeking their meat from God, move with so slow and indolent a grace that it would not be hard to imagine it were a studied thing. With unbeating wings they sidle down the wind, and the scream wells slowly from their throats.—Alan Devoe, *Down to Earth*

(2) *Incidental description in a narrative creates an authentic setting.* It makes events seem real by providing graphic, vivid impressions of characters and scenes. Fiction, biography, and historical writing all profit from competent use of incidental description. Here are two passages that help give the reader of Ralph Ellison's *Invisible Man* the feeling of "I was there." In your own words, how would you sum up the contrast between the two settings?

We stopped before an expensive-looking building in a strange part of the city. I could see the word *Chthonian* on the storm awning stretched above the walk as I got out with the others and went swiftly toward a lobby lighted by dim bulbs set behind frosted glass, going past the uniformed doorman with an uncanny sense of familiarity; feeling now, as we entered a soundproof elevator and shot away at a mile a minute, that I had been through it all before. Then we were stopping with a gentle bounce and I was uncertain whether we had gone up or down.

I looked past their heads into a small crowded room of men and women sitting in folding chairs, to the front where a slender woman in a rusty black robe played passionate boogie-woogie on an upright piano along with a young man wearing a skull cap who struck righteous riffs from an electric guitar which was connected to an amplifier that hung from the ceiling above a gleaming white and gold pulpit.

(3) *Effective descriptive details make for graphic illustration in prose of opinion and argument.* They help a writer explain and convince by linking ideas to the world of experience. In the following paragraph, the author talks about her mother's work as a seamstress at a Ford plant. Note how weak the word *fatiguing* would be without the telling detail that follows it:

My mother works a tight eight-hour day, with half an hour for lunch; the routine is so demanding that she has nothing left for herself. As fatiguing as the job is (her index finger is swollen to more than twice its natural size from tugging on the "decking" and her eyes are similarly injured from staring eight hours a day at a moving needle) . . . yet she does all her own housework when she leaves the shop, including floor scrubbing, window washing, and other heavy duties.—Patricia Cayo Sexton, "Speaking for the Working Class Wife," *Harper's*

EXERCISES

A. Write three sentences, each a *one-sentence portrait of a different person.* Pack each sentence with specific, concrete detail. Try to make your readers see the person by the time they have finished reading each sentence. Use the following student-written sentences as models:

1. A sad little man with a scraggly beard and a shabby coat was walking along the curb, selling rooter buttons.
2. A sour middle-aged woman with frowsy hair and wearing a faded chenille bathrobe leaned out of a tenement window, wondering what was making the neighbor's dog bark.
3. A contented old man with a dirty, shabby, stained uniform was humming an old hymn as he cleaned the long red carpet that led to the office.

B. Write three sentences, each a capsule description that captures the *characteristic atmosphere of a place*—a hotel, dormitory, city hall, police headquarters, or the like. Here are possible models:

1. The doctor's office is filled with the sound of magazines being flipped through, along with sniffles and coughs.

2. The mortuary was an eerie place that was so quiet you could hear yourself breathing.
3. The dance studio represents a discipline with its polished hardwood floors and mirrors, both reflecting the graceful movements of the class.
4. The Military Park is a soup-stained hostelry, its onetime elegance worn at the cuffs, the carpets trod thin by Rotarian feet.

C. Write down half a dozen phrases that bring to mind the most characteristic *sights, sounds, and smells* of one of the following: registration day, a football game, a political rally, a rodeo, a circus, Sunday morning in church.

2. THE NEED FOR DETAIL

A good observer has an eye for striking, revealing details. Words like "interesting," "impressive," "beautiful," or "exciting" merely sum up a general impression. They do not help a reader *share* in the excitement, or become impressed in turn. The writer has to show what *made* a building impressive, or what *makes* the desert beautiful, or what *makes* a pawn shop interesting.

General and Specific

Fill in specific detail. The basic attitude of an effective writer is: "I won't just tell you about it—I'll take you there." The writer who merely gives us the "general idea" often leaves us dissatisfied. We need the specifics that make us say: "Yes—I get the picture." Make it a practice to move in for the closer look:

GENERAL IMPRESSION: Leaving the bright, burning sunlight and entering the dark, gloomy old hotel, I see a cheap, sleazy Old West flophouse decor.

A CLOSER LOOK: The gold-and-crystal chandelier that I expected to see swinging from the twenty-foot ceiling is, in reality, made from pinewood and tin cans. The carpet is a worn, cotton-braided oval. The floor surrounding it is nothing more than plain, gray, right-off-the-sidewalk concrete. The furniture in the lobby is close to what is expected at this point: old, scratchy horsehair, very uncomfortable—overstuffed couches and chairs with tacky little antimacassars covering the worst of the worn spots—all a bilious shade of purple. The front desk is a poor imitation of a step-up-and-order bar found in the saloon of a bad "B" western. All of this leads to the expectation that the clerk working the desk will have a face that hasn't been repaired since the accident, and that he will probably be forty pounds overweight and dressed to match the tacky decor.

Sensory Detail

Choose details that appeal to the reader's senses. Sensory details make writing **concrete**: They appeal to the reader's sense of sight, hearing, taste, smell, and touch. Would you agree that in each of the following pairs the concrete version helps us share in how it felt to be there?

BARE: The person walking down the path behind the house cannot help noticing the many spiders and other insects that are always present.

CONCRETE: Spiders, large black ones with red markings, stretch their webs across the path to catch the flies humming and buzzing in the afternoon sun.

BARE: Stacking hay is one of the dirtiest and most uncomfortable jobs I know.

CONCRETE: The hay is burned crisp and with every jab of the fork black dust flies out; it sticks on the wet arms and face, this sharp chaff, and under the collar it grits against raw sunburn.

BARE: I always passed the neighborhood saloon with an instinctive feeling of dislike.

CONCRETE: Through the doorway of the saloon, in the dim light, I could see people sitting around a small round table. As I stood there in the hot, humid evening, the rancid smell of smoke, liquor, and garbage turned my stomach.

Relevant Detail

Make your descriptive detail add up. Details become significant when they become part of a larger picture. Effective detail is relevant to a larger purpose. Here are the kinds of questions that can guide you in your selection of detail:

(1) *What is distinctive about what I want to describe?* Describing a Gothic cathedral, we are likely to stress the features that make it different from a Roman basilica or a Greek temple: the pointed arches, the filigreed spires, everything that makes for airiness, height, and upward thrust. Writing about modern skyscrapers, we are likely to stress what makes for their boxy, flat-topped quality; the absence of the cornices, Aztec towers, and the like, that cap similar buildings from earlier decades.

(2) *What is the overall effect I am trying to produce?* Details become relevant when they help to build up one **dominant impression**. In your own words, what is the overall effect that the italicized phrases in the following passage keep building up?

In that instant, in too short a time, one would have thought, even for the bullet to get there, *a mysterious, terrible change had come over the elephant*. He neither stirred nor fell, but every line of his body had altered. He looked suddenly *stricken, shrunken, immensely old*, as though the frightful impact of the bullet had *paralysed* him without knocking him down. At last, after what seemed a long time—it might have been five seconds, I dare say—he *sagged flabbily to his knees*. His mouth *slobbered*. An enormous *senility* seemed to have settled upon him. One could have imagined him *thousands of years old*. I fired again into the same spot. At the second shot he did not collapse but climbed *with desperate slowness* to his feet and stood *weakly* upright, with *legs sagging* and *head drooping*. I fired a third time. That was the shot that did for him. You could see the agony of it jolt his whole body and knock *the last remnant of strength* from his legs. But in falling he seemed for a moment to rise, for as his hind legs *collapsed* beneath him he seemed to tower upwards *like a huge rock toppling*, his trunk reaching skywards like a tree. He trumpeted, for the first and only time. And then down he came, his belly towards me, with a crash that seemed to shake the ground even where I lay.—George Orwell, *Shooting an Elephant and Other Essays*

(3) *What is the point I am trying to make?* As a thoughtful observer, you do not merely take in data the way a tape recorder registers sounds. You draw conclusions about what you see and hear. In the following passage about a trip to Utah, descriptive detail supports a major point:

Farther along we came to a cool moist cave beneath a great ledge of overhanging rock, like the opening of a giant clamshell. At the inmost recess, where the sloping roof came down to the dirt floor, lay a spring-fed pool, with maidenhair fern growing in the crevices above it, as it might have grown in a mist-filled mountain gorge. The contrast between the cave's microclimate and the arid heat outside underscored the obvious fact, which we sometimes forget in the East, that *water is life*.—Paul Brooks, "Canyonlands," *Atlantic*

EXERCISES

A. Study the following description of a city street. Answer the questions that follow it.

Fourteenth Street

Fourteenth Street is well into winter. Mays and Klein's are displaying heavy, overpriced woolen coats. At five o'clock the women from Con Ed, wearing their photo IDs, seem to be more interested in pulling wads of curtains and draperies off display tables than in going right home. The man with the stall off Seventh Avenue with the brown-and-white rabbit fur coats that hung there all summer is looking just a bit less unpleasant in November. The poor Puerto Rican women who shop 14th Street because it reminds them of Santurce, Puerto Rico, are sifting through racks of shabbily constructed clothing and shoes that are no bargain. Blasting out of music stores, one hears the all-pervasive Latin music. A young man

from the Partido Socialista Puertor-
riqueño hands out leaflets announcing
a demonstration to support the inclu-
sion of Puerto Rico in the United Nations' list of colonies (in several
months of walking 14th Street and its
environs, this is the first manifestation
of the Partido or Pro-Independence
movement I've seen).

Outside his building at 231 Second Avenue (14th at Second), Dr.
Massaro continues to explain that his
building, the one with the water-rotted
foundation, is still, literally, cracking
apart and nothing is being done by
either the landlord or the city, despite
the years of written complaints. The
residents of the 14th Street tenements
near the East River complain less audibly; they simply wait for the next inevitable fatal fire. . . . David, a young
man who plugs his guitar and amps
into a street light behind the Con Ed
plant in order to have a place to practice, worries quietly and good-
humoredly about the coming of the
cold weather. The two homeless
families I've seen living out of parked
cars on 13th Street, way east, and in
SoHo, move on.

If on weekdays 14th Street most
resembles Santurce, Puerto Rico
(Mira! Venta Especial!), Sunday
mornings 14th Street becomes an evo-
cation of almost any quietly stirring
city: the muted sounds of cars ac-
celerating, conversations quiet as actors whispering in the wings of a small
theater. Old women sit spread-legged

on front stoops. A little girl walks by
on her way to church, the metal taps on
her black patent-plastic shoes hitting
the sidewalk with a peculiar sharp,
light percussion that brings back
memories of other little girls walking,
dressed up, on other earlier city
sidewalks.

In front of the Salvation Army
Headquarters between the Avenue of
the Americas and Seventh Avenue
South (General William Booth's Army
of the poor directly facing the concrete
fortress of an army of the not-so-poor,
the middle-class weekend soldiers of
the National Guard), the boys from
Captain Doreen Scott's Sunday School
class are showing off, gently hammering the sides of their old yellow school
bus, bragging about the recording
studio off the Salvation Army auditorium ("Didja see it? And they got
rock concerts here . . . The Regenera-
tions . . . Ugh!"). Down the block, at
Zeus Souvlaki, a smiling man in dirty
white overalls washes the awning.

Toward noon, the long-hairs begin
to emerge from West 14th Street lofts.
The sounds of the street get louder.
Well-dressed women from Fifth Avenue apartments wheel pampered
babies over the geologic fault that runs
like a pretty metaphor beneath 14th
Street.

Fourteenth Street continues, always, to seethe with energy. It works
its way into one's consciousness like
the scratch of a street cat.—Anne
Schneider, *New York*

1. Are there any details here that make you say: "I can see it (or hear it) in front of
   me"? Are there any details here that make you say: "This I would not have
   expected"? Point out authentic details that get the reader close to "what is
   there."
2. Does any general pattern emerge from the details? Sum up in your own words
   the overall impression that emerges from this account.

B. Spend some time getting acquainted with a major downtown street, or with a neighborhood usually bypassed by suburban shoppers and commuters. Take mental or written notes. Be the *camera eye*—simply take in what is there. Write a description that is rich in authentic detail. Simply register your impressions as fully as you can—try to keep out all comment, all editorializing on your part.

C. Write three *"detail first"* sentences in which several descriptive details are funneled into a general impression. You may use the following student-written sentences as models:

1. Red, white, and blue banners; crowds of people cheering, booing; men with tired eyes, smiling and shaking hand after hand: *This is a political rally.*
2. Crowds of people, machines clanging, bells ringing, lights flashing, kids running to one then another: This is an arcade.
3. The portrait captured Lincoln's lanky ungainliness; the ill-at-ease, though re-signed, submission to the crackling stiff formal shirt; the unruly hair, resisting brush or comb—*the complete lack of pomposity in Lincoln's nature.*
4. The peeling paint, the squawking gulls, the pungent odors, the creaking sounds of the waterlogged hulls: a wharf.

D. We often use a *short* sentence to sum up. We often use a *longer*, more elaborate sentence to fill in details. Study this one-two pattern in each of the following pairs of student-written sentences. Write several similar pairs that give "the short and the long of it."

1. A crowd of people is getting ready as the bus approaches. There is some confusion as everyone tries to calculate exactly where the bus will stop so as to be the first to embark.
2. From the tops of tall buildings that block out much of the sunlight, pigeons watch the street. Occasionally, one will spring out in flight, as if pushed by one of its comrades; there is a desperate flutter of its wings as it returns to its home base.
3. A man pauses in front of half a dozen rusty old newspaper stands, debating where to drop his coins. He carefully studies each box, apparently reading each exposed page; then, fumbling, his fingers too thick to handle the coins, he finally drops them in, lifts up the cover of the box, retrieves his paper, and departs.

E. Choose three of the following. For each, write a one-sentence description stressing the *distinctive features* that would help the reader tell

- a Siamese cat from other cats;
- a trout from other fish;
- a robin from other birds;
- a mule from a horse;
- a clarinet from an oboe;
- a banjo from a guitar.

3.   FINDING THE RIGHT WORD

We cannot share what we have observed unless we can put it into words. Effective descriptive language is like a clean window, giving us a clear look at the outside world.

Specific Words

Know things by their names. Use words that are accurate, specific, informative. Instead of using *thing, gadget,* or *contraption,* use *lid, lever, valve, tube,* or *coil.* The author of the following passage was a close observer. Note how often he uses the right specific word for things, creatures, or movements. Point out as many examples as you can:

> There are hotter places than a hayfield, but I doubt if there is another place where as many things remind you of the heat. In the next field, the corn is yellow, the blades are rolled tight for lack of water. A buzzard hangs becalmed above the field; his shadow creeps along the hillside. Brown grasshoppers clatter out of the dead grass as you walk. Sometimes they fly against your face and hang clawing at an eyebrow. Swarms of gnats swirl along the ground. Yellow nit-flies sing above the lathering horses and swing down to sting them under the jaw and to make them tangle the lines and shy. (Student paper)

Note: Specific words may become too **technical** for the general reader. Briefly *explain* a technical term that the reader is not likely to know. Or *prefer* the less technical term when two words both adequately describe the same thing: *lady slipper* rather than *Cypripedium* as the name of a plant; *tree-dwelling ape* rather than *arboreal primate* to identify a kind of animal.

Concrete Words

Use words that appeal to our senses. Concrete words do not merely convey information but conjure up a picture. They call to mind sounds, textures, odors, and flavors. *Speak* is merely a convenient all-purpose term. To make us visualize an actual speaker, use a word like *chat, mumble, coo, whisper, shout, rant, quip, jeer, scold, brag, bluster, drone, stammer,* or *blurt.* A word like *mumble* makes us imagine a person actually mumbling; the word helps us see and hear.

Here are some other all-purpose words with the more concrete choices that could take their place:

GENERAL	CONCRETE
walk	stride, march, slink, trot, shuffle, drag
sit	slump, squat, lounge, hunch, crouch
take	seize, grab, pounce on, grip
cry	weep, sob, sigh, bawl
throw	hurl, pitch, toss, dump, flip

Point out concrete words in the following passage. What does each word make you *see*? What sounds do some of the words make you *hear*?

Nick laid the bottle full of jumping grasshoppers against a pine trunk. Rapidly he mixed some buckwheat flour with water and stirred it smooth, one cup of flour, one cup of water. He put a handful of coffee in the pot and dipped a lump of grease out of a can and slid it sputtering across the hot skillet. On the smoking skillet he poured smoothly the buckwheat batter. It spread like lava, the grease spitting sharply. Around the edges the buckwheat cake began to firm, then brown, then crisp. The surface was bubbling slowly to porousness. Nick pushed under the browned under surface with a fresh pine chip. He shook the skillet sideways and the cake was loose on the surface. I won't try and flop it, he thought. He slid the chip of clean wood all the way under the cake, and flopped it over onto its face. It sputtered in the pan.—Ernest Hemingway, "Big Two-Hearted River"

Figurative Language

Use figurative language to stretch the resources of language. When we do not have a specific and concrete word for something, we try to tell the reader what it is *like*. We compare the shape of a blimp to that of a huge cigar, the shape of an imported car to that of a beetle. Figurative language makes use of such similarities, exploiting them in shorthand comparisons:

• A **simile** is a compressed but still explicit comparison, introduced by *as* or *like* ("The great fantastic arch of the Delaware River bridge loomed ahead of me *like a preposterous giant's toy*").

• A **metaphor** is an implied comparison, using one thing as the equivalent of another ("The candidate *surfed* to the speaker's table on a nice *wave* of applause").

• A common kind of metaphor involves **personification**, giving human qualities to objects or ideas ("The sound of the passing cars was *a steady whisper out of the throat of the night*").

Look at the following passages. Where and how does figurative language help us see, hear, and feel?

I just saunter into the electric eye in my white shirt ironed the night before, and the door heaves itself open, and outside the sunshine is skating around on the asphalt. (John Updike)

When they are on the alert, a flock of sparrows, or pigeons, or cedar-birds, or snowbuntings, or blackbirds, will all take flight as if there was but one bird, instead of a hundred. The same impulse seizes every individual bird at the same instant, as if they were sprung by electricity. . . . A brood of young partridges in the woods will start up like an explosion, every brown particle and fragment hurled into the air at the same instant. (John Burroughs)

The whales rise and breathe all around us, sometimes just ten or fifteen feet away, making us jump and gasp. They are so close we can see their twin blowholes, like high-set nostrils, and the individual patterns of parasitic barnacles on their backs. We can hear the inhalation phase of their blow, the breathy resonance of the great lungs a little like the compressed and magnified sound of your own breath in a snorkel, with sometimes a slight whistle. (Annie Gottlieb)

EXERCISES

A. A British writer discussing the "vocabulary of the future" predicted that "man will be less in touch with the natural world" and that "as more and more land comes under cultivation, the ability to distinguish between the forms of wild life is bound to diminish and eventually die. . . . The general term *bird* will swallow the swallow, the finch, the green linnet. *Vegetation* will have to serve for most of the varieties of green life—plant and weed alike." What *names of animals and plants* do you know that the city dweller may no longer be sure of? Choose one of the following categories and explain, in one sentence each, *six* names that you consider worth preserving: birds, game, fish, trees, flowers, weeds.

B. In one sentence each, explain six *technical terms* that you would have to use in describing the characteristic features of one of the following: this year's women's fashions; one of the traditional styles of architecture (classic, Romanesque, Gothic, baroque); one of the major schools, traditional or modern, of painting.

C. Point out the uses of *figurative language* in each of the following. What does each make us see or hear? What makes each example effective?

1. There is a huge mass of rubble on one corner. Thick and heavy blocks of cement are scattered and piled in a place where a building once stood. A crane extends upward into the sky, like a giraffe reaching for green leaves on the small branches at the top of the tree. (Student paper)
2. A distant airplane, a delta wing out of a nightmare, made a gliding shadow on the creek's bottom that looked like a stingray cruising upstream. (Annie Dillard)
3. Many men can chord a guitar, but perhaps this man was a picker. There you have something—the deep chords beating, beating, while the melody runs on the strings like little footsteps. (John Steinbeck)
4. He lay down in his shirt and breeches on the bed and blew out the candle. Heat stood in the room like an enemy. (Graham Greene)

5. Cornelia's voice staggered and bumped like a cart in a bad road. (Katherine Anne Porter)

D. Study the *use of language* in the following passages. How does each author use words to make the reader see, hear, and feel? Discuss each author's use of specific words, concrete words, and figurative language. How apt, expressive, or effective is the use of words? What makes the passage unusual, striking, distinctive?

1. My car coasts to a stop on the corner, and there, glaring at me like an emaciated sentry, the parking meter stands, demanding to be fed. A haggard old man, his white hair plastered to his skull, squeaks by on his antique Schwinn, oblivious to the rain and the roaring traffic. The buildings--squat, ugly, monoto- nous--provide a dreary background as the people hurry to get out of the suddenly furious downpour. As a bus stops ahead of me on the street, a swarm of people appear as if by magic from the surrounding cover. Their quick movements signal the start of the race for the best seats. The loser is a large woman who almost misses the bus entirely. A sudden gust of wind tugs at the wires that crisscross the street and rattles the stoplight. Finally the rain drives me back to the comfort of my car, and I join the facelss flow of traffic as it rumbles down the street. (Student theme)

2. To get there you follow Highway 58, going northeast out of the city, and it is a good highway and new. Or was new, that day we went up it. You look up the highway and it is straight for miles, coming at you, with the black line down the center coming at and at you, black and slick and tarry-shining against the white of the slab, and the heat dazzles up from the white slab so that only the black line is clear, coming at you with the whine of the tires, and if you don't quit staring at that line and don't take a few deep breaths and slap yourself hard on the back of the neck you'll hypnotize yourself and you'll come to just at the moment when the right front wheel hooks over into the black dirt shoulder off the slab, and you'll try to jerk her back on but you can't because the slab is high like a curb, and maybe you'll try to reach to turn off the ignition just as she starts the dive. . . .

But if you wake up in time and don't hook your wheel off the slab, you'll go whipping on into the dazzle and now and then a car will come at you steady out of the dazzle and will pass you with a snatching sound as though God-Almighty had ripped a tin roof loose with his bare hands. Way off ahead of you, at the horizon where the cotton fields are blurred into the light, the slab will glitter and gleam like water, as though the road were flooded. You'll go whipping toward it, but it will always be ahead of you, that bright, flooded place, like a mirage.—Robert Penn Warren, *All the King's Men*

3. The stream wound its burrow into the jungle. Already they had forgotten how the mouth appeared in sunlight. Their ears were filled with the quick frenetic

rustling of insects and animals, the thin screeching rage of mosquitoes and the raucous babbling of monkeys and parakeets. They sweated terribly; although they had marched only a few hundred yards, the languid air gave them no nourishment, and black stains of moisture spread on their uniforms wherever the pack straps made contact. In the early morning, the jungle was exuding its fog drip; about their legs the waist-high mists skittered apart for the passage of their bodies, and closed again sluggishly, leisurely, like a slug revolving in its cell. For the men at the point of the column every step demanded an inordinate effort of will. They shivered with revulsion, halted often to catch their breath. The jungle dripped wetly about them everywhere; the groves of bamboo trees grew down to the river edge, their lacy delicate foliage lost in the welter of vines and trees. The brush mounted on the tree trunks, grew over their heads; the black river silt embedded itself in the roots of the bushes and between the pebbles under their feet. The water trickled over the stream bank tinkling pleasantly, but it was lost in the harsh uprooted cries of the jungle birds, the thrumming of the insects.—Norman Mailer, *The Naked and the Dead*

E. Study the way the following paragraph carries through the same figurative analogy. Then write a similar descriptive paragraph making use of such a *sustained metaphor*.

Squatting in the middle of the field, the threshing machine was a weird-looking mass of rumbling wheels, spouts, and conveyers. A metal rack with a conveyer extended from one end of the machine. Bundles of oats thrown onto this belt crept to the *mouth* of the machine and suddenly disappeared within the huge *belly* of the thresher. Inside, meshing steel separated the grain from the stalks and hulls and sent them into separate compartments. Scooping up the grain, a second conveyer belt *spewed* it from the spout in a golden stream that filled the wagon waiting below, while the straw and hulls were blown through a large funnel extending twelve to fifteen feet beyond the rear of the machine. The funnel was periodically cranked up as the straw stack was built to a conical peak. So our harvest machine *ate* its way through the morning; and at noon, when the air was suddenly still, all that remained of the field were two straw piles and a bin full of grain.

4. ORGANIZING THE DESCRIPTIVE THEME

Compared with argument or narration, description often is only *loosely* organized. Some of the best descriptive writing is found in journals, diaries, travel notes—which record the changing observations of the author from day to day. Yet even in the kind of description that offers us great variety, individual sketches and some longer passages will have the unified impact of successfully organized writing.

Here are sample patterns for short sketches and longer descriptive themes of your own:

Tracing the Pattern

Make your description trace a definite pattern in space or time. Description easily becomes too static. There are many things for readers to look at, but in the end they do not feel that they have made any headway or covered ground. Put things in motion: Give your description a definite course to follow. Trace the source of a river through a valley. Follow the course of a hike from the valley floor through the green foothills into the dry sierras. Trace a walk from the outskirts of town to a central landmark. Follow the course of a souvenir peddler through a crowded stadium.

The following paper describes the scene at a Lake Michigan beach as a drowning victim is given artificial respiration. Note how the paper moves through three plausible stages:

An Incident at the Beach

Focus on the victim	The woman looked as though she was lifeless. Appearing as though she were some form of statuary caked with wet sand, her body lay in a motionless prone position. . . .
Focus on the rescuer	A young man was desperately trying to restore her normal breathing pattern. His whole suntanned body moved rhythmically up and down in the cycle of artificial respiration. . . .
Focus on bystanders	The drowning seemed no more than an attractive diversion for many of the people on the beach. A graying middle-aged man was instructing his wife to stay and watch the food while he was taking the children "to have us a look." . . .

The Key Idea

Use a key sentence as a program for a piece of descriptive writing. This pattern applies the familiar "thesis-and-support" scheme to descriptive writing. The thesis sentence sums up the dominant impression or overall effect that the paper is trying to convey. Such a thesis sentence, stated at the end of a short introduction (or, in a short sketch, as the very first sentence) gives clear direction to the description that follows. The writer can simply ask himself: Do the details I am using *reinforce* the overall effect?

Here is the beginning of a descriptive sketch in which the initial thesis sentence sums up a *prevailing mood*:

Tropical fish create an atmosphere of peace and relaxation. It is soothing to observe some of the fish *hanging motionless* in the water, as if suspended by a fine thread, while the angler fish *glide silently* across the tank. . . .

Then and Now

Use comparison and contrast for the purposes of descriptive writing. Change is one of the most effective ways of making us take notice: the highway where we used to play in the fields; the cluttered commercial buildings where orchards used to be; the concrete office building that replaced a wooden Victorian mansion; the glass-and-steel palace that superseded the turreted old City Hall.

The following passage records the kind of experience that provides promising material for a "then-and-now" paper:

> I went down from this ancient grave place eighty or ninety rods to the site of the Van Velsor homestead, where my mother was born (1795), and where every spot had been familiar to me as a child and youth (1825–40). Then stood there a long, rambling, dark-gray, shingle-sided house, with sheds, pens, a great barn, and much open road-space. Now of all those not a vestige left; all had been pulled down, erased, and the plow and harrow passed over foundations, road-spaces and everything, for many summers; fenced in at present, and grain and clover growing like any other fine fields. Only a big hole from the cellar, with some little heaps of broken stone, green with grass and weeds, identified the place. Even the copious old brook and spring seemed to have mostly dwindled away. The whole scene, with what it aroused, memories of my young days there half a century ago, the vast kitchen and ample fireplace and the sitting-room adjoining, the plain furniture, the meals, the house full of merry people, my grandmother Amy's sweet old face in its Quaker cap, my grandfather "the Major," jovial, red, stout, with sonorous voice and characteristic physiognomy, with the actual sights themselves, made the most pronounced half-day's experience of my whole jaunt.—Walt Whitman, *Specimen Days*

The "Detail-First" Paper

Let your details build up to the main point. The "detail-first" sketch or paper turns the usual thesis-and-support pattern upside down. It first provides the related details, making them *build up* to the intended effect or key point. The key sentence, or thesis sentence, then appears at the end—after it has been earned, so to speak.

Writing with "detail first" is modeled on the actual process of observation. Authentic observation *starts* with detail and then gradually funnels it into general impressions or conclusions. Can you see the funnel effect in the following "detail-first" passages?

> When he was done shaking hands with me, the Judge smoothed back his thick, black mane, cut off square at the collar, like a senator's, put one hand in his pocket, played with the half-dozen emblems and charms on his watch chain with the other, teetered from his heels to his toes two or three times, lifted his head, smiled at me like I was the biggest pleasure he'd had in years, and drew a great,

deep breath, like he was about to start an oration. I'd seen him go through all that when all he finally said was, "How-do-you-do?" to some lady he wasn't sure he hadn't met before. *The Judge had a lot of public manner.*—Walter Van Tilburg Clark, *The Ox-Bow Incident*

Throughout the press conference, the public address system kept going off and on, with raucous squeaks of feedback anguish. A few minutes before the candidate's arrival, a hotel crew had arrived with ladders and stapling guns to fasten some bunting to the molding. Now a worker returned to retrieve a forgotten ladder. As he left, a swash of bunting collapsed like a broken wing. One of the closed-circuit TV receivers went berserk, rolling the candidate's image endlessly up and off the screen. *It was, in brief, an utterly amateur staging.*

REVIEW EXERCISE

Study the following sampling of student-written impressions of a downtown street. Point out details that might make a reader say "well observed!" or "true to life!" Point out uses of concrete or figurative language.

The Camera Eye

A young man is hurrying down the street, his umbrella clicking on the sidewalk. . . . An old lady stops to put her mantilla on before she drags herself and her grocery basket into St. Joseph's.

Massive white pillars, stained glass windows, and silver domes are what I notice first.   When I look more closely, I see that the pillars are chipped and worn and the sidewalk and steps are spattered with bird droppings and chewing gum. . . . The empty and abandoned Budget Store brings back happy childhood memories: Riding the elevators up and down and having the 66 cent special at the basement fountain when the store bore a different name and was very popular.

On the corner, there was a condemned thrift shop with a painting on the wall that had a tree on it and some writing saying, "If you love me, feed my sheep."

The owner is sweeping in front of his shop. . . . He cautiously sweeps the dirt off into the street, stroking the broom slowly along the sidewalk so he won't miss a speck of dirt.

De la Rosa market stands here, with a scent re-
sembling a mixture of baked goods, Italian sauce,
cheeses and beer. . . . Noontime, and the simulated
platters of turkey, ham, beef and sausage, along with
the neon lights, draw people into the Garden City
Hofbrau (middle-class raincoats and umbrellas only—
the moth-eaten sweaters, baggy pants, and torn shoes
migrate to Sandra's Cafe).

Further up the street, the style of the buildings changes—automatic doors activated by someone
simply stepping in front of the door. Mirrored windows reflect the landscaping across the street.

A hearse is parked in front of the church. A
few feet in front of the hearse, a telephone service
truck is parked. The manhole cover is off, and a
huge vacuum-cleaner-type hose is stretched down inside. Presently, the pallbearers emerge and file
slowly down the steps to the waiting car. Instead of
a huge crowd of mourners, only a few follow. The
policeman is waiting to escort the procession to the
cemetery. Every few seconds his radio bleeps, and
all is silent again. The two morticians stand talking together animatedly. One is standing hand in
pocket leaning against the parking meter.

Something that especially caught my eye was a
dark, spooky-looking garage of parked cars. They
were all parked in a row, with a light that swung on
a cord from the center of the ceiling. The light
reflected on every car window and gave the garage a
lonely appearance.

Some local boys lean toward me and unconvincing-
ly ask me for a cigarette, as though this was a programmed question that they ask any likely looking
person. . . . Several teenagers are hanging around
the pawn shop with their black leather jackets contemplating the knives.

THEME TOPICS 2

1. Write a paper in the form of *journal entries* or *traveler's notes*. Make the length of your notes vary from short thumbnail sketches to full paragraphs. Choose one of the following as the subject of your notes: a camp, a jail, an amusement park, a construction site, a factory. Rely on fresh, authentic observation to hold the reader's interest.

2. Write one paragraph each about two buildings representing *different styles of architecture*: a skyscraper fifty years old and one recently completed, a church in the city and one in the suburbs, the oldest and the most modern building on campus. Concentrate on *distinctive* detail.

3. What is the closest you can come to firsthand observation of a natural setting, unspoiled by human hands? Write about a stretch of beach, a lake, a mountain, a patch of forest, or the like. Draw on authentic firsthand observation. Try to trace a definite pattern in space or in time.

4. Write a paper in which you develop a *dominant impression* derived from your observation of the crowd at a bus terminal, a rock concert, a country fair, a church picnic, the scene of an accident, or a political rally. State the dominant impression in your first sentence.

5. Write a *"detail-first"* sketch of a person, a room, or a building. Select details that build up to a general effect or key point, and state the intended effect or point in your last sentence.

6. Write a *"then-and-now"* paper about a scene or a place you know well: a downtown area before and after redevelopment; a factory before and after automation; a farm, a section of town, or a waterfront that has either been upgraded or gone downhill.

7. Describe a place or a scene that turned out *differently from what you had been led to expect*: a national monument, an often-visited city, a famous site, a ghetto, a scenic wonder. Concentrate on re-creating your own authentic, firsthand impression.

8. How closely do you look at photographic records of other cultures? How well can you *reconstruct* how one of the following places looked and sounded and felt to a person living there: the Roman forum, an Indian village or city before the arrival of Columbus, a medieval town in Europe? Write as if you were a native and a contemporary recording a familiar scene.

Personal Experience

CHAPTER THREE

1. **The Uses of Autobiography**

2. **Words and Experience**
   Involving the Reader
   Being Yourself

3. **Organizing the Autobiographical Theme**
   The Incident with a Point
   The Study in Contrasts
   The Unifying Theme
   The Process of Growing Up

1. THE USES OF AUTOBIOGRAPHY

We write what we know. And only the most impersonal part of what we know is what we learn from textbooks. What we know in the most real sense of the word is what we have lived. Writing that relies on this kind of knowledge is **autobiography**. In autobiographical writing, we write from personal experience. We take stock of where we come from, what we are, and where we are going.

Autobiographical writing prepares a writer to draw on personal experience for several important purposes:

(1) *Firsthand experience makes writing real.* Much writing is unreal because it remains too impersonal. The following sentiments do not *sound* like anybody; they read like a recorded announcement from the dean's office:

> A willing mind is all the more easily trained. The student who comes to college with little or no intention of training his mind does not long remain among his newfound friends. With his failure to meet the intellectual challenge, he is asked to leave and is quickly replaced by the earnest, more conscientious newcomer.

Contrast the following autobiographical passage, which gives us a sense of real people moving onto a real campus:

> Its high, iron-runged, Gothic gate, which swung open on this day to receive the stream of cars laden with luggage, tennis rackets, phonographs, lamps, and musical instruments, was for most of us outlanders, still in our neat cloche hats and careful little traveling suits, a threshold to possibility.—Mary McCarthy, "The Vassar Girl"

(2) *Personal experience provides evidence with which to back up the writer's claims or assertions.* The most convincing answer to the question "How do you know?" is "I know *from experience*." Notice how the account of an actual incident gives substance to the following paragraph:

> A lively street always has both its users and watchers. Last year I was in the Lower East Side of Manhattan, waiting for a bus on a street full of errand goers, children playing, and loiterers on the stoops. In a minute or so a woman opened a third-floor tenement window, vigorously yoo-hooed at me, and shouted down that "The bus doesn't run here on Saturdays!" Then she directed me around the corner. This woman was one of thousands of New Yorkers who casually take care of the streets. They notice strangers. They observe everything going on. If they need to take action, whether to direct a stranger or to call the police, they do so.—Jane Jacobs, "Violence in the City Streets," *Harper's*

(3) *An account of firsthand experience has a chance of getting the reader involved.* A sociologist's analysis of hidden prejudice will leave us better informed. But it will not stir our sympathies or enlist our support as effectively as a single authentic incident from a writer's own experience:

> I and two Negro acquaintances, all of us well past thirty, and looking it, were in the bar of Chicago's O'Hare Airport several months ago, and the bartender refused to serve us, because, he said, we looked too young. It took a vast amount of patience not to strangle him, and great insistence and some luck to get the manager, who defended his bartender on the ground that he was "new" and had not yet, presumably, learned how to distinguish between a Negro boy of twenty and a Negro "boy" of thirty-seven.—James Baldwin, *The Fire Next Time*

EXERCISE

The following are brief excerpts from autobiographical passages by well-known writers. Prepare to answer questions like the following: What kind of person wrote the passage? How close do you feel to the person? Why? Is there any point where you want to say: "This is the way it is," or "This is life"? Where and why? If you were asked to read more autobiographical writing by one of these four writers, which one would you choose, and why?

1. My first notebook was a Big Five tablet, given to me by my mother with the sensible suggestion that I stop whining and learn to amuse myself by writing down my thoughts. She returned the tablet to me a few years ago; the first entry is an account of a woman who believed herself to be freezing to death in the Arctic night, only to find, when day broke, that she had stumbled onto the Sahara Desert, where she would die of the heat before lunch. I have no idea what turn of a five-year-old's mind could have prompted so insistently ironic and exotic a story, but it does reveal a certain predilection for the extreme which has dogged me into adult life.—Joan Didion, *Slouching Towards Bethlehem*

2. I had forgotten, in the rage of my growing up, how proud my father had been of me when I was little. Apparently, I had a voice and my father had liked to show me off before the members of the church. I had forgotten what he had looked like when he was pleased but now I remembered that he had always been grinning with pleasure when my solos ended. I even remembered certain expressions on his face when he teased my mother—had he loved her? I would never know. And when had it all begun to change? For now it seemed that he had not always been cruel. I remembered being taken for a haircut and scraping my knee on the footrest of the barber's chair and I remembered my father's face as he soothed my crying and applied the stinging iodine. Then I remembered our fights, fights which had been of the worst possible kind because my technique had been silence.

I remembered the one time in all our life together when we had really spoken to each other.

It was on a Sunday and it must have been shortly before I left home. We were walking, just the two of us, in our usual silence, to or from church. I was in high school and had been doing a lot of writing and I was, at about this time, the editor of the high school magazine. But I had also been a Young Minister and had been preaching from the pulpit. Lately, I had been taking fewer engagements and preached as rarely as possible. It was said in the church, quite truthfully, that I was "cooling off."

My father asked me abruptly, "You'd rather write than preach, wouldn't you?"

I was astonished at his question—because it was a real question. I answered, "Yes."

That was all we said. It was awful to remember that that was all we had *ever* said.—James Baldwin, *Notes of a Native Son*

3. We, the children who were on the receiving end, knew that our mothers' self-sacrifice existed mostly in their minds. We were constantly exhorted to be grateful for the gift of life. Next to the redemption, for which we could never hope to be sufficiently grateful, although we had no very clear idea of why we needed anyone to die for us in the first place, we had to be grateful for the gift of life. The nuns pointed out that the commandment to love our parents followed immediately upon the commandment about loving God, and because they themselves were *in loco parentis* and living solely for God and their neighbor we ought to be grateful for that too. But children are pragmatic. We could see that our mothers blackmailed us with self-sacrifice, even if we did not know whether or not they might have been great opera stars or the toasts of the town if they had not borne us. In our intractable moments we pointed out that we had not asked to be born, or even to go to an expensive school. We knew that they must have had motives of their own for what they did with and to us. The notion of our parents' self-sacrifice filled us not with gratitude, but with confusion and guilt. We wanted them to be happy yet they were sad and deprived, and it was our fault.—Germaine Greer, *The Female Eunuch*

4. Throughout my life I have longed to feel that oneness with large bodies of human beings that is experienced by the members of enthusiastic crowds. The longing has often been strong enough to lead me into self-deception. I have imagined myself in turn a Liberal, a Socialist, or a Pacifist, but I have never been any of these things, in any profound sense. Always the skeptical intellect, when I have most wished it silent, has whispered doubts to me, has cut me off from the facile enthusiasms of others, and has transported me into a desolate solitude. During the War, while I worked with Quakers, nonresisters, and Socialists, while I was willing to accept the unpopularity and the inconvenience belonging to unpopular opinions, I would tell the Quakers that I thought many wars in history had been justified, and the Socialists that I dreaded the tyranny of the State. They would look askance at me and while continuing to accept my help would feel that I was not one of them.—Bertrand Russell, *Autobiography, 1914–1944*

2. WORDS AND EXPERIENCE

Most people know us only in one of our official functions: as students, as patients, as sales clerks, as teachers. When we write about ourselves, they have a chance to come to know us as people. What does it take to make your readers feel that they are coming to know you as a person?

Involving the Reader

Give your reader a look at authentic firsthand experience. Let your readers take a look at things that actually happened. Give them a close-up view of real people. Let your readers share in what you thought and felt. Do the following to involve the reader in actual firsthand experience:

(1) *Make the reader share in the actual sights and sounds.* Study the following account of the kind of people an author remembered from his childhood. In your own words, restate what he tells us about their appearance, gestures, talk, and attitudes:

> Once there was a lot of sound in my grandmother's house, a lot of coming and going, feasting and talk. The summers there were full of excitement and reunion. The Kiowas are a summer people; they abide the cold and keep to themselves; but when the season turns and the land becomes warm and vital, they cannot hold still; an old love of going returns upon them. The aged visitors who came to my grandmother's house when I was a child were made of lean and leather, and they bore themselves upright. They wore great black hats and bright ample shirts that shook in the wind. They rubbed fat upon their hair and wound their braids with strips of colored cloth. Some of them painted their faces and carried the scars of old and cherished enmities. They were an old council of warlords, come to remind and be reminded of who they were. Their wives and daughters served them well. The women might indulge themselves; gossip was at once the mark and compensation of their servitude. They made loud and elaborate talk among themselves, full of jest and gesture, fright and false alarm. They went abroad in fringed and flowered shawls, bright beadwork, and German silver.—N. Scott Momaday, *The Way to Rainy Mountain*

(2) *Do not just talk about attitudes and feelings: act them out.* Do not just tell us about people; show us what they do and say. Study the following brief account of an autobiographical incident. What feelings play a major role in the account, and how are we made to share in them?

Going Away

It was a sunny Saturday afternoon. I had spent a nice day at the park with Robin, the little boy I had been working with for several years. Robin was seven years old, an active brown-haired, brown-eyed little boy with deep emotional problems. He had grown much over the past few years; he was finally beginning to open up and beginning to talk. He had even started showing some emotions. As I drove him home after an enjoyable but tiresome day at the park, I remembered it was only five days until I would be leaving for school. I had talked to Robin about my leaving for several months; we both knew today would be our last day together. As we drove along a narrow road, I broke the silence by saying, "I'm going to miss you, Robbie." Robin looked at me with those big brown eyes and began crying. The sobbing gave way to screaming. His feet kicked the glove compartment of my small car, and his small but sturdy fists pounded the window. I put an arm around him and tried to comfort him by telling him that I'd come back to visit. His small body became rigid; he arched his back like a cat preparing to pounce on its victim. He pulled at his hair.

I pulled to the side of the road and tried to comfort him. He fought viciously, as if I had deceived him. I repeated over and over that I would come visit him. The screaming stopped, the fighting ceased, and his body went limp from exhaustion. I gathered his body in my arms and cradled him. He let me comfort him, too upset to fight anymore.

(3) *Do justice to problems and contradictions.* Real people have failures as well as successes. They have mixed feelings and divided loyalties. If you always filter out things that are unflattering or upsetting, you will be writing about a cardboard hero rather than a real person.

What makes the following passage more frank, more real, than what other people might have told us about the same experience?

My school days were not all golden. In my senior high-school year, I became deeply unsettled, by life and literature, and came to reject the whole scheme of things, including the silly data the school had poured into me and the monster they had tried to make me—competitive, aggressive, snobbish. My family was bewildered, as was everyone else including myself, but had no way of helping as my grades dropped from all A's to failures. I've never been the same since. Though I've developed a genuine passion for learning, it has been on my own terms, and what I have learned and done has been guided almost exclusively by my own stubborn will. Naturally enough, this caused serious problems for me in school from time to time. If assignments appealed to me, I did them—if they didn't, I didn't. . . . Moreover, I never received a cent of tuition aid, being too proud, uninformed about how to do it, and uncertain about the future to apply for scholarships or even loans.—Patricia Cayo Sexton, "Speaking for the Working Class Wife," *Harper's*

Being Yourself

Try to keep words from coming between you and the reader. Ideally, writers of autobiographical material would talk to us directly and naturally about who they are and what they have experienced. But in practice people are often trying to do other things at the same time. They may want to impress us, or make themselves look good. They may be on the defensive, trying to protect themselves against criticism or ridicule.

Remember the following advice when trying to find a direct and natural style:

(1) *Avoid cant.* Modern readers are suspicious of fake enthusiasm and fashionable poses. If a person meets "wonderful" people and has a "wonderful" time everywhere, the word *wonderful* becomes meaningless. If a person always finds everything other people do "absurd," it becomes hard to tell the difference between what is sensible and what is idiotic. **Cant** keeps us from expressing our own honest feelings; it makes us substitute attitudes that are merely fashionable, or that seem expected in a given group or situation.

(2) *Steer clear of sentimentality.* Don't expect your reader to get tearful automatically over children, newlyweds, and puppies. When your subject calls for emotion, make it arise as directly as you can from the concrete situation. Look at the following autobiographical passage. What were the child's feelings? What does the writer do to make the reader *share* those feelings?

> The word was my agony. The word that for others was so effortless and so neutral, so unburdened, so simple, so exact, I had first to meditate in advance, to see if I could make it, like a plumber fitting together odd lengths and shapes of pipe. I was always preparing words I could speak, storing them away, choosing between them. And often, when the word did come from my mouth in its great and terrible birth, quailing and bleeding as if forced through a thornbush, I would not be able to look the others in the face, and would walk out in silence, the infinitely echoing silence behind my back, to say it all clearly back to myself as I walked in the streets.—Alfred Kazin, *A Walker in the City*

(3) *Do without clichés.* **Clichés** are ready-made phrases that come to us all in one piece, already glued together and ready to be pasted up with others of the same kind. People who ask us to "face reality," or not to be "a sore loser," or to look for "the silver lining" are not talking to us as individuals. They had these phrases all *made up* long before we appeared on the scene. Whenever you can, use

fresh, authentic figurative language to help you communicate your own actual feelings and attitudes.

What is fresh or different about the way the following passages express attitudes, feelings, motives? Try your hand at writing three or four similar sentences about feelings or states of mind that you have recently experienced.

> She would look for dark spots in his character and drill away at them as relentlessly as a dentist at a cavity. (Mary McCarthy)
>
> "I couldn't beat the system. . . ." He was speaking more rapidly and confidently . . . he was cutting the cloth to fit his faults, as everyone did at some time or other. (John P. Marquand)
>
> He was like a piece of rare and delicate china which was always being saved from breaking and which finally fell. (Alice Walker)

EXERCISES

A. Write a paragraph in which you recreate the most *typical atmosphere* of your early childhood. Try to make your reader see the setting and the people. Try to involve the reader in the typical sights, sounds, gestures, talk, attitudes.

B. Select a general term for a personal quality or a personal feeling. Choose a term like *apprehension, frustration, grief, rudeness, poise, shyness,* or *happiness.* Write a paragraph in which your reader can see the term acted out.

C. Study the following student-written passages. Answer these questions and defend your answers:

- Which of the passages would you consider overstated, overdone? Which would you consider understated, played down? Which would you consider just right?

- Which of the passages would you consider the most sincere? Which would you consider least sincere?

1. I heard rumors and sayings of how college life would be: the classes, the excitement, and the ideas put into your mind; the lectures, the sayings of the professor; the flunk-outs, the dropouts--all these were brought to my attention. Then my opportunity as a student and an individual in this world opened my eyes to this wondrous happening. Now I am going through the same experience that many people have gone through before. The busy halls, the walking people, the bicycle riders, the easy-goers--all play a part in college life. New ideas, a different ap-

proach, parties, and clubs--these are some of the
things that I expected. Now that I've reached the
same level of about a million more people it's up to
me to compete. Competing and communication play a
vital role in college life. To stand on his own, to
control himself, this is what makes a college student
successful.

2. We talked about racism in our class today, and
I really wish that people could speak what they
wanted to. I saw people hanging their heads and
people shaking their heads, but not many people said
what they thought. Feelings come from deep down inside, and a typical class is not close enough to
criticize this very touchy area. I could see and
feel as we were talking that everyone felt pressures
that affected what was said and felt. I don't think
anybody really revealed his real feelings of prejudice. I admire the blacks not only for what they
have gained but also for what they want to achieve.
Most of all I wish that the fear between blacks and
whites would be eliminated.

3. When a surfer looks at the sea, he feels the
power of the waves and a surge of independence over-
comes him. The surfer sees the sea as a challenge to
his surfboard, and he accepts this challenge with all
his skill, for he knows he must win or else he may
lose his game of life.

4. Then I heard people screaming that there was a
man trapped under the front tire of the other car. I
found Jack, who was completely stunned by the whole
event. He told me that he put on the brakes at the
intersection and that the brakes had failed. He just
couldn't stop the car. Within minutes the police and
ambulance arrived, and the car was tediously lifted
off the trapped, quiet man. I observed a girl sitting
in the ambulance, and I realized that she also had
been riding in the other car.

5. As I walk down the hard sidewalk, the sunlight

is behind me, and I stare blindly into my dark
shadow. A group of people pass me talking happily
among themselves. It seems as if they are in a
moving box, and I can only see the walls. I smile,
but there are no windows to see me through. A
gusty cold wind blows and has crept into my mind.
A dark concrete building looms ominously above me.
No lights, no colors, just gray unfinished concrete.
My mind is cold; I feel the hollowness, the hurt,
but cannot rid myself of these bitter feelings.

D. Study the letters written by people with personal or emotional problems in
a question-and-answer column in a newspaper or magazine. Can you generalize
about these letters—their candor, their tone? How useful or responsible is the advice these people receive?

3. ORGANIZING THE AUTOBIOGRAPHICAL THEME

Ordinary experience is miscellaneous, one thing after another.
Autobiographical writing easily becomes rambling. Try to avoid a
loose "and-then . . . and-then" sequence. Good autobiographical
writing is more than the unedited record of the past. It has a point.
Make your paper serve a unifying purpose: Use it to pinpoint a problem. Use it to trace an important contrast. Use it to chronicle an
important change in your point of view.

Here are sample patterns for a unified autobiographical theme:

The Incident with a Point

Concentrate on a single meaningful incident. For instance, focus
on an episode in which a false impression is first created and then
corrected. Or make an incident reveal a character trait you had long
suspected. The point made is most convincing when it *emerges*
naturally and vividly from incident. The basic pattern of such a
paper is "This-is-what-happened-and-this-is-what-it-means."

The more naturally the point emerges from the event, the less
likely the reader is to object to it as the tacked-on "moral of the
tale." Can you show how the student's main point emerges from the
following autobiographical sketch? (What *is* the main point?)

Enjoy

My father is a ten-gallon-hat man, big and tall. At home, when he opened a bag of potato chips, he never ate any himself; he gave them to me: This was satisfaction, knowing I was happy. My brothers and I could never enjoy ourselves enough for him. "Enjoy life while you can. Have fun," he would say. "Don't study so hard."

Sometimes I carried my books home, wearing them between my shirt and my chest, and then hid with them and some crackers in the attic next to the grayed windows with light filtering through and down upon me. The attic smelled of stale dry air. There I could lie and read.

Then my father would roar up the stairs. "Why don't you go play baseball? Enjoy yourself!"

I stood up without answering.

"Your mother said you were playing baseball, but I said I'd find you reading!"

I studied his watch.

"I worked hard, studied long hours, and got little sleep all my life. Saturday is not a day to study. Hah?"

I couldn't say anything.

"What's the matter, cat got your tongue? Don't you feel good? You want to lay down?"

"I want to go outside and enjoy myself," I finally said. Instead of taking it up or carrying it any further, he would let it drop.

My father had worked hard all his life. He never had any time to enjoy life until he was older. For these reasons he always wanted me to enjoy life.

The Study in Contrasts

Work out a major conflict or a major contrast. Much autobiographical writing attempts to come to terms with conflicting influences in the author's life. Young people are often pulled in contradictory directions by friends, parents, teachers, and their own inclinations. A well-focused paper may work out a contrast between two such conflicting forces:

- a businesslike father and a sensitive, artistic mother (or vice versa);

- the foreign customs of immigrant parents and the Americanizing influence of school;

- two teachers that strongly influenced the writer but represented strongly opposed views of life;

- a strongly religious family but friends with a different outlook.

The Unifying Theme

Trace the common thread in a series of experiences. At a given stage in our lives, a major new interest may develop; a problem may loom large. Such an interest or problem can provide the common thread for experiences dissimilar on the surface. It can thus become the focus for a paper that traces the common element in *several related incidents*.

In the following excerpt from a magazine article, can you see how the italicized passages strike the recurrent note that helps the author unify autobiographical detail?

I was a *strong patriot*, a peppy, idealistic fellow living in a walkup near Union Square. I *had hitchhiked all over America*, dragging my suitcase to forty-three states. I'd seen the Snake and the Rio Grande and San Diego and Aberdeen, Wash. In fact I'd turned down a trip to Europe in order to go out and see more. And so in the evening I often went to the Square to hear the accents of the soapbox speakers, *scanning the Kentucky and wheat-belt faces*. It seemed the whole country was represented there, old men of every occupation, scallop-boat men and soybean farmers. The Communists spoke under an equestrian statue—"under the horse's ass," as they said. Early birds saved the platform for them and they scheduled themselves: first a small, dedicated Jewish bookkeeper who spoke seriously from notes; after him, a rangy Dos Passos Communist *with Idaho still in his voice* and the vocal cords of a Wobbly organizer; . . . last, an emotive, fair-minded Russian, a family man with an earthy, demonstrative face who rode up from Delancey Street on his bicycle with a white terrier running alongside. . . .

The other speakers hadn't the training or the podium but they did their best—a prototype black nationalist, a hollering atheist, a thin Catholic proselytizer and retired businessman who lived on West 72nd Street. He tore his voice shouting at all of them. They brought up the Inquisition so many times that at last he started defending it. There were also a couple of opera singers, a vaudeville comedian, and a pacifist who knelt on the pavement after every pugnacious remark that he made. . . .

I loved Steinbeck and Dos Passos and, though my blood beat at the stories of injustice I was told, it was mainly the faces I came to see, *the map of the continent*, from the tunafish cannery where I'd worked one July to the Platte River that I'd hitchhiked along.——Edward Hoagland, "The Draft Card Gesture," *Commentary*

The Process of Growing Up

Trace one important stage in the process of growing up. As autobiographical writing becomes more ambitious, it goes beyond limited topics and begins to confront its larger underlying subject. That subject is a process of growth. We look back at what we once were and ponder what we have become. In the more serious kind of autobiographical paper, we map *one important stage in the process* of gradual change that has shaped our personality.

Read the following student paper. How would you describe the phase of growing up that this paper deals with?

A Change of Places

I lived in a neighborhood that respectable white people like to think does not exist. Ninety percent of its people were poor blacks. The rest, like me, were poor whites. I was a minority. All my friends were black, as were my enemies. I lived by their standards, and, consequently, I felt the pains of being different. Whenever we played games, my name was not Dick, but "Milky," or "Sugar," or that old standby "Whitey." If a new club was formed in the neighborhood, I was always left out because I couldn't be trusted with any secrets. If I made a new friend and he asked me to come play at his house, I had to prepare myself for that same chilling, motherly line, "You can't have any friends in, Georgie, because your father is sleeping, and you'd better come in anyway because it's time to eat." Whenever I got into a fight with another kid, I knew that there would be no help from any of my friends, because I was white and they were black, and the bonds of color were much stronger than the ties of friendship. I had to stand alone.

My soul was not that of a young child, in those days. As a matter of survival, I had encased myself in a callus of bitter acceptance. Smiles became a strange, bewildering phenomenon to the muscles of my face. The usual childhood tears were never able to find an escape route through my eyes. Crying is not allowed when one is a minority, for one doesn't show his feelings, or else his weaknesses may be exposed. And so I existed, very cold and all alone.

But my father, unlike the other fathers in that neighborhood, was able to increase his income enough to take us out and into a new environment. Left behind were those cluttered streets and crowded apartment buildings, and those cold black faces. I soon found myself in a new world, a world of front lawns, and pastel-colored toilet bowls, and two-car garages. As for the people, they were not black, as I had expected them to be, but white like me. For a while then, I was happy. But then a black family moved into our neighborhood, and they had a boy my age. He was a raisin in a sugar bowl, and he knew it. He was cold and lonely as I had been, and I remembered that awful feeling that I had left behind.

EXERCISES

A. Write an "I-was-there" paragraph about an incident that has been, or is likely to be, misrepresented or misinterpreted. For instance, write about the crucial stage of a quarrel, a classroom incident, or an accident.

B. Write a one-paragraph theme describing an incident that revealed something significant about the character of a friend or relative. Sum up the point of the episode in a key sentence placed at the end of the paragraph.

C. Read the following autobiographical paper. After you finish it, write down your candid reaction to this student's story. Later, compare your own reaction with those of your classmates.

A Lot of Growing Up to Do

Although I don't remember my childhood years, I can account for what has been told me by my parents. Since I was the youngest of my family with two older sisters, I was brought up being given everything I ever wanted. My family moved to a small three-bedroom home when I was three. Our house wasn't the quietest place to live. Of course my older sisters both teased me for as long as I can remember. But always mom and dad favored me since I was their "baby." I loved my neighborhood as the years went by until we moved about ten miles away. I was used to the old park with the big slide and the muddy baseball field. But the new home became my favorite. The outside was well kept by my dad, and the inside was kept to perfection by my mom. She always was dad's favorite housekeeper and cook. My life up until the fifth grade was what you would call normal for my age. It wasn't until March of the sixth grade that my life seemed to change abruptly.

My mom had always been sick with a heart condition since she was married. One early morning, I heard her coughing inside my parents' bedroom, so I jumped out of bed to see what the matter was. My father was leaning over my mother trying to pump her heart. I was crying and yelling at my father to call an ambulance. While we waited for one to come, I helped my mother dress. She could hardly breathe. After it had finally come, my sisters got up and asked where everyone was. I was explaining to them what happened when the phone rang. I can still remember the five words dad spoke so clearly to me: "Kathy, she didn't make it."

Facing people I knew on the streets was one of the problems I learned to face after my mother died. We all grew older, each helping around the house. When I was in the ninth grade, my oldest sister got married and moved to the East. So now I was left alone most of the time while my dad and sister worked. I had no mother to watch over me and discipline me. I knew I was still spoiled but too young to realize how much dad still treated me as the "baby." Three years later, my father remarried, marrying a young widow with three daughters and a son. My other sister at first lived with us, until she married a year later. My stepmother would not move into our house, so my dad and I had to move all our belongings to her house about two miles away. I can remember crying myself to sleep at night, thinking of the great times I had when it was just the "five of us."

My father remarried to give me a mother, someone who could bring me up as a fine young lady. I never could understand why he did except for this reason, but I didn't let it bother me as long as he was happy. This attitude towards his new marriage had changed absolutely after I had lived in the new house for a year. Having been brought up by my sister for two years, I felt as though I didn't need a mother.

My stepmother and I just didn't get along. She disliked my sisters and myself. At first my father decided to bring me up alone and have my stepmother bring up her children, but this plan didn't work for obvious reasons. You can't have a family living under two rulers. So my stepmother would restrict me in any way she could. I tried hard for years to treat her as a mother, but it was worthless. Everything I said went in one ear and out the other. She was strict with her children, whereas my father did spoil me, so that I was used to being treated leniently. I admit I had a lot of growing up to do, but it was impossible to grow up with her standing over me with evil eyes. My father tried always to make me feel better, knowing I felt uneasy living with a strange family. But it never helped ease the tension which built up inside me.

The problem was that I had already been brought up by my real mother. Then she came along and tried to change my whole way of life. I can remember one incident when we got into a big argument. She disliked my dog and made me give him away. My heart was broken for months, and I resented her for that for a long time. This is why I am away at college right now, to keep peace in my family. Right now my father is alone with their family and I keep in touch with him very often. He knows how I feel about going home, and he understands. Every time I set foot in "her" home, I get jumped on for the littlest things.

I guess to me home life wasn't the best because of my situation. The sad part is that I did grow up, but instead of getting closer to my stepmother, I grew further and further away from her. The fact is that we will never get along only because from the very beginning she resented me as a new daughter, and I resented a "new" mother. She seemed to want my father all to herself and would become very jealous to see the love I received from him.

I will always realize how much my dad loved me to do the thing he did and for my sake mostly. But why did things turn out the way they did in my home? Why did my mother have to "not make it"? Why couldn't I get along with my stepmother, or why did I have to be the "baby" all my life? These questions I may someday answer, but for now I am thankful for my dad and my sisters who love me very much and care for me. My real mother will never be forgotten, but as I continue to grow up and meet new people, I will begin to understand why things happen, and why situations like mine ever exist.

THEME TOPICS 3

1. Write an *"I-was-there" paper* to set the record straight on an event to which you were an eyewitness, or in which you were a major participant. Try not to talk *about* the event but to show how it really happened.

2. Write a paper focused on a *single incident* that taught you something about a matter that up to then you had only *heard about*: juvenile delinquency, drug use, race prejudice, poverty, crime in the streets, the authoritarian personality, intolerance, or the like. Make the point of the incident emerge clearly toward the end of the paper.

3. Work out a *comparison and contrast* between two people who strongly influenced you: parents, relatives, teachers, friends, idols. Limit yourself to a few key features and illustrate in authentic detail.

4. Have you ever felt divided loyalties? Have you ever felt caught between conflicting or opposed standards? Have you ever felt torn between advice or influences from two strongly opposed sources? Discuss the *contrast or conflict* in detail.

5. Trace *a major theme* in your upbringing or past history through several related incidents. For instance, write about a challenge or problem that has played a major role in your life. Or write about a strong interest or commitment you developed. Or write about a kind of person that you gradually came to know and understand.

6. Write a paper focused on an important *change* in your outlook—a change in attitude toward someone important in your life or toward a public figure; a changed attitude toward a group, institution, tradition, or kind of work; a basic change in your ambitions, expectations, ideals, or beliefs.

7. It has become a cliché to talk about the generation gap, with young people expected to reject the "complacent" views of their elders. In what area, or in what way, did the generation gap become most real to you, or to close friends?

8. Psychologists and counselors have been much concerned with frustration and depression experienced by young people. What has your own experience taught you about their causes and their cure?

Opinion

CHAPTER FOUR

1. **A Matter of Opinion**

2. **Opinions Worth Writing Down**
     Fact and Inference
     Identifying an Issue
     Forming an Opinion
     Changing Your Mind

3. **The Opinions of Others**
     Cross-Examining Your Witnesses
     Questioning Conventional Views
     Staying Clear of Verbal Traps

4. **Organizing the Essay of Opinion**
     Defending a Thesis
     The "Yes, But" Paper
     The Change of Mind

1. A MATTER OF OPINION

Most writing in one way or another expresses the author's opinions. It shows how people interpret what they have observed. When we read an "essay of opinion," we are aware of the *person* who is selecting data, who is appraising a situation, who is making judgments. We do not ask a person's opinion on how far it is from Philadelphia to Baltimore. For such questions, we rely for answers on records or measuring instruments that tell the same story to different observers. We do ask for people's opinions on subjects like the generation gap, abortion, hairstyles, or violence on the screen. We know that on these subjects people hold different views.

How do people form their opinions? How do they get from firsthand experience to ideas about things of general concern? Much of a person's thinking used to be shaped by tradition: Custom provided the answers to such questions as what kind of person to marry and when. The thinking of many people has always conformed to that of the group: They thought more or less what everybody else thought. Some people easily absorb the prejudices of their elders; others are easily swayed by fads or slogans.

However, writing that is worth reading does not just repeat familiar ideas—ready-made, secondhand. In an essay of opinion, there is an implied promise that the writer has something fresh to say. There is also an implied promise that the writer's ideas will not just be arbitrary. Instead, they will be anchored in some way to common experience or available evidence. In writing devoted to opinion, you want to let your readers know where you stand. But you also want them to respect and if possible share your views. To make them respect your opinion, you have to show them not only *what* you think but also *why*.

EXERCISES

A. Read the following passages. What kind of person wrote each passage? How do you know? For each passage, sketch out a *different* opinion that might be held by a person with a different point of view.

1. I can't think of a better definition of hell than to live in the inner city of some American metropolis and be forced to watch all the crime dramas on the air with their sick parade of loonies hiding in every darkened alley just outside the door waiting to maim and kill for vengeance, money, or amusement. The total effect of this season's outrageous number of crime "entertainments" cannot help leaving an overwhelming impression of fear and suspicion of others instead of a feeling of love and understanding. (Terrence O'Flaherty)

2. There is a special kind of impiety abroad, and the top of the iceberg is the religious, or more properly the antireligious, joke. A magazine, available on the newsstands, features a blasphemous, altogether vile caricature of the Incarnation by which the Christian community is guided, and inspired. I wrote once that no one should be permitted to put on a Broadway musical on the theme of Buchenwald, pointing out that to do something that insensitive at the expense of the Jewish people is to cut bonds of affection to one another in so decisive a way as to make us strangers to ourselves. (William F. Buckley, Jr.)

3. In sports the end in view is not success independent of physical equipment; it is rather the attainment of perfection within the limitations of each physical type. The featherweight boxing champion is as much of a champion as is the heavyweight. The woman skiing champion is not the inferior of the faster male champion; they belong to two different classes. It is precisely the female athletes who, being positively interested in their own game, feel themselves least handicapped in comparison with the male. (Simone de Beauvoir)

4. A controversial columnist for *The Washington Post* has been making a great stink about the function of the Center, which he maintains is to entertain an elite minority. The management is responding by booking some jazz groups and enough black artists to make the place look integrated. From the initial list, it is clear that they don't want to attract the kind of a rock audience that just might tear the place apart. This is temporizing. Opera, ballet, symphony concerts and repertory recitals do appeal to a limited audience, and the overwhelming preponderance of the people who attend and perform in them are whites of the middle and upper classes. (A music critic)

B. Write a paragraph in which you take a definite stand. Start your paragraph with a statement like the following: "I believe in _____ because _____ " or "I object to_____ because _____. In the first blank in the sentence, fill in one of the following topics:

- large families
- stronger support for the U.S. military
- stricter speed limits
- rent controls
- religion in the schools
- health foods
- financial aid to minority students
- more financial support for women's sports

Use the rest of your paragraph to present your most important reason or reasons.

2.   OPINIONS WORTH WRITING DOWN

What does it take to make a reader take your opinions seriously? When you ask for someone's serious attention, the opinion you offer should be your *considered* opinion. It should show that you have wrestled with the subject and, if necessary, changed your mind. It should show that you have considered objections and made the necessary adjustments in your own position. The kind of writing that will make a reader think is the end result of a process. Opinions worth listening to are the result of exploration and discovery. Writing an essay of opinion gives us a chance to make up our minds.

Fact and Inference

Distinguish between observable facts and the conclusions you draw from them. Ideally, a fact is something we can verify by direct observation or measurement. We can see a car in a ditch; we can measure skid marks; we can take an injured passenger's pulse. The more factual a police report is, the more it stresses exact time and location; the exact extent of damage done to the car; the observable condition of the victim. When we conclude that there has been an accident, we take a large step away from fact to **inference**. We infer something we have not actually observed. To help support our inference, we would probably look for the testimony of eyewitnesses who actually saw a car spin around, or the like.

The closer they stay to the facts, the better the chance that two competent observers will bring back the same data. We would be surprised if two police officers disagreed violently on the length of the skid marks. But we are not surprised when we hear two different *interpretations* of the same facts. Even though our inference about an accident stayed close to the facts, an insurance adjuster might investigate the chance that the accident was staged to defraud his company.

The farther our inferences move beyond direct observation, the more chances there are for them to differ from those of others. If we were to take a sampling of opinion from motorists who stopped at the scene of the accident, we would encounter many inferences that come close to merely being *one person's view*:

- The type of car involved in the accident is unsafe.
- People in the age group of the victim tend to be careless drivers.
- Speed limits in this state are too high.
- The driver was probably drunk.

The opinions you present to your reader will be inferences, resting on a more or less factual foundation. Your most basic task is to reassure your readers that the superstructure of inference that you are erecting is founded in observations that they themselves could share or verify. To make the reader respect your opinion, observe the following advice:

(1) *Keep your inferences close to the facts you present.* The more freely you editorialize, the more difficult you make your basic task: to give solid substance to one major point at a time. In each of the following pairs, both passages offer an interpretation of available facts. But the first version goes too far too fast. The second version has a better chance of carrying the reader along:

DEBATABLE: The voters of the fifth district expressed their resentment of Republican policies by sending a Democrat to Washington.

MORE FACTUAL: Though voter registration in the fifth district is 58 percent Republican, a majority of the voters voted for a Democratic candidate. The results show a sizable crossover to the Democratic side by normally Republican voters.

DEBATABLE: Without provocation, the police attacked the demonstrators, beating boys and girls alike.

MORE FACTUAL: After a plate glass window was broken, the police moved in to disperse the demonstrators. In the ensuing melee, a dozen students were injured. Three boys and two girls were treated at the Student Health Service for cuts and bruises.

(2) *Be content to leave moot points unresolved.* Often, an issue is too large, the facts too contradictory, for us to form a sound opinion. We may have hunches or preferences, but we do not expect the reader to accept these on our mere say-so. Opinionated people can be recognized by the firm stand they take on such debatable subjects. Here are some subjects on which a writer with a respect for facts hesitates to make emphatic pronouncements:

• What are the results of *permissiveness* in child rearing? Does it make children on the whole more natural, well-adjusted people? Or does it spoil children, making it impossible for them to accept or respect authority?

• What is the long-range effect of constant exposure to *violence through the mass media*? Does it provide a healthy outlet, or is it an incitement to imitation?

(3) *Consider every statement of opinion as a promise to the reader.* Much factual information is complete in its own terms: "It is now six

o'clock." The response, if any, is simply "Correct." But a statement of opinion is a different matter: "It is too late for college freshmen to start learning a foreign language." The predictable response is: "What makes you think so?" The mere statement is an implied promise to supply the data, the facts, the arguments that would make the reader think so too.

Identifying an Issue

Identify an issue open enough to allow for differences of opinion and limited enough to be explored in a short paper. Your first task in writing an essay of opinion is to raise a question that will make the reader want to know your answer. Even when you are writing on an assigned topic, it will be part of your job to identify, within the general area suggested by the topic, an issue that will arouse and focus the reader's attention.

What, for instance, are issues on your own campus? You might find some of the following by reading the student newspaper or listening to a campus debate: Does a college administration have a right to regulate where and how students live? Does a student health service have the right to refuse services on moral grounds? Should colleges abolish failing grades? Should there be special courses for minority students—and if so, what kind? Is athletic competition between schools an anachronism?

Here is an outline for an essay of opinion dealing with one of these issues:

THESIS: Athletics deserves a place in American higher education.
SUPPORT: I. Even in the so-called "spectator sports," athletes set a standard of *physical fitness* that serves as a model to others.
              I. Though too much lip service has been paid to "character building" through sports, athletics *does* build qualities like *determination and perseverance*.
            III. Colleges help train athletes that greatly enhance the *prestige of our country* in international competition.

This outline reveals several qualities that make an essay of opinion worth writing:

• *The thesis has been, or is likely to be, contested.* Teachers and students who equate "academic" with "intellectual" have strongly attacked collegiate athletics as a sideshow distracting from the true purposes of higher education.

• *Something is at stake.* A threatened de-emphasis on athletics jeopardizes jobs, scholarships, career opportunities for the future, as well as alumni loyalty to their alma mater.

• *The issue can be argued in relatively objective terms.* The paper can be based on something more solid than "I happen to like it" or "I happen to think this is true." The writer can appeal to the reader's own observation of possible alternatives and results.

Forming an Opinion

Let your opinion take shape in the process of gathering and organizing your material. Ideally, an opinion is the result of a process of investigation. Rather than find facts to fit a preconceived opinion, we develop an opinion to fit the facts we have found. Thus, most of what makes a paper substantial takes place *before* we actually start writing. Ideally, when asked for an opinion on a key issue, we would say: "I don't know, but I am willing to *find out.*"

Suppose you want to cut through familiar clichés and stereotypes to form your own opinion concerning race relations in this country. You decide to investigate the experiences and attitudes of students of your own generation. The following is the result of a week's interviewing you have done of students on your own campus. On the basis of this limited sample, what tentative opinions would you form concerning the present state of race relations in America? What does the future hold? (Compare your conclusions with those reached by your classmates. Can you reach any kind of consensus?)

1. Prejudice and discrimination seem to be slowly fading out of our society. On radio and television, there are many shows with members of minorities in them. In department store catalogues, models are usually white, black, and Asian. There are more blacks in college now than there were ten years ago. There are also more black teachers. In sports, there never were black coaches or managers before. But some years ago, the first black manager in baseball was named by the Cleveland Indians. Black coaches made their appearance in pro basketball. People seem to keep their prejudices inside themselves more these days. We don't see prejudice out in the open anymore.

2. Discrimination toward Asian-Americans today is usually so unobvious that people of Asian ancestry may not be able to recognize the prejudices against them. I, personally, am very sensitive to verbal reactions. There is always the question, "What are you?" The mere fact of being questioned makes me stiffen with resentment at the ignorance of those who

felt that they had to ask. There have been times
when I have been completely at a loss for words on
how to reply. I could answer, "American," "Japanese," and "Japanese-American," but somehow I feel
unnatural and placed in an awkward situation. I do
not consider myself totally American, because of obvious visible differences, nor do I think of myself
as Japanese, since I was not brought up with the
strict traditions and culture. Being thought of as
a member of a minority makes me slightly uncomfortable, and responding to that question has made me
sometimes regret my existence. I am a person, just
like everyone else. I want to be considered an
American living in America, but there is always
present my Asian past. I'm very proud of my ancestors' traditions and culture. My ancestors have
struggled hard to become Americanized. During World
War II, when they were placed in relocation camps,
they tried hard to prove that they were Americans.
When they finally won the battle for their identity,
some of the discrimination against them was removed.
They have kept the Japanese language and ceremonies
in their lives, and this has made my search for an
American identity a difficult struggle.

3. Every black person learns to steel himself for when he finds racial prejudice. As soon as he forgets, something like this happens: When I went to a big
department store to buy something really slick with the accumulated loot from my
birthday and a month of baby-sitting, a lady about sixty years old would not ring up
on the register the items I wanted to buy until all the other people were taken care
of. At first I didn't realize what she was doing until she snatched my things, rang
them up, and wadded them in a bag. Then she abruptly turned away.

4. Why is there this negative attitude toward people and things? When I was a small child, every
stranger that came up to me I would shy away from.
This reaction is really never outgrown. When one
gets right down to it, it is basically a fear inside
me. When I see a group of black students in my dorm,
my first reaction is to get away as fast as possible
or else they might say or do something to hurt me. I
also noticed the hostile attitude shown toward me by
the black girls in my dorm.

5. I heard a valedictorian give her speech on how equal and fair our peaceful town was. She was almost laughed off the podium. In the graduation exercise, we are allowed to sit by our friends and, in general, pretty much where we wanted. Why then did the black kids sit in the last three rows and the Mexican-Americans in little clusters here and there? And the parents were in the same situation in the audience. Sure, some blacks were congratulated by important white citizens— those that were outstanding in football and basketball were "good luck" graduates, but what about those that strove for high academic standing? Who were they? This made me think of my relations with my black friends. Lucy was a songleader and captain of our girls' basketball team. We sat near each other in English. If we were talking while the teacher was, and got caught, I would get the reprimand. After the third or fourth time (we liked to talk), Lucy began to notice it too. The teacher was trying to be so fair that the black kids in our class were never wrong.

Changing Your Mind

Change your mind in the light of new evidence. In practice, we seldom approach a subject with a completely open mind. Often we bring to it opinions based on hearsay or previous experience. Even when we treat the subject as an open question, we will soon form first guesses and tentative hypotheses. The test of open-mindedness is our willingness to *modify* first impressions as it becomes necessary.

Here are some examples of the kind of change of mind that is necessary for the development of opinions worth paying attention to:

PREVIOUS OPINION: People on welfare are loafers who prefer the easy money of welfare to honest hard work.

RESULTS OF INQUIRY: Of the about eight million on relief, more than two million, mostly women, are 65 or over; more than 700,000 are totally blind or disabled; almost four million are children whose parents cannot support them; about one million are their mothers; about 100,000 are their physically or mentally incapacitated fathers. Less than 100,000 are "able-bodied men."

ADJUSTED OPINION: The great majority of those on relief are either too young, too old, too sick, or too disabled to be self-supporting.

PREVIOUS OPINION: In a capitalistic society like ours, economic power is in the hands of a few individuals of great wealth.

RESULTS OF INQUIRY: Few large corporations are now run by their owners; those like Du Pont, where, for many generations, a talented family has had a decisive influence on the enterprise it owns, are becoming a rarity. Typically the power lies with the professional managers. These make elaborate obeisance to the stockholders. But they select the Board of Directors, which the stockholders then dutifully elect, and in equally solemn ritual the Board then selects the management that selected it. In some cases, for example the Standard Oil Company of New Jersey, once dominated by the first Rockefeller, the Board consists exclusively of managers selected by the managers who were selected by the Board. . . .

Some of the worst cases of corporate misfortune in recent times have been those in which the owners of the capital have managed to use their power to keep the professionals out. In the thirties and early forties the elder Henry Ford used his power as the sole owner of the Ford Motor Company to remain in command. It is now freely acknowledged that the company suffered severely as a result. Following his death the management was professionalized and much improved. The great merchandising house of Montgomery Ward under Sewell Avery provided a parallel example.—John Kenneth Galbraith, *The Liberal Hour*

ADJUSTED OPINION: Much of the effective economic power in our society is exercised not by stockholders but by a professional class of salaried managers serving as executives of large corporations.

When you find yourself changing your opinion, you are learning something about your subject. Far from destroying their confidence in your judgment as a writer, evidence of open-mindedness reassures your readers that you are using your mind.

EXERCISES

A. We are often told that today's students are apathetic about the political and social issues of our time. How true is this charge? Identify three major issues that you think people of your generation care about. Rank them in order of importance: What is the Number One issue for people of your age today? What is next in importance? In a few sentences each, explain what is involved or what is at stake. (Your instructor may ask you to write a paper presenting your position on one of these issues.)

B. An American college president said recently: "This is a time of single-issue politics. . . . The growing tendency of voters to judge a candidate on the basis of his or her position on only one issue—be it abortion, tax reform, or capital punishment—threatens representative government and typifies the danger an ill-educated electorate poses in times of stress." (Adele Simmons, "Harvard Flunks the Test," *Harper's*) What, in your own words, is the problem that concerned this writer? Have you seen evidence that it exists? How serious is it?

C. Read the following statements on the status of women in contemporary society. What are the opinions of each writer? How are they founded or on what are they based? How do they compare with your opinions on the same subject?

1. Not all the skills that are necessary for learning mathematics are learned in school. Measuring, computing, and manipulating objects that have dimensions and

dynamic properties of their own are part of the everyday life of children. Children who miss out on these experiences may not be well primed for math in school.

Feminists have complained for a long time that playing with dolls is one way of convincing impressionable little girls that they may only be mothers or housewives—or, as in the case of the Barbie doll, "pinup girls"—when they grow up. But doll-playing may have even more serious consequences for little girls than that. Do girls find out about gravity and distance and shapes and sizes playing with dolls? Probably not.

A curious boy, if his parents are tolerant, will have taken apart a number of household and play objects by the time he is ten, and, if his parents are lucky, he may even have put them back together again. In all of this he is learning things that will be useful in physics and math. Taking parts out that have to go back in requires some examination of form. Building something that stays up or at least stays put for some time involves working with structure.

Sports is another source of math-related concepts for children which tends to favor boys. Getting to first base on a not very well hit grounder is a lesson in time, speed, and distance. Intercepting a football thrown through the air requires some rapid intuitive eye calculations based on the ball's direction, speed, and trajectory. Since physics is partly concerned with velocities, trajectories, and collisions of objects, much of the math taught to prepare a student for physics deals with relationships and formulas that can be used to express motion and acceleration.—Sheila Tobias, "Who's Afraid of Math, and Why?" *Atlantic*

2. The police department usually does not like to answer calls for "domestic problems." They do not feel that such a minor thing as a husband beating his wife is worth taking any risks for. When I talked with several police officers regarding this subject, they smirked and replied, "If a husband is beating his wife then she probably deserved it." When a battered wife is admitted to a hospital, her physical condition can be attended to, but nothing is done about her emotional problem. After treatment she either has to return to her husband or take refuge at a center for battered women. These centers are usually overcrowded and are temporary as there is not enough public funding. She can file for a divorce or bring charges against her husband, but the case may not come to court for three or four months or even longer. In the meantime she is subjected to her husband's abuse. The majority of women do not file charges against their husbands because of their economic dependence; they often do not know any other way to live. Often the woman is more afraid of being on her own than she is of her husband. The Housing Authority reports that many landlords will not rent an apartment to a woman with children and no husband. In talking to several battered wives, I was told their husbands usually apologize and justify their actions by saying they have quite a bit of pressure, such as the fear of losing their jobs, and the worry of not being able to pay the bills and support their families. Their wives usually accept these reasons. (Student theme)

3. I think all single women should learn self-defense. I hold a purple belt in karate, which I got after I was sexually abused by four boys while teaching in Harlem. When a situation in a city gets to the place where police cannot or will not do their jobs, and the judges permit the scum of the earth to walk the streets, then one has to take one's defense in her own hands, just like in the Old West. (Interview)

D. In recent years, the relationship between the police and the community has often been an emotion-charged and politically explosive issue. Suppose you have been appointed to a citizens' commission charged with making recommendations for improved relations in this area. As a first step, you have been asked to do an honest accounting of the personal experiences and observations that have helped shape your own opinions on the subject. Concentrate on major experiences or incidents. Be as *honest and objective* as you can. If you have been strongly influenced by reports in the media, try to make allowance for any bias or distortion; concentrate on the *factual* content of the reports. (Be prepared to compare your account with similar accounts prepared by your classmates.)

E. A prominent speaker at a convention of professional journalists said that "to the true newsman, partisanship is the original sin":

It is this striving for objectivity that places the journalist apart from society today; it is this struggle for objectivity that keeps him awake at night as he wrestles with the facts; . . . a journalist deals in facts, and they continually come back to haunt him—because facts are often contradictory.

Examine the *news reports* in several recent issues of a major newspaper. Can you cite specific examples of respect for "contradictory" facts? Can you cite facts that a partisan spokesman might have refused to recognize?

F. Study the proportion of *fact and inference* in a series of *columns or editorials* in a major newspaper. Are the facts to which editorial opinion is anchored kept clearly in view? Would you call the editors opinionated or open-minded? Use specific evidence to support your conclusions.

3.   THE OPINIONS OF OTHERS

We do not form our opinions in a vacuum. When trying to make up our own minds, we constantly have to come to terms with the opinions of others. On many subjects, we merely adopt, or adapt, the opinion of parents, teachers, or friends. We find ourselves echoing opinions that we have not examined. If we want to know our own minds, we have to become critical of opinions that are the result of mere hearsay or mere tradition.

Cross-Examining Your Witnesses

Sift the testimony of authorities. Alert readers do not believe everything they are told, but neither are they cynical about everything they see in print. The following pointers will help you to profit from *authoritative* opinion:

• Discount the testimony of *interested parties*. If a coach talks about the character-building virtues of football, we do not expect an objective study of the actual moral growth of the players. When writing about alcoholism in your home town, you will be as skeptical of material put out by the whisky companies as of pamphlets distributed by the Women's Temperance Society.

• Guard against excessive reliance on any *single source*. When you try to form an opinion about teachers' salaries, pay attention to the arguments of teachers, administrators, government officials, and taxpayers alike. Even when you can draw on the impartial outside expert, compare the views of another expert equally competent. This way you will become alert to contradictions that result from professional rivalries or doctrinaire attachment to theory. You can identify the areas on which there is solid agreement.

• Try to identify the *factual basis* for judgments and projections. Look for hard facts and figures:

> Attorneys have 4.5 percent less income now than ten years ago, professors have 13.8 percent less, and civil servants 1.8 percent less. However, truck drivers earned 17.3 percent more in terms of real income, automobile mechanics 16 percent, and maintenance machinists 13.1 percent. "While a truck driver once averaged only 52 percent of the income of a lawyer, today he averages 63 percent," according to the report of the Labor, Employment, and Consumer Affairs Committee.

Questioning Conventional Views

Question opinions that seem to be everybody's and nobody's at the same time. In examining our opinions we often come up against ideas with obscure credentials. The more uncertain their origin, the more thoroughly we need to investigate them before we make them our own. Examine your writing especially for the following:

Stereotypes   Stereotypes provide us with prepackaged attitudes toward a whole group of people or things. Familiar stereotypes are the bungling bureaucrat, the ivory-tower intellectual, the money-grubbing businessman, the corrupt politician. A familiar stereotype in American political journalism is the windbag member of Congress—"illiterate hacks whose fancy vests are spotted with gravy, and whose speeches, hypocritical, unctuous, and slovenly, are spotted also with the gravy of political patronage." (Mary McCarthy)

The unfairness of stereotypes is obvious to the person at the receiving end: the American who hears his European visitor hold forth on the superficial smiles of Americans; the woman who hears a junior executive hold forth on the emotional instability of women employees. A fair writer tests stereotypes and revises them as necessary:

It was the habit of proponents for the repeal of the Eighteenth Amendment during the 1920s to dub Prohibitionists "Puritans," and cartoonists made the nation familiar with an image of the Puritan: a gaunt, lank-haired killjoy, wearing a black steeple hat and compounding for sins he was inclined to by damning those to which he had no mind. Yet any acquaintance with the Puritans of the seventeenth century will reveal at once, not only that they did not wear such hats, but also that they attired themselves in all the hues of the rainbow, and furthermore that in their daily life they imbibed what seem to us prodigious quantities of alcoholic beverages, with never the slightest inkling that they were doing anything sinful. True, they opposed drinking to excess, and ministers preached lengthy sermons condemning intoxication, but at such pious ceremonies as the ordination of new ministers the bill for rum, wine, and beer consumed by the congregation was often staggering.—Perry Miller and Thomas Johnson, *The Puritans*

Prejudice Prejudices are hostile preconceptions, usually widely shared, and sometimes handed on from generation to generation. Prejudice makes a stereotype the basis for systematic exclusion or discrimination. Prejudice enables people to feel superior to others who may be, and often are, their moral and intellectual betters. Negative judgments on representatives of a faith, race, or nationality easily seem to proceed from prejudice.

Staying Clear of Verbal Traps

Keep ready-made phrases from channeling your thinking. On most subjects we write about, we encounter convenient verbal formulas that sum up a key idea. But such phrases often commit us to more than we are ready for. They often say more than our own exploration of the matter warrants. They often carry with them a set of built-in attitudes—and keep us from developing our own.

Check your writing for ready-made formulas:

Pregummed Labels Be wary of repeating formulas that are becoming catchwords—suggesting a definite point of view that may or may not be the same as yours. Would you agree that each of the following labels carries with it its own set of ready-made attitudes? Can you spell these out?

law and order
crime in the streets
centralized federal bureaucracy
white power structure
fiscal responsibility
law-abiding citizen

alien ideologies
hard-core pornography
senseless violence
credibility gap
police brutality

Slogans   A powerful slogan brings an important idea into clear focus. Often a slogan expresses effectively what we may have only vaguely felt: "Less is more," "Small is beautiful." Decades later, American schools still show the impact of the slogans of progressive education: "Learn by doing," "Teach the whole child," "Teach children, not subjects." Though such slogans can help break down fossilized systems of ideas, they in turn set our thinking in a new mold. They are a great comfort to one-track minds. Many familiar slogans are devices for *warding off* new ideas: "You can't change human nature," "The mind is not a muscle," "Peace with honor."

EXERCISES

A. Find three recent magazine articles that reassess the role of one of the following: President Kennedy, President Truman, President Johnson, President Nixon. From each article, copy a central paragraph or two that seems to sum up the author's opinion of the president. What differences are there in the authors' estimates of the man? How do you explain them? Which author's judgment are you most inclined to trust? Why?

B. What do the authors of the following passages do to attack or modify *stereotypes*? How familiar, how strong, or how current are the stereotypes involved?

1. "This-here is a internal combustion engine," Joe said. Lee said quietly, "So young to be so erudite." The boy swung around toward him, scowling. "What did you say?" he demanded, and he asked Adam, "What did the Chink say?"

Lee spread his hands and smiled blandly. "Say velly smaht fella," he observed quietly. "Mebbe go college. Velly wise."—John Steinbeck, *East of Eden*

2. What is imputed to Americans is an abject dependence on material possessions, an image of happiness as packaged by the manufacturer, content in a can. This view of American life is strongly urged by advertising agencies. We know the "others," of course, because we meet them every week in full force in *The New Yorker* or the *Saturday Evening Post*, those brightly colored families of dedicated consumers, waiting in unison on the porch for the dealer to deliver the new car, gobbling the new cereal ("Gee, Mom, is it good for you too?"), lining up to bank their paychecks, or fearfully anticipating the industrial accident and the insurance check that will "compensate" for it. We meet them also, more troll-like underground, in the subway placards, in the ferociously complacent One-A-Day family, and we hear their courtiers sing to them on the radio of Ivory or Supersuds. The thing, however, that repels us in these advertisements is their naïve falsity to life. Who are these advertising men kidding, besides the European tourist? Between the tired, sad, gentle faces of the subway riders and the grinning Holy Families of the Ad-Mass, there exists no possibility of even a wishful identification. . . . It is true that America produces and consumes more cars, soap, and bathtubs than any other nation, but we live among these objects rather than by them. Americans build skyscrapers; Le Corbusier worships them. Ehrenburg, our Soviet critic, fell in love

with the Check-O-Mat in American railway stations, writing home paragraphs of song to this gadget—while deploring American materialism. When an American heiress wants to buy a man, she at once crosses the Atlantic. The only really materialistic people I have ever met have been Europeans.—Mary McCarthy, "America the Beautiful," *Commentary*

3. The white policeman standing on a Harlem street corner finds himself at the very center of the revolution now occurring in the world. He is not prepared for it—naturally, nobody is—and, what is possibly much more to the point, he is exposed, as few white people are, to the anguish of the black people around him. Even if he is gifted with the merest mustard grain of imagination, something must seep in. He cannot avoid observing that some of the children, in spite of their color, remind him of children he has known and loved, perhaps even of his own children. He knows that he certainly does not want *his* children living this way. He can retreat from his uneasiness in only one direction: into a callousness which very shortly becomes second nature. He becomes more callous, the population becomes more hostile, the situation grows more tense, and the police force is increased. One day, to everyone's astonishment, someone drops a match in the powder keg and everything blows up. (James Baldwin)

C. *Prejudice* is easy to denounce but hard to fight. Read the following account of fruit workers, written by a farmer's daughter. Is there any way of affecting the writer's prejudices? Write a letter in which you try.

Caring for fruit trees and harvesting the crops at times requires the help of many men. I have worked alongside drunkards, prostitutes, and men literally from skid row. These people are generally the epitome of laziness, foul language, and deceit. I have frequently found fruit boxes with leaves or dirt filled in to provide a cushion for the few peaches on top. I have seen workers gather discarded fruit from the ground, or even cheat among themselves by claiming another's stock. The area in which the fruit workers live is typically rundown, dirty and depressing. These people don't care; it is the way they were brought up, and for most of them, this is the way they will live until they die. I knew families on welfare who worked harvesting crops during the summer and spent the time drinking during the winter. The more kids they produce, the more money flows in for cars, color TV, and drinks. What an easy life!

D. Prepare a report in which you examine the *verbal formulas* of one: (1) environmentalists; (2) women's liberation; (3) left-wing campus politics; (4) chamber of commerce promotion; (5) an aggressive labor union. Look for promising material in published speeches or debates, editorials, pamphlets, leaflets, letters to the editor, and the like.

4. ORGANIZING THE ESSAY OF OPINION

Writing an essay of opinion breaks up into two major (though overlapping) stages: working out the matter to the writer's own satisfaction, and then presenting the results effectively to the reader.

Here are strategies of organization that will help you present your opinions effectively to your reader:

Defending a Thesis

To make your point as clear and emphatic as possible, state your thesis early and devote the rest of the paper to defending it. The essay of opinion presents the most typical opportunities for the **thesis-and-support** paper. (See also Chapter One.) Such a paper from the beginning clearly focuses the writer's and the reader's attention on the point at issue. The reader is protected against a rambling "some-thoughts-I-want-to-share-with-you" approach.

In writing this kind of paper, you would typically present your opinion as the central idea at the end of a short introduction. You would then support it by devoting the rest of the paper to one or more of the following:

- several detailed *examples* (or sometimes *one* key example examined at length);
- one or more *case histories*;
- *precedents* offering convincing parallels to the current situation;
- the probable *consequences* or benefits;
- the testimony of *experts*.

Here are some opinions, staying close to the student's own experience, that might provide the unifying thesis to be defended in a "thesis-and-support" paper:

Living in a fraternity and pursuing a highly competitive field of study are rapidly becoming mutually exclusive.

For the children of recent immigrants from rural Mexico, the transition to the Anglo school causes difficulties that most teachers neither understand nor know how to handle.

A job gives a married woman something to talk about and someone to talk to; it gives her life a focused interest and an organized purpose.

Here is a possible scheme for a paper supporting such a thesis:

THESIS: The prestige of sororities is declining on today's campuses.
  I. Declining number of rushees
 II. Declining amount of space given to sororities in campus newspapers
III. Adverse comments by student leaders

The "Yes, But" Paper

To establish common ground, present but then modify a generally accepted opinion. The "yes, but" paper shows a decent respect for the opinions of others. It reassures the readers that they are not going to be frontally assaulted. At the same time, it involves both writer and reader in the kind of process by which opinions are actually formed.

Here is a possible outline for a magazine article using the "yes, but" pattern:

I. COMMON VIEW: Much of the American press is owned by conservative Republicans, biased against the liberal or progressive elements in American politics. (References to several famous presslords are offered in support.)

II. COMPLICATIONS: Reporters and editors often seem to be people of liberal sympathies. For example,
  A. Republican presidential candidates have at times bitterly complained about hostile treatment by reporters.
  B. Southern conservatives often attack the "left-wing" press.
  C. Initial press coverage of revolutionary movements (for instance, Castro) has often been sympathetic.

III. ADJUSTED VIEW: Like other American institutions, the American press functions as the result of compromise between conflicting interests and opposing views.

The "yes, but" approach is ideal for correcting stereotypes, for enlarging the reader's horizons. By agreeing with the probable views of your readers at the start, you keep them from erecting their defenses. Putting them in an assenting mood, you have a chance of making them receptive to the different or the new.

The Change of Mind

Make your statement of opinion dramatic rather than static by tracing an important change in your views. Ideas come to life when the author is seen as someone searching for truth. A writer with unpopular views may gain a sympathetic hearing by an honest account of earlier assumptions and later changes in outlook.

Here is a possible outline for a paper tracing an important change of mind:

I. EARLIER VIEW: Coming from a conservative business family, I used to be convinced that big government more and more determines the course of the individual's life.

II. CONTRARY EVIDENCE:
    A. Acquaintance with local politics has convinced me of the power of big private organizations—unions, chambers of commerce, the AMA—to bring about or to block change.
    B. Working with members of minority groups has made me familiar with some of the set social patterns and attitudes hard for any government to change.
    C. Service in the army and study at a big university have shown me the force of mere custom and tradition.
III. NEW VIEW: Government is often helpless in trying to change the patterns that determine our lives.

REVIEW EXERCISE

Read the following slightly shortened version of a student paper. Where and how does the author relate her opinions to her experience? Where and how does she use authorities? Where and how does she counteract prejudice, stereotypes, verbal formulas? Does she employ any verbal formulas of her own? (Your instructor may ask you to write a reply to this paper.)

The Struggle for Women's Equality

In recent years, women have become more aware of their worth as human beings. For years we have been treated as second-class citizens, valued only as sex objects and slaves. But a change is taking place. Tired of our low status, women have taken on the struggle for our equality.

Our struggle begins in early childhood. As "young ladies," we were told to act proper and prim: Little girls do not fight or yell. The rhymes we learned told of girls made of "sugar and spice and everything nice," while fairy tales said we would be swept off our feet by Prince Charming. For Christmas and birthdays we were given dolls, toy ovens, and tea sets, all the paraphernalia needed for good little homemakers. Boys at this stage were free to be mischievous, aggressive, and a little bit naughty.

As a result of our childhood environment, we were programmed to be modest and obedient. We believed the father should be "leader of the family." He's "physically stronger." The woman is the "homemaker." Brainwashed with this ideology, some women still refuse to open their minds to realize how we have been discriminated against.

I grew up with the same belief. Woman's main
purpose on earth is to cook, sew, clean, and serve.
But, after a year in college, I have changed my outlook on the role women have been playing in our
society. I have become more aware of the injustice
done to women and more concerned with the future liberation movement. My awakening began after a series of
unpleasant dates. The guys have the attitude that we
are here for their pleasure. They do not consider
women as living, breathing, thinking beings but as sex
objects. Most of my dates were very similar. He would
be quite friendly at first, saying, "You look nice"—
I was wearing blue jeans and an old T-shirt. All the
time, though, he was thinking how he could get me up
to his apartment. We go to his place to listen to his
new album. Once there, the fun really begins! The nice
guy turns into a vampire. It is not fun being mauled
by a six-foot-two body! Eventually he gets around to
asking me the invariable question, "How 'bout spending
the night with me?" When I refuse his nice offer, he
takes me home. He never calls me again.
     Besides being sex objects, women are categorized
as man hunters. The men believe the only reason we
came to college is to get a "MRS" degree. To a small
degree, it is true. I have heard a few girls talk of
their husband hunting. However, there is a larger percentage of women working for a B.S. degree rather than
a MRS degree. Men do not want to believe we are here
for the same reason they are, to acquire an education.
We must prove that we are here to learn a trade, by
putting women power in all fields of study and to gain
recognition for hard and outstanding work.
     We must also prove that in a biased world, women
are willing to work hard to achieve their equality. As
Michael Korda says in an article on "The Single Girl's
Search for Herself in the Big City,"

> Women have never been presented with an easy
> entry into adult society that a middle-class
> background and a college education gave to
> the American male. The young woman, unless
> she marries at twenty, is subjected to low
> wages, spiritual torment, and physical threat.

A hundred years have transferred our savage
tribal initiation rights from the man to
women, created a world in which she is expected to earn her freedom and independence
by experiencing loneliness, poverty, the
boredom of meaningless work, the humiliation
of being chained to a typewriter after working four years for a B.A. degree.

As late as ten years ago, a Presidential commission on the status of women reported that women earned
up to 40 percent less than men on the same jobs. In
chemistry, for instance, women with Ph.D.s earned less
than men who could offer only B.A.s. I myself found
discrimination in the office I worked in last summer.
The office manager, a male, was relieved of his job.
Instead of hiring someone new, the management gave his
duties to one of the secretaries. She received a raise
in salary, but her salary was still not equal to that
of the former office manager. The secretary was capable of running the office. She was in charge whenever the office manager was absent. But because she
was a woman, she was not given the title of office
manager or the same salary the man received, even
though she did the same job.
    Why must we suffer because we are women? We are
trained as well as men. We can do the same jobs as
men. Fortune magazine's "Top 500" have included a
woman who is a vice-president of a major American bank
and a woman biophysicist and leading researcher for
the Honeywell Corporation. The women of the U.S. Olym-
pic team have also shown their excellence. The excuse
of women not being equal to men is invalid. We are
equal and it is up to us to prove it. As Julie Ellis
says in Revolt of the Second Sex, we must be determined to play in a game so fixed that to win we have
to "look like a girl, act like a lady, think like a
man, and work like a dog."

THEME TOPICS 4

1. A student said of the rulebook given to her as she entered a women's college: "It said what a young lady may not *wear*. That's so superficial, it makes me sick." Does a college have any business regulating the dress, appearance, or manners of its students? Why, or why not?

2. The mass media are often accused of accentuating the negative. They are blamed for playing up everything that is unjust or sick in American society. What is *your* opinion? Give detailed examples to support your view.

3. A sociology professor has said, "Our schools, both high schools and colleges, teach sentimental rubbish in their marriage and family courses. . . . If taught honestly, these courses would alert the teenager and young adult to the realities of matrimonial life in the United States and try to advise them on how to survive marriage if they insist on that hazardous venture." To judge from your experience, how honest or how relevant are such courses?

4. Is intercollegiate athletic competition an anachronism in today's society? Does it perpetuate an image of American higher education as remote from the real problems and challenges of contemporary America?

5. Is it true that American teachers do not encourage, or even tolerate, dissent in their classes? Is it the better part of wisdom for the student to tell teachers what they want to hear?

6. How much truth is there in the stereotype? Select one that you at one time shared or still in part share: the welfare chiseler, the militaristic ex-marine, the bookworm, the back-slapping Rotarian, the authoritarian father, or the like. Show how much or how little truth there is in the stereotyped picture.

7. On subjects like the following, people do not easily change their minds: divorce, interracial marriage, homosexuality, child abuse, integrated schools. On which of these do *you* have a fairly strong personal opinion? State your opinion as your thesis early in the paper. Then give an honest accounting of how you developed your opinion.

8. A magazine put this query to 1,000 readers: "What should an unmarried pregnant teenager do?" Forty-one percent said the girl should have the baby, then put it up for adoption; 27 percent said get an abortion; 23 percent said marry the boy and keep the child; and 9 percent said keep the child, but don't marry. What do you think of these responses? What would your answer have been, and why?

9. In the early seventies, about 50 percent of college freshmen felt "there is too much concern in the courts for the rights of criminals." By the end of the decade, the proportion had grown to 65 percent. What explains this shift in attitude? Where do *you* stand?

Definition

CHAPTER FIVE

1. **The Need for Definition**
   Relative Words
   Vague Words
   Ambiguous Words
   Overlapping Terms
   Specialized Terms

2. **Getting Down to Cases**

3. **Formulating and Supporting Definitions**
   Dictionary Definitions
   Formal Definitions
   Aids to Definition

4. **Writing an Extended Definition**
   The History of a Term
   Providing the Key
   Finding the Common Denominator
   Drawing the Line

1. THE NEED FOR DEFINITION

One of the most common questions people want to ask a writer is: "What do you mean?" What do you mean—an "honorable solution? What do you mean—"premeditated"? What do you mean—"guided democracy"? We challenge words and phrases that don't tell us enough. We question words that promise more than the writer is willing to deliver.

When you write on a serious subject, you want your reader to see that the words you use are not just words. When you use a term like "social justice," your reader wants to know what the term means in practice. What does it include, and what does it spare out? When you define such a term, you take time to spell out its exact meaning. You mark off the territory it covers. You make sure the reader can say: "I see what you mean."

Here are kinds of words that often need definition:

Relative Words

Many words cover a range of meaning. Their exact meaning depends on circumstances: "Hot" may mean 95 degrees or 9,500 degrees. A "large" sum of money may suggest $500 to you and $500,000 to your next-door neighbor. To make such words less relative, we may have to indicate a precise point on the scale. Look at the kinds of questions we encounter when we deal with relative words. What would your first tentative answer be to questions like the following?

- How intelligent does a boy have to be before we classify him as "gifted"?
- How severely handicapped would he have to be before we would classify him as "retarded"?
- Suppose you were asked to estimate how many Americans are poor. Where would you draw the "poverty line"?

Vague Words

Many familiar terms cover too much ground. Here are some statements with vague terms that call for definition. How would you answer the questions in parentheses?

VAGUE: A military academy does more than the typical public school to build a student's *character.* (What character traits does the writer have in mind? When and how are they demonstrated by graduates of military academies?)

VAGUE: New educational programs will be developed in close *consultation* with representatives of the student body. (Who should select the representatives? How and when should they be consulted? Should they have a chance to propose programs of their own? Should they be allowed to vote on anything? How much should their vote count?)

Ambiguous Words

Some terms have several different, and at times contradictory, meanings. We all learn to manage words that do double duty: *sense* means both "sense perception" and "intelligence." Context helps us choose the right meaning: Having a "sixth sense" is like having another sense organ keener than the eye, or more far-ranging than the ear. When we "talk sense," we talk intelligently.

But with some words *either* of two possible meanings might fit the context. What exactly is meant by "national honor"? One of the meanings of *honor* is implied in the expression "to honor a person." This meaning centers on recognition, esteem, prestige, reputation. The other is implied in an expression like "an honorable person." This meaning centers on the person's own standard of conduct. We might call the first external honor and the second internal honor. Which of the two meanings do you think is at work in each of the following sentences? Where is it hard to tell?

> There's no honor among thieves.
> Jean's name has been put back on the honor roll.
> A knight valued honor above all.
> In some countries, a woman that has been raped is considered dishonored.
> The school abandoned its honor code.

Overlapping Terms

We often need to mark a word off from another word that covers some of the same ground. The law, for instance, often asks people to make fine distinctions—between murder and homicide, or between ordinary carelessness and gross negligence. Here are other questions that ask us to draw the line between two closely related words:

- When does a *committed* person become a *fanatic?*
- When do *fair profits* become *excess profits?*
- When does a *practical* person become an *opportunist?*

Specialized Terms

Much serious writing makes specialized use of terms that have a more general meaning in everyday use. In popular journalism, for instance, the term *tragedy* usually means "disaster," any event involving fatal loss or great suffering. Drama critics use the term in its more technical sense of "a serious play having a disastrous or unhappy ending." They may define tragedy as "a play about a great person who brings about his or her own downfall."

EXERCISES

A. What is the meaning of the words italicized in the following sentences? Compare your answers with those of your classmates. Do you find it easy or difficult to pin down the meaning of these words?

1. When I meet a person, I try to be interested and express an interest through a warm handshake and a *sincere* smile.
2. Her family are nice people, but they have absolutely no *class*.
3. He was good-looking, but I soon found he was very *shallow*.
4. I voted today for the first time in a presidential election. It was no big thing to me, but my mother reacted as if it were the biggest event in my life and hers. Mothers sometimes are quite *sentimental* about first occurrences.
5. The trouble with my high school teachers was that they used absolutely no *psychology*. They tried to argue recalcitrant students into changing their ways, instead of cracking down.
6. We should send criminals to jail not for punishment but for *rehabilitation*.
7. He claimed to feel love for her but it was just *infatuation*.
8. The jury was asked to decide if the accused had been temporarily *insane*.
9. Modern democracies are built on the principle of government by *consent*.
10. People in my part of the country have always been suspicious of *radical* change.

B. In each of the following passages, a writer uses a familiar term in a personal way. How would *you* use the term? What does the writer stress that you wouldn't? What is left out that you would include?

1. Sharing a *culture* (in the anthropological sense) means reacting in the same way to something without having to think about or mention the matter: Attitudes are "automatic." Obviously, a society can go too far in enculturating its members, and in fact the more serious and persistent dangers have probably been in that direction. On the other hand, if people in a society share nothing, if everything has to be argued before decision or action is possible, and if consensus is rarely achieved because its members hold so little in common, a society has difficulty giving the individual those benefits that make having a society worthwhile.

2. By a *generation* I mean that reaction against the fathers which seems to occur about three times in a century. It is distinguished by a set of ideas, inherited in a moderated form from the madmen and outlaws of the generation before; if it is a real generation, it has its own leaders and spokesmen, and it draws into its orbit those born just before it and just after, whose ideas are less clear-cut and defiant. (F. Scott Fitzgerald)

3. An *anarchist* believes that the primary goal of all legitimate organization is individual freedom, that is, self-sovereignty. Individual participation in any organization ought to be voluntary. It is voluntary only if there is right of secession with resources.

4. The vision of Latin America as part of the *Third World* is oversimple. . . . It's enough to reflect that we are Christians, we are Spanish and Portuguese and gained our independence with the tools of French and English ideas. . . . Of course we are part of the Third World if we think in economic and social terms; however, in historical terms we are part of the civilization of the West. (Octavio Paz)

C. In your own words, explain the distinction made in the following paragraph between two overlapping words. Then write a similar paragraph that will help your reader draw the line between the words in one of the following pairs: *pride—arrogance*; *privacy—secrecy*; *dissent—disobedience*; *force—violence*.

Assertive behavior is, as we see it, the golden mean between *aggressiveness*, at one extreme, and *nonassertiveness*, at the other. "Assertive" is never to be confused with "aggressive." . . . The intent of assertive behavior is to communicate honestly and directly. The intent of aggressive behavior is to dominate, to get your own way at the expense of others. The intent of nonassertive behavior is to avoid conflict altogether, which usually means that you have to subordinate your wishes to those of others. When we are aggressive we are insensitive to others' rights, and we express ourselves in ways that demean, humiliate, or coerce them. When we are nonassertive we are natural victims for the aggressor. We either don't tell others what we want and think, or we try to get what we want through devious means. We let others choose for us and infringe on our rights. When we are assertive we make choices for ourselves without harming or being harmed by others.—Lynn Z. Bloom, Karen Coburn, and Joan Pearlman, *The New Assertive Woman*

2.   GETTING DOWN TO CASES

The general principle for successful definition applies to all successful writing: *Anchor the general to concrete reference.* Give substance to abstract terms by relating them to people, places, and events. **Abstract** terms are extremely general words that "draw us away" from reality—and often become just words. Notice how the writer in the following example anchors the general term *work* to her account of a character who throughout her essay serves as an example of what hard, lifelong work means:

Whenever I think of the word "work" I first think of my Aunt Clara. Next I think of the hymn we used to sing so often in our North Dakota village church: *Work, for the night is coming, / Work in the noonday sun. / Work, for the night is coming, / When man's work is done.* The logic of those verses has always eluded me, but their meaning has always been mysteriously clear, perhaps because I knew my Aunt Clara and so many others almost like her. Because I knew my Aunt Clara I am astounded at the number of people who seem to think of work as an abstraction—like Truth or Beauty.—Lois Phillips Hudson, "'Work, for the Night Is Coming,'" *The Reporter*

The more general a term, the greater our need to climb down the abstraction ladder till we can see actual people, actual events.

When we define any important term, our first order of business is to "get down to cases." To find out what terms like *justice* and *freedom* mean in our society, we have to look at how these concepts actually affect our lives. What, specifically, can I be summoned to court for, and put in jail, perhaps for years on end? What, as a teacher, or preacher, or truck driver, am I free to do? And when and where do I start running into signs that say NO TRESPASSING or NO VACANCY or WAIT ON THE OTHER SIDE OF THIS LINE?

Suppose a visitor from a distant land had asked you: "If the Statue of Liberty could talk, what would she tell me about freedom in your country?" Here are the kinds of questions you might explore as you try to give concrete substance to the abstract term *freedom*:

(1) What *specific freedoms* would you include? These might include the following:

• *Freedom of movement.*   The slave, the deportee, and the inmate of a labor camp are denied the fundamental freedom to move on. They are not free to "grab a train and ride."

• *Free choice of employment.*   The government that sends intellectuals to work on farms, the employers that blacklist political undesirables, the union that reserves apprenticeships for nephews of members, the college department that does not hire women—all these restrict our opportunities to find satisfying, productive work of our own choice.

• *Freedom of artistic creation.*   How much regulation of literature and the arts is there on political, religious, or moral grounds? How much banning, blacklisting, or censorship is there? How much hunting for heresy, pornography, "degenerate art," alien ideologies, counter-revolutionary writers?

(2) What *basic limitations* on freedom do you accept as necessary? We have zoning laws, traffic regulations, health controls, and criminal statutes to regulate many kinds of public and private conduct. What limitations can we impose on logging firms, strip miners, drug manufacturers, and pesticide sprayers and still have a free society?

(3) What *procedures* for implementing the necessary restrictions do you approve? Does the person who runs into restrictions or prohibitions have any recourse? Does the individual who is up against government authority have any opportunity for appeal and review? And when these restrictions were imposed in the first place, did they

have the consent of the majority? Was there any consideration of minority interests and dissenting views?

A meaningful definition of freedom would have to *pull together* the results of this kind of exploration. Your definition would probably stress the idea of *personal choice*. A free society would provide the largest possible scope for your choice of job, mate, friends, place to live, hobbies, religion, and forms of creative expression. You might further want to stress the idea of *due process*—the idea that the restrictions that affect our lives should not be imposed arbitrarily by the authorities.

During your exploration of your key term, the case histories and test cases you examine would be the raw data. By studying a full sampling of these, you would try to find any common pattern. In a paper devoted to a definition of the central term, the case histories and test cases would appear as *examples* to back up your general findings. They would provide the evidence that you are talking about your key term as it actually operates in the world outside.

EXERCISES

A. A writer with an eye for the concrete defined sewage as "whatever goes down the drain in home, factory, or office." In one sentence each, write a similar "down-to-earth" definition for three of the following: credit, prestige, glamor, influence.

B. The president of a large urban college asked himself what we mean by "urban." Here is part of his answer. How, and how successfully, does it give concrete substance to an abstract sociological term?

The urban society means crowded neighborhoods, poor housing, sometimes shacks on the fringes of the city inhabited by the fringes of humanity, more often fine old houses, tottering with age, wrinkled and cross-veined with partition. . . . Urban means poverty, hunger, disease, rats; it means unemployment, placement below skills, welfare and dependence perpetuated now to the third generation. . . . Urban means the decay of the central city, the moving out of business, the proliferation of "For Rent" signs, the boarding up of windows, the transformation of pride to embarrassment. . . . What once was city is now largely deteriorating buildings, empty stores, buildings about to empty themselves, and open spaces where buildings once stood.

Using the above passage as a model, write a paragraph in which you give concrete substance to one of the following terms: *downtown, suburbia, rural, slum, metropolitan*.

C. Study the way the following paragraph gives concrete substance to a familiar term. What is that term? How would you define it in your own words? What effect does the author achieve by *not* stating the term at the very beginning?

It was an old black man in Atlanta who looked into my eyes and directed me into my first segregated bus. I have spent a long time thinking about that man. I never saw him again. I cannot describe the look which passed between us, as I asked him for directions, but it made me think, at once, of Shakespeare's "the oldest have borne most." It made me think of the blues: *Now, when a woman gets the blues, Lord, she hangs her head and cries. But when a man gets the blues, Lord, he grabs a train and rides.* It was borne in on me, suddenly, just why these men had so often been grabbing freight trains as the evening sun went down. And it was, perhaps, because I was getting on a segregated bus, and wondering how Negroes had borne this and other indignities for so long, that this man so struck me. He seemed to know what I was feeling. His eyes seemed to say that what I was feeling he had been feeling, at much higher pressure, all his life. But my eyes would never see the hell his eyes had seen. And this hell was, simply, that he had never in his life owned anything, not his wife, not his house, not his child, which could not, at any instant, be taken from him by the power of white people. This is what paternalism means.—James Baldwin, *Nobody Knows My Name*

D. Use the above paragraph by James Baldwin as a model. Write a paragraph of your own in which you first describe *one extended incident* or experience that made a familiar term meaningful for you. Then present the abstract term that the experience illustrates. Choose one of the following terms: *fairness, pluralism, respect, integrity, bigotry, the work ethic, colonialism.*

E. Study the following test cases. In each case, how would "justice" best be served? Can you define justice in such a way that your definition will fit all (or most) of these test cases? Which does it fit best? Which least? Why?

1. A candidate for school board did not decide to run until the last minute. He went down to the city council office and turned in his application with some information about his experience. The people in the office accepted his application but refused to print the information about the candidate on the sample ballots to be mailed out. He needed some three hundred dollars to pay for the printing. He pleaded for an extension so as to go and borrow the money, but his request was refused. One point here is that you have to have a good amount of money even to participate in local politics.

2. A large ship with many passengers is going down in the middle of the ocean. Only two lifeboats are usable, and some passengers must be left behind. The captain orders that lots will be drawn to select those to be left behind. Women, children, and married men whose wives are with them are exempted from taking part in the drawing. Is it just that certain people do not have to take the risk of being excluded from the lifeboats so others can survive?

3. Those who work are rewarded. As a violinist, I know that if I don't practice and seriously concentrate on playing well I will not be a successful violinist. Having talent is the springboard; using it is the test. But what if an untalented person who works hard competes with a talented person who works much less? The rewards would probably go to the talented person, who has something to work with.

4. Vigilante justice deals with criminals who might be treated too leniently by the judicial system. In our own town, kidnappers abducted and killed the child of a department store owner and were publicly lynched by a mob for it. My father tells me that federal marshals knew about it and arrived in time to disperse the crowd of onlookers and cut the bodies down.

5. After stealing food from a local grocery, a young lad is apprehended by the police and taken downtown to jail. It is illegal to steal food, but it is not illegal to starve. So the hungry young lad is given a criminal record and sent home hungry still. Justice has been done.

3.   FORMULATING AND SUPPORTING DEFINITIONS

A meaningful definition is the result of investigation. It sums up what we found out about a term. How do we pull together the results of our investigation? How do we present them to the reader?

Dictionary Definitions

Take into account but do not simply repeat a dictionary definition. Dictionary definitions are most useful when they give a reliable, exact account of a technical term:

> **ka·lei·do·scope.** an optical instrument in which bits of glass, beads, etc., held loosely at the end of a rotating tube, are shown in continually changing symmetrical forms by reflection in two or more mirrors set at angles to each other.

—The Random House Dictionary

What your dictionary tells you about the uses or the history of a word may help you bring an important term into focus:

The word *ecology* has its root in the Greek word *oikos* meaning "house" or "home." Our future success depends upon the recognition that household management in this wider sense is the most backward branch of technology and therefore the one most urgently in need of development. An entirely new technology is required, one founded on ecology in much the same way as medicine is founded on physiology. If this new technology is accepted, I shall be completely confident of our ability to put and keep our house in order.—Sir Peter Medawar, "Man: The Technological Animal," *Smithsonian Magazine*

When you quote a dictionary definition, make sure you relate it to *your own* investigation of the subject. Show how it fits in with your own discussion of the term. Show how it would have to be filled in, or broadened, or otherwise modified.

Formal Definitions

A *formal definition first places a term in a larger class and then sums up distinctive features.* It makes you sort out the parts of a definition into two types of information. First, you list things that classify the term to be defined as a member of a group, or **class**. Second, you list features that distinguish the term to be defined from other members of the same group. Thus, a formal definition of *horse* first places horses in the general category of four-legged mammals that have solid hoofs and feed on grass or grain. It then points out characteristics that distinguish horses from other animals in the same general category. Here are some examples of formal definition:

TERM TO BE DEFINED	CLASS	DIFFERENTIATION
An Autobiography	is the story of a person's life,	written by that person.
Oligarchy	is a form of government	in which power lies in the hands of a few.
A Martyr	is someone who suffers persecution	for refusing to renounce his or her faith.

This simple formula proves useful for several reasons: It focuses on essentials and yet can be packed with relevant *information:*

A Faun	is a Roman wood god	who is half man and half goat.

It trains us to take in the important *nuances:*

To Double-cross	is to betray someone	whom we have deliberately impressed with our trustworthiness or loyalty.

Several precautions have to be observed if a formal definition is to be informative. Check your definitions for the following:

(1) *The class in which a term is placed may be too inclusive.* Classifying a cello as "a musical instrument" is less informative than classifying it as "a string instrument of the violin family." Classifying an epic as "a type of literature" is less informative than classifying it as "a long narrative poem."

(2) *The definition may place the term in a group without supplying adequate differentiation.* Defining *Puritanism* as "the religion of the

Puritans" makes it clear that we are dealing with a religion but does not tell us what kind. Defining *tragedy* as "a play concerned with a tragic situation" clarifies the meaning somewhat but leaves the key term undefined. Definitions that repeat the key term in a slightly different guise are called **circular definitions**.

(3) *The distinctive features may not adequately rule out things that are similar or closely related.* This is the weakness of a definition of *patriot* as "a person who promotes the best interests of the country." This definition does not exclude the person who serves the country for the sake of gain or personal glory. Adding the words *zealously* and *unselfishly* to the definition would make it more discriminating.

(4) *A definition may be too restrictive.* A definition referring to a *senator* as "an elected representative of a state" would exclude the minority of senators who are not elected but appointed.

(5) *A definition may merely offer another term covering approximately the same area of meaning.* **Synonyms** are useful when they provide a familiar equivalent for an unfamiliar or difficult term, such as "double meaning" for *ambiguity*. But a writer makes little headway by explaining that *just* means "right in action or judgment," or that *equitable* means "fair or equal."

Aids to Definition

Do what is necessary to help make your definition clear and convincing. A formal definition is designed to sum up rather than to explain or convince. To drive home a definition, you have to answer questions like the following: How would this actually work? How did this term get this meaning? How is this term different from terms that are closely related?

(1) *If necessary, use distinctive labels to clear up the ambiguities of a broad term.* For example, distinguish between "direct democracy" and "representative democracy." Look at how Paul Goodman, in *Growing Up Absurd*, used the term "participatory democracy":

> What the American young do know, being themselves pushed around, itemized and processed, is that they have a right to a say in what affects them. They believe in democracy, which they have to call "participatory democracy," to distinguish it from double-talk democracy. . . . they want the opportunity to be responsible, to initiate and decide, instead of being mere personnel.

(2) *Use comparison and contrast with closely related terms.* What contrasting term does the author of the following passage bring in to

help explain the social role of taboos? How does the contrast help us understand the key term?

> When we examine how any society works, it becomes clear that it is precisely the basic taboos—the deeply and intensely felt prohibitions against "unthinkable" behavior—that keep the social system in balance. Laws are an expression of principles concerning things we can and do think about, and they can be changed as our perception of the world changes. But a taboo, even against taking a human life, may or may not be formulated in legal terms in some societies; the taboo lies much deeper in our consciousness, and by prohibiting certain forms of behavior also affirms what we hold most precious in our human relationships. Taboos break down in periods of profound change and are re-created in new forms during periods of transition.—Margaret Mead, "We Need Taboos," *Redbook*

(3) *Pay attention not only to what something is but to how it is produced, how it works, what its results are.* Children's definitions stay close to this level of "How does it work?" and "What does it do?" ("A genius is a fellow who gets into trouble. Then some moron comes along and gets blamed.") Scientists, engineers, business people, and politicians all expect from a definition an account of essential causes, functions, and effects. A physicist looks for an **operational definition**, showing how a given phenomenon can be experimentally reproduced.

(4) *Keep a stipulated meaning clearly in view to prevent confusion.* Terms like *liberal* and *liberalism* have a long and confusing history, and a number of different current meanings. *Liberalism* used to mean a political doctrine favoring free enterprise, but is now usually taken to mean the opposite. To cut through the thicket of conflicting meanings and associations, a writer may have to stipulate clearly the meaning of *liberalism* "as used here."

EXERCISES

A. If necessary, rewrite the following definitions to make them more exact or more informative. Explain what made the original version inexact or uninformative.

1. A barometer is an instrument used in predicting the weather.
2. Classical music is the type of music played in concert halls.
3. A sorority is a private association that provides separate dormitory facilities with a distinctive Greek letter name for selected female college students.
4. Tyranny is rule by a tyrant.
5. Jazz is a form of strongly rhythmic music played by black musicians.
6. Islam is the religion of the Muslims.
7. A strike means that workers leave their jobs in order to get higher pay.
8. An alien is a person born in another country.
9. Pacifism makes people refuse military service in times of war.
10. A plebiscite is a method of giving the public a voice in political decisions.

B. Sometimes a short, informal definition gets to the point better than a long roundabout account could. Look at the following *capsule definitions*. How well do they hit the target? Can you state the point of each in a more detailed and formal fashion?

Flirtation	attention without intention
Prejudice	being down on somebody you are not up on
Authoritarianism	authority stripped of its rightfulness (Milton Mayer)
Intuition	knowing without being told—just *knowing* it

Try your hand at your own capsule definition of one of the above and some of the following:

optimism	love	frustration	expediency	subculture
sarcasm	inferiority complex		good taste	snobbery

C. How accurately can you distinguish between the two key terms in each of the following passages? Define each term so as to set it off clearly from the other.

1. Some talk about discipline but really mean *self-discipline*; others talk about discipline but really mean *regimentation*. (Olga Conolly)
2. The young people today are much closer in their views on civil rights to the abolitionists of a century ago than they are to yesterday's liberals. The oppression of black people is to them a *sin* rather than a *wrong*.
3. "Yes," a student said to me, "I want to be *intelligent*, but I don't want to be a detached, emotionless *intellectual*."
4. Many people today hold strong religious *beliefs* while rejecting *dogma*.
5. The author described her father as "a tough, taciturn, *uneducated* man but also a deeply *learned* and handsome one."

D. Study the following two sample passages, both devoted to definition. What was the major intention or purpose of each writer? Summarize the author's definition of the key term in your own words. What procedure did each writer follow? What means did she use?

1. Patriotism, dictionary-defined, means the act of loving, supporting, and defending a country. Definite ways of expressing this support are associated with the word. Flag-displaying, fighting for the cause, and celebrating the Fourth of July--all are common examples of patriotism. But patriotism soon loses any value and becomes ritualistic if no analysis of these actions occurs. True patriotism cannot be blind allegiance to tradition and the status quo. Obviously, constructive criticism is essential to the existence of our democracy. Therefore, our deepest care and concern is shown when we exercise the right to be critical and take initiative to modify the system. This idea of critical observation has been part of our democratic system since it began. The Declaration of

Independence is built on the idea that the people
ought to revolt or instigate change in the government
if it is not fulfilling the people's ideals of what
it should be. More recently, we have seen this criticism apparent in opposition to the Vietnam War and
the crimes of high officials in Watergate. Awareness
of inequality has generated movements for gaining individual rights for minorities and women. Our allegiance is toward a country which allows free examination
of the government and specializes in preserving individual rights. True patriotism examines the governing
principles and supports them only after close examination of their truth and merit. In America, patriotism
stems from the right to take that closer look.
(Student theme)

2. The woman of the future, who is really being born today, will be a woman
completely free of guilt for creating and for her self-development. She will be a
woman in harmony with her own strength, not necessarily called masculine, or
eccentric, or something unnatural. I imagine she will be very tranquil about her
strength and her serenity, a woman who will know how to talk to children and to
the men who sometimes fear her. Man has been uneasy about this self-evolution of
woman, but he need not be—because, instead of having a dependent, he will have
a partner. He will have someone who will not make him feel that every day he has
to go into battle against the world to support a wife and child, or a childlike wife.
The woman of the future will never try to live vicariously through the man, and
urge and push him to despair, to fulfill something that she should really be doing
herself. So that is my first image—she is not aggressive, she is serene, she is sure,
she is confident, she is able to develop her skills, she is able to ask for space for
herself.—Anaïs Nin, *In Favor of the Sensitive Man*

4.   WRITING AN EXTENDED DEFINITION

Writing a whole paper that defines a single important term gives
you a chance to become fully aware of words as words. It makes you
ponder the relationship between words and experience, and between
words and ideas. Here are some possible patterns for a theme devoted
to definition:

The History of a Term

Explain a word by tracing its development. Often the best way to
clarify a confusing term is to trace major stages in its history. College dictionaries provide at least some historical information. In
taking history classes or studying books by historians, our attention

often focuses on the terms that label major ideas or movements. Here is an outline of a paper that would shed light on changing meanings of the word *democracy*:

We the People

I.   Ideally, democracy gives people a direct voice and vote in the common business of the community.
     A.   The Greek beginnings
     B.   Early town meetings
     C.   Modern workers' councils

II. In practice, participation in the political process is often indirect and ineffectual.
     A.   Parliamentary democracy
     B.   Checks and balances

III. In modern "popular democracies," an authoritarian leadership claims to exercise power in the name of the people.

Providing the Key

Make your definition of a term the thesis that the rest of the paper will support. By modeling an extended definition on the thesis-and-support paper, you can answer the question that may be uppermost in the reader's mind: "What is the clue? What is the secret?" For instance, you may have concluded that the key element in a narrow-minded person's makeup is quickness to *judge*—to make judgments that put others in the wrong and the speaker in the right. You state this key element as your definition of narrow-mindedness early in the paper. The rest of your paper shows how well your definition fits actual examples of narrow-mindedness.

Here is a rough scheme for a similar paper on romantic love:

THESIS: Romantic love is a love *strong enough to overcome for-midable obstacles.* It makes a lover persevere in an apparently hopeless passion. It makes lovers go against the opposition of parents, church, and state. . . .

FIRST EXAMPLE: The most striking representative of the persevering lover is the knight of the *medieval romance.* . . .

SECOND EXAMPLE: The most famous example of all but hopeless and yet persevering passion are Shakespeare's young lovers in *Romeo and Juliet.* . . .

THIRD EXAMPLE: In *modern literature,* . . .

Finding the Common Denominator

Make your reader participate in the search. When you write about a term like *fairness*, your readers may prove suspicious of ready-made rulings on what is fair or unfair. You might get a more respectful hearing if you took the stance of the impartial observer, approaching the subject with an open mind. You could take your readers through a series of test cases, each raising an issue of fair play. You could ask what these cases have in common.

Here is a rough scheme for the kind of paper that would ask the reader to join in the search for the common denominator:

FIRST TEST CASE:	An honor code states that it is not "fair" to cheat.
SECOND TEST CASE:	According to a newspaper story, a mother considered it "fair" to steal food for her starving children.
THIRD TEST CASE:	A tennis player considers it "fair" to let an opponent find his or her footing after stumbling.
FOURTH TEST CASE:	Students consider it "unfair" to penalize a sick student for failure to take a test.
COMMON DENOMINATOR:	Fair play makes us impose limits on competition—and sometimes *suspend* normal limits—in order to assure greater equality of opportunity. It shows our desire to "give everybody a chance."

Drawing the Line

Define a term by setting it off from a more familiar term to which it is closely related. Systematic comparison and contrast with a familiar synonym or near synonym is often the best way to clarify a term that may be blurry in the reader's mind. Look at the way the author of the following excerpts draws the line between protest and resistance:

DEFINITION OF FIRST TERM:	To protest is to speak out against. You let it be known that you do not like a certain action of another. To protest is an act of intellectual commitment. It is to say, "Sir, I protest" when you are slapped in the face. . . .
FIRST EXAMPLE:	To protest is to play a game. You go to a demonstration, listen to speeches, wave signs, and go home to see if you got on television. . . .
SECOND EXAMPLE:	There are many toys in the game of protest. There is the picket line. Originally a picket line was formed by striking workers to keep strike-breakers out. If anyone tried to cross that picket line, the strikers tried to kill him. Today you get a permit from the police to protest. . . .
DEFINITION OF SECOND TERM:	To resist is to say NO! without qualification or explanation. . . .

FIRST EXAMPLE: To resist is not only to say I won't go. It is to say, I'll make
                        sure nobody else goes, either. . . .

SECOND EXAMPLE: To resist is to not go to jail when sentenced, but only
                        when caught and surrounded and there is no other choice. . . .

REVIEW EXERCISE

Study the following extended definition of conservatism. Identify the major
elements of conservatism that the author discusses. Describe the order she follows
or the strategy she adopts in presenting these elements. Sum up the overall definition of conservatism that emerges from this selection. In one sentence each, define
some of the other key terms used: *liberal, nostalgia, tradition, élite, raw democracy,
quixotic*. (Your instructor may ask you to write one paragraph each about conservatism and liberalism as seen by this author.)

One autumn Saturday afternoon I was
listening to the radio when the station
switched to the Dartmouth-Harvard
game. The game had not begun, and
the announcer was rambling on about
the nip in the air, the autumn colors,
past games, this year's players, their
names and hometowns—a seminostal-
gic discourse that, despite an aversion
for football talk, I found unexpectedly
moving. Autumn, a new crop of
players, New England: The world was
on a steady keel after all. I could not
remember having felt that quiet sense
of cycle, of ongoing life and the past
floating so serenely to the surface, in a
long time.

That morning, anyway, I felt like
a conservative.

I am not a conservative. I think
the government not only should try to,
but can, improve life for its citizens;
yet for the first time I've begun to understand the value of tradition, both
for the counterpoint it can provide to
the Left and for the different perspective it offers on the drift rightward of
the electorate.

Two elementary attitudes underlie
the conservative tradition. The first is
a passionate sense of the need to
conserve—the land, the culture, the
institutions, codes of behavior—and

to revere and protect those elements
that constitute "civilization." The
conservative looks to the enduring
values of the past—to holding on to
what we've got—in forming his political positions, rather than to alluring,
idealistic visions of what the future
could be.

The second attitude is a cautious
view of raw democracy, or direct rep-
resentational government. The conservative believes firmly in the rights
of minorities and those institutions
that protect minorities from the whims
of the majority, such as the Supreme
Court—an elite, appointed body—
and the Constitution, particularly the
First Amendment. The concern behind this attitude is less for racial,
ethnic or religious groups than for intellectual minorities—the educated
elite—to which conservatives have
always belonged.

These institutions that restrain the
mass will are precious in the conservative view, not just because they protect the few from being trampled by
the many, but also because they protect the majority from its own mistakes. This awareness that the majority can often be wrong (so easily
forgotten by social crusaders) produces
a mental habit. Conservatives tend to

be automatically uncomfortable with any idea or trend that smacks of mob psychology—anything that gains a swift and wide popularity—to the point of appearing to enjoy embracing unpopular positions and dropping wet blankets on the emotional political moods to which this country is prone.

An outgrowth of these attitudes—and one with particular value—is the humor that the skeptical turn of the conservative mind can bring to bear on the confused, disaster-prone but unreservedly grand schemes for the betterment of mankind, which the quixotic and too often humorless liberal is forever earnestly pressing to perpetrate.—Susannah Lessard, "The Real Conservatism." *The Washington Monthly*

THEME TOPICS 5

1. Some words point to important issues in our society, but when these words are repeated over and over people get tired of them nevertheless. About which of the following do you feel most strongly that the word is more than just a cliché? Show what the word or expression means and why it is important:

   bureaucracy   law and order   permissiveness   exploitation
   assimilation   nonviolence   alienation

2. Write an extended definition of one of the following terms: *respectability, sentimentality, cynicism, expediency*. Try to identify a key element and sum it up early in your paper. Support your definition with authentic examples from your own observation, experience, and reading.

3. What is true charity, true courage, true maturity, or true patriotism? Choose one of these. Write a paper in which you examine several key examples to find the common element. Sum up the common denominator at the end of your paper.

4. Write a paper that would help your reader see the difference between the two members of one of the following pairs. How are the two terms related? What sets them apart? Choose one:

   Culture and popular culture
   Professional and amateur sports
   Humor and satire

5. Some familiar terms have been the subject of long and confused arguments among lawmakers, lawyers, and judges: *equal opportunity, integration, pornography, obscenity*. Choose one of these terms and write a paper in which you make your reader join in the search for the common denominator.

6. Some words have had a long history and are rich in sometimes contradictory meanings and associations. Choose one of the following: *Puritanism, liberal, romantic love*. Write a paper in which you help your reader understand some of the major uses and associations of the word.

7. We often hear it said that "human rights" are more important than "property rights." In what kind of situations does the phrase *human rights* occur? What is meant or should be meant by the term? Where do human rights start, and where do they end?

8. Write a paper that defines an ideal or a goal for the future. Choose one of the following: What is your vision of the ideal woman (or man) of the future? Or, what is your vision of an ideal marriage?

Argument

CHAPTER SIX

1. **Writing and Thinking**

2. **How We Generalize**
   The Uses of Induction
   Effective Generalizations
   Hasty Generalization

3. **Thinking the Matter Through**
   Valid Deductions
   Checking Your Premises
   Interpreting Statistics
   Avoiding Common Fallacies

4. **Structuring an Argument**
   The Inductive Paper
   The Pro-and-Con Paper
   Analyzing Cause and Effect
   Analyzing Alternatives

1. WRITING AND THINKING

In a structured argument, we try to convince the reader by presenting our reasoning step by step. When we become serious about an issue, we soon find that it is not enough to turn to a reader and say: "This is what I think—take it or leave it." To hold our own in serious discussion, we have to show that we have thought the matter through. We try to take the reader along by laying out our reasoning one step at a time.

One of the most basic questions readers ask of us is "How does this follow? How did you get from A to B?" Our readers want to see where they are asked to go, and why. They want to see the connection. They want to be sure that the leaps they are supposed to take are not too big, or the turns in the wrong direction.

Here are some typical statements that make a reader say: "How did we get here?"

> Most women who work would rather stay home raising a family.
> ("How do you know? Has anyone recently polled these women? Are you generalizing from two or three examples?")
>
> The same basic rule applies to the budget of a family and the budget of a nation: If either continually practices deficit spending, bankruptcy eventually follows.
> ("But aren't there some important differences between the economics of a family and of a whole nation?")
>
> The right of private citizens to own guns is guaranteed by the Second Amendment to the U.S. Constitution.
> ("What exactly does it say? Does everyone agree with your interpretation?")

When readers challenge us in this fashion, it becomes necessary for us to argue our case. We show how we reached our conclusions. We make clear how we arrived at a general rule, and how we decided whether it applies to a specific instance. We show how we decided which cases are alike and which are different. We show how we examined causes or analyzed alternatives.

In much of the writing we do, we present the *results* of our thinking. We present a thesis, a definition, or a program for action, and then support it with examples, reasons, precedents. But when we seriously try to change the reader's mind, we may have to lead up to the intended conclusion through the *actual steps in the argument*. We turn to our readers as if to say: "This is how it looks if you examine the matter calmly and objectively, and if you think it through to its logical conclusion."

EXERCISE

Study the following statements. Which of them make you say: "I agree"? (How would you argue in *support* of the writer?) Which of them make you say: "I would like to take issue with that"? (On what grounds would you *challenge* the writer?)

1. Americans have always believed in education as the road to opportunity. Most parents have always believed that the schools would make it possible for their children to have better lives than they had had themselves.
2. The government has ways to prevent people from entering the country illegally, but Americans are too soft-hearted to put these into practice.
3. Public colleges are financed through taxes. They therefore should provide the kind of education that taxpayers want them to provide.
4. Juveniles don't have voting rights, nor can they go to the neighborhood bar and buy a beer. If they are not given adult rights, why should they be punished like adults, because they commit the same crimes that adults do?
5. There are certain four-letter or Anglo-Saxon words that we could not accept in a campus magazine. Our standards, as a university, are naturally high. This is our main restriction: No four-letter words.
6. A law is passed by the majority of the people before it becomes a law; therefore, everyone should obey the laws.
7. The language of the Second Amendment is crystal clear: "A well-regulated militia being necessary to the security of a free state, the right of the people to keep and bear arms shall not be infringed." This language has nothing, but nothing, to do with guns for sport, or guns for target practice, or mail order guns, or guns for private collections. It protects the right to bear arms for members of individual state *militias* only.
8. Where there is smoke there is fire. If a public official comes under attack for stealing public funds, it is a good sign that some kind of wrongdoing has been committed. Officials accused of dishonesty should be removed from their jobs before they can do any further harm.
9. College students are interested in learning all they can while in college. Unlike high school, college is not required by law; therefore, a person who goes to college is going because of a desire to further his or her education.
10. Alcoholism is a terrible disease; therefore, beer should not be sold on college campuses.

2. HOW WE GENERALIZE

To generalize means to find the common element in different situations. A group of educators studying high school curricula may find that the senior class in the first high school they visit is, among other activities, reading *Macbeth*. In the next school, a senior honors section is scheduled to read *Macbeth* later in the year. In the third or fourth school visited, the senior class is studying *Hamlet*. If this pattern persists, the educators' final report will generalize that high school seniors in the area visited usually study a Shakespeare play, often *Macbeth*.

This process of drawing general conclusions from individual observations is known as **induction**, or inductive reasoning. Without
inductive reasoning, each observation would remain a mere isolated
fact. Each additional example would remain new and unpredictable. Induction pulls different observations together. It makes data
add up. The generalizations it produces tell us what to expect. If we
have no reliable generalizations about what mushrooms are edible,
our cooking will have to proceed by trial and error—with possibly
fatal results.

The Uses of Induction

Reasoning that aims at finding a common element has many
applications. Here are three of the most common:

(1) *Induction makes us find the common pattern linking individual instances.* It makes us conclude that the "hot pursuit" of juvenile
offenders by police cars is a grave danger to life and property. The
same kind of induction is at work when we correlate data: We read
that in one of our industries 18 percent of the skilled workers are
women, 15 percent of the executives, 12 percent of the technicians, 3
percent of the lawyers. We conclude that women in this field have
only a small share of highly skilled and responsible work.

(2) *Induction makes us classify things as members of the same
category.* Whales may look and act like huge fish. But the zoologist
can list many *shared features* that make us classify them with other
mammals. They breathe like many land animals; they give birth to
live offspring; they nurse their young. The more such points of contact there are, the more convincing the **classification**.

(3) *Induction helps us account for related facts.* Notice how we
construct a **hypothesis** to account for a puzzling state of affairs:

FACT 1:   The house across the street has shown no signs of life in some days;
FACT 2:   Some rolled-up, rain-soaked newspapers lie on the front steps;
FACT 3:   The grass needs cutting badly;
FACT 4:   Visitors who ring the doorbell get no answer; . . .
              Therefore:

CONCLUSION: The people across the street are away on a trip.—Monroe C.
              Beardsley, *Thinking Straight*

All the clues in this example seem to point in a common direction:

Houses show no sign of life *when the owner is away*.
Newspapers remain on the steps *when the owner is away*.
Lawns remain uncut *when the owner is away*.
[And so on.]

How probable our hypothesis is depends on the nature and number of the clues. We have to be careful not to ignore clues that point in *other* directions.

Effective Generalizations

Anchor your generalizations firmly to representative examples. Make your reader see the connection between your generalization and the observations or experiences from which they were derived. Ideally, you should back up every generalization with a fair sampling of the evidence behind it. For an effective writer, presenting solid examples for general statements has become second nature:

> *Americans* are a sententious people and *are taught at an early age to moralize.* They learn it in Sunday school. They learn it from Poor Richard—at least they did so in my time. In Chicago during the twenties we were filled up with Poor Richard: "Little strokes fell great oaks." "Plough deep while sluggards sleep." These formulas seemed true and sound. Longfellow, whom we had to memorize by the yard, was also strongly affirmative: "Life is real! Life is earnest! And the grave is not its goal." And finally there was "The Chambered Nautilus"; "Build thee more stately mansions, O my soul."—Saul Bellow, "The Writer as Moralist," *Atlantic*

Here are the most common ways to establish the vital link between general assertions and their sources:

(1) *Back up your generalization with a solid listing of facts and figures.* It's hard to argue with a statement as well supported as the following:

> *Apart from the grim human cost of war, the mere economic cost of war has always been staggering.* The cost of killing a single man in the war between Athens and Sparta 2,300 years ago has been estimated at the equivalent of $50. During the Roman wars the price of a single death was supposed to have come to something in excess of $100. By the American War for Independence that cost had climbed to $600. During the American War between the States, the figure had been multiplied almost ten times and was more than $5,000. The estimated cost for killing one man in World War I was about $26,000; for World War II it was $65,000.

For reasons of strategy, a writer may marshal the supporting facts first and then lead into the generalization they are meant to support:

Two hundred years ago, the average U.S. citizen had a life span of between 35 and 45 years and an annual income of around $200. Indeed, as late as 1910, our average life expectancy was 47 years. Yet in 1975, the average life span in the United States was 72 years and per capita income was about $5000. *Significantly, the key ingredient in this remarkable achievement was technology, and chemical technology was a star contributor.* One hundred and twenty-six of the 500 most important technological advances over a 20-year period were chemical in nature and an additional 76 had strong chemical input, according to a 1974 National Science Board report to Congress.—C. A. I. Goring, "Nature Isn't That Benign," *World*

(2) *Make strategic use of outstanding familiar examples.* Give readers a chance to relate what you say to their own experience or memory:

The average athlete begins to wonder when his career is going to end almost as soon as he starts it. He knows that it either can be shortened with devastating swiftness by an injury, or eventually reach the point at which the great skills begin to erode. As time goes on, and the broadcasters begin to refer to the athlete as a "veteran" and the club begins to use high draft choices to acquire young collegians to groom for his position, the player has to decide whether to cut it clean and retire at the top—as Rocky Marciano, the heavyweight champion, did—or wait for some sad moment—Willie Mays stumbling around in the outfield reaches of Candlestick Park—when the evidence is clear not only to oneself but to one's peers that the time is up.—George Plimpton, "The Final Season," *Harper's*

(3) *Choose authentic examples that will strike the reader as typical or representative.* For many readers, the quotation in the following passage will have a convincing, authentic ring:

Hate letters are a fact of life for anyone whose name appears in print or whose face is seen on television or whose voice is heard on radio. They are terribly disturbing—but after the first few, you begin to catch on to the fact that they have nothing whatever to do with you (or your book) but are sheer projections on the part of their writers. They are often unsigned. They often begin with sentences like: "My mother was a lady who never used four-letter words and ——s like you are what's rotting America and weakening our morale [*sic*] fiber. . . ." They are often misspelled and ungrammatical, and full of mixed metaphors and malapropisms.— Erica Jong, "The Writer as Guru," *New York*

Avoid two common weaknesses:

• *Avoid the example that is striking but atypical.* It is tempting to document the American need for "constant expensive amusement" by citing slot machines installed in its toilet booths by a gambling casino in Nevada. But many readers will feel: "You are not talking about *me.*" There must be a better example than a reference to a place that caters to the *un*usual, that promises Americans what they do *not* typically get at home.

• *Avoid the sample that is too narrow or too weighted to be representative.* You cannot reach a general conclusion about the attitude of college professors toward their students by observing a Latin professor about to retire, a part-time Greek instructor, and a graduate student who plans to teach Hebrew. At the least, you will have to branch out into other specialties: science, engineering, English. Ideally, you would sample teachers of different opinions and backgrounds. A small sample, carefully chosen to cover different possibilities, can be more representative than a large sample favoring one type of person.

Hasty Generalization

Revise hasty generalizations. We have a natural tendency toward drawing general conclusions that are superficial or premature. We think we see the general picture when we really see only a few pieces of the puzzle. Each of the following passages shows the writer in the process of "jumping to a conclusion." What makes the inductive leap too big in each case?

Every week we read newspaper reports of some college hiring a professor who holds Marxist views. We are turning our colleges into centers of indoctrination in the Marxist view of economics and history.

Every young black I have talked to has rejected the materialistic ideals of middle-class America. Blacks today no longer aspire to becoming black counterparts of the organization men of white suburbia.

Writers like Carl Sandburg and e. e. cummings rejected traditional meter and rhyme. The modern poet rejects traditional poetic form.

Remember the following advice:

(1) *Scale down sweeping generalizations like the following:*

SWEEPING: Armenians are an exceptionally gifted people.
CAUTIOUS: A number of Armenians have done exceptional work in music and art.

SWEEPING: Americans are the most generous people on earth.
CAUTIOUS: Over the years, Americans have given impressive support to private charity and to such government programs as foreign aid.

(2) *Use labels like* typical, normal, *or* average *cautiously.* No one wants to be a typical freshman, a typical Republican, a typical Jew.

An experienced writer uses such labels very cautiously, if at all. Notice how the author of the following passage presents his generalizations as tentative first impressions, how he explains terms that might prove misleading or offensive:

> American women are particularly conspicuous to the European observer. *They strike him first* as being *generally* better groomed and better dressed than their European sisters, *even if* they rarely show individual and critical taste. *Then they strike him* as being more sure of themselves than are the women of any other nation, even those of Northern Europe. *There seems to be* little hesitation and shyness, even in a very young American girl. American women, to the European, *may even seem* "tough," *not in the sense that* they are vulgar in any way, *but in the sense that* they are both resilient and forthright. These are qualities which the European is accustomed to find only among men.—Gunnar D. Kumlien, "America: Image and Reality," *Commonweal*

(3) *Do not move on such a high level of abstraction that you will have trouble getting down to earth.* In the following example, note how far we have to move down the abstraction ladder before we reach something that readers could see with their own eyes:

VERY GENERAL:	The younger generation has no morals.
LESS GENERAL:	Students are careless in their conduct.
LESS GENERAL:	College students present a casual appearance.
LESS GENERAL:	Freshmen dress casually.
SPECIFIC:	Betty came to class in her bare feet.

The various levels of generalization form a pyramid. There are countless concrete, factual observations at the bottom ("My feet are blistered"). There are a limited number of sweeping general pronouncements at the top ("We are born to suffer"). Some writers are most at home on the ground level, talking about individuals. Others are most at home in the clouds, generalizing about life and existence. The most instructive kind of writing moves in the space between. It presents generalizations large enough to be of interest and yet limited enough to be tied to specific examples.

EXERCISES

A. Write three sentences in which a generalization emerges from detail presented earlier in the sentence. Use the following as a model:

> Dogs bark at the door to be let in; rabbits thump to call each other; the cooing of doves and the growl of a wolf defending his kill *are unequivocal signs of feelings and intentions to be reckoned with by other creatures.* (Susanne Langer)

B. Examine the generalizations in the following passages. On what level of generalization does the author move? Which generalizations would you *challenge*, and on what grounds? Which generalizations could you *buttress* with evidence of your own? How would you scale down generalizations that are too sweeping?

1. For the current generation of students, the importance of athletics is rapidly becoming null.

2. Single men are the nation's leading social problem. Within the same age groups, they are fifteen times more likely than married men—and about twenty times more likely than single women—to be incarcerated in prisons or institutions for the criminally insane. They constitute the vast majority of violent criminals and suicides. They earn less money than single women, don't pay their bills, or observe speed limits when drunk.

3. Young people today consider World War II as merely another meaningless war, to be blamed not on Hitler and Hirohito but on the older generation.

4. A stable society is made up of stable individuals. An individual can be stable (generally speaking) only if she or he was raised in a stable atmosphere, that is, a stable family environment. A family does not necessarily have to consist of a mother-father-children group. Any situation that gives the child love, understanding, and a certain degree of discipline can serve as a family.

5. Students see a bureaucratic educational system whose teachers are remote and uninterested in them; whose administrators never listen seriously to their views on issues (housing, academic problems, regulations, student activities) which vitally affect them; and in whose classrooms they are expected not to participate but merely to listen.

6. Any white person who owns anything is under siege. Particularly if he's not young. A mansion or a one-room apartment, a Mercedes or a secondhand compact, if he owns anything, he is hated. The class war seems to be coming to the knife-edge, but as Marx didn't quite foresee, it's not only a war between haves and have-nots, it's also a war between generations and races. The white poor hate the white nonpoor. (How many city people have had their country places broken into lately? Friends of mine, with a small house on a remote mountain road, have arrived three times in the last six months to discover thefts.) The young rob the nonyoung, and justify this "ripping off" on moral, almost evangelist grounds. And as for races, the brute fact—in New York, at least—is that every white person is an animal in a game preserve whom nonwhites can hunt at their pleasure.—Stanley Kauffmann, "On Films," *The New Republic*

7. Seems our mad quest for material objects is a national characteristic. We constantly desire more than we know rationally we need. But instead of curbing our desires, as mature persons seemingly should, we let our desires command us. We allow ourselves to fall into the most outrageous financial arrangements in order to finance all the material goods we feel are essential for the "good life." Of course these goods usually supply no real satisfaction and, paradoxically, their attainment seems usually to be followed by an even greater desire for more possessions—a kind of fever.

8. People like killers. (Ionesco)

C. The following generalizations are from an article about what college students look for when thinking about a future job. In the light of your own acquaintance with students, are this author's conclusions what you would expect? How would you challenge or change the author's generalizations? Do your own informal survey of students' attitudes toward future careers. What questions would you ask to bring out their true feelings? How much of a cross section would you feel obliged to interview? How would you make your sample representative? (Your instructor will tell you whether to present the results of your survey as an oral or as a written report.)

Students are most explicit, placement officers report, about what they *don't* want. They don't want to work for a big company. They don't want to work on a regular schedule. They don't want to work in the city. They don't want to sell. They don't want money or prestige as much as their elders do. And they don't want a job that forecloses their options . . . which is to say that a lot of them aren't properly thrilled by the prospect of a good, steady job with a future.

What they *do* want, placement officers agree, comes out only under probing. They want to work in small groups offering rewarding personal "interaction," to borrow a term from college psychology courses. They want work over which they have a lot of control ("make my own decisions"). They want to be creative and express themselves. They want work that allows them freedom to live as they please (flexible hours, no dress code). Most important, they want work that really matters, and since most of their life experience has been academic, it is not surprising that their definition of meaningful work grows out of the courses they've taken: cleaning up the environment, helping the poor, promoting international understanding, writing and researching, the arts.—Caroline Bird, "The Job Market," *New York*

D. The following excerpt is from an assessment of students' political attitudes first published in an independent student daily. (Which of the generalizations would you question? On what grounds? Which would you tend to accept?) Conduct your own *informal survey* of students' political attitudes. Make up half a dozen questions designed to bring out candid responses on areas of special interest to you: race, radicalism, business ethics, the environment, the military, or the like. Question or interview a sample of students on your campus. What tentative generalizations can you formulate after listening to them? Present and support your findings in a final report. Make use of short verbatim quotations to give your report an authentic flavor. (Be prepared to compare your results with those obtained by your classmates.)

Students care more, are more concerned, more resolutely hostile to the major institutions of society than they have ever been in recent history. In the early sixties, the vast majority of students thought that while America may have made some mistakes, for the most part its history was one of singular goodness. Unique among national histories, America had never had a bad president, a country blessed with an unbroken line of great men on white horses. Today most any college student will tell you that the case is more of a succession of white men on great horses.

3. THINKING THE MATTER THROUGH

Much argument starts from common ground. It starts from assumptions shared by writer and reader. It then moves step by step to a conclusion that the writer claims these shared assumptions justify. The kind of thinking that "draws out" conclusions from shared assumptions is called deductive reasoning, or **deduction**. Deductive reasoning starts from what we already know. It applies our knowledge to the solution of specific problems, to the analysis of particular instances. Here is the kind of deductive reasoning that is behind many everyday decisions:

> All the people selling encyclopedias look well dressed.
> I'm wearing a crumpled T-shirt.
> Maybe I better change before I apply for the job.

> Several writers I have read resented being called "boy."
> I use the word "boy" a lot in talking to people.
> Maybe I better watch that word in talking to my friends.

As you can see from these examples, induction and deduction are two sides of the same coin. Induction helps us develop the generalizations and classifications that map out our world for us. Deduction helps us apply these general guidelines to the particular problem, to the case at hand.

To judge if a logical conclusion is justified, we can try to line it up as the final step in a deductive argument. Such an argument proceeds as follows:

FIRST PREMISE: All *members of the Pegasus Club* are English majors.
SECOND PREMISE: Claire Benton is a *member of the Pegasus Club*.
CONCLUSION: Claire Benton is an English major.

A deductive argument moving from two initial assumptions to a conclusion is called a **syllogism**. The statements representing what we already know are called **premises**. Syllogistic reasoning deduces conclusions that follow from accepted premises. The common term ("member of the Pegasus Club") accounts for the partial overlapping of the two premises and thus makes a conclusion possible. It is called the **middle term.** Here are some additional syllogisms, with the middle terms italicized:

FIRST PREMISE: No *round-headed Irishmen* are eligible to join the Phi Beta Gamma Fraternity.
SECOND PREMISE: I am a *round-headed Irishman*.
CONCLUSION: I am not eligible to join the Phi Beta Gamma Fraternity.

FIRST PREMISE: Only *seniors* can be elected to the student court.
SECOND PREMISE: Gerald is not a *senior*.
CONCLUSION: Gerald cannot be elected to the student court.

Valid Deductions

When you apply a generalization to specific instances, pay special attention to its scope. There is an important difference in scope between the following two statements:

NONEXCLUSIVE: *All* Maoists quote the sayings of Chairman Mao.

EXCLUSIVE: *Only* Maoists quote the sayings of Chairman Mao.

The first generalization includes all Maoists, but it does not *exclude* anybody else. When we hear someone quoting Mao, we would say to ourselves: "This person could be a Maoist—or *somebody else* who studies the thoughts of Chairman Mao (maybe to *take issue* with them)." The second generalization is much more restrictive. Every time we hear someone quote Mao, we would say: "Aha! A Maoist!"

We call a deduction **valid** if it draws only those conclusions that are justified by the premises. To draw valid conclusions, we must remember that a generalization may apply to some members of a group but not all. It may apply to all members of a group and no one else, or to all members of a group and others also. *Assuming the premises to be true*, the following arguments would result in the following justified conclusions:

FIRST PREMISE: Some redheads are passionate.

SECOND PREMISE: Horace is a redhead.

CONCLUSION: Horace *may or may not be* passionate.
                    (The greater the percentage of passionate people among redheads, the stronger the likelihood that Horace is passionate.)

FIRST PREMISE: All redheads are passionate.

SECOND PREMISE: Horace is a redhead.

CONCLUSION: Horace is passionate.
                    (A statement true of *all* members of a group applies to each individual member.)

FIRST PREMISE: All redheads are passionate.

SECOND PREMISE: Horace is passionate.

CONCLUSION: Horace *may or may not be* a redhead.
                    (Horace shares *one* quality with all members of the group "redheads," but that does not make him a member of the group.)

FIRST PREMISE:	Only redheads are passionate.
SECOND PREMISE:	Horace is passionate.
CONCLUSION:	Horace is a redhead. (Horace has a quality possessed *only* by redheads; it therefore identifies him as a member of the group.)

FIRST PREMISE:	No redheads are passionate.
SECOND PREMISE:	Horace is a redhead.
CONCLUSION:	Horace is not passionate. (A quality *ruled out* for all members of a group is ruled out for each individual member.)

FIRST PREMISE:	No redheads are passionate.
SECOND PREMISE:	Horace is not a redhead.
CONCLUSION:	Horace *may or may not be* passionate. (When both premises are negative, neither an affirmative nor a negative conclusion can be drawn.)

Note: Logicians sort out arguments such as these into two types. The first is the true syllogism, in which a definite conclusion *necessarily* follows from the premises. If the premises are true, and the logical operations valid, the conclusion is necessarily true. The second type leads to a merely *probable* conclusion. It allows more or less reliable prediction. In your writing, you will seldom present generalizations that start with "all" or "no" and thus can function as the first premise in a true syllogism. More typically, you will be drawing probable conclusions from generalizations neither all-inclusive nor all-exclusive.

Checking Your Premises

Examine the premises on which you base your arguments. Any argument based on previous knowledge can be no more accurate than that previous knowledge itself. If it starts from unreliable assumptions, the argument itself may be technically valid. It may proceed "according to the rules." But the results would still be untrue. Even when the logical machinery is operating correctly, it cannot produce true results from misleading information.

When you present an argument like the following, your reader may challenge one of your premises rather than your conclusion:

Students learn best in a relaxed, permissive atmosphere.
The present system of exams induces tensions and anxieties.
Therefore, exams work against true learning.

(But is it *true* that a relaxed atmosphere is best for learning? Do not at least some people perform better under pressure?)

To make sure you do not argue from shaky premises, try to bring **hidden premises** into the open. When important assumptions are not stated, readers feel frustrated: They may find it hard to agree or disagree with something that is only in the background, never really put into words. Here are some arguments with their hidden assumptions spelled out. Would you *accept* the hidden premise in each case?

PREMISE: Jones is a fascist.
CONCLUSION: Don't listen to him.
HIDDEN PREMISE: Fascists are not worth listening to.

PREMISE: Professor Metcalf is from a middle-class background.
CONCLUSION: He cannot be expected to sympathize with the poor.
HIDDEN PREMISE: People always take over the attitudes of their parents.

Note: Some arguments merely restate the initial assumptions. **Circular arguments** merely *seem* to move from premise to conclusion. But in fact they tread water. How far does the following argument get from the initial assumption?

True ability will always assert itself.
People of true ability see to it that their talents are recognized.
Therefore, true ability will not want for recognition.

Interpreting Statistics

When you base logical arguments on statistical figures, make sure you understand the information they provide. Statistical figures have something solid about them and are a powerful tool of persuasion. However, unless you interpret them cautiously, they may lead you to make claims they do not justify.

Suppose a set of statistics indicates that the average income of the twenty families living in Blueberry Park is $25,000—a figure that is said to represent an increase of 100 percent during the last two decades. These figures might conjure up a picture of twenty well-to-do families. But perhaps most of the twenty families earn $3,000 a year and live in shacks, while the twentieth family earns $400,000 and lives in a mansion on the hill. The reported increase offers similar problems of interpretation. It may be an increase in dollar earnings, which could be largely nullified by a corresponding increase in the cost of living. It could be an increase in actual purchasing power as determined by the cost of basic commodities.

When you cite statistics, show that you understand the assumptions and procedures of the statistician. When you wish to quote the data provided by an intelligence test, find out what kinds of intelligence the test measures and what measurements it applies. If the results of the test are described in terms of norms, medians, and percentiles, make sure that you understand the technical terms before you start quoting the figures.

Avoiding Common Fallacies

Look out for common logical fallacies. To take an argument to a logical conclusion, we have to move patiently from step to step. To make the reader follow, we have to lay out the argument clearly and make the reader see that each step is justified. Many common **fallacies** are the result of an argument proceeding too quickly. A fallacy is a familiar and predictable way that a logical argument can go wrong. Many fallacies are examples of short-cut thinking. Guard against short cuts like the following:

Oversimplification   When we look for the solution to an urgent problem, we welcome a quick and simple answer. Often the simple answer is not the right one. Suppose we ask: "Why is public transportation in such a sorry state? Why do we hear so many complaints about inadequate commuter trains, poor bus service, nonexistent transportation for the aged or the young?" One answer may well be the economic interest of car makers and oil companies. Whatever puts more cars on the roads may well be good for General Motors. But we *oversimplify* if we ignore other factors. For instance, many people prefer to use their own cars, no matter what dire warnings they hear about congestion or pollution or fuel shortages.

We call an argument that ignores possible complications **simplistic**. Here is the kind of writing that deliberately guards against oversimplification:

> . . . Few poor countries are without a minority of exceedingly rich. And it is difficult to understand why an Andean or Middle Eastern peasant should seek to enhance his income by irrigation, improved seed, or acceptable livestock when he knows that anything in excess of subsistence will be appropriated by the landlord, tax collector, moneylender, or merchant. Yet the world has much poverty without evident exploiters. In India and Pakistan there are millions of small landowning peasants who are very poor but whose poverty cannot be related to the enrichment of any landlord, moneylender, tax collector, or other visible oppressor.

. . . Low income allows of no saving. Without saving there is nothing to invest. Without investment there can be no economic advance, and so poverty is self-perpetuating. *Yet* in several countries of the Middle East, as also in South America—Venezuela is particularly a case in point—oil provides a rich source of revenue and capital is not scarce. But the vast majority of the people remain exceedingly poor.—John Kenneth Galbraith, "The Poverty of Nations," *Atlantic*

Post Hoc Fallacy A second event following closely after another is not necessarily a result of the first. We naturally look for immediate, clear-cut causes. Often the result is the *post hoc* fallacy, from Latin *post hoc ergo propter hoc*: "*after* this, therefore *because* of this." We eat potato salad and return home violently ill—cause and effect? A party-goer smokes marijuana and has a bad accident on the way home—cause and effect? A young man proposes to a woman after he learns of her recent inheritance—cause and effect? What would it take to make you say "yes" or "very likely" in answer to each of these questions? What other possible causes might have to be considered?

False Dilemma A true dilemma leaves us only two ways out, both undesirable. A false dilemma presents us with two ways out, while the author is trying to block our view of the third. An ad might offer worried parents a choice between buying a home encyclopedia and allowing their children to grow up ignorant. A third alternative is to trust in the educational efforts of the schools.

To resist the "either-or" fallacy, we have to remember that often there are *more* than two sides to an issue. We encounter many suspect "either-or" alternatives: "Conservatism vs. Liberalism," "Socialism vs. Free Enterprise," "Censorship vs. Freedom of Thought," "Traditional vs. Modern Education." What does the author of the following passage do to keep his readers from "either-or" thinking?

It is all very well to say that a reporter collects the news and that the news consists of facts. The truth is that, in our world, the facts are infinitely many and that no reporter could collect them all, no newspaper could print them all, and nobody could read them all. We have to select *some* facts rather than others, and in doing that we are using not only our legs, but our selective judgment of what is interesting or important, or both. . . .

Because we are newspapermen in the American liberal tradition, the way we interpret the news is not by fitting the facts to a dogma. It is by proposing theories or hypotheses, which are then tested by trial and error. We put forward the most plausible interpretation we can think of, the most plausible picture into which the raw news fits, and then we wait to see whether the later news fits into the interpretation.—Walter Lippmann, "The Job of the Washington Correspondent," *Atlantic*

False Analogy   Just as there is a difference between *after* and *because*, there is a difference between *similar* and *alike*. People may have seen a land boom end in a spectacular crash. They watch the real estate prices shoot up again, noting many factors at work that remind them of the earlier boom. Noting the similarities, they may confidently wait for a crash—that may never come. In spite of the many similarities, there may also be important *differences* between the two situations.

To use an analogy to advantage, make sure you realize *where it breaks down*. Analogies are most valuable when used for explanation and illustration. For instance, we might compare the human brain to a telephone switchboard or to an electronic calculator. The switchboard analogy could explain how the brain sorts out the many incoming impressions and establishes relevant connections. But in order not to mislead the reader, we should also point out some of the things that make a brain different from a machine. For instance, a brain is not produced in a factory. It is largely self-directing, and it suffers from quirks and ailments more mysterious than a short circuit.

Rationalization   Hesitate to adopt simply the most flattering or the least damaging hypothesis. What do you say to people who make statements like the following?

> I failed algebra. That teacher always had it in for me.

> My father finally resigned from the diplomatic service. His superiors never did like his outspoken political views.

> Misleading IQ tests can really hurt a person. I was tagged as "low IQ" in high school, even though it is well known that IQ measurements are extremely unreliable.

EXERCISES

A. Which of the following arguments seem to reach a logically justified conclusion? Which seem to illustrate a familiar fallacy or logical weakness?

1. George is above the national average in intelligence. But he is below the national average in reading ability. Above-average intelligence is no guarantee that a student will be an above-average reader.
2. George is above the national average in intelligence. But he is below the national average in reading ability. Therefore, the school's system of teaching reading must be defective.
3. Wars must be understood in economic terms. Wars are started by have-not nations against those who have. It's as simple as that.

4. Today a columnist of the *Washington Post* criticized the Democratic leadership in Congress. She must be a Republican.
5. In periods of rapid expansion, the American economy gorges on time payments and capital investment. It needs to chew this cud sufficiently before it resumes eating. Therefore, recessions are a natural and organic part of the business cycle.
6. All members of the imperial bodyguard had to be at least six feet tall. Kim's grandfather was a member of the guard. He must have been very tall.
7. All members of the imperial bodyguard had to be at least six feet tall. Kim's grandfather was rejected when he tried to join the guard. He must have been too short.
8. A large piece of man is still irrational animal, with a frightening capacity for destruction. Technology increases man's power. Therefore, the more powerful the technology, the greater man's capacity for destruction.
9. John does not believe in baptism. He must be an atheist.
10. Haven't we advanced farther and faster than any other nation in the past one hundred and eighty years? Isn't our standard of living the highest in the world? Since we are governed under a two-party system and since we enjoy the highest standard of living under this system, it certainly follows that attempts to form a third major party in the United States should be discouraged.

B. Study the following passages. Which of them would make you say: "I agree with your conclusion"? Where you can, spell out the assumptions on which an argument rests. Which premises do you find acceptable, and why? Where would you challenge the logic by which an argument proceeds, and why?

1. My feeling about discrimination is that everyone is equal. If I am not hired for a job because I lack the necessary skills, or because I do not have the necessary experience, I will not get angry. I will not object if a black man or woman is hired instead of me. But that man or woman better have the skills I lack or better qualifications than I do. Otherwise, the employer would be guilty of reverse discrimination.

2. Teenagers are not adults, so why should they be judged as adults? There's a big difference between a sixteen-year-old juvenile and a twenty-six-year-old adult. If a teenager has committed a crime, there is a possibility he or she can change for the better with the proper help. If juvenile delinquents aren't given the proper help they need, society will make it harder for them to adjust to their problems and harder for itself. If a boy in trouble doesn't understand what he has done, why he is being punished, and how he can deal with his problems, then how will prison help him? There are many different reasons why teenagers commit crimes: Many are filled with hatred in their minds; some want attention; others come from families that desperately need money. These and other problems need to be dealt with on an individual level. Sending a fifteen-year-old to the state penitentiary will not solve these problems.

3. Nobody in Japan is permitted to own a pistol except police officers. In one recent year, Japan had 37 murders by firearms. The United States has twice the population of Japan. There were 4,954 murders by firearms here in the same year. Our present laws allowing private citizens to own guns are responsible for this tremendous difference.

4. Colleges should not set up facilities to accommodate political rallies or debates. For colleges are not intended to be institutions for the advancement of

aspiring political leaders, but to prepare our young citizens for their place in society. I am not against voicing our opinions; in fact, I feel that we are extremely fortunate to be able to express our views openly. Nevertheless, there is no place for the luxury of such provisions on campus. The money needed to build a hall or a meeting place could be put to better use in the addition of new classrooms or laboratories. Students should be studying while they are fresh—later or when they take a break they may read about political events in the paper. An employer will look at the grade point average, not at views on a bygone political issue.

C. Explain the kind of argument used in the following passage. How convincing is the argument?

The Tragedy of the Commons

Under a system of private property, the men who own property recognize their responsibility to care for it, for if they don't they will eventually suffer. A farmer, for instance, will allow no more cattle in a pasture than its carrying capacity justifies. If he overloads it, erosion sets in, weeds take over, and he loses the use of the pasture.

If a pasture becomes a commons open to all, the right of each to use it may not be matched by a corresponding responsibility to protect it. Asking everyone to use it with discretion will hardly do, for the considerate herdsman who refrains from overloading the commons suffers more than a selfish one who says his needs are greater. If everyone would restrain himself, all would be well; but it takes only one less than everyone to ruin a system of voluntary restraint. In a crowded world of less than perfect human beings, mutual ruin is inevitable if there are no controls. This is the tragedy of the commons.

One of the major tasks of education today should be the creation of such an acute awareness of the dangers of the commons that people will recognize its many varieties. For example, the air and water have become polluted because they are treated as commons. Further growth in the population or per capita conversion of natural resources into pollutants will only make the problem worse. The same holds true for the fish of the oceans. Fishing fleets have nearly disappeared in many parts of the world; technological improvements in the art of fishing are hastening the day of complete ruin. Only the replacement of the system of the commons with a responsible system of control will save the land, air, water and oceanic fisheries.—Garrett Hardin, "Lifeboat Ethics," *Psychology Today*

D. Report as fully as you can on the hidden premises or unstated assumptions in a political speech, an editorial, or a letter to the editors of a newspaper or magazine.

4. STRUCTURING AN ARGUMENT

Much forceful writing carries us along because it suggests determination, a sense of purpose. We feel that the groundwork is being done for conclusions to be reached in due time. Each paragraph is a link in a chain; each point being established is necessary as a step in the argument as a whole.

These patterns of organization follow the order of a logical argument:

The Inductive Paper

Use the inductive approach to overcome the resistance of a skeptical or hostile audience. An inductive paper presents examples, case histories, or evidence and then draws a general conclusion. Inductive order is especially effective when a writer has to overcome prejudice or distrust. It keeps readers from saying too early: "I don't believe it!" Instead, they find themselves paying attention to the evidence, and perhaps step by little step changing their minds. Spend most of your time "letting the evidence speak for itself":

A Time of Progress

FIRST SET OF FACTS: (Economics)	The median income of nonwhite families rose from 55 percent of that of white families in 1950 to 63 percent twenty years later. . . .
SECOND SET: (Education)	Whereas in 1947 black adult Americans completed 34 percent fewer years of schooling than the entire population, by 1969 this difference had narrowed to 19 percent; and, for persons in the age bracket from twenty-five to twenty-nine years, it had nearly vanished. . . .
THIRD SET: (Health)	The differences between the life expectancies at birth of the two races diminished significantly during the postwar era. . . .
FOURTH SET: (Politics)	The steadily rising proportion of black citizens that were registered and voted in elections and of blacks in public office showed a narrowing of the political gap. . . .
FIFTH SET: (Self-Image)	Blacks themselves overwhelmingly believed that conditions were improving for their race in this country, as sociologist Gary T. Marx reported in his book *Protest and Prejudice*. . . .
AUTHOR'S CONCLUSION:	All these facts demonstrate measurable postwar progress of American blacks toward economic and political equality. . . .

The Pro-and-Con Paper

Weigh the pro and con to reach a balanced conclusion. The great advantage of the pro-and-con paper is that it treats an issue as a genuine issue—as an open question worth thinking about. Instead of presenting an open-and-shut case, it appeals to the readers' intelligence. A writer may first discuss the advantages of a proposal or a program, and then the disadvantages. A writer may first discuss arguments in support of a new method or approach, and then look at possible objections. Pro-and-con papers are often effective because they make possible an exceptionally clear overall scheme:

Learning More About Less

I. FIRST STEP: A familiar idea is confirmed:
Much emphasis today is put on courses that will help students in a future career (detailed illustrations).

II. SECOND STEP: An objection is stated:
But responsible citizens must be able to recognize competence and quackery in fields other than their own (detailed illustrations).

III. THIRD STEP: A balanced conclusion is drawn:
Therefore, students need at least some required courses that give them a basic understanding of some important disciplines outside their own fields.

The formal lining up and playing off against each other of opposites is known as the **dialectic** method. The dialectic process makes us move from narrow or one-sided views to a larger perspective. It starts with a strong statement of one extreme, the **thesis**. This statement in turn provokes a counterstatement, or **antithesis**. An attempt to reconcile or balance the two statements produces the resolution, or **synthesis**.

Can you see the dialectic process at work in the following excerpt, adapted from a discussion of American military power?

THESIS: The United States has the physical potential—both human and material—for implementing even greater international commitments than those we have hitherto assumed. Our population includes more than 16 million young men between the ages of eighteen and thirty, and we have the industrial potential to equip whatever armed forces we raise with more firepower than any other nation of the world. . . .

ANTITHESIS: What is missing, of course, is the will. Americans value their private comforts and pleasures, and are unwilling to make the sacrifices that are necessary for the success of imperial ventures. Young men are not volunteering to fight for manifestly destined causes these days. Our citizens look upon their personal incomes as sacred vessels, not to be tapped by the tax collector for ambitious expenditures on armaments. . . .

SYNTHESIS: Thus to say that our power is "limited" is really to admit that the citizens of America are unwilling to devote more than a minor fraction of their population or their prosperity to the enterprise of empire.

The *result* of the dialectic method typically is to produce balanced views. But it reaches these views as the result of a confrontation. We would expect yawns if we were to announce that the great early political leaders of the United States were only human. But we might create some interest if we first sketched the moral paragons of schoolbook and patriotic speech: honest George Washington, thrifty Ben Franklin. We could then counter by taking the reader through the debunker's gallery of American leaders: a disciplinarian Washington, a slave-holding Jefferson, a Franklin peopling the world with illegitimate children. We could then work toward a balanced view of people with quite human failings and yet setting *political* precedents of great importance for modern times.

Analyzing Cause and Effect

Trace a chain of causes and effects. In analyzing a current problem, we are often trying to disentangle the various causes that have helped create it. We can clarify matters by presenting the major causes in historical order, or in order of importance. Once the major causes and effects are sorted out, the reader might be ready to listen to possible solutions.

Here is an outline of a magazine article that sorts out major causes, shows their effects, and points toward desirable remedies:

Bald Eagles at Bay

STATEMENT OF PROBLEM:	It is believed that when the bald eagle became the nation's symbol in 1782, there were nesting pairs in each of the present 49 mainland states. But in the summer of 1973, only 627 active nests were found in the lower 48 states. South of Alaska, the United States may have only about 1,000 breeding pairs left. . . .
FIRST MAJOR CAUSE:	According to students of the bald eagle, its precarious position is traceable to a variety of causes. One, *habitat destruction,* has confronted the eagles since colonial days. Forests are cleared and replaced with villages, cities, highways, and summer homes, and the eagles must go. . . .
SECOND MAJOR CAUSE:	*Acts of violence* are another of the major reasons for the disappearance of the national bird. Too often, guns are pointed at eagles even though they are fully protected by federal law. . . .
THIRD MAJOR CAUSE:	But the biggest eagle killers of all in recent times are probably such *agricultural poisons* as DDT, dieldrin, and other chlorinated hydrocarbons. These accumulate in wildlife food chains and eagles, being at the top of the food pyramid, build up particularly high levels. . . .
CURRENT REMEDIES:	Those who have worked with the bald eagle look hopefully at evidence of a growing public determination to rescue the magnificent bird. Ranchers in Florida, and tree farmers in many other places, now maintain private sanctuaries to protect active eagle nests. . . .—George Laycock, *National Wildlife*

Analyzing Alternatives

Examine and eliminate undesirable alternatives. To make people accept one of several options, we have to show that it is preferable to the others. We can do so by first examining the less desirable alternatives and finding them wanting. Our readers will then be ready for our own more acceptable choice. This strategy helps to make people accept the "lesser evil," or an untried new approach.

The following excerpt from an article on population control proceeds by examining alternatives. (What do you think the writer might be leading up to?)

There are many different methods of achieving limitation of births. . . .

FIRST
ALTERNATIVE:
Abortion is undoubtedly preferable to infanticide, though we know too little about the physiological and psychological damage which it may cause to recommend it without serious qualms. . . .

SECOND
ALTERNATIVE:
Contraception certainly seems preferable to abortion, and indeed the moral objection to contraception in principle seems to be confined to a single major branch of the Christian church. Even here the difference in practice between this church and the rest of society is much smaller than the difference in precept. Contraception, however, also has its problems, and it is by no means an automatic solution to the problem of population control. . . .

THIRD
ALTERNATIVE:
The fact that we must recognize is that it is social institutions which are dominant in determining the ability of society to control its population, not the mere physiology of reproduction. A classic example of this proposition is Ireland. . . .The population of Ireland has increased very little in over a hundred years, partly as a result of continued emigration, but more as a result of limitation of births. In this case the limitation was achieved through *late marriages* and the imposition of a strongly *puritan ethic* · upon the young people. . . .—Kenneth E. Boulding, *The Meaning of the Twentieth Century*

EXERCISES

A. Choose a subject on which you have strong feelings. Choose a subject where you are strongly aware of views different from or *opposed to* yours. For instance, you might choose a subject like abortion, "no growth" policies, affirmative action, or equal funding for men's and women's sports. Write a paragraph in which you describe as fully and fairly as you can a view opposed to yours.

B. Opinion polls and surveys often include a category for "Undecided." Select four or five problems or issues on which you are undecided because of *contradictory* evidence or opposed influences on your thinking. About each, write a brief summary statement on the following model:

> On the one hand, I strongly believe in ————————————— . On the
> other hand, I am also aware of ————————————— .

C. Sometimes we feel that people are too *limited* in their perception of the causes that have contributed to a problem. Sometimes we feel that people are not *resourceful* enough in thinking of the full range of options or alternatives open to them in solving a problem. Choose a topic where this limited view seems to you especially common or obvious. Outline the full range of possible causes or alternatives.

D. Study the following student-written argument. Answer the following questions: What if any seems to be the writer's basic premise? What is the overall plan of organization? What use did the writer make of examples? What use did the writer make of analogies? How clear and convincing is the writer's argument as a whole?

Staying Free

When alone, no one is compelled to consider the welfare of others in making decisions. On the proverbial desert island, we would be free to take any license we wished. If smoking were satisfying to us, we would smoke. If drinking were pleasing to us, we would drink. If taking drugs were gratifying to us, we would take drugs. If killing ourselves were to seem the best course, we would kill ourselves. Our range of choice would be limited only by the limits of our *physical* resources. Within the range of what is physically possible, we would have complete freedom to do whatever we wish. Where is the person who is not envious of such freedom?

There is one consideration that lessens this envy. For if we begin to smoke, we may soon feel the need to smoke more. If we begin to drink, we may not be able to stop. If we begin to take drugs, we may come under an absolute compulsion to take more. And if we kill ourselves, we are forever dead. It is much as in a game of chess, when one player has fallen into an opponent's trap. Then, though at the beginning he had complete freedom, he has no choice in his play, and in the end he is checkmated. Freedom, to be truly freedom, must be self-perpetuating.

If we are not to diminish by our actions the amount of freedom we have, how can we act? Any decision would limit the number of available alternatives and thus would ultimately lead to a loss of freedom.

Fortunately, it is possible to look at this situation in a more positive light. Freedom may be understood as a choice among creative possibilities. The concern is only that the choices be creative, that they do not rob us of paths or pursuits we know to be good. Freedom is not an end in itself; it must be a tool for producing good. The ideal is not so much to be *free* to do whatever we please. Rather, it is to be *free for* doing what we know, or think, we should.

THEME TOPICS 6

1. George Orwell said that the American ideal was the "he-man, the tough guy, the gorilla who puts everything right by socking everybody else on the jaw." To

judge from current popular entertainment, how true would such a comment be today? Watch current television serials built around male characters. What type seems to predominate? Are there any competing major types or runners-up? Use detailed evidence from shows you have watched. Present your material *inductively*—present your general conclusions at the end.

2. Here is a description of the parent generation from an independent student newspaper: "Our parents created suburbia, a religious faith in technology and appeasement morality. They raised the rate of divorce, built (and feared) large organizations; then they sat back in their padded chairs watching TV, drinking beer, and saying to our probing questions: 'Children, you can't fight city hall!'" Write an *inductive paper* in which you present your own general conclusions about the parent generation. Try to make your portrait as fair and balanced as you can.

3. Identify one major common trend in the treatment of minorities in current movies or television programs. Present a broad range of *representative examples*.

4. Write a *pro-and-con* paper on one of the following topics. In the first part of your paper, present the arguments or evidence on one side. In the second part, present the arguments or evidence on the opposing side. Reach a balanced conclusion in the final part of your paper. Choose *one*:

   • Should the major aim of American public schools be to promote one common language and one common culture? (Where do you stand on "assimilation" vs. "pluralism"?)

   • Should the United States grant more aid to poor countries in order to help them fight starvation and disease? (Are you for or against increased "foreign aid"?)

   • Should the United States take steps to limit future immigration—legal or illegal—to this country? (Where do you stand on the issue of "liberal" immigration policies?)

5. Write a paper in which you analyze *the major causes* of one of the following: poor performance by students in their school work; road accidents; marital problems and divorce. Choose a topic that allows you to draw on authentic material from your observation, experience, or reading.

6. Write a paper in which you analyze *major alternatives* for achieving one of the following goals: freer access to college education; a more integrated society; improved career opportunities for women; avoidance of armed conflict.

7. Argue as fully as you can your position on one of the following issues. Try to make your reader see as fully as you can the assumptions on which your argument rests and the steps by which it proceeds.

   • Should a newspaper represent the opinions of its journalists, its publishers, its advertisers, or its public?

   • Should a college have the right to bar undesirable or controversial speakers?

   • Should college professors be allowed to bring their own political views into the classroom?

- Is there any justification for censorship of the arts?
- Should we protect the environment by a "no-growth" policy?

Persuasion

CHAPTER SEVEN

1. **You and Your Reader**

2. **The Tools of Persuasion**
   Taking a Stand
   Dramatizing the Issue
   Appealing to Emotions
   Aids to Persuasion
   The Limits of Persuasion

3. **The Language of Persuasion**
   Denotation and Connotation
   The Power of Words
   Statement and Implication

4. **The Strategies of Persuasion**
   The Common Cause
   Persuading by Degrees
   The Cause Célèbre
   Refuting Objections

1. YOU AND YOUR READER

We write to be read. Sooner or later we ask ourselves: "Is anybody listening? What does it take to get a hearing? What does it take to make a real *difference* in the way my readers think and behave?" The more we care about the reader's reactions, the more important such questions become. In writing devoted to persuasion, producing the desired effect on the reader has become the writer's central purpose.

Persuasion aims at producing results. Its effectiveness can often be judged by tangible consequences: products sold, bond issues passed, officials forced to resign or to mend their ways. But the results of persuasion are equally important when they are harder to measure: attitudes hardened or changed, expectations created or doubts raised.

What does it take to persuade a reluctant reader? Remember the following guidelines:

(1) *Know your reader*. Readers are people with a history and with minds of their own. Every writer has to ask: "What basic information do I have to fill in? What basic commitments do I have to reckon with? What am I up against?"

What do you think you would be up against in each of the following situations?

- Explaining a police officer's job to a minority group audience
- Trying to get an audience of business executives to support free tuition at public colleges
- Discussing American business interests in South America with a South American student

(2) *Meet the reader halfway*. A striking characteristic of truly persuasive speakers is patience. They judge carefully what the audience is ready for. They hold back important points until the time is ripe.

Can you show how the authors of the following passages are going out of their way to meet their readers?

The sins of omission and commission of the over-thirty generation (if it makes any sense to speak in such general terms) are many and serious: So it has always been and so it will always be. But unless one is willing to compare reality only with utopia, then the nation into which these young people are entering as adults cannot be simply or reasonably characterized as a "sick society." It is, among many other things, a nation that enjoys and has always enjoyed more political, cultural, and religious freedom than any—or almost any—other society, past or present; it is a nation with an economy of almost unbelievable productivity; and it is a nation that has, since having leadership thrust upon it, generally played an honorable role in international affairs.—William Gerberding, "Liberals and Radicals," *The Reporter*

The abuse meted out to presidents has a healthily scurrilous element. Some commentators see it as a guarantee that Americans will never accept a real dictator: Their natural irreverence protects them against such psychological radiation. But the scurrility has a hysterical tinge. John F. Kennedy may not have deserved all the praise that was heaped upon him: He certainly did not deserve the corrosive denunciations that were circulating before his death.—Marcus Cunliffe, "A Defective Institution?" *Commentary*

(3) *Be prepared to follow through.* The reader's misconceptions and prejudices are not going to crumble at a single blast from the writer's trumpet. In writing to persuade, you have to identify your target carefully. You have to work up your subject to know its opportunities and its pitfalls. You have to gather enough ammunition to break down the reader's apathy or resistance.

EXERCISE

Study the following passages as examples of writing aimed at persuasion. Answer the following questions about each: What is the author's target? What is the method or the ammunition used by the author? What kind of audience would provide the ideal readers for each passage? (What kind of person would be the *wrong* reader for each passage?)

1. Consider this question from a standardized group IQ test. "No garden is without its _____." The desired answer is one of these five: "sun - rain - tool - work - weeds." A child who happens to know the expression will recognize the missing word (weeds) and complete the sentence "correctly." If he doesn't have that piece of information, he'll have to figure out the answer. He might explain to a tester, "It isn't 'tools' because I once planted a garden with my hands." But there is no tester to tell. He might continue, "I don't know how to choose between sun and rain, so I won't use either one." Again there's no tester to hear his reasoning. "So it's either 'work' or 'weeds.'" Another pause. "Well, if a gardener worked hard, maybe he wouldn't have any weeds—but, if he doesn't work at all, he won't have any garden!" Triumphantly, the clever, logical, analytical young mind has selected—the wrong answer!

When a computer grades that test, "work" will simply be marked wrong, and no one will be there to explain the thought process to the computer. Nor will anyone point out the differences between the child who has personal experience with gardens and the child whose closest contact may be the city park, ten blocks away from his fire escape.—Arlene Silberman, "The Tests That Cheat Our Children," *McCall's*

2. I have never been able to understand (and this always brings card-carrying liberals to their feet in horror) why tapped telephone conversations are inadmissible in court. What is the difference between an overheard telephone conversation and any other kind? What are you all saying on your telephones you're so ashamed of?

If a cop overheard Joe Smith say on the telephone that he planned to mow down John Doakes with a shotgun in Piccadilly Circus at high noon on Tuesday and John Doakes thereupon fell mortally diseased by shotgun pellets at high noon (or even at 12:01) Tuesday, why can't the jury be told?

Because, the lawyers tell you indignantly, the jury might be influenced. They might indeed.

I have never understood—to voice another legal heresy—why the jury can't be told that the defendant, who is on trial for raping a little girl, has been convicted four times and indicted twelve other times for the same offense. Again the lawyers say it might influence the jury. Well, it bloody well ought to.

All lawyers I have met would secretly like to make truth itself inadmissible as being a little too blinding for the feeble mental equipment of the rest of us.—John Crosby, "Button Your Lip," *This World*

3. The impact of steadily rising tuition on what might be called the heartland of the population—the working and lower-middle class—is a matter for serious concern. It should be seen as a warning that the retreat from the educational commitment is turning into a rout.

When even low-cost public institutions require an annual investment for tuition, room, and board approaching $3,000 for one child in college, the family in the $10,000-to-$15,000 income bracket is on the point of being squeezed out. Attendance at the elite colleges will become virtually impossible for youths from such homes. Thus, only a select few from the poverty level and the very rich will find it possible to attend. Higher education, which has scored significant triumphs in assuring upward mobility and preventing the stratification of American society, is in danger of being forced to move in the opposite direction—to restratify America.—Fred M. Hechinger, "Murder in Academe," *Saturday Review*

2. THE TOOLS OF PERSUASION

Much effective persuasion is the result of trial and error. A speaker discovers what catches fire with listeners. A writer over the years builds up an audience and starts appealing directly to their tested loyalties. Nevertheless, some basic techniques, some basic tools, are used over and over by men and women who have learned how to persuade.

Taking a Stand

Make sure that your readers get the message. To do justice to a difficult subject, we have to weigh the pros and cons. To defuse a hot controversial subject, we have to be diplomatic. But ultimately the reader wants an answer to a basic question: "What do you want me to believe? What do you want me to do?"

A persuasive writer has to make sure that the message gets through to the reader. The first requirement for effective persuasion is the ability to speak out. When the time comes, a persuasive writer knows how to take a stand:

> Of all the drug problems afflicting the world, heroin is the most deadly and the one that most seriously affects American young people. Once addicted, the heroin user needs about $35 a day to maintain the habit. The males steal and rob. The women become shoplifters and prostitutes.—Horace Sutton, "Drugs: Ten Years to Doomsday?" *Saturday Review*

> Do not, I say to today's women, please do not mistake sensitivity for weakness. This was the mistake which almost doomed our culture. Violence was mistaken for power, and the misuse of power for strength. The subjection is still true in the films, in the theater, in the media. . . . Let us start the new regime of honesty, of trust, abolishment of false roles in our personal relationships, and it will eventually affect the world's history as well as women's development.—Anaïs Nin, *In Favor of the Sensitive Man*

Dramatizing the Issue

Translate abstract issues into personal or human terms. Grave issues have *general* significance; they may seem far from the reader's personal experience. The statistics of misfortune and injustice, however grim, are also *impersonal*. Accident statistics can make us shudder, but they do not jolt us as witnessing a single actual accident does. The fate of a single individual can fire our imagination the way large figures cannot. When statistics about violence in our cities fall on deaf ears, a single horrible event, involving someone widely loved or admired, can dramatize the issue.

Does the following passage in any way change your mind about "crime in the streets"? How? Why?

> One block farther south, that same gray afternoon, I saw two young hoodlums accost an old black man who seemed to be something of an anachronism in his stained red tie and black fedora. The old man waved his trembling fists at them while some younger men gathered around and laughed at him. I could not hear what the two hoodlums said, but whatever it was elicited a loud cackle from the sidewalk loiterers, much slapping of the palms and cries of "right on!" The old man hobbled off, sure in the knowledge that if anyone decided to kill him right there because the color of his tie was offensive to that person's eye, he would die, helpless, alone on the Harlem sidewalk and in full view of his fellow blacks. When I ran up to him and asked him what was going on, he looked at me with his eyes pinched in terror and said: "Don't kill me, please. Don't kill me."
>
> It is this fatalism, this absolute belief that one stands alone in the face of one's attackers, that is most eroding to the spirit of all our Harlems. And it is quite easy to see where this slow disintegration of commonality leads. How can we get together to spell out our political aims, to worship and to organize if every time a black man ventures out of his home he must look behind every garbage can for a potential ambusher? How can we measure our progress if each man runs away from his

brother, fearing, through experience, that on every black ghetto street there is the possibility of death?—Orde Coombs, "Fear and Trembling in Black Streets," *New York*

Appealing to Emotions

Get the reader emotionally involved. A persuasive writer must appeal effectively to the reader's standards and motives. It's not enough for the reader to say "That is very interesting" or "That's good to know." When necessary, the persuasive writer must be able to arouse the readers' emotions—their aspirations, their fears, their indignation, their loyalties.

Assume you are part of the white audience to which the Reverend Martin Luther King directed his "Letter from Birmingham Jail." Study the following excerpt. How is the author trying to reach you? To what standards does he appeal? Where does he come closest to home? Where and how do you get emotionally involved?

I guess it is easy for those who have never felt the stinging darts of segregation to say wait. But when you have seen vicious mobs lynch your mothers and fathers at will and drown your sisters and brothers at whim; when you have seen hate-filled policemen curse, kick, brutalize, and even kill your black brothers and sisters with impunity; when you see the vast majority of your twenty million Negro brothers smothering in an airtight cage of poverty in the midst of an affluent society; when you suddenly find your tongue twisted and your speech stammering as you seek to explain to your six-year-old daughter why she can't go to the public amusement park that has just been advertised on television, and see tears welling up in her little eyes when she is told that Funtown is closed to colored children, and see the depressing clouds of inferiority begin to form in her little mental sky, and see her begin to distort her little personality by unconsciously developing a bitterness toward white people; when you have to concoct an answer for a five-year-old son asking in agonizing pathos: "Daddy, why do white people treat colored people so mean?"; when you take a cross-country drive and find it necessary to sleep night after night in the uncomfortable corners of your automobile because no motel will accept you; . . . when you are harried by day and haunted by night by the fact that you are a Negro, living constantly at tiptoe stance never quite knowing what to expect next, and plagued with inner fears and outer resentments; when you are forever fighting a degenerating sense of "nobodiness";—then you will understand why we find it difficult to wait. There comes a time when the cup of endurance runs over, and men are no longer willing to be plunged into an abyss of injustice where they experience the bleakness of corroding despair. . . .—Martin Luther King, *Why We Can't Wait*

Aids to Persuasion

Persuasive writers know how to make their side appear in a good light, and they know how to show up the weaknesses of the opposition. How many of the following aids to persuasion do you recognize?

The Strategic Comparison   Comparisons can change our perspective. They can help a writer magnify or belittle a problem. With what effect is a comparison used in the following passage?

When a child cannot remain with its parents, the best substitute is a permanent, long-term adoptive relationship in which the child becomes part of a new family. But our present system of foster care is a failure. One reason is the inadequate level of support payments to foster parents. These are as low as $90 a month in Texas, $32 a week in Connecticut—or lower than the $35 a week normally charged in most areas by kennels for care of a dog.

Insider's Testimony   Readers tend to listen to testimony from the "front lines," from people "who have been there":

Narcotics agents would sooner deal with a heroin addict who is docile and compliant than with confirmed marijuana users who grow rash beyond the limits of reason and daring beyond the borders of judgment. "You pull a gun on them," says one seasoned agent with whom I toured the heavily infected drug neighborhoods in New York, "and they will say, 'Go ahead and shoot, you can't hurt me.'"

The Bandwagon Effect   When everybody seems to be moving in the right direction, the lone opponent can be made to feel out of step:

Today, capital punishment has fallen into near international disuse. Over thirty nations, including Great Britain and the USSR, have completely abolished the death penalty. In this country, numerous states have completely abolished the death sentence. . . .

The Confused Opposition   In probing for weaknesses, a persuasive writer is likely to seize on contradictions in opposing arguments. How serious would you consider the contradiction pointed out by the author of the following passage?

Correctional facilities should be designed to rehabilitate and resocialize people, so that when released they will have a good chance to cope with the free society, and so that they will have the training needed for a fair chance at a job. The way things are now, we condemn people for committing abnormal acts in society. Then we put them in prison, the most abnormal of societies.

The Limits of Persuasion

Persuasive devices defeat their own purpose if the reader feels pushed or manipulated. Your readers want to feel that you are appealing to their own honest judgment. You can antagonize critical readers simply by trying too hard to persuade.

Avoid the following in your writing:

(1) *Avoid routine exaggeration.* There is always the temptation to state a weak position forcefully in the hope that its weakness will not be apparent. Editorials, speeches, and advertisements are full of **superlatives**, absolute claims to superiority or singularity: "the biggest," "the best," "available now for the first time," "threatening us with utter extinction," "fatal to our most cherished institutions," "unparalleled in recorded history."

Remember: Where everything is emphasized, nothing is emphasized. Tone down sweeping charges and exaggerated claims. Whenever you write in an angry or enthusiastic mood, put the result aside for a sober second reading.

(2) *Keep slanting from discrediting your writing with a fair-minded reader.* We slant material if we always select from several true statements the ones most favorable to our cause. A lawyer defending a client may describe him as a veteran, a homeowner, and a father of three children. A lawyer representing the plaintiff may describe the same man as an ex-convict, a man twice divorced, and a heavy drinker. Both descriptions may be truthful, but each creates an entirely different picture.

(3) *Do not abuse emotional appeals.* Readers with a mind of their own do not like to be wheedled, bullied, or threatened. Some people represent every minor departure from their own views as a national disaster. Too often and too rashly they predict runaway inflation, depression, or tyranny. They appeal to such ideals as love of country in support of every minor project or conviction. Many (says e. e. cummings) "unflinchingly applaud all / songs containing the words country home and / mother." But many also object to the use of such words to put a halo effect on the passing causes of the day.

(4) *Do not evade the issue by dealing in personalities.* The argument **ad hominem**, directed "at the person," shifts attention from the merit of ideas to the merits of their advocates. Instead of refuting an economist's analysis of economic trends, critics may let it be known that the person is being sued for divorce or once failed in business. Such tactics boomerang with a responsible audience. (Sometimes, of course, a person's background or conduct *is* the issue. In that case, make sure your reader can see the *relevance* of any personal remarks.)

EXERCISES

A. Study the following examples of persuasive writing. Describe the methods of persuasion or the aids to persuasion used by each writer. Which of these samples do you find most persuasive, and which least? Why?

1. In Manteca, Cal., eight-year-old Dawn Quintal was attacked and killed by a 200-pound St. Bernard as she watched building construction work near her home. In Fort Worth, Tex., infant Johnny Patterson was fatally mauled by a German shepherd despite his mother's efforts to drive the dog away. In Jersey City, N.J., when Herbert Russell, six, didn't come home for supper, his grandmother called the police. Two German shepherds, trained as guard dogs, had burrowed beneath the fence where they were guarding contracting equipment and killed the boy. The dogs stood guard over the body and had to be killed before it could be retrieved.

All these tragedies were the result of guard dogs or attack dogs becoming mixed up about their jobs. (Guard dogs are trained to keep intruders out of a territory; attack dogs, to attack on command of their master. Both are trained to be nasty.) A neighbor of mine, for example, had two Doberman pinschers that were trained as attack dogs. He kept them under excellent control, but they were still the terror of the neighborhood. The man died, and when his wife returned from the funeral, the dogs killed her on her front porch. Dogs such as these—often used to guard construction or industrial sites and trained to attack all intruders—are clearly a danger in the hands of the general public.—Richard A. Wolters, "The Good and Bad About Guard Dogs," *Parade*

2. Modern pesticides have helped Americans achieve the world's highest dietary standards. They have increased crop yields in nations that at one time knew only starvation. Yet while pesticides are constantly being painted as environmental killers, little attention is paid to the toxic qualities of naturally occurring chemicals. Consider that each of us consumes each year 40 mg of pesticides compared with 40,000 to 400,000 mg of caffeine (depending on whether we drink one cup or ten cups of coffee a day). Caffeine has an acute toxicity of about 100mg per kilogram of body weight, which makes it substantially more toxic than most pesticides. The yearly consumption level of all pesticides is 1,000 times safer than that of caffeine consumed by a moderate coffee drinker. Botulism toxins formed in improperly canned foods are at least 50,000 times more poisonous than our most toxic pesticide, yet I have heard no suggestions that we prohibit home canning. Properly managed, of course, home canning is completely safe, as are the human-made chemicals that benefit all our lives.

3. The proponents of specialization and career education insist that they want only what is best for each youngster. . . . It is one of the ironies of the new trend that vocationalism is particularly counterproductive in an uncertain economy, when jobs are both scarce and changeable. It makes slim indeed the chances of picking the right specialization years in advance of actual entry into the labor market. The writer of a recent article in *The New York Times Magazine* extravagantly extolling the virtues of New York's Aviation High School appeared unaware of its own ultimate contradiction: Only 6 members of last June's 515-member graduating class reported that they had found jobs in the aviation industry. The primary reason for youth unemployment is not lack of training but lack of jobs.—Fred M. Hechinger, "Murder in Academe," *Saturday Review*

4. The British official policy with delinquents is still based on hate—making them move at the double, granting hardly any leisure, demanding obedience (the worst of the seven deadly virtues), administering punishment. In short, wayward adolescents are treated with the very attitudes that made them delinquent to begin with. Delinquents are always deprived of love, and only love can save them.

But how can there be love in an institution with strict laws that foster fear of authority? Hence my open prison would be founded on—I'd better not use the word love—it is becoming a dirty four-letter word—*approval*, approval meaning to be on the side of the sick offender.

Years ago I read an American book about a prison warden who had appointed a murderer, a lifer, as head of the shoemaking department. The warden sent him out to study the latest machinery in factories. The prisoner returned with a full report.

Said the warden: "Why didn't you slip off when you were free?"

The convict scratched his head. "Dunno, warden, I guess it was because you trusted me."

The chances are that if the warden had said: "I trust you to return," the prisoner would have gone off, for by so saying the warden would have revealed that he did not trust him. If all prison wardens had that man's humanity and good sense, prisons would not be the hell they are today.—A. S. Neill, "Punishment Never Cures Anything," *Cosmopolitan*

B. Study the following passage by an author who is expert at steering the reactions of his readers. *What* does the author want his readers to think and feel? *How*, in detail, does he achieve his aim? (Your instructor may ask you to rewrite the passage so that it will describe the same basic situation but produce the opposite, or at least a sharply different, effect.)

Before the ambulance arrived, the police were there. They came strolling into the classroom with their legs apart, as if they remembered ancestors who rode the plains. Their mouths were heavy in thought. They had noses like salamis, red and mottled with fat. They were angry at the weather, at the crowd, and especially at the prostrate man at our feet. . . . They stared at him in the classic pose—one cop with a hand resting lightly on the butt of his gun and the other on his butt, the younger cop with lips so pouted that his breath made a snuffling sound in his nose. They both had head colds. Their Ford was pulled up on the snow-covered lawn outside, with raw muddled marks of tread in the soft dirt. When the snow melted, there would be wounded streaks in the grass. The cab driver closed his eyes under the finicking, distasteful examination. At last one spoke: "See your driver's license."

The cab driver made a clumsy gesture towards his pocket. The cop bent and went into the pocket. He flipped open the wallet, glanced briefly at the photographs and cash, glanced at me, and then began lip-reading the license.—Herbert Gold, *The Age of Happy Problems*

3. THE LANGUAGE OF PERSUASION

Part of the secret of persuasive writing is skillful use of language—often in ways of which the reader is unaware. While seeming to convey information, language can at the same time convey the writer's preferences and dislikes. Persuasive writing relies heavily on **emotive language**, on words charged with attitudes and emotions. Whatever the actual data presented, or the causes and effects analyzed, the writer is likely to keep up a steady drumfire of words designed to shape the reader's reactions.

Look at the following phrases from an article on the urban crisis. What is your normal spontaneous reaction to each of the italicized words?

antisocial allocation of transportation funds
irresponsible *self-seeking* of large corporations
pressure from *lobbyists*
metropolitan *chaos*
vested interests
segregated, bureaucratic high-rise projects
speculators robbing the public

Denotation and Connotation

Become aware of favorable and unfavorable connotations. In discussing the meaning of words, we can separate "what is out there" from the attitudes, preferences, or emotions of the speaker. *Dog* simply points to a certain kind of animal "out there." *Mutt* carries along a low opinion of dogs. It calls to mind dogs that are noisy, fat, sloppy, sniveling, and likely to get in the way. *Hound* carries along a more favorable opinion. It may make us think of dogs that are sleek, clean, powerful, fast.

The part of the meaning that points "out there" is the **denotation** of a word. The attitude or emotion that a word suggests is its **connotation**. *Leader* has favorable, flattering connotations. *Demagogue* has unfavorable, derogatory connotations. We can often pair such "plus words" and "minus words" in order to bring out the attitudes they suggest. For instance, what is the difference between *courageous* and *reckless, loyal* and *servile, tolerant* and *indiscriminate, devout* and *sanctimonious*? How do you react to *conciliation* as against *compromise, grant-in-aid* as against *handout, diplomatic* as against *expedient*?

In each of the following sets, can you see that all three terms might be applied to the same person? What attitudes do the different choices bring into play?

COMPLIMENTARY	DEROGATORY	NEUTRAL
public servant	bureaucrat	government employee
financier	speculator	investor
law officer	cop	police
legislative consultant	lobbyist	representative of group interests
stage personality	ham	actor
manufacturer's representative	huckster	sales personnel
labor leader	union boss	union official
captain of industry	tycoon	business success
investigator	spy	detective
captive	jailbird	prisoner
soldier of fortune	hired killer	mercenary

Remember the following points about emotionally charged language:

(1) *Words with strong connotations bring into play a wide range of associations.* *Dagger* simply denotes a short weapon for stabbing, but it connotes treachery. *Sword* denotes a somewhat longer weapon; it connotes valor, chivalrous adventure.

(2) *Some strongly charged words produce an almost automatic response.* If we refer to the killing of John Doe as the "murder" of John Doe, the word *murder* will cause an almost automatic reaction of horror, disgust, and violent disapproval. If we speak of the "execution" of John Doe, the killing will sound more respectable and official. To "liquidate" one's political opposition makes killing sound businesslike and scientific; "exterminate" or "eradicate" makes it sound as though one were getting rid of vermin.

(3) *Emotive language provides clues to the preferences and commitments of a writer.* We reveal our sympathies by the words we use to identify issues and personalities. An editorial writer who speaks of "labor strongmen," "labor politicians," and "union bosses" is not likely to be a champion of organized labor. Changes in vocabulary are often a symptom of changes in attitude. Changing moral standards are reflected in gradual shifts from *vicious* to *antisocial* to *maladjusted*; from *perversion* to *abnormality* to *deviation*; from *modest* to *shy* to *inhibited*. Paying attention to the values implied in such words is one way of reading between the lines.

The Power of Words

Respect the power and the limitations of emotional language. Emotionally charged language has a powerful effect when the person using it is attuned to the feelings of the audience. There is a powerful sense of vindication when someone uses words that verbalize what the audience feels. With the right kind of audience, passages like the following can promote a strong sense of solidarity:

I am going to ask you to begin your study of democracy by considering it first as a big balloon, filled with gas or hot air, and sent up so that you shall be kept looking up at the sky whilst other people are picking your pockets. (George Bernard Shaw)

As women, we should be aware of how idealization serves oppression. Throughout much of our literature, fanciful constructs of the ideal female, her character and psychology, have obscured the limitations suffered by actual women. (Lillian S. Robinson)

Emotions, however, are personal and subjective. Emotionally charged language produces emotional reactions—not always those intended by the writer. Remember:

(1) *Emotional language polarizes attitudes.* It can fire up the enthusiasm of readers inclined to agree with you, but it will also make your opposition more hostile. A passage like the following will please people who deplore "leftist" tendencies, but among the people attacked it is likely to increase the very hostility the writer deplores:

Because of their *dogmatism, violence, disrespect for the rights of others*, intellectual *rigidity*, belief in *class hostility* and *social insurrection*, and *animosity* toward the American political system, the *"anti-Americans"* of the Left have severed all connections with the *accommodating, cooperative* nature of American liberalism. (Letter to the editor)

(2) *The routine use of loaded words makes writing sound biased or insincere.* Many journalists and public figures habitually use one set of terms when reporting the activities of their favorite "statesman," another set of terms when reporting those of an opposition "politician." Statesman knows, understands, is aware of, is firmly convinced. Politician guesses, theorizes, speculates, or suspects. Statesman gravely points out, forthrightly declares, bluntly states, eloquently sets forth. Politician sputters, proclaims, alleges, or asserts. Statesman consults with his advisers, reaffirms basic convic-

tions, and finds solutions. Politician listens to his cronies, hunts for issues, and jumps to conclusions. Statesman presents a sound program, guards basic rights, and works for the good of the nation. Politician indulges in utopian dreams, caters to special interests, and plays politics.

(3) *When overused, strong language loses its sting.* Terms like *reactionary*, *radical*, *Fascist*, and *Communist* have so often served as ignorant abuse that they have lost their power to influence a thoughtful reader. A fuller glossary of used-up vilifiers might include *leftist*, *fellow traveler*, *do-gooder*, *militarist*, *aggressor*, *appeasement*, *decadent*, and *Uncle Tom*. (Add your own favorites to this list.)

Statement and Implication

Feel responsible for what you hint as well as for what you state outright. Much persuasive language exploits the difference between statement and **implication**. Mentioning two things together can suggest a causal relationship: "He is Irish and drinks a great deal" (because he is Irish?). The mere fact that something is mentioned at all can suggest that it is newsworthy. "Salvex is now 100 percent pure" suggests that purity is important. "Salvex now contains *three* active ingredients" suggests that impurity is important.

Here are some uses of implication that many readers find evasive or annoying:

Innuendo   Suggestion becomes innuendo when it hints things that the writer or the speaker is unable and unwilling to defend. The legislator who says "Most college professors are loyal, competent Americans" is seldom prepared to substantiate charges against that minority of college professors who, by implication, are disloyal and incompetent.

Vague Charges   Implied charges are often left deliberately vague, so that the victim has little chance to refute them. "Scientist So-and-So associated with Communists" might damage So-and-So's career and reputation. It may, however, mean many different things: He may have met a Communist or two at a cocktail party. He may have had long arguments with Communist fellow scientists. We want to know: "What is the charge?"

Loaded Allusions   An editorial writer may have been blaming the opposition party for being too friendly toward a foreign power. His last sentence reads, "If we listen to these people, we may be engulfed by disaster, without so much as a Trojan horse for a souvenir." What exactly is implied in the allusion to the "Trojan horse"?

Rhetorical Questions   The rhetorical question has a built-in answer. It *seems* to leave the decision up to the reader, but it is worded in such a way that only one answer is possible: "Would you recommend a teacher who doesn't care whether his students succeed or fail?" It is hard to answer "yes" to such a question.

An occasional rhetorical question can serve to dramatize an important point. However, when rhetorical questions are used to cover up a scarcity of good arguments, they easily become annoying. Do not try to settle difficult issues by asking: "If the government can send an eighteen-year-old boy to war, can it deprive him of the right to vote?" or "Can a law that goes against the desires of millions of citizens be called just and fair?" An impatient reader is likely to reply: "Well, can it? If not, why not?"

EXERCISES

A. Spell out as fully as you can the *attitudes implied or suggested* by the words italicized in the following passages. Then rewrite three of the passages so that the language used will suggest a different point of view.

EXAMPLE:
(Original)   Last night, vandals defaced a patriotic monument by smearing yellow paint over a statue of the father of our country.
(Rewrite)   Some youngsters out for a lark last night painted a yellow mustache on a weatherbeaten statue of George Washington.

1. The President *trimmed* $8 billion from the budget, and the *howls* went up from the *afflicted*.
2. *Going after* students as formerly politicians went after labor and farmers, the candidate was being *pawed* by the *adoring*.
3. The *ritualistic* "anticop" attitude of many liberals is *sophomoric* and *escapist*.
4. Because he doubted the wisdom of *backdoor entry* into World War II, he was *tarred* as a Nazi.
5. The governor refused to *turn her back* on a trusted subordinate involved in *legal difficulties*.
6. To preserve the inculcation of *reverence* in your public schools may not be possible under the *regime* of the present chief justice.
7. Students are politically *disenfranchised*. They are, it is true, allowed to have a *toy government* of their own. It is a government run for the most part by *Uncle Toms* and concerned principally with *trivia*.
8. The *intelligentsia's* affinity for left-wing politics results from the fact that Ameri-

can conservatism is an intellectual wilderness, populated by *Babbitts* and ex-*plebeians* who have acquired *split-level homes*.
9. The real estate operators are interested in *speculation*, the city planners in votes and *graft*. The building trades *cannily* see to it that their own numbers remain few, their methods *antiquated*, and their rewards high.
10. Immense sums of public money have been wasted to create *reeking swamps* in *once green valleys* where hundreds of people had *farms, schools, churches, plans, and hopes*.

B. Examine the differences in attitude suggested by the *changes in the wording* of the following passages. Write three similar sets on topics of your own choice.

1. Jones was a portly man with a healthy glow in his cheeks.
   Jones was a stout man with a ruddy complexion.
   Jones was a pudgy man with a complexion like a boiled lobster.
2. Her father was unemployed and received relief payments from the county welfare department.
   Instead of working, her father lived on government handouts.
   Her father was out of work and had to accept help from the county.
3. The school board fired Mr. Smith for insubordination.
   The school board dismissed Mr. Smith for refusing to answer questions about his home life.
   The school board deprived Mr. Smith of his job for resisting their attempts to pry into his private affairs.
4. An economy-minded legislature has called a halt to additional spending.
   A penny-pinching legislature has refused to appropriate adequate funds.
   The legislature has cut the budget submitted by the governor by approximately 3 percent.
5. Former prisoners were continually spied upon even after their return to civilian life.
   Ex-convicts were kept under surveillance after their release from penal institutions.
   Criminals were carefully watched as a potential menace to society.

C. Study the way language is used in the following passages to steer the reactions of the reader. Where are the "plus words"—words designed to cause a strong favorable reaction? Where are the "minus words"—words designed to make you shy away, take a dim view, or view with alarm? In your words, what is the message, stated or implied, of each author? How do *you* react? Why?

1. No euphemisms, however numerous or skillfully employed, can obscure the inevitable impact of strip-mining, because stripping is a total assault upon the land. It uproots and destroys every plant and drives out every creature. Some flora and fauna may return but, initially at least, none escapes. The dozer and power shovel go to the bottom of the mineral vein. In Montana and Wyoming the over-burden may be twenty-five feet thick and the coal may extend down in a solid black ledge from eighty to one hundred and fifty feet. Once the overburden is pushed aside, the coal is exposed and loosened by explosives. After the fuel has been lifted out and hauled away, a yawning void remains. If the overburden is shoved into the pit and spread out on the floor—and if seeds are sowed and take

root—someone will own a field at the bottom of a man-made abyss.—Harry M. Caudill, "There Is No Land to Spare," *Atlantic*

   2. Once Washington's birthday denoted the long, drawn-out, uphill struggle for national independence. Lincoln's birthday commemorated an agony of battle for unity and equality. But what message does Presidents' Day—the amalgam of the two—deliver? To me, it announces a weakening of national fiber, a decline in the atmosphere of American life. By itself the fusion of the two holidays expresses a changed attitude toward work. Two dates traditional to the national heritage have been virtually scrubbed from the calendar to make way for more time off. Taking it easy has been legitimized by most of the "enlightened" movements developed in the 1960s. Minority groups have joined in that sentiment. Despite the pressing need of their followers for employment, the leaders are constantly condemning "dead end" jobs. Hence the widespread demand for illegal workers from Mexico and other parts of Latin America.—Joseph Kraft, "Washington Insight"

   3. Dams that throttle the Colorado River, tourism in Telluride and suburban sprawl blurring Phoenix into Tucson, bounty hunters and government coyote-poisoners, automobiles that defile the wilderness while they slacken the human body and spirit, all the tacky trash of commercial "civilization"—these are the targets of [the author's] irritable humor. . . . Against them he poses the mysterious magnificence of desert and mountain and the saving vitality of "human bodies and human wit . . . united in purpose, independent in action."—Annie Gottlieb, "Putting Down Roots," *Quest*

   4. We live in a society where "anything goes."
The consequences are manifested in a society of
escapists, gripped in history's greatest pleasure
binge, in cravings for luxury and ease, in materialistic money-worship. "Anything goes" shows itself
in entertainment obsessed with sex-ploitation and
violence. We have our "anything-to-make-a-buck"
business ethic, our New Morality or better our New
Immorality, our loose-living subculture, our white-
collar thief, and our shoplifting junkies. Our commercial society shouts and screams its materialistic
goals and values at every corner, on our billboards,
with nearly every flip of a magazine page, with many
a TV broadcast. "Indulge yourself," "you owe it to
yourself," "buy now, pay later" is the song sung by
a self-indulgent society. When an entire nation
seems to have nothing but the pursuit of money,
gadgetry, pleasure, escape, and thrills as its
national goals, that nation is in serious trouble.
(Student theme)

   D. Readers occasionally give eloquent expression to their emotions when canceling a subscription to a publication that has in some way failed or offended them. Here are some excerpts from such letters of cancelation after a news-magazine had published a feature story on a movie considered unusually daring in its treatment of sex:

> Since you have stooped to pimping for B-rated peep-show-type movies, please cancel my subscription to your magazine.
>
> Minutes after your magazine arrived, I threw it in the refuse can, whereupon the rest of the garbage got out and walked away.
>
> Where have all the flowers gone? They have wilted into a stinking pile of compost, nurtured by irresponsibility, disrespect, laziness, greed and moral decay, exemplified by your feature story.

Has any publication recently incurred your displeasure? Write two versions of an imaginary letter canceling your subscription. In the first version, express your feelings as freely and abusively as you please. In the second version, try to be respectful and persuasive in the style of people "who reason together."

E. Study samples of *advertising* for a nationally known product or company. Select a full-page ad and examine the methods of persuasion used, paying special attention to the use of emotive language. Your instructor may ask you to provide a copy of the ad.

4. THE STRATEGIES OF PERSUASION

To change someone's mind (or vote), we have to give serious thought to our overall strategy. Where are we going to start? What is going to be the key element of our attack? Where are we going to concentrate our effort, so as not to scatter our fire?

Here are some overall strategies that can give unity and direction to a persuasive paper:

The Common Cause

Appeal to a common interest or shared conviction that will bring the reader over to your side. When we expect readers to change their minds on an important issue, we are not likely to succeed unless we can appeal to a strong common motive or commitment. That common motive may be a gut feeling like a dislike of high taxes or a distrust of government interference. Or it may be an ideal like equality of opportunity or compassion for the unfortunate.

Study the following excerpted version of a student paper. In how many different ways does the author appeal to the reader's sense of justice?

Capital Punishment: Relic of the Past

Capital punishment is a barbaric, pointless anachronism from the primitive period of our history. In medieval times, the death sentence was the usual form of punishment for nearly all felonies. In the 1700s and early 1800s, English law listed 160 offenses as punishable by death. One thirteen-year-old British boy in 1801 was even hanged for stealing a spoon.

Capital punishment is applied to some groups in society more than to others. Minority racial groups are hit hardest by this imbalance of justice. Between 1930 and 1959, 3,666 prisoners were put to death. Of these, 1972 were blacks; 42 were from other minority racial groups. That makes 2,014 of the total, almost two-thirds, from minority racial groups. . . .

Then, too, wealthy people seldom receive the death penalty because they can afford better counsel. All of the people executed in the United States in 1964 were represented by court-appointed attorneys. A former governor of California stated, "As for the poor of all races, it is clear we execute them in disproportionate numbers, because they lack the resources to retain the most skillful counsel or to press their cases to the ultimate. . . ."

Finally, the death penalty can wrongfully execute an innocent man. There are documented cases of this happening. Dr. Hugo Adam Bedau, author of the book *The Death Penalty in America*, states, "I have abstracted 74 cases occurring in the United States since 1893, in which a wrongful conviction of criminal homicide has been alleged and in most cases, proved beyond doubt; 8 probably erroneous executions and an additional 23 erroneous death sentences have been discovered. . . ."

A governor working for the abolition of the death penalty in his own state summed up my feelings in this statement: "I oppose capital punishment because it is more vengeful than punitive; because it is more an act of hate than of justice. We kill the murderer because we fear him, not because he is beyond rehabilitation or control. We kill him not for his crime but in the blind hope that others may not commit his crime."

Persuading by Degrees

Lead up by easy stages to what your reader will find difficult to accept. A persuasive writer will often move

- from the simple to the difficult;
- from the familiar to the new;
- from the safe to the controversial.

By taking on the easier points first, you can establish a pattern of assent. You can get your audience to feel: "This writer sounds like a reasonable person. I'll see where the argument leads." Can you see how the following paper on "tolerance" gradually leads the reader from the trivial and familiar to the significant and controversial?

Your Space and Mine

I. The most basic quality of a tolerant person is *patience*. A teacher must be tolerant when the person being taught to play tennis or run a mimeographing machine gets the same simple operation wrong for the fourth time.

II. A tolerant person demonstrates tolerance by *willingness to live and let live*. Someone who is tolerant has learned to put up with noisy neighbors, dogs running over the lawn, a radio blaring on the beach.

III. But the true test of a tolerant person is *willingness to listen and to learn*— the willingness of a strongly religious student to listen to an astronomer's lecture denying supernatural existence, the willingness of a no-nonsense science major to look at the evidence for extrasensory perception.

The Cause Célèbre

Concentrate on one major test case in order to bring an important issue into focus. To the persuasive writer, one striking case, dramatizing the issue, is worth a thousand anonymous ones, reflected in statistical percentages. In nineteenth-century France, much anti-Semitism was of the country club and officers' mess variety—practiced by eminently respectable people. To discredit their complacency became possible through the Dreyfus affair, the case of a Jewish officer convicted of treason but cleared after years of bitter controversy. In Germany after World War II, it took the story of Anne Frank to make many Germans fully realize the enormity of the Nazi crimes.

An effective persuasive writer will often build a case entirely or in part on a single striking instance. The foe of capital punishment may devote all or most of the argument to the detailed examination of a *cause célèbre*, someone executed after years of legal battle and bitter debate.

Refuting Objections

Attack opposed views likely to carry much weight with your reader. Often, more positive arguments would be unavailing, because basic misconceptions on the part of the reader might not have been touched. Though the writer might make a strong case *for* his point of view, the stubborn reader would say, "That is all very well, but . . ."

Sometimes, a whole paper or article may be devoted to attacking obstacles to reform, or views blocking the acceptance of a new idea. More often an attack on the opposition is only one part of a larger strategy. In the following excerpted theme, positive arguments in favor of dissent, and its defense against the most important objections, combine to give shape to the paper as a whole:

The Importance of Dissent

Appeal to a Common Cause

    The right to dissent, to disagree and differ in opinion, is one of the most precious rights of an American citizen. . . .

Appeal to Historical Precedent

    It was the exercise of dissent that first led the American colonists to assert their independence in the revolutionary war. . . .

First Objection Refuted

    It is sometimes made to seem as if the right of dissent is claimed mainly by self-important people who must always make known their own views. But the true purpose of dissent is not to indulge those who want to speak their minds, but to help "prevent error and discover truth.". . .

Second Objection Refuted

    Many find dissent distasteful because it is disorderly and disruptive; because it is often shrill or unmannerly. But it is universally painful to have to rethink established premises. . . .

Third Objection Refuted

    Probably the most significant objection to dissent is that it is unpatriotic in a time of crisis. Dissent is said to weaken our nation in external conflicts because it gives opponents the impression that the American people are divided. But, in the words of one U.S. senator, our country has "rarely been far from a crisis of sufficient magnitude" for someone to call for the suspension of dissent. . . .

Appeal to Authority

    The importance of dissent was well summed up by John Stuart Mill: "If all mankind minus one were of one opinion, and only one person were of a contrary opinion, mankind would be no more justified in silencing that one person than he . . . would be justified in silencing mankind."

REVIEW EXERCISES

    A. Write an account of an *individual case* that strongly influenced your views on an important issue.

    B. Write a brief outline of a speech, a lecture, or an article that you found especially effective in *leading the audience up* to the major point(s) aimed at by the author.

    C. How persuasive is the following *letter to the editor*? How would you describe the overall strategy of the author? Point out in detail the features that you consider most effective and those you consider least effective. How much depends on the audience?

A Life with Guns

When I was seven, happiness was a toy six-shooter, with which I banged around the neighborhood and felt as powerful as Tom Mix.

When I was eleven, Christmas brought a Daisy Air Rifle with which I promptly killed a few sparrows, and almost shot out a playmate's eye while playing cops and robbers. When I was fourteen I graduated to a .22 rifle, which was deadly on songbirds, but which consistently missed the bounding local jackrabbits. At fifteen I began collecting old unfireable guns and miscellaneous cartridges. I daydreamed of what could be killed with this or that bullet, and felt vicariously potent.

I don't think I was an uncharacteristic product of the American culture—a culture which has made folk heroes of not only Daniel Boone and Kit Carson, but also Billy the Kid and Bonnie and Clyde.

Modern anthropologists have become aware that our prehuman primate ancestors were not tree-dwelling vegetarians like present-day apes, but ground-dwelling, weapon-using carnivores. Our heritage then is aggression, and it is hard to change our ingrained instincts in a few thousand years of semicivilization. In America, having no history of battles won with sword or bow, the gun has been our aggressive tool. With it we killed off the buffalo and the Indians, conquered a continent and fought some wars. And guns are still our "thing." Boys still grow up as I did, steeped in Wyatt Earp.

I still feel this romantic attachment for the things. I occasionally still daydream of defending my home from some dastardly criminal with my trusty Colt. But this is unrealistic—it is a dream. The day of the frontier is past, and guns no longer represent security. Rather they are the symbol of the murderer, the robber, the rioter, the suicide.

We have seen ostensible "hunting" rifles used to kill a president, Martin Luther King, and thousands of lesser folk. It is said that guns would not kill if there were not people to shoot them. It could also be said that people would rarely kill if they lacked the weapons to do so. There is no prospect of our being able to recognize and adequately deal with the potential killers among us in the near future. A more practical solution for the present is to remove the primary method of homicide—the gun.

But there is a more pressing threat than even the sniper or assassin. Blacks after two centuries of exploitation are openly rebellious, and, given the weapons, their youth could ignite the most bloody revolution this country has seen since the Civil War. On the other side there are the white racists arming in fear, and the militant right wingers storing up arsenals against the omnipresent Communists that pervade their paranoid world.

The measures so far suggested or adopted to control guns are ludicrously inadequate. Registration will accomplish little or nothing. In spite of my lifelong infatuation with the things, reason tells me that guns must be eradicated from our cities.

What I would propose is that there be state or even national laws that guns be illegal anywhere that there is no legitimate use for them. Except in the hands of law enforcement personnel, guns would be kept locked up at target ranges and at depositories in hunting areas. They could be checked out only for those acceptable uses. The ramification of this proposal is that the mere possession of an unauthorized gun in a city would be cause for arrest.

To the anticipated argument that this would breach the Second Amendment, it should be pointed out that the right to bear arms refers to a "well-regulated militia." None of our gun-carrying civilian organizations, white or black, can be seriously considered such.

THEME TOPICS 7

1. Write a letter to the editor in which you criticize an institution, a custom, or a practice of which you disapprove. Try to make your letter as persuasive as you can for a typical newspaper reader, or for a large representative cross section of the newspaper audience.

2. In recent years, Americans have become used to a constant stream of warnings about dangers to their health, well-being, or happiness. There have been campaigns against drug abuse, alcoholism, cigarette smoking, food additives, consumer fraud, and the like. Write a paper in which you sound the alarm about one such danger that you think has been ignored or treated too lightly. Try to convince the jaded, skeptical newspaper reader or television viewer.

3. We often hear it said that many young people have lost interest or confidence in the political process. Write a paper in which you try to persuade young people to become politically involved. Or write a paper in which you defend their lack of involvement.

4. Argue the case *for or against* one of the following in a paper addressed to an audience strongly committed to the opposite point of view: capital punishment; use of state lotteries to help finance public education; pacifism; gun control; legalized abortion; community care for the mentally ill.

5. Write a brief article for a student newspaper or magazine in which you argue a cause *unpopular* with many students. For instance, say something *good* about the "value system" of their parents or about a "paternalistic" administration. Find a topic on which you can write with conviction.

6. Have you ever felt that one of the following groups is at times *misrepresented* by people who are part of the academic community? Have you ever felt moved to come to the defense of business people, military officers, Southern politicians, state legislators, the "mass audience," advertisers? Come to the defense in a paper addressed to students and teachers that might attend a typical discussion session on campus.

7. James Baldwin said in *Nobody Knows My Name*,

   . . . when we think of the American boy, we don't usually think of a Spanish, Turkish, a Greek, or a Mexican type, still less of an Oriental type. We usually think of someone who is kind of a cross between the Teuton and the Celt, and I think it is interesting to consider what this image suggests. Outrageous as this image is, in most cases, it is the national self-image. It is an image which suggests hard work and good clean fun and chastity and piety and success. It leaves out of account, of course, most of the people in the country, and most of the facts of life, and there is not much point in discussing those virtues it suggests, which are mainly honored in the breach. The point is that it has almost nothing to do with what or who an American really is.

Write a paper in which you persuade your audience to abandon a misleading or inadequate "national self-image," or to accept a more adequate picture of "what or who an American really is."

Tone and Style

CHAPTER EIGHT

1. **The Personal Voice**

2. **Setting the Right Tone**
   Formal Writing
   Informal Writing

3. **The Elements of Style**
   The Right Word
   The Graphic Image
   Appropriate Emphasis
   A Fresh Point of View

4. **Writing with the Lighter Touch**
   The Uses of Humor
   Irony and Sarcasm
   Satire
   Parody

1. THE PERSONAL VOICE

Style makes writing come to life. It makes the difference between writing that is dull and gray and writing that has force or vitality. In effective expository writing, style does not call attention to itself. It serves the author's purpose; it enhances the author's message.

When style serves its purpose effectively, what is said and how it is said become hard to separate. Nevertheless, you can make your writing more effective by aiming at the following general qualities:

(1) *Effective style has a fresh, pointed quality.* It does not just string together ready-made phrases. It shows the sharpening or heightening that takes place when someone takes a fresh, independent look. Passages like the following make us pay attention because they make their point in the author's own words:

I came from an ivy-covered mansion of Catholic mind *school-boarded with planks of piety.*

In my own house I was never left in the care of baby-sitters or left behind while my parents vacationed. But then my parents never traveled, never went anywhere. *Neglect would have been too expensive a luxury.* (Patricia Cayo Sexton)

(2) *Effective style shows the commitment of the writer.* It does not stay on the same even level; it has more than one register. It grows emphatic or even eloquent as the writer takes up things that really matter. Passages like the following make us feel that the author *cared* about the subject:

As more and more people have painful reason to know, the press has a nasty kind of power, the same kind of power a bully has; that of hurting somebody smaller and weaker than himself. . . . Journalists themselves generally have a horror of being interviewed, "written up," or even noticed by the press; they know too well from their own experience how inept and cruel a distortion the result is likely to be—even in photographs—which, in the lying phrase, "cannot lie." (T. S. Matthews)

She was an intelligent, articulate, well-educated, handsome, enterprising, eccentric, and fearless woman: Her mind had never been narrow or fettered; she was physically courageous, traveled alone on the public transport of the mid-1800s, and had strong opinions on most subjects. (Margaret Drabble about Jane Carlyle)

(3) *Effective style has individuality.* It makes us feel that we are hearing the personal voice of the author. It makes us feel that what we are reading was written by a human being—sensitive or brash,

solemn or lighthearted. In passages like the following we hear echoes of the author's personal voice:

> I wear my hat as I please inside and out. (Walt Whitman)

> If it all blew up, if it all came to so little, if our efforts, our loves, our crimes added up to no more than a sudden extinction in a minute, in a moment, if we had not even time before the bomb (as civilians did once) to throw one quick look at some face, some trinket, some child for which one had love, well, one could not complain. That was our fate. That was what we deserved. (Norman Mailer)

> People who should know tell us that during the Paleolithic Age man's store of knowledge doubled every 100,000 years, give or take a month or two. Even then it didn't amount to much. Man learned to build fires, say, and then in another 100,000 years he learned to put fires out. That sort of thing. (Patrick Butler)

EXERCISE

What makes each of the following sentences different from humdrum averaged-out prose? What gives it an individual touch? Your instructor may ask you to select three of these and for each write a sentence of your own imitating it as closely as you can.

1. The forward guywire of our mast began to sing under the wind, a deep and yet penetrating tone like the lowest string of an incredible bullfiddle. (John Steinbeck)
2. The role of the U.S. Commission on Civil Rights is to move the U.S. government forward, inch by agonizing inch, on civil rights. (Elizabeth Brenner Drew)
3. I was gratified to be able to answer promptly, and I did. I said I didn't know. (Mark Twain)
4. The poet who does not share in the struggles of the oppressed and humiliated is not a poet but merely a mannikin for the shop windows of elegant stores for the rich. (Pablo Neruda)
5. The day arrived when he warned his companion that he could hold out—or hold in—no longer. (Henry James)
6. The bank, as will happen in Vermont, was right across the street, and we found there the ball-point instruments usual in local temples of deposit, insultingly chained to their tuberous sockets. (John Updike)
7. She wasn't given to thinking very far, but she did a lot of intelligent feeling. (Walter Van Tilburg Clark)
8. The human back can become the seat of more aches and pains than are registered in books for the composite anatomy of a regiment. It is a limited area, but it can become the theater of innumerable muscular conflicts, tangles, wrenches, knots, and other comforts. (Stephen Crane)
9. The historic function of the American public school, and especially of the high school, has been to serve as a social and economic ladder—though today's school personnel, referring to a more passive clientele, sometimes think of it as an escalator. (Edgar Z. Friedenberg)
10. He sat forward nervously on his chair; and she knew herself to be acting the Ancient Mariner, but her dignity would not allow her to hurry. (Mary McCarthy)

2. SETTING THE RIGHT TONE

In expository writing, the element of style that we are likely to notice first is tone. **Tone** reflects the writer's *attitude* toward the subject and the reader. Speaking to a friend in need of help, we can give much the same advice in a nagging or in a quietly encouraging tone. Similarly, a writer can vary tone to express patience or exasperation, amusement or resentment.

The most obvious differences in tone are due to the level of formality or informality on which the writer moves. At one extreme is the dignified, impersonal, polished style appropriate to the **formal** discussion of serious issues. At the other extreme is the chatty, personal, improvised style appropriate to **informal** letters among friends. A formal style signals that we want the reader to pay serious attention. An informal style signals that the reader may expect to be amused or entertained.

Formality is a matter of degree. Just as it is possible to be overdressed at a party, so it is possible to be too stiffly formal in a piece of writing. But it is also possible to be so casual as to suggest "I don't care." Usually, we can place a statement on a *scale of informality*:

VERY FORMAL: In our society, performance is a primary determinant of status.

LESS FORMAL: What an individual can deliver more than anything else determines how far he can go in our society.

VERY INFORMAL: You have to come through if you want to make it in this society.

In your own writing, you will have to avoid two extremes. The first is a stiff pseudoscholarly jargon, in which an outing is a "recreational activity" and a college an "institution of higher learning." The other extreme is breezy informality misapplied to subjects that deserve serious attention. In a serious paper about the dilemmas of college education, it is inappropriate to refer to teachers as "Prof" and "Doc," to fellow students as "kids," to campus policemen as "the fuzz."

Formal Writing

Serious writing is formal without being stuffy or unnatural. A formal style does not use "big words" to impress the reader. It uses the less common word where it makes possible distinctions or associations passed over in casual talk. The best formal writing uses much

of the *common stock* of the language as well as resources not usually
drawn on in everyday speech. The words in the following list are
likely to appear only in formal writing:

WORD	GENERAL MEANING	SPECIAL ASSOCIATIONS
arduous	difficult	so difficult as to require strenuous or dedicated effort
felicitous	appropriate	exceptionally fitting, as if by a lucky or marvelous coincidence
incongruous	out of place	sticking out in a weird or ridiculous fashion
lucid	clear	making something exceptionally clear that might otherwise have been muddy or obscure
precarious	risky	already tottering on the brink
spurious	false	claiming to be authentic but actually completely fake
serene	peaceful	so peaceful as to calm the spirit and make us especially happy and contented

Closely related to the scope of vocabulary is the range of **allusion** and comparison. Writers using a formal style are likely to
draw freely on references to history, literature, the fine arts. They
may expect their readers to know what a "utopia" is, what
"Napoleonic airs" are, or how an "interregnum" comes about.

The sentences and paragraphs of formal writing are usually
more elaborate, or at least more carefully planned, than ordinary
conversation. The following two sentences illustrate several features
that help make formal writing different from improvised speech:

> Many critics through the years have pointed out that almost all antiwar novels
> and motion pictures are, in fact, prowar. Blood and mud and terror and rape and an
> all-pervading anxiety are precisely what is attractive about war—in the safety of
> fiction—to those who, in our overprotected lives, are suffering from tedium vitae
> and human self-alienation. (Kenneth Rexroth)

Notice how the writer has carefully balanced opposites ("anti-
war . . . prowar"). He has lined up a long series of related terms
("blood and mud and terror and rape and an all-pervading anxi-
ety"). He has worked important comments into an already elaborate
sentence without breaking its rhythm or muddying its meaning
("—in the safety of fiction—"; "in our overprotected lives").

The following sample passages range from formal to moderately
formal:

Formal

Western capitalism has not been aristocratic, proletarian, or leisured. It has been the bourgeois economic order. Without reducing all of its complexity to a single historic strand, one can say that it was dominated by the ethic, and even religion, of work. To this day, the West believes that a man establishes his worth in the eyes of his neighbor, and even before God, through industry and drudgery and saving. In its most acutely American form, as the poet William Carlos Williams once observed, this attitude asserts itself in the conversational opening, "What do you do?" This question follows immediately upon an exchange of names between strangers, it establishes much of the substance of their talk, it is the quickest means of identification. One is, it implies, what one does. One is one's work.

What, then, would happen if technology rendered work and the work ethic decadent?—Michael Harrington, *The Accidental Century*

This author is writing seriously and formally about some of the major forces shaping our society. Many of the words he uses are more frequently found on the printed page than in casual conversation: *bourgeois, ethic, acutely, asserts, substance, render, decadent*. The sentences are carefully constructed, making use of careful parallelism ("This question follows ... it establishes ... it is ..."). The author uses the impersonal pronoun *one* rather than the direct *you*.

Moderately Formal

It happens to be a fact that all classic works without exception deal directly or indirectly with problems of conduct. That is their great virtue for school use. Not that they teach a plain goody-goody morality, but that they show and discuss and solve dilemmas that a shipping clerk or an athlete can be made to understand. For this understanding, the discussion of any classic *must be superficial*. If you dive below the surface with your pupil you drown him. Certain teachers are always terrified of superficiality; they seem to think other teachers will scoff or that the dead author will scold. Let them remind themselves that their colleagues' profundity would strike the great author as either surface scratching or pedantry; and let them remember that for every reader there is a time when a given book is being read for the first time.—Jacques Barzun, *Teacher in America*

The author is writing about a subject close to his personal experience. He is using a formal style with informal touches. He uses the conversational phrase ("it happens to be a fact that ..."), the occasional colloquialism ("goody-goody morality"), the informal *you*. His metaphors have a homely, familiar quality ("if you dive ... you drown him"; "surface scratching"). But he does not *limit* himself to the familiar, the simple. His vocabulary ranges beyond the conversational: *terrified of superficiality, scoff, colleagues' profundity, pedantry*. His sentences are deliberate and effective. They repeatedly become insistent ("show and discuss and solve"; "let them remind themselves . . ."; "let them remember . . .").

Note: Formal English is *edited* English. It shows the standardizing influence of editing designed to make it generally acceptable to educated readers. In matters of usage, it is likely to observe the traditional distinctions between *who* and *whom*, *like* and *as*, *if he was* and *if he were*. (See the handbook chapter on grammatical usage, and the glossary of usage, for a discussion of many of these.)

Informal Writing

Informal writing can be casual or entertaining without being brash. Informal writing of this kind may make occasional use of the folksy, **colloquial** phrase. It occasionally uses **slang**, usually in tongue-in-cheek fashion. Its range of reference and allusion is likely to be that of patio, garage, and playing field rather than that of library or study. Its sentence structure and its punctuation sometimes suggest the pauses, ramblings, and afterthoughts of speech. It tends to be subjective; it makes room for personal impressions, reminiscences, and whims. It often tells the reader as much about the author as about the subject.

The following selection illustrates an *informal style*:

> Advertising is relatively a Johnny-come-lately. It did not exist in the mass-market form that we know much before World War I, and did not exist in any form at all before the late nineteenth century.
>
> But before advertising, there were newspapers and magazines. They were very much as we know them today, except of course that the pages were filled with news instead of paid hustle. Since they had almost no other source of revenue, the publications of that time lived or died by the reader's penny spent, and charged an honest price; if a publication cost five cents to produce, you can bet a publisher charged at least five cents for it, and hoped like hell that what his paper had to say was interesting enough to get enough people to pony up their nickels. It is no coincidence that the great muckraking magazines of American legend flourished under these game conditions; he who pays the piper calls the tune, and the only paymaster was their readers, who apparently liked what the muckrakers were playing.—Warren Hinckle, "The Adman Who Hated Advertising," *Atlantic*

The author is expressing personal feelings of alternate amusement and anger. He writes in a distinctly informal style, fit for the "insider" who is not awed by his subject. He in fact does not intend to treat the people and policies discussed very respectfully. There are folksy conversational expressions ("Johnny-come-lately"; "he who pays the piper . . .") and some outright slang ("hustle," "pony up"). The loosely built sentences move on like those of a fast talker, with frequent uses of *and* to string thoughts together. Pronouns are personal and familiar ("*we* know"; "*you* can bet"). The occasional touch of profanity ("hope like hell") helps give the passage its informal, casual quality.

EXERCISES

A. How *formal or informal* is the style of each of the following passages? Examine word choice, allusions, sentence structure, and degree of objectivity. (How appropriate is the style of each passage to its subject matter?)

1. I cannot remember who it was who said that a family was a dictatorship ruled over by its sickest member—he certainly could not have known my grandfather—but it was some such symbol he must have had in mind when he made the remark, for my grandfather, whom I adored, towered over my first seven years like an Everest of Victorian tyranny. He was, in many ways, quite an extraordinary man, and his effect on me in those early and crucial years was, I suppose, incalculable. I am certain I still bear the marks. He was a cigarmaker by trade, and he worked side by side on the same bench with his closest friend, Samuel Gompers. Together they hatched out the first early dream of an American Federation of Labor, and for a while it was a tossup as to who would lead the crusade, my grandfather or Samuel Gompers. The family legend is that they quarreled bitterly and their friendship ended on the somewhat comic grounds of who was to carry the briefcase in to union meetings—the one briefcase they owned between them. I am quite prepared to believe this story as not entirely apocryphal. It sounds, indeed, very much like my grandfather, and exactly the way he was likely to behave.— Moss Hart, *Act One*

2. There are rumors that when dying of the thirst you can save soul *and* body by extracting water from the barrel cactus, but this is a dubious proposition and I don't know anyone who has made the experiment. It might be possible in the low desert of Arizona where the barrel cactus will often grow as high as a man and big around as a beer keg. In Utah a similar species of cactus grows no more than a foot up and bristles with needles curved like fishhooks. To even get close to this devilish plant you need leather gloves and a machete, or at least a big hunting knife. Slice off the top and you find inside not a little tun of precious water but only the green pulpy core of the living plant. To get a few drops of liquid from that you would have to hack the cactus into manageable chunks and wring what water you could from each piece. Meanwhile you are sweating badly from the labor and the exasperation, dehydrating rapidly, doomed anyway. You'd actually be better off to stay at home with the TV and a case of beer. If this happy thought arrives too late, relax and enjoy your demise as best you can; it's the only one you are likely to know. See those big, black, scrawny wings far above, waiting? Console yourself with the thought that within only a few hours, if all goes well, your human flesh will be working its way through the gizzard of a buzzard, your essence transformed into the fierce greedy eyes and unimaginable consciousness of the vulture—you too will soar on motionless wings far above the ruck and the rack of human existence, part of the Oneness of the One.—Edward Abbey, "The West's Land of Surprises," *Harper's*

3. There are more people than ever before, at least in the sense of mutations in our national botany, and this is probably due to mobility—cross-fertilization. Take as an example a gangster who was in the slot machine racket, decided to go straight and became a laundromat king, sent his daughter to Bennington, where she married a poet-in-residence or a professor of modern linguistic philosophy. There are three characters already sketched out in that sentence and all of them brand-new: the father, the daughter, and the son-in-law. Imagine what one of the old writers might have made of the wedding and the reception afterward at the 21 Club. The laundromat king or his equivalent is easy to meet in America; there are hundreds of him. . . . People speak of the lack of tradition or of manners as having a bad effect on the American novel, but the self-made man is a far richer figure, from the novelist's point of view, than the man of inherited wealth, who is likely to be a mannered shadow.—Mary McCarthy, "Characters in Fiction," *Partisan Review*

B. What is the *range of formality* that you encounter on the editorial page (and in related matter) of a major newspaper? Are there editorials or columns written in a very formal style? Are there others more informal? Provide examples.

C. Examine the level of formality in the following passages from student newspapers or student magazines. Which is the *most formal*? Which is the *most informal*? Which is in-between? Point out specific evidence.

1. We seem as a result to be an unsatisfied, uneasy people, living in a society which has a crazy, frenetic quality. A drive down a freeway at night is all one needs to confirm this. The sight of thousands of human beings hurtling through the night, each sealed in a steel capsule, cannot but instill in the observer the feeling of aimless urgency which seems to characterize our society. It is as if there is a basic need to stay in constant motion, to be always *active* (a favorite word in advertising). It is as if we know instinctively that if the cars were ever to stop, or the televisions to be silenced, or the insane longing after material goods to abate, our society would deflate like a punctured tire, so unsubstantial are the institutions upon which it rests.

2. I got busted for smoking tea. Can you believe that? I was at home having fits for another cigarette but couldn't find one anywhere in the house. I got one of my mother's tea bags and opened it and rolled a teagarette. Finally I had something to smoke. I looked at the clock, and it was time for me to leave for practice. So I caught the bus on Broadway, not thinking of the teagarette I was smoking. When I got off the bus, this pig grabbed me and asked, "What is that you are smoking?" I said it was tea, and he said he would have to arrest me because he thought it was grass. I was locked behind bars—oh Jesus, I was behind real bars. I stayed there for three hours before it was announced that I had been smoking tea. The law doesn't prohibit tea smoking.

3. A man is born into this world strong and free. He says, "I will," and like St. George is prepared to slay his dragon. He has worlds to conquer but before he is able to say, "I am strong and brave and free," he finds that those worlds he wished to conquer have vanished and he feels relieved to be able to conquer his own castle. What beast or foe could have possibly devoured his strength? What could have possibly crushed his shining armor into a heap of scrap metal? How could this have happened?

How, indeed. How, indeed, could he have avoided it when at so tender an age he was overrun by a mass of "Thou shalts" and "Thou shalt nots." Society, like the great Borgia, poured poison from her ring into the lad's wine cup and he became hollow. Thou shalt not eat with thy fingers, little one. Thy shalt not color with thy crayons on mother's wall, little one. Thou shalt go to school little one and thou shalt go to college. Thou shalt get a nine-to-five job, little one, and go home each night and be shackled to the dungeon with thy family. Thou shalt pay thy bills and thou shalt not try to free thyself by committing suicide. So, the lad listens and becomes another machine used for the betterment of society.

3. THE ELEMENTS OF STYLE

Effective style makes us say: "Well said!" Effective writers do not just get a message across in routine fashion. They know how to make us pay attention. They know how to make a point sink in. They know how to make us remember.

The Right Word

Develop a love and respect for words. Effective writers provide the verbal handles that help us think about a subject, that help us sum up an idea. They know how to choose a word or a phrase that helps us remember a major point. Notice how frequently a writer like Julian Huxley uses a well-chosen, memorable phrase to help a major point sink in:

> Billions of dollars are spent every year on outer space research—much of it merely for the sake of prestige, in an effort to get to Mars before somebody else—as against a few millions on exploring the "inner space" of the human mind; . . . hundreds of millions on "death control" through medical science as against four or five millions on birth control and reproduction.
> In the natural sciences, man has learned the technique of "reality thinking"—of accepting the facts and phenomena of external nature and trying to understand them objectively, without bias.
> . . . We must rigorously prevent the horrible unplanned spread of what is neither city nor suburb nor country town, but "slurb"—a compound of slum, suburbia, and urban sprawl, which has already blighted southern California and much of the Atlantic seaboard.

Language is more than a neutral code. Each word has its own shape, sound, history, associations. *Squander* is not just another word for *waste*. *Toil* is not just another word for *work*. A good writer has a feeling for nuance, for words that are closely related and yet different:

> The choice of the word "roots" for the latest passage in the quest for an American identity may be unconsciously significant. . . . roots have not only an origin, but a function: to nourish by being anchored in a particular soil. (Annie Gottlieb)

Look at the following passages. What is each author saying? What differences in meaning set the italicized words apart?

The way to be *safe* is never to be *secure*. (Benjamin Franklin)

The new head of the Central Intelligence Agency, who looks more like a man of the *cloth* than of the *cloak*, does not make friends easily.

For the gifted young woman today, such a life . . . is not a *destiny* but a *fate*. (Mary McCarthy)

He has *imitators* by the score, but no *competition*.

The Graphic Image

Translate the abstract into the concrete. Good writing is graphic. The effective writer moves almost habitually from idea to image, from states of mind to gestures and actions that act them out, from figures to demonstrations of what they mean:

The world's population is increasing by over sixty million a year—the equivalent of a good-sized town every day of the year, and of nearly twelve baseball teams (with coach) every minute of the day.

Notice how quickly and naturally the authors of the following passages move from general terms like *habit* and *critic* to things we can see:

Habit is habit and not to be flung out of the window by any man but coaxed downstairs a step at a time. (Mark Twain)

When books pass in review like the procession of animals in a shooting gallery. . . . the critic has only one second in which to load and aim and shoot and may well be pardoned if he mistakes rabbits for tigers, eagles for barnyard fowls, or misses altogether and wastes his shot upon some peaceful cow grazing in a further field. (Virginia Woolf)

Appropriate Emphasis

Know how to emphasize what is important. Effective writers know how to make things stand out. They know how to sum up, how to state briefly and directly something that they want the reader to remember. Each of the following statements is brief and to the point, and therefore memorable:

Official war propaganda, with its disgusting hypocrisy and self-righteousness, tends to make thinking people sympathize with the enemy. (George Orwell)

The price the immigrants paid to get into America was that they had to become Americans. (LeRoi Jones)

Here are ways you can make your writing more forceful, more emphatic:

(1) Employ a *full range* of resources. Effective writers know how to soft-pedal, how to play down:

> Although we know very little about deterrence, it seems probable that the prospect of punishment does dissuade some people from the commission of some crimes.

But they also know how to come on strong:

> The same [reason] must be given for the failure of the system of criminal justice. We as a people do not care to put the necessary intellectual and financial resources into the job. We are therefore an easy prey for snake-oil salesmen who tell us that if we will only stop "coddling criminals" we shall be secure. (Robert M. Hutchins)

(2) Help key ideas sink in by drawing clear lines, by *lining up opposites* for clear-cut contrast. An **antithesis** is a clear-cut opposite; it can help bring major choices or major issues into focus. What examples of a clear-cut lining up of opposites can you find in the following excerpt from a letter to the editor?

> "Depressed" individuals are not "oppressed" by conditions of the real world (except, of course, in extreme instances) but rather by private demons which are "in their heads." There is nothing embarrassing, degrading, or repellent about this fact and one should not attempt to shy away from it by using society as a scapegoat. American civilization at the present time is a far cry from paradise. Yet millions of individuals—including those most oppressed (blacks, Indians, and women)—have managed to cope with their situation and to seek alternatives to it. There is not a sliver of clinical evidence to prove that emotional illnesses such as paranoia are caused by the ills of society.

(3) Use *deliberate repetition* to drive home a point. The writer of the following passage keeps hammering away at his central idea till the reader cannot help saying: "Yes—I get the point!"

> Color is the first thing Black people in america become aware of. You are born into a world that has given color meaning and color becomes the single most determining factor of your existence. Color determines where you live, how you live and, under certain circumstances, if you will live. Color determines your friends, your education, your mother's and father's jobs, where you play, what you play and, more importantly, what you think of yourself. (H. Rap Brown)

Cumulative repetition gradually builds up to a climax. It gradually gets the reader ready for the major point. Parallel sentence structure helps the writer set up a cumulative pattern in the following passage:

> Many a businessman feels himself the prisoner of his business and the commodities he sells; he has a feeling of fraudulency about his product and a secret contempt for it. *He hates his customers,* who force him to put up a show in order to sell. *He hates his competitors* because they are a threat; his employees as well as his superiors, because he is in a constant competitive fight with them. *Most important of all, he hates himself,* because he sees his life passing by, without making any sense beyond the momentary intoxication of success.—Erich Fromm, *The Sane Society*

A Fresh Point of View

Write from a fresh personal perspective. Show your willingness to take a new look. In the following passage, how is the point of view adopted by the author different from what we are used to? What does his unusual point of view help the writer show and emphasize?

> The present state of things on the planet Earth would be rather a puzzle to an observer from another planet. If he landed in the United States, the most conspicuous animals in sight would be automobiles, and if he examined these vigorous hard-shelled creatures, he would find that each contains one or more soft, feeble organisms that appear notably helpless when removed from their shells. He would decide, after talking with these defenseless creatures, that they have no independent existence. Few of them have anything to do with the production or transportation of food. They need clothing and shelter, but do not produce them for themselves. They are dependent on their distant fellows in thousands of complex ways. When isolated, they usually die—just like worker ants that wander helplessly and hopelessly if separated from their colony.—Jonathan Norton Leonard, *Flight into Space*

The impact and meaning of what we write changes with the stance we adopt toward people and events. The "impartial reporter" writes with the attitude of "I just work here. I report what I see." The "involved observer" writes as a sympathetic spectator, asking us to care, to take sides. The "accuser" writes as judge and jury, exposing and condemning wrongdoing.

You can identify the stance of an author by imagining yourself asking him: "Where are *you* in this picture?" Can you see the changes in perspective as you move from one of the following passages to the next?

> Some guys went to see the dean and raised a little hell in his office.
> There were close to two hundred policemen and they were fully dressed in riot gear—faceless, blue creatures with shiny helmets and badges.
> Rioting students invaded the administration building and vandalized the dean's office.

EXERCISES

A. The following passage uses many words that have exceptionally rich overtones and associations. Select six of these words. Discuss their meanings and associations as fully as you can.

The economic history of west Texas . . . from the beginning has pitted big outside capital and the quick-profit motive against the modest aims and indigenous care of working men who know and love the land. And it is finally the realities, not the myths, of cowboy life that impress: the taciturn, gallant, baffled masculinity, with its periodic outbursts of drunken violence, balanced by the truly maternal care of the cowboy for his cows; the fierce, independent pride balanced by the tradition of "neighboring," the mutual lending of helping hands; the discipline and compassion of a cowboy's wife—a complement that only a woman writer could have noted; and above all the competent, experiential knowledge, honed to the fineness of instinct, which attunes the cowboy to the needs of living things.—Annie Gottlieb, "Putting Down Roots," *Quest*

B. What is each of the following authors saying? How does he or she translate the abstract into the concrete?

1. The young, of course, are always questioning values, knocking the status quo about, considering shibboleths to see if they are pronounceable. (Edward Albee)
2. The academic curriculum consists of shards of a predemocratic academic culture. (Edgar Z. Friedenberg)
3. The principal effect of our material well-being has been to set the children's teeth on edge. (James Baldwin)
4. The black slums are ringed by a white noose of suburbs.
5. We went back to New Orleans to stay with my father's sisters for six months each year. I was thus moved from school in New York to school in New Orleans without care for the season or the quality of the school. This constant need for adjustment in two very different worlds made formal education into a kind of frantic tennis game, sometimes played with children whose strokes had force and brilliance, sometimes with those who could barely hold the racket. (Lillian Hellman)

C. Study the following sentence as an example of how a writer can take us from a general term *(passivity)* to a graphic picture that makes the term concrete. Write *three* similar sentences of your own. Some possible general terms: *sensitivity, callousness, hyperactive, sensationalism, sentimentality.*

The phrase "mass culture" conveys emotional overtones of passivity: It suggests someone *eating peanuts at a baseball game.* (Northrop Frye)

D. Study the way the authors of the following sentences have balanced off opposites. Choose *three* of these as model sentences. For each, write a very similar sentence on a subject of your own choice.

1. The idols of every campus generation have always been *against* everything and *for* nothing. (Peter F. Drucker)

2. The playful use of long or learned words is a one-sided game *boring the reader* more than it *pleases the writer.* (H. W. Fowler)
3. The quality of *strength lined with tenderness* is an unbeatable combination, as are *intelligence and necessity when unblunted by formal education.* (Maya Angelou)
4. Democracy substitutes *selection by the incompetent many* for *appointment by the corrupt few.* (G.B. Shaw)

   E. What elements of an effective style can you point out in the following passages?

   1. Much traditional literature reflects an opposition between conjugal love with its tame domesticity and extramarital love with its immoral pleasures. Often, the hero or heroine has to choose between love without marriage and marriage without love. It is this cross-wiring of elements that accounts for the tragic outcome of love.

   2. The volume of solid matter discharged annually into the world's waters amounts to over sixty-five cubic miles—equivalent to a mountain with twenty-thousand-foot vertical sides and a flat top of over sixteen square miles. This includes so much sewage that bathing in many lakes, including even the Lake of Geneva, and on numerous sea beaches has become either disgusting, dangerous to health, or both. Our vaunted Affluent Society is rapidly turning into an Effluent Society. Meanwhile, rubbish dumps and used automobiles are polluting the land; automobile exhausts, domestic smoke, and industrial fumes are polluting the air; and pesticides and herbicides are killing off our birds, our wild flowers, and our butterflies. The net result is that nature is being wounded, man's environment desecrated, and the world's resources of enjoyment and interest demolished or destroyed.
   Here is an obvious case where quality of life and living must take precedence over quantity of production and profit. Compulsory measures against pollution, whatever they may cost, are as necessary as are compulsory vaccination or compulsory quarantine against disease.—Julian Huxley, "The Crisis in Man's Destiny"

   3. A major point of the liberation movement is freedom of choice: freedom of man and woman as individuals to pursue the life that they most want to live. And if a woman enjoys a purely domestic role, she has every right to it.
   But for a great many it is not enough. We do not want to spend our days without men, without the formulation and execution of ideas, without the use of what special talents or skills we have, whether for science or art, for engineering or business, for journalism or technology, for philosophy or broadcasting, for government or law. And whether men like it or not, the universities of this nation are turning out more and more women who are prepared to use their skills and demand that they be used without fear, favor, or discrimination. Many of us—perhaps most of us—want to live with men and bear their children—no more, hopefully, than two. And even, perhaps, none.
   Society forgets that not all women are naturally maternal. And all of us must know by now that the large family is no more a blessing than the childless couple is a crime. In fact, the woman who is a copious breeder is doing infinitely more harm than good to this suffocating planet and its crowded broods.
   The rest of us really want more men in our lives, not fewer. We want their comradeship at work as well as their company at home. We refuse a life that forces us to live ten hours of every weekday confined to the company of children and

women.—Marya Mannes, "How Men Will Benefit from the Women's Power Revolution"

4.   WRITING WITH THE LIGHTER TOUCH

An effective writer does not treat solemn and trivial matters with the same deadly seriousness. Evidence of a writer's sense of humor gives writing a human touch. Things become truly grim when writer and reader lose sight of what might be ridiculous about their subject, or about themselves.

The Uses of Humor

Use humor to put your readers at ease and break down their reserve. Some of the most readable writing combines a basic seriousness with touches of dry wit:

There is another possibility to be taken account of, which is that of manufacturing food chemically. There seems no good reason why we should continue to grow our food laboriously in soil and allow ourselves to be dependent on the vagaries of sun and rain. Why not make beefsteaks in factories? And flour in workshops? I dare say that food made in this way would not taste very nice, but in time people would get used to it and a little "real" food would still be produced for wedding feasts and the banquets of heads of states. Some very rich men would occasionally issue invitations saying in one corner, "Decorations will be worn" and in the other corner, "Real peas."—Bertrand Russell, "The Next Eighty Years," *Saturday Review*

The writer who wants to be serious without being dull makes at least some use of **verbal humor**. Verbal humor can be quite unintentional ("There are several million alcoholics in the world. This is a staggering number"). When it is intentional, writers make use of unexpected twists in their choice of words ("Bear it like a man, even if you feel it like an ass"—G. B. Shaw). They line up contrasting ideas in parallel form for antithetical heightening.

Here are some other familiar devices of verbal humor:

(1) A **paradox** is an apparent contradiction; it goes "counter to what people think." A paradox at first seems absurd but then turns out to *contain a valid point*. "When peace breaks out" is a paradoxical phrase. We usually speak of war, rather than peace, as "breaking out," but on second thought we may agree that the arrival of genuine peace would be as momentous as the outbreak of open war. The apparent contradiction of a well-turned paradox annoys the literal-minded but delights more nimble-witted readers:

To be natural is such a very difficult pose to keep up. (Oscar Wilde)

(2) The **pun** exploits ambiguity, or similarity between two words, to make the same word suggest *two different but equally possible meanings*. A writer is punning when he accuses a college president of having an "edifice complex"; when she speaks of a congested bridge as "the car-strangled spanner."

Irony and Sarcasm

In using irony, make your ironical intention clear to the reader. **Irony** exploits the comic juxtaposition of things that don't go together. Verbal irony uses statements that mean the opposite of what they seem to say. A student is likely to be ironical when saying, "I just love to write my English themes!" or "How I enjoy dormitory food!"

How does a writer show an ironical intention? What the reader knows about the *New York Times* is enough to make the following statement ironical:

> We had an engineer officer who wrote confidential letters to the Office of Naval Intelligence requesting emergency security checks on officers who read the *New York Times*.

The clues to irony are more clearly built into the text itself when a writer says, "Bill's political ideas happened to correspond exactly to those of the employer he worked for at a given time." The wholeheartedness of Bill's agreement with his employers, combined with the opportune changes in his convictions, is obviously *not* a coincidence; the word *happened* is therefore being used ironically.

Special uses of irony are as follows:

(1) Irony can be indulgent, as when Mary McCarthy describes the spirit of Vassar College as "the passion for public service coupled with a yearning for the limelight." But irony can also become *bitter, cutting, insulting*. Irony turned sour becomes **sarcasm**:

> At the university every great treatise is postponed until its author attains impartial judgment and perfect knowledge. If a horse could wait as long for its shoes and would pay for them in advance, our blacksmiths would all be college dons. (G. B. Shaw)

(2) **Understatement** achieves an ironical effect by *belittling something that is of serious importance to the speaker*, as when a man with double pneumonia says, "I don't feel quite as sprightly as I

might wish." In the following passage, a familiar point gains fresh impact through vast understatement:

> Among the enterprises currently attracting the energies of man, one of considerable moment is his effort to launch himself across space. A second, less grand, less costly, *but perhaps not less important*, is the effort to improve the position of *those who will stay behind*.—John Kenneth Galbraith, "The Poverty of Nations," *Atlantic*

(3) Similar in effect to verbal irony is **irony of situation**. Not only the writer's statements or opinions but also the *details and events* described may go counter to expectation. We can ridicule what is pompous by pointing out the shabby rear of a building with an imposing façade. An easy prey of this kind of irony is the person whose theory points one way and whose practice another: the traffic-safety expert who has an accident, or the marriage counselor who is sued for divorce.

Satire

Experiment with using satire as a means of persuasion. When you make systematic use of humor, irony, or sarcasm to attack something you disapprove of, you are employing **satire**. Satire criticizes shortcomings by holding them up to ridicule and scorn.

The following passage is satirical in intention:

> Harvard (across the river in Cambridge) and Boston are two ends of one mustache. Harvard is now so large and international it has altogether avoided the whimsical stagnation of Boston. But the two places need each other, as we knowingly say of a mismatched couple. Without the faculty, the visitors, the events that Harvard brings to the life here, Boston would be intolerable to anyone except genealogists, antique dealers, and those who find repletion in a closed local society. Unfortunately, Harvard, like Boston, has "tradition" and in America this always carries with it the risk of a special staleness of attitude, and of pride, incredibly and comically swollen like the traits of hypocrisy, selfishness, or lust in the old dramas. At Harvard some of the vices of "society" exist, of Boston society that is— arrogance and the blinding dazzle of being, *being at Harvard*.—Elizabeth Hardwick, "Boston: The Lost Ideal," *Harper's*

The author's target is stagnation, a "closed society," "tradition," staleness, snobbery. Her aim is to make her target look comical, "whimsical." Her method is to use details and analogies that are comical and belittling at the same time: "two ends of one mustache," "mismatched couple," "genealogists, antique dealers." She makes use of satirical exaggeration ("incredibly . . . swollen"); she mimics the people she attacks ("*being at Harvard*").

In writing a satirical paper, try to keep satire from becoming a mere indiscriminate flailing out. A satirical paper is most effective when it clearly implies the positive standards by which its target is judged. For instance, a paper on hunting, no matter how merciless in its attack upon hunters, can have a constructive purpose. The reader can be made to realize that the author is, indirectly, setting up two basic requirements: minimum competence in the handling of firearms and a respect for human life strong enough to keep the hunter from firing at just anything that moves.

Parody

Experiment with writing that mimics the way someone else writes or talks. A **parody** is a comic imitation, exaggerating traits that are vulnerable to ridicule. (A good parody requires loving attention to the original, and often becomes a kind of backhanded tribute to what is being parodied.) Here is a parody of a gushy, pseudo-glamorous style:

> Oh, to be young and come to New York and move into your first loft and look at the world with eyes that light up even the rotting fire-escape railings, even the buckling pressed-tin squares on the ceiling, even the sheet-metal shower stall with its belly dents and rusting seams, the soot granules embedded like blackheads in the dry rot of the window frames, the basin with the copper-green dripping-spigot stains in the cracks at the bottom, the door with its crowbar-notch history of twenty-five years of break-ins, the canvas-bottom chairs that cut off the circulation in the sural arteries of the leg, the indomitable roach that appears every morning in silhouette on the cord of the hot plate, the doomed yucca straining for light on the windowsill, the two cats nobody ever housebroke, the garbage trucks with the grinder whine, the leather freaks and health-shoe geeks, . . . the herds of Uptown Boutique bohemians who arrive every weekend by radio-call cab—oh, to be young and in New York and to have eyes that light up all things with the sweetest and most golden glow!—Tom Wolfe, "Sweet Mysteries of Life," *Harper's*

EXERCISES

A. Point out and discuss uses of humor, irony, and paradox in the following passages.

1. A recent increase in rapes in Israel occasioned discussion in the Israeli legislature about a curfew for women to keep them off the streets after a certain hour. Whereupon Golda Meir suggested that perhaps what they needed instead was a curfew for men.

2. The Post Pavilion is now under the management of a New York firm which has found out that, with rock concerts, you can pack them in, and that with kids you can dispense with the amenities. I recently attended a symphonic program there, and found my seats floating in a pool of vomit which had been left there at a

rock matinee that had drawn a crowd of 14,000. The usher told me that they would not clean up the vomit because the vomit-cleaner-upper was not working that day, and added that if I moved to another seat, I might get kicked out.—Robert Evett, in *The New Republic*

3. Scientists, noting that whales exhibit more rapid growth than other mammals, have speculated that we may one day be forced to cultivate our great cetaceans to meet a world food crisis. When you consider that during a year's captivity at Sea World a young gray whale gained 10,000 pounds and grew 9 feet, this is a comforting thought.

Unfortunately these concepts are offensive to our well-fed society, although folks seem to feel no guilt at all about enjoying a "Big Mac" or buying beefsteak in plastic-wrapped packages. The stockyard scene, the plight of hothouse-raised, hormone-stuffed chickens and force-fed geese seldom concern us for long. Yet we pride ourselves on our compassion for sea mammals. Some of my Eskimo friends suggest that perhaps the best way to bring their point home would be to have every American personally kill and butcher one animal for his own consumption annually.—Lael Morgan, "Let the Eskimos Hunt," *Newsweek*

B. Readers of American magazines and newspapers are familiar with satirical attacks on various aspects of American popular culture or popular entertainment. Study the following example. What is the author's major target—where or how does it become clear? What methods does she employ, and how effective are they? (How justified to you think they are?)

The sport that wears the undisputed crown of vapidity is auto racing. Nowhere else in the realm of muscular activity is there such carefully constructed waste of time, money, and life.

This weekend, the city of Indianapolis is hosting approximately 500,000 people to create a two-day saturnalia out of the annual celebration of grease, gasoline, and death. To be sure, many look upon the trek to the Indy 500 as a sort of Midwest Ft. Lauderdale for celebrating the end of school. Thousands of college kids in camper vans descend on the city to drink, play, and toast complexions paled by too many hours in the library. They are the harmless infield spectators.

But the stands inside the Indy Speedway will be filled on Monday with hundreds of thousands of real racing fans. I can't help but think of them as sports vultures who come to watch the 500-mile race on the highway of death to nowhere, hoping that the monotony of watching cars flick by at speeds in excess of 190 mph will be relieved by mechanical—and human—catastrophe.

The beltway around Indianapolis is staked with grim white crosses, mute reminders to travelers of the fatal consequence of a too-heavy foot on the accelerator.

In 1966 there was a 16-car crash on the first lap, but—as auto racing fans triumphantly point out—no fatalities. It is a sport like Russian roulette—like rolling for snake eyes with your life on the line. Watching the race from the Indy grandstand is a little like watching hyperactive hamsters tread a cage wheel. The cars fly by like brightly painted berserk vacuum cleaners sucking the ground.

A sport that exists on the alluring promise of blood and death is no sport. It is a morbid vigil for human destruction.—Joan Ryan, "Grease, Gasoline, and Death," *Washington Post*

C. What, in detail, gives the following passage from *Time* its characteristic *Time*style quality? Your instructor may ask you to write the first two paragraphs of a *Time*style obituary on one of the following: Lincoln, Hitler, J. F. Kennedy, General Custer, Trotsky, Gandhi, or Captain Cook.

CRIME

Double-Dealer's Death

The rubout was executed neat Chicago gangland style. Two armed men —wearing ski masks and carrying a walkie-talkie to get word from a lookout —slithered into Rose's Sandwich Shop on the hairy, scary West Side. "Up against the wall!" they ordered the eight people inside. One of the gunmen then shoved a twelve-gauge shotgun under the chin of Richard Cain, 49. The hit man fired two blasts, blowing away Cain's handsome face. The killers quickly fled, accompanied by what witnesses later said was a mysterious "woman in blue."

Thus ended Cain's remarkable double-dealing life as a policeman and mobster. Cain was a Chicago detective in the 1950s, and later became chief investigator in the Cook County sheriff's office. In the mid-1960s he was dismissed from the sheriff's office for concocting a phony drug raid, and he became the chief operative of Chicago Mafia Overlord Momo Salvatore (Sam) Giancana. In 1966 Giancana left Chicago for Mexico to avoid federal heat and counseled the Chicago syndicate from his exile; Cain was a trusted aide.

THEME TOPICS 8

1. Write an informal letter to a friend about your difficulties in adjusting to college life.

2. Write a humorous paper on a subject usually treated with too much glum seriousness.

3. Write an ironical endorsement of a product or a policy that you disapprove of. Make sure your reader is aware of your ironical intention.

4. Write a parody of a type of speech, lecture, editorial, poem, short story, or play that annoys or amuses you. Or do an excerpt from a script for a parody of a type of movie or television show.

5. Write a satirical paper on some familiar part of the American scene. For instance, select some feature of popular culture or popular entertainment with which you are especially familiar.

6. Write a paper about the current scene as you would imagine it if written by one of the following in a characteristic style: a blues singer, a gospel singer, a modern jazz musician, a Shakespearean actor, a Baptist preacher, a disc jockey for a Country-and-Western station.

7. Study the manner and technique of an author who has attracted your notice because of a distinctive style. Modeling your style on the writer's, write a composition on a subject of your own choice.

8. Select an object that to you symbolizes a set of attitudes or a way of life—the motorcycle, the guitar, blue jeans, bare feet, the hunting rifle, the three-piece suit. Write to illustrate the set of attitudes involved, suiting your style to the interests and feelings expressed.

The Research Paper

CHAPTER NINE

1. **Getting Started**

2. **Going to the Sources**
   General Reference Works
   Specialized Reference Works
   Library Catalogs
   Bibliography Cards
   Evaluating Your Sources

3. **From Notes to the First Draft**
   Taking Notes
   Using Your Notes
   Organizing Your Notes
   Revising the First Draft

4. **Footnotes and Bibliographies**
   Footnotes
   First References
   Later References
   Abbreviations
   Final Bibliography

1. GETTING STARTED

When you write a research paper, you write for a reader who wants to *know*. Your job is to find reliable and up-to-date sources of information or evidence on a given subject. You then assemble, interpret, and correlate material from your several different sources.
Remember the following guidelines:

(1) *Stay away from highly technical subjects.* Recent discoveries about the nature of the universe or about the biochemistry of our bodies make fascinating topics, but you may soon need more knowledge of physics or mathematics than you and your reader can command.

(2) *Center your paper on one limited aspect of a more general subject.* Limit your area until you arrive at something that you can explore in detail. "The early history of American universities" is a general subject area. "The training of Puritan divines at Harvard" is a specific subject.

(3) *Make detailed use of several different sources.* Avoid subjects that would tempt you to summarize information from one main source. Avoid subjects that you find conclusively treated in a textbook or encyclopedia.

(4) *Stay close to the evidence you present.* When you write a research paper, the stance you adopt toward your audience is: "Here is the evidence. This is where I found it. You are welcome to verify these sources and to check these facts."

The finished research paper differs from the ordinary theme in outward form. It includes **documentation**: It fully identifies sources, usually in footnotes. It often lists them again in a bibliography, a final alphabetical listing of sources consulted during the project. The author of a research paper makes sources and procedures available for inspection and review. The reader can check the sources—to see if they were quoted correctly, or if the evidence was selected fairly.
Documentation helps the writer avoid **plagiarism**. Writers who plagiarize take over the results of someone else's research or investigation without acknowledgment. It is true that many facts and ideas are common property and need not be credited to any specific source. Major historical dates and events, key ideas of major scientific or philosophical movements—these are generally accessible in reference books. However, identify your source whenever you use

information recently discovered or collected. Show your source whenever you adopt someone's characteristic, personal point of view. Never copy whole sentences or paragraphs without making it clear that you are quoting another writer.

Here are some general areas for research:

1. The history of dictionary making: the principles and practices of lexicographers like Samuel Johnson or Noah Webster; the history of the *Oxford English Dictionary*; the reception of Webster's *Third New International.*
2. Bilingualism: problems encountered by French Canadians or Spanish-speaking Americans; assimilation vs. the preservation of a separate linguistic and cultural tradition; the schooling provided for children who speak a different language at home.
3. The history of the American Indian: early contacts with whites; wars, treaties, and reservations; the role of church and missionary; assimilation vs. self-identity.
4. The current state of prison reform: current conditions in American jails; retribution vs. rehabilitation; treatment of juveniles.
5. Changing attitudes toward age and aging: the shift from a youth culture toward an aging society; society's image and self-image of senior citizens; early vs. late retirement.
6. Alternative sources of energy: fission and fusion; oil and other fossil fuels vs. solar energy.
7. Saving the animals: wildlife in your state then and now; shrinking habitats for major endangered species; national and international conservationist efforts.
8. Censorship: public pressures encountered by artists and writers; the role of religious or patriotic groups; defining pornography or obscenity; the role of lawgivers and courts.
9. The self-image of the young black in white society as reflected in the writings of one or more black authors: Richard Wright, James Baldwin, Ralph Ellison, LeRoi Jones, Lorraine Hansberry, Maya Angelou, Alexander Haley.
10. The public reception of a controversial author: Henrik Ibsen, D. H. Lawrence, Gertrude Stein, Henry Miller, Sylvia Plath, Kurt Vonnegut, Joyce Carol Oates; changing standards of public taste and morals.

2.   GOING TO THE SOURCES

The experienced investigator knows where to look. Writing a research paper gives you a chance to find your way around a library and to get acquainted with its resources.

General Reference Works

Learn to use the reference tools available to every investigator.

Encyclopedias   An encyclopedia is a good place to start—but not to finish—your investigation. The encyclopedia provides a convenient summary of what is generally known on your subject. The purpose of your investigation is to go *beyond* the encyclopedia—to take a closer firsthand look.

• The *Encyclopaedia Britannica*, now an American publication, is the most authoritative of the general encyclopedias. It provides extended articles on general subjects, with exceptionally full bibliographies at the ends of articles. It is brought up to date each year by the *Britannica Book of the Year*. (Although you would normally consult the most up-to-date version, you will occasionally find references to scholarly articles in earlier editions.)

• The *Encyclopedia Americana* is sometimes recommended for science and biography. General subjects are broken up into short articles, arranged alphabetically. The annual supplement is the *Americana Annual*.

• *Collier's Encyclopedia* is another multivolume general encyclopedia, written in a more popular style.

• The one-volume *Columbia Encyclopedia* provides a bird's-eye view. It serves well for a quick check of people and places.

Bibliographies At the end of many encyclopedia entries you will find a short bibliography, a list of important books and other sources of information. The encyclopedia may list only very general books, but these in turn will often contain more detailed bibliographical listings or direct you to book-length bibliographies. Any general survey of a subject is likely to provide information about more detailed studies. College textbooks often provide a short bibliography at the end of each chapter.

Take up first those books that a bibliography labels "standard," "indispensable," or "the best introduction" to your subject. If the bibliographies you have consulted merely *list* books, take up those that are most frequently mentioned. Study their tables of contents, prefaces, introductory or concluding chapters. Find out what each book is trying to do and whether all or parts of it would be useful for your project.

Note: The *Book Review Digest* contains short selections from book reviews written shortly after publication of the book reviewed. These can give you an idea of the intention and importance of books on subjects of general interest.

Periodical Indexes When writing on a current problem, you may have to rely mainly on articles in both general and technical magazines. The card catalog of your library lists magazines but not individual magazine articles. You will have to find the latter in the **periodical indexes**. These are published in monthly or semimonthly installments and then combined in huge volumes, each listing articles for a period of one or more years.

• The *Readers' Guide to Periodical Literature* indexes magazines written for the general reader. If you are writing on American policy in the Near East, the *Readers' Guide* may direct you to speeches by government officials reprinted in a publication like *U.S. News & World Report*. It may direct you to discussions of American foreign policy in such magazines as *Newsweek* and *New Republic*.

Here is a sample entry from the *Readers' Guide*. Note that you would have found this magazine article under the subject heading "Adult Education." The article was written by B. Farber, is called "Mother Goes Back to School," and appeared in *Parents Magazine*:

> ADULT education
>   Mother goes back to school. B. Farber. il
>   Parents Mag 49:46-7+ Ja '74

(Further information included: The article appears in the issue for January 1974. The issue is part of Volume 49. The main part of the article appears on pages 46 and 47, but it is continued elsewhere. The article is illustrated.)

• The *Social Sciences Index* (formerly *International Index*) lists articles in more scholarly magazines. If you are looking for important studies of the black community, this index will direct you to articles in sociological and psychological journals.

• The *Humanities Index*. For the years 1965–1973, this index was combined with the *Social Sciences Index*.

Note: Whatever index or bibliography you use, read its introductory pages and study its list of abbreviations. *Study the list of the periodicals indexed*—it may not include a magazine that you have seen mentioned elsewhere and that you know to be important. Look at sample entries to study the listing of individual articles (usually by subject) and the system of cross references.

Specialized Reference Works

Use the reference tools of a special area of study. Every major area, such as education, history, or art, has its own specialized reference guides: yearbooks, specialized encyclopedias, dictionaries of names and technical terms, general bibliographies. To find specialized reference works relevant to your research project, turn to Constance M. Winchell's *Guide to Reference Books*, or another general guide to reference works.

Biography   In addition to the biographical entries in the major encyclopedias, most libraries have ample material for this kind of project.

• *Who's Who in America*, a biographical dictionary of notable living men and women, provides a brief summary of dates and details on important contemporaries.

• The *Dictionary of American Biography* (*DAB*) contains a more detailed account of the lives of important persons. (The British counterparts of these two volumes are *Who's Who* and the *Dictionary of National Biography*.)

• The *Biography Index* is a guide to biographical material in books *and* magazines. By consulting both recent and earlier volumes, you can compile a comprehensive bibliography of material on the married life of George Washington or on the evangelistic campaigns of Billy Graham.

Literature   A library project on a subject from literary history may deal with an author's schooling or early reading, recurrent themes in the books of a well-known novelist, the contemporary reputation of a nineteenth-century American poet.

• The fifteen-volume *Cambridge History of English Literature* and the *Cambridge Bibliography of English Literature* provide comprehensive information about English authors and literary movements.

• The Spiller-Thorp-Johnson-Canby *Literary History of the United States*, with its supplementary bibliographies, lists as its contributors an impressive roster of contemporary American literary scholars.

• *Harper's Dictionary of Classical Literature and Antiquities* is a comprehensive scholarly guide to Greek and Roman history and civilization. (Robert Graves' *The Greek Myths* and Edith Hamilton's *Mythology*, both available as paperbacks, provide an introduction to famous names and stories.)

Current Events   A number of special reference guides are useful for papers on a political subject or on current events.

• *Facts on File* is a weekly digest of world news, with an annual index. It gives a summary of news reports and comments with excerpts from important documents and speeches. It can serve as a convenient review of day-to-day happenings in politics, foreign affairs, entertainment, sports, science, and education.

• The *New York Times Index* (published since 1913) is a guide to news stories published in the *New York Times*. Look up an event or a controversy in this index to find the approximate dates for relevant articles in other newspapers and magazines.

• The annual index to the *Monthly Catalog of the United States Government Publications* lists reports and documents published by all branches of the federal government.

Library Catalogs

Learn to make efficient use of the card catalog. Your research projects will ordinarily be geared to the resources of your college library. Its central card catalog is a complete alphabetical index of the materials available to you. In most card catalogs, the same book is listed several times: by *author* (under the author's last name), by *title* (under the first word of the title, not counting *The*, *A*, or *An*), and by *subject*.

An **author card** will look like this:

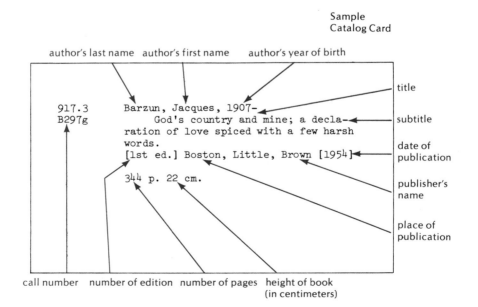

Sample
Catalog Card

Look for the following clues to the nature of the book:

- *the number or description of the edition.* If the catalog lists both the original edition and another one marked "2nd ed." or "Rev. ed.," you will generally choose the one that is most nearly up to date.

- *the name and location of the publisher.* For instance, a book published by a university press is likely to be a scholarly or specialized study. The *date of publication is* especially important for books on scientific, technological, or medical subjects, where older information is often out of date.

- *the number of pages* (with the number of introductory pages given as a lower-case Roman numeral). It shows whether the book is a short pamphlet or a full-scale treatment of the subject. If the book contains *illustrations* or a *bibliography*, the card will carry a notation to that effect.

Often, a card lists the several major *subject headings* under which the book can be found. For instance, a catalog card for a sociological study of a town in the Middle West may carry the following notation concerning various headings under which the study is listed:

1. U.S.—Social conditions.   2. Cities and Towns—U.S.   3. Cost and standard of living—U.S.   4. U.S.—Religion.   5. Social surveys.   6. Community life.

Subject cards can direct you to many books that are relevant to your topic. Look for subject headings under which books on your topic might be listed. Books on progressive education might appear under *Education—Aims and Objectives,* under *Education—Experimental Methods,* or under *Educational Psychology.* Books on the Civil War might appear under *U.S.—History—Civil War,* under *U.S. —History—Military,* under *Slavery in the United States,* or under *Abolitionists.*

Once you decide that you should consult a book, copy its call number. The **call number** directs you, or the librarian, to the shelf where the book is located. Your library may use either of two numbering systems: the Library of Congress system or the Dewey decimal system. The **Library of Congress system** divides books into categories identified by letters of the alphabet. It then uses additional letters and numerals to subdivide each main category. For instance, the call number of a book on religion would start with a capital *B*; the call number of a book on education starts with a capital *L*. The **Dewey decimal system** uses numerals to identify the main categories. For instance, 400–499 covers books on language; 800–899 covers books on literature. The 800 range is then further subdivided into American literature (810–819), English literature (820–829), and so on. Additional numerals and letters distinguish among individual authors and among individual works by the same author.

Note: Most libraries have a separate, compact catalog for all periodicals to which the library subscribes. For each periodical it indicates the location of recent issues (often on the shelves of a separate periodical room) as well as of back issues (usually in bound volumes in the book stacks of the library).

Bibliography Cards

Make your own card catalog of promising materials. Include a separate note card for each book, pamphlet, or magazine article you intend to use. Your instructor may suggest a minimum number of sources to consult. On each bibliography card, include the library call number or the place in the library where the publication is to be found. (This information is for your own use. Do *not* include it in your finished paper.)

A bibliography card for a book will look like this:

```
HV       Mitford, Jessica
947      Kind and Usual Punishment: The
M58          Prison Business
1973     New York: Random House, 1973
```

Put the author's *last name first* to facilitate alphabetizing. If a work has been collected or arranged by a person other than the author you may start with that person's name, followed by "ed." for "editor." Ordinarily, however, the name of an editor or of a translator (followed by "trans.") appears on a separate line below the title. If an article in an encyclopedia is identified only by the author's initials, you may be able to find the full name by checking the initials against a list of contributors.

Start a new line for the *full title of the publication*, including a subtitle, if any. Underline the title of a book, pamphlet, or other work published as a separate entity. (Underlining in a typed manuscript corresponds to italics in print.) Put the title of an article or short poem in quotation marks and underline the title of the magazine or collection in which it appears.

Use a separate line for the *facts of publication*. For a book or pamphlet these may include:

(1) The *number or description of the edition* (unless a book has not been re-edited since publication).

(2) The *number of volumes* (if a work consists of several, and all are relevant to your investigation).

(3) The *place of publication* (usually the location of the main office of the publishing house, or of the first branch office listed if several are given).

(4) The *name of the publisher*.

(5) The *date of publication* (which can usually be inferred from the copyright date, found on the reverse side of the title page).

(6) The *number of the specific volume used* (if only one of several volumes is relevant to your investigation).

A bibliography card for an article may look like this:

```
Periodical    Schorer, Mark
Room             "D. H. Lawrence: Then, During, Now"
                 The Atlantic, 233 (March 1974), 84-88

       The author, one of Lawrence's biographers,
    traces Lawrence's reputation as a writer from its
    low point at the time of his death to its present
    "position of primacy among great twentieth-century
    prose writers in English."
```

For a magazine or newspaper article, the facts of publication ordinarily do *not* include the name of the publisher and the place of publication (though the latter is sometimes needed to identify a small-town journal). The pages of most professional or technical magazines are numbered consecutively through the several issues making up one **volume**, usually the issues published during one year. For an article in such a magazine, record the *number of the volume* (in arabic numerals), the *date of the issue,* and the *page numbers of the article.* For articles in other magazines and in newspapers, record the date of the issue and the page numbers. If the pages in separate sections of a newspaper are not numbered consecutively, identify the section where the article is to be found.

Note: The above bibliography card for an article is an example of an **annotated card**. When you annotate your cards, you include brief reminders concerning your sources. You may want to note whether an article is written in a very technical or very popular style. You may want to note that a book has a glossary of technical terms, or a convenient summary of historical facts.

Evaluating Your Sources

Learn to choose authoritative sources and to evaluate conflicting evidence. Every investigator tries to find sources that are reliable and truly informative. When confronted with conflicting testimony, ask: Who is talking? How does this writer know? What is this author trying to prove? What side is he or she on? When you evaluate your sources, consider points like the following:

(1) *Is the author an authority on this subject?* If you can, find out whether a book was written by an economist whose specialty is Russian agriculture or by a columnist who spent four weeks surveying Russian agriculture from the windows of a train.

(2) *Is the work a thorough study or a sketchy survey of the topic?* Is it short on opinion and long on evidence? Does it weigh the findings of other authorities, or ignore them?

(3) *Does the author settle important questions by going to primary sources?* **Primary sources** are legal documents, letters, diaries, eyewitness reports, transcripts of speeches and interviews, reports on experiments, statistical surveys, and the like. They take us close to unedited firsthand facts. They are often more reliable than *sec-*

ondary sources—other authors' accounts and interpretations of primary materials.

(4) *Is the author's treatment balanced or one-sided?* An early phase in the history of the American labor movement is likely to be treated one way in the success story of a famous industrialist. It will be treated another way in the biography of a labor leader. An objective historian will weigh both pro-business and pro-labor views.

(5) *Is the work recent enough to have profited from current scholarship?* If it was originally published ten or twenty years ago, is the current version a revised edition? Consider the possibility that an author's views may have been invalidated by new findings and changing theories in a rapidly expanding field of study.

EXERCISES

A. Select one of the following subjects and compare its treatment in a general encyclopedia and in one of the more specialized reference works listed below. Choose one: atonality, surrealism, cybernetics, Zen, ESP, Savonarola, Hercules, Jacobins, Gestalt psychology, the Maccabees, Pan.

1. *Grove's Dictionary of Music and Musicians*
2. *Standard Dictionary of Folklore, Mythology and Legend*
3. *Comprehensive Dictionary of Psychological and Psychoanalytic Terms*
4. *Standard Jewish Encyclopedia*
5. *New Catholic Encyclopedia*
6. *Van Nostrand's Scientific Encyclopedia*
7. *Cambridge Medieval History*
8. *Cambridge Modern History*
9. *McGraw-Hill Dictionary of Art*
10. *Concise Encyclopedia of Living Faiths*

B. In the *Readers' Guide, Social Science Index,* or *Humanities Index,* find an article on one of the subjects listed below. Report on the intention of the author, level of difficulty of the article, and the author's use of sources. Choose one of the following general subjects:

- Supersonic aircraft

- Reevaluations of the CIA or FBI

- Freud and his disciples

- Birth rates and the schools

- Dissent in the Soviet Union

- Estimates of the world's fuel supply

- Testing in our public schools

C. Through the card catalog of your college library, find one of the following books. Study its preface, table of contents, bibliography (if any), and any other introductory or concluding sections. Study its treatment of selected entries or of one or two limited topics. Then prepare a brief report on the intention, scope, and possible usefulness of the book. Choose one:

1. H. L. Mencken, *The American Language*
2. Leo Rosten, *The Joys of Yiddish*
3. G. M. Trevelyan, *History of England*
4. Edgar Z. Friedenberg, *Coming of Age in America*
5. Kenneth Rexroth, *Classics Revisited*
6. Norma Lorre Goodrich, *Ancient Myths*
7. Margaret Mead, *Male and Female*
8. Alden T. Vaughan, *New England Frontier: Puritans and Indians*
9. Robert Coles, *Children of Crisis*
10. Thomas Pyles, *The Origin and Development of the English Language*
11. S. I. Hayakawa, *Language in Thought and Action*
12. Margaret M. Bryant, *Current American Usage*
13. Linda Goodman, *Sun Signs*
14. Joseph Campbell, *The Hero with a Thousand Faces*
15. Simone de Beauvoir, *The Second Sex*

D. Study the arrangement of cards in the central card catalog of your college library in order to answer the following questions:

1. What are the major subdivisions for subject cards under the heading "Education"?
2. Where would you find a book by an author named John McMillan (under *Mc*, *Mac*, *Mi*?), George St. John (under *St.*, *Sa*, *Jo*?), Antoine de Saint-Exupéry (under *De*, *Sa*, *St.*?)?
3. Do subject cards for books on the Civil War precede or follow cards for books on the War of Independence? Is the arrangement alphabetical or chronological?
4. Are books about George Washington listed before or after books about the State of Washington, or about Washington, D.C.?
5. Check under *John Keats*: What is the relative order of the author's individual works, his collected works, and books about the author?

3.   FROM NOTES TO THE FIRST DRAFT

In putting a research paper together, you face two major tasks. You collect material that bears on the question you are trying to answer, on the issue you are trying to explore. You then sort out and arrange these materials in a coherent presentation, supporting the conclusions that your investigation has made you reach.

Taking Notes

Take accurate notes to serve as raw material for your first draft. For a short research report, you may be able to take notes on ordinary sheets of writing paper. But for a longer research paper, 3″ x 5″ or 4″ x 6″ note cards will enable you to *shuffle* and arrange your information as the overall pattern of your paper takes shape. Remember:

- Make sure *author and title of your source* (in shortened form) appear on each card, along with exact page numbers. Use the tentative subdivisions of your paper as the common heading for each group of related cards.

- Use each card for a *single piece of information*, for a single quotation, or for closely related material. This way you won't have to split up the material on the card later, to use in different parts of your paper.

- Include the kind of *specific detail* that you will need to support generalizations: selected examples, statistical figures, definitions of difficult terms.

- Make sure the material you select is *representative* of the source—not taken out of context. The person you quote should be able to say: "Yes, I'll stand behind that. That's more or less what I meant."

In taking notes, do not simply copy big chunks of material. *Adapt* the material to suit your purposes as you go along. Normally, you will be using several major techniques:

(1) *Summarize background information; condense lengthy arguments.* Here is a note card that condenses several pages of introductory information in John G. Neihardt's book *Black Elk Speaks*:

```
Last Battles

      In the fall of 1930, a field agent helped Nei-
hardt meet Black Elk, a holy man of the Oglala Sioux
who was a second cousin to chief Crazy Horse.  Black
Elk was nearly blind and knew no English.  Neihardt,
speaking to him through an interpreter, gained his
confidence partly by respecting the holy man's long
silences.  In the spring of 1931, Black Elk took many
days to tell his life story, including the story of
his share in the defeat of General Custer, which
Black Elk witnessed as a young warrior.

Neihardt, Black Elk, pp. vii-xi
```

(2) *Paraphrase much of the material that you are going to use.* In a **paraphrase**, we put information and ideas into our own words. This way we can emphasize what is most directly useful. We can cut down on what is less important. At the same time, we show that we have *made sense* of what we have read. The following sample note card paraphrases an author's statement and support of one key point:

```
Rehabilitation

     Trades or vocational skills taught in today's
prisons are often outdated or unrealistic. In one
case, a New York medium security prison provided de-
tainees with a course in operating diesel trucks. The
course was very popular and was supported by local
charitable organizations. Ironically, after their re-
lease the prisoners found that the law prohibited
them from obtaining a Class One driver's license for
more than five years in most cases. In the interim,
many returned to the professions that had put them
behind bars in the first place. As a result, over
half returned to prison.

Menniger, "Doing True Justice," p. 6
```

(3) *Make strategic use of brief, well-chosen, direct quotations.* When we quote **verbatim**, we quote directly word for word. Quote characteristic or striking phrases. Quote sentences that sum up well a step in an argument. Look for sentences that show well the point of view or intentions of the quoted author. Apt, brief, direct quotations give your writing an authentic touch; they show that you are staying close to the firsthand sources:

```
Indian Education

     Indian children were put in crowded boarding
schools and fed at the cost of 11 cents a day (with
their diet supplemented by food that could be grown
on school farms). From the fifth grade up, children
put in half a day's labor on the school farm. They
were taught "vanishing trades of little or no eco-
nomic importance."

"Breaking Faith," p. 240
```

(4) *Use more extended direct quotation for key passages.* Quote at some length to let the original author sum up a major argument. Quote the exact words when an author takes a stand on a difficult or controversial issue:

```
Federal Policy

     "From the very beginnings of this nation, the
chief issue around which federal Indian policy has
revolved has been, not how to assimilate the Indian
nations whose lands we usurped, but how best to
transfer Indian lands and resources to non-Indians."

Van de Mark, "Raid on the Reservations," p. 49
```

Note: In the actual finished paper, quotations running to several sentences, or to a paragraph or more, are usually set off as **block quotations.** (See chart, "Punctuating Quotations," on page 215.) Use such long quotations *sparingly*. Excerpt or break up quotations beyond paragraph length to keep the reader from merely skimming them or passing them by. (See P 6c.)

Using Your Notes

Learn how to work the material from your note cards into your own text. To keep your text moving smoothly, remember the following:

(1) *Link quoted and paraphrased material clearly to its source.* Where necessary, put in tags like "According to the governor . . ." or "As Erich Fromm has observed, . . ." When you quote several authors, make sure references like "he" or "she" or "the writer" point clearly to the one you have in mind.

(2) *Steer your readers by telling them what the point of a quotation is or why you quote it.* Prepare the reader to look for a key point:

According to William G. Nagel in his book *The New Red Barn*, we neglect our penal system because *it deals mainly with people of low social and economic status*. We neglect the prison population because they are mostly people who *do not count in our society*: "The generally unsatisfactory condition of the correctional process reflects the lowly status of the people caught in it. . . . As long as the majority of offenders are poor, uneducated, and from minority groups, the correctional slice of the federal budget will remain small, and the overall response will be repressive."[2]

(3) *Know how to quote key words and phrases as part of your own sentences.* When a quotation becomes part of a sentence of your own, fit it into the grammatical pattern of your own sentence—without changing the wording of the part quoted directly:

INDIVIDUAL
NOTE CARDS:

Hamlet as thinker

"Hamlet's character is the prevalence of the abstracting and generalizing habit over the practical. He does not want courage, skill, will, or opportunity; but every incident sets him thinking; . . . I have a smack of Hamlet myself, if I may say so."
                                  4

Hamlet as thinker

According to Coleridge (1818?), Shakespeare meant to show the need for a healthy balance between observation and thought, between reality and the world of imagination. "In Hamlet this balance is disturbed: his thoughts, and the images of his fancy, are far more vivid than his actual perceptions . . . Hence we see a great, an almost enormous, intellectual activity, and a proportionate aversion to real action . . . he vacillates from sensibility, and procrastinates from thought."   5

in Smith,

Hamlet as thinker

           1
"It is we who are Hamlet." . . . Whoever has become thoughtful and melancholy through his own mishaps or those of others; whoever has borne about with him the clouded brow of reflection, and thought himself 'too much i' th' sun;' . . . whose powers of action have been eaten up by thought, he to whom the universe seems infinite and himself nothing; . . . this is the true Hamlet."   (3)   2

Hazlitt, Characters of Sh.'s Plays (1817) in Smith, pp. 287-88

WRONG: Pope Pius described a just war in this way: "If it has been forced upon one by an evident and extremely grave injustice that in no way can be avoided."

RIGHT: Pope Pius stated that a war is just "if it has been forced upon one by an evident and extremely grave injustice that in no way can be avoided."

(4) *Learn how to combine material from your notes.* A paragraph in your finished paper will often combine material from several different note cards. Don't simply stitch the patches together. Spell out the conclusion that the evidence on your cards points to. Then *select* the material from your cards that will best back up your general point. Study the way material from the accompanying note cards on p. 212 has been selected to serve as evidence in a coherent paragraph.

COMBINED PARAGRAPH:

The Romantic critics saw in Hamlet a man paralyzed by thought. They saw in him a reflection of their own temperament: a love for solitude, an extreme sensitivity, a tendency to be kept from effective action by melancholy reflections. "It is we who are Hamlet," said William Hazlitt. The true Hamlet is someone "whose powers of action have been eaten up by thought"--"whoever has become thoughtful and melancholy through his own mishaps or those of others; whoever has borne about with him the clouded brow of reflection, and thought himself 'too much i' th' sun.'"[7] Coleridge, who said "I have a smack of Hamlet myself," saw in Hamlet a lack of balance between thought and reality--"a great, an almost enormous, intellectual activity, and a proportionate aversion to real action."[8]

Organizing Your Notes

As your paper begins to assume definite shape, remember the following advice:

(1) *Group together note cards that contain related material.* Often a group of cards will record details pointing to a common generalization. Several cards will contain evidence backing up the same major point. Often a group of cards will record related causes combining to produce a common result. Two related groups of cards may contain parallel sets of data for detailed comparison.

(2) *Work toward a unifying thesis.* Ask yourself: "What is this paper as a whole going to tell the reader?" Suppose you are writing a paper on the present state of gambling in the United States. Your problem will be to keep your paper from becoming a repository of miscellaneous facts about gambling laws, famous gamblers, different games of chance, and tourist life in Las Vegas. To unify your paper, you might concentrate on the legal aspects of gambling. You could then review in some detail the laws of Nevada as exceptions to antigambling laws in other states, the legal status of horse and dog races, the question of lotteries and games conducted for charitable purposes. Everything you say in the paper could support one single major point:

THESIS: Gambling laws in the United States are paradoxical and unpredictable.

To give clear direction to your paper, state the thesis early—at the end of a brief introduction.

(3) *Work out a definite overall strategy.* When writing about interpretations of Hamlet's character, do not simply give a survey following straight chronological order. Instead, try to identify three or four major schools of thought. Group together critics interested in the *lone* Hamlet, listening to him most intently in his monologues and solitary musings. Group together critics interested in the *social* Hamlet and absorbed by his playacting and verbal fencing. Group together critics interested in the *child* Hamlet, listening, in psychoanalyst's fashion, for hints of his early psychological history.

(4) *Write a preliminary outline.* Formulate a tentative thesis sentence summarizing the conclusion that your paper seems to suggest.

Punctuating Quotations
An Overview (See also P 6)

DIRECT QUOTATION—A sentence or more directly quoted: quotation marks, introduced by a comma or colon

As Doris and David Jonas point out in *Young Till We Die,* old ideas about the dignity of age are fading fast: "Youthful culture is now cherished, and the elderly strive to fit in. . . . We impose upon our elderly the duty of acting and appearing young without giving them the privileges accorded to those who are indeed young."[3]

PARAPHRASE—Indirect quotation: *no* quotation marks, *no* comma or colon

According to Carol Katz, a special bond and a special love exist between the very young and the very old. Both of these groups are separated from the practical, businesslike working world of middle-aged people.

SHORT QUOTATION—Quoted words or phrases becoming part of a larger sentence: quotation marks, *no* comma or colon

Americans have always had faith that the next generation will do better than the last. Like Horace Mann, they have considered education the "great equalizer" and the "balance wheel" of society.

BLOCK QUOTATION—Long quoted passages indented and set off if they run to more than four or five lines: indent ten spaces for the whole quotation, *no* quotation marks

A recent article in *Psychology Today* claims that most young children today have distorted ideas about older people:

> Most children have little contact with old people. Their grandparents may be thousands of miles away or in nursing homes seldom visited. As a result, young children's feelings about the elderly and about getting old tend to be negative and stereotyped.[7]

LINES OF POETRY—When two or three lines of poetry appear as part of the running text, a slash shows where each new line starts:

As Juliet says, it is his name that is her enemy: "That which we call a rose, / By any other word would smell as sweet."

But usually we set of two or more lines as a block quotation, centered on the page:

Emily Dickinson often sums up a contradiction in startlingly simple words:

> In this short Life
> That only lasts an hour
> How much—how little—is
> Within our power.

Your outline and your thesis sentence will enable you to decide which of your note cards contain irrelevant material and should be set aside. They will also help you to decide in which areas your notes need to be supplemented by further reading. A definitive outline preceding the final paper usually shows whether the paper has a unifying purpose, whether the major subdivisions of the paper contribute to that purpose, and whether unrelated odds and ends have been eliminated. (For forms of outlines, see Chapter One, "The Whole Theme.")

Revising the First Draft

Allow time for a final rewriting of your first draft. A first draft usually makes jerky reading. Important explanations may be missing. Links may be missing from one section to the next. Awkward repetition or backtracking may slow down the reader. In your final revision, do the following:

• Check for *clear overall intention*. Make sure your main points are not merely implied but clearly and fully stated. State them preferably at the beginning of the paper following your introduction. Or, if more appropriate, state them toward the end of the paper in the form of a summary.

• Check for *adequate support*. Make sure you have the details and examples that your reader would accept as adequate evidence for your major points.

• Check for adequate *interpretation*. Many papers suffer from too much quotation, too much summary, and not enough explanation and comparison. Examine key terms to see whether they need to be more fully defined. Explain terms like *Hellenistic, psychosomatic*, or *lingua franca*.

• Check for *coherence*. Make your reader see the relationship between different parts of your paper. Anticipate and answer the questions of a reader mired in a mass of details: "How did this get in here?" "Why do I have to study this particular set of statistics?" Make sure there is a clear **transition**, implied or stated, from paragraph to paragraph.

• Check for clear *attribution*. Make sure all material directly quoted is clearly identified. (See chart on page 215.)

EXERCISES

A. Select a magazine article or a chapter in a book on one of the general topics listed below. Assume that you are extracting information or opinions for use in a larger research project. Prepare five note cards illustrating the various techniques of note-taking. Choose one:

- the history of advertising
- secret wartime codes and how to break them
- the history of photography
- the Long March
- Hollywood's early stars
- the Cherokee nation
- the suffragette movement
- rape and the law

B. After finishing the first draft of a research paper, write a *one-page abstract* that spells out the thesis and summarizes the argument. (Your instructor may ask you to submit a *preliminary* summary of findings at an earlier stage of your investigation.)

4. FOOTNOTES AND BIBLIOGRAPHIES

Documentation enables your readers to identify, trace, and check your sources. Its purpose is to provide exact and comprehensive information in condensed form.

Footnotes

Use footnotes to show the source of facts, opinions, and examples. Use them not only when you quote an author directly, but also when you merely paraphrase or summarize what someone said.[1] A footnote is *not* necessary when the author has merely repeated something that is widely known or believed:

NO FOOTNOTE: George Washington was elected to the Virginia assembly in 1758. (This is "common knowledge," the kind of fact likely to be recorded in public documents and found in many history books.)

---

[1] Not all footnotes serve exclusively for documentation. **Explanatory footnotes,** of which this note is an illustration, may define technical terms unfamiliar only to some of the readers. They may provide information not necessary to the main trend of the argument.

FOOTNOTE: Samuel Eliot Morison describes Washington as "an eager and bold
              experimenter" in new agricultural methods.[17]
              (This is a judgment the historian made on the basis of firsthand inves-
              tigation. The text already mentions his name; the footnote, not re-
              printed here, will give the exact source.)

Number your footnotes consecutively. Place the raised **footnote
number** outside whatever punctuation goes with the sentence or
paragraph. Indent the footnote itself like a paragraph, and start it
with the raised footnote number. Normally, capitalize the first word
and use a period or other end punctuation at the end. In your typed
manuscript, *single-space* your footnotes and put them in one of three
positions:

• Between two unbroken lines *immediately below the line of typed
material* to which they belong.[2]

_____

    [2] Even when a different system of placing foot-
notes is required in the final paper, students may
find the system of which this footnote is an illustration the most convenient one to follow in the
first draft. It prevents errors when footnotes have
to be renumbered because of changes in the manuscript.

_____

• *At the bottom of the page*, separated from the text by an unbroken
line or triple spacing. To estimate the amount of space required at
the bottom of the page, you may have to type your footnotes on a
separate sheet of paper first.

• On a separate sheet *at the end of your paper*. This system is usually required when a manuscript is submitted for publication.

First References

Fully identify a source the first time you refer to it. The most common type of footnote gives full information about a source the first
time it is mentioned or drawn on in the text. The following sample
footnotes illustrate the standard form for such a first reference, as
well as the most important variations.

(1) *Standard reference to a book.* Give the author's full name, putting the first name *first*. After a comma, add the title of the book—*underlined* in typescript (italicized in print). Give the facts of publication in parentheses. (Include place of publication, name of publisher, date of publication.) After a comma, add the page reference ("p." for single page; "pp." for several pages: pp. 163–65).

> ⁷ Mary McCarthy, <u>Memoirs of a Catholic Girlhood</u> (New York: Harcourt, 1957), p. 23.

> ⁴ Neil Postman and Charles Weingartner, <u>Teaching as a Subversive Activity</u> (New York: Delacorte, 1969), pp. 158–59.

(2) *Newspaper or magazine article.* Enclose the title of the article in quotation marks; underline the title of the newspaper or magazine: "How to Deep-Freeze Bait," *The Fisherman's Monthly*. Give the date of issue, separated from what precedes and follows by commas. If a magazine provides a volume number, give it as an Arabic numeral, enclose the date in parentheses, and give the page reference *without* using "p." or "pp.": 15 (Sept. 1975), 47.

> ³ "U.S. Asked to Aid Youth Exchanges," <u>New York Times</u>, 15 June 1978, p. 8, col. 1.

> ⁷ Kenneth F. Weaver, "The Promise and Peril of Nuclear Energy," <u>National Geographic</u>, 155 (April 1979), 466.

(3) *Partial footnote.* If the text of your paper has given the author's full name, start your footnote with the title. (Do the same even if your text has given both name and title.) If your text attributes a quotation about American dialects to its author, the footnote might look like this:

> ² <u>American English</u> (New York: Oxford Univ. Press, 1958), p. 17.

(4) *Work with subtitle.* Separate the subtitle from the title by a colon unless the original has other punctuation. Underline the subtitle of a book. Enclose both the title and the subtitle of an article in the same set of quotation marks:

[11] Bruno Bettelheim, <u>The Uses of Enchantment:</u>
<u>The Meaning and Importance of Fairy Tales</u> (New York:
Knopf, 1976), p. 65.

[6] Sarah Schmidt, "From Ghetto to University: The
Jewish Experience in the Public School," <u>American</u>
<u>Educator,</u> Spring 1978, p. 23.

(5) *Edited or translated work.* Insert the editor's or translator's
name after the title, separating it from the title by a comma. Use the
abbreviation "ed." or "trans." The editor's name may come *first* if
the author is unknown, if the editor has collected the work of different authors, or if the editor has brought together an author's work
from different sources.

[2] H. L. Mencken, <u>The Vintage Mencken,</u> ed.
Alistair Cooke (New York: Vintage, 1956), p. 49.

[4] Alice Griffin, ed., <u>Rebels and Lovers:</u>
<u>Shakespeare's Young Heroes and Heroines</u> (New York:
New York Univ. Press, 1976), p. 80.

[6] Konrad Lorenz, <u>On Aggression,</u> trans. Marjorie
Kerr Wilson (New York: Harcourt, 1966), p. 7.

(6) *Revised editions.* If a work has been brought up to date since
its original publication, give the number of the edition you are using. Place it before the facts of publication. Separate it from what
precedes it by a comma.

[2] Albert C. Baugh, <u>A History of the English Lan-</u>
<u>guage,</u> 2nd ed. (New York: Appleton, 1957), pp. 7-8.

[11] M. B. Forman, ed., <u>The Letters of John Keats,</u>
3rd ed. (London: Milford, 1948), pp. 67-68.

(7) *Work published in several volumes.* Show the number of the
volume you are quoting. Use a capital Roman numeral. Insert it
after the facts of publication, and separate it from what precedes
and follows it by commas. Remember that after a volume number
"p." and "pp." are omitted.

[3] Virginia Woolf, The Diary of Virginia Woolf
(New York: Harcourt, 1977), I, 17.

(8) *Article in a collection.* Identify fully both the article and the collection of which it is a part.

[4] Carl R. Rogers, "Two Divergent Trends," in
Existential Psychology, ed. Rollo May (New York:
Random House, 1969), p. 87.

(9) *Encyclopedia entry.* Page numbers and facts of publication are unnecessary for *short* entries appearing in alphabetical order in well-known encyclopedias or dictionaries. Date or number of the edition used, however, is sometimes included because of the frequent revisions of major encyclopedias.

[2] M. J. Politis, "Greek Music," Encyclopedia
Americana, 1956.

[4] "Drama," Encyclopaedia Britannica, 1958, VII,
596.

(10) *Bible or literary classic.* References to the Bible usually identify only book, chapter, and verse. The name of a book of the Bible is *not* underlined or put in quotation marks. References to a Shakespeare play available in many different editions may specify act, scene, and line:

[4] Judges 13:5.   or   [4] Judges xiii.5.

[3] Hamlet II.ii.311-22.

Note: You will have to specify the edition used if textual variations are important, as with a new translation of the Bible. No identification is necessary for well-known or proverbial lines: "To be or not to be"; "The quality of mercy is not strained"; "They also serve who only stand and wait."

(11) *Quotations at second hand.* Make it clear that you are not quoting from the original or complete text:

⁵ William Archer, letter of October 18, 1883, to his brother Charles; quoted in Henrik Ibsen, <u>Ghosts</u>, ed. Kai Jurgensen and Robert Schenkkan (New York: Avon, 1965), p. 135.

(12) *Pamphlets and unpublished material.* Indicate the nature and source of materials other than books and magazines: mimeographed pamphlet, unpublished doctoral dissertation, and the like. Start with the title if no author or editor is identified. Use quotation marks to enclose unpublished titles.

⁶ Walter G. Friedrich, ed., "A Modern Grammar Chrestomathy" (Valparaiso, Indiana, mimeo., 1961), p. 12.

⁷ U. Fuller Schmaltz, "The <u>Weltschmerz</u> of Charles Addams," Diss. Columbia 1969, p. 7.

⁸ <u>Grape Harvesting</u> (Sacramento: California Department of Viticulture, 1980), pp. 8-9.

Later References

Keep subsequent references short but clear. There is no need to repeat the full name and title, or the facts of publication. Here are the most common possibilities:

(1) *Shortened reference.* Once you have fully identified a book, use the author's last name to identify it in later footnotes. Separate the name from the page reference by a comma.

¹¹ Baugh, p. 9.

When you are using *several works by the same author,* use the author's last name and a shortened form of the title:

¹¹ Baugh, <u>History</u>, p. 9.

(2) *One footnote for several quotations.* Avoid long strings of footnotes giving different page references to the same work. If several quotations from the same work follow one another in the same

paragraph of your paper, incorporate the page references in a single footnote. Use this method only when *no* quotations from another source intervene.

¹³ Harrison, pp. 8-9, 12, 17.

(3) *Page references in the text.* If all or most of your references are to a single work, you may put page references in parentheses in the body of your text: (p. 37). Identify the source in your first footnote and explain your procedure:

¹ Jerome S. Bruner, <u>On Knowing: Essays for the Left Hand</u> (New York: Atheneum, 1965), p. 3. All page references in the text of this paper are to this source.

(4) *Latin abbreviations.* A different system for shortened reference is frequently found in earlier scholarship but is rarely used today. Instead of repeating, in a shortened form, the author's name or the title, the writer used *ibid.*, an abbreviation of Latin *ibidem*, "in the same place." When used by itself, without a page reference, it means "in the last publication cited, on the same page." When used with a page reference, it means "in the last publication cited, on the page indicated." Like other Latin abbreviations used in footnotes, *ibid.* is no longer commonly italicized. It can refer only to *the last source cited*.

¹ G. B. Harrison, <u>Introducing Shakespeare</u> (Harmondsworth, Middlesex: Penguin Books, 1939), p. 28.

² Ibid., p. 37.

If a reference to a *different* work has intervened, the author's name is followed by *op. cit.*, short for *opere citato*, "in the work already cited." (This abbreviation cannot be used when several works by the same author have already been cited.)

¹ G. B. Harrison, <u>Introducing Shakespeare</u> (Harmondsworth, Middlesex: Penguin, 1947), p. 28.

² B. Ifor Evans, <u>A Short History of English Drama</u> (Harmondsworth, Middlesex: Penguin, 1948), pp. 51-69.

³ Harrison, op. cit., p. 37.

Abbreviations

Know common abbreviations used in footnotes in scholarly books and articles. You will encounter a number of abbreviations and technical terms in addition to those you will regularly use in your own work. The meaning of many of these will be clear from their context or position: *anon.* for "anonymous," *ch.* and *chs.* for "chapter" and "chapters," *col.* and *cols.* for "column" and "columns," *l.* and *ll.* for "line" and "lines," *n.* and *nn.* for "note" and "notes." Others are not self-explanatory:

©	copyright (© 1961 by John W. Gardner)
c. or ca.	Latin *circa*, "approximately"; used for approximate dates and figures (c. 1952)
cf.	Latin *confer*, "compare"; often used for **cross references** instead of see; "consult for further relevant material" (Cf. Ecclesiastes xii.12)
et al.	Latin *et alii*, "and others"; used in references to books by several authors (G. S. Harrison et al.)
f., ff.	"and the following page," "and the following pages" (See pp. 16 ff.)
loc. cit.	Latin *loco citato*, "in the place cited"; used without page reference (Baugh, loc. cit.)
MS, MSS	manuscript, manuscripts
n.d.	"no date," date of publication unknown

passim	Latin for "throughout"; "in various places in the work under discussion" (See pp. 54–56 et passim)
rpt.	"reprint"; a current reprinting of an older book
q.v.	Latin *quod vide,* "which you should consult"

Final Bibliography

In your final bibliography, include all the information needed to identify a source when first cited. Its main purpose is to describe in one single alphabetical list all sources you have used. You may include sources that you have found helpful but have not actually quoted in your paper.

Entries in the bibliography differ from footnotes as follows:

(1) The *last name of the author comes first.* This order applies only to the first author listed when a book has several authors. (The bibliography is an *alphabetical* listing.)

Shaw, Bernard. The Quintessence of Ibsenism, 3rd ed. New York: Hill, 1957.

(If *no name of author or editor is known to you,* list the publication alphabetically by the first letter of the title, not counting "The," "A," or "An.")

(2) *Major breaks are shown by periods.* The full name of the author is separated from what follows by a period. The facts of publication for a book are not enclosed in parentheses and are separated from what precedes and what follows by periods.

(3) *Entries for books do not include page references.* Entries for parts of books or items in magazines give the *inclusive page numbers* for the whole selection:

Granville-Barker, Harley. "When Ibsen Split the English Stage in Two." Literary Digest, 28 April 1928, pp. 24–25.

(4) *The author's name is not repeated if you list several publications by the same author.* Substitute a line made of ten hyphens for the name in the second and later entries.

Ibsen, Henrik. <u>Four Great Plays by Ibsen</u>. New York:
    Dutton, 1959.

----------. <u>Ghosts</u>. Trans. Kai Jurgensen and Robert
    Schenkkan. New York: Avon, 1965.

----------. <u>Three Plays</u>. Trans. Una Ellis-Fermor.
    Harmondsworth, Middlesex: Penguin, 1950.

Note: In a typed manuscript, single-space each individual item but leave a double space between items. Indent five spaces for the *second* and for subsequent lines of each item.
    The following might be sample entries from a final bibliography for a paper on photography as social document. Study the different kinds of entries. (See also the bibliography at the end of the sample research paper.)

Bibliography

Capa, Cornell, ed. <u>The Concerned Photographer</u>,
    Vol. II. New York: Grossman, 1972.

Capa, Robert. <u>Images of War</u>. New York: Grossman,
    n.d.

Dillard, Annie. "Sight into Insight." <u>Harper's</u>,
    248 (Feb. 1974), 39-46.

Eisenstaedt, Alfred. <u>The Eye of Eisenstaedt</u>. New
    York: Viking, 1969.

Gernsheim, Helmut, and Alison Gernsheim. <u>Creative</u>
    <u>Photography: 1826 to the Present</u>. Detroit:
    Wayne State Univ. Press, 1963.

Nairn, Ian. <u>The American Landscape: A Critical View</u>.
    New York: Random House, 1965.

"A Photographer's Odyssey." The Oakland Herald,
    26 Aug. 1974, p. 9, col. 3.

Sontag, Susan. On Photography. New York: Farrar,
    Straus & Giroux, 1977.

EXERCISES

A. Interpret the information provided in the following footnotes:

6 C. E. Silberman, Crisis in the Classroom: The
Remaking of American Education (New York: Random
House, 1970), p. 26.

3 Robert E. Spiller et al., Literary History of
the United States, rev. ed. (New York: Macmillan,
1953), p. 1343.

1 William McGuire, ed., "The Freud/Jung Letters,"
Psychology Today, 7 (Feb. 1974), 41.

9 Euripides, The Trojan Women, trans. Richmond
Lattimore, in Greek Plays in Modern Translation, ed.
Dudley Fitts (New York: Dial, 1947), p. 161.

4 "Prison System Breaking Down?" U.S. News and
World Report, 11 Aug. 1967, p. 61.

8 Kenneth Muir, ed., Collected Poems of Sir
Thomas Wyatt (Cambridge, Mass: Harvard Univ. Press,
1950), p. xx.

7 1 Corinthians iii. 18-20.

13 Simone Weil, "The Iliad, or The Poem of Force,"
trans. Mary McCarthy, in The Mint, ed. Geoffrey
Grigson, No. 2 (1948), p. 85.

12 Cf. The Complete Works of William Hazlitt,
ed. P. P. Howe (London: Dent, 1932), XI, 88 ff.

   [8] Paul Goodman, "The New Reformation," New York
Times Magazine, 14 Sept. 1969, p. 14.

   B. Find and evaluate three major sources for a research report on changing attitudes toward one of the following: (1) nuclear safety; (2) prison reform; (3) age and aging. Your sources should include

   • one book from the college or public library;
   • one magazine article indexed in the *Readers' Guide*;
   • one current magazine article.

Do the following:

1. On a sheet of paper, draw three rectangles each the size of a *bibliography card*. Fill these in with full bibliographical information for your three sources. Include call numbers.
2. On a second sheet of paper, present one *key quotation* from each of these three sources. (Each should be at least one longer sentence or several sentences.) Introduce each quotation with a statement that helps explain its point and its importance. Below each quotation, draw a line the way you would at the bottom of a page to separate text from footnotes. Below the line, write a *footnote* that identifies the source and gives the page number.
3. On a third sheet of paper, alphabetize your sources and present them as a final *bibliography*.

REVIEW EXERCISE: SAMPLE RESEARCH PAPER

   Study the following sample research paper. Pay special attention to the way the author has adapted and worked into the text a variety of quoted material. Compare the different kinds of footnotes used. Contrast the way sources are identified in the footnotes and in the final bibliography. How successful has the author been in meeting the standards outlined in the preceding chapter?

Aging in America:

Is the Best Yet to Be?

by

Barbara Johnston

English 2, Section 5

May 11, 1980

OUTLINE

THESIS: American society needs to change its assessment of
what aging is and how the aged should be treated.

Introduction: The questioning of youth-worship

    I. Old age: "A time whose topic has come"

      A. Our older population

      B. Growth statistics on the aging movement

    II. Contradictory voices on the subject of age

    III. Areas of general agreement

      A. The rejection of old stereotypes

        1. Description of the stereotypes

        2. How the stereotypes harm everyone

        3. How research and group pressure are
destroying the stereotypes

      B. The aged as leaders of the movement

      C. The demand for choices

        1. Choice in relationships

        2. Choice in education

        3. Choice in employment

Conclusion: The idea of life as a continuum

In a famous poem, Robert Browning said, "Grow old along with me! / The best is yet to be."[1] — lines of poetry — Traditionally, American culture has not found this sentiment either comforting or believable. The idea that old age can be the "golden years" has been voiced by many but believed by few. A spot check of American magazines over the past decades reveals that Americans are a people obsessed with youth. The covers of magazines abound with titles such as "How to Stay Forever Young," "You Don't Have to Get Old," and "Closing in on the Fountain of Youth." Cosmetic firms make millions of dollars annually, peddling creams and cover-ups that promise to hide lines and wrinkles, those "telltale signs of aging," and hair dyes that will cover gray hair for both men and women. Soft drink companies sell drinks by claiming that use of their product will identify a person as a member of the "Now Generation," shown usually as suntanned adolescents, playing tag on a beach.

Recently, thoughtful people have begun to question America's worship of youth and fear of age. Increasingly, our popular magazines give space to vigorous defenders and advocates of the aged:

> There is no change, normally, in intelligence
> and little in memory. Any blunting we do see

---

[1] "Rabbi Ben Ezra," ll. 1-2.

2

> in the absence of actual disease commonly
> results not from age but from put-downs,
> boredom, and exasperation. . . . Wasting
> 20 percent of the population doesn't seem
> to be in anyone's interest, especially since
> everyone eventually joins that 20 percent.[2]

excerpted
block
quotation

"Old age is a time whose topic has come," says David Fischer in an article entitled "Aging: The Issue of the 1980's."[3] While modern writers and thinkers frequently disagree about the nature of and solution to the problem of aging, one common idea stands out: American society needs to change its assessment of what aging is and how the aged should be treated.

Statistics show that significant changes are taking place. The percentage of older people in our population has grown and is continuing to grow rapidly. In 1900, those over 65 made up some 4 percent of the nation's population. Today they make up over 10 percent. They are 16 percent of the voting-age population. Some predict that those over 65 will soon make up 15 percent of the nation's people.[4] Those who are studying these changes conclude that today we have an unprece-

summary
of
statistics

---

[2] Dr. Alex Comfort, "Old Age: Facts and Fancies," Saturday Evening Post, 249 (Mar. 1977), 45.

article with
subtitle and
volume no.

[3] New Republic, 179, (2 Dec. 1978), 31.

[4] Shana Alexander, "Getting Old in Kids' Country," Newsweek, 84 (11 Nov. 1974), 124.

standard
footnote
for article

3

dented situation: "Large numbers of retired persons, reasonably healthy, geographically separated from their families,
and relying on social insurance programs for a living income
are a comparatively new phenomenon in this nation."[5]

direct quotation for key idea

The statement just quoted is from a journal called the
Gerontologist. The very existence of such a journal shows
that important changes have begun to take place. Gerontology,
the field of research and service created to understand and
aid older people, has only recently had significant impact.
The first public commission on aging was founded by the State
of Massachusetts in 1909. Today there exist some 1,300 public
agencies related to aging. In the universities, the formal
study of gerontology barely existed before World War II. Today a national directory lists more than 1,275 educational
programs on aging. There are many voluntary associations for
older people: in Denver, the Soroptimist Club Denture Effort;
in Minneapolis, a "senior-owned" drugstore cooperative; in
New Orleans, the "Repairs on Wheels" home maintenance group;
in California, the "Rent-a-Granny" employment service, and so
on. Political groups, too, have grown. Founded only twenty

summary of information

---

[5] David A. Peterson, Chuck Powell, and Lawne Robertson,
"Aging in America: Toward the Year 2000," Gerontologist,
16 (June 1976), 364.

4

years ago, The American Association of Retired Persons (AARP)
today has nine million members. Together with the National
Retired Teachers Association, The National Council of Senior
Citizens, The Gray Panthers, and several other groups, it
makes up a powerful "gray lobby" in Washington. In summing
up, one observer said, "To find lobbying skills equal to
those of organizations that represent the elderly, you have
to go to someone with a gun—the weapons contractors or the
National Rifle Association."[6]

It would be a mistake, however, to assume that these
statistics represent a unified movement with singleness of
purpose. The ferment that is taking place in our attitudes
toward aging is characterized by contradictory voices.
Rarely is there even agreement over precisely what aging is.
The Encyclopaedia Britannica defines aging as "the sequential
or progressive change in an organism that leads to an in-   partial quote
creased risk of debility, disease, and death."[7] Many today
would take issue with such a definition, arguing that debility
and disease are not necessary probabilities linked to aging.
Gerontologist Alex Comfort, for instance, writes, "Modern re-

---

[6] Quoted in Fischer, "Aging," New Republic, p. 33.

[7] "Aging," Encyclopaedia Britannica, 1974, I, 299.   encyclopedia article

5

search indicates that a high proportion of the mental and attitudinal changes seen in 'old' people are not biological effects of aging. They are the results of role playing."[8] Some researchers are beginning to argue that even death itself is unnecessary. The authors of the book No More Dying assert that medical research is on the verge of conquering death.[9] A recent article in the Smithsonian sets forth the opinion that an anti-aging drug is just around the corner and that "the fixed life span of human beings is neither absolute nor immutable. It will be up to us to choose how long to live."[10] The strong conflicting claims surrounding aging may be evidence that major and lasting changes in attitudes are ahead:

> Vivian Gornick tells us, for example, that "America is one of the worst countries in the world in which to grow old," while Merrill Clark insists that it is really one of the best. We are variously informed that things have never been worse, and never better; that we need more government action and less of it; that the "plight" of the old is pitiable in the extreme, and that pity itself is part of the problem.

partial quote

block quotation

---

[8] A Good Age (New York: Simon & Schuster, 1976), p. 11.

[9] Jib Fowles, "The Impending Society of Immortals," Futurist, 12 (June 1978), 176.

[10] Albert Rosenfeld, "In Only 50 Years We May Add Centuries to Our Lives—If We Choose to Do So," Smithsonian, 7 (Oct. 1976), 41.

6

> It isn't easy to make sense of so many and
> such varied opinions. But an interesting pattern
> begins to emerge if we study them <u>historically</u>,
> as events in their own right. The great diver-
> sity of contemporary interest in aging becomes
> a unity of sorts if we understand it as <u>move-
> ment</u>, both in the general sense of something
> that is changing through time, and more speci-
> fically as the latest of the great American
> reform movements, whose history is repeating in
> new and important ways.[11]

When any great reform movement begins to stir up set ways

of thinking, confusion and contradiction are bound to result.

But it is also possible to find areas of general agreement

within a movement, and we can pick out some general trends

today in the changing attitudes toward aging.

First of all, most people who have thought in any depth

on the subject agree that the traditional stereotypes of old

people have been mostly destructive, to young and old alike.

They have distorted reality, and, by portraying old age as

either ridiculous or awesome, have had the effect of dehuman-

izing the aged. Simone de Beauvoir writes:

> The purified image of themselves that society
> offers the aged is that of the white-haired and
> venerable sage, rich in experience, planing
> high above the common state of mankind: If they
> vary from this, they fall below it. The counter-
> part of the first image is that of the old fool
> in his dotage, a laughing stock for children.

---

[11] Fischer, pp. 31-32.

7

> In any case, either by their virtue or by
> their degradation, they stand outside human-
> ity.[12]

Research on the way old people are portrayed in children's

books supports what Simone de Beauvior is saying. Edward F.

Ansello, associate director of the Center on Aging at the

University of Maryland, and doctoral student Joyce Letzler

collected data on the portrayal of old people in juvenile

picture books and easy readers. They found that three-fourths

of them have no discernible function or position. For the

most part, they talk rather than act, and their actions are

dull and routine. Oldsters, they found, are not portrayed as

flesh-and-blood characters, as problem solvers, or as self-

sufficient persons. They went back as far as Beatrix Potter

and Kate Greenaway and found that even in the earlier chil-

dren's literature most old characters were portrayed as

"either passive bores or aggressive witches and wizards."[13]   ]partial quote

It is not just the old who are harmed by such stereo-

types. By falling victim to prejudice against the old, we

are harming ourselves because the "they" will most certainly

---

[12] The Coming of Age, trans. Patrick O'Brian (New York:]translated book
G. P. Putnam's, 1972), p. 4.

[13] Henrietta Wexler, "Ageism in Children's Books,"
American Education, 14 (July 1978), 29.

8

before long become "we." The person who ridicules old age rarely has the last laugh. Alex Comfort believes that the stereotypes we accept as young people about age exact a high price from us later on in life.

> Lies about aging are especially hard to expose. When society penalized blacks, or Jews, or women, the victims lived with prejudice all their lives—and some of them had had time to debrainwash themselves and to fight back, building a basis of civil rights on which others could stand. The trouble is that we aren't born old. Society's prejudices indoctrinate us before they hit us. . . . On this basis we obligingly drown ourselves as persons when the clock points to the appropriate age.[14]

Modern research is blasting these old sterotypes. On the basis of seven years of studies of older people at the University of Chicago, Bernice Neugarten believes that real people simply do not fit our societal notions about them: Most old people are not lonely, neglected, or senile. She writes:

> For example, old persons do not become isolated and neglected by their families, although both generations prefer separate households. Old persons are not dumped into mental hospitals by cruel or indifferent children. They are not necessarily lonely or desolate if they live alone. Few of them ever show signs of mental deterioration or senility, and only a small proportion ever become mentally ill.[15]

---

[14] Comfort, A Good Age, pp. 10-11.]second reference

[15] "Grow Old Along with Me! The Best is Yet to Be," in Growing Old, ed. Gordon Moss and Walter Moss (New York: Simon & Schuster, 1975), p. 114.

9

Neugarten believes that even the terms "old" and "young" involve distorting stereotypes since chronological age is a poor
basis for categorizing people. She says, "In a society as
complex as ours, with increasing social permissiveness for
people to follow their own bents, a good case can be made
that—despite the counterpressures that create conformity—
increased differentiation occurs over the life cycle."[16] In
other words, instead of growing more alike as they get older,
people become more distinct and individualized, and the group
referred to as "the old" is really just a social fiction.

Research is not the only thing breaking down the stereotypes. Efforts to change the images of old people as presented by the media and by textbooks are having an effect.
For instance, the Gray Panthers, a powerful group dedicated to
the fight against discrimination based on age, have formed a
"Media Watch." Volunteers monitor television programs and   paraphrase
file complaints about those that foster negative images
of old people. The Panthers have complained about negative
stereotypes of old folks in certain comedy routines and the
absence of older emcees and news anchor people.[17] Consistent

---

[16] Neugarten, in <u>Growing Old</u>, p. 116.   second
                                                                 reference
[17] Rebecca Blalock, "Gray Panthers: Work of Maggie Kuhn,"
<u>Saturday Evening Post</u>, 251 (Mar. 1979), 127.

10

pressure on networks and publishers has been getting
results.

In discussing the areas of common agreement in today's
aging movement, it is worthwhile to note that the aged themselves are in the forefront of the movement, leading the way.
This is in sharp contrast to past decades when the aged were
looked at as the objects rather than the agents of reform.
Leafing through issues of popular magazines from the forties
and fifties, we find titles like "Food We Eat: Feeding Grandfather and Grandmother," "What Old Person Do You Have to Support?", "Baby Grandpa," "Encourage the Old," and "Use Old
People Wisely." Such titles show that the reading audience
was assumed to be young or middle-aged. Apparently few older
people were assumed to be among the readers. Instead, the
articles are directed to a younger audience interested in the
care and feeding of old people. Today entire publications are
directed at an older audience, such as Fifty Plus and Retired
Living. Maggie Kuhn, founder of the Gray Panthers, is representative of these new senior leaders. Forced into retirement
after twenty-five years of service with the Presbyterian
Church, she rebelled and set out to organize other old people
against mandatory retirement. She serves on countless committees and task forces, delivers about 200 lectures a year,

11

pickets, lobbies, marches, and is not timid about confronting
HUD officials, nursing home administrators, or TV celebrities.
She says: "This is a new age, an age of sweeping change and
liberation, of self-determination; a new kind of freedom for   key
                                                                quotation
all of us who dare to take risks. And I see us as a new breed
of old people."[18]

The common theme in what this "new breed of old people"
are demanding is freedom to choose: to choose relationships,
to choose to work, to choose to learn. The emphasis has
switched from security to freedom of choice:

> The goal of old age security has not been
> reached for all Americans, but it is increas-
> ingly submerged in a larger and more complex
> purpose, which is not one of providing secur-
> ity for the aged, but promoting autonomy
> throughout the aging process. Material means
> are, of course, necessary for autonomy but not
> sufficient to that end. Autonomy requires an
> extension of possibilities for making choices
> in the world.[19]

Older people today want the freedom to choose their
own relationships. The popular stereotype is that of the
old person clinging tenaciously to relatives. But Alex
Comfort says that the real need of older people is not so
much for relatives as it is for friends, chosen rela-

---

[18] Quoted in Blalock, p. 34.

[19] Fischer, p. 34.

12

tionships.[20] Maggie Kuhn has nothing but contempt for age-
segregated "sun-fun" communities and thinks they are for people who have "given up, copped out."[21] Many share the view

quoted phrases

that segregating people by age is harmful to people of all
ages. It prohibits cross-generational sharing. Kuhn prefers
inter-generational living and shares a house with two women,
ages 30 and 35, and a man, age 25. The trend today is toward
freedom to choose relationships without special regard to age.

Another choice being demanded by older people today is
the option to learn. In an article entitled "Education's Gray
Boom," Edith Roth writes, "Because older adults are increasing
faster than any other segment of the population, educational
programs that attend to their special needs are spreading like
crabgrass."[22] She outlines some of the new educational pro-

striking short quote

grams available to older people, among which are DOVES (Dedicated Older Volunteers in Educational Services), a group of
3,400 trained volunteers who work as teacher aides and tutors
in the Los Angeles Unified School District; and Elderhostel, a
program that opens up college campuses to older adults for

---

[20] A Good Age, p. 172.

[21] Quoted in Blalock, p. 34.

[22] "Education's Gray Broom," American Education, 14 (July 1978), 6.

13

fifteen weeks out of the year and offers a variety of college
courses to elders at reasonable prices. Older people, who
frequently lack formal education, have proved themselves capable of doing college-level work. Says Roth:

> Reports from numerous education programs show
> that life itself has taught most oldsters
> enough so that their learning skills are plenty
> sharp if they are able to study what truly in-
> terests them. The idea that capacity for
> learning shrinks with the years is an outworn
> notion that has been generally discarded; in
> effect, the reverse is true for those who have
> learned the skills of survival.[23]

By far, though, the most vocal demand being made by elders is the right to work. The trend over the last few decades
had been toward earlier and earlier mandatory retirement. In
1900 people over 65 made up 36 percent of the labor force.
Today, only 14 percent are over 65. Projecting on the basis
of this trend, a recent report to a Senate Subcommittee indicated that increasing mechanization might mean that in twenty-
five years the economic life of most blue-collar workers would
be twenty years.[24] In other words, people might be forced to
retire at age 39. Alex Comfort, among others, finds this outrageous:

---

[23] Roth, p. 6.

[24] Comfort, _A Good Age_, p. 14.

14

> Forty-year retirement contracts are things of
> the past. Thirty-year contracts are on the way
> out—roll on the twenty-year contracts! As
> this happens, if we let it happen, one of two
> things will occur. Either we reprogram society
> to find new engagement for the people it dumps,
> or we declare them unpeople and discover a
> stack of bogus-science grounds for believing
> that ineptitude, nonhumanness, dependency,
> unintelligence, and lack of dignity start at
> age 39.[25]

Recent surveys have shown that many who are forced to retire would like to continue working. According to one survey,
more than half of today's employees would prefer to continue
working past their normal retirement age.[26] Real progress has
been made in the campaign against forced retirement. On January 1, 1979, Civil Rights for Older Americans went into effect,
prohibiting discrimination based on age in any federally
funded programs. At the same time, another law went into effect that lifted the mandatory retirement age from 65 to 70
for those in private industry.

Beneath the demand for greater freedom of choice for
older people is a deeper demand: that we begin to see life,
not as a series of segments, but as a continuous aging process.
It asks that we stop regarding old age as a stage with fixed

---

[25] Comfort, A Good Age, p. 14.

[26] "Early Retirement Rejected by Many," Christian Science
Monitor, 24 Apr. 1979, p. 19, col. 4.] newspaper article

15

boundaries and begin to measure life by learning instead of
time. Old age does not hit a person suddenly, like a catastrophe. Instead, life as a continuum means that a person
gradually learns and grows through the years, changing, yet
maintaining his or her identity.

The idea of life as a continuum, rather than a sequence
of separate stages, each with its set of age-imposed limitations, can be a freeing concept. The implication is that
learning and meaningful activity are lifelong, if one chooses
it to be so. Kuhn observes: "Education has traditionally been
deemed for the young. Work is for the middle years, and leisure for the later years. Life, which is a continuum, has
been chopped up into age-segmented pieces. Instead, education, meaningful work, and leisure should all be lifelong
experiences."[27]

strong final
quotation

---

[27] Quoted in Blalock, p. 32.

16

BIBLIOGRAPHY

"Aging." <u>Encyclopaedia Britannica</u>. 1974, I, 299-304.   ⎤encyclopedia
⎦article

Alexander, Shana. "Getting Old in Kids' Country." <u>News-</u> ⎤standard
<u>week</u>, 84 (11 Nov. 1974), 124. ⎦entry: magazine

Blalock, Rebecca. "Gray Panthers: Work of Maggie Kuhn."
<u>Saturday Evening Post</u>, 251 (March 1979), 32. ⎤subtitle

Browning, Robert. <u>Poetical Works</u>. London: Oxford Univ. ⎤standard
Press, 1967. ⎦entry: book

Comfort, Alex. <u>A Good Age</u>. New York: Simon & Schuster, 1976.
----------. "Old Age: Facts and Fancies." <u>Saturday Evening</u> same author
<u>Post</u>. 249 (Mar. 1977), 45.

de Beauvoir, Simone. <u>The Coming of Age</u>. Trans. Patrick
O'Brian. New York: G. P. Putnam's, 1972.

"Early Retirement Rejected by Many." <u>Christian Science Moni-</u> ⎤anonymous
<u>tor</u>, 24 Apr. 1979, p. 19, col. 4. ⎦article

Fischer, David Hackett. "Aging: The Issue of the 1980's."
<u>New Republic</u>, 179 (2 Dec. 1979), 31-36.

Fowles, Jib. "The Impending Society of Immortals." <u>Futurist</u>,
12 (June 1978), 175-81.

Neugarten, Bernice. "Grow Old Along with Me! The Best Is Yet ⎤article in
to Be." In <u>Growing Old</u>. Ed. Gordon Moss and Walter Moss. ⎦collection
New York: Simon & Schuster, 1975.

Peterson, David A., Chuck Powell, and Lawne Robertson. "Aging ⎤several
in America: Toward the Year 2000." <u>Gerontologist</u>, 16 ⎦authors
(June 1976), 264-75.

Rosenfeld, Albert. "In Only 50 Years We May Add Centuries to
Our Lives—If We Choose to Do So." <u>Smithsonian</u>, 7
(Oct. 1976), 40-47.

Roth, Edith Brill. "Education's Gray Boom." <u>American Educa-</u> ⎤inclusive
<u>tion</u>, 14 (July 1978), 6-11. ⎦page numbers

Wexler, Henrietta. "Ageism in Children's Books." <u>American</u>
<u>Education</u>, 14 (July 1978), 29.

Writing About Literature

CHAPTER TEN

1. **The Responsive Reader**

2. **Kinds of Critical Papers**
    Explication
    Studying a Character
    The Central Symbol
    Tracing the Theme
    Defining a Critical Term

3. **Organizing the Critical Essay**
    Focusing on a Major Issue
    Following Logical Order
    Comparison and Contrast

1. THE RESPONSIVE READER

When you write about a piece of imaginative literature, you try to explain to your reader what you make of a poem, a short story, a play. The most basic requirement for a paper of this kind is your *careful reading of the work itself*. Whether your readers agree with you or not, they must feel: "This person has read the text." No matter how you argue or classify, your paper should always come back to the actual poem or story. Quote from it. Talk in detail about characters and events. Show in detail how the poem or story is put together.

Remember the following guidelines:

(1) *Use the author's own words.* Literary language is rich in personality and rich in meaning. Much of this richness is lost in a paraphrase. Make ample use of striking, revealing, memorable quotations. Study the following excerpt from a student paper. Look at the way it brings to life a character from a play by using numerous *short* quotations from the play itself.

Lady Macbeth

Lady Macbeth has long been recognized as the prime mover of her husband's actions. Without her prompting, Banquo might have enjoyed ripe old age. But in order to aid her husband, she must step out of the traditional feminine role, for she realizes—perhaps unconsciously—that popular tradition will not permit a woman the attributes necessary for such grisly deeds: fortitude, purposefulness, and a strong stomach. Therefore, she must metamorphosize into a male. She is hardly on stage when she beseeches the darker spirits to "unsex me here / And fill me . . . top full of direst cruelty . . . And take my milk for gall" (*Macbeth*, I.v.). Thus, metaphorically, Lady Macbeth becomes male, and her husband will assume many attributes of the female.

There are many passages illustrating the exchange of sex roles between this murderous couple. The recurrence of milk-and-babe imagery is quite striking: Macbeth is "too full o' the milk of human kindness" (I.v.) to murder for a throne. Pity "like a new-born babe" (I.vii.) would stay his hand. On the other hand, his wife, to underscore her resoluteness, vows she would have unhesitatingly snatched the "babe that milks me" (I.vii.) from her breast and "dash'd the brains out, had I sworn as you / Have done to this." She is astonishingly capable and stout-hearted. As her husband notes, "her undaunted mettle should compose / Nothing but males" (I.vii.). She dismisses his "flaws and starts" as childish (III.iv.). His heightened sensitivity reminds her of "a woman's story at a winter's fire" (III.iv.). She quails only at performing the deed herself, explaining, "Had he not resembled / My father as he slept, I had done't" (II.ii.).

(2) *Respond to the way a piece of literature develops.* A work of literature is not something static and finished that we take in all at one time. A novel develops gradually; it takes shape as the plot un-

folds. What a play has to say is acted out: Contrasting characters set up major conflicts. Conflicting motives or divided loyalties create tension or suspense. We *live through* what happens when such a conflict is acted out.

Even a short poem *takes shape*. As you read the following poem, ask yourself: What is happening? How does the poem develop? What does it make you feel? What does it make you think?

The Opening

Seed said to Flower:
You are too rich and wide.
You spend too soon and loosely
That grave and spacious beauty
I keep secret, inside.
You will die of your pride.

Flower said to Seed: Each opens, gladly
Or in defeat. Clenched close,
You hold a hidden rose
That will break you to be
Free of your dark modesty.

—Jon Swan

(3) *Explain your likes and dislikes.* Our reaction to a work of literature is a very personal thing. Something may disturb us profoundly but leave other people cold. Something may shock us but strike others as ordinary. To make a reader understand our reactions, we try to explain how we feel, and why. If we use terms like *sentimental* or *escapist,* we do not just use them as labels to paste on what we dislike. We try to explain and justify the standards we apply.

Note: When we encounter something new or different, we are often too quick to criticize, to judge, to reject. To get out of a work what it has to offer, we have to approach it as a reader, not as a judge. The ideal reader, Virginia Woolf once said, is the author's "fellow-worker and accomplice." We have to say to ourselves: "Let me see what this author is trying to do. Let me try to understand. Let me try to get into the spirit of the thing."

EXERCISE

Read the following poem. What is it all about? How do you react to the poem? Present and explain your reactions as fully and as candidly as you can.

The Chariot

Because I could not stop for Death,
He kindly stopped for me;
The carriage held but just ourselves
And Immortality.

We slowly drove, he knew no haste,
And I had put away
My labor, and my leisure too,
For his civility.

We passed the school, where children strove
At recess, in the ring;
We passed the fields of gazing grain,
We passed the setting sun.

Or rather, he passed us;
The dews grew quivering and chill,
For only gossamer my gown,
My tippet only tulle.

We paused before a house that seemed
A swelling of the ground;
The roof was scarcely visible,
The cornice in the ground.

Since then 'tis centuries, and yet
Feels shorter than the day
I first surmised the horses' heads
Were toward eternity.

—Emily Dickinson

2. KINDS OF CRITICAL PAPERS

What a literary work means to the reader is not a simple prose statement like "Modern humanity is alienated from its environment." The meaning of a poem or a play is not simply something we are told. It is something that we are made to *take in*, something in which we become involved. A poem presents images that appeal to our senses. A story or a play presents characters and events that appeal to our emotions. As a result, the question *"What* does it mean?"* turns into *"How* does it mean?" How does the author make us experience the feelings, the attitudes, the ideas that make up our response to a poem, a story, or a play?

Each of the following kinds of papers focuses on one major question we can ask when we try to get at what and how a work means.

Explication

Trace the full meaning and implications of the writer's language. The poet—and to a lesser degree other imaginative writers—says "much in little." We must be patient enough to listen for the full implications of a word, a phrase, a figure of speech. At its most businesslike, critical writing simply answers the question "What does it say?"

Here is a shortened version of a student paper devoted to **explication**—to spelling out the full meaning of key words and phrases:

Thought

An essential part of Richard Wilbur's poem "Mind" is the simile "the mind is like a bat," which is developed throughout the poem. When I think of a bat, I think of a creature who lives in darkness, who is confined by a cave. The blind bat protects himself from colliding into the cave walls by a delicate sensory system. Perhaps, unknowingly, he sends out sound waves which bounce back from obstacles in his path and thereby avoids destruction. Wilbur draws a parallel between the bat's method for self-preservation and the mind's: "Contriving by a kind of senseless wit / Not to conclude against a wall of stone." The paradox of "senseless wit" suggests an irrationality. Yet "wit" refers to intelligence. This may imply the unconscious mind. The unconscious mind acts in continual adjustment against reality's threatening barriers. Wilbur enhances the allusion between the mind and the unconscious with these lines: "It has no need to falter or explore; / Darkly it knows what obstacles are there." This seems to express the unconscious mind's awareness of its deepest fears or "obstacles." But in the concluding lines the author differentiates the mind from a bat: ". . . That in the very happiest intellection / A graceful error may correct the cave." If the bat commits "a graceful error," he may well die. The mind, however, performing in like manner may discover that a wall was an illusion. The mind may "correct the cave," or man may change his perception of his environment. The bat will stay in his cave of darkness. The mind can grow out of its confines.

Studying a Character

Write a coherent account (or trace the contradictions) of a character in fiction or drama. A paper of this kind makes you bring together from *different* parts of a story or play the evidence that helps you understand a fictional person. That evidence may be of different kinds. In the traditional novel of the kind Charles Dickens and George Eliot write, the **omniscient** author may tell us what his characters *think* as well as what they say and do. In later fiction, like that of Henry James or William Faulkner, we may see a character only through the eyes of an outside **reflector**. We may have to *infer* thoughts and motives on the basis of puzzling or contradictory behavior. In a Shakespeare play, we soon learn to listen not only to what a character says but also to what *other* people say about the character.

The following excerpted paper provides a model for a theme studying a character:

A Typical Boy

It is not surprising that Thomas E. Adams' story "Sled" appears in an anthology under the heading "The Beginnings of Awareness." It would be stretching a point to say that the boy in the story grows up and becomes an adult. He *does* become aware of what it is like to be mean (as all people are at some time) and what it is like to feel remorse for that meanness. . . .

At the beginning of the story the boy is thoroughly typical and believable. He has had a quarrel with his sister, calling her a liar, and his mother is demanding that he apologize. The boy resists and at last apologizes half-heartedly and rather belligerently so that he can go outside to slide on his new sled. Following his apology this bit of dialogue occurs:

> "Put your hat on," his mother said without looking at him.
> His face, toward the door, screwed and tightened with disgust. "Aw Ma."
> "Put it on."
> "Aw Ma, it's not that cold out."
> "Put it on."
> "Honest Ma, it's not that cold out."
> "Are you going to put your hat on, or are you going to stay and help with the dishes?"
> He sighed. "All right," he said, "I'll put it on.". . .

Several other details in the story serve to develop the picture of a typical boy: for example, his delight in the newness and strength of his sled, his great care in running to start a slide, his amazement when he realizes that the sled is irreparably broken, and his coming very close to crying about what to him is a considerable loss. . . .

But the most convincing episode comes at the end of the story when the boy offers his sister a chance to slide on the broken sled, knowing that she will take a spill. He still harbors a grudge against her and is taking his revenge. When he realizes, however, that his sister has been hurt, and that his action has really been a piece of cruel deception, he is immediately sorry. Probably the boy could not, in his own mind, have put the matter quite so clearly; and his somewhat dim realization comes through in his awkward efforts to make his sister feel better.

> "It'll be all right," he said. He felt that he ought to do something but he did not move. "I can get it soldered. Don't worry about it.". . .

When the boy knows from the extinguishing of the grocery-store light that it is seven o'clock and that he must go home, he does not return a totally changed person. He has learned something, to be sure, and he has grown up a little. And he has reacted to the experience as a boy would.

The Central Symbol

Trace the role of a symbol that is central to the work as a whole.
Symbols are objects that have a significance beyond themselves. In
T. S. Eliot's "The Waste Land," the dry rock "where the sun beats"
and the life-giving water that we yearn for in vain become symbols
for the aridity of modern life. The "dry bones," the "dead tree," the
"empty cisterns" in the poem all echo the idea of life that has with-
ered or dried up.

Even when a symbol is not actually repeated, it can play a central role because it sums up many of the meanings that a work has
been developing. Toward the end of Arthur Miller's *Death of a
Salesman*, Willy Loman, defeated and alone, is blundering about in
his dark backyard planting seeds. That futile gesture sums up much
of what we have learned about Willy in the course of the play: his
delight in making plans for the future; his happiness in doing useful
things with his hands; his refusal to face up to the things that will
make his happy plans come to nothing.

Examining a central symbol makes us look at a poem, short
story, or play *as a whole*. The last stanza of Robert Frost's "Stopping
by Woods on a Snowy Evening" reads as follows:

> The woods are lovely, dark and deep.
> But I have promises to keep,
> And miles to go before I sleep,
> And miles to go before I sleep.

Are we justified in seeing in the dark lovely woods a symbol of
restful, peaceful death? Such a symbolic interpretation is supported
by many details *earlier in the poem*. The woods are dark and filling
up with snow—and both darkness and snow are hostile to ordinary
purposeful activity, that is, to ordinary life. The traveler has stopped
"without a farmhouse near," between "the woods and frozen lake."
He is, thus, far from a village or other center of human activity. His
horse acts as if stopping there "is some mistake," since in ordinary
life people are usually "getting somewhere." The traveler has to
choose between "promises" that keep him going into the future and
the "easy wind" and "downy flake" that suggest rest, sleep. Though
the symbolic meaning of the dark woods is not spelled out in the
poem, the woods do appear throughout the poem as the opposite of
life and of going on into the future.

Tracing the Theme

Trace the underlying theme that gives unity to a work as a whole.
When we state the **theme** of a poem, short story, or play, we try to
sum up a key idea that helps to give it shape and direction. A true
theme is not simply a "lesson for today" tacked on at the end. It
may be nowhere directly stated but may gradually become clear as
we think about the whole poem, story, or play.

Sometimes the author of the literary work comes close to summing up the major theme in one or more *thematic passages*. We encounter such a thematic passage when Linda says of her husband in
Death of a Salesman,

> I don't say he's a great man. Willy Loman never made a lot of money. His
> name was never in the paper. He's not the finest character that ever lived. But he's
> a human being, and a terrible thing is happening to him. So attention must be paid.
> He's not to be allowed to fall into his grave like an old dog. Attention, attention
> must be finally paid to such a person.

Looking back over the play as a whole, we realize that it does
indeed ask us to "pay attention" to an ordinary individual. It is
about a man who is outwardly a "failure" and yet entitled to our
respect as a human being.

Sometimes we are alerted to the underlying theme by a *key term*
that appears at crucial points. In *Macbeth*, the phrase "vaulting *ambition*" contains such a term, echoing in the play elsewhere. Is the
play as a whole concerned with seduction by, and the price to be
paid for, ambition? A paper tracing the role of this key term is
bound to strengthen our understanding of the whole play.

In writing about a major theme, we have to show how it is
reflected in the work as a whole. We have to relate different elements of the story or play to its overall meaning. The following excerpt is from a discussion of a major theme in Shakespeare's *Romeo
and Juliet*. The critic claims that the love between the two young
lovers "sets them apart from the rest of the world." Notice how the
critic makes familiar details from the play serve her thesis:

> *Romeo and Juliet* has always been one of Shakespeare's most popular plays;
> audiences in every age group seem to find the hero and heroine irresistibly sym-
> pathetic as they struggle to attain love in a hostile world. The opening scene intro-
> duces us to that world, a brawling society in which hatred between two
> families—Capulet and Montague—erupts in the street: Servant cudgels servant,
> gentleman duels with gentleman, Montague abuses Capulet. It is a materialistic

society, where money and position are a major concern in marriage arrangements; the Capulets are pleased with Paris's "noble parentage" and "fair demesnes" (domains) and the Nurse brags of Juliet's dowery: "... he that can lay hold of her / Shall have the chinks" (coin). It bustles with the petty activities of daily life. The fighting crowd in the street and the dancing couples at Capulet's party represent the world from which Romeo and Juliet withdraw to seek a happiness bound solely by each other's presence. As soon as they meet, they are oblivious to everyone else. Their love develops in isolation from the society whose blood feud finally destroys that love.—Alice Griffin, *Rebels and Lovers*

Defining a Critical Term

Apply an important critical term to a key example. Critical terms help us find our way. They guide our expectations. They help us put into words important differences and similarities. We would find it hard to talk about drama if we did not have terms like *tragedy, comedy, farce, theater of the absurd, protagonist, subplot,* or *dénouement.*

When you apply a term like *tragedy* or *farce* to a single major play, you sharpen your sense of the term; you put it to the test. The following excerpts are from a paper that works out its answer to the question asked in its title:

Death of a Salesman—a Tragedy?

Raising the Question

Ever since Willy Loman trudged into his living room and set down his heavy sample satchel in the first stage production of *Death of a Salesman,* critics have been arguing whether or not Arthur Miller's creation is a tragedy. Some maintain the play is a tragedy of the common man, with Willy Loman as the tragic hero. Others hold that the play does not fit the requirements of true tragedy and that Willy Loman is incapable of being tragic let alone any other type of hero at all. . . .

DEFINITION
First Criterion

There exists a great deal of unity among great tragedies as to the effect they work on their audiences. The Greeks used the words *pity, fear, catharsis* to classify this effect. Tragedy fills its audience with pity for the tragic hero. This pity is not patronizing but implies equality, a sharing of grief. The word *fear* is not restricted to fright or terror but includes anxious concern, awe, reverence, and apprehension. . . .

Second Criterion

Though the point has been overly emphasized through the years, it is necessary that the tragic hero possess some *tragic flaw* which shapes his actions and helps bring about his eventual downfall. We assume that the hero has free will; and we look in his or her character for a flaw that begins the chain of events leading to ruin. . . .

Third Criterion

In the agony, humiliation, and suffering of defeat, the hero invariably reaches a point of *increased self-awareness.* The hero or heroine is able to look back and see the steps leading to disaster. . . .

APPLICATION
First Criterion

Miller certainly achieves the effects of *pity and fear* on his audience. . . .

Second
Criterion

Certainly, Willy Loman possesses a *tragic flaw,* if not several. But this flaw is not a personal characteristic coming from his own nature, but rather it is a burden given to him by society. Willy believed in the American Dream because he was brought up to do so. . . .

Third
Criterion

Willy, finally, never enters into the period of *self-realization* characteristic of true tragedy. If the play were tragic, Willy would realize in the last act that "he had all the wrong dreams." But this conception remained beyond him. He died considering himself a greater man, worth more dead than he was alive. . . .

Summing up
the Answer

By the definition and evidence presented, it is evident that *Death of a Salesman* is not a tragedy. The beauty and stunning effect of tragedy cannot be maintained without the tragic hero's bitter recognition of his true self.

EXERCISES

A. In one paragraph, explain in as much detail as you can the *implications and associations* that contribute to the full meaning of *one* of the following passages from Shakespeare's sonnets and plays:

1.   O, how shall summer's honey breath hold out
       Against the wreckful siege of battering days,
       When rocks impregnable are not so stout,
       Nor gates of steel so strong, but Time decays?
                                   (Sonnet 65)

2.   That time of year thou mayest in me behold
       When yellow leaves, or none, or few, do hang
       Upon those boughs which shake against the cold,
       Bare ruined choirs, where late the sweet birds sang.
                                   (Sonnet 73)

3.   Love's not Time's fool, though rosy lips and cheeks
       Within his bending sickle's compass come;
       Love alters not with his brief hours and weeks,
       But bears it out even to the edge of doom.
                                   (Sonnet 116)

4.   O, she doth teach the torches to burn bright!
       It seems she hangs upon the cheek of night
       Like a rich jewel in an Ethiop's ear—
       Beauty too rich for use, for earth too dear!
                                   (*Romeo and Juliet,* I.v)

B. Write a paragraph describing a *central character* of a play as seen through the eyes of a minor figure. For instance, have Polonius describe Hamlet; have Desdemona's father describe Othello; have the friar describe Romeo or Juliet.

C. Write a paragraph examining the role of the bird used as the *central symbol* in one of the following poems: Shelley's "The Skylark"; Keats's "Ode to a Nightingale"; Whitman's "Out of the Cradle Endlessly Rocking." Or write about a modern poem that uses an animal as a central symbol.

D. The following excerpt sums up a modern reader's interpretation of a famous Victorian novel: Charlotte Brontë's *Jane Eyre*. In your own words, restate the central theme that the critic finds in the novel. Then show how many major elements from the novel she ties in with her summing up of the author's major theme.

Coming to her husband in economic independence and by her free choice, Jane can become a wife without sacrificing a grain of her Jane Eyre-ity. Charlotte Brontë sets up the possibility of this relationship in the early passages of the Thornfield episode, the verbal sparring of this couple who so robustly refuse to act out the patterns of romantic, Gothic fiction. We believe in the erotic and intellectual sympathy of this marriage because it has been prepared by the woman's refusal to accept it under circumstances which were mythic, romantic, or sexually oppressive. . . . It is clear that Charlotte Brontë believes that human relations require something quite different: a transaction between people which is "without painful shame or damping humiliation" and in which nobody is made into an object for the use of anybody else.

In telling the tale of Jane Eyre, Charlotte Brontë was quite conscious, as she informed her publisher, that she was not telling a moral tale. Jane is not bound by orthodoxy, though superficially she is a creature of her time and place. As a child, she rejects the sacredness of adult authority. As a woman, she insists on regulating her conduct by the pulse of her own integrity. She will not live with Rochester as his dependent mistress because she knows that relationship would become destructive to her. She would live unmarried with St. John as an independent co-worker; it is he who insists this would be immoral. The beauty and depth of the novel lie in part in its depiction of alternatives—to convention and traditional piety, yes, but also to social and cultural reflexes internalized within the female psyche.—Adrienne Rich, "The Temptations of a Motherless Woman"

E. Select a *thematic passage* from a play you have read or seen performed. Defend your choice by showing how the passage sums up (or anticipates) major developments in the play.

F. The following passage from an introduction to poetry defines three important *critical terms*. Find one or more illustrations for each of these terms in a poem by William Blake, John Keats, or a modern poet of your choice. (Or your instructor may provide a copy of a poem.)

Image, metaphor, and symbol shade into each other and are sometimes difficult to distinguish. In general, however, an image means only what it is; a metaphor means something else than what it is; and a symbol means what it is and something more too. If I say that a shaggy brown dog was rubbing its back against a white picket fence, I am talking about nothing but a dog and am therefore presenting an image; if I say, "Some dirty dog stole my wallet at the party," I am not talking about a dog at all, and am therefore using a metaphor; but if I say, "You can't teach an old dog new tricks," I am talking not only about dogs but about living creatures of any species, and am therefore speaking symbolically.—Laurence Perrine, *Sound and Sense*

3.   ORGANIZING THE CRITICAL ESSAY

As you experiment with longer or more ambitious critical papers, employ strategies like the following to help you organize your writing.

Focusing on a Major Issue

Focus on one major critical problem or issue. The richer a poem or a story, the more tempted we are to call attention to this and that. As a result, writing about literature easily becomes *impressionistic:* The writer points to something beautiful here, something interesting there. To keep a critical essay from rambling, ask, "What question am I trying to answer in this paper? What is the issue that I am going to focus on? What is the problem that I am trying to solve?"

The following discussion of an author focuses on the issue of "realism" vs. "sentimentality":

Kate Chopin: Precursor of Modern Literature

Of the writers of the late nineteenth century, Kate Chopin is one that unfortunately has received very little recognition. It is only very recently that her writings have been collected and appraised as precursors of modern twentieth-century literature. "The Story of an Hour" and "A Pair of Silk Stockings" are two of her short stories that especially exemplify the traits of the realistic tradition.

One trend of the realistic writer has been to portray characters and common events of a bourgeois society. In "A Pair of Silk Stockings," the protagonist, Mrs. Sommers, is an ordinary middle-class housewife. The main action centers upon her unexpected possession of fifteen dollars and the means by which she spends it in one day. The main character of "The Story of an Hour" is also a middle-class woman, although the situation, which concerns her reaction

to the false news of her husband's death, is somewhat
more tragic.
        The crucial, distinctive characteristic, how-
ever, of realistic literature is not the focus on
common people and events but the manner in which the
subjects are treated, with a basic lack of sentimentality and idealism. The most striking element in
Kate Chopin's stories is the almost ruthless attempt
on the part of the author to present a true picture
of society as she sees it, ugly though it may be.
In "A Pair of Silk Stockings," unaltruistic feelings
of selfishness and competition are revealed in such
a way as would, and presumably did, shock complacent
Victorian readers. Little Mrs. Sommers at first enter-
tains generous plans to spend all of the fifteen
dollars on new clothes for her children: "The vision
of her little brood looking fresh and dainty and new
for once in their lives excited her and made her
restless and wakeful with anticipation." But, ironically, once at the shops, she indulges in buying herself a pair of silk stockings, and then, carried away
by the sense of luxury and not once hindered by a
guilty conscience, goes on to spend the entire sum
on herself.
        Materialism in society is well depicted by the
scene of the mad rush of shoppers at the bargaining
counter. Mrs. Sommers, herself, "could stand for
hours making her way inch by inch toward the desired
object that was selling below cost." . . .

Following Logical Order

Follow a logical rather than a merely chronological order. The
weakest kind of critical essay is merely a summary of plot. The
writer simply follows the action of a novel from chapter to chapter,
or the plot of a play from act to act and from scene to scene. The
paper tells us what happened, but not why it happened or what it
means.

Often the best way to show that you have a grasp of the whole
poem, play, or story is to *abandon* chronological order as a major
principle of organization. Instead, bring to bear, on a given point,
evidence from different parts of the same work. As with other kinds
of writing, try to arrange your material for a critical paper under

several *logical* headings. Suppose you are writing about a play dealing with the alienation of a young romantic hero. Look at the way
the following rough outline sets up four major facets of the hero's
alienation:

THESIS: Haunted by feelings of inadequacy and guilt, the central character of the
play fails to find spiritual fulfillment in God, man, or nature.
 I. His sense of guilt (bringing together the various hints about the character's past
to show what light they shed on his guilt feelings)
 II. His rejection of religion (interpreting the various encounters of the character
with advocates of religious orthodoxy)
 III. His alienation from society (tracing a common pattern in the character's relationships with other people)
 IV. His disillusionment with nature (tracing the character's progression from a quest
for kindred and benign influence in nature to a view of nature as beautiful but
impersonal, indifferent, inhuman)

Comparison and Contrast

*Use comparison and contrast to alert the reader to significant fea-
tures.* Striking similarities between two works can alert us to things
that are important in both. Striking differences between two works
make us aware of what makes each distinctive. Use either of two
major strategies for organizing your comparison:

• Here is a possible scheme for a **point-by-point** comparison of
two major Shakespearean characters:

Brutus and Macbeth may *appear, on superficial examination, to be very differ-*
ent: One is an idealistic ancient Roman senator, the other a selfish and ambitious
medieval Scottish nobleman; one publicly assassinates a decadent and vain dictator
in order to restore the republican form of government; the other stealthily murders a
good and generous king in order to usurp the throne.
 On closer examination, however, Brutus and Macbeth do turn out to *have*
something important in common. . . .
 Both Brutus and Macbeth seem to feel that the act of murder they are contemplating is *unnatural* and therefore horrible. . . .
 These "horrible imaginings" suffered by Brutus and Macbeth in contemplating
murder upset the natural balance of their faculties and cause *inner strife and disor-*
der. . . .
 The strife and disorder in the small world of the two speakers parallels and
mirrors the strife and disorder that will result *in the large world of society and*
nature from the destruction of established authority.

• Here, in excerpted form, is a model paper devoted to a **parallel-**
order comparison of the speakers in two well-known poems:

To Move or Not to Move

THESIS

Tennyson's "Ulysses" and T. S. Eliot's "The Love Song of J. Alfred Prufrock" are both monologues uttered by the speakers at crucial moments in their lives: Ulysses, the mythical aging Greek king of Ithaca, has decided to embark on his final voyage. J. Alfred Prufrock, a balding middle-aged bachelor in what passes in twentieth-century America for high society, is trying to decide on visiting a lady to propose to her or to proposition her. . . . Although the monologues are spoken in superficially similar situations, they differ fundamentally in the attitude of the speaker towards adventure represented by the voyage in one and by the visit in the other.

I. Ulysses
  A. Audience

  B. Eager desire
     for voyage

  C. Heroic
     attitude

Ulysses' monologue dealing with the voyage he has decided to make is addressed partly to himself and partly to his followers. He states that, although he has roamed the known world, he "cannot rest from travel" and be content to live out his days as a king, husband, and father performing safe but routine duties; and that he is "yearning in desire" to make a final voyage into the unknown "beyond the sunset, and the baths / Of all the western stars." He states, further, that he is aware of the dangers posed "by the dark, broad seas" whose "deep moans round with many voices," but that he is willing to face these dangers for the sake of what he may discover and learn regardless of the outcome. . . . Ulysses' attitude towards the adventure of the voyage is courageous expectancy reflecting a heroic view of life. He remarks that by embarking on this dangerous voyage to an uncertain destination he and his followers can still do some "work of noble note" appropriate to their famous past, and he implies that he lived fully—"enjoyed greatly" and "suffered greatly"—on previous voyages and that he is going on his last voyage to return to this kind of life. . . .

II. Prufrock
  A. Audience

  B. Reluctance
     to visit

  C. Unheroic
     attitude

Prufrock's monologue dealing with his attempts to decide on the visit is addressed only to himself; his scattered remarks about his fear of being unmasked and made to look ridiculous suggest that he would not willingly reveal himself to another living creature. He acknowledges that he is dissatisfied and unfulfilled by the "evenings, mornings, afternoons" spent in the safe but meaningless routine of high society; that he is lonely—like the "men in shirtsleeves" whom he has seen "leaning out of windows" in the slums—and yearns desperately for companionship. Yet he confesses that he is afraid of making the visit and putting the "overwhelming question" to the lady, since he is uncertain whether she will accept him or reject him. . . . Prufrock's attitude towards the adventure of the visit is fearful expectancy reflecting a nonheroic view of life. . . . By the end of his "love song," he has decided to forgo the "dangerous" visit to an unpredictable lady and to live out his days, figuratively, on the beach—correctly attired, careful of his diet, hair parted behind to conceal "a bald spot in the middle"—watching the mermaids who "ride seaward on the waves" and hearing them sing, yet knowing that they will not sing to him. . . .

THEME TOPICS 10

1. Poets that have been widely read by college students in recent years include Richard Brautigan, Sylvia Plath, and Nikki Giovanni. From their poems, select one that means something special to you, or that you would like to take issue with. Write a paper about the poem.

2. Write a character study of a secondary but important character in a major play you have read: Creon in *Antigone*; Lady Macbeth in *Macbeth*; Claudius in *Hamlet*; Desdemona in *Othello*.

3. Discuss the role of a central symbol in a poem by William Blake, Emily Dickinson, Robinson Jeffers, D. H. Lawrence, or a modern poet of your choice. Or, discuss the role of a central symbol in a short story by Stephen Crane, Ernest Hemingway, John Steinbeck, Willa Cather, Eudora Welty, or another more recent writer.

4. Trace the role of a key term or concept in a Shakespeare play; for instance, "love" in *Romeo and Juliet*, "honor" in *Henry IV, Part One*, "nature" in *King Lear*.

5. Compare and contrast two poems dealing with a similar topic or the same subject matter: the same animal, city, mythological figure, legendary hero or event. Or compare and contrast a Greek tragic heroine, such as Antigone, Electra, or Medea, with the heroine of a modern drama, such as Ibsen's Nora or Hedda Gabler.

6. In recent years, women have criticized male authors of short stories and novels for being "unable to portray women convincingly." Select *one* male author that you know well. Defend him or find him guilty of the charge.

7. Examine the treatment of the theme of alienation from society in *one* of the following: James Joyce, *A Portrait of the Artist as a Young Man*; Albert Camus, *The Stranger*; Ralph Ellison, *Invisible Man*; Kurt Vonnegut, *Slaughterhouse Five*; Sylvia Plath, *The Bell Jar*.

8. In recent decades, readers and audiences have responded warmly to novels and plays in which authors examine their ethnic or cultural roots. Discuss the major theme of a book like the following: Chinua Achebe's novel *Things Fall Apart*; Lorraine Hansberry's play *Raisin in the Sun*; Elia Kazan's *America, America*.

9. Discuss fully a poem in which you find strongly contradictory or opposing elements. For instance, discuss a poem by Emily Dickinson, e. e. cummings, May Swenson, Gwendolyn Brooks, or another poet of your choice.

Part Two
The Writer's Tools

11   Words

12   Sentences

13   Paragraphs

Words

CHAPTER ELEVEN

D 1 College Dictionaries
   a Synonyms and Antonyms
   b Denotation and Connotation
   c Context
   d Grammatical Labels
   e Idiom

D 2 Word History
   a Latin and Greek
   b Borrowings from Other Sources

D 3 Varieties of Usage
   a Nonstandard Words
   b Informal Words
   c Slang

D 4 Words in Limited Use
   a Regional Labels
   b Obsolete and Archaic
   c Neologisms
   d Subject Labels

D 5 Expressive Language
   a Accurate Words
   b Specific Words
   c Figurative Words
   d Fresh Words

D 6 Directness
   a Redundancy
   b Euphemisms
   c Jargon
   d Flowery Diction

Good writers know the power of words. They marvel at the resources of language and exploit them in their work. They are aware of the different uses to which a word is put, and the different effects it may have on a reader. They are always looking for words that will help them say what they want to say more clearly, more directly. They look for words that are fresh and vigorous rather than stale and tired. The following chapter is designed to help you improve your command of vocabulary and diction; that is, of word resources and word choice.

D 1   COLLEGE DICTIONARIES

To make the best use of your dictionary, familiarize yourself fully with how it provides information.

College dictionaries provide information not only on the full range of meaning of a word but also on its history, implications, and possible limitations. The ideal dictionary would tell the users in plain English what they want to know. In practice, dictionaries try to give information that is technically accurate and yet intelligible to the reader who needs help.

The following dictionaries are widely recommended:

• *Webster's New World Dictionary* (NWD) makes a special effort to explain the meanings of words simply and clearly, using "the simplest language consistent with accuracy and fullness." Historical information *precedes* current meanings, so that the reader is given a sense of how a word developed. Lists of idioms provide an excellent guide to how a word is used in characteristic phrases. Throughout, informal and slang uses of words are so labeled. Sample entry:

> **bi·o·de·grad·a·ble** (-di grā′də b′l) *adj.* [BIO- + DEGRAD(E) + -ABLE] capable of being readily decomposed by biological means, esp. by bacterial action: said of some detergents with reference to disposal in sewage

• *Webster's New Collegiate Dictionary* is published by the G. & C. Merriam Company, whose collection of several million citation slips has been called "the national archives of the language." The *Collegiate* is based on *Webster's Third New International Dictionary*, the most authoritative and comprehensive unabridged dictionary of current American English. Historical information precedes meanings, which are presented in the order of their development. The Merriam-Webster dictionaries have abandoned the practice of label-

vocabulary entry pronunciation syllabication dots	**beau·ty** (byōō′tē), *n., pl.* **-ties** for 2–6. **1.** a quality that is present in a thing or person giving intense aesthetic pleasure or deep satisfaction to the senses or the mind. **2.** an attractive, well-formed girl or woman. **3.** a beautiful thing, as a work of art, building, etc. **4.** Often, **beauties.** that which is beautiful in nature or in some natural or artificial environment. **5.** a particular advantage: *One of the beauties of this medicine is the absence of aftereffects.* **6.** a person or thing that excels or is remarkable of its kind: *His black eye was a beauty.* [ME *be(a)ute* < OF *beaute*; r. ME *bealte* < OF, var. of *beltet* < VL **bellitāt-* (s. of **bellitās*) = L *bell(us)* fine + *-itāt- -ITY*]
synonym lists	**—Syn. 1.** loveliness, pulchritude, comeliness, fairness, attractiveness. **2.** belle. **—Ant. 1.** ugliness.
part of speech and inflected forms	**be·gin** (bi gin′), *v.*, **be·gan, be·gun, be·gin·ning.** **—v.i. 1.** to proceed to perform the first or earliest part of some action; commence or start. **2.** to come into existence; originate: *The custom began during the Civil War.* **—v.t. 3.** to proceed to perform the first or earliest part of (some action): *Begin the job tomorrow.* **4.** to originate; be the originator of: *Civic leaders began the reform movement.*
etymology	[ME *beginn(en)*, OE *beginnan* = *be- BE- + -ginnan* to begin, perh. orig. to open, akin to YAWN] **—be·gin′ner,** *n.*
synonym study	**—Syn. 3.** BEGIN, COMMENCE, INITIATE, START (when followed by noun or gerund) refer to setting into motion or progress something that continues for some time. BEGIN is the common term: *to begin knitting a sweater.* COMMENCE is a more formal word, often suggesting a more prolonged or elaborate beginning: *to commence proceedings in court.* INITIATE implies an active and often ingenious first act in a new field: *to initiate a new procedure.* START means to make a first move or to set out on a course of action: *to start paving a street.* **4.** inaugurate, initiate.
antonym	**—Ant. 1.** end.
	be·la·bor (bi lā′bər), *v.t.* **1.** to discuss, work at, or worry about for an unreasonable amount of time: *He kept belaboring the point long after we had agreed.* **2.** to scorn or ridicule persistently. **3.** *Archaic.* to beat vigorously. Also, *Brit.,*
variant spelling	**be·la′bour.**
hyphenated entry	**belles-lettres** (*Fr.* bel le′tR³), *n.pl.* literature regarded as a fine art, esp. as having a purely aesthetic function. [< F: lit., fine letters] **—bel·let·rist** (bel le′trist), *n.* **—bel·let·ris·tic** (bel′li tris′tik), *adj.* **—Syn.** See **literature.**
word element	**bene-,** an element occurring in loan words from Latin where it meant "well": *benediction.* [comb. form of *bene* (adv.) well]
	be·neath (bi nēth′, -nēth′), *adv.* **1.** below; in or to a lower place, position, state, or the like. **2.** underneath: *heaven above and the earth beneath.* **—prep. 3.** below; under: *beneath the same roof.* **4.** further down than; underneath; lower in place than: *the first drawer beneath the top one.* **5.** inferior in position, rank, power, etc.: *A captain is beneath a major.* **6.** unworthy of; below the level or dignity of: *beneath contempt.*
consecutive definition numbers	
usage note	**bent¹** (bent), *adj.* **1.** curved or crooked: *a bent bow; a bent stick.* **2.** determined, set, or resolved (usually fol. by *on*): *to be bent on buying a new car.*
example contexts	**bet·ter¹** (bet′ər), *adj., compar. of* **good** *with* **best** *as superl.* **1.** of superior quality or excellence: *a better coat.* **2.** morally superior; more virtuous: *He's no better than a thief.* **3.** of superior value, use, fitness, desirability, acceptableness, etc.: *a better time for action.* **4.** larger; greater: *the better part of a lifetime.* **5.** improved in health; healthier: *Is your mother better?* **—adv., compar. of** **well** *with* **best** *as superl.* **6.** in a more excellent way or manner: *to behave better.* **7.** to a greater degree; more completely or thoroughly: *I probably know him better than anyone else.* **8.** more: *I walked better than a mile to town.* **9. better off, a.** in better circumstances. **b.** more fortunate; happier. **10. go (someone) one better,** to exceed another's effort; be superior to. **11. had better,** would be wiser or more reasonable to; ought to: *We had better stay indoors today.* **12. think better of,** to reconsider and decide more favorably or wisely: *She was tempted to make a sarcastic retort, but thought better of it.* **—v.t. 13.** to make better; improve; increase the good qualities of. **14.** to improve upon; surpass; exceed: *We have bettered last year's production record.* **15. better oneself,** to improve one's social standing, financial position, or education. **—n. 16.** that which has greater excellence: *the better of two choices.* **17.** Usually, **betters.** those superior to one in wisdom, social position, etc. **18. for the better,** in a way that is an improvement: *His health changed for the better.* **19. get the better of, a.** to get an advantage over. **b.** to prevail against. [ME *bettre,* OE *betera;* c. OHG *bezziro* (G *besser*), Goth *batiza = bat-* (akin to BOOT²) + *-iza* comp. suffix] **—Syn. 13.** amend; advance, promote. See **improve.**
idiomatic phrases	

Explanation of Dictionary Entries (From *Random House Dictionary*) ing words informal as too arbitrary or subjective. They make only sparing use of the label "slang." Unlike the NWD, the *Collegiate* lists names of people and places in separate indexes at the end of the book. Sample entry:

> **ex·po·sé** *or* **ex·po·se** \ˌek-spō-'zā, -spə-\ *n* [F *exposé*, fr. pp. of *ex-poser*] **1** : a formal recital or exposition of facts : STATEMENT **2** : an exposure of something discreditable ⟨a newspaper ∼ of crime conditions⟩

• *The Random House College Dictionary* caters to the preferences of conservative teachers. Thus, both informal English and slang are marked. Usage notes recognize many traditional caveats and restrictions. The most frequently encountered meanings of a word come first. Like *Webster's Collegiate,* this dictionary is based on a larger unabridged dictionary. Sample entry:

> **e·lite** (i lēt′, ā lēt′), *n.* **1.** (*often construed as pl.*) the choice or best of anything considered collectively, esp. of a group or class of persons: *the elite of the intellectual community.* **2.** (*construed as pl.*) persons of the highest class: *Only the elite were there.* **3.** a group of persons exercising the major share of authority or control within a larger organization: *the power elite in the U.S.* **4.** a type, approximately 10-point and having 12 characters to the inch, widely used in typewriters. Cf. **pica**¹. —*adj.* **5.** representing the choicest or best. Also, **é·lite′.** [< F *élite,* OF *e*(*s*)*lite,* n. use of fem. of *e*(*s*)*lit* ptp. of *e*(*s*)*lire* to choose; see ELECT]

• *The American Heritage Dictionary* aims at providing a "sensible" (moderately conservative) guide to edited English. It presents word meanings in a "natural flow" from a central meaning and gives exceptionally full treatment to word history. Sample entry:

> **mod·ule** (mŏj′ōol, mŏd′yōol) *n.* **1.** A standard or unit of measurement. **2.** *Architecture.* **a.** The part of a construction used as a standard to which the rest is proportioned. **b.** A uniform structural component used repeatedly in a building. **3.** *Electronics.* A self-contained assembly of electronic components and circuitry, such as a stage in a computer. **4.** *Aerospace.* A self-contained unit of a spacecraft that performs a specific task or class of tasks in support of the major function of the craft. [Latin *modulus,* MODULUS.] —**mod′u·lar** *adj.*

D 1a   Synonyms and Antonyms   *d*

Use the dictionary to help you distinguish between closely related terms.

Often, a dictionary indicates meaning by a **synonym**, a word that has nearly the same meaning as the word you are looking up. Thus, your dictionary may give "sad" or "mournful" as a synonym for *elegiac,* or "instructive" as a synonym for *didactic.* Often, your dictionary will explain a word by giving an **antonym**, a word of approximately opposite meaning. *Desultory* is the opposite of "methodical." *Hackneyed* is the opposite of "fresh" or "original."

Synonyms are seldom simply interchangeable. Their areas of meaning overlap, but at the same time there are subtle differences. *Burn, char, scorch, sear,* and *singe* all refer to the results of exposure to extreme heat, but whether a piece of meat is charred or merely seared makes a difference to the person who has it for dinner.

Look at the way the following entry tries to distinguish among words like *feeling, passion,* and *emotion.* How would you state the differences in your own words?

> *SYN.*—**feeling,** when unqualified in the context, refers to any of the subjective reactions, pleasurable or unpleasurable, that one may have to a situation and usually connotes an absence of reasoning *[I can't trust my own feelings]*; **emotion** implies an intense feeling with physical as well as mental manifestations *[her breast heaved with emotion]*; **passion** refers to a strong or overpowering emotion, connoting especially sexual love or intense anger; **sentiment** applies to a feeling, often a tender one, accompanied by some thought or reasoning *[what are your sentiments in this matter?]*

From *Webster's New World Dictionary*

D 1b   Denotation and Connotation   *d*

Use the dictionary as a guide to the associations of words.

Many words **denote**—that is, point out or refer to—very nearly the same objects or qualities. At the same time, they **connote**—that is, suggest or imply—different attitudes on the part of the speaker. *Cheap* and *inexpensive* both mean low in price. However, we may call an article "cheap" to suggest that we consider it shoddy or inferior; we may call it "inexpensive" to suggest that we consider it a good bargain. *Unwise* and *foolish* both indicate a lack of wisdom. However, calling a proposal "unwise" suggests a certain amount of respect for the person who made it; "foolish" suggests ridicule and contempt.

Here is how a dictionary handles the connotations of synonyms of *plan*:

> *SYN.*—**plan** refers to any detailed method, formulated beforehand, for doing or making something *[vacation plans]*; **design** stresses the final outcome of a plan and implies the use of skill or craft, sometimes in an unfavorable sense, in executing or arranging this *[it was his design to separate us]*; **project** implies the use of enterprise or imagination in formulating an ambitious or extensive plan *[a housing project]*; **scheme,** a less definite term than the preceding, often connotes either an impractical, visionary plan or an underhanded intrigue *[a scheme to embezzle the funds]*

From *Webster's New World Dictionary*

D 1c Context

d

Use the dictionary as a guide to the context where a given meaning is appropriate.

If we really want to know a word, we have to know how it is used in **context**. The context of a word may be another word ("*square* meal"), a whole sentence or paragraph ("*Square* your precepts with your practice"), a whole article or book (a treatment of squares in a book on plane geometry), or a situation (a police officer directing a pedestrian to a square).

Here is an entry showing a word used in different contexts:

> **apt** (apt), *adj.* **1.** inclined; disposed; given; prone: *too apt to slander others.* **2.** likely: *Am I apt to find him at home?* **3.** unusually intelligent; quick to learn: *an apt pupil.* **4.** suited to the purpose or occasion: *an apt metaphor.*

From *The Random House College Dictionary*

In an unfamiliar context, familiar words may have a new or different meaning. For instance, an author praising modesty and thrift may describe them as "homely virtues." Looking up the word, you will find that its original meaning is "associated with the home." Favorable associations of domestic life account for such meanings as "simple," "unpretentious," "intimate." Unfavorable associations account for such meanings as "crude," "unpolished," "ugly."

D 1d Grammatical Labels

id

Use the dictionary as a guide to the functions a word serves in a sentence.

For instance, *human* is usually labeled both as an **adjective** (adj.) and as a **noun** (n.), with some indication that the latter use ("a human" rather than "a human being") is not generally accepted as appropriate to written English. *Annoy* is labeled a **transitive verb** (v.t.); it is incomplete without an object. In other words, we usually annoy somebody or something; we don't just annoy. *Set* also is usually transitive ("*set* the bowl on the table"), but it is labeled **intransitive** (v.i.) when applied to one of the celestial bodies. In other words, the sun doesn't set anybody or anything; it just sets.

D 1e Idiom

Use the dictionary as a guide to idiomatic phrases.

A word often combines with other words in a set expression that becomes the habitual way of conveying a certain idea. Such expressions are called **idioms**. To write idiomatic English, you have to develop an ear for individual phrases and ways of saying things. For instance, we *do* a certain type of work, *hold* a job or position, *follow* a trade, *pursue* an occupation, and *engage in* a line of business.

Study the following list of idiomatic phrases all using the word *mind*. Can you think of half a dozen similar phrases all using the word *eye*, or the word *hand*?

> **—bear** (or **keep**) **in mind** to remember **—be in one's right mind** to be mentally well; be sane **—be of one mind** to have the same opinion or desire **—be of two minds** to be undecided or irresolute **—☆blow one's mind** [Slang] to undergo the hallucinations, etc. caused by, or as by, psychedelic drugs **—call to mind** 1. to remember 2. to be a reminder of **—change one's mind** 1. to change one's opinion 2. to change one's intention, purpose, or wish **—give (someone) a piece of one's mind** to criticize or rebuke (someone) sharply **—have a (good or great) mind to** to feel (strongly) inclined to **—have half a mind to** to be somewhat inclined to **—have in mind** 1. to remember 2. to think of 3. to intend; purpose **—know one's own mind** to know one's own real thoughts, desires, etc. **—make up one's mind** to form a definite opinion or decision **—meeting of (the) minds** an agreement **—never mind** don't be concerned; it doesn't matter **—on one's mind** 1. occupying one's thoughts 2. worrying one **—out of one's mind** 1. mentally ill; insane 2. frantic (*with* worry, grief, etc.) **—put in mind** to remind **—set one's mind on** to be determined on or determinedly desirous of **—take one's mind off** to stop one from thinking about; turn one's attention from **—to one's mind** in one's opinion

From *Webster's New World Dictionary*

A special problem for inexperienced writers is the idiomatic use of **prepositions**. The following list reviews idiomatic uses of some common prepositions:

abide *by* (a decision)
abstain *from* (voting)
accuse *of* (a crime)
acquiesce *in* (an injustice)
adhere *to* (a promise)
admit *of* (conflicting interpretations)
agree *with* (a person), *to* (a proposal), *on* (a course of action)
alarmed *at* (the news)
apologize *for* (a mistake)
aspire *to* (distinction)
assent *to* (a proposal)
attend *to* (one's business)
avail oneself *of* (an opportunity)
capable *of* (an action)
charge *with* (an offense)

collide *with* (a car)
compatible *with* (recognized standards)
comply *with* (a request)
concur *with* (someone), *in* (an opinion)
confide *in* or *to* (someone)
conform *to* (specifications)
deficient *in* (strength)
delight *in* (mischief)
deprive *of* (a privilege)
derived *from* (a source)
die *of* or *from* (a disease)
disappointed *in* (someone's performance)
dissent *from* (a majority opinion)

dissuade *from* (doing something foolish)
divest *of* (responsibility)
find fault *with* (a course)
identical *with* (something looked for)
ignorant *of* (a fact)
inconsistent *with* (sound procedure)
independent *of* (outside help)
indifferent *to* (praise or blame)
infer *from* (evidence)
inferior *to* (a rival product)
insist *on* (accuracy)
interfere *with* (a performance), *in* (someone else's affairs)
jealous *of* (others)
long *for* (recognition)
object *to* (a proposal)
oblivious *of* (warnings)
part *with* (possessions)

partial *to* (flattery)
participate *in* (activities)
persevere *in* (a task)
pertain *to* (a subject)
preferable *to* (an alternative)
prevail *on* (someone to do something)
prevent someone *from* (an action)
refrain *from* (wrongdoing)
rejoice *at* (good news)
required *of* (all members)
resolve *on* (a course of action)
rich *in* (resources)
short *of* (cash)
secede *from* (the Union)
succeed *in* (an attempt)
superior *to* (an alternative)
threaten *with* (legal action)
wait *for* (developments), *on* (a guest)

EXERCISES

A. Compare *three* college dictionaries by investigating the following:

1. Read the definitions of *cliché*, *kitsch*, *graffiti*, *gobbledygook*, and *guru*. What do they say? Are they clear and informative?
2. Study the order of meanings for *coy*, *nice*, *operate*. How does the order differ, and why?
3. Compare the treatment of synonyms (if any) for *dogmatic*, *prompt*, and *train* (v.).
4. What and where are you told about Dreyfus, Prometheus, Niels Bohr, Tierra del Fuego, Susan B. Anthony?
5. How does the dictionary deal with *Aryan*, *dago*, *dame*, *nazi*?

B. What's new in dictionaries? How up to date, or how far behind, is your dictionary in its coverage of the following words? For those that are missing, write a short definition that would help a dictionary editor bring the dictionary up to date.

aerospace	chicano	paparazzo
airbag	cosmonaut	residuals
anchorman	holding pattern	schlock
black muslim	hydrofoil	skydiving
bluegrass	kibbutz	tax shelter
body stocking	minibike	tokenism
buzz word	payload	unisex

C. Study the synonyms in the following sets. What meaning do all three words have in common? How do they differ? Which are differences in connotation?

1. gaze—stare—ogle
2. settlement—compromise—deal

3. loyalty—allegiance—commitment
4. obedient—docile—obsequious
5. revolt—revolution—mutiny
6. intelligent—clever—shrewd
7. juvenile—youngster—adolescent
8. severe—strict—punitive
9. imaginary—fantastic—visionary
10. fatherly—paternal—paternalistic

D. How does your dictionary distinguish among the changing meanings of each of the following words? Show how context determines your choice of the meaning appropriate in each phrase.

1. *bay* leaves, at *bay*, *bayed* at the moon, *bay* window, bomb *bay*, a breeze from the *bay*
2. *head* of lettuce, *head* the procession, a *head* of steam, *heads* or tails, over the listeners' *heads*, went to his *head*, *heads* of government, *head* off complaints, not have a *head* for figures
3. car of recent *make*, *make* the beds, *make* money, *make* excuses, *makes* my blood boil, *make* a speech, *makes* easy reading, *made* him a sergeant
4. *repair* a car, *repaired* to the meeting, in good *repair*, *repair* the damage
5. *straight* to the point, *straight* alcohol, *straight* party line, the comedian's *straight* man, *straight* hair, thinking *straight*

E. Check your answers to the following questions by consulting your dictionary:

1. Is *incompetent* used as a noun?
2. Which of the following words are used as verbs: *admonition*, *loan*, *lord*, *magistrate*, *minister*, *sacrilege*, *spirit*, *war*?
3. Are the following words used as adjectives: *animate*, *predominate*, *very*?
4. What idiomatic prepositions go with the following words when they are used as verbs: *glory*, *care*, *marvel*?
5. Are the following used as intransitive verbs: *entertain*, *censure*, *promote*?

F. Find any unidiomatic use of prepositions. Write a more appropriate preposition after the number of each unsatisfactory sentence.

1. To seek a good grade at someone else's expense would be a violation to our standards of conduct.
2. Politicians must learn to refrain from making hasty statements.
3. During the past fifty years, deaths caused by highway accidents have been more numerous than those incurred from two world wars and the war in Korea.
4. Plans for cost reduction have been put to action by different agencies of the federal government.
5. Several families volunteered to take care for the children of flood victims.
6. Most of the people on our mailing list complied with our request.
7. The present board will never assent to a radical revision of the charter.
8. Only the prompt help of the neighbors prevented the fire of becoming a major disaster.

9. During the first years of marriage we had to deprive ourselves from many things that other people take for granted.
10. The arrival of the ship to its destination caused general rejoicing.
11. Though I support Mr. Finchley's candidacy, I take exception with some of his statements.
12. We will not hesitate to expose businesses that deprive their employees from these benefits.
13. The new ordinance was identical with one tried out and rejected in another city.
14. The government seemed indifferent to the suffering caused by its actions.
15. As an instrument of the popular will, the Senate suffers from defects inherent to its constitution.

D 2   WORD HISTORY

Let the history of a word help you understand its uses, meanings, and associations.

College dictionaries often summarize the **etymology** of a word. They briefly trace its origin and history. Your dictionary is likely to relate the word *lock* to corresponding words in earlier English (ME. = Middle English; AS. = Anglo-Saxon or Old English), in other Germanic languages (G. = German; ON. = Old Norse or Early Scandinavian), and in the common parent language of most European languages (IE. = Indo-European). Here is the etymology of a word that came into English from Latin by way of Italian and French:

> **pop·u·lace** \\'päp-yə-ləs\\ *n* [MF, fr. It *popolaccio* rabble, pejorative of *popolo* the people, fr. L *populus*] **1** : the common people : MASSES **2** : POPULATION

From *Webster's New Collegiate Dictionary*

In addition to tracing words to other languages, the etymologist is concerned with **semantic** change—gradual changes in meaning. The most complete record of such changes is the unabridged *New English Dictionary on Historical Principles*, reissued in 1933 as the *Oxford English Dictionary* (OED). This monumental reference work gives the earliest date a word occurs and then provides quotations tracing its development down through the centuries.

The most extensive changes in vocabulary come about through contacts between different cultures. Armed conquest, colonial expansion, and international trade make words move from one language to the other. Roughly three-fourths of the words in your dictionary came into English from foreign sources. When the Anglo-Saxon tribes came to England from continental Europe during the period between A.D. 450 and 600, they spoke Germanic dialects, close to the dialects from which modern Dutch and German are derived. The American tourist coming to Germany can still easily recognize the German equivalents of *arm*, *drink*, *father*, *fish*, *hand*, or *house*. However, the basic Germanic vocabulary of **Anglo-Saxon** or **Old English** was enriched and modified by words from other languages throughout early English history.

D 2a   Latin and Greek

Know some of the most common Latin and Greek roots.

English has borrowed heavily from Latin and Greek. Latin had been the language of the Roman empire. It became the official language of the Roman Catholic Church, which established itself in England in the seventh century and remained the supreme spiritual authority until the sixteenth century. English early absorbed Latin words related to the Scriptures and to the doctrines and ritual of the church, such as *altar*, *candle*, *chalice*, *mass*, *palm*, *pope*, *shrine*, *relic*, and *rule*. Other early borrowings were related to church administration, the everyday life of monks and the clergy, and the church-controlled medieval system of education.

Greek was the language of the literature, philosophy, and science of ancient Hellenic culture, flourishing both in Greece proper and in other parts of the Mediterranean world. Either in the original Greek or in Latin translation, this body of knowledge exercised a continuous influence on Western civilization during the Middle Ages and Renaissance. Modern philosophical, scientific, and technological terminology draws heavily on Latin and Greek roots. Examples of words absorbed either directly from Greek or from Greek through Latin are: *anonymous*, *atmosphere*, *catastrophe*, *chaos*, *climax*, *crisis*, *enthusiasm*, and *skeleton*. Examples of words absorbed from Latin are: *contempt*, *gesture*, *history*, *incredible*, *index*, *individual*, *intellect*, *legal*, *mechanical*, and *rational*.

(1) *Latin and Greek roots.* Knowledge of a common Latin or Greek root often provides the key to a puzzling word. For instance, the Greek root *phys-* usually refers to the body or to material things. The Greek root *psych-* usually refers to the mind or the soul. This distinction explains *physician* (heals the body) and *psychiatrist* (heals the mind), *physiology* (study of bodily functions) and *psychology* (study of mental functions), *physical* (characteristic of material reality) and *psychic* (going beyond material reality).

Here is a brief list of common Latin and Greek roots. Explain how each root is used in the sample words given for it:

ROOT	MEANING	EXAMPLES
arch-	*rule*	monarchy, anarchy, matriarch
auto-	*self*	autocratic, autonomy, automation
capit-	*head*	capital, per capita, decapitate
carn-	*flesh*	carnivorous, incarnation, carnival
chron-	*time*	chronological, synchronize, anachronism
culp-	*fault*	culpable, culprit, exculpate
doc-	*teach*	docile, doctrine, indoctrinate
graph-	*write*	autograph, graphic, seismograph
hydr-	*water*	dehydrate, hydraulic, hydrogen
jur-	*swear*	conjure, juror, perjury
man-	*hand*	manacle, manual, manufacture
port-	*carry*	portable, exports, deportation
phon-	*sound*	euphony, phonograph, symphony
terr-	*land*	inter, terrestrial, subterranean
urb-	*city*	suburb, urban, urbane
verb-	*word*	verbal, verbiage, verbose
vit-	*life*	vitality, vitamin, revitalize
vol-	*wish*	volition, involuntary, volunteer

(2) *Common prefixes and suffixes.* Especially useful is a knowledge of the most common Latin and Greek **prefixes** and **suffixes**—syllables attached at the beginning or at the end of a word to modify its meaning. A common prefix like *sub-*, meaning "below" or "beneath," helps to explain not only *substandard* and *subconscious* but also *submarine* (below the sea) and *subterranean* (beneath the surface, underground). The suffix *-cide* means "killer" or "killing" in *homicide* (of a human being), *suicide* (of oneself), *fratricide* (of a brother), *parricide* (of a parent), and *insecticide* (of insects).

Here is a brief list of Latin and Greek prefixes:

PREFIX	MEANING	EXAMPLES
bene-	*good*	benefactor, benefit, benevolent
bi-	*two*	bicycle, bilateral, bisect
contra-	*against*	contraband, contradict, contravene
ex-	*out, out of*	exclude, exhale, expel
extra-	*outside*	extraordinary, extravagant, extrovert
omni-	*all*	omnipotent, omnipresent, omniscient
per-	*through*	percolate, perforate, permeate
pre-	*before*	preamble, precedent, prefix
poly-	*many*	polygamy, polysyllabic, polytheistic
re-	*back*	recall, recede, revoke, retract
tele-	*distant*	telegraph, telepathy, telephone
trans-	*across, beyond*	transatlantic, transmit, transcend

D 2b Borrowings from Other Sources

Recognize some of the sources of the English vocabulary.

Here are some kinds of historical information that you will find in a good dictionary:

(1) *Thousands of words were absorbed into English from French.* England was conquered by the French-speaking Normans in the years following 1066. At the beginning of the so-called **Middle English** period, about 1150, the Norman conquerors owned most of the land and controlled the most important offices in state and church. The language of law, administration, and literature was French. When the native English of the conquered people gradually reestablished itself, thousands of French words were retained. Many of these words were associated with the political and military role of the aristocratic Norman overlords: *castle, court, glory, mansion, noble, prince, prison, privilege, servant, treason, treasure, war.* But hundreds of other words absorbed into Middle English were everyday words like *avoid, branch, chair, demand, desire, disease, envy, praise, table, uncle.*

Note: Many French words passed into English through the hands of English poets who found them in medieval French poetry and romance. Some of these words preserve a poetic and often old-fashioned flavor: *chevalier* for "knight," *damsel* for "girl," *fealty* for "loyalty," *paramour* for "sweetheart," *travail* for "toil."

(2) *A number of foreign languages have influenced the vocabularies of special fields of interest.* Since the consolidation of **Modern English** (about 1500), many words have come into English from French, Italian, Spanish, and various other sources. French elegance, artistry, and military organization gave us words like *apartment, ballet, battalion, cadet, caress, corps, façade, infantry, negligee, patrol.* Italian opera and symphonic music provided terms like *cantata, concert, falsetto, sonata, solo, soprano, violin.* From Spain, which pioneered in the discovery and exploitation of new continents, came words like *alligator, banana, cannibal, cocoa, mosquito, Negro, potato, tobacco,* and *tomato,* some of them absorbed into Spanish from New World sources.

(3) *Modern English has a number of foreign words in different stages of assimilation.* If they are still felt to be foreign rather than English, your dictionary may put a special symbol in front of them, or label them "French," "Italian," or whatever is appropriate. How does your dictionary handle the following Russian words: *troika, tovarich, apparatchik?*

EXERCISES

A. Find the original meaning of each of the following words: *attenuate, circumlocution, disaster, egregious, immigrant, paradise, philosophy, premise, recalcitrant, republic*. How does the original meaning help explain the current use of each word?

B. Report on the history of *five* of the following. What language does each term come from? How did it acquire its current meaning?

carnival	Halloween	police
crescendo	laissez faire	propaganda
cynic	millennium	pundit
dollar	nirvana	utopia
ecology	pogrom	vaudeville

C. Explain the meaning of the common element in each of the following sets. How does the common element help explain each word in the set?

1. anesthetic—anarchy—anemic
2. antibiotic—biography—biology
3. audio-visual—audition—inaudible
4. biennial—centennial—perennial
5. century—centipede—percentage
6. cosmic—cosmopolitan—microcosm
7. disunity—discord—dissent
8. eugenics-eulogy-euphonious
9. heterogeneous—heterosexual—heterodox
10. magnify—magnificent—magnitude
11. prelude—interlude—ludicrous
12. synchronize—symphony—sympathy

D. Indicate the basic meaning of each Latin and Greek prefix used in the following words: *ambivalent, antedate, antipathy, circumvent, concord, hypersensitive, international, introvert, malpractice, multimillionaire, neofascist, postgraduate, pseudoscientific, retroactive, semitropical, ultramodern, unilateral.*

E. What are the meanings of the following expressions? How many of them does your dictionary consider foreign rather than English? *Ad hoc, aficionado, blitz, corpus delicti, coup de grace, cum laude, de jure, El Dorado, ersatz, eureka, fait accompli, habeas corpus, hara-kiri, hoi polloi, quod erat demonstrandum, tour de force.*

D 3   VARIETIES OF USAGE

Recognize words that are appropriate only to certain situations or limited to specific uses.

Dictionaries use **restrictive labels** to show that a word is used only under certain circumstances, or that it will seem out of place in the wrong situation. In the following dictionary entry, six of the nine numbered meanings of *brass* carry restrictive labels:

brass (bras, bräs), *n.* **1.** any of various metal alloys consisting mainly of copper and zinc. **2.** an article made of such an alloy. **3.** *Mach.* a partial lining of soft metal for a bearing. **4.** *Music.* **a.** an instrument of the trumpet or horn family. **b.** such instruments collectively. **5.** *Brit.* **a.** a memorial tablet or plaque incised with an effigy, coat of arms, or the like. **b.** *Slang.* money. **6.** *Furniture.* any piece of ornamental or functional hardware. **7.** *U.S. Slang.* **a.** high-ranking military officers. **b.** any very important officials. **8.** *Informal.* excessive assurance; impudence; effrontery. —*adj.* **9.** of or pertaining to brass. [ME *bras,* OE *bræs;* c. OFris *bres* copper, MLG *bras* metal] —**brass′ish,** *adj.*

> subject label
> geographic label
>
> usage label

From *The Random House College Dictionary*

D 3a   Nonstandard Words   *NS*

Recognize words that suggest nonstandard speech rather than educated usage.

Usage labels provide a guide when roughly synonymous choices have different associations. One choice may suggest the folk speech of street and neighborhood ("nohow"); the other may suggest the standard English of school and office ("not at all"). Words like *anywheres* and *nohow* are either not listed in your dictionary at all or labeled illiterate or **nonstandard**. Like nonstandard grammatical patterns, they are often associated with low social standing or a lack of formal education.

> See **G 2a** for more on nonstandard English.

D 3b   Informal Words   *inf*

Recognize words that are too informal for serious writing.

People use informal language when at ease and with their friends. As a result, it tends to sound relaxed and folksy. But people who are comfortable in sports clothes over the weekend put on business clothes when going to the office on Monday morning. Similarly, a writer has to be able to use formal language in formal situations. Some dictionaries label informal words **colloquial**. The word does *not* mean "local" but "characteristic of informal speech."

Varieties of Usage

INFORMAL	FORMAL	INFORMAL	FORMAL
boss	superior	kid	child
brainy	intelligent	mean	ill-natured
bug	germ	skimpy	meager
faze	disconcert	sloppy	untidy
flunk	fail	snoop	pry
folks	relatives	snooze	nap
hunch	premonition	splurge	spend lavishly
job	position	stump	baffle

Other familiar words are generally acceptable in one sense but informal in another. Informal are *alibi* in the sense of "excuse," *aggravate* in the sense of "annoy," *funny* in the sense of "strange," and *mad* in the sense of "angry."

Informal language uses qualifiers like *kind of* (hard), *sort of* (easy), *a lot*, *lots*; abbreviated forms like *ad*, *bike*, *exam*, *gym*, *phone*. It uses many **phrasal** verbs, verbs that combine a short basic verb with one or more prepositions: *check up on*, *chip in*, *come up with*, *cut out* (noise), *get across* (a point), *take in* (a show), *take up with* (a person). Informal English usually contains a liberal sprinkling of catchall words like *nice*, *cute*, *great*, *awful*, *wonderful*, or *terrible*. It is fond of **figurative expressions** like *have a ball*, *polish the apple*, *shoot the breeze*, *hit the road*.

Informal expressions can set a casual, leisurely tone:

> There was a broad streak of mischief in Mencken. He was forever *cooking up* imaginary organizations, having *fake* handbills printed, inventing exercises in pure nonsense.—Philip M. Wagner, "Mencken Remembered," *The American Scholar*

But informal English can also suggest that you are not taking your subject (or your reader) seriously enough.

D 3c   Slang   *sl*

Use slang only in the most informal kinds of writing or for special effects.

No one can fix the exact point at which informal language shades over into slang. Generally, slang is more drastic in its disregard for what makes language formal and dignified. It often has a vigor missing in more pedestrian diction. The figurative expressions it substitutes for less imaginative formal terms are often apt: *blowhard*, *gumshoe*, *drunk tank*, *downer*, *spaced out*, *whirlybird*. Often a slang expression has no very satisfactory formal equivalent: *come-on, eyewash, runaround, stuffed shirt.* Nevertheless, most slang is too crude, extravagant, or disrespectful for use in writing. Avoid expressions like the following: *beat one's brains out, blow one's top, chew the fat, fly off the handle, hit the ceiling, lay an egg.*

TOO SLANGY: What *folks have dumped on marriage* in the way of expectations, selfish interests, and *kinky kicks* needs prompt removal if the institution is to survive.

TOO SLANGY: People didn't live as long, so a spouse could safely assume that the partner would *kick the bucket* in five or ten years and the *one still breathing could have another go at it.*

Note: The humor in slang is often callous. Calling a person "fatso" or "skinny" or "bonehead" may be funny, but it also suggests a lack of tact or respect.

EXERCISES

A. Which of the following expressions would you expect to carry *restrictive labels?* Check your answers with the help of your dictionary.

Bad-mouth, Brownie point, go Dutch, goof off, hang-up, highfalutin, jalopy, mooch, narc, nit-picking, persnickety, shyster, skin flick, windbag.

B. Arrange the expressions in each group in order *from the most formal to the most informal.* Be prepared to defend your decisions. (Your instructor may ask you to check your own judgments against those of your dictionary.)

1. live it up, live on little, live up to a promise
2. dress up for a party, dress down an offender, dress a wound
3. dream up a scheme, a cherished dream, dreamboat
4. tear up the bill, tear into someone, that tears it
5. hook up the microphone, got him off the hook, did it on his own hook
6. crack a book, her voice cracked, crack down on crime
7. have a go at it, go through with it, go for broke
8. skip town, skip a grade, children skipping down the path
9. deal cards, make a deal, big deal!
10. sweat shirt, sweat out a decision, no sweat

C. Much slang comes and goes. Which of the following are still current? Select five and write a sentence or two about each to help a dictionary editor complete a coverage of recent slang.

cop-out	mickey mouse	uptight
rap	jive	bread
jock	blast	the man
gyp	busted	yak
rip-off	dude	flaky
bummer	zonked	put-down

D. Point out *informal words and slang*. Suggest a more formal replacement for each informal expression.

1. Travelers who wish to see the true Paris should not go at a time when it is swamped by tourists.
2. Modern medicine has found ways of licking many dread diseases.
3. Psychologists have discovered that many young people get a kick out of cutting up in front of a group.
4. I liked this book because it shows guts to stand up for what is right.
5. When the refugees were told that the train was going to leave in ten minutes, there was a mad rush to the station.
6. Parents only confuse a child by bawling him out every time he commits a minor mistake.
7. When Lovelace fails to suggest a definite date for the wedding, Clarissa begins to suspect that he is only pulling her leg.
8. Sent to size up our new allies, he found most of them in good shape.
9. The concert was scheduled to start at eight o'clock, but unfortunately the soloist did not show up.
10. In view of the late hour, we decided we better shove off and get some shut-eye.

E. Observe the language used by your friends or fellow students to find *six current slang expressions* not listed in your dictionary. Define them and explain their use. Indicate what, if anything, they reveal about the speaker's attitude.

D 4 WORDS IN LIMITED USE   *d*

Recognize words that have only regional currency or are no longer in general use.

Dictionaries use restrictive labels to show that a word is not current throughout the English-speaking world, or not current at this time, or familiar mainly to specialists.

D 4a   Regional Labels

Notice geographic labels for words in use mainly in one region.

During the centuries before travel, books, and finally radio and television exercised their standardizing influence, languages gradually developed regional varieties. Sometimes, as in the case of German and Dutch, they grew far enough apart to become separate languages.

Here are the types of regional variation that you are likely to encounter:

(1) *Vocabulary differs somewhat from one English-speaking country to another.* American travelers in England notice the British uses of *tram, lorry, lift, torch, wireless, fortnight.* Here is a passage with many British terms:

> A scale or two adhered to the *fishmonger's* marble slab; the *pastrycook's* glass shelves showed a range of interesting crumbs; the *fruiterer* filled a long-standing void with fans of cardboard bananas and a "Dig for Victory" placard; the *greengrocer's* crates had been emptied of all but earth by those who had somehow failed to dig hard enough. . . . In the *confectioner's* windows the ribbons bleached on dummy boxes of chocolate among flyblown cutouts of prewar blondes. *Newsagents* without newspapers gave out in angry red chalk that they had no matches either.—Elizabeth Bowen, *The Heat of the Day*

(2) *Like most European languages, British English varies greatly from area to area.* Such regional varieties within a country are called **dialects**. Students of English literature usually encounter some dialect writing. For instance, a poet to whom a girl is a "bonny lass," a church a "kirk," and a landowner a "laird" is using one of the dialects of Scotland and Northern England rather than standard British English.

(3) *American speech shows some regional differences.* By and large, the intermingling of settlers from many areas and the rapid growth of mass media have kept these American dialects from drifting very far apart. Here are some of the words that your dictionary may mark dialectal: *dogie, poke* (bag), *reckon* (suppose), *tote* (carry), *you all.*

D 4b Obsolete and Archaic

Know how dictionaries label words no longer in common use.

Some words, or meanings of words, have gone out of use altogether. They are called **obsolete**. Examples of obsolete meanings are *coy* (quiet), *curious* (careful), and *nice* (foolish). Some words or meanings are no longer in common use but still occur in special contexts. Such words and meanings are called **archaic**. The King James version of the Bible preserves many archaisms that were in common use in seventeenth-century England: *thou* and *thee, brethren, kine* (cattle).

In the following dictionary entry, five of the numbered meanings of *brave* are labeled obsolete:

brave (brāv) *adj.* **brav·er, brav·est 1.** Having or showing courage; intrepid; courageous. **2.** Making a fine display; elegant; showy. **3.** *Obs.* Excellent. — *v.* **braved, brav·ing** *v.t.* **1.** To meet or face with courage and fortitude: to *brave* danger. **2.** To defy; challenge: to *brave* the heavens. **3.** *Obs.* To make splendid. — *v.i.* **4.** *Obs.* To boast. — *n.* **1.** A man of courage. **2.** A North American Indian warrior. **3.** *Obs.* A bully; bravo. **4.** *Obs.* A boast or defiance.

From *Standard College Dictionary*

Here are some archaisms familiar to readers of poetry and historical fiction:

anon	(at once)	fere	(companion)
brand	(sword)	forsooth	(truly)
childe	(aristocratic youth)	methinks	(it seems)
erst	(formerly)	rood	(cross)
fain	(glad or gladly)	sprite	(ghost)

D 4c   Neologisms

Be cautious in using words that have recently come into the language.

Lexicographers, who at one time resisted the introduction of new words, now compete in their coverage of **neologisms**, or newly coined expressions. Many new words serve a need and rapidly become accepted: *bookmobile, cybernetics, astronaut, fallout, supersonic, transistor*. But many other coined words make conservative readers squirm. Avoid copywriters' words like the following:

jumboize	paperamics	outdoorsman
moisturize	usership	

Many new words are part of an impersonal *bureaucratic jargon* that lacks the life and color of real language. Memos and reports often use words made up, on the model of *escapee, personalize, finalize, socioeconomic*. (See **D 6c**.)

D 4d   Subject Labels

Watch for technical terms that are not likely to be familiar to outsiders.

Labels like *Law*, *Naut.* (nautical), or *Mach.* (machinery) are called subject labels. The **technical terminology** or, on a less formal level, the shoptalk of a trade or profession requires explanation in writing for the general reader. Math students will have no difficulty with *set*, *natural number*, *integer*, *rational number*, and *number sentence*. But others would want these terms explained.

EXERCISES

A. Which of the following words have regional or dialect uses? (And where are they used?) Which of these words (or which of their uses) are archaic? Which are obsolete?

bloke	cove	hackney
bonnet	dogie	petrol
boot	favor	quid
bower	gentle	thorpe
complected	goober	trolley
costermonger	goodman	tube
coulee		

B. E. B. White, in an article on Maine speech, discussed the following expressions among others: *tunk* a wedge, *soft* weather, *dozy* wood, people *from away*, a *snug* pasture, *gunkhole*, *nooning*. Write a paper in which you discuss a number of expressions that you associate with a specific region or group of people. For instance, investigate dialect features that set your own native speech apart from that of a region where you now live.

C. The following words have all gained wide currency in recent years. Choose five of these. Explain briefly what each means and why it has become familiar.

printout	fast-breeder	bleep
subculture	peak load	replay
sexism	elitist	multiethnic
transplant	laser	recycle

D. Discuss the use of newly coined words in current advertising. Show which of these you think may eventually become standard English and explain why.

E. What special fields of interest do the following technical terms represent? Which of the terms would you expect the average high school graduate to know: *a priori*, *brochure*, *calorie*, *camshaft*, *crochet*, *de facto*, *denouement*, *graupel*, *lien*, *plinth*, *solstice*, *sonata*, *sprit*, *symbiosis*, *tachistoscope*, *thyroid*, *transubstantiation*, *valence*, *venire*, *ventricle*.

F. A student investigating post office shoptalk discussed the following terms: *swing room*, *star route*, *merry-go-round*, *Tour Three*, *fat stock*, *confetti*, *shedders*, *scheme man*, *nixie clerk*. Investigate and report on post office shoptalk in your area. Are any of the same terms in use? Are any of the terms recorded in general or specialized dictionaries? Or conduct a similar investigation of shoptalk in one of the following areas: railroading, trucking, flying.

D 5 EXPRESSIVE LANGUAGE   *d*

Use the exact words needed to carry your intended meaning.

Effective writing is clear, fresh, graphic, and concrete. Learn to revise your writing for more effective, more expressive word choice.

D 5a   Accurate Words

Aim at accurate words and exact shades of meaning.

Hastily written words often express the intended meaning almost but not quite:

HASTY: *The news* about widespread corruption was first *exposed* by the local press.

REVISED: The news about widespread corruption first *appeared* in the local press. (Evildoers or shortcomings are "exposed," but news about evildoers is "printed," "presented," or "reported.")

Check your papers for the following:

(1) Watch out for words easily *confused* because closely related in sound or meaning.

The work was sheer *trudgery* (should be *drudgery*).
Similar choices *affront* every student (should be *confront*).
He grew up in a *staple* environment (should be *stable*).

(2) Watch out for *garbled idioms:*

GARBLED: Unemployment *played* an important *factor.*
SHOULD BE: Unemployment *played* an important *role.*

GARBLED: Many young people have *lost their appeal for* fraternities.
SHOULD BE: Fraternities have *lost their appeal* for many people.

(3) Watch out for words with the wrong *connotation:*

INEXACT: Life in the suburbs *subjects* a family to the beauties of nature.

REVISED: Life in the suburbs *brings* a family *closer* to the beauties of nature. (The connotations of *subject* are unfavorable; it implies that we are exposed to something unwillingly.)

D 5b Specific Words

Use specific, informative words.

Instead of a colorless, general word like *building*, use a more expressive word like *barn, mansion, warehouse, bungalow, tenement, shack, workshop,* or *cabin. Tenement* carries more information than *building*. It also comes closer to concrete experience, making it possible for the reader to visualize an actual structure. When words remain unnecessarily general, readers are too far removed from what they can see, hear, and feel.

GENERAL: All the animals of the farm joined in singing "Beasts of England."

SPECIFIC: The whole farm *burst* out into "Beasts of England" in tremendous unison. The cows *lowed* it, the dogs *whined* it, the sheep *bleated* it, the horses *whinnied* it, the ducks *quacked* it. (George Orwell)

Good writers have at their fingertips the right word for specific objects, shapes, sounds, textures, motions:

sand crabs, *wriggling* and *scuttling* . . . heavy little creatures, shaped like *scarabs*, with *gray-mottled* shells and orange underparts . . . (John Steinbeck)

a big, squarish *frame house* that had once been white, decorated with *cupolas* and *spires* and *scrolled* balconies in the heavily lightsome style of the seventies . . . (William Faulkner)

D 5c Figurative Words

Use figurative expressions to make writing graphic and colorful.

Figurative language exploits the similarities between things. A compressed comparison introduced by *as* or *like* is called a **simile**. An implied comparison that uses one thing as the equivalent of another is called a **metaphor**. Literally, *monkey* refers to a small, long-tailed animal. Figuratively, it may mean a person who, like a monkey, is agile, mischievous, imitative, or playful.

Fresh, well-chosen figurative expressions catch our attention and make us see the point:

In this movie, "understanding" is sprinkled onto both sides of the conflict like meat tenderizer. (Peter Rainer)

Getting complete sentences out of him was like trying to put together *Homo sapiens* from a few bones in a cave. (Anita Strickland)

Remember the following advice:

(1) *Figurative expressions should be apt.* The implied analogy must fit:

APT: Putting the hubcap back on the rim is *like putting an undersized lid on an oversized jar.* (As one side of the hubcap is pounded into place, the opposite side pops out.)

INEPT: Lacking the ignition of advertising, our economic engine would run at a slower pace. (An engine without ignition would not run at a slower pace; it would just be dead.)

(2) *Figurative expressions should be consistent.* When several figurative expressions appear closely together, they should blend into a harmonious whole rather than clash because of contradictory associations. Avoid the **mixed metaphor**:

CONSISTENT: Fame cannot spread wide or endure long that is not *rooted* in nature, and *manured* by art. (Samuel Johnson)

MIXED: America's colleges are the *key* to national survival, and the future of the country lies in their *hands.* (Keys do not have hands.)

MIXED: Enriched programs give the good student a chance to *dig* deeper into the large *sea* of knowledge. (Most people do their digging on solid ground rather than at sea.)

(3) *Figurative expressions should not call excessive attention to themselves.* Avoid metaphors that are strained enough to become distracting.

EXTRAVAGANT: When the average overmothered college student is removed from parental control, the severance of the umbilical cord causes him or her to bleed to death, psychologically speaking.

D 5d   Fresh Words

Phrase ideas freshly in your own words.

Many phrases that may once have been striking have become trite through overuse. Such tired phrases are called **clichés**. They make the yawning reader feel that nothing new is being said and that there is little point in paying attention.

TRITE: He was always *wrapped up* in his own thoughts and feelings.

FRESH: Only the *cocoon* of his own thoughts and feelings existed for him.

TRITE: The dean let us have it, *straight from the shoulder.*

FRESH: The dean spoke to us directly and urgently, *like a scout just returned from the enemy camp.*

To the cliché expert, ignorance is always "abysmal," fortitude "intestinal," and necessity "dire." Daylight is always "broad," silence "ominous," and old age "ripe." People make a "clean break" and engage in "honest toil" till the "bitter end." They make things "crystal clear"; they wait "with bated breath"; they work "by the sweat of their brow."

Avoid clichés like the following:

believe it or not	last but not least
better late than never	the last straw
beyond the shadow of a doubt	let's face it
bolt out of the blue	malice aforethought
burn the midnight oil	nature's glory
couldn't care less	off the beaten track
crying shame	pride and joy
dire straits	proud owner
easier said than done	rear its ugly head
the facts of life	rude awakening
few and far between	a shot in the arm
fine and dandy	sink or swim
the finer things	a snare and a delusion
first and foremost	sneaking suspicion
free and easy	something tells me
get in there and fight	straight and narrow
good time was had by all	strike while the iron is hot
green with envy	tender mercies
in one fell swoop	to all intents and purposes
in the last analysis	truer words were never spoken
it goes without saying	truth is stranger than fiction
it stands to reason	up in arms

EXERCISES

A. Make sure you can distinguish between the confusing words in the following pairs: *antic—antique; biography—bibliography; clique—cliché; connive—conspire; difference--deference; ethical—ethnic; feudalism—fatalism; gentle—genteel; literal—literary—literate; manners—mannerisms; sensible—sensitive; specie—species.*

B. Write down a *more accurate* word for the word italicized in each sentence.

1. Diane had only a small knowledge of the problem *coherent* in being a woman.
2. Justice prevails when a criminal is *righteously* punished for wrongdoing.
3. The March of Dimes was originally organized to help those *inflicted* with infantile paralysis.
4. My parents were idealists and tried to raise healthy, *opinionated* children.
5. By *defying* to participate in saluting the flag, people are showing disrespect to our country.

6. Abortion is quickly becoming more acceptable but still considered by many *immortal*.
7. In my *analogy* of this essay, I hope to show its strengths and weaknesses.
8. Our next *fiascle* took place in Hollywood.
9. My dilemma is whether to describe the three incidents separately or *incarcerate* them all in one short story.
10. He tried for years to win the *disparaging* strife against alcohol.
11. Many references to his early life *percolate through* Eliot's poetry.
12. The chairman *contributed* the low attendance to poor publicity.
13. A good listener can listen to teachers and retain the knowledge they have *expelled*.
14. Sick people can no longer pay for their hospital costs without a tremendous *drain* being put on their families.
15. Thorough reforms would be hard to *induce upon* our society.

C. How many different figurative expressions can you find in the following passage?

The sixties was the decade when the frightened cry of "Timber!" was everywhere in the unclean air of publishing. The flow of competitive daily newspapers dried up, and magazines great and small fell like the trees chopped down for the paper to print them. Now that the flagship *Life* has joined its lessers in the Sargasso Sea of bestilled publications, some conventional wisdom prevails as to how American publishing became trapped in such an economic rathole: spiraling production costs, quadrupling postage rates, blood-sucking competition for advertising dollars from television, the general malaise of the economy, mass circulations sustained at uneconomical cut rates, the decline of print, et cetera. None of these reasons, to my way of thinking, explains the big picture.—Warren Hinckle, "The Adman Who Hated Advertising," *Atlantic*

D. Look at the use of figurative expressions in the following sentences. Which work well to help the author make a point? Which are mixed or overdone? Which are borderline? (Your instructor may ask you to find more apt figurative expressions to replace the unsatisfactory ones.)

1. Frustration and depression will take over our minds the way bacteria do our bodies if we do not harness them.
2. The new law is a carefully tossed salad of penalties and incentives.
3. Modern society is like a mobile: Disturb it here and it jiggles over there, too. Because every facet of life involves energy, energy policy disturbs everything at once.
4. The story told by Poe's biographers was a tale told by idiots, in which incredible oceans of slushy sentimentality broke in waves of froth over the submerged rocks of fact.
5. The producer and director of the movie have tapped a sensitive nerve in their audiences like a bunch of wildcatters hitting a pool of oil.
6. The president will run down his batteries if he continues issuing high-voltage announcements about energy "catastrophe."
7. When I moved to the new school, many new faces dotted this horizon of experience.

8. Slapping on a price freeze to stop inflation could become a one-way street to a Pandora's box of problems.
9. To be the son of a great man can be a disadvantage; it is like living next to a huge monument.
10. This cat was in our driveway when the kiss of death took him by surprise.
11. Education is certainly not a precise instrument. When you increase the supply, you don't get the same immediate effect as when you press on the accelerator of your automobile.
12. College can supply the appropriate building blocks that make it easier to grow up in the tough world of today.
13. We sat in a circle on the floor, pouring out the paths and roads we had traveled since we graduated.
14. An industrial world thinks it wants only a pinch of intelligence to season a great plateful of mechanical aptitudes. (Jacques Barzun)
15. I was dismayed to find that the place associated with my favorite childhood memories had succumbed to the clutch of change.

E. Rewrite the following sentences to *eliminate clichés*. Try to make your phrasing fresh enough to revive the reader's attention.

1. They will have to get his signature by hook or by crook.
2. Catching the street-corner pusher has become small potatoes. The major effort is now international, and it is a pathway strewn with political pitfalls.
3. Cleopatra squeezes Antony under her thumb, while Octavia pulls the rug from under him in front of Caesar and his troops.
4. After one more defeat, she will have to throw in the sponge.
5. The reporter swallowed their story hook, line, and sinker.
6. The typical organization man knows which side his bread is buttered on.
7. Party platforms never get down to brass tacks.
8. In trying to revitalize our neighborhoods, appealing to self-interest is our best bet.
9. When we are asked to change administrations in the midst of a serious international crisis, we should remember that it is unwise to change horses in midstream.
10. The opposing candidate is a Johnny-come-lately who entered the campaign only at the urging of influential backers.

D 6   DIRECTNESS

Know how to be blunt and direct.

At times, a writer will be deliberately indirect for tactical reasons. More common is the kind of careless indirectness that for no good reason slows down the reader.

D 6a   Redundancy

Avoid wordiness.

The most easily spotted kind of wordiness is redundancy, or unnecessary duplication. The phrase *basic fundamentals* is redundant

because *basic* and *fundamental* mean nearly the same thing. In the
following sentences one or the other way of expressing the same idea
should be omitted:

> We left *in the morning* at about six o'clock A.M.
> *As a rule,* the weather was *usually* warm.
> There is more to it than *seems apparent.*
> *Physically,* he has not grown much in *height.*
> *In my opinion, I think* you are right.

Here are some sources of wordiness other than direct duplication:

(1) *All-purpose nouns* like *situation, angle, factor, aspect, line,* or
element are often mere padding:

PADDED: When I first came to Smith College, *there was a situation where* some
            students lived in better housing than others.
CONCISE: When I first came to Smith College, some students lived in better hous-
            ing than others.

PADDED: Another *aspect* that needs to be considered is the consumer relations
            angle.
CONCISE: We should also consider consumer relations.

(2) *Roundabout transitions* sometimes take the place of simple
phrases like *for example, however,* and *therefore:*

WORDY: *In considering this situation we must also take into account the fact
            that* other students do not feel this way.
ECONOMICAL: Others, *however,* do not feel this way.

WORDY: *Taking these factors into consideration, we must conclude that* your
            request is unjustified.
ECONOMICAL: *Therefore,* your request seems to us unjustified.

(3) *Introductory phrases* like *the fact that* or *the question whether*
can often be trimmed without loss:

WORDY: *The question of whether* churches should unite agitates people of
            many denominations.
ECONOMICAL: *Whether* churches should unite agitates people of many denomina-
            tions.

D 6b Euphemisms   *d*

Prefer plain English to euphemisms and weasel words.

Much roundabout diction results from the desire to be elegant. Refined or impressive names for unpleasant or prosaic things are known as **euphemisms.** The most familiar euphemisms are those for elementary facts of human existence:

(birth)	*blessed event, new arrival*
(pregnancy)	*to be expecting, to be in a family way*
(age)	*senior citizens, the elderly*
(death)	*pass on, expire, the deceased, mortal remains, memorial park*

Euphemisms are "beautiful words"—words more beautiful than what they stand for. Often they are required by politeness or tact. When referring to people you respect, you will prefer *stout* to *fat*, *intoxicated* to *drunk*, and *remains* to *corpse*. Often, however, euphemisms mislead, or even deliberately deceive. Plumbers become "sanitary engineers," file clerks "research consultants," undertakers "funeral directors," translators "language facilitators," and fortune tellers "clairvoyant readers." In much public-relations prose and political propaganda, euphemisms cover up facts that the reader is entitled to know: *straitened financial circumstances* for "bankruptcy"; *planned withdrawal* for "disorganized retreat"; *resettlement* for "forcible removal."

EUPHEMISM	BLUNT
immoderate use of intoxicants	heavy drinking
lack of proper health habits	dirt
deteriorating residential section	slum

D 6c Jargon   *d*

Do not try to impress your reader with pretentious pseudoscientific language.

Much inflated diction results from a writer's using two highbrow words where one lowbrow word would do. **Jargon** tries to make the trivial seem important. It cultivates an impressive pseudoscientific air by using indirect, impersonal constructions and technical-sounding Latin and Greek terms.

JARGON:	Procedures were instituted with a view toward the implementation of the conclusions reached.
PLAIN ENGLISH:	We started to put our ideas into practice.

JARGON:	Careful consideration of relevant data is imperative before the procedure most conducive toward a realization of the desired outcomes can be determined.
PLAIN ENGLISH:	Look before you leap.

Jargon addicts say "Reference was made" rather than "I mentioned"; "the hypothesis suggests itself" rather than "I think." They are fond of "factors," "phases," "aspects," "criteria," "data," "facets," "phenomena," "structures," "levels," and "strata." In each of the following pairs, avoid the "big word" if the simpler word will do:

FANCY	SIMPLE
ameliorate	improve
magnitude	size
interrelationship	relation
methodology	methods
residence	home
maximize	develop fully
insightful	intelligent
preadolescence	childhood

Obviously, many scientific and scholarly subjects call for language that is technical, precise, impersonal. Jargon is the *unnecessary* use of technical language in order to borrow the prestige of science and scholarship.

D 6d   Flowery Diction   *d*

Avoid language that is flowery or overdone.

Flowery and extravagant diction interferes with a writer's doing justice to a subject. Flowery diction results from an attempt to give a poetic varnish to prose. Some writers cannot resist the temptation to call a police officer a "minion of the law," an Irishman a "native of the Emerald Isle," a colonist who served in the War of Independence a "gallant warrior defending our infant republic."

FLOWERY:	The respite from study was devoted to a sojourn at the ancestral mansion.
PLAIN ENGLISH:	I spent my vacation at the house of my grandparents.
FLOWERY:	The visitor proved a harbinger of glad tidings.
PLAIN ENGLISH:	The visitor brought good news.

Do not imitate writers who habitually prefer the fancy word to the plain word, the elegant flourish to the blunt phrase. Here is a brief list of words that can make your writing seem affected:

FLOWERY	PLAIN		FLOWERY	PLAIN
astound	amaze		nuptials	wedding
betrothal	engagement		obsequies	funeral
commence	begin		presage	predict
demise	death		pulchritude	beauty
emolument	pay, reward		vernal	springlike
eschew	avoid		vista	view

EXERCISES

A. What makes each of the following sentences wordy? Rewrite each sentence to eliminate wordiness.

1. The war against alcohol lasts enduringly forever.
2. Mormons fleeing persecution founded the beginning of our community.
3. In due time, a new fad will eventually replace this current craze.
4. The central nucleus of the tribe was based around the institution of the family.
5. I feel that I have the personality of a happy, smiling type of person.
6. Some of today's popular music seems to revert back to music popular thirty years ago.
7. The weather bureau announced that at times there would be occasional rain.
8. The reason that married students have high grades academically is that they have a definite goal in the future to come.
9. In the modern world of this day and age, economical operation has become an indispensable condition for business success.
10. I felt honored and lucky to have a chance of taking advantage of the opportunity of getting a good education.

B. Investigate the *current use of euphemisms* in one major area, such as education, medicine, or the funeral industry. Examine such euphemisms for intention, appropriateness, effect.

C. Translate the following examples of jargon into plain English.

1. I sincerely believe that the government should divulge more on the subject of socialism and its cohorts, because its impetus has reached a frightening momentum.
2. In camp, cooking is done over open fires, with the main dietary intake consisting of black beans and rice.
3. To be frank about it, today an inadequacy can bring about the ruination of a person in later life when it happens in education.
4. Being in social situations in Washington subjected me to some embarrassing instances due to my deficiency in etiquette, which was superfluous at home because of its nonexistence.

5. The English language and its use have become very important factors in corre-
lation with communication to large audiences.

6. In these two books, there are basic differences in character representation that
are accountable only in terms of the individual authors involved.

7. Further insight into the article discovered that the writing insinuated a connection between the conviction of the accused and his working-class background.

8. Advertisements similar to those of Certs and Ultra-Brite are creating a fallacy in
the real cause of a person's sex appeal.

9. The fact that we are products of our environmental frame of reference ensures
that each of us has deeply ingrained within the fiber of our being preconceived
ideas that influence our thoughts, actions, and reactions.

10. We say we believe in democracy while denying the partaking of its first fruits,
justice and equality, to diverse members of our society. This is true in many
aspects of our lives, but especially so in the context of racial prejudice.

   D. Study the language used by your favorite *sports writer, fashion analyst,* or
society editor. Write a brief report, providing samples of characteristic diction.

Sentences

CHAPTER TWELVE

S 1 Sentence Building
  a Effective Predication
  b Effective Coordination
  c Effective Subordination
  d Effective Modifiers

S 2 Sentence Variety
  a Sentence Length
  b Varied Word Order

S 3 Awkward Construction
  a Deadwood
  b Awkward Passive
  c Impersonal Constructions
  d Excessive Subordination
  e Awkward Modifiers

S 4 Repetition
  a Awkward Repetition
  b Emphatic Repetition
  c Parallel Structure

A writer's most basic tool is the sentence. The English sentence gives the writer a tremendous range of *choice*. At one extreme is the short, bare-facts sentence that records events as they happen without comment, one thing at a time:

> Manuel lay back. They had something over his face. It was all familiar. He inhaled deeply. He felt very tired. He was very, very tired. They took the thing away from his face. (Ernest Hemingway)

At the other extreme is the leisurely long sentence that follows up an idea as different details come to mind:

> She liked a simple life and simple people, and would have been happier, I think, if she had stayed in the backlands of Alabama riding wild on the horses she so often talked about, not so lifelong lonely for the black men and women who had taught her the only religion she ever knew. (Lillian Hellman)

Between the two extremes is the kind of sentence that carries most of the message in effective prose: clearly focused on the main idea, including the necessary details, and showing clearly how its major parts are related. Each of the following is the kind of well-built sentence that makes us want to comment: "Well said!"

> A trim, clear-eyed, self-assured woman, she sometimes runs the five miles to and from her office at the Institute of Medical Sciences.
> Courage is not the absence of fear; it's the control over fear. (Dickie Chapelle)
> What makes democratic politics different from most other professions is that, occasionally, the politician has a duty to risk his job by performing it conscientiously. (George W. Will)

When you work on sentence style, you focus on what helps your sentences carry their message. You work on what makes sentences *effective*. You practice writing sentences that come right to the point. You practice choosing among the available sentence resources those that are right for the job.

> See **G 1** for a review of basic sentence elements.

S 1 SENTENCE BUILDING

Write sentences that clearly signal important relationships.

Many simple sentences are built on the "Who does what?" model. When such a sentence moves with few or no modifiers from subject to verb and from there to any complements, we are likely to encounter few problems of clarity or proper perspective:

> *My friend waited* outside the restaurant.
> *The relatives* of the deceased *crowded the room.*
> *The heavens declare the glory* of God.

Learn how to keep your sentences equally clear and direct when they carry more, and more complicated, information.

S 1a   Effective Predication   *st*

Rewrite weak sentences on the "Who does what?" model.

Try to make the subject name the key agent. Then make the predicate state the key point:

WEAK:
One crucial factor in the current revolution in our social structure *is the relationship* between the white policeman and the black community. (Subject and predicate carry little of the meaning.)

STRONGER:
The white policeman standing on a Harlem street corner *finds himself* at the very center of the revolution now occurring in the world.— James Baldwin, *Nobody Knows My Name* (The "crucial factor"—the *policeman*—is now the subject of the sentence.)

Watch out especially for the following:

(1) Look for sentences in which nouns ending in *-ment, -ion, -ism*, and the like, serve as the subject of the sentence. Often these refer to actions, events, and activities that could be more vigorously expressed by a verb. Make the agent or "doer" the subject of the sentence:

WEAK:
Violent *arguments* frequently *took place.*

REVISED:
We often *argued* violently.

WEAK:
A certain element of confusion *was present.*

REVISED:
The speaker confused us.

WEAK:
A criticism which is prevalent against modern poetry *is that its appeal is* only to the supersophisticated.

REVISED:
Many critics complain that *modern poetry appeals* only to the supersophisticated.

(2) To make the subject and predicate of a main clause carry your main point, *eliminate tag statements* like "The simple fact is

that . . ." and "the question now confronting us is whether . . ."

WEAK: *The question* now confronting us *is* whether we should yield to intimida-
          tion, and thus encourage other groups to resort to the same tactics.
REVISED: *Should we yield* to intimidation, and thus encourage other groups to
          resort to the same tactics?

S 1b   Effective Coordination   *st*

Use coordination when two ideas are about equally important.

When we coordinate two things, we make them work together.
In sentences like the following, both clauses are about equally relevant to the general trend of the report or argument. A simple *and* or
but coordinates the two ideas:

> We tried to locate the files, *but* we were unsuccessful.
> Matthew was a subeditor on a large London newspaper, *and* Susan worked in
> an advertising firm. (Doris Lessing)
> Our press is essentially provincial in this country, *and* except for a few syndi-
> cated columnists the reputation of our newspaper reporters is mainly local.

A simple *and* is also appropriate when events follow each other as
they happen, without emphasis on cause and effect or other logical
relations:

> There was a shock, *and* he felt himself go up in the air. He pushed on the
> sword as he went up and over, *and* it flew out of his hand. He hit the ground
> *and* the bull was on him.—Ernest Hemingway, "The Undefeated"

Excessive coordination results from the overuse of *and*. Note that
it merely says "more of same," without showing any specific relationship. Avoid *and* when it merely makes a sentence ramble on,
without preparing the reader for what is coming:

RAMBLING: A member of the reserve has to participate in weekly drills, *and* he
           may be called up in emergencies, which came as an unpleasant sur-
           prise to me, *and* you would do better to stay away from it.

If you doubt the appropriateness of a coordinating connective
like *and* or *but*, test the sentence by inserting a parenthetical
"equally important":

EFFECTIVE: Under one of the plans, a reservist spends only six months on active
            duty, *but* [equally important] he remains in the ready reserve for seven
            and one-half years.

S 1c Effective Subordination   *sub*

Use subordination when details, reasons, or qualifications accompany a main point.

Subordinating connectives (*when, while, since, because, if, though*) and relative pronouns (*who, which,* and *that*) add a **dependent** clause to the main clause. They can make the material they subordinate seem less important. They fit well when the main clause states a major point, with the dependent clauses establishing relations in place, time, or logic:

> The edge of the cape was wet with blood *where* it had swept along the bull's back as he went by.—Ernest Hemingway, "The Undefeated"

Subordination helps us make the main idea stand out in a larger combined sentence:

SIMPLE: The term *democracy* originated in ancient Greece. Different people have used it to describe quite different political systems. Usually the person who uses the word thinks it has only one meaning.

COMBINED: *Democracy,* a term that originated in ancient Greece, *has been used to describe quite different political systems,* though the person who uses it usually thinks it has only one meaning.

Remember the following points:

(1) *Effective subordination clarifies relationships in a sentence.* Merely placed next to each other, the following two statements may seem disjointed: "Kroger organized a counterfeiting ring. He had studied printing in Germany." When one is subordinated to the other, the connection between them becomes more obvious:

EFFECTIVE: Kroger, *who had studied printing in Germany,* organized a counterfeiting ring.

(2) *Unskillful subordination blurs emphasis.* "I was ten when we moved to Alaska" focuses the reader's attention on you and your age. "When I was ten, *we moved to Alaska*" focuses the reader's attention on Alaska. **Upside-down subordination** results when the wrong item seems to stand out. When tucked away in a subordinate part of a sentence, important information may catch the reader unaware and, as a result, have an ironic effect. Avoid upside-down subordination when no irony is intended:

UPSIDE-DOWN: The salary was considered good by local standards, *though* it was not enough to feed and clothe my family.

IMPROVED: *Though* considered good by local standards, my salary was not enough to feed and clothe my family.

UPSIDE-DOWN: He had a completely accident-free record up to the last day of his employment, *when* he stepped on a power line and almost lost his life.

IMPROVED: On the last day of his employment, *after* ten years without a single accident, he stepped on a power line and almost lost his life.

S 1d   Effective Modifiers   *sub*

Use modifiers to help a sentence carry added freight.

A skillful writer often uses modifying words and phrases where an inexperienced writer might use separate clauses. Observe the tightening of relationships in the following pairs:

LOOSE: I lay on the couch in the kitchen. I was reading *The Last Days of Pompeii*. How I wished I could have been there.

COMPACT: I lay on the couch in the kitchen, reading *The Last Days of Pompeii*, and wishing I were there. (Alice Munro)

LOOSE: We caught two bass. We hauled them in briskly, as though they were mackerel. After we pulled them over the side of the boat, we stunned them with a blow on the back of the head.

COMPACT: We caught two bass, *hauling them in briskly* as though they were mackerel, *pulling them over the side of the boat* in a businesslike manner without any landing net, and *stunning them with a blow on the back of the head*. (E. B. White)

The following sentences, from a bullfighting story by Ernest Hemingway, illustrate the effective use of one or more modifiers *at different positions* in the sentence:

• Breaking up subject and verb:

The horse, *lifted and gored*, crashed over with the bull driving into him.
Manuel, *facing the bull, having turned with him each charge*, offered the cape with his two hands.

• At the end of the sentence:

Manuel walked towards him, *watching his feet*.
The bull was hooking wildly, *jumping like a trout, all four feet off the ground*.

- **At the beginning of the sentence:**

  Now, *facing the bull*, he was conscious of many things at the same time.
  Heads up, swinging with the music, their right arms swinging free, they stepped out.

- **More than one position:**

  The bull, *in full gallop*, pivoted and charged the cape, *his head down*, *his tail rising*.

EXERCISES

A. Write five simple short sentences built on the "Who does what?" model. Then *add* to each sentence, building up relevant details. Use the following sentences as possible models:

1. A girl plays "Silent Night."
   A small skinny girl plays "Silent Night" with two fingers on an untuned piano in a garage.
2. A dog zigzags.
   A dog, tail held high, zigzags among the tailless creatures in search of its master.
3. The *News* condemned the violence.
   The *Amsterdam News*, the nation's largest black newspaper, condemned the night's violence as criminal, outrageous, and damnable.
4. Creative people have produced.
   Using their dreams alone, creative people have produced fiction, inventions, scientific discoveries, and solutions to complex problems. (Jean Houston)
5. The movement was attempting to win.
   The women's movement was attempting to win the right to vote by changing every single state constitution (in 1912, nine states had woman suffrage). (Ann Pincus)

B. Rewrite the following sentences for *more effective predication*. If possible, make the subject and the predicate tell the reader who does what.

1. Vigorous discussions of current political events often took place among the customers.
2. It is very probable that intimidation of witnesses will result from such threatening remarks.
3. A recent development is the encouragement of new technology for extracting oil by the Canadian government.
4. There has been much support among voters for rent control measures of different kinds.
5. A conscientious teacher's satisfaction is incomplete unless she reaches a full realization of her goals.
6. As the result of unruly demonstrations, repeated interruptions of the committee's deliberations took place.
7. The conclusion is inevitable that considerable impairment of our country's military strength has come about as the result of these cuts.

8. A plan for safe driving is of no use if the cooperation of the individual driver is not present.
9. The pressure of society to conform is so great that the student is in constant awareness of its presence.
10. The contribution of the alumni to the growth of the college will be in proportion to their information about its educational needs.

C. Rewrite the following passages, making effective use of *subordination* or *modifiers*.

1. Campus elections are ridiculous. Nobody qualified runs. I refuse to have anything to do with them.
2. Piloting a boat is easy. It is like driving a car. The controls are about the same.
3. The monkey family is large. It includes monkeys, baboons, lemurs, and apes. The animals in the monkey family are closely related to humans. They are imitative. They can be trained to perform simple tasks. However, their intelligence is low.
4. My father came from a wealthy family, and my mother came from a very poor home, and it was strange that she held the purse strings in the family.
5. Many high school teachers follow a textbook word for word, and they go over each page until everyone understands it. In college, many teachers just tell the student to read the textbook, and then they start giving lectures on the material covered in the text, but they don't follow it word for word.

D. Study the following model sentences. They make exceptionally full use of the *sentence resources* that we can draw on to help load a sentence with information. For each of the model sentences, write a sentence of your own on a subject of your own choice. As much as you can, follow the sentence structure of the original. Try to come close—you need not follow the model sentence in every detail.

MODEL 1: Your photographs will be more artistic if you use the film that has chromatic balance.

IMITATION: Your checks will be more welcome if you draw them on an account that has money in it.

MODEL 2: Everyone is a moon and has a dark side which he never shows to anybody. (Mark Twain)

MODEL 3: Lonnie wore the composed, polite appreciative expression that was her disguise in the presence of grown-ups. (Alice Munro)

MODEL 4: Sitting in the study hall, she opened the lid of the desk and changed the number pasted up inside from seventy-seven to seventy-six.

MODEL 5: The fullback held the ball lightly in front of him, his knees pumping high, his hips twisting as he ran toward the end zone.

S 2 SENTENCE VARIETY   *var*

Keep your sentences from becoming plodding and monotonous.

An effective writer uses sentences of different length and structure for variety and emphasis.

S 2a Sentence Length

Use short sentences to sum up a point; use long sentences for detailed explanation and support.

A short sentence is often appropriate for summing up a key idea or for giving pointed advice. The following short sentences are quotable, emphatic, to the point:

> Economy is the art of making the most of life. (G. B. Shaw)
> You should write, first of all, to please yourself. (Doris Lessing)

A long elaborate sentence is often appropriate for detailed description, explanation, or argument. The following sentences are carefully worked out, with all details in place, and all ifs and buts fully stated:

> As the pastor paused to gather his thoughts—hair falling to the wrong side of its part, tie clashing more loudly than last week, and his smile slightly twisting his face—he seemed a little more human to us all.
> There will never be a really free and enlightened State until the State comes to recognize the individual as a higher and independent power, from which all its own power and authority are derived, and treats him accordingly.—Thoreau, "Civil Disobedience"

Remember the following points:

(1) *Avoid excessive use of short, isolated sentences.* They can easily make your writing sound immature:

CHOPPY: Many teachers can give students information. Very few can inspire students to learn. Information is of little use to students. Soon they will leave college. Then they will forget what they have memorized. They must be inspired to learn on their own.

IMPROVED: Many teachers can give students information, but few can inspire them to learn. When students leave college, the information they have memorized will be of little use and will soon be forgotten. What they need most is the ability to learn on their own.

(2) *Learn how to make a short summary sentence and a long elaborating sentence work together.* We often use a short pointed sentence as the opening sentence or topic sentence of a paragraph. Then we follow up in longer sentences that fill in details:

> *Newspapers give a distorted view of life.* They overemphasize the unusual, such as a mother giving birth to quintuplets, the development of a Christmas tree that grows its own decorative cones, the minting of two pennies which were only half-engraved, gang fights, teenage drinking, or riots. . . .

(3) *Occasionally make your reader stop short at a concise, memorable statement of an important point.* A short sentence can be especially effective if it sets off an important conclusion or a key observation at the end of a passage. Notice the emphatic short sentences in the following passages:

> With the great growth in leisure-time activities, millions of Americans are turning to water sports: fishing, swimming, water skiing, and skin diving. *Clean water exhilarates and relaxes.*—Vance Packard, "America the Beautiful—and Its Desecraters," *Atlantic*
>
> Bennett was always facing the wonder of the actualities of living. It was wonderful to him that we live as we do, that time will pass and change us, that we will die and perhaps die painfully, that life is what it is. *He never decorates or embroiders. He is wholly materialistic. Common sense is the salt of his plate.*—John Van Druten, "My Debt to Arnold Bennett," *Saturday Review*

S 2b   Varied Word Order

Vary normal word order to keep your sentences from being too much alike.

Though most of your sentences will follow the subject-verb sequence, there will usually be enough variety in the remaining sentence elements to prevent tiring repetition. Monotony is most likely to result when a number of sentences start with the same subject, especially a pronoun like *I* or *he* or *she*:

MONOTONOUS: A good example of a topic drawn from personal experience is a bus accident I once had. I wrote a paper about this experience of mine. I remembered the events that took place during the accident. I could describe them well. After all, I had experienced them. It was a shocking experience. I will never forget it. The facts stand out in my memory because it was so shocking.

(1) *Make a modifier that usually occurs later in the sentence precede the subject.* The **introductory modifier** can bring variety into a group of plodding sentences:

VARIED: He reversed the direction of the canoe. *After a few seconds* he stopped paddling. *Slowly* he made the canoe drift to the bank. *When within a yard of the shore,* he grabbed one of the overhanging branches.

VARIED: The Trans World Terminal stems from the work of contemporary architects like Corbusier of France and Nervi of Italy, masters of the curve in concrete. *Like a true eagle,* this building is all curves and muscle, no right angles. *Built of reinforced concrete,* the whole structure swoops and turns and rises.—Ken Macrorie, "Arriving and Departing," *The Reporter*

(2) *Shift a complement to a more emphatic initial position.* The **introductory complement** is normal in exclamations beginning with *what* or *how*: *"What stories* that man told!" *"What a liar* you are!" *"How true* that is!" In other sentences, this turning around (or **inversion**) of the usual pattern is especially effective when it takes up something mentioned earlier:

EFFECTIVE: The committee has asked me to resign. *That* I will never do.

EFFECTIVE: Mr. Schlumpf fried two small pieces of fish. *One of these* he fed to his cat. *The other* he ate himself.

EFFECTIVE: We really should not resent being called paupers. *Paupers* we are, and *paupers* we shall remain.

Note: Like other attention-getting devices, the introductory complement sometimes attracts attention to the speaker rather than to what he or she is saying. Sometimes the construction smacks of old-fashioned oratory:

More patient wife a husband never had.
Gone are the days of my youth.
Such deeds of glory we shall see no more.

(3) *Shift the predicate of the main clause toward the end.* Work some of the modifiers into the sentence earlier. Such treatment may strengthen a sentence especially if a **final modifier** is a belated qualification or concession, unexpectedly weakening the main point:

WEAK: Richard Wagner became one of the most successful composers of all time in spite of the jeers of his contemporaries. (This version may make your readers remember the jeers rather than the man's success.)

IMPROVED: Richard Wagner, *though jeered at by his contemporaries,* became one of the most successful composers of all time.

Note: A **loose** sentence finishes one major statement *early* but then leads on to further points or further detail. It is an expandable or cumulative sentence that looks as if it had been built in stages:

LOOSE: *Comedy usually moves toward a happy ending,* and the normal response of the audience to a happy ending is "this should be," which sounds like a moral judgment. (Northrop Frye)

In a **periodic** sentence, an essential part of the main statement is *held in suspense* until the end. The sentence ends when the main statement ends. Everything else is worked into the sentence along the way:

Sentence Variety

PERIODIC: *Comedy, though often showing us cranks or eccentrics, nevertheless aims its ridicule,* as many critics have said, *at common failings of human nature.*

EXERCISES

A. Choose five of the following short, memorable statements as *model sentences*. For each, write a sentence of your own that follows as closely as possible the structure of the original. (Sample imitations follow two of the model sentences.)

MODEL 1:   Love is as necessary to human beings as food and shelter. (Aldous Huxley)

MODEL 2:   The man with a new idea is a crank until the new idea succeeds. (Mark Twain)

IMITATION: The person with two-inch soles is considered crazy until two-inch soles become fashionable.

MODEL 3:   Those who cut their own wood are twice warmed.

MODEL 4:   A nail that sticks out will be hammered down. (Japanese saying)

MODEL 5:   Curiosity, like all other desires, produces pain as well as pleasure. (Samuel Johnson)

IMITATION: Marriage, like many other institutions, brings restrictions as well as benefits.

MODEL 6:   Work expands so as to fill the time available for its completion. (C. Northcote Parkinson)

MODEL 7:   Perversity is the muse of modern literature. (Susan Sontag)

B. Study the following examples of *long, elaborate* sentences carrying along many details. Choose three of these as model sentences. For each, write a similar sentence of your own, carrying nearly as much freight as the original. (You need not follow the structure of the original in all details.)

1. (a news event) On an early January day in 1968, a volcanic eruption pushed some steaming rocks above the surface waters of the South Pacific, adding a new island to the remote Tonga Archipelago.
2. (a snapshot of a person) A dirty long-haired young man in a faded army fatigue jacket, weary from walking, reached through the barbed-wire fence to pet a mud-covered Jersey milk cow grazing in a field alongside the country road.
3. (a sentence that traces a process) We begin as children; we mature; we leave the parental nest; we give birth to children who, in turn, grow up, leave and begin the process all over again. (Alvin Toffler)
4. (a sentence that explains an important requirement) An interview need not be an ambush to be good, but it should set up a situation in which the subject can be surprised by what he says—that is, a situation in which he has to do some audible thinking. (Richard Todd)

C. Study the following example of how a *short summary* sentence and a *long elaborating* sentence can work together. Then write three pairs of your own that similarly give your reader "the long and the short of it."

Training is everything. The peach was once a bitter almond; cauliflower is nothing but cabbage with a college education. (Mark Twain)

D. Describe the variations in sentence style in the following passages. Describe the functions performed or the effects produced by sentences of different *length*. Point out variations in *word order*.

1. Why conform to a group? Why throw away your birthright for a Greek pin or a peace button, for security and nonentity? This goes especially for the typical college student, who merely wants to do what "everyone else is doing." What everyone else is doing isn't best. It's merely common. One of the synonyms of "common" is "vulgar."
2. The dictionary can neither snicker nor fulminate. It records. It will offend many, no doubt, to find the expression *wise up,* meaning to inform or to become informed, listed in the Third International with no restricting label. To my aging ears it still sounds like slang. But the evidence—quotations from the *Kiplinger Washington Letter* and the *Wall Street Journal*—convinces me that it is I who am out of step, lagging behind. (Bergen Evans)
3. Some people believe that it is easier today for a woman to achieve whatever she wants simply because the idea that all fields are open to women is more widely accepted, and therefore many more opportunities exist. But this is only partly true. Having chosen what she wants to become, a woman must be prepared to commit herself over a long period to reach her goal. She must work hard and be ready to meet the unexpected; and she must face the fact that she will have to put up with a lot to make her dreams come true. (Margaret Mead)

S 3   AWKWARD CONSTRUCTION   *awk*

Avoid constructions that make for an indirect, awkward, wooden style.

Effective sentences may be long and complicated, as long as the words and structural relationships convey meaning clearly and directly. On the other hand, the grammatical equipment even in short sentences may become so heavy that it interferes with communication.

S 3a   Deadwood

Prune your sentences of deadwood.

Often a sentence runs more smoothly after it has been trimmed down. Avoid unnecessary *there are*'s and *who were*'s:

AWKWARD: *There are* many farmers in the area *who* are planning to attend the meeting *which is* scheduled for next Friday.

BETTER: Many farmers in the area plan to attend the meeting scheduled for next Friday.

Other sentences can be cleared of deadwood by effective use of pronouns:

AWKWARD: A child of preschool age often shows a desire to read, but *the child's* parents often ignore this *desire*.

BETTER: Often a child of preschool age shows a desire to read—*which his* parents ignore.

Some connectives, prepositions, and pronouns are unnecessary or unnecessarily heavy:

AWKWARD: I wrote little, *because of the fact that* my childhood had been *an* uneventful *one*.

BETTER: I wrote little, because my childhood had been uneventful.

S 3b Awkward Passive

Avoid the passive when it makes sentences awkward or roundabout.

An active sentence is modeled on the "agent-action-target" relationship: "The woodcutter *felled* the tree." A passive sentence reverses this perspective and looks at the action from the point of view of the original subject: "The tree *was felled* by the woodcutter." As a result, the passive is appropriate when the target or result of an action seems *more important than the performer*:

The unpretentious monarchs of Scandinavia and the Low Countries are respectfully accepted by their sober subjects.—Kingsley Martin, "Strange Interlude," *Atlantic*

Among the Ibo, *the art of conversation* is regarded very highly, and proverbs are the palm oil with which *words* are eaten.—Chinua Achebe, *Things Fall Apart*

The passive is also appropriate when the doer or performer of an action is *beside the point* or *hard to identify*:

Some of John's brain cells *were damaged* when he was a small child.

In World War II, millions of people *were driven* from their homes.

Do not *overuse* the passive under the mistaken impression that it will make your sentences more formal or impressive. Learn to convert weak passives back to the active:

WEAK PASSIVE: Although Bradley Hall *is* regularly *populated* by students, close study of the building as a structure *is* seldom *undertaken*.

ACTIVE: The students *passing* through Bradley Hall seldom *pause to study* its structure.

WEAK PASSIVE: My experiences at writing *were* greatly *increased* due to two large essays due each week.

ACTIVE: I *wrote* more than ever, *having to turn in* two long essays each week.

Since the doer or performer is often *omitted* from a passive sentence, we may find it hard to identify the person responsible for an action or idea:

EVASIVE: A plan for popular election of Supreme Court justices *is* now *being advanced*. (By whom?)

EVASIVE: The racial problem is clearly one that *could and should have been solved* long ago. (By whom?)

On *shifts* to the passive, see **G 10c.**

S 3c   Impersonal Constructions

Revise impersonal constructions to make your sentences more direct.

The impersonal *one*, the *it* without antecedent, and *there-is* or *there-are* sentences are most appropriate when the people or forces behind an action are of secondary importance. We naturally say "it rains" or "it snows"—what matters is the process, not its causes. Guard against the *unnecessary* use of such constructions:

(1) The **impersonal one** is often a tiresome substitute for the people concerned, especially if their identity is indirectly revealed by modifiers:

ROUNDABOUT: *When teaching, one* should be patient.
DIRECT: *Teachers* should be patient.

ROUNDABOUT: *As a father, one* should not spoil his children.
DIRECT: *Fathers* should not spoil their children.

ROUNDABOUT: *If one is a citizen of a democracy, she* should exercise her voting rights.
DIRECT: *A citizen of a democracy* should vote.

(2) In **it-is** and **there-is** sentences, the first two words are mere props, which can make the sentences sound lame and indecisive. Sometimes, the main topic of a sentence receives needed emphasis if it is introduced by *it is* or *there is*:

EMPHATIC: It is *his competence* that we question—not his honesty.

More often, however, the reshuffling of sentence elements made necessary by *it is* or *there is* causes awkwardness:

AWKWARD: In 1958, *there was* a strike participated in by five thousand union members.

DIRECT: In 1958, five thousand union members went on strike.

S 3d   Excessive Subordination

Avoid overburdened sentences caused by excessive subordination.

Excessive subordination causes various types of overburdened sentences. One common type *dovetails* several dependent clauses into each other, thus making a subordinating connective follow another subordinating connective or a relative pronoun. The resulting **that-if**, **if-because**, **which-when** constructions are often awkward:

AWKWARD: I think *that if* there were less emphasis on conformity in high school, college students would be better prepared for independent thinking.

IMPROVED: In my opinion, college students would be better prepared for independent thinking *if* there were less emphasis on conformity in high school.

Look out for the following:

(1) *Avoid "house-that-Jack-built" sentences.* Several dependent clauses of the same type follow each other, making the sentence trail off into a confusing succession of modifiers:

AWKWARD: When I was in Mexico City, I visited Jean, *who* was living with a Mexican girl *who* posed for the local artists, *who* are usually too poor to pay their rent, let alone the model's fee.

IMPROVED: When I was in Mexico City, I visited Jean. She was living with a Mexican girl *who* posed for the local artists but seldom received any money for her work. Most artists there are too poor to pay their rent, let alone the model's fee.

(2) *Avoid having too many similar dependent clauses delay the main clause:*

AWKWARD: When a child is constantly watched *when* he is born and *while* he is a baby, the reason is that his mother wants to see whether he is developing as her books say he should.

IMPROVED: Some mothers constantly watch young children to see whether they are developing as the books say they should.

(3) *Avoid seesaw sentences.* These start with a dependent clause, proceed to the main clause, and then add a *second dependent clause* that in a confusing way qualifies the meaning of the first:

CONFUSING: *Because many teenagers marry hastily,* their marriages end in divorce, *because they are too immature to face adult responsibilities.*

CLEARER: Many teenagers are too immature to face adult responsibilities. They marry hastily, and often their marriages end in divorce.

S 3e   Awkward Modifiers

Keep disproportionately heavy modifiers from breaking up the pattern of a clause.

Lengthy appositives, verbal phrases, or dependent clauses sometimes separate elements that belong together:

AWKWARD: The pilot told his friends that he had flown Clinton Morris, *a resident of New York City sought by the government for income tax evasion,* out of the United States.

AWKWARD: The club treasurer, *being* the son of a father constantly *stressing* the importance of *maintaining* a proper sense of the value of money, refused to pay our expenses.

EXERCISES

A. Which of the following sentences seem clear and well built? Which seem awkward, overburdened, or confusing? (Your instructor may ask you to revise the weak sentences.)

1. Saturday mornings used to be my best time for studying, because I knew nothing was due the next morning (which was Sunday), until I started working.
2. From across the dinner-littered dining table, my father blinks myopically and asserts that current conflicts are no different from any other conflicts and that my dissent is no different from what his dissent used to be.

3. Motorists are quickly informed of the whereabouts of restaurants, motels, and, of course, speed traps set by the police, by other CB operators.
4. The dreary weather, mainly rain, that never seemed to stop, and my problems with my parents, which were serious, upset me.
5. The Texas-born, Boston-trained lawyer, who has rung up many firsts in just three years on Capitol Hill, has plain-spoken her way to national prominence.
6. A child's first impressions of people and places shape the course of her future life, frequently.
7. All electric appliances, far from being labor-saving devices, are new forms of work, decentralized and made available to everybody. (Marshall McLuhan)
8. Knowing the right answers is sometimes less important than asking the right questions.
9. As we left the city, we approached a range of hills which seemed like giant waves which were about to break.
10. If someone is exercising his slightly off-key singing voice and a friend mockingly plugs her ears and winces in agony, the singer might well take the gesture as a personal insult if he didn't have a sense of humor.

B. Rewrite each of the following sentences to make them less awkward or more direct.

1. There are many ways in which a student who is interested in meeting a foreign student may come to know one.
2. From small incidents, like receiving too much change and pocketing it, to larger issues, like cheating on a test, a lifelong pattern may be established.
3. The camp counselor, talking on and on and without noticing anything wrong or hearing the laughter, finally turned around.
4. If any experimenting endangering human lives is to be done by the government, the voters should be consulted first.
5. When information about summer school is received, the necessary deadlines may be ones that have already passed.

S 4 REPETITION

rep

Learn to make effective use of repetition and parallelism.

Unintentional repetition can make a passage sound clumsy. Deliberate repetition can emphasize important points and give continuity to a sentence or a paragraph.

S 4a Awkward Repetition

Avoid unintentional repetition of sounds, syllables, words, or phrases.

Carelessly repeated sounds or sentence elements grate on the reader's ears.

AWKWARD: Commercials seldom make for entertain*ing* and relax*ing* listen*ing*.

BETTER: Commercials seldom entertain and relax the listener.

AWKWARD: Close examina*tion* of the results of the investiga*tion* led to a reorgani-*zation* of the department.

BETTER: Close study of the results of the inquiry led to a reorganization of the department.

AWKWARD: We listened to an account *of* the customs *of* the inhabitants *of* the village.

BETTER: We listened to an account of the villagers' customs.

Unintentional repetition is especially annoying when the similarity in sound covers up a *shift in meaning or relationship*:

My father lost his savings during the depression because he had *banked on* [better: "relied on"] the well-established reputation of our hometown *bank*.

S 4b   Emphatic Repetition

Use intentional repetition for clarity and continuity.

A writer may repeat important words and phrases for emphasis:

EMPHATIC: When I returned to State, *I studied* as I have never studied since. *I studied* before classes. *I studied* after classes. *I studied* till English, history, and zoology merged into one blurry mass of incoherent erudition.

EMPHATIC: In my mother's world, *no one ever* shrugged his shoulders; *no one* was *ever* bored and lazy; *no one* was *ever* cynical; *no one ever* laughed.—Alfred Kazin, "The Bitter 30's," *Atlantic*

Notice the cumulative effect of intentional repetition in the following passage from Stephen Crane's "The Open Boat":

In the meantime, the oiler *rowed,* and then the correspondent *rowed,* and then the oiler *rowed.* Gray-faced and bowed forward, they mechanically, turn by turn, plied the leaden oars.

S 4c   Parallel Structure

Use parallel structure to help channel the reader's attention.

Parallel structure pulls together related ideas through the repetition of similar grammatical patterns. The following passages make effective use of parallelism:

The only advice, indeed, that one person can give another about reading is
to take no advice,
to follow your own instincts,
to use your own reason,
to come to your own conclusions. (Virginia Woolf)

The air must be pure
if we are to breathe;
the soil must be arable
if we are to eat;
the water must be clean
if we are to drink.

The more things you love,
the more you are interested in,
the more you enjoy,
the more you are indignant about—
the more you have left when anything happens. (Ethel Barrymore)

Remember:

(1) *Parallel structure helps us line up related ideas in a sentence or in a paragraph:*

Together we planned the house, *together we* built it, and *together we* watched it go up in smoke.
I have *thought* about their remarks, *tried* to put myself in their place, *considered* their point of view. (Nora Ephron)
It was much worse for them, *they tell me.* They had a terrible time of it, *they assure me.* I don't know how lucky I was, *they say.* (Nora Ephron)

(2) *Parallel structure helps us line up different ideas for comparison or contrast:*

Her remarks provoked much comment, *self-righteous from her enemies, apologetic from her friends.*
Whereas *it is desirable that* the old *should treat with respect* the wishes of the young, *it is not desirable that* the young *should treat with respect* the wishes of the old.

We call the neat balancing of two direct opposites an **antithesis**. Note the antithetical style of the following passage:

India *is a poetic nation, yet it demands* new electrical plants. It *is a mystical nation, yet it wants* new roads. It *is* traditionally *a peaceful nation, yet it could,* if misled, *inflame* Asia.—James A. Michener, "Portraits for the Future," *Saturday Review*

(3) *Parallel structure helps us make a series of parallel sentences*

build up to a **climax**. Notice how the author of the following passage starts with fairly harmless generalities and leads up to a specific point dear to his heart:

> The future *is not for* little men with little minds. It *is not for* men without vision who fear progress. It *is not for* timid men who early were frightened by the story of Frankenstein. And it *is not for* those arch reactionaries who seek to shatter big enterprise and to force American industry back into the puny production patterns of its nineteenth-century infancy.

On *faulty* parallelism, see **G 10d**.

EXERCISES

A. Study the use of repetition and parallelism in the following passages. Choose three of these as model sentences. For each, write a passage of your own on a subject of your own choice. Follow the structure of the original as closely as possible.

1. Studies serve for delight, for ornament, and for ability. (Sir Francis Bacon)
   SAMPLE IMITATION: Cars serve for transportation, for relaxation, and for ostentation.
2. It is in vain to say human beings ought to be satisfied with tranquility: They must have action, and they will make it if they cannot find it. (Charlotte Brontë)
3. Women feel just as men feel; they need exercise for their faculties, and a field for their efforts as much as their brothers do; they suffer from too rigid a restraint too absolute a stagnation, precisely as men would suffer. (Charlotte Brontë)
4. Young people believe that by remaining individuals, by avoiding the marriage vows, by living together only as long as love lasts, they will avoid the togetherness demanded of the married; they will avoid the staleness of being taken for granted.
5. While there is a lower class, I am in it; while there is a criminal element, I am of it; while there is a soul in prison, I am not free. (Eugene Debs)

B. Point out any features that make for effective sentence style. Examine such features as sentence length, variety, emphasis. Point out any special or unusual effects.

1. We go to our libraries in order to read and take advantage of the experiences of others. I think we all realize that not every written word in a library is entirely true. Many different authors have here written what they think, what they have experienced, what they believe is true, and sometimes what they wish were true. Some are wrong, a few are right, and many are neither entirely wrong nor entirely right.

2. This is not a Utopian tract. Some of those who complain about the quality of our national life seem to be dreaming of a world in which everyone without exception has talent, taste, judgment and an unswerving allegiance to excellence. Such dreams are pleasant but unprofitable. The problem is to achieve some measure of excellence *in this society*, with all its beloved and exasperating clutter, with all its exciting and debilitating confusion of standards, with all the stubborn problems that won't be solved and the equally stubborn ones that might be.—John W. Gardner, *Excellence*
3. We are informed that marriage should be a place where we can grow, find ourselves, be ourselves. Interestingly, we cannot be entirely ourselves even with our best friends. Some decorum, some courtesy, some selflessness are demanded. As for finding myself, I think I already know where I am. I'm grown up; I have responsibilities; I am in the middle of a lifelong marriage; I am hanging in there, sometimes enduring, sometimes enjoying.—Suzanne Britt Jordan, "My Turn," *Newsweek*

Paragraphs

CHAPTER THIRTEEN

O 1 The Well-Made Paragraph
    a   The Topic Sentence
    b   Relevant Detail
    c   Transition
    d   Recurrent Terms

O 2 Organizing the Paragraph
    a   The All-Purpose Paragraph
    b   Paragraphs with a Special Purpose
    c   Paragraphs with a Special Strategy

In a newspaper article, a paragraph break may occur after every long sentence, and after every group of two or three short ones. In dialogue, a paragraph break conventionally signals a change from one speaker to another. In writing that explains things or argues with the reader, the paragraph is the basic unit: The expository paragraph *does justice to one major point*. It presents an important idea or an important step in an argument. It does not just state an idea but supports or defends it as well.

O 1   THE WELL-MADE PARAGRAPH

Write the kind of solid paragraph that presents and develops one key idea.

A well-written paragraph has a point. It offers supporting material that makes the reader take the point seriously. It provides the signals that help the reader see what kind of material is offered in support and in what order.

O 1a   The Topic Sentence   *coh*

Use a topic sentence to focus a paragraph clearly on one major point.

A **topic sentence** sums up a central idea:

TOPIC SENTENCE: Women have always been stuck with the sewing.

TOPIC SENTENCE: Some of the job areas most popular with students are very small.

TOPIC SENTENCE: Loading and unloading grain from ships and barges was an arduous and dangerous business.

In a well-focused paragraph, all or most of what follows backs up such an initial statement. How many separate examples does the author of each of the following paragraphs use to "follow through"?

SAMPLE PARAGRAPH 1

Women have always been stuck with the sewing. The connection is there in Greek myth and legend—the Three Fates are women, and one of them cuts the thread of life. Ariadne used thread to save Theseus from the Labyrinth. In Homer, Penelope, famous for her patience, used weaving to put off her unwelcome suitors. American Indian women chewed hides and sewed them with bone needles. Farm women, weighed down with huge families and no servants, spent hours stitching—*after* all the other household work was done. Even in their leisure time they quilted while they socialized. James Fenimore Cooper read novels to his wife in the evening while she sewed.

SAMPLE PARAGRAPH 2

Some of the job areas most popular with students are very small. Only 1,000 foresters will be hired this year, although perhaps twice as many students got forestry degrees. Only 2,700 new architects will be needed to design all the buildings sprouting on the landscape, and almost twice that number graduated last year. Everyone wants to design things, but according to the Department of Labor, only about 300 industrial designers are added to the labor force during an average year. Landscape architecture is appealing, too, because it combines creativity with outdoor work, but only 600 are expected to find jobs in the field this year.

SAMPLE PARAGRAPH 3

Loading and unloading grain from ships and barges was an arduous and dangerous business. One had to walk through mounds of rye or corn up to the knees, an exercise which makes running along a sandy beach seem like a cakewalk. Grain dust used to fill the hold, making a smokescreen so thick a worker couldn't recognize a fellow worker at twenty feet. The occasional pier rats were so big from eating grain and chasing it down with the polluted Hudson they could have pulled Cinderella's carriage.

In writing or revising a theme, remember:

(1) *A good topic sentence gives unity to a paragraph.* It can point out a logical connection you previously missed or ignored:

RAMBLING: San Francisco is a city of beautiful parks and public buildings. Golden Gate Park, with its spacious lawns and graceful ponds, enjoys international fame. The city's bohemian section became the national headquarters for jazz-age poetry and philosophy. Every tourist must visit Fisherman's Wharf and Coit Tower. The city is famed for its cultural events and conventions.

UNIFIED: *Tourists and convention managers are irresistibly attracted to San Francisco.* Miles of varied waterfront, spacious parks, and impressive public buildings contribute to the city's unique appearance and cosmopolitan atmosphere. Fisherman's Wharf, with its seafood smells and colorful shops, attracts sightseeing crowds. Coit Tower affords a spectacular view of bay and city. Golden Gate Park, with its spacious lawns and graceful ponds, enjoys international fame.

(2) *A good topic sentence gives clear direction to a paragraph.* Can you see how the topic sentence in each of the following examples steers the paragraph in a different direction? What additional details would you expect in each of these paragraphs?

VERSION 1: *The dormitory reminds me of a third-class hotel.* Each room has the same set of unimaginative furnishings: the same pale red chest of drawers, the same light brown desks. . . .

VERSION 2: *The dormitory reminds me of a big office building.* People who half know each other pass in the hall with impersonal friendliness. . . .

The Well-Made Paragraph

VERSION 3:   *The dormitory reminds me of a prison.* The study room is enclosed by windows with lines on them, giving the student a penned-in feeling. . . .

(3) *In the theme as a whole, a good topic sentence moves the presentation or the argument ahead one essential step.* Then the rest of the paragraph fills in, illustrates, and supports the point made. Then the next topic sentence again takes a step forward. Part of an article on the influence of television on political campaigns might proceed like this:

Smile—You're on Camera

STEP 1:   *Television continues to change the look of political conventions.* Speeches are fewer and shorter. Sweaty orators, bellowing and waving their arms for an hour or more, have yielded almost completely to Tele-PrompTer readers, younger and brisker, some of them very slick and many of them no fun. Both parties have shortened sign-waving, chanting demonstrations. . . .

STEP 2:   While many of the changes may be for the best, *there is something synthetic about this new kind of convention.* There is a lack of spontaneity, a sense of stuffy self-consciousness. There is something unreal about seeing a well-known newscaster starting across the floor to interview a delegate and getting stopped for an autograph. . . .

STEP 3:   Nevertheless, *television coverage of conventions manages to get across to us a great deal about the way our political system works.* We are still a nation of disparate parts. The conventions are the occasions that bring various coalitions together every four years to pull and haul at one another; to test old power centers and form new ones; to compromise and, yes, to raise a little hell together in a carnival atmosphere. . . .

O 1b   Relevant Detail   *dev*

Strengthen skimpy paragraphs by supplying relevant detail.

A good topic sentence pulls together a mass of closely related material. Notice how much detail has been brought together in the following paragraph. Notice how directly it *ties in* with the major point the author is trying to make about Latin American culture:

Latin American culture has been and is a dynamic element in the development of our own. It has, for example, furnished more than 2000 place names to the United States postal directory. Its languages have influenced American English, as such simple examples as "rodeo" and "vamoose" indicate. Its customs are part of our "Westerns" on television. Its housing, its music, its dances, its scenery, its ruins and its romance have been imitated and admired in the United States. One-third of the continental area of this republic was for a long period, as modern history goes, under the governance of Spanish viceroys or of Mexico. The largest single Christian church in the United States is identical with the dominant church in Latin America.—Howard Mumford Jones, "Goals for Americans," *Saturday Evening Post*

In many weak paragraphs, the supporting material remains *too thin*. In revising such paragraphs, build them up by providing additional relevant detail. Notice how the following passage becomes more authentic through the filling in of detail from the author's experience:

THIN: I like politicians. I have spent a lot of time in their company. Mostly, I have reported their doings, but on occasion I have assisted them. On the whole, they have proved better company than any other professional group I have had a chance to know well.

AUTHENTIC: I like politicians. *Ever since I started work as a city-hall reporter in New Mexico some thirty years ago,* I have spent a lot of time in their company—*in smoke-filled rooms, jails, campaign trains, shabby courthouse offices, Senate cloakrooms, and the White House itself.* Mostly I've been reporting their doings, but on occasion I have served them *as speech writer, district leader, campaign choreboy, and civil servant.* On the whole, they have proved better company than any other professional group I've had a chance to know well—*including writers, soldiers, businessmen, doctors, and academics.*—John Fischer, "Please Don't Bite the Politicians," *Harper's*

Build up relevant material in support of your topic sentence until the reader feels like saying: "Enough! I'll grant you have a point." Try the following to make sure that your paragraphs are *developed* adequately:

(1) *Follow up a major example with several parallel ones.* Often, a detailed first example helps clarify the point. Then, several additional examples show how generally it applies. Show how the following paragraph illustrates this pattern:

Many Americans mindlessly oppose hunting, even in cases where animal populations are dangerously high. In some areas of Alaska wolves have become so prolific they are running out of hunting ground and prey heavily on moose, deer, and occasionally dogs. In the past, game managers curbed wolf populations by trapping and aerial hunting without wiping out the species. Still, whenever they propose to do this nowadays, they receive tens of thousands of letters of protest. Growing deer populations in parts of California threaten to starve themselves out. Sea-otter colonies, burgeoning along the Pacific coast, are fast running out of fodder, too, as well as putting commercial fishermen out of business.—Lael Morgan, "Let the Eskimos Hunt," *Newsweek*

(2) *Use one exceptionally detailed example to drive home a point.* Sometimes one striking example or summarized case history is re-

membered where more routine examples would be forgotten. Study the following example:

> Outside the arctic, which is my second home, *I find little comprehension of the remarkable skill, work, and endurance it takes for Eskimos to live off the land and sea in one of the world's most inhospitable climes.* The whale has traditionally been, and still is, a large and important part of the Eskimo diet. Even today, natives usually hunt it as their ancestors did—paddling up to the quarry in homemade driftwood-framed sealskin boats, then dispatching the giant with a hand-thrust harpoon or shoulder gun, the design of which was patented in the 1800s. As part of the hunt ritual, the Eskimos return the whale's skull to the sea to appease the spirit of the magnificent beast. Since bowheads are fairly wily, weigh a ton a foot and sometimes grow to be 60 feet long, the crews require considerable courage. Their primitive method of hunting definitely limits the take which, until 1978, was unrestricted by law.—Lael Morgan, "Let the Eskimos Hunt," *Newsweek*

(3) *Practice building up detail in a* **multiple-example** *paragraph.* Here is a paragraph that makes exceptionally ample use of relevant examples. How many can you identify?

> *A person's touch makes what the other senses take in more real to the memory.* A wood carving appeals to the touch with deep grooves and parts that are rough as well as parts that are smooth. The fingers can interpret the richness of brocade and the rough warmth of wool. An ancient book becomes even older when one feels the fragile pages. A puppy tugging wildly at a leash feels like energy. Winter is felt in the hastily prepared snowball and the pine boughs that are brittle in the sharp air. A child must feel a hot stove before it becomes a thing to avoid touching. The energy of the sun becomes more apparent when one focuses a magnifying glass on one's fingers. A baby chick is something altogether new when one holds the cottonlike ball of feathers and feels its nervous heartbeat. An oil painting is only paint and canvas until one touches the swirls made by the artist's brush. A rose is only a flower until one holds it and pulls the petals from the intricate pattern. The surface of a rock is only light and shadow until one feels its ridges and ripples. Touching helps one to see and hear more clearly.

(4) *Give priority to supporting detail by practicing the* **examples-first** *paragraph.* When you reverse the usual order from topic sentence to supporting detail, you force yourself to provide the relevant examples that in the end will add up to a well-earned generalization:

> The shops of the border town are filled with many souvenirs, "piñatas," pottery, bullhorns, and "serapes," all made from cheap material and decorated in a gaudy manner which the tourist thinks is true Mexican folk art. Tourists are everywhere, haggling with the shopkeepers, eager to get something for nothing, carrying huge packages and boxes filled with the treasures bought at the many shops. Car horns blare at the people who are too entranced with the sights to watch where they are going. Raucous tunes pour from the nightclubs, open in broad day-

O 1c

light. Few children are seen in the town, but some boys swim in the Rio Grande and dive to retrieve the coins that tourists throw as they cross the bridge above. People come for a cheap thrill, a quick divorce, cheap liquor. *A border town is the tourist's Mexico, a gaudy caricature of the real country.*

O 1c Transition

Use transitional expressions to help your reader follow from step to step.

Transitional phrases help the reader who wants to know: "Where are you headed?" *For instance, for example*, or *to illustrate* takes the reader from a general point to a specific example. *Similarly, furthermore, moreover*, and *in addition* prepare the reader to continue the same line of thought. *However, but, on the contrary, on the other hand*, and *by contrast* signal that the argument is turning around: Objections or complications are about to follow.

Look at the italicized transitional expressions in the following paragraphs. In your own words, can you explain how each moves the paragraph forward one step?

PARAGRAPH 1

Many animals are capable of emitting meaningful sounds. Hens, *for instance*, warn their chicks of impending danger. *Similarly*, dogs growl at strangers to express distrust or hostility. Most of our pets, *in fact*, have a "vocabulary" of differentiated sounds to express hunger, pain, or satisfaction.

PARAGRAPH 2

Most of us are less tolerant than we think. *It is true that* we tend to be tolerant of things sufficiently remote, such as Buddhism or impressionist painting. *But* we lose our tempers quickly when confronted with minor irritations. My friends, *at any rate*, will rage at drivers who block their way, at acquaintances who are late for appointments, or at manufacturers of mechanisms that break down.

PARAGRAPH 3

The fact that "intelligence" is a noun shouldn't delude us into believing that it names some single attribute we can attach a number to, like "height." *In life*, we face a variety of tasks and environments. Intelligence takes many forms: A machinist suggests a new production technique, a family manages in spite of inflation, a hustler helps build a huge conglomerate. *Similarly*, how intelligent a person's behavior is will vary with time. Why should we suppose that these changes are fluctuations from some fixed, basic level? *Most important*, what people of almost any IQ can learn or do depends on what they want to do and on what kind of education and training they are given.

PARAGRAPH 4

All the frontier industrial countries except Russia received massive waves of emigrants from Europe. They *therefore* had a more rapid population growth than their industrializing predecessors had experienced. As frontier countries with great room for expansion, *however*, they were also characterized by considerable internal migration and continuing new opportunities. *As a result* their birth rates remained comparatively high. In the decade from 1950 to 1960, with continued immigration, these countries grew in population at an average rate of 2.13 percent a year, compared with 1.76 percent for the rest of the world.— Kingsley Davis, "Population," *Scientific American*

O 1d   Recurrent Terms   *coh*

Use recurrent or related terms to help hold a paragraph together.

In a well-focused paragraph, the same central term and various synonyms of it may come up several times. Such **recurrent terms** show that the paragraph is focused on a major idea. They help the reader concentrate on a major point or a key issue. In the following excerpt, notice the network of terms that relate to the idea of change:

It is an ominous fact that in the long chain of evolution the latest link, man, has suddenly acquired alchemic powers to *alter* whatever he touches. No other species before has been able to *change* more than a tiny fraction of his habitat. Now there is but a tiny fraction that he has *left unchanged*. A bulldozer *undoes* in an hour the work of a million years. . . .—Paul Brooks, "Canyonlands," *Atlantic*

Notice how many words and phrases in the following paragraph echo the author's central point—the Victorian tendency to *avoid* discussion of sex:

In Victorian times, when the *denial* of sexual impulses, feelings, and drives was the mode and one *would not talk* about sex in polite company, an aura of sanctifying *repulsiveness* surrounded the whole topic. Males and females dealt with each other as though neither possessed sexual organs. William James, that redoubtable crusader who was far ahead of his time on every other topic, treated sex with the *polite aversion* characteristic of the turn of the century. In the whole two volumes of his epoch-making *Principles of Psychology*, only one page is devoted to sex, at the end of which he adds, "These details are a little *unpleasant to discuss*. . . ." But William Blake's warning a century before Victorianism, that "He who desires but acts not, breeds pestilence," was amply demonstrated by the later psychotherapists. Freud, a Victorian who did look at sex, was right in his description of the morass of neurotic symptoms which resulted from *cutting off* so vital a part of the human body and the self.—Rollo May, *Love and Will*

EXERCISES

A. Study each of the following *topic sentences*. What kind of paragraph does it make you expect? How do you think the paragraph would be developed? What is the author's major point or intention? (Your instructor may ask you to write the paragraph that would follow up one or more of these topic sentences.)

1. Good friends of our family, after eighteen years of marriage, are getting a "civilized" divorce.
2. The rate of high school students going on to college has tripled during the last twenty years.
3. The modern "mature" style is for parents to punish a misbehaving child *after* they have cooled off.
4. Customs officials at an airport know how to make the traveler feel like a criminal.
5. When I went through high school, there were too many elective courses with little academic content.
6. The traditional American car has many features that have nothing to do with providing cheap and efficient transportation.
7. A major industry can shape the environment and determine the quality of life of a whole town.
8. The average person encounters many causes of frustration every day.
9. The student who causes trouble at school often has seen little but trouble at home.
10. Violence in movies is getting more realistic.

B. For each of the following paragraphs, state the key idea *in your own words*. Point out the details or examples that support it. Point out any transitional expressions and show how they help move the paragraph forward. Point out any recurrent or related terms.

1. All the evidence indicates that the population upsurge in the underdeveloped countries is not helping them to advance economically. On the contrary, it may well be interfering with their economic growth. A surplus of labor on the farms holds back the mechanization of agriculture. A rapid rise in the number of people to be maintained uses up income that might otherwise be utilized for long-term investment in education, equipment, and other capital needs. To put it in concrete terms, it is difficult to give a child the basic education it needs to become an engineer when it is one of eight children of an illiterate farmer who must support the family with the produce of two acres of ground.—Kingsley Davis, "Population," *Scientific American*

2. My personal Mexican-ness eventually produced serious problems for me. Upon entering grade school I learned English rapidly and rather well, always ranking either first or second in my class; yet the hard core of me remained stubbornly Mexican. This chauvinism may have been a reaction to the constant racial prejudice we encountered on all sides. The neighborhood cops were always running us off the streets and calling us "dirty greasers," and most of our teachers frankly regarded us as totally inferior. I still remember the galling disdain of my sixth-grade teacher, whose constant mimicking of our heavily accented speech drove me to a desperate study of *Webster's Dictionary* in the hope of acquiring a vocabulary

larger than hers. Sadly enough, I succeeded only too well, and for the next few years I spoke the most ridiculous high-flown rhetoric in the Denver public schools. One of my favorite words was "indubitably" and it must have driven everyone mad. I finally got rid of my accent by constantly reciting "Peter Piper picked a peck of pickled peppers" with little round pebbles in my mouth.—Enrique Hank Lopez, "Back to Bachimba," *Horizon*

3. Our democracy would be in trouble without quality public education. Public schools are the driving force behind the high levels of social and economic opportunity in the United States. Fourteen percent of the people in the top leadership positions of our country come from the lowest socioeconomic groups—substantially higher than other countries, where those rates hover around 3 to 4 percent. About 50 percent of working males are in jobs with a higher occupational status than their parents. Researchers have found that the occupational, educational, and income levels of previously low-income white ethnic and Asian minorities (such as Jews, Poles, Irish, Slavs, Italians, Japanese, and Chinese) are now equal to whites of native parentage—a tremendous change over the past decades.—Louis Honig, Jr., "The Case for Public Education," *San Francisco Chronicle*

4. What must be even more surprising is the thinness of coverage right here at home in the center of our national news, Washington. Washington has a very large press corps. The roster of the National Press Club is substantial, and the State Department auditorium is easily filled by a glamour press conference. The trouble is that most of the Washington press corps runs as a herd, concentrating on the "big" story of the day to the neglect of much else. The news services have large staffs, and a few papers priding themselves on their national news maintain bureaus ranging from a half-dozen full-time correspondents to three times that number. But most of the so-called bureaus in Washington are one-reporter affairs. Except for an hour of gossip at the Press Club or at one of the other informal meeting places, and for what a lonesome reporter picks up from the home congressional delegation, and the steady stream of inspired handouts, the average Washington reporter never gets beneath the surface of the day's one obvious story.—Philip M. Wagner, "What Makes a Really Good Newspaper," *Harper's*

5. With a few splendid exceptions, professional reviewers do not really read books. They are in the book *business*. And that makes a big difference. They are so bored and so jaded with the sheer volume of books which pass through their hands that if they manage to respond freshly to one, it's nothing short of a miracle. They tend to regard all books as guilty until proven innocent. But readers are different. They regard each book with optimism. They expect their lives to be changed—and often write to tell me that they were.

C. Choose one of the following statements. Complete it two different ways, each time filling in a *different comparison*. Use each of the two statements as a topic sentence. For each, write the complete paragraph filling in the examples or details that follow through. Choose one:

A college is like _____ .
A big city is like _____ .
A small town is like _____ .

D. Write a *multiple-example* paragraph about a type of person, a type of building, or a type of art. Pack the paragraph with as many different examples of the same basic trait or for the same basic point as you can.

E. Study the following *examples-first* paragraph. Write a similar paragraph about something you have had a chance to observe on the social, political, or educational scene. Build up your examples first and then funnel them into your general point.

Black Africans sweeping the streets of Paris; Algerians and Italians working on the high-speed assembly lines of the vast Renault auto plant; Turkish waiters in the cafes of Hamburg; Portuguese laborers at the construction sites on the outskirts of Geneva; Indians and Pakistanis driving busses through the heart of London—all over Western Europe, millions of immigrants from the poorer southern end of the Continent, from North and Central Africa, from Asia Minor and the Middle East, from South Asia and the Caribbean, are doing the vital but back-breaking work that the native-born are glad to leave them, despite widespread complaints that "the foreigners are coming here to eat our bread and take our jobs. . . ." As it was put by one European economist, "The immigrants increasingly play the role of a basic industrial proletariat in the West European economies, while the native-born citizens comprise the 'new working class' of technicians, managers, and supervisors."—Schofield Coryell, "New Grapes of Wrath," *Ramparts*

F. From a recent theme, select a paragraph that could be improved by use of a clear topic sentence, fuller building up of examples, and the like. Hand in both the "Before" and the "After" version.

O 2   ORGANIZING THE PARAGRAPH

Give your paragraphs an overall pattern the reader can follow.

You can keep your readers moving along if your paragraphs give them a sense of direction. To help you in revising a rambling paragraph, ask yourself: "Could I outline the structure of this paragraph? Does it serve some overall purpose? Is it shaped by some overall strategy?"

O 2a   The All-Purpose Paragraph   *coh*

Organize the typical expository paragraph by going from statement through explanation to illustration.

A topic sentence has its strongest impact if it is brief and to the point. Often, your next step will be to explain and elaborate. You may have to explain some of your key terms; you may have to show how a process works. Then, as a third step, you provide the examples, the illustrations, that support your key point. Sometimes, as an optional fourth step, a writer reinforces the main point by *restating* it in a "clincher sentence" at the end.

Notice how the following paragraphs vary the basic pattern of *statement—explanation—illustration*. (Here and in later examples, words and phrases that help give continuity to the paragraph have been italicized.)

PARAGRAPH 1

Key idea	The deep sea has its *stars,* and perhaps here and there an
Detailed restatement	eerie and transient equivalent of *moonlight,* for the mysterious *phenomenon of luminescence* is displayed by perhaps half of all the fishes that live in dimly lit or darkened waters, and by many
First example	of the lower forms as well. Many fishes carry *luminous torches* that can be turned on or off at will, presumably helping them find
Second example	or pursue their prey. Others have *rows of lights* over their bodies, in patterns that vary from species to species and may be a sort of recognition mark or badge by which the bearer can be known as friend or enemy. The deep-sea squid ejects a spurt of fluid that
Third example	becomes a *luminous cloud,* the counterpart of the "ink" of his shallow-water relative.—Rachel Carson, *The Sea Around Us*

PARAGRAPH 2

Key question	Where do the terms of businesese come from? Most, *of course,* are hand-me-downs from former generations of business people,
Key idea	*but* many are the fruit of cross-fertilization with other jargons. Business people who castigate government bureaucrats, *for example,*
First set of examples	are at the same time apt to be activating, expediting, implementing, effectuating, optimizing, minimizing, and maximizing—and at all levels and echelons within the framework of broad policy
Second set of examples	areas. *Similarly,* though amused by the long-hairs and the social scientists, they are beginning to speak knowingly of projective techniques, social dynamics, depth interviewing, *and* sometime soon, if they keep up at this rate, they will probably appropriate that hall-
Restatement of key idea	mark of the sound sociological paper, "insightful." Businesese, *in fact,* has very nearly become the great common meeting ground of the jargons.—William H. Whyte, "The Language of Business," *Fortune*

PARAGRAPH 3

Key idea	Every time a man unburdens his heart to a stranger he reaffirms the *love* that unites humanity. To be sure, he is unpacking his *heart*

Explanation	with words, but at the same time he is encouraged to expect *interest* and *sympathy,* and he usually gets it. His interlocutor feels unable to impose his own standards on his confidant's behavior; for once he feels *how another man feels.* It is not always sorrow and squalor
Example from personal experience	that is passed on in this way but sometimes joy and pride. I remember a truck driver telling me once about his wife, how sexy and clever and loving she was, and how beautiful. He showed me a photograph of her and I blushed for guilt because I had expected something plastic and I saw a woman by trendy standards plain, fat, and ill-clad. Half the point in reading novels and seeing plays and
More general application	films is to exercise the *faculty of sympathy* with our own kind, so often obliterated in the multifarious controls and compulsions of actual social existence.—Germaine Greer, *The Female Eunuch*

O 2b   Paragraphs with a Special Purpose   *coh*

Make your readers see a clear pattern in paragraphs that serve a special purpose.

Often the organization of a paragraph is determined by its special purpose: to describe a step in a process, to compare two related things, or to choose between alternatives.

Study the way a different overall purpose helps structure each of the following sample paragraphs:

(1) *Tracing a* **process** *in time:*

Beginnings	The orphanage across the street is torn down, a city housing project *begins to rise* in its place, and on the marvelous vacant lot next to the old orphanage they are building a playground. Much
Later developments	excitement and anticipation as *Opening Day draws near.* Mayor LaGuardia himself comes to dedicate this great gesture of public benevolence. He speaks of neighborliness and borrowing cups of sugar, and of the playground he says that children of all races, colors, and creeds will learn to live together in harmony. *A week later,* some of us are swatting flies on the playground's inadequate little ball field. A gang of Negro kids, pretty much our own age, enter from the other side and order us out of the park. We refuse, proudly and indignantly, with superb masculine fervor. There is a fight, they win, and we retreat, half whimpering, half with bravado. My first nauseating experience of cowardice. And my first appalled realization that there are people in the world who do not seem to be afraid of anything, who act as though they have nothing to lose. *Thereafter* the playground becomes a battleground, sometimes quiet, sometimes the scene of athletic competition between Them and Us. But
End result	rocks are thrown as often as baseballs. *Gradually* we abandon the place and use the streets instead. The streets are safer, though we do not admit this to ourselves. We are not, after all, sissies—that most dreaded epithet of an American boyhood.—Norman Podhoretz, *Doings and Undoings*

(2) *Examining* **cause and effect:**

Key idea

Cause
(with specific
examples)

Effect
(with specific
examples)

Europeans with time-honored experience in the technique of painlessly extracting cash from foreigners' pockets have correctly gauged that Americans like to travel abroad provided they don't really have to leave home. *They've seen* the U.S. armed forces and U.S. oil companies spend millions to give their personnel the illusion of living in a European or African suburbia filled with shopping centers, post exchanges, movie houses, ice-cream parlors, juke boxes, and American-style parking lots. *Smart promoters now give* the American abroad exactly what he wants. Hotel rooms are furnished to please him, meal hours drastically advanced to suit the American habit of eating dinner at 6 P.M., arrangements made to satisfy the Americans' affection for crowds, action, and noise.— Joseph Wechsberg, "The American Abroad," *Atlantic*

(3) *Working out a* **comparison or contrast:**

Key idea
(linked to
preceding step in
discussion)

First subtopic
(situation in
Alger's books)

Second subtopic
(contrasting
situation today)

Just as Alger's view of money as something to be made and kept no longer generally operates, [neither] does his view of how it should be given away. There is a great deal of "charity" in Alger, but *it is always man-to-man, even palm-to-palm.* It is a gesture in the tradition of the New Testament, a retail transaction between two individuals, spiritual in essence, monetary in form. The adjective that comes first to mind when we think of it is "Christian." *The adjective that comes first to mind when we think of charity today is "organized."* Via drives, community chests, red feathers, we can give more away more quickly. At the same time the primitive-Christian heart of the process, man-to-man giving, is weakened. Warmheartedness is communized.— Clifton Fadiman, "Party of One," *Holiday*

(4) *Choosing among* **alternatives:**

First alternative
examined and
rejected

Second alternative
presented and
supported

History shows that wars between cities, states, and geographic regions cease once the originally independent units have amalgamated under the leadership of a single government with the power of making and enforcing laws that are binding upon individuals. *One might reason on this basis that* if all of the industrialized and semiindustrialized regions of the world were to federate under a common government, the probability of another war would be greatly decreased. It seems likely that this conclusion would be valid if the resultant federation were as complete as was the federation formed by the original thirteen colonies in America. *On the other hand,* it is extremely unlikely that such a highly centralized federation could come into existence at the present time; nationalistic feelings of individual men and groups of men, and conflicts of economic interests, are too strong to permit rapid transition. *Also,* those nations which have high per capita reserves of resources and high per capita production would be most reluctant to delegate their sovereignties to higher authority and to abandon the economic barriers that now exist.—Harrison Brown, *The Challenge of Man's Future*

O 2c   Paragraphs with a Special Strategy   *coh*

Experiment with strategies that channel the reader's attention.

Like a larger composition, a paragraph can employ strategies designed to capture the readers' attention and hold their interest. Try some of the following:

(1) *Anticipate the questions of the curious reader.* In presenting information, especially, avoid the effect of merely presenting miscellaneous facts. The following paragraph might have been put together to answer questions somewhat in the order an interested reader would ask them:

What evidence?	Comets strew debris behind them in interplanetary space. *Some of it is seen* from the earth as the zodiacal light, which is visible as a glow in the eastern sky before sunrise and in the western sky after sunset. (It is brightest in the tropics.) Much of the zodiacal light near the plane of the earth's orbit is sunlight scattered by fine dust left behind by comets. Under ideal observing
Where else observed?	conditions cometary dust *also appears* as the Gegenschein, or counterglow: a faint luminous patch in the night sky in a direc-
How produced?	tion opposite that of the sun. Comets need to *contribute about 10 tons of dust per second* to the inner solar system in order to maintain this level of illumination. Over a period of several thousand
What becomes of it?	years *the particles are gradually broken down* by collisions with other particles, or are blown away by solar radiation.—Fred L. Whipple, "The Nature of Comets," *Scientific American*

(2) *Make the reader follow you to a desired conclusion.* In dealing with a difficult or controversial subject, you may first want to present details or facts for the reader to think about. Sometimes you may want to "let the facts speak for themselves." At other times, you may want to draw the desired conclusion at the end. Such a paragraph follows **inductive order**. What conclusion did the writer of the following paragraph want his readers to reach? Why didn't he state it bluntly at the beginning?

A very imaginative black comedian named Richard Pryor appeared briefly on national television in his own show. He offended a great many people, and his show was canceled after only a few weeks. But I remember one episode that may emphasize my own group's confusion about its historical experience. This was a satiric takeoff on the popular television movie *Roots*, and Pryor played an African tribal historian who was selling trinkets and impromptu history to black American tourists. One tourist, a middle-class man, approached the tribal historian and said, "I want you to tell me who my great-great-granddaddy was." The African handed him a picture. The black American looked at it and said, "But that's a *white* man!" The tribal historian said, "That's right." Then the tourist said, "Well, I want you to tell me where I'm from." The historian looked hard at him and said, "You're from Cleveland." I think I was trying very hard in my book to say the same thing, but not just to black people.—James Alan McPherson, "On Becoming an American Writer," *Atlantic*

(3) *Arrange material in a climactic order.* Go from the unimportant to the important, from the optional to the essential:

Random impressions   The morning sun was streaming through the crevices of the canvas when the man awoke. A warm glow pervaded the whole atmosphere of the marquee, and a single big blue fly buzzed musically round and round it. Besides the buzz of the fly there was not a sound. He looked about—at the benches—at the table supported by trestles—at his basket of tools—at the stove where the furmity had been boiled—at the empty basins—at some shed grains of wheat—at the corks which dotted the grassy floor. Among the odds and ends he

Crucial detail   discerned a little shining object, and picked it up. *It was his wife's ring.*—Thomas Hardy, *The Mayor of Casterbridge*

EXERCISES

A. How were the following paragraphs put together? Chart the purposes or the strategies that helped shape each paragraph. Point out any major directional signals or clues to the author's intention. Point out anything that makes a paragraph different or unusual.

1. Animals are always realists. They have intelligence in varying degrees— chickens are stupid, elephants are said to be very clever—but, bright or foolish, animals react only to reality. They may be fooled by appearance, by pictures or reflections, but once they know them as such, they promptly lose interest. Distance and darkness and silence are not fearful to them, filled with voices or forms, or invisible presences. Sheep in the pasture do not seem to fear phantom sheep beyond the fence, mice don't look for mouse goblins in the clock, birds do not worship a divine thunderbird.—Susanne K. Langer, "The Prince of Creation," *Fortune*

2. Baseball does not pay its officials nearly as well as basketball does. In basketball, an NBA official with ten years' experience may make perhaps $600 per game, with over eighty games on the schedule. The official would make over $45,000 a season. In baseball, an umpire with ten years in the majors until recently made closer to $200 a game, with a schedule of about 160 games. The umpire's salary would work out to about two-thirds that of the other official. Some of the fringe benefits are hard to compare, such as who gets first-class air fare and the like. Anyway, what is fair in each case is in the eye of the beholder—a judgment call, as it were.

3. I was spending most of my time with a group from an orphanage down the block. I guess the orphan group was no more attractive than any other, but to be an orphan seemed to me desirable and a self-made piece of independence. In any case, the orphans were more interesting to me than my schoolmates, and if they played rougher they complained less. Frances, a dark beauty of my age, queened it over the others because her father had been killed by the Mafia. Miriam, small and wiry, regularly stole my allowance from the red purse my aunt had given me, and the one time I protested she beat me up. Louis Calda was religious and spoke to me about it. Pancho was dark, sad, and to me, a poet because once he said, "Yo te amo."—Lillian Hellman, *An Unfinished Woman*

4. To my mind, Henry James and Edith Wharton are the two great American masters of the novel. Most of our celebrated writers have not been, properly speaking, novelists at all. Hawthorne and Melville wrote romances. Hemingway and Crane and Fitzgerald were essentially short story writers (a literary form which Americans have always excelled at). Mark Twain was a memoirist. William Dean Howells was indeed a true novelist, but as Edith Wharton remarked (they were friendly acquaintances), Howells's "incurable moral timidity . . . again and again checked him on the verge of a masterpiece."—Gore Vidal, "In Praise of Edith Wharton," *Atlantic*

5. There was in those days a great deal of optimism, shared by all levels of the black community. Besides a certain reverence for the benign intentions of the federal government, there was a belief in the idea of progress, nourished, I think now, by the determination of older people not to pass on to the next generation too many stories about racial conflict, their own frustrations and failures. They censored a great deal. It was as if they had made basic and binding agreements with themselves, or with their ancestors, that for the consideration represented by their silence on certain points they expected to receive, from either Providence or a munificent federal government, some future service or remuneration, the form of which would be left to the beneficiaries of their silence. And maybe because they did tell us less than they knew, many of us were less informed than we might have been. On the other hand, because of this same silence many of us remained free enough of the influence of negative stories to take chances, be ridiculous, perhaps even try to form our own positive stories out of whatever our own experiences provided. Though ours was a limited world, it was one rich in possibilities for the future.—James Alan McPherson, "On Becoming an American Writer," *Atlantic*

6. Recent census figures show that 53.7 percent of the college-age children of families with incomes of $15,000 and more were attending college. The proportion went downhill in direct relation to earnings until it reached a low of 12.7 percent for the same age group from poverty-level homes. In the past years, moreover, the percentage of college attendance among youths from lower-middle-class families has declined sharply. If this trend continues, young Americans from the old, established college "class" will increasingly dominate the campuses. Instead of helping to broaden the socioeconomic mix of the nation's leadership, higher education will then revert to its original restrictive function—to give children of inherited wealth an ever larger share of society's controlling positions.

7. Immigration, exile, the tides of the Atlantic, the killing breath of famine, the murderous streets of Belfast had brought our parents to New York. We were to be the children of the second chance, living proof that a man can start over in his life and make something valuable out of that effort. But most of the time that second chance had become warped by some grasping obsession with property. We began

to visit friends who kept china closets filled with dishes that you were supposed to look at and admire but never sully with the fruits of the earth. People bought cars and two-family houses, and the dime-a-week insurance man vanished somewhere, and nobody needed credit at the corner grocery store anymore. The coal stove gave way to steam heat.—Pete Hamill, "Notes on the New Irish," *New York*

B. Study the following student-written paragraphs and describe the way they are organized. Then write your own set of paragraphs using the following starter sentences:

"Advertising is full of _____ ."
"We often forget that there are two kinds of _____ ."
"My classes always possessed at least one _____ ."

1. Advertising is full of indoctrination that helps keep women in their place. Women are to be soft for men, smell good for men, and cook for them and their families. Billboards lining the streets and highways picture faultless figures, clinging panty-hose, and phony makeup: perfect females, each strand of hair faithfully in place, with a roll of paper towels or bottle of dishwashing liquid in their hands. Magazines are filled with ads which imply that females should try to be pleasing for men: "The fragrance which can shake your world . . . and his."

2. We often forget that there are two basic kinds of crime. By taking action against crime, we hope to soothe a basic paranoia of our society. We fear being stolen from, or cheated. Also we fear death or personal injury. These are the crimes involving two parties, a criminal and a victim. But our society also reacts to someone offending against our personal morality. Because of this we have laws against homosexuality, drunkenness, obscene publications, and lately, the usage of narcotics. These crimes involve only one party, the "criminal." We thus have two quite different kinds of criminal behavior: the crimes involving a victim, versus the crimes without victims.

3. My classes always possessed at least one uncompromising conservative with very forceful opinions, so that it created a right-wing atmosphere from which my ears never rested. For example, one girl was a strong-headed Republican, a dedicated Mormon, and was teetering on the edge of John Birchism. She had a great reverence for the flag and her country, but hated certain peoples that existed in her great America—blacks, Mexicans, Jews, and so on. She was a staunch supporter of white supremacy, with the school whitened beyond salvation to her pleasure. Her heroes were men like Richard Nixon and Ronald Reagan, while she detested even hearing the names of people like Martin Luther King.

C. Write a paragraph about one *process* or one major *cause-and-effect relationship* of special concern to people worried about the environment. Trace the process or the relationship involved as clearly as you can. Fill in specific examples or details.

D. Write a paragraph about an episode, an experiment, or a situation, but let the details speak for themselves. Try to make sure the *implied conclusion* emerges strongly from the details or examples without your actually stating it. Then let your fellow students suggest a possible topic sentence for the paragraph. How close do they come to the idea you had in mind?

Part Three
A Reference Handbook

14   Grammar and Usage

15   Punctuation

16   Mechanics and Spelling

17   Glossary of Usage

18   Practical Prose Forms

Grammar and Usage

CHAPTER FOURTEEN

G 1   A Bird's-Eye View of Grammar
    a   Grammatical Devices
    b   Basic Sentence Elements
    c   Modifiers
    d   Joining Clauses
    e   Appositives and Verbals

G 2   Grammar and Usage
    a   Standard and Nonstandard
    b   Formal and Informal

G 3   Agreement
    a   Irregular Plurals
    b   Confusing Singulars and Plurals
    c   Compound Subjects
    d   Blind Agreement
    e   Agreement After *There* and *It*
    f   Agreement After *Who*, *Which*, and *That*
    g   Logical Agreement

G 4   Verb Forms
    a   Irregular Verbs
    b   *Lie*, *Sit*, and *Rise*

G 5   Pronoun Reference
    a   Ambiguous Reference
    b   Reference to Modifiers
    c   Vague *This* and *Which*
    d   Implied Antecedents
    e   Indefinite Antecedents

G 6   Pronoun Case
    a   Subject and Object Forms
    b   *Who* and *Whom*

G 7   Modifiers
    a   Adjectives and Adverbs
    b   Misplaced Modifiers

G 8 Confused Sentences
    a   Omission and Duplication
    b   Mixed Construction
    c   Faulty Predication
    d   Faulty Equation
    e   Faulty Appositives

G 9 Incomplete Constructions
    a   Incomplete Comparison
    b   Contraction of Coordinate Elements

G 10 Consistency
    a   Shifts in Tense
    b   Shifts in Reference
    c   Shifts to the Passive
    d   Faulty Parallelism

Grammar is the system by which words combine into larger units to convey ideas and information. Current textbooks for school and college draw on the contributions of three major approaches to the study of grammar:

(1) *Traditional school grammar* long dominated the teaching of grammar in the schools but today survives mainly in modernized versions. Traditional grammar approached grammatical study through a systematic survey of eight **parts of speech**: noun, pronoun, verb, adjective, adverb, conjunction, preposition, interjection. It relied to some extent on *meaning-based* definitions. The sentence was defined as a "complete thought." The noun was defined as the name of a person, idea, or thing; the verb was defined as expressing action or state of being.

(2) *Structural grammar* stressed the concrete, observable features that make up the signaling system of the language. What turns a jumbled list of words (practice—type—Mary—afternoon) into a sentence like "Mary practices her typing in the afternoon"? One obvious signal is **word order**—the arrangement of words in the sentence. Another type of signal is the use of **inflections**—the -s of *practices*, the -ing of *typing*. A third type of signal is the use of **function words**—*in, the*. Structural grammar aimed at developing the student's sentence sense by the study of the most common **sentence patterns**:

Subject – Verb:	Dogs bark.
Subject – Verb – Object:	Canadians like tea.
Subject – Verb – Indirect Object – Object:	Music gives people pleasure.
Subject – Verb – Object – Object Complement:	Linda called Bert a pest.
Subject – Linking Verb – Noun:	Hubert is a madman.
Subject – Linking Verb – Adjective:	Hubert is mad.
Subject – Verb – Object – Adjective:	Noise drove Hubert mad.

(3) *Transformational grammar* looked beyond the "surface" features investigated by earlier grammars. It tried to formulate the rules by which grammatical structures are generated. The basic procedure of transformational grammar is to identify first the **source sentences** from which more complex structures derive. These would be such simple statement patterns as "Jean eats," "John makes tacos," "The tacos are good." We then look at the **transformations** that change these sentences to statements about the past, or questions, or negative statements, or the like:

John made tacos.
Did Jean eat?
John does not make tacos.
The tacos were made by John.

Additional transformations help us add to one simple statement ("John made tacos") material from another ("The tacos are good"). By adding material from a second source, we produce sentences like the following:

John made *good* tacos.
John made tacos, *which Jean ate*.
Jean eats *when John makes tacos*.

The following chapter does not attempt to provide a complete grammar of the English sentence. It provides a *writer's* grammar, which aims at helping a writer identify the forms and constructions that are appropriate for written English.

G 1   A BIRD'S-EYE VIEW OF GRAMMAR

Grammar is the study of how words work together in a sentence.

Words convey only fragmentary meanings as long as they are loosely strung together. Tourists abroad can make some crude sense to foreigners after picking up some important words. Foreign visitors to the United States can make some headway by taking words from a dictionary. But they will not be speaking English until they can work words into meaningful patterns like the following:

ACTOR	ACTION VERB	TARGET	
The agent	scrutinized	my passport.	

SENDER	ACTION VERB	ADDRESS	MISSIVE
The travel bureau	sent	me	a brochure.

ACTOR	ACTION VERB	TARGET	LABEL
Maurice	called	the trip	a disaster.

G 1a   Grammatical Devices

Study the grammatical devices that help give meaning to a succession of words.

In the typical written sentence, inflections, word order, and function words combine to help the reader select among the possible meanings of words and to work those words into a meaningful sequence:

• **Inflections** are *changes in the form of a word*. Inflections signal the differences in meaning between the sentences in each of the following pairs:

Stops annoy*ed* our passenger.
Stop annoy*ing* our passenger.
The physician stud*ied* burns.
The physician's study burn*ed*.

The endings spelled *s*, *ed*, and *ing* are the inflections most frequently used in English. Some languages, such as Latin and German, rely heavily on inflections. Originally, English was close to German in number and importance of inflected forms. Through the centuries, however, English has shed many of these. Modern English relies mainly on other grammatical devices.

• A second major grammatical device is **word order**. *Different arrangements of words in a sentence produce different meanings*. Compare the sentences in the following pairs:

Craig was looking for *a police officer*.
A police officer was looking for *Craig*.
A *tramp* called *the mayor* a *liar*.
A *liar* called *the mayor* a *tramp*.
He ate *only* the steak.
He ate the *only* steak.

• A third major grammatical device is the use of *words whose main function is to clarify relationships among other words*. Many modern grammarians group these words together as **function words**. Function words account for the differences in meaning in the following pairs:

> George set *a* poor example.
> George set *the* poor *an* example.
> He left his friends the estate.
> He left *with* his friends *for* the estate.

G 1b   Basic Sentence Elements

Study the basic building blocks of the English sentence.

Grammarians assign words to major word classes (or **parts of speech**) according to the functions they perform. The same word may serve different functions, and belong to different word classes, in different sentences. The word *light* performs a different function in each of the following:

> Turn off the *light*.
> Let's *light* a candle.
> She had *light* hair.
> The water was *light* blue.

(1) *The basic model of the English sentence consists of only two major elements.* A complete sentence normally has at least a **subject** and a **predicate**:

SUBJECT	PREDICATE
The boy	reads.
A car	stopped.
Dogs	bark.

The most important part of the subject is usually a **noun**: *car, student, bulldog, college, education*. We use nouns to name or classify things, places, people, animals, concepts. The consumer looking up entries in the Sears catalog, the chemist giving names to new plastics, the advertiser naming new products—all rely on the naming function of the noun.

Here are the most important formal and structural features of nouns:

• They occur in typical noun positions: *"Dogs* bark," "I like *dogs,"* and "for my *dogs."*

• Their appearance is often signaled by noun markers such as *a*, *an*, and *the* (**articles**); *this*, *these*, *that*, and *those* (**demonstrative pronouns**); or *my*, *our*, and *your* (**possessive pronouns**). Modern grammars group these noun markers together as **determiners**.

• They typically add the inflectional *-s* to refer to more than one (**plural**); *boys, dogs, cars, ideas, preparations*. But note irregular plurals like *children* and *oxen* and unmarked plurals like *deer, sheep, offspring*. Some nouns normally occur only in the **singular**: *chaos, courage, rice*.

• They often show noun-forming endings (**suffixes**) like *-acy, -age, -ance, -dom, -ness, -hood*: *literacy, bondage, importance, wisdom, happiness, brotherhood*.

The place of nouns may be taken by noun substitutes, such as the **personal pronouns**:

He	reads.
It	stopped.
They	bark.

See **G 5** for an overview of pronouns.

The predicate, the second major part of a simple sentence, makes a statement about the subject. (Sometimes the predicate asks a question about the subject.) The most important word, or group of words, in the predicate is the **verb**: *reads, stopped, has left, will return, is reprimanded, has been elected*. The verb signals the performance of an action, the occurrence of an event, or the presence of a condition. A noun may *name* an action: *theft, movement, investigation*. A verb refers to present, future, past, or possible performance: *steals, has moved, may investigate*.

Here are the most important formal and structural features of verbs:

• They occur in typical verb positions: "Let's *eat*," "*Eat* your cereal," and "Big fishes *eat* little fishes."

• In the present tense, most verbs add *-s* when *he, she*, or *it* could substitute for the subject (**third-person singular**): "He *eats*," "She *writes*," "It *surprises* me." Many verbs have a separate inflected form for past tense: *eat—ate, sing—sang, ask—asked, investigate—investigated*. Verbs are words that can show a change *in time* by a change in the word itself: *steals* (now), *stole* (then); *lie* (now), *lied* (then).

• Typical verb-forming suffixes are *-ize* and *-en*: organi*ze*, redd*en*, sharp*en*.

• In verb forms consisting of several words, a limited number of **auxiliaries** occur. If there are several auxiliaries, they typically appear in the following order: first, a modal, if any—*will (would), shall (should), can (could), may (might)*; second, a form of *have*, if any *(has, had)*; third, a form of *be (is, am, are, was, were, be, been)*. Here are some of the resulting combinations:

MODAL	HAVE	BE	MAIN VERB
can			happen
	has		arrived
could	have		called
		is	waiting
may		be	canceled
will	have	been	sold
should	have	been	revised

(2) *In several typical sentence patterns, the predicate is completed by one or more complements.* **Complements** (or completers) become essential parts of the basic structure. An action verb may carry its action across to a target or result (**direct object**):

SUBJECT	ACTION VERB	OBJECT
The student	reads	a book.
Dudley	made	sandals.
A storm	had delayed	the plane.

An action verb like *give, send,* or *write* may carry the pattern first to the destination (**indirect object**) and then go on to what was given, or sent (direct object):

SUBJECT	VERB	INDIRECT OBJECT	OBJECT
Hannah	gave	the travelers	directions.
My aunt	will send	us	the money.
The boy	wrote	his parents	a letter.

A verb like *name, elect,* or *call* may carry the pattern first to a direct object and then pin a label on the direct object. (The second completer is then called an **object complement**.)

SUBJECT	VERB	OBJECT	OBJECT COMPLEMENT
Eric	called	his friend	a liar.
The voters	elected	Carter	President.
The mayor	made	Jim	his assistant.

In other sentences, the verb is a **linking verb**, which introduces a description of the subject. A linking verb pins a label on the subject. The label may be a noun:

SUBJECT	LINKING VERB	NOUN
Schnoogle	is	a custodian.
He	may be	your brother.

Or the label may be an adjective:

SUBJECT	LINKING VERB	ADJECTIVE
The price	seemed	reasonable.
The food	tasted	good.

> For more on adjectives, see **G 1c.**

(3) *Several simple transformations rearrange (and sometimes omit or expand) basic sentence elements.* Thus, the **passive** makes the original *object* the subject of a new sentence. The original subject appears after *by* at the end of the pattern, or is omitted altogether. The verb is changed to its passive form, which uses the auxiliary *be* and the past participle (see **G 4**). The resulting pattern reverses the more common actor-action sequence by making the receiver, the target, or the result of the action the subject of the sentence.

SUBJECT	PASSIVE VERB	
The book	was read	(by the student).
A letter	has been sent	(by my friend).

A second transformation changes the verb to the form used in requests or commands (**imperative**) and omits the subject:

VERB	COMPLEMENT
Shut	the door.
Be	my friend.
Keep	quiet.

A third transformation introduces an initial *there* and postpones the subject:

	VERB	SUBJECT
There	is	hope.
There	was	no time.
There	were	few survivors.

G 1c Modifiers

Study the elements we use to flesh out the basic patterns.

The typical sentence contains words, or groups of words, that *develop, restrict, or otherwise modify* the meaning of the basic sentence elements. Such **modifiers** can be roughly divided into two main groups: those that modify nouns (or noun equivalents) and those that modify other parts of a sentence.

(1) All of the modifiers italicized in the following examples modify the noun *dog* and thus belong in the first group:

A *shaggy* dog barred my way.
A *big, yellow* dog was chewing the rug.
A dog *wearing a muzzle* emerged from the door.
A *police* dog tracked me down.
A dog *with droopy eyes* dozed in the sun.

Of these modifiers, the first three (*shaggy, big, yellow*) are true adjectives. An **adjective** occurs in typical adjective positions: "a *reasonable* price," "The price is *reasonable*," "a very *reasonable* price." Most adjectives have distinctive forms for use in comparisons: *small—smaller—smallest; good—better—best; reasonable—more reasonable—most reasonable*. Suffixes that help us derive adjectives from other words are *-ic, -ish, -ive,* and *-ous: basic, foolish, expensive, courageous*. In traditional grammar, however, any modifier that modifies a noun is said to *function* as an adjective.

(2) The second group of modifiers is illustrated in the following sentences:

The bell rang *twice*.
Suddenly the bell rang.
The bell rang *loudly*.
The bell rang *at intervals*.

Twice, suddenly, and *loudly* belong to a class of words called **adverbs**. Many of these show the *-ly* ending. *At intervals* is not formally an adverb, but in traditional grammar it is said to serve an adverbial function.

See **G 7a** for problems with adverb forms.

(3) Combinations introduced by *with, at, on,* and similar words may modify either nouns or other parts of a sentence:

A Bird's-Eye View of Grammar

The girl *from Chicago* disappeared.	(adjective function)
The girl disappeared *from Chicago*.	(adverbial function)

With, *at*, *on*, and *from* are **prepositions**. They tie a noun (or equivalent) to the rest of the sentence. Other common prepositions are *about*, *by*, *during*, *in*, *of*, *through*, *to*, *under*, *until*, and *without*. A preposition plus the noun it introduces is a prepositional phrase.

G 1d   Joining Clauses

Recognize the units that make up the larger combined sentence.

When several subject-predicate groups combine, they need to be distinguished from the sentence as a whole. They are traditionally called **clauses**. The following sentences illustrate different ways of joining one clause to another:

My brother proposed to Elvira;	*however,*	she dislikes him.
My brother proposed to Elvira,	*but*	she dislikes him.
My brother proposed to Elvira,	*though*	she dislikes him.
My brother proposed to Elvira,	*who*	dislikes him.

Know the different kinds of clauses:

(1) **Independent** *clauses are self-sufficient enough to stand by themselves.* They *could* be punctuated as complete separate sentences. They are still considered independent when they are joined to another independent clause by an adverbial connective or by a coordinating connective. **Adverbial connectives** are such words as *however*, *therefore*, *moreover*, *nevertheless*, and *besides*. **Coordinating connectives** (coordinators, for short) are such words as *and*, *but*, and *for*. A complete sentence contains at least one independent clause.

ADVERBIAL:	Congress passed the law; *however,* the president vetoed it.
ADVERBIAL:	I think; *therefore,* I am.
COORDINATOR:	Jim caught the pass, *and* the crowd roared.
COORDINATOR:	We waited in the rain, *but* the bus never came.

See **P 2b** and **P 2c** for punctuation of independent clauses.

(2) **Dependent** *clauses are subordinated to the main clause.* Like a two-wheel trailer, they cannot normally function by themselves. They are joined to the main clause by a subordinating connective or a relative pronoun. **Subordinating connectives** (subordinators) are

words like *if, when, while, as, unless, where, because, though, although*, and *whereas*. **Relative pronouns** are *who (whom, whose)*, *which*, and *that*:

SUBORDINATOR: You get a special discount *if* you buy your ticket now.
SUBORDINATOR: You will be arrested *unless* you pay the fine.

RELATIVE: The tickets had gone to people *who* had signed up early.
RELATIVE: The company shut down the reactor, *which* had been built in 1972.

Dependent clauses can be considered as modifiers. Those introduced by subordinating connectives usually, though not always, serve adverbial functions: "The bell rang *when I started to answer.*" Those introduced by relative pronouns usually serve adjective functions: "The bell *that had startled me* had ceased to ring." A dependent clause alone cannot be a complete sentence:

FRAGMENT: *Although* I've never tried it.
FRAGMENT: *Which* reminds me of another teacher.

Note: The relative pronouns *whom* and *that* are often omitted:

The speaker [*whom*] *we had invited* failed to appear.
The support [*that*] *we received* was inadequate.

See **P 2d** for punctuation of dependent clauses.

---

(3) *A special type of dependent clause, rather than being joined to the main clause, replaces one of its nouns.* Such a clause-within-a-clause is called a **noun clause**. Noun clauses often start with words like *who, what, why, where,* and *how*:

NOUN: *The thief* returned my documents.
NOUN CLAUSE: *Whoever stole my wallet* returned my documents.

NOUN: He was excited by *the news*.
NOUN CLAUSE: He was excited by *what he had heard*.

That, frequently used as a relative pronoun, is also used to introduce a noun clause:

Osbert denied *that he had forged the check*.
That Osbert forged the check has not been proved.

G 1e   Appositives and Verbals

Recognize special sentence resources like appositives and verbals.

We can greatly extend our sentence resources by putting familiar sentence elements to special uses. Many of the words we use do double duty; they serve more than one kind of purpose. For instance, know special uses of nouns and verbs:

(1) *Recognize nouns used as modifiers.* A noun alone often replaces an adjective that modifies another noun: a *group* effort, our new *track* coach, a special *sales* tax. But a noun may also come *after* another noun to modify that noun and bring added information into the sentence. We call such an added noun an **appositive.** The appositive may bring its own determiner (*a, the, our*) along with it, and it may in turn be modifed by other material:

> Her best friend, *a sophomore,* finished second.
> The book was about Margaret Mead, *the world-famous anthropologist.*
> Aunt Minnie, *a vigorous woman of fifty-five,* had come in to help. (Dorothy Canfield Fisher)

See **G 8e** on faulty appositives.

(2) *Know the difference between verbs and verbals.* **Verbals** are parts of verbs or special forms of verbs, but they cannot by themselves be the complete verb of a sentence. For instance, "he *writing*" or "the letter *written*" are not complete sentences. We would have to add an auxiliary to turn each verbal into a complete verb: "He *was writing*"; "The letter *had been written.*"

Two kinds of verbals can take the place of a noun in a sentence. The first of these are the *to* forms, or **infinitives.** The second are the *-ing* forms, called **verbal nouns** (or gerunds) when used instead of a noun. In the following examples, infinitives and verbal nouns serve as subjects or complements, taking the place of nouns:

SUBJECT	VERB	COMPLETER
Speeding	causes	accidents.
He	refused	*to pay.*
Teachers	discourage	*cheating.*

Though used instead of nouns, such verbals do keep important features of verbs. For instance, they are often followed by objects:

Studying *grammar*	inspires	me.
Joan	refused	to pay *her dues.*
Courtesy	forbids	calling *a police officer a cop.*

Two kinds of verbals can take the place of an adjective and serve as a modifier. The first are forms like *burning, falling, hiding* (**present participles**). The second are forms like *burnt, fallen,* and *hidden* (**past participles**).

> The spectators fled the *burning* hall.
> *Fallen* leaves make me feel sad.
> She looked for *hidden* meanings.

Again, such verbals may carry along other material, making up a verbal phrase:

> *Hiding in the cellar,* he heard the officers *searching the house.*
> Nobody had found the papers *hidden in the attic.*

Note: Infinitives have many other uses besides taking the place of nouns. For instance, we use them in combinations like the following:

> We *ought to* go.
> It is *going to* rain.
> Aliens *had to* register.
> I was *about to* call you.

We also use infinitives to modify various other parts of a sentence:

> We were looking for a place *to stay.*
> The truck driver was ready *to leave.*
> The thing *to do* is to stay calm.

See **G 7b** for problems with dangling or misplaced verbals.

EXERCISES

A. In the following sentences, identify the basic elements in each clause. Describe the function and grammatical category of as many other elements as you can. Point out distinctive grammatical features.

1. The water in the bowl was purple, and the goldfish were gulping for air.
2. Throughout the length of the valley, the river's course widens and narrows by turns.

3. In recent years, sport parachuting has enjoyed a small boom.
4. The only means of access was to hack one's way through hundreds of miles of jungle.
5. He painted with the suppleness of an artist who wanted a deep union with nature.
6. Many customs were common to both sides of the Rio Grande when the river became a frontier.
7. Recipes for happiness cannot be exported without being modified.
8. Uncle Alfred complained that outboard motors had driven off the fish.
9. Avoiding traffic police is easy if they ride in specially marked cars.
10. Fritz annoyed the neighbors by blowing the bugle his father had brought back from France.
11. What maintains one vice would bring up two children. (Benjamin Franklin)
12. When you are lost in the woods, remember your Indian lore.

B. Study the following sets of three sentences. The first five sets show different ways basic sentence elements combine to make up a simple English sentence. The last five sets show sentences that combine information from two or more simple statements. In each set, two of the sentences are very similar in their basic structure—in the way they have been put together. The remaining sentence is different. Write the letter for the different sentence after the number of the set.

1. (a) The school board has banned our humor magazine.
   (b) Malnutrition had become a national menace.
   (c) Bromo-Seltzer will cure that headache.
2. (a) The father gave the pair his blessing.
   (b) The Russian authorities denied his wife a passport.
   (c) Her actions kept the voters happy.
3. (a) Corruption was common in high places.
   (b) The apartment was searched by the police.
   (c) His sister looked different without her wig.
4. (a) Leonard lent strangers money.
   (b) The voters elected the actor governor.
   (c) My parents named their child Miranda.
5. (a) Charitable people give generously to charities.
   (b) Please contribute freely to our special fund.
   (c) My father contributed reluctantly to the heart fund.
6. (a) A man who kicks his dog will beat his child.
   (b) You can't tell by the looks of a cat how far it can jump.
   (c) Cars that use much gasoline drain our resources.
7. (a) He can count to twenty after he takes his shoes off.
   (b) If you save one person from hunger, you work a miracle.
   (c) When the cat leaves the house, the mice have a ball.
8. (a) Children love excitement, but they also need stability.
   (b) She had a perfect alibi, which made things easy for her lawyer.
   (c) Sewage pollutes the water, and exhaust fumes poison the air.
9. (a) He had forgotten where he hid the money.
   (b) She owned the car that had stalled in the driveway.
   (c) We had found a mechanic who worked on Sundays.
10. (a) If she is there when I come home from work, I'll call you.
    (b) If you are hungry, we should meet at a place where we can eat.
    (c) When the session ended, they agreed on times when they would meet again.

C. The following *sentence-building* exercise tests your ability to recognize and use a variety of familiar building blocks for the English sentence.

1. Look at the way the italicized words add information to the two sample sentences. Fill in similar modifiers in the blank spaces left in the next two sentences. (The added elements are adjectives and adverbs.)

    EXAMPLES: The *handsome* cowboy *slowly* mounted his *magnificent* horse.

    The *tired* detective *again* questioned the *uncooperative* suspect.

    YOUR TURN: The ————————— gentleman ————————— proposed to the ————————— lady.

    The ————————— traveler ————————— asked the ————————— guide ————————— questions.

2. Look at the way the italicized words add information to the two sample sentences. Fill in similar modifiers in the blank spaces left in the next two sentences. (The added elements are prepositional phrases.)

    EXAMPLES: The girl *in the Cadillac* approached the locked gate *at high speed*.

    At the other end of the swamp, Leroi was wrestling *with a huge alligator*.

    YOUR TURN: The stranger ————————— had hidden the suitcase —————————.

    ————————— the news ————————— had wiped out the fortune —————————.

3. Look at the way the italicized words add information to the two sample sentences. Fill in similar modifiers in the blank spaces left in the next two sentences. (The added elements are appositives.)

    EXAMPLES: Godzilla, *the fire-breathing reptile,* was fighting two giant caterpillars.

    Clark Gable, *an unforgettable screen star,* played in "Gone with the Wind," *a great but controversial movie.*

    YOUR TURN: Marilyn Monroe, —————————, experienced both success and failure in Hollywood, —————————.

    Tarzan, —————————, travels through the forest with Cheetah, —————————.

4. Look at the way the italicized words add information to the two sample sentences. Fill in similar modifiers in the blank spaces left in the next two sentences. (The added elements are verbal phrases.)

    EXAMPLES: The man *holding the gun* had stopped, *taking careful aim at the animal.*

    Fighting the storm, the little boat, *lifted by each wave,* plowed on.

    YOUR TURN: The girls ————————— mobbed the rock star —————————.

_____, the woman _____ waved
to her audience.

D. Study the way the following simple S-V-O sentences have been built up by
a variety of modifiers. Then write three S-V-O sentences of your own—first the
bare-bones version, then a version using a variety of modifiers to help the sentence
carry additional freight.

1. A man introduces the judges.
   A young man wearing a frilly red dinner jacket introduces the judges.
2. A lady presents a rose.
   A young lady with lipstick on her teeth presents a rose to Reeves.
3. A man monitors the questions.
   A young man named Tony, who is considerably more sure of himself than he
   has reason to be, monitors the questions.

E. Write three *pairs* that each consist of two simple source sentences. Then
illustrate different ways of working the material in each pair into a more complicated sentence. Example:

SEPARATE: The guests had departed. Alvin tidied the room.

COMBINED: After the guests had departed, Alvin tidied the room.
                      Alvin tidied the room, for the guests had departed.
                      The guests had departed, so Alvin tidied the room.
                      The guests having departed, Alvin tidied the room.

G 2   GRAMMAR AND USAGE

Use the kind of English that is right for serious writing.

The language that educated adults use in serious conversation
and in writing differs from the language they use when not on their
best behavior. Students learn early that often they should say "is
not" rather than "ain't," "can hardly wait" rather than "can't hardly
wait," and "this kind of car" rather than "these kind of cars." Differences such as these are differences in **usage**. The study of usage
investigates *choices among alternative words, word forms, and constructions*. Effective writers have learned to make the choices that
will prove acceptable to their readers.

G 2a   Standard and Nonstandard   *NS*

Know how to use the kind of English that has social and cul-
tural prestige.

Standard English is the language of education, journalism, and
government. You will use it in your written work except when you

record or deliberately imitate **nonstandard** speech. Nonstandard speakers have often had relatively little formal education. Their jobs may require little reading of instructions or writing of reports. They may have had few dealings with teachers, lawyers, journalists, and other presumably highly literate persons.

Here are some forms and constructions of nonstandard English:

VERB FORMS:	he *don't,* you *was,* I *says; knowed, growed;* I *seen* him
PRONOUN FORMS:	*hisself, theirself; this here* book, *that there* car; *them* boys
CONNECTIVES:	*without* you pay the rent; *on account of* he was sick; *being as* she couldn't come
DOUBLE NEGATIVES:	we *don't* have *no* time; a little rain *never* hurt *no* one

Nonstandard English is the natural speech in many a home and on many a blue-collar job. Standard English is essential to success in school and office. Many of the features of nonstandard speech stand out and seem clearly out of place in writing. It is true that some expressions are on the borderline between nonstandard and standard. Expressions like *off of* and *irregardless,* widely considered nonstandard, are frequently heard in the speech of educated people. In your *writing,* however, a simple principle applies: When in doubt, be safe. Readers who consider you half-educated because you use *irregardless* will seldom give you a chance to prove them wrong.

Note: See the Glossary of Usage for items like the following:

as	*hadn't ought to*
being as	*learn*
couple of	*used to could*
double comparative	*without*
double negative	

G 2b   Formal and Informal   *inf*

Use different kinds of standard English for different occasions.

We use relatively **informal** English in casual conversation, but also in writing designed to sound chatty or familiar. We find relatively **formal** English in books on serious subjects and articles in serious magazines. We hear relatively formal English in lectures, speeches, and discussions.

Here are some features of informal English:

CONTRACTIONS:	*don't, doesn't, isn't, won't, can't; I'm, you've, they're*
CONVERSATIONAL TAGS:	*well, . . . ; why, . . . ; now, . . .*
PRONOUN FORMS:	it's *me,* that's *him; who* did you invite

PRONOUN REFERENCE: everybody took *theirs;* somebody left *their* gloves
INTENSIFIERS: *so* glad, *such* a surprise; *real* miserable, *awful* fast

In *informal* English, our sentences often keep some of the loose, improvised quality of speech. We may start one pattern and then shift to another in midsentence. We may rethink what we are saying while we are saying it. In *formal* English, grammatical relationships in a sentence are carefully and accurately worked out: Predicates logically fit their subjects; modifiers are clearly related to what they modify. The advice given in this chapter is designed to help you write formal English—English appropriate for serious writing but not so extremely formal as to become stilted or affected.

Note: See the Glossary of Usage on the following items:

apt/liable	*like I said*
between/among	*most everybody*
blame on	possessives with verbal nouns
can and *may*	preposition at the end of a sentence
cannot help but	*providing*
couple of	*reason is because*
different than	*shall/will*
due to	split infinitives
each other/one another	*these kind*
get hit	*used to/didn't use to*
it's me	*where at*
less/fewer	*you* with indefinite reference

For a discussion of formal and informal words, see **D 3.**

DIAGNOSTIC TEST

Look at the blank in each of the following sentences. Of the three possible choices that follow the sentence, which would be right for serious written English? Put the letter for the right choice after the number of the sentence.

1. If she had had a chance, she would have _____ to college.
   a. went   b. gone   c. going
2. A new judge took over and _____ him to appear in court.
   a. orders   b. order   c. ordered
3. She went to the bank, but _____ denied her the loan.
   a. it   b. they   c. them
4. In my school, there _____ not enough things to hold my interest.
   a. was   b. were   c. being
5. Many students do not take their education _____.
   a. real serious b. really serious   c. really seriously
6. My best friends are those _____ have a sense of humor.
   a. who   b. which   c. whom

7. When we lost, I was upset because I _____ very hard.
    a. working   b. have worked   c. had worked
8. There was much ill feeling between _____ and his mother.
    a. he   b. him   c. hisself
9. As you enter, the first thing that _____ is a large poster.
    a. is seen   b. you saw   c. you see
10. Average drivers became more aware of how much gas _____
    used.
    a. you   b. they   c. one
11. We read several articles about _____ kind of accident.
    a. this   b. these   c. them
12. Miraculously, last week's explosion _____ no real harm.
    a. done   b. did   c. doing
13. When _____ a bike, thoughtless motorists are a constant menace.
    a. riding   b. you riding   c. you are riding
14. Vacationers were warned to watch out for sharks and _____
    gradually.
    a. should tan   b. to tan   c. tanning
15. Eskimos always _____ and still are hunting whales for food.
    a. have   b. have hunted   c. had
16. The accuracy of her predictions _____ always amazed us.
    a. has   b. have   c. having
17. My aunt and her daughters knew how to take care of _____ .
    a. themself   b. themselves   c. theirselves
18. None of my brothers did _____ in high school.
    a. very well   b. very good   c. real good
19. No growth is a new and strange concept for _____ Americans.
    a. us   b. we   c. ourself
20. The boy and the girl in the front seat _____ hit by flying debris.
    a. being   b. was   c. were

G 3   AGREEMENT

agr

Make the subject and its verb agree in number.

Most nouns and pronouns have one form for one of a kind (**singular**), another form for more than one (**plural**). Often, verbs also offer us two choices: *is/are, was/were, has/have, asks/ask*. When subject and verb are both either singular or plural, they are said to agree in number. To make the verb agree with its subject, we choose the matching form.

SINGULAR	PLURAL
The boy *goes* home.	The boys *go* home.
Love *makes* fools.	Fools *make* love.
My friend *was* pleased.	My friends *were* pleased.

See **G 5e** for agreement of a pronoun with its antecedent.

G 3a   Irregular Plurals

Know which nouns borrowed from other languages preserve irregular plurals.

Most English nouns use the familiar -*s* plural (cars, buildings, trees, books, petitions). But some words borrowed from Greek and Latin have irregular plural forms:

SINGULAR	PLURAL	SINGULAR	PLURAL
crisis	crises	criterion	criteria
thesis	theses	phenomenon	phenomena
analysis	analyses	medium	media
hypothesis	hypotheses	stimulus	stimuli

Note the following:

• "Data" are items of information, and "bacteria" are very small organisms. The singular forms of these two words (*datum* and *bacterium*) are rarely used, with the result that *data* now often occurs as a singular.

• A boy who graduates from college becomes an "alumn*us*," a girl an "alumn*a*." Several male graduates would call themselves "alumn*i*," several female graduates "alumn*ae*."

• The following anglicized plurals are becoming acceptable: "ind*exes*" rather than "ind*ices*," "curriculu*ms*" rather than "curricul*a*," and "formul*as*" rather than "formul*ae*."

G 3b   Confusing Singulars and Plurals

Know how to handle expressions not clearly either singular or plural.

Agreement problems may result when form points one way and meaning the other. Remember:

(1) *Each, neither, either*, and *everyone* (**indefinite pronouns**) may seem to point to more than one person or thing. But they are treated as singulars in formal written English:

SINGULAR: Each of the students *is* going to receive a diploma.
SINGULAR: Either of the plans *sounds* all right.

A number of is treated as a plural if it means "several" or "many":

PLURAL: A number of people *were* standing in the hallway.

(2) Expressions showing quantity may be treated as singulars even when they seem plural in form. They are singular if the sentence is concerned with *the whole amount* rather than with the individual units:

> In those days two dollars *was* much money.
> It is the most imperative social truth of our age that about one-third of the world is rich and two-thirds of the world *is* poor.—C. P. Snow, "On Magnanimity," *Harper's*

(3) Words like *audience, committee, family, group, jury, police,* and *team* are **collective nouns**. We use these as singulars when we are thinking of the group as a whole. We sometimes use them as plurals when we are thinking of the individual members of the group:

SINGULAR: The family *is* a crucial social unit.

PLURAL: The family *were* seated around the dinner table.

(4) Words ending in *-ics* look like plurals but are often singular. Singular are *aeronautics, mathematics, physics,* and similar words that identify a branch of knowledge or field of study:

SINGULAR: Mathematics *is* an indispensable tool of modern science.

Other words ending in *-ics* are singular in some senses and plural in others. We say "Statistics *doesn't* appeal to me" when speaking of the *science* of statistics. We say "Statistics *don't* convince me" when speaking of statistical *data*.

G 3c   Compound Subjects

Check for agreement in clauses that contain more than one subject.

After a **compound subject**, the verb may be plural even if each of the subjects is singular when taken by itself:

> Tom and Sue *don't* smoke.
> Hiking and canoeing are fun.

And actually adds one possible subject to another. *Or* merely gives us a choice between two possible subjects (each of which may be singular). We say "Both his father and his mother *are* to blame" but

"Either his father or his mother *is* to blame."
Note some special difficulties:

(1) *As well as, together with,* and *in addition to* do not add one subject to another. They merely show that what is said about the subject applies *also* to other things or persons:

Aunt Martha, together with her six children, *is* leaving town.

(2) Two nouns joined by *and* may be merely different parts of the *description of a single thing or person*:

Pork and beans *is* one of my favorite dishes.
My closest friend and associate *was* a cocker spaniel.

(3) In some sentences, an *or*, an *either . . . or*, or a *neither . . . nor* gives the reader a *choice between a singular subject and a plural one*. Make the verb of such a sentence agree with the subject closer to it:

Either laziness or excessive social obligations *have kept* him from his work.

G 3d   Blind Agreement

Do not make the verb agree with a word that stands in front of it but is not its subject.

Avoid **blind agreement**. Check especially for *a plural noun* that comes between a singular subject and its verb. Beware of faulty agreement whenever the subject of a sentence is one thing singled out among several, one quality shared by several members of a group, or one action affecting different things or persons:

SINGULAR: Only one of my friends *was* ready in time.
(not "*were* ready")

SINGULAR: The usefulness of these remedies *has been* questioned.
(not "*have been* questioned")

SINGULAR: Understanding the opponent's motives *is* important.
(not "*are* important")

When for some reason *the subject follows the verb*, do not make the verb agree with a stray noun that stands in front of it:

PLURAL: Sleeping in the cradle *were* two rosy-cheeked infants.
(Who was sleeping? The infants *were* sleeping.)

PLURAL: In the very first chapter *occur* several incredible incidents.
(What occurs? Incidents *occur*.)

G 3e   Agreement After *There* and *It*

**Check for agreement in sentences starting with "there is,"
"there are," "it is," and the like.**

After *there*, the verb agrees with the **postponed subject**—with
whatever is "there":

SINGULAR: There *was* much *work* to be done.
PLURAL: There *were* scattered *rumblings* of dissent.

In formal usage, the plural verb is required even when followed
by a compound subject of which each part is singular:

> On the crown of the hill, there *are* a miniature plaza, miniature cathedral, and
> miniature governor's palace.—Arnold J. Toynbee, "The Mayan Mystery," At-
> lantic

Note: It is a pronoun and can function as the subject. After *it*, the
verb is *always* singular:

> It's your last chance.
> It *was* the Joneses.

G 3f   Agreement After *Who*, *Which*, and *That*

**Check for agreement problems caused by relationships among
several clauses.**

Who, which, and *that* often serve as subjects in **adjective
clauses**—that is, dependent clauses that modify a noun or pronoun.
The verb following the *who, which,* or *that* agrees with the *word
being modified*:

SINGULAR: I hate a person who *stares* at me.
PLURAL: I hate people who *stare* at me.

Note: Watch for agreement in combinations like "one of those
who *know*" and "one of those who *believe*." Look at the contrast in
the following pair:

PLURAL: Jean is one of *those girls who go* to college for an education. (Many
              girls *go* to college for an education—and Jean is one of them.)
SINGULAR: Jean is the *only one* of those girls *who goes* to college for an educa-
              tion. (One girl *goes* to college for an education—the others don't.)

G 3g   Logical Agreement

Where meaning requires it, observe agreement in other sentence elements in addition to verbs.

Often, you have to carry through agreement in number from the subject not only to the verb but also to the remainder of the sentence.

ILLOGICAL: Average newspaper *readers* go through their whole *life* knowing a little about everything but nothing well.

REVISED: Average newspaper *readers* go through their whole *lives* knowing a little about everything but nothing well.

ILLOGICAL: My more studious *friends* are wise like *an owl* and always look up to higher things.

REVISED: My more studious *friends* are wise like *owls* and always look up to higher things.

See **G 5e** for agreement of pronoun and antecedent.

See the Glossary of Usage on *these kind*.

EXERCISES

A. In each of the following sentences, solve an agreement problem by changing a single word—usually the verb or first auxiliary. Write the changed form of the word after the number of the sentence.

1. Each of these activities are equally exciting.
2. Much work, skill, and knowledge is involved in assembling a successful exhibit.
3. The description of his appearance and manners hint at his hidden emotions.
4. For these men, the years spent in the armed forces has been a waste of time.
5. My sister and older brother belongs to my mother's church.
6. As one walks farther up the street, the style of the buildings change.
7. The responsibilities of the future lies in our hands.
8. In the display window, there is two old sewing machines and a tailor's dummy dressed in a faded white dress.
9. The deep thinkers among the students attempt to solve all the world's problems by the use of their powerful mind.
10. The weak chemical bonds among oxygen atoms in ozone allows the molecule to break apart.
11. Many crime shows make the viewer feel tough by association and boosts their egos.
12. Youth or good health alone are not enough to assure someone's happiness.

13. There are a daily diet of banal news stories which viewers are expected to be entertained by.
14. The qualifications for a sales representative is much different from those for a manager.
15. That kind of television drama with nonstop action, fast dialogue, and no message bore me to tears.
16. I am not one of those who believes in indiscriminate force to restore law and order.
17. A sharp increase in thefts are occurring on the beaches and in the campgrounds of this area.
18. The general attitude of the people I asked were very evasive.
19. The political science courses one takes in college often shows that the nation's great thinkers were people with human failings.
20. One of the first situations that challenge the reader's stereotypes arise as Elisa is working at a drive-in restaurant.

B. Choose the right forms, paying special attention to common sources of faulty agreement. Put the number of the right form after the number of the sentence.

1. In many of my classes the attitude of the students *(1) was / (2) were* very poor.
2. The benefits that the city has derived from its new industries *(3) is / (4) are* negligible.
3. Cooking, as well as sewing or cleaning, *(5) has / (6) have* always bored me.
4. I was raised in a home where smoking and excessive drinking *(7) was / (8) were* not permitted.
5. Getting along with one's neighbors *(9) is / (10) are* not always easy.
6. The qualities that we look for in a spouse *(11) is / (12) are* determined in part by our family backgrounds.
7. The World's Fair dazzled everyone who *(13) was / (14) were* there.
8. The ability to talk about something other than money and children *(15) is / (16) are* important if a marriage is to last.
9. Colleges have to make provision for students who are below average academically but who nevertheless *(17) wants / (18) want* a college education.
10. Using words like *dichotomy* and *schizophrenia (19) is / (20) are* no sign of superior intelligence.
11. He was one of those hosts who *(21) makes / (22) make* no attempt to entertain the guests.
12. His father felt that five dollars *(23) was / (24) were* more than sufficient as a monthly allowance.
13. According to the judge, neither of the witnesses *(25) was / (26) were* guilty of perjury.
14. We soon realized that our supply of food and fuel *(27) was / (28) were* dangerously low.
15. Weapons like the bow and arrow, the spear, or the knife *(29) was / (30) were* among the first major human inventions.

C. In a college dictionary, look up the plural forms of the following nouns: *antenna, appendix, beau, cactus, cello, cherub, nucleus, oasis, stigma, vertebra.* Check whether the following forms are singular or plural or both: *addenda, agenda, apparatus, candelabra, deer, dice, Saturnalia, series, species, strata.*

G 4 VERB FORMS *v*

Use verb forms appropriate to serious written English.

The most important verb forms are those traditionally grouped together to form the system of tenses. The **tenses** of a verb are *forms that show different relationships of events in time:*

ACTIVE VERBS

	NORMAL	PROGRESSIVE
Present	I ask	I am asking
Past	I asked	I was asking
Future	I shall (will) ask	I shall be asking
Perfect	I have asked	I have been asking
Past Perfect	I had asked	I had been asking
Future Perfect	I shall (will) have asked	I shall have been asking

PASSIVE VERBS

Present	I am asked	I am being asked
Past	I was asked	I was being asked
Future	I shall (will) be asked	————
Perfect	I have been asked	————
Past Perfect	I had been asked	————
Future Perfect	I shall (will) have been asked	————

In studying this chart, note the following points:

(1) Most English verbs, the *regular verbs*, have two basic forms. The first form is the plain form of the verb (*consent, smoke, depart, investigate, organize*). Standing by itself, it can form the **present tense**. This "simple present" may point to something happening now, something done regularly or habitually, or something about to happen in the immediate future:

> We *consent.*
> I *smoke* a pack a day.
> They *depart* tonight.

(2) The plain form can combine with *will* or *shall* in the **future tense:**

> He *will* talk to you later.

(3) The plain form plus *-ing* makes up the present participle. This form is used in the various tenses of the **progressive** construction. The progressive construction normally shows an action or event in progress, still going on:

> We *are considering* your request.
> Her cousin *was painting* the house.

(4) The second basic form of a verb can stand by itself as the **past tense**. It shows that an action took place in the past and came to an end in the past. To form this "simple past," regular verbs add *-ed* or *-d* to the plain form:

> He *consented*.
> We *asked* him.
> They *investigated* him thoroughly.

(5) Regular verbs make the *-ed* form do double duty as a verbal (past participle) combining with the various forms of *have* to make up the **perfect tenses**. The present perfect ("I *have considered* your request") describes something that may have happened in the fairly recent past and that has a bearing on the present. The past perfect ("I *had considered* his request very carefully") describes something that had already happened when *other* events in the past took place.

See **G 10a** for sequence of tenses and shifts in tense.

G 4a   Irregular Verbs

Know the standard forms of irregular verbs.

Irregular verbs often have not two but three basic forms. The simple past is often different from the past participle: *run—ran—run; know—knew—known; go—went—gone*. Pay special attention to verbs whose basic forms are *confusing in spelling or in sound*. Here is a brief list:

PRESENT	PAST	PERFECT
begin	began	have begun
bend	bent	have bent
blow	blew	have blown
break	broke	have broken
bring	brought	have brought
burst	burst	have burst
choose	chose	have chosen

come	came	have come
deal	dealt	have dealt
dig	dug	have dug
do	did	have done
draw	drew	have drawn
drink	drank	have drunk
drive	drove	have driven
eat	ate	have eaten
fall	fell	have fallen
flee	fled	have fled
fly	flew	have flown
freeze	froze	have frozen
go	went	have gone
grow	grew	have grown
know	knew	have known
lead	led	have led
run	ran	have run
see	saw	have seen
send	sent	have sent
sing	sang	have sung
speak	spoke	have spoken
swim	swam	have swum
take	took	have taken
throw	threw	have thrown
wear	wore	have worn
write	wrote	have written

Remember the following points:

(1) The third of the three forms is the one used after *have* (*has, had*). It is also the one used after *be* (*am, was, were*, etc.) in all passive verbs:

PERFECT: She *had* already *written* to the manager.
                 You *should have thrown* it out long ago.

PASSIVE: The bicycle *was stolen* during the night.
                 The bolt *had been worn* out.

(2) Sometimes you have a choice of *two acceptable* forms:

They gracefully *dived* (or *dove*) into the pool.
She *dreamed* (or *dreamt*) of a vacation in the sun.
He *lighted* (or *lit*) his cigarette.
Your prediction *has proved* (or *has proven*) wrong.
The ship *sank* (or *sunk*) within minutes.
Business *thrived* (or *throve*) as never before.
The sleepers *waked* (or *woke*) refreshed.

(3) Sometimes we have two different forms with *different meanings*. For instance, "The picture was *hung*" but "The prisoner *was hanged*." "The sun *shone*" but "I *shined* my shoes."

G 4b *Lie*, *Sit*, and *Rise*

Know the standard forms of lie, sit, and rise.

Some verbs have doubles just different enough to be confusing:

(1) *Lie—lay—lain* shows somebody or something situated somewhere. The same basic forms are used in the combination *lie down*:

PRESENT: On hot days the animals *lie* in the shade.
PAST: A letter *lay* on the floor.
PERFECT: They *have lain down*.

Lay—laid—laid indicates that somebody is placing something somewhere. Use it when you can substitute *place* or *put*:

I wish I *could lay* my hands on him.
The weary travelers *laid down* their burdens.
You *should have laid aside* some money for emergencies.

(2) *Sit—sat—sat* shows that someone is seated. *Sit down* follows the same scheme:

Though he told me that he seldom *sat* while at work, he *has sat* for an hour exactly where he *sat down* when he looked for a place to *sit*.

Set—set—set, one of the few verbs with only one basic form, belongs with *lay* as a possible substitute for *place* or *put*. You, yourself, *sit*, or *sit down;* you *set*, or *set down*, something else:

When you *have set* the alarm, *set* it down by the cot I *set* up.

(3) *Rise—rose—risen* means "get up" or "go up." *Raise— raised—raised* refers to lifting something or *making* it go up:

Since you *rose* this morning, the tax rate *has risen* ten cents.
Though they are always *raising* prices, they have not *raised* the salaries of the employees.

EXERCISES

A. What form of the word in parentheses would be right for the blank space in each of the following sentences? Put the right form after the number of the sentence. (Use a single word each time.)

1. (steal)   Several sticks of dynamite had been _____ from the shed.
2. (throw)   We spotted the swimmer and _____ him a lifeline.
3. (tear)   Someone had _____ open the envelope.
4. (go)   He might have _____ in someone else's car.
5. (choose)   Last year, the party _____ a new leader.
6. (know)   Without the ad, she would not have _____ about the job.
7. (drive)   The car has been _____ too fast and too carelessly.
8. (see)   Several years ago, we _____ a road company production of *Hair*.
9. (break)   Her cabin had been _____ into several times.
10. (grow)   Everything had _____ well in the moist climate.

B. Choose the right verb forms for formal written English. Put the number for the right forms after the number of each sentence.

1. If a teacher *(1) lays / (2) lies* a hand on an unruly student, he or she is likely to be sued by the student's parents.
2. In discussions touching on religious issues, many perplexing questions can be *(3) raised / (4) risen*.
3. After the class *(5) sat / (6) set* down, the teacher wanted to know who had *(7) wrote / (8) written* "The Student's Lament."
4. The picture showed two elderly gentlemen *(9) setting / (10) sitting* at a table and playing chess.
5. While my cousins *(11) swam / (12) swum* in the clear, cold water, I *(13) sat / (14) set* in the canoe watching them.
6. While *(15) setting / (16) sitting* up a new filing system, we must have *(17) mislaid / (18) mislain* your letter.
7. The report has been *(19) laying / (20) lying* on her desk all summer; at least I saw it *(21) lay / (22) lie* there last week.
8. When I *(23) saw / (24) seen* the deserted entrance, I *(25) knew / (26) knowed* that the performance had already *(27) began / (28) begun*.
9. The park department finally *(29) sat up / (30) set up* benches for visitors who might want to *(31) set down / (32) sit down*.
10. Satisfied with the conditions *(33) sat / (34) set* by the negotiators, the rebels *(35) laid down / (36) lay down* their arms.

G 5   PRONOUN REFERENCE   *ref*

To make a pronoun stand for the right noun, place the right pronoun in the right position.

Pronouns often take the place of something mentioned earlier. When you use a pronoun like *he*, *it*, or *this*, it should be clear to your reader who or what *he*, *it*, or *this* is. A pronoun has to refer clearly to its **antecedent**, the thing or person that "went before."

G 5a Ambiguous Reference

Do not let a pronoun point to more than one possible antecedent.

Look at the use of *he* and *him* in the following example: "Jim was friendly to my brother because *he* wanted *him* to be *his* best man." Who was getting married, and who was going to be best man? The sentence is **ambiguous**; it confuses the reader because of an unintended double meaning. You may have to rearrange the material in such a sentence:

AMBIGUOUS: After Mother brought Sue back from the game, we took pictures of her.

CLEAR: We took pictures of *Sue* after Mother brought *her* back from the game.

CLEAR: We took pictures of *Mother* after *she* brought Sue back from the game.

If a *they* follows two plural nouns, you can sometimes avoid ambiguity by *making one of them singular*. (Similarly, one of two singular nouns might be changed into a plural.)

AMBIGUOUS: *Students* like *science teachers* because *they* are realistic and practical.

CLEAR: A *student* usually likes *science teachers* because *they* are realistic and practical.
(*They* can no longer be mistakenly referred to *students*.)

Note: The *farther removed* a pronoun is from its antecedent, the greater the danger of ambiguous reference. Do not make a reader go back through several sentences in a paragraph to check what *he*, *this*, or *they* stands for.

G 5b Reference to Modifiers

Make pronouns refer to one of the basic elements of a sentence rather than to a modifier.

The following sentence would sound absurd: "During the summer, Grandfather worked on a river boat, but in the winter *it* usually froze over." The *it* seems to refer to the boat, but boats do not

KINDS OF PRONOUNS An Overview		
personal pronouns	SUBJECT FORM	OBJECT FORM
	I you he she it we you they	me you him her it us you them
possessive pronouns	FIRST SET	SECOND SET
	my your his her its our your their	mine yours his hers its ours yours theirs
reflexive pronouns (also "intensive" pronouns)	SINGULAR	PLURAL
	myself yourself himself herself itself	ourselves yourselves themselves
demonstrative pronouns ("pointing" pronouns)	SINGULAR	PLURAL
	this that	these those
indefinite pronouns	everybody (everyone), everything somebody (someone), something nobody (no one), nothing anybody (anyone), anything one	
relative pronouns	who (whom, whose) which that	
interrogative pronouns ("question" pronouns)	who (whom, whose) which what	

freeze over. Similarly absurd sentences may result when a pronoun is expected to refer to a possessive:

AMBIGUOUS: I reached for the *horse's* bridle, but *it* ran away. (The bridle seems to be running away.)

CLEAR: The *horse* ran away after I reached for *its* bridle.
(The possessive has been changed to a pronoun, and the noun put where it is needed to prevent confusion.)

Note: Reference to a possessive accounts for the awkwardness of sentences like the following: "In *John Steinbeck's* novel *The Grapes of Wrath*, he describes the plight of the marginal farmer." Better: "In *his* novel... *John Steinbeck* describes ...'"

G 5c   Vague *This* and *Which*

Avoid ambiguity caused by idea reference.

Vague idea reference results when a *this* or *which* refers to the overall idea expressed in the preceding statement:

AMBIGUOUS: I knew that Bob was cheating, but the other students were not aware of *this*.
(Were they unaware of the *cheating*, or of my *knowing* about it?)

A vague *this* can be easily supplemented: "this assumption," "this outrage." A vague *which* is more difficult to improve. You may find it easier to do without it:

AMBIGUOUS: I have received only one letter, *which* frightens me.

CLEAR: Receiving only one letter frightened me.

CLEAR: The letter (the only one I received) frightened me.

G 5d   Implied Antecedents

Eliminate indirect reference.

In informal conversation, we often make a pronoun point to something that we have not actually mentioned. We expect its identity *to be understood*. We say, "In London, *they* have a great deal of fog." *They* means "Londoners" or "the people living in London." In writing, spell out the implied antecedent.

Avoid the orphaned *it* or *they*, which refers to an implied idea in sentences like the following:

AMBIGUOUS: My mother was a musician; therefore, I have also chosen *it* as my profession.
(The *it* stands not for "musician" but for "music.")

REVISED: My mother was a *musician*; therefore, I have also chosen *music* as my profession.

AMBIGUOUS: The prisoner's hands were manacled to a chain around his waist, but *they* were removed at the courtroom door.
(What was removed? The prisoner's hands?)

REVISED: The prisoner's hands were manacled to a chain around his waist, but *the manacles* were removed at the courtroom door.

G 5e Indefinite Antecedents

In formal usage, treat indefinite expressions that are singular in form as singular antecedents.

Informal English often switches to a plural pronoun after expressions that are technically singular:

INFORMAL: *Everybody* I knew was getting more serious about *their* future career.

INFORMAL: *A person* can be successful if *they* set realistic goals for *themselves*.

Handbooks used to require the singular pronoun *he*, or *him*, or *his* in such sentences: "*Everybody* received *his* copy of the test." In recent years, many people have pointed out that *he or she* or *his or her* would usually be more accurate in such situations: "*Everybody* received *his or her* copy of the test." Since the double pronoun can make a sentence awkward, the best solution is often to make the original expression plural in form as well as in meaning:

FORMAL: *All my friends* were getting more serious about *their* future careers.

FORMAL: *People* can be successful if *they* set realistic goals for *themselves*.

Watch for the following:

(1) Look out for the **indefinite pronouns**—*everybody* (*everyone*), *somebody* (*someone*), *nobody* (*no one*), *anybody* (*anyone*), *one*. If you use one of these, treat it consistently as a singular:

RIGHT: *Everybody* on the team did *her* best.

RIGHT: *Nobody* should meddle in affairs that are none of *his* or *her* business.

RIGHT: It was part of the knight's code that *one* must value *his* (or *one's*) honor more than life.

RIGHT: *Someone* had left *her* (or *his*) car parked in the driveway.

(2) Treat as singular expressions like *a person, an individual, the typical student,* or *an average American.* These may seem to refer to more than one person, but they are singular in form:

FAULTY: A *person* can never be too careful about *their* use of language.

REVISED: A *person* can never be too careful about *his or her* use of language.

FAULTY: A *student* is here in college to study, but *they* are usually poorly prepared for this task.

REVISED: A *student* is here in college to study, but *he* (or *she*) is usually poorly prepared for this task.

Note: None started as the equivalent of "no one," but today either singular or plural forms after it are acceptable:

None of the students *has his* (or *her*) books ready [or "*have their* books ready"].

On shifts in pronoun reference, see **G 10b**.

EXERCISES

A. In each of the following sentences, you can solve a problem of pronoun reference by changing one single pronoun. Write the changed pronoun after the number of the sentence.

1. Universities provide many services to the community surrounding it.
2. Each woman has their own reason for getting an education.
3. The bear feeds primarily on roots; to attack livestock, they would have to be desperate.
4. All his clothes looked tailor-made, and it gave him an air of distinction.
5. Women medical students are still a minority, although admission policies are now more favorable toward her.
6. In most cases, given time, the new brother will learn their responsibilities quickly.
7. A girl who follows my advice should find themselves doing well in school.

8. Everyone entered in the men's singles had proved themselves in tough competition.
9. Our society, while asserting the rights of the individual, did not practice what they preached.
10. No one in my father's fraternity had ever forgotten their old friends.

B. Check pronoun reference in the following sentences. Write S for satisfactory or U for unsatisfactory after the number of each sentence. (Be prepared to explain what is wrong with each unsatisfactory sentence and how it could be revised.)

1. Each person runs differently, depending on their body size.
2. Good advice and much practice can help debaters improve their style.
3. The average individual respects the wishes of the group because they hate to be considered odd.
4. My father is extremely intelligent, though he does not always express it in a verbal form.
5. Although most Americans were in support of the Allies, they tried to remain neutral.
6. Our teachers told us we should learn for our future and not for the grades.
7. I feel bad when I'm in a market and they look at me as if I were a criminal.
8. The uniformed guards look very official, but they are employed by a private company.
9. Since Mary's father coaches the basketball team, she tried to attend some of them.
10. We always assumed that someone's religion was his or her own business.
11. People must learn to have faith in themselves.
12. The English taught in elementary school included a weekly spelling test, but they did little to improve my oral use of language.
13. Newspapers give prominence to youths who get into trouble, which pins a bad label on all young people.
14. Average students often need more explanation than they get in class.
15. Everyone wants to be the sole owner of their property.
16. In order for a person to be an individual, he or she must be themself.
17. The book's title sounded interesting, but when I read it I found it boring.
18. Teachers should have longer office hours so they can help their students.
19. In today's world, the sight of a parent spending enough time with their child is rare indeed.
20. When a person leaves home and goes to school, they are on their own.

G 6 PRONOUN CASE   *pr*

Use the right pronoun forms for written English.

Some pronouns have different forms, used depending on the function of the pronoun in the sentence. *I* and *he* are **subject forms**, identifying the person that the predicate says something about. *Me* and *him* are **object forms**, identifying the object of a verb or preposition. Only half-a-dozen pronouns have a separate object form:

I—me; *we—us*; *he—him*; *she—her*; *they—them*; *who—whom*. These differences in form are traditionally called differences in **case**.

SUBJECT	OBJECT	OBJECT OF PREPOSITION
I congratulated	*him.*	
He recommended	*me*	to *them.*
They prejudiced	*her*	against *me.*

A third possible form typically indicates that the object of an action is the same as the performer. *Himself, themselves, myself, ourselves*, and similar forms are **reflexive forms**:

> He cut *himself.*
> They asked *themselves* what had gone wrong.
> We introduced *ourselves* to the interviewer.

They are also used as **intensives**, for emphasis:

> The dean told me so *herself.*
> We should also weigh the testimony of the accused men *themselves.*

G 6a   Subject and Object Forms

Use the right pronoun forms for subject and object.

Formal use of these forms differs from what we commonly hear in informal and nonstandard speech.

(1) Choose the standard form when a pronoun is *one of several subjects or objects*:

SUBJECT: My brother and *I* [not "*me* and my brother"] were reading comic books. (Who was reading? *I* was reading.)

OBJECT: She asked my brother and *me* [not "my brother and *I*"] to dry the dishes. (Whom did she ask? She asked *me*.)

(2) Be careful with *pronoun-noun combinations* like *we girls —us girls* or *we Americans—us Americans*:

SUBJECT: *We* scouts are always eager to help. (*We* are eager.)

OBJECT: He told *us* scouts to keep up the good work. (He told *us*).

(3) Use object forms as required *after prepositions* (with *her*; because of *him*; for *me*). Use the object form for a pronoun that is the second or third object in a prepositional phrase:

OBJECT: This kind of thing can happen to you and *me* [not "to you and *I*"].

OBJECT: I knew there was something between you and *her* [not "between you and *she*"].

(4) Use the right pronoun after *as* and *than*. Often the part of the sentence they start has been shortened. Fill in enough of what is missing to see whether the pronoun would be used as subject or object:

SUBJECT: He is as tall as *I* (am).
           His sister was smarter than *he* (was).

OBJECT: I owe you as much as (I owe) *them*.
           I like her better than (I like) *him*.

(5) In formal usage, use subject forms *after linking verbs*. These introduce not an object of an action but a description of the subject:

The only ones not invited were *she* and a girl with measles.

The need for this use of the subject form seldom arises except after "it is," "it was," "it must be," and so on. (See the Glossary of Usage for *it's me / it is I*.)

Note: Formal English used to avoid the reflexive pronoun as a substitute for the plain subject form or object form:

SAFE: My friend and *I* [not "and *myself*"] were the last ones to leave.

SAFE: I asked both his friend and *him* [not "and *himself*"] to come over after dinner.

G 6b   *Who* and *Whom*

Know how to use *who* and *whom*.

Who and *whom* are easily confused because their function in a sentence is not always obvious. Furthermore, *who* is increasingly replacing *whom* in speech.

SPOKEN: Tell me *who you are thinking of.*

WRITTEN: It is good for the sanity of all of us to have *someone whom we continue to think of* as Mister even though we address him by his given name.—
           Philip M. Wagner, "Mencken Remembered," *The American Scholar*

Observe the following guidelines in your writing:

(1) When *who* or *whom* occurs *at the beginning of a question,*

who asks a question about the subject. *Whom* asks a question about an object:

SUBJECT: *Who* did it? *He* did.
OBJECT: *Whom* did you meet? I met *him*.
OBJECT: To *whom* should I write? To *him*.

In more complicated questions, it may not be obvious whether a *who* asks about a subject or about an object. However, the *he*-or-*him* test will always work:

> *Who* do you think will win? (I think *he* will win.)
> *Whom* did you expect to come? (I expected *him* to come.)

(2) *Who* and *whom* may *introduce dependent clauses*. To apply the *he*-or-*him* test to a dependent clause, separate it from the rest of the sentence:

SUBJECT: Ask her / *who* wrote the letter.
          (*He* wrote the letter.)
SUBJECT: We approached the man / *who* was waiting.
          (*He* was waiting.)
SUBJECT: Here is a nickel for / *whoever* gets there first.
          (*He* gets there first.)
OBJECT: *Whom* we should invite / is a difficult question.
          (We should invite *him*.)
OBJECT: She knew my brother, / *whom* I rarely see.
          (I rarely see *him*.)
OBJECT: He knew few people / on *whom* he could rely.
          (He could rely on *them*.)

> See the Glossary of Usage for *who, which,* and *that.*

EXERCISES

A. Which of the italicized pronoun forms are right for written English? Which are inappropriate?

1. A teacher should not be condescending just because *he* knows more than *us* students.
2. Jack constantly enriched the conversation of my friends and *I* with brilliant comments.
3. People *who* are asked to "play *themselves*" in a movie often find that a good actor can portray their type more effectively than *them*.

4. My brother and *I* had no respect for the people with *whom* we worked, and soon we had no respect for *ourselves*.
5. I am tired of the rumors about a rift between the board and *I*.
6. People *whom* I had not seen for months or *whom* I knew very slightly telephoned to advise *me* to get off the newly formed committee.
7. People *who* cannot suffer can never grow up, can never discover *who* they are. (James Baldwin)
8. Grandmother disapproved of John, *who she* felt lacked some of the qualities of a gentleman.
9. Every reader occasionally encounters a fictional character with *whom* he can immediately identify.
10. Giles would argue for hours with *whoever* was willing to listen to *him*.

B. In each of the following sentences, change one pronoun to the form that is right for written English. Write the changed form after the number of the sentence.

1. After dinner, us children would go to the first floor to play, explore, and talk.
2. When my mother punished my sister and I, she always suffered more than we did.
3. My cousin, who I had not seen for several years, worked there and knew how to get things done.
4. My sister is better than me at learning foreign languages.
5. I stopped at Jane's house because I had some letters for she and her mother.
6. I recognize the man's face; it was him who started the riot.
7. Every year, my parents take my sister and I on a camping trip.
8. This information should remain strictly between you and I.
9. The new ruler surrounded himself with subordinates on who he could rely.
10. Visitors from outer space might smile at the technology that us Earthlings possess.

G 7 MODIFIERS

Check the form and position of modifiers.

Modifiers help us build up bare-bones sentences. Modifiers range all the way from single words to long prepositional or verbal phrases:

ADJECTIVES:	The *dutiful* son married the *wealthy* girl.
ADVERBS:	Jean will *probably* leave *early*.
PREP. PHRASE:	A woman *in overalls* was standing *on a ladder*.
VERBAL PHRASE:	The man *waiting in the dark doorway* was an old friend.

G 7a Adjectives and Adverbs   *adv*

In formal English, use the distinctive adverb form.

Adjectives modify nouns. They tell us which one or what kind:

the *dutiful* son, a *difficult* exam, an *easy* answer, the *angry* driver. After a linking verb an adjective points back to the subject; it pins a label on the subject:

ADJECTIVE: These bottles are *empty*. (*empty* bottles)
The speaker seemed *nervous*. (a *nervous* speaker)
The rains have been *heavy*. (*heavy* rains)

The most common linking verb is *be* (*am, is, are, was, were, has been,* and so on). Here are some other verbs that may function as linking verbs and may then be followed by adjectives:

Genevieve *turned* pale.
The heat *grew* oppressive.
He *became* rich overnight.
Your fears *will prove* silly.
The accused *remained* silent.

Honeysuckle *smells* sweet.
The soup *tasted* flat.
His hands *felt* moist.
Sirens *sound* scary.
Your friend *looks* ill.

Adverbs modify verbs. They tell us where, when, and how something is done:

WHERE?   We ate *outside*.
The guests went *upstairs*.

WHEN?   The bus will leave *soon*.
Your brother called *yesterday*.

HOW?   The engine ran *smoothly*.
She answered *reluctantly*.
We lifted the lid *cautiously*.

Remember:

(1) *Whenever you have a choice, use the distinctive adverb form to modify a verb.* Very often, we can turn an adjective into an adverb by adding the *-ly* ending: *bright—brightly, cheerful—cheerfully, considerable—considerably, frequent—frequently, happy—happily, rapid—rapidly, rare—rarely, single—singly.* Use the distinctive adverb form to tell the reader how something was done, or how something happened:

ADVERB: The inspectors examined every part *carefully*.

ADVERB: We have changed the original design *considerably*.

ADVERB: No one took the new policy *seriously*.

Note: Some adverbs, such as *fast, much, thus,* and *well,* have no distinctive ending. Some words ending in *-ly* are not adverbs but adjectives: a *friendly* talk, a *lonely* life, a *leisurely* drive.

(2) *Make sure to use* well *and* badly *as adverbs instead of* good *and* bad. *Good* and *bad* used as adverbs are commonly heard in informal speech but are widely considered nonstandard. In formal English, "I don't hear so good" would be "I don't hear *well*." "I write pretty bad" would be "I write *badly*."

OBJECTIONABLE: This morning, the motor was running *good*.

FORMAL: This morning, the motor was running *well*.

The adverb *well*, however, may do double duty as an adjective, in the sense of "healthy," "not ill": "He looks *well*"; "I don't feel *well*."

(3) *Avoid informal adverbs like* slow, quick, *and* loud. Formal usage prefers "talks *loudly*" to "talks loud," "go *slowly*" to "go slow," or "come *quickly*" to "come quick," though both the long form and the short form of these adverbs have long been standard English.

(4) *Use adverbs to modify other modifiers.* In formal usage, use the adverb form to modify either an adjective or another adverb. In the phrase "our *usually* polite waiter," *usually* is an adverb modifying the adjective *polite*.

ADVERB+ADJECTIVE: a surprising*ly* beautiful bird
                            a hopeless*ly* retarded student
                            an impressive*ly* versatile actor

ADVERB+ADVERB: You sang admirab*ly* well.
                            He answered surprising*ly* fast.
                            She worked incredib*ly* hard.

(5) *Avoid informal expressions like* real scared, awful expensive, *and* pretty good. Many everyday expressions use adjective forms instead of adverb forms as informal **intensifiers**: "He speaks *awful* fast." "Dean Howard is *real* popular." "I am *dreadful* sorry." Substitute a formal intensifier like *really*, *very*, *fairly*, or *extremely*:

FORMAL: Dean Howard is *extremely* popular.

FORMAL: The city hall is *fairly* old.

G 7b   Misplaced Modifiers

$\mathcal{MM}, \mathcal{DM}$

Place modifiers so that they point clearly to what they modify.

Notice the changes in meaning that result from changes in the position of modifiers:

ADVERB: The car *almost* broke down on every trip we took.
               (It never quite did.)
               The car broke down on *almost* every trip we took.
               (It did frequently.)

PREP. PHRASE: The man *with the ax* opened the door.
               The man opened the door *with the ax.*

VERBAL: Jerry married a wealthy woman *yearning for high social status.*
               Yearning for high social status, Jerry married a wealthy woman.

Watch out for the following:

(1) Misplaced modifiers *seem to point to the wrong part of the sentence.* Usually you can simply shift the modifier to a more appropriate position, though you may sometimes have to recast the sentence as a whole:

MISPLACED: I looked at the tree I had felled *with my hands in my pockets.*
               (It is hard to fell trees with your hands in your pockets.)
REVISED: *With my hands in my pockets,* I looked at the tree I had felled.

MISPLACED: *Being made of stone,* the builder expected the house to stand for a century.
               (They called him Old Stoneface, no doubt.)
REVISED: Since *the house* was made of stone, the builder expected it to stand for a century.

(2) A dangling modifier *is left dangling—what it points to is not part of the sentence.* A dangling modifier is usually a verbal—a *to* form (infinitive) or *-ing* form (participle). Revise by bringing back into the sentence what the verbal is supposed to modify:

DANGLING: *To do well in college,* good grades are essential.
REVISED: To do well in college, a *student* needs good grades.

DANGLING: Often, *after convincing a girl to finish school,* she finds few openings in the field of her choice.
REVISED: Often, after *her friends* have convinced her to finish school, a girl finds few openings in the field of her choice.

(3) *A* **squinting modifier** *seems to point two ways at once:*

SQUINTING: I feel *subconsciously* Hamlet wanted to die.
             (Are you talking about *your* subconscious feelings—or Hamlet's?)
REVISED: I feel that Hamlet *subconsciously* wanted to die.

Note: Some verbal phrases are not intended to modify any one part of the main sentence. These are called **absolute constructions**. The most common ones are the many generally acceptable expressions that *clarify the attitude or intention of the speaker*:

Generally speaking, traffic is getting worse rather than better.
They had numerous children—seven, *to be exact.*
Considering the location, the house is not a bad bargain.

Formal English, more frequently than informal English, uses verbals that *carry their own subjects along with them*:

The air being warm, we left our coats in the car.
Escape being impossible, we prepared for the worst.

EXERCISES

A. Check form and position of modifiers in each of the following sentences. After the number of the sentence, write *S* for satisfactory or *U* for unsatisfactory. (Be prepared to explain how you would revise unsatisfactory sentences.)

1. The counselor tried hard to treat everyone fair and equal.
2. He was hit by a rotten egg walking back to the dorm.
3. Brushing the aides aside, the reporter insisted on the promised interview with the senator.
4. All the girls performed admirably, but Judy did exceptionally well.
5. No matter what dish George prepared, it tasted flat.
6. Having walked for four hours, the car looked wonderful.
7. Whenever my parents fight, they try to talk quiet but usually fail.
8. The children were becoming less cautious and more brave on their bicycles.
9. The pay was good, but the food was awful bad.
10. To play tennis properly, the racket must be held firmly.
11. The survey was as complete as the time allowed.
12. When cooking Chinese food, the vegetables have to be very fresh and crisp.
13. We opened the door very cautious and looked around.
14. Being forever late to meetings, the committee had finished its business before I arrived.
15. Such magazines as *Argosy, Adventure,* and *True* have on their covers brightly colored pictures of men fighting wars or hunting in wild country.

B. In each of the following sentences, one word should be changed to the distinctive adverb form. Write the changed word after the number of the sentence.

1. When the witness began to talk, she spoke nervously and very defensive.
2. He was tired and unable to think logical.
3. I read the questions as careful as the time allowed.
4. Toward the end of the story, the events unfold very sudden as they sometimes do in real life.
5. My father regarded life more serious than most people do.
6. Macbeth interpreted the prophecies of the weird sisters very literal.
7. During the time Judy spent in France, her French improved considerable.
8. I had to talk fast and furious before the householder could slam the door in my face.
9. An experienced cryptographer can decipher a simple code very easy.
10. My father didn't do very good in school because he had to work on my grandfather's farm.

C. Rewrite each of the following sentences to eliminate unsatisfactory position of modifiers.

1. Having run for an hour, the food tasted great.
2. The car was towed away by John, having exploded on Interstate 59.
3. Unsure of my future, the army was waiting for me.
4. After ringing for fifteen minutes, the president's secretary answered the phone.
5. Several reporters sat with coffee cups discussing the day's events.
6. After graduating from high school, my parents asked me what I planned to do.
7. When traveling during the night without sufficient lighting, other motorists will have difficulty seeing the vehicle.
8. These magazines appeal to immature readers with stories about torrid love affairs.
9. Sometimes a student studies only so that she can prove in class the professor is wrong just to be showing off.
10. I just wrote to my family for the first time since I came here on the back of a postcard.

G 8   CONFUSED SENTENCES   *st*

Avoid garbled sentences resulting from hasty writing, inaccurate copying, or careless typing.

Revise confusing sentences. Even when the reader can make out the intended meaning, he or she will be annoyed at being temporarily misled or tripped up.

G 8a   Omission and Duplication

Check your sentences for omitted or duplicated elements.

Make sure you have written each sentence in full. Do not leave out minor sentence elements like *a, the, has, be,* or *am.* Make sure you have not awkwardly repeated minor elements, especially connectives like *that* or *when*:

> I think *that* because he is ill (*that*) he will not come.
> When school starts in the fall (*that is when*) most parents sigh with relief.

Many hastily written sentences lack some essential part:

HASTY: After my sister moved to Ohio, her little girl contracted polio, but did not cause paralysis.
(It was not *the girl* that didn't cause paralysis, but the disease.)

REVISED: After my sister moved to Ohio, her little girl contracted polio, but fortunately *the disease* did not cause paralysis.

G 8b   Mixed Construction

Do not confuse different ways of expressing the same idea.

The experienced writer will try out various possible constructions and select the one that seems to fit best. The inexperienced writer may plunge ahead, confusing the various possibilities. The result is known as **mixed construction**:

MIXED: In case of emergency should be reported to the head office.

CONSISTENT: *In case of emergency, report* to the head office.

CONSISTENT: *Emergencies should be reported* to the head office.

MIXED: The department manager *rejected him to be* one of her assistants.

CONSISTENT: The department manager *rejected his application.*

CONSISTENT: The department manager *did not want him to be* one of her assistants.

Note: In informal English, an adverbial clause starting with *because* sometimes appears as the subject of a verb. Formal English requires a noun clause starting with *that*:

MIXED: The course was canceled *because of* not enough students registered.

CONSISTENT: The course was canceled *because not enough students registered.*

CONSISTENT: The course was canceled *because of insufficient enrollment.*

MIXED: *Because people enjoy watching a light comedy* does not mean that our society is in a state of decay.

CONSISTENT: *That people enjoy watching a light comedy* does not mean that our society is in a state of decay.

G 8c Faulty Predication

Make sure that what the predicate says can logically apply to the subject.

Suppose you say, *"The choice* of our new home *was selected* by my mother." What was actually selected? Not a choice, but a home.

LOGICAL: The choice *was made* by my mother.
LOGICAL: *The home* was selected by my mother.
FAULTY: At the beginning of the year, *the participation* in club activities is always *overcrowded.*
           (The meetings—not the participation—are overcrowded, though the fact that many people participate is the reason for the overcrowding.)
LOGICAL: At the beginning of the year, *our club meetings* are always overcrowded.

G 8d Faulty Equation

Use a linking verb to equate two things that are logically equal.

In informal English, such equations are often loose and illogical. "His job *is* a mail carrier" is illogical because a mail carrier is a person, not a job. Formal English would require *"He* is a mail carrier" or "His job is *that of* a mail carrier."

FAULTY: A *student* going to college to become educated is as valid a reason as going to college to become a dentist or a lawyer.
           (A student is a reason?)
REVISED: A *student's* going to college . . .
           (Going to college to become educated is a reason.)

A common type of faulty equation makes a linking verb introduce an **adverbial clause.** Children, for instance, will say, "A zoo is *when you go to look at animals."* "When you go to look at animals" is not logically a description of a zoo; normally it would indicate *when* an action takes place or a condition occurs.

FAULTY: Punishment is *when you are told to stand in the corner.*
SATISFACTORY: When you are told to stand in the corner, you are being punished.
SATISFACTORY: Punishment is a means of keeping children out of mischief.

Linking verbs often cause faulty equation when they introduce **prepositional phrases** that would normally show the circumstances of an action. Use an infinitive (or similar noun equivalent) instead:

Our only hope *is to convince* your parents [not *"is by convincing* your parents"].

Their method of selection *was to question* the candidates carefully [not *"was by questioning* the candidates"].

G 8e   Faulty Appositives

Make sure that your appositives can be equated with the nouns they modify.

An **appositive** is a noun placed next to another noun: "John, *a sophomore*, came to see me." Here, John and the sophomore are identical. However, it does not make sense to say, "There was only *one telephone call*, *a friend* of yours." A friend can *make* a telephone call, but we would not say that he *is* one.

FAULTY: We have only one *vacancy*, *a mathematics teacher*.
           (A teacher is not a vacancy, and a vacancy is not a teacher.)

REVISED: We have only one *vacancy*, a *position* for a mathematics teacher.
           (What is actually vacant is a *position* for a teacher.)

EXERCISES

A. Check the following sentences for examples of hasty writing, mixed construction, faulty predication, and faulty appositives. Label each sentence S (satisfactory) or U (unsatisfactory). Be prepared to explain how you would revise unsatisfactory sentences.

1. In an era of dwindling resources, we will all have to give up conveniences to which we are used to.
2. Divorce is the official, legal termination of a marriage.
3. Parents view sex as sacred and should be reserved for marriage alone.
4. By cutting the number of jurors in half greatly reduces the time used in selecting a jury.
5. He was watched by the owner, a little man who peeped over the counter with a wrinkled face.
6. Committing suicide in the story pointed out that the weak cannot survive in this world.
7. Scientists know how to distill drinking water from salt water, but the cost of such a project is too unprofitable.
8. One good example of romantic love triumphing against odds is when there is an interracial marriage.
9. I saw him eat three hot dogs and drank three cokes.
10. I suddenly realized that we were no longer on level ground and that the road was tilting upward on great concrete stilts.
11. In my experience, the older a man is, the more chivalrous and the more gallantry he possesses.
12. Nowadays, the idea of love is begun at a very tender age.

13. One major reason for increased job opportunities for women is the threat of successful law suits against companies that discriminate.
14. Because little of the pledged money actually came in, the repertory company had to give up its experiment.
15. My father first met his business partner in the army, for whom he drove a jeep and was his immediate supervisor.

   B. Revise each of the following confused sentences.

1. Usually, it takes a minimum of effort and concentration to watch TV than it does to read a book.
2. She tried to promote peace among each individual.
3. The individual pieces of this complex problem makes it nearly impossible for anyone to find the solution.
4. Our government, both state and federal, are bound by the Constitution to educate the citizenry.
5. Typical playground equipment fails to keep in mind the needs of children.
6. A woman is more likely to understand another woman's feeling better than a man.
7. The players up for the team were about even in ability and was a hard decision to make.
8. A person who fails in various things might give him an inferior feeling.
9. Radical opinions are too biased and will not accept realistic compromise.
10. Assimilation is when we try to make everyone as similar as possible.

G 9   INCOMPLETE CONSTRUCTIONS   *st*

In formal English, spell out relationships merely implied in various informal constructions.

In written English, we avoid shortcuts common in informal speech. Check constructions like the following for logical completeness.

G 9a   Incomplete Comparison

Complete incomplete comparisons.

Normally, *more*, *better*, and *whiter*, the **comparative forms**, establish a comparison between at least two elements:

> Carpenters make more money than *teachers*.
> Half a *loaf* is better than a *slice*.

Most, *best*, and *whitest*, the **superlative forms**, establish a comparison within a group of at least three elements:

The annual classic at Le Mans is the most dangerous *automobile race in Europe*.

In formal English, observe the following guidelines:

(1) *Spell out what is being compared with what.* Watch for incomplete comparisons resulting from the use of *more* and *the most* as intensifiers: "That girl has *more* luck" (than who or than what?). "I had *the most* wonderful experience" (of the day? of the year? of a lifetime?). "I saw *the most* exciting play" (the most exciting play of the season? the most exciting play ever produced?).

(2) *Compare things that are really comparable.* Revise sentences like the following: "The *fur* was as soft as a *kitten*." Actually, the *fur* was as soft as a *kitten's* (fur), or as soft as *that* of a kitten. Check for logical balance in sentences like the following:

ILLOGICAL: *Her personality* was unlike *most other girls* I have known in the past.

LOGICAL: *Her personality* was unlike *that* of most other girls I have known.

ILLOGICAL: The *teachings* of Horatio Alger reached a wider audience than *Whitman.*

LOGICAL: The *teachings* of Horatio Alger reached a wider audience *than those* of Whitman.—Saul Bellow, "The Writer as Moralist," *Atlantic*

(3) *Clarify three-cornered comparisons.* Some comparisons mention *three* comparable items without making it clear which two are being compared:

CONFUSING: We distrusted the *oil companies* more than the *Arabs.*

CLEAR: We distrusted the oil companies more than *we did* the Arabs.

CLEAR: We distrusted the oil companies more than the Arabs *did.*

See the Glossary of Usage for informal *so* and *such*.

G 9b   Contraction of Coordinate Elements

In telescoping coordinate elements, omit only identical items.

When several items of the same kind are coordinated by a connective like *and* or *but*, we often leave out forms that would cause unnecessary duplication. When we leave out too much, we may cause truncated sentences. Check for excessive omission in the following situations:

(1) *Check for completeness when one of several verbs in a sentence appears in a shortened form.* Fill in the complete forms first and omit only identical items. In "It *can be done* and *will be done*," the *be done* after *can* is identical with that after *will*. You can therefore omit it and say: "It *can* and *will be done*." But avoid "It *can* and *has been done*." The complete forms are *can be done* and *has been done*.

INCOMPLETE: The patient *was given* an injection and the instruments *made* ready.

COMPLETE: The patient *was given* an injection, and the instruments *were made* ready.

(2) *Check for unsatisfactory telescoping in double-barreled comparisons.* These are comparisons of the *as-good-if-not-better* type: "My theme is as good if not better than yours." The complete forms would be *as good as* and *better than*. Formal English would require "My theme is as good *as*, if not better *than*, yours." Less awkward and equally acceptable is shifting the second part of the comparison to the end of the sentence:

My theme is as good as yours, *if not better.*

(3) *Check several linked prepositional phrases.* Keep prepositions that are not identical but merely express a similar relationship:

SATISFACTORY: I have great *admiration and respect* for him.
                 (Taken up separately, the two prepositions would prove identical: "admiration *for* him" and "respect *for* him.")

UNSATISFACTORY: I have great *respect and faith* in her.
                 (Taken up separately, the two phrases would require different prepositions: "respect *for* her" and "faith *in* her.")

Notice the use of different prepositions in the following examples:

She was jealous *of* but fascinated *by* her rival.
His behavior during the trial adds *to* rather than detracts *from* my admiration for him.

EXERCISES

A. Check the following sentences for incomplete constructions. Label each sentence *S* (satisfactory) or *U* (unsatisfactory). Be prepared to explain how you would revise unsatisfactory sentences.

1. In much of Europe, American films are more popular than any other country.
2. Children on the whole understand other children better than adults.

3. The light at the intersection of Sixth and Grove will turn green exactly six seconds after the intersection of Wright and Grove.
4. Our present prison system does neither prevent nor deter people from returning to crime.
5. Children seem to like the so-called adult Westerns as much as adults do.
6. Unlike America, traveling abroad is a rare luxury in many foreign countries.
7. Marsha never has and never will succeed in making her restaurant something more than a place to eat food.
8. The United States has more television sets to the square mile than any other country in the world.
9. Year after year, American colleges produce more physical education teachers than mathematics.
10. The secretary of state usually attracts more criticism than any member of the President's cabinet.
11. Critics of our schools must realize that they can and are doing great harm by indiscriminate attacks.
12. Unlike a track coach, history teachers seldom have newspaper articles written about them when their students do exceptional work.
13. Most young children learn a second language more readily than an older person does.
14. The impact of American books, magazines, and comics in Great Britain is much greater than British publications in the United States.
15. A good background in the liberal arts is excellent preparation for such practical professions as engineers and lawyers.

B. Make each of the following sentences more complete by rewriting the italicized part. Write the rewritten part after the number of the sentence.

1. People today use more resources and live longer *than the previous century.*
2. *Juries have always and will always be swayed* by the eloquence of a lawyer.
3. An older person's need for love is *as big as a child.*
4. Taxpayers are already *familiar and hostile to the usual explanations.*
5. The population of China is already *bigger than any country.*
6. *The club had in the past and was still barring* certain kinds of people from membership.
7. I thought the Sears Building in Chicago was *as tall or taller than any building in New York City.*
8. People in show business *seem to have more bad luck.*
9. The statistics for rape are much less complete *than robberies or similar crimes.*
10. Few of my friends were *preoccupied or even interested in making a living.*

G 10 CONSISTENCY

Do not confuse your readers by shifts in tense, reference, or grammatical perspective.

The need for consistency makes a writer guard against confusing shifts in perspective. Like a road full of unexpected twists and turns, sentences that lack consistency slow down and confuse the reader.

G 10a   Shifts in Tense   *sf*

Be consistent in your use of verb forms that show the relationship of events in time.

Verbs are words that have a built-in reference to time: We *agree*
(now). We *agreed* (then). The forms that show time relationships are
called **tense** forms.

> For an overview of verb tenses, see **G 4**.

Watch out for confusing shifts in time:

(1) *Avoid shifting from past to present.* Do not switch to the present when something becomes so real that it seems to be happening
in front of you:

SHIFT: We *disembarked* at noon and fought our way through the jungle in the
sultry afternoon heat. Suddenly, there *is* a tiger! I *aim* my rifle and *pull* the
trigger! Nothing *happens*—the gun *wasn't* loaded.

Tell the whole story as though it were happening now: "We *disem-
bark* . . . *fight* our way . . . one of them *saves* me." Or, describe *everything* in the past.

(2) *Avoid shifts in perspective when two events happen at different
times or during different periods.* Look at the time sequence in the
following: "When I *saw* the *F* on my report card, I *was* terribly disappointed, because I *studied* very hard." If studying hard was a matter of past history by the time the student received his grade, the
sequence of tenses would be more accurate like this:

CONSISTENT: I *was* disappointed, because I *had studied* very hard.

Formed with *have* or *has*, the **present perfect** indicates that
something has happened prior to events taking place *now*: "He *has
finished* his supper and *is getting* up." Formed with *had*, the **past
perfect** indicates that something happened in the relatively distant
past, prior to *other* events in the past: "He *had finished* his supper
and *was getting* up." A confusing shift results when a writer disre-
gards these relations:

SHIFT: Last March, the secretary of the air force told the committee what *has happened* to air transport in this country.

CONSISTENT: Last March, the secretary of the air force told the committee what *had happened* to air transport in this country.
(The secretary could not have told the committee then what *has happened* up to the present time.)

(3) *Avoid shifts resulting from failure to observe the distinction between direct and indirect quotation.* What the speaker felt or observed at the time would be in the present tense in direct quotation: He said, "I *feel* fine." It would be in the past tense in indirect quotation: He said that he *felt* fine. What the speaker felt *before* he spoke would occur in the past (or perhaps in the present perfect) when quoted directly: He said, "I *felt* fine." It would occur in the past perfect when quoted indirectly: He said that he *had felt* fine.

Failure to adjust the tenses in indirect quotations can lead to sentences like the following:

SHIFT: Her husband admitted that he *was* [should be *"had been"*] a confirmed bachelor.

SHIFT: Mr. Chamberlain said that there *will be* [should be *"would be"*] peace in our time.

Note: When *a statement made in the past states a general truth*, the present tense is plausible:

Galileo said that the earth *moves* and that the sun *is* fixed; the Inquisition said that the earth *is* fixed and the sun *moves*; and Newtonian astronomers, adopting an absolute theory of space, said that both the sun and the earth *move.*—A. N. Whitehead, *Science and the Modern World*

(4) *Avoid inconsistent combinations between forms dealing with possible events.* In the following sentences, note the differences between factual reference to a possibility and the **conditional**, which makes the same possibility seem less probable, or contrary to fact:

SHIFT: If they *come* to this country, the government *would* offer them asylum.

FACTUAL: If they *come* to this country, the government *will* offer them asylum.

CONDITIONAL: If they *came* to this country, the government *would* offer them asylum.

G 10b   Shifts in Reference   *sf*

Be consistent in the way you refer to yourself and others.

The least ambiguous pronoun you can use to refer to yourself is of course *I*, *me*, or *my* (**first person singular**). Writers who want to speak directly to their readers can call them *you* (**second person singular** and **plural**). They can use *we* to refer to both the readers and themselves:

> You will agree that *we* must do everything in our power.
> As *you* no doubt remember, *we* have witnessed several similar incidents during the past year.

But *you* also appears as an informal equivalent of *one* or *a person*, referring not so much to the reader as to people in general:

FORMAL: *One* cannot be too careful.
INFORMAL: *You* can't be too careful.

Confusion results when we shift to the indefinite, generalized *you* after we have already identified the person involved: "I don't want to be a famous actress. *I* would rather lead my own life without people always knowing what *you* are doing." The easiest way to avoid this kind of shift is to use *you* only to mean "you, the reader":

CONSISTENT: *I* want to lead *my* own life without people always knowing what *I* am doing.

Similar in effect to shifts to *you* are shifts to the **imperative**, the request form of verbs: "*Come* in." "*Put* it down." "*Leave* him alone." Imperatives are most appropriate in directions or instructions. They startle the reader when they suddenly break into ordinary prose:

SHIFT: High schools *should stop* educating all students at the same rate. *Give* aptitude tests for placement and then *separate* the students accordingly.

CONSISTENT: High schools *should stop* educating all students at the same rate. They *should give* aptitude tests for placement and then *separate* the students accordingly.

G 10c   Shifts to the Passive   *sf*

Avoid shifting to the passive when the person in question is still the active element in the sentence.

Some sentences confuse the reader by shifting from an **active** construction ("*He built* the house") to a **passive** one ("*The house was built* by him"):

INCONSISTENT: He *returned* to the office as soon as *his lunch had been eaten.* (This sounds as though his lunch might have been eaten by somebody else.)

CONSISTENT: He *returned* to the office as soon as he *had eaten* his lunch.

Unsatisfactory shifts to the passive are especially frequent after an impersonal *one* or *you*:

INCONSISTENT: As *you scan* the area of your backyard, a small patch of uninhabited earth *is located.*

CONSISTENT: As *you scan* your backyard, *you locate* a small patch of earth.

G 10d   Faulty Parallelism   *FP*

Use parallel grammatical structure for elements serving the same function in a sentence.

Sentence elements joined by *and*, *or*, and *but* have to be **parallel**. They have to fit into the same grammatical category. If you put an *and* after *body*, the reader expects another noun: "body and *chassis*," "body and *soul*." If you put an *and* after *swore*, he expects another verb: "swore and *affirmed*," "swore and *raved*." The same principle applies to other elements:

INFINITIVES: Two things that a successful advertisement must accomplish are *to be noticed* and *to be remembered.*

PARTICIPLES: I can still see my aunt *striding* into the corral, *cornering* a cow against a fencepost, *balancing* herself on a one-legged milking stool, and *butting* her head into the cow's belly.

CLAUSES: The young people *who brood* in their rooms, *who forget* to come down to the dining hall, and *who burst out* in fits of irrationality are not worrying about who will win the great game.—Oscar Handlin, "Are the Colleges Killing Education?" *Atlantic*

Faulty parallelism results when the second element does not fit the expected pattern. For instance, *"ignorant* and *a miser"* is off balance because it joins an adjective and a noun. You could change *ignorant* to a noun ("He was an *ignoramus* and a miser") or *miser* to an adjective ("He was ignorant and *miserly"*).

FAULTY: My grandfather liked *the country* and *to walk* in the fields.
PARALLEL: My grandfather liked *to live* in the country and *to walk* in the fields.

FAULTY: She told me of *her plans* and *that she was leaving*.
PARALLEL: She *informed* me of her plans and *told* me that she was leaving.

Look especially for the following:

(1) *Avoid linking a noun with an adjective as the modifier of another noun:*

FAULTY: The schools must serve *personal and society* needs as they evolve.
PARALLEL: The schools must serve *personal and social* needs as they evolve.

(2) *Check for parallelism when using paired connectives.* These are words like *either ... or, neither ... nor, not only ... but also,* and *whether ... or:*

FAULTY: I used to find him either *on the porch* or *dozing* in the living room.
PARALLEL: I used to find him either *sitting* on the porch or *dozing* in the living room.

FAULTY: We wondered whether *to believe* him or *should we try* to verify his story.
PARALLEL: We wondered whether we should *believe* him or *try* to verify his story.

(3) *Avoid faulty parallelism in a series of three or more elements.* Do not lead your readers into what looks like a conventional series only to make the last element snap out of the expected pattern:

Consistency

FAULTY: He liked to *swim, relax,* and *everything peaceful.*
PARALLEL: He liked *swimming, relaxation,* and peaceful *surroundings.*

If the elements in a faulty series are not really parallel in *meaning*, the revision might break up the series altogether:

FAULTY: My new friend was *polite, studious,* and *an only child.*
PARALLEL: My new friend was a *gentleman, a scholar,* and *an only child.*
BROKEN UP: My new friend, *an only child,* was a gentleman and a scholar.

(4) *Repeat structural links as needed to reinforce parallel structure.* Repeating a preposition like *for* or *to,* or a connective like *when* or *whether,* can help you improve parallelism in a sentence:

FAULTY: The story focuses on whether *the old man will capture* the large beautiful fish or *will the fish elude* him.
PARALLEL: The story focuses on *whether* the old man will capture the large beautiful fish or *whether* the fish will elude him.

EXERCISES

A. Check the following passages for unnecessary or confusing shifts in perspective. Label each sentence S (satisfactory) or U (unsatisfactory). Be prepared to explain how you would revise unsatisfactory sentences.

1. Things like this make a person face reality and wonder what your destiny could possibly be.
2. We gathered some old rags, and a bucket and soap were placed near the car.
3. The harder I push, the tighter I grip the wrench, the more the blood dripped from my scraped knuckles, and the angrier I became.
4. The more I think about capital punishment, the more one question kept entering my mind.
5. It was soon discovered by the students that if you didn't work fast you were put in the slow learning group.
6. Suddenly the sky darkens, a breeze springs up, and a premonitory rumble rolls across the lake.
7. Only when one faces the decision of whether to have an abortion can you really feel what a tough issue it is.
8. A true gentleman behaves the way he does because courtesy has to him become second nature.

9. As the world grew dark, he dreams of a place he will never see.
10. To the early Christians, endurance meant seeing one's loved ones thrown to wild beasts without losing faith in your God.
11. Parents must take an active interest in what their children are doing. Coach a ball team or be a counselor to a scout group.
12. As I walk by the shop, the owner, not having anything to do, was looking out of the window.
13. The police were warning us that if the crowd did not calm down arrests will be made.
14. My favorite television program was already in progress. Right in the middle of a dramatic scene, the station goes off the air.
15. Millions of people every day rush off to jobs they detest.

B. Check the following sentences for parallel structure. Label each sentence *S* for satisfactory, or *FP* for faulty parallelism. Be prepared to explain how you would revise the unsatisfactory sentences.

1. Her parents kept telling her Joe was poor, lazy, and his hair was too long.
2. The affluent American has a large income, a nice house, and lives in the nice part of town.
3. The book made me remember the bombings, the dismembered bodies, and the fire and fury of war.
4. The boy described how he was beaten by his masters, taken advantage of by the older servants, and the meager meals of bread and porridge he received.
5. To most readers, the word *home* suggests security and comfort as well as a place to live.
6. The success of a television program depends on how well the program has been advertised, the actors taking part, and is it comedy or serious drama.
7. Students come to college to have fun, find a husband or wife, get away from home, and many other ridiculous reasons.
8. Objective tests can never be a true measure of a student's ability or an accurate prediction of future success.
9. My father thought that girls should not go to dances, see boys only in the company of a chaperone, and many other old-fashioned prejudices.
10. In many gangster movies, the hero deceives the police, moves in the best society, and shows brazen courage when finally cornered by the police.

C. Make each of the following sentences more consistent by rewriting the italicized part. Write the rewritten part after the number of the sentence.

1. I had been waiting for more than three hours *when finally help arrives.*
2. During the summer, they planned to hitchhike, stop at interesting places, *and taking side trips whenever they felt like it.*
3. The rain fell for thirteen days; *then suddenly the sun shines.*
4. People wonder at times *if others try to make you feel bad on purpose.*
5. Teenagers assert their independence through the way they dress, comb their hair, *and their tastes in music.*
6. He blamed me for not giving him a chance to succeed *and I ruined his big chance for him.*

Consistency

7. We are not qualified to speak of good *if evil has never been examined.*
8. She got her opinions by listening to her teachers *and then evaluate their ideas.*
9. If voters understood the true extent of environmental pollution, *they will vote for the necessary cleanup measures.*
10. Few newspaper readers understand the subtle ways *in which advertisers appeal to your fears and prejudices.*

Punctuation

CHAPTER FIFTEEN

P 1 End Punctuation
    a   Sentences and Fragments
    b   Exclamations and Questions

P 2 Linking Punctuation
    a   Comma Splice
    b   Coordinating Connectives
    c   Adverbial Connectives
    d   Subordinating Connectives

P 3 Punctuating Modifiers
    a   Unnecessary Commas
    b   Restrictive and Nonrestrictive
    c   Sentence Modifiers

P 4 Coordination
    a   Series
    b   Coordinate Adjectives
    c   Dates and Addresses
    d   Repetition and Contrast

P 5 Parenthetic Elements
    a   Dashes
    b   Parentheses
    c   Commas for Parenthetic Elements

P 6 Quotation
    a   Direct Quotation
    b   Terminal Marks in Quotations
    c   Insertions and Omissions
    d   Indirect Quotation
    e   Words Set Off from Context

PUNCTUATION MARKS
Reference Chart

COMMA

before coordinating connectives	P 2b
with nonrestrictive adverbial clauses	P 2d
after introductory adverbial clauses	P 2d
with nonrestrictive modifiers (other than adverbial clauses)	P 3b
after introductory modifiers (other than adverbial clauses)	P 3c
with adverbial connectives	P 2c
with *especially, namely, for example*, and so on	P 1a
with *after all, of course*, and other sentence modifiers	P 3c
between items in a series	P 4a
in a series of parallel clauses	P 2a
between coordinate adjectives	P 4b
with dates and addresses, and so on	P 4c
with direct address and other parenthetic elements	P 5c
between repeated or contrasted elements	P 4d
with quotations	P 6a

SEMICOLON

between closely related sentences	P 2a
before adverbial connectives	P 2c
before coordinating connectives between clauses containing commas	P 2b
in a series with items containing commas	P 4a

COLON

to introduce a list or explanation	P 1a
to introduce a formal quotation	P 6a

PERIOD

at end of sentence	P 1a
ellipsis	P 6c
with abbreviations	M 2

DASH

break in thought	P 1a, P 5a
before summary at end of sentence	P 5a

QUOTATION MARKS

with quotations	P 6a
quotation within quotation	P 6a
with terminal marks	P 6b
with slang or technical terms	P 6e
to set off titles	M 1d

EXCLAMATION MARK	P 1b
QUESTION MARK	P 1b
PARENTHESES	P 5b

When we speak, we do more than put the right words together in the right order. We pause at the right times and raise our voices for emphasis. To the structures and forms of the written sentence, speech adds **intonation**: differences in timing, pitch, and stress that make our words mean what we want them to mean. When writing, we use punctuation marks for similar purposes.

Punctuation marks may separate groups of words from each other. They may establish different kinds of connection between them. For instance, punctuation may show two closely related groups of words to be a general statement followed by detailed explanation:

The room was full of noisy people: ranchers, merchants, and lawyers.

It may show them to be an important statement followed by additional information:

Richard inherited his uncle's estate, which had been in the family since 1832.

DIAGNOSTIC TEST

Look at the blank in each of the following sentences. Of the three possible choices that follow the sentence, which would be right for serious written English? Put the letter for the right choice after the number of the sentence.

1. The weather had _____ was raining heavily.
   a. changed it   b. changed, it   c. changed; it
2. Our friends had a fishing _____ converted navy boat.
   a. trawler, a   b. trawler. A   c. trawler; a
3. The offer has _____ we are returning your check.
   a. expired therefore   b. expired; therefore,   c. expired, therefore,
4. We put everything in the back of the _____ wear,
   fishing gear, and coils of rope.
   a. truck, rain   b. truck: rain   c. truck. Rain
5. Lillian _____ as a playwright, also wrote *An Unfinished Woman.*
   a. Hellman, known   b. Hellman known   c. Hellman; known
6. Dudley had been the second _____ the first.
   a. child not   b. child; not   c. child, not
7. We had moved to _____ when I was three.
   a. El Paso, Texas,   b. El Paso Texas   c. El Paso Texas,
8. An attendant came in and asked: "Who is _____.
   a. next?   b. next"?   c. next?"
9. The handicapped were _____ new legislation.
   a. helped. By   b. helped by   c. helped; by

10. She encouraged her daughters to take difficult _____ math.
    a. subjects, such as   b. subjects. Such as   c. subjects, such as,
11. "Be careful," my aunt _____ cannot be trusted."
    a. said, she   b. said, "she   c. said. "She
12. Traditional cars—big, showy, _____ on the way out.
    a. uneconomical were   b. uneconomical—were   c. uneconomical, were
13. We lived in a small _____ of the people were farmers.
    a. town most   b. town; most   c. town, most
14. To speed up _____ sent the money in advance.
    a. delivery, we   b. delivery we   c. delivery; we
15. The store sold fishing supplies: _____ and beer.
    a. bait, tackle,   b. bait tackle   c. bait; tackle
16. According to the biographer, "Walt Whitman always dreamed of 'the true _____
    a. America."   b. America".   c. America.'"
17. There will be no diplomas for _____ fail the new tests. tests.
    a. students, who   b. students. Who   c. students who
18. People applying for _____ to fill in long forms.
    a. loans have   b. loans, have   c. loans; have
19. Who first said, "Less is _____
    a. more?"   b. more"?   c. more."
20. Many settlers had _____ the first year was over.
    a. died. Before   b. died, before   c. died before

P 1   END PUNCTUATION

Use end punctuation to mark off complete sentences.

End punctuation brings what we are saying to a complete stop. We use it to separate complete sentences—units that can stand by themselves. Here are three kinds of complete sentences:

STATEMENTS: We hear much about solar energy.
               Many Canadians speak French.
               Space probes have landed on Venus.
QUESTIONS: Do our big cities have a future?
               Why has your policy changed?
               What should we do next?
REQUESTS: Send in your coupon now!
               Turn down the radio!
               Sell real estate in your spare time!

P 1a   Sentences and Fragments   *frag*

Use the period at the end of a simple statement.

A complete statement normally needs at least a subject and a complete verb. Look at the complete verbs that help turn each of the following into a separate sentence:

Linda *works* downtown.
My insurance *will pay* for the damage.
Her friends *are studying* in the library.
My baggage *was left* behind.

Do not use a period to set off a unit that is not a complete sentence but merely a sentence fragment. Do not use the period between two complete sentences, thus producing a fused sentence:

COMPLETE: He is gone. *He left for Alaska.*
FRAGMENT: He left yesterday. *For Alaska.*
FUSED: You won't find him *he left for Alaska.*

Most fragments merely put down in writing the many fragmentary sentences we hear in informal speech. The most common kind adds an afterthought to the main statement. Each of the following typical sentence fragments adds an explanation or a comment:

FRAGMENT: I left home. *To go to college.*
FRAGMENT: They pulled up in their new car. *A gray Mercedes.*
FRAGMENT: The office was closed. *Because of a strike.*

We can sort out such fragments as follows:

ADJECTIVES AND ADVERBS: Early in the morning.
                            Late as usual.
                            Beautiful but dangerous.

PREPOSITIONAL PHRASES: In an old station wagon.
                            For my brothers and me.
                            Without a valid permit.

APPOSITIVES: Her ex-husband.
                            A dear old friend.
                            The next turn after this.

VERBALS: Basking in the sun.
                            Being a holiday.
                            Having studied all night.
                            Written on a napkin.

All of these fragments lack either a subject, or all or part of the verb. An additional type of fragment has its own subject and verb. But it starts with a connective that *subordinates* a clause to something else: *if, because, whereas, though, unless,* and the like. Or it starts with a relative pronoun: *who, which,* and *that.*

SUBORDINATOR:	*If* you arrive in time.
	Because the motor was running.
	Whereas Lyle pays all her own bills.
RELATIVE:	*Which* had never happened before.
	Who lived in the house next door.

Do the following to eliminate sentence fragments:

(1) *Try joining the fragment to the main statement without any punctuation at all.* Whenever a fragment is pointed out to you, try first to connect it with the main idea in such a way that the sentence flows smoothly, without interruption:

FRAGMENT:	Be sure to be there. *At seven o'clock.*
REVISED:	Be sure to be there *at seven o'clock.*
FRAGMENT:	He bought a used car. *In spite of my warnings.*
REVISED:	He bought a used car *in spite of my warnings.*
FRAGMENT:	His sister had gone back to school. *To study medicine.*
REVISED:	His sister had gone back to school *to study medicine.*

Note: Most prepositional phrases and infinitives can be joined to the main statement this way without a break. However, many other additions require a slight break, signaled by a **comma**:

He collected South American snakes, *beautiful but dangerous.*
We had coffee with Henry, *a dear old friend.*
I slept through most of the day, *having worked all night.*

See **P 2** and **P 3** for situations that require a comma.

(2) *Use a* **dash** *to show a definite break in thought:*

These are my relatives—*a motley crew.*
He would close his eyes and talk into the dictaphone—*a very strange way to write an English theme.*

For more on uses of the dash, see **P 5a.**

(3) *Use a* **colon** *or transitional expression to bring in an explanatory afterthought.* Use the colon to introduce a list or description of something that has already been mentioned in a more general way:

> We have two excellent players this year: *Phil and Tom.*
> They served an old-fashioned breakfast: *fishballs, brown bread, and baked beans.*
> Your friend lacks an essential quality: *tact.*

Added explanations or examples often follow expressions like *especially, such as, namely,* or *for example.* When they introduce material that is not a complete sentence, these expressions usually come after a **comma**:

> He took courses in the humanities, *such as French Literature and The Russian Novel.*
> Plato and Aristotle wrote in the same language, *namely Greek.*

Note: In formal usage, another comma often keeps *namely, for example, for instance,* and *that is* separate from what they introduce:

> Professor Miller objected to my system of punctuating, for example, my use of dashes.

(4) *Turn the fragment into a separate statement.* If the fragment cannot become part of the preceding statement, you may have to develop it into a complete separate sentence:

FRAGMENT: He appealed to a higher court. *Being a futile effort.*
REVISED: He appealed to a higher court. *The effort was futile.*

Note: Experienced writers use permissible fragments for special effects. The following examples illustrate the most common of these:

• *Common transitional expressions:*

> *So much for* past developments. *Now for* a look at our present problems.

• *Answers to questions,* suggesting the give-and-take of conversation:

> What did we gain? *Nothing.*

• *Descriptive passages,* especially when designed to give a static, pictorial effect:

We stood in the hot dry night air at one in the morning, waiting for a train at an Arizona station. *Nothing but the purple arc of sky and at the end of the platform the silhouette of a cottonwood tree lapped by a hot breeze. The stars big as sunflowers.* —Alistair Cooke, *One Man's America*

- **Narrative passages suggesting** *random, disconnected thought*:

There he is: the brother. *Image of him. Haunting face.* —James Joyce, *Ulysses*

- **Afterthoughts delayed for** *ironic effect*:

Man is the only animal that blushes. *Or needs to.* (Mark Twain)

Many teachers discourage their students from experimenting with such incomplete sentences.

P 1b Exclamations and Questions ◢℗

Signal exclamations and questions by adding the appropriate marks.

Use the exclamation mark to give an utterance *unusual emphasis*. Such utterances range from a groan, curse, or shout to an order or a command. The **exclamation mark** can signal excitement, insistence, surprise, indignation, or fear:

Ouch!
Silence! Get up! Close the book!
He loves me!
And this man wants to be president!

Use the question mark whenever an utterance is worded *as a request for information*. Whenever you raise your voice inquiringly at the end of something you say, you should terminate the written equivalent with a **question mark** (*He sent you a check?*). Not all questions, however, are marked by intonation:

Who are you?
What did he want?

Do not forget to use question marks at the end of questions that are long or involved:

How is the student who enters college as a freshman supposed to find her way through the maze of instructions and regulations printed in small print in the college catalog?

EXERCISES

A. In which of the following passages is the second unit a sentence fragment? Write *frag* after the number of each such passage. In which of the following passages is the second unit a complete separate sentence? Write *S* for satisfactory after the number.

1. The United States has always been a rich country. Free from serious starvation problems and devastating diseases.
2. Christmas time in prison is a sad time. Grimy walls like any other time of the year.
3. The cry for law and order has changed nothing. Crimes are still as numerous as before.
4. Americans were considered materialists. Interested only in money.
5. The story begins like a typical short story. A story about a small town having a drawing once a year.
6. The smart students bragged about their grades. The athletic stars treated other people as inferiors.
7. The article is aimed at the twenty- to twenty-seven-year-old group. Male and female college juniors, seniors, and recent graduates trying to find employment with little luck.
8. Moviegoers are tired of sex and violence. They can get those on the evening news.
9. The school was very poor. Most of the time we shared books.
10. I want to be able to write a good essay. Something with facts and important details.
11. She left school after two years. To take over her father's business.
12. Many minority students went out for sports. Because it gave them their only real chance.
13. People used to grow up in larger families. For example, a family consisting of parents, grandparents, and three or four children.
14. The place was called the loft. It was a big room at the top of the building.
15. We got a new teacher. She was a deeply concerned and dedicated woman.
16. The veterinarian told us the animal died of a heart attack. While he was preparing to operate.
17. A regulation target resembles an upside-down saucer. Measuring no more than five inches in diameter.
18. She simply could not satisfy anybody's standards. Not those of her superiors and not those of her co-workers.
19. The ocean has always beckoned to people. Daring them to risk all to sail the seas.
20. Felipe has never washed a dish in his life. He does not mind cooking.

B. Check the following for sentence fragments and other problems with end punctuation. Rewrite the italicized part of each example, adding or changing punctuation as necessary. (Use a period followed by a capital letter to separate two complete sentences.)

1. There were jobs for *the newcomers the rent was reasonable*.
2. That morning I *had been late. Because of the wait in the bus line*.
3. The mother had hiked *down into the valley. To get help*.

4. They were studying the marvels of *Indian architecture. Such as Aztec pyramids and Mayan temples.*
5. Men once had clearly *defined roles. Hunting and fishing.*
6. One woman was a *jockey the other woman interviewed was a commercial pilot.*
7. We tried a new *sales technique. With good results.*
8. What good does it do to kill *a person for taking someone else's life.*
9. He was attacking his *favorite target. Public money for private schools.*
10. American schools are neglecting the major languages *of the modern world. Especially Russian and Chinese.*
11. When will people realize that the *resources of this planet are not inexhaustible.*
12. Her favorite authors were always experimenting with *impossible new ideas. For example, robots with human emotions.*
13. In the old sentimental stories, the desperate unwed mother would *leave her child on someone's doorstep. In a wicker basket.*
14. He began to consider *the unthinkable. Turning himself in.*
15. The prime suspect had spent the evening *conducting a symphony orchestra. A perfect alibi.*

P 2   LINKING PUNCTUATION

Use commas or semicolons as required when several clauses combine in a larger sentence.

Several short statements may combine to become part of a larger sentence. We call each sub-sentence in the new combined sentence a **clause**. Independent clauses are still self-contained. They could easily be separated again by a period. Dependent clauses have been linked in a more permanent way. They would sound incomplete if separated from the main clause.

P 2a   Comma Splice   *CS*

Use the semicolon between complete sentences that are closely related.

A **semicolon** may replace the period between two complete sentences. Often two statements go together as related pieces of information. Or they line up related ideas for contrast. When a semicolon replaces the period, the first word of the second statement is *not* capitalized:

Sunshine was everywhere; orchards were in bloom.

Some librarians circulate books; others hoard them.

The queen is not allowed to wear a crown; nothing less than a halo will suffice.—Kingsley Martin, "Strange Interlude," *Atlantic*

Remember:

(1) *Do not use a comma alone to join two clauses.* Notice that there is no connective between the two clauses in each of the following pairs. The clauses remain "independent." A **comma splice** runs on from one independent clause to the next with only a comma to keep them apart:

COMMA SPLICE: I loved London, it is a wonderful city.
REVISED: I loved London; it is a wonderful city.

COMMA SPLICE: Carol is twenty-eight years old, she might go back to school.
REVISED: Carol is twenty-eight years old; she might go back to school.

(2) *Never merely put two independent clauses next to each other without any punctuation.* A **fused sentence** results when two such clauses are simply run together without a connective:

FUSED: I am not sick or anything I just like to sit in a chair and think.
REVISED: I am not sick; I just like to sit in a chair and think.

(3) *Use commas if you wish in order to separate three or more parallel clauses.* Note that the clauses in the following examples are closely related in meaning and similar in structure:

Be brief, be blunt, be gone.
Students in India demonstrate against the use of English, African nationalists protest against the use of French, young Israelis have no use for the languages once spoken by their parents.

Note: Some of the best modern writers use the comma between *two* clauses when the logical connection or similarity in structure is especially close. For instance, there may be a *carefully balanced contrast*:

Rage cannot be hidden, it can only be dissembled.—James Baldwin, *Notes of a Native Son*
Today Kleist gives pleasure, most of Goethe is a classroom bore.—Susan Sontag, *Against Interpretation*

Many conservative teachers and editors object to this practice; avoid it in your own writing.

P 2b   Coordinating Connectives

Use a comma when a coordinator links two clauses.

Coordinating connectives typically require a comma. *And, but, for, or, nor, so,* and *yet* link two clauses without making the one more important than the other. They are typically preceded by a **comma**:

> The bell finally rang, *and* George rushed out of the room.
> She saw me, *but* she did not recognize me.
> We went inside, *for* it had started to rain.
> You had better apologize, *or* she will not speak to you again.

Notice the reversal of subject and verb after *nor*:

> We cannot through the courts force parents to be kind, *nor can we force* men to be wise by the pressure of committees. —Dan Lacy, "Obscenity and Censorship," *The Christian Century*

Do not use the comma with these connectives when they merely join two words or two phrases (came in *and* sat down, tired *but* happy, for cash *or* on credit).

Notice the following variations:

(1) *And, but,* and *or* often appear without a comma *when the clauses they join are short. Yet* and *so* are frequently used with a **semicolon**:

> The wind was blowing *and* the water was cold.
> The critics praised Oliver's work; *yet* no one bought his paintings.

(2) Any coordinating connective may be used with a semicolon between *clauses that already contain commas* or that are unusually long:

> Now in the Big Bend the river encounters mountains in a new and extraordinary way; *for* they lie, chain after chain of them, directly across its way. —Paul Horgan, "Pages from a Rio Grande Notebook," *New York Times Book Review*

(3) Coordinating connectives leave the clauses they join self-sufficient or independent grammatically. Thus, the clauses they connect may still be kept separate from each other by a **period**:

> I called your office twice. *But* nobody answered. *So* I left without you.

P 2c   Adverbial Connectives   ;/

Use a semicolon with adverbial connectives.

Adverbial connectives are words like *therefore, however, neverthe-less, consequently, hence, accordingly, moreover, furthermore, besides, indeed,* and *in fact.* (The older term for these words is **conjunctive adverb.**) The two statements they join are often linked by a **semico-lon** rather than by a period. A period, nevertheless, would still be possible and acceptable.

> Business was improving; *therefore*, we changed our plans.
> Business was improving. *Therefore*, we changed our plans.
> The hall was nearly empty; *nevertheless*, the curtain rose on time.
> The hall was nearly empty. *Nevertheless*, the curtain rose on time.

Remember:

(1) *Do not use just a comma with adverbial connectives.* If a comma replaces the semicolon, the sentence turns into a comma splice:

COMMA SPLICE: French Canadians insisted on preserving their language, there-fore federal employees were being taught French.

REVISED: French Canadians insisted on preserving their language; there-fore, federal employees were being taught French.

(2) *Put the semicolon at the point where the two statements join, regardless of the position of the connective.* The adverbial connective itself often appears *later* in the second clause:

> Attendance is compulsory; *therefore*, the students have no choice.
> Attendance is compulsory; the students, *therefore*, have no choice.
> Attendance is compulsory; the students have no choice, *therefore*.

Use this possible shift in position to help you identify members of this group. They share their freedom of movement with adverbs (and are therefore called *"adverbial* connectives" or "connective *adverbs"*).

(3) *In formal writing, separate the connective from the rest of the second statement by* **commas.** You then have to make sure that there is a punctuation mark both before and after the connective:

FORMAL: We liked the area; the food, *however*, was impossible.

Note: These additional commas are *optional*. Informal writing and journalistic writing tend toward **open punctuation**, using fewer commas than formal writing does. Accordingly, the authors of popular books and magazine articles tend not to separate adverbial connectives from the rest of a clause.

P 2d Subordinating Connectives   *p*

Use commas or no punctuation as required with subordinators.

Subordinating connectives are words like *if*, *when*, and *because*. An *if* or a *because* changes a self-sufficient, independent clause into a **dependent clause**, which normally cannot stand by itself. "If I were in charge" does not become a complete sentence until you answer the question "If you were in charge, *then what?*" Beware of dependent clauses added to a main statement as an afterthought:

FRAGMENT: He failed the test. *Because he did not study.*
REVISED: He failed the test *because he did not study.*

Subordinators normally start dependent clauses that tell us when, where, why, or how (adverbial clauses). Here is a list of subordinators, sorted out according to the kind of information they bring into a sentence:

TIME AND PLACE: when, whenever, while, before, after, since, until, as long
                      as, where, wherever
REASON OR CONDITION: because, if, unless, provided
CONTRAST: though, although, whereas, no matter how

In some situations, subordinators require no punctuation. In others, they require commas. Observe the following guidelines:

(1) *Do not separate restrictive adverbial clauses from the rest of the sentence.* Adverbial clauses usually restrict or limit the meaning of the main clause. Suppose an employer tells you, "I'll raise everyone's wages *after I strike oil.*" Without the proviso about striking oil, the sentence would sound like an immediate promise of more money. With the proviso, it means that you will get more money only by a remote chance. When they *follow* the main clause, such **restrictive** clauses are not set off by punctuation:

NO COMMA: I consulted my notes *before I spoke.*
             Do not sign anything *until you hear from me.*
             We cannot keep you on the team *unless you improve.*

(2) *Set off nonrestrictive adverbial clauses.* Occasionally, the time, place, or condition for an action or event is already indicated in the main clause. In that case, the dependent clause may merely *elaborate* on the information already given. Such dependent clauses are called **nonrestrictive**. They are separated from the main clause by a **comma**:

COMMA: Bats were well developed *as far back as the Eocene, when our ancestors were still in the trees.*

Some subordinates introduce either restrictive or nonrestrictive material, depending on the meaning of the sentence:

NO COMMA: Why are you going to town?
I am going to town *because I want to do some shopping.*
(The reason for your trip is the essential part of the sentence.)

COMMA: What are you going to do?
I am going to town, because I want to do some shopping.
(The reason for your trip is added, nonrestrictive explanation.)

(3) *Set off an adverbial clause that establishes a contrast. Though, although,* and *whereas* usually introduce nonrestrictive material and as a result require a comma. Rather than adding essential qualification, these words establish a *contrast* between the statements they connect:

I like the work, *though the salary is low.*
Her friend wore a sports shirt and slacks, *whereas the other men wore tuxedos.*

Combinations like *whether or not* and *no matter how* show that the main statement is true *regardless*:

We are canceling the lease, *whether you like it or not.*
She will never forgive you, *no matter what you do.*

(4) *Set off an adverbial clause that precedes the main clause.* With a subordinating connective, you can reverse the order of the two statements that it joins. After an introductory adverbial clause, a **comma** normally indicates where the main clause starts:

Vote for me *if you trust me.*
If you trust me, vote for me.
I drove more slowly *after I noticed the police car.*
After I noticed the police car, I drove more slowly.

Linking Punctuation

Note: Some connectives belong to different groups depending on their meaning in the sentence. *However* is normally an adverbial connective and requires a semicolon. It sometimes takes the place of the subordinating connective *no matter how* and requires a comma:

> I cannot please him; *however, I am trying hard.*
> I cannot please him, *however hard I try.*

Though, normally a subordinator, is used in informal English as an adverbial connective placed in the middle or at the end of a clause:

> I felt entitled to more freedom; *my parents, though, didn't agree with me.*

See **P 3a** for noun clauses, **P 3b** for relative clauses.

EXERCISES

A. Each of the following sentences consists of two independent clauses. In each case, the two clauses simply stand next to each other, without a connective. Write down the last word of the first clause and the first word of the second, with a semicolon to join them.

EXAMPLE: His hair was very neat every strand was in place. (Answer) neat; every

1. A pawnshop is on the ground floor above it is a hotel.
2. The old man has stepped out of the lobby he's walking down the street.
3. I enjoy running as opposed to other sports it becomes an almost unconscious act.
4. People were shouting ridiculous commands everyone with a flashlight began directing traffic.
5. The building has two stories there are two big display windows on the ground floor.
6. At first we were afraid later we learned to trust each other.
7. Poverty is a major problem in our world it is found in every city in the United States.
8. The church is usually completely quiet a few people come in to pray.
9. John wasn't going to school anymore he was a photographer.
10. Being an officer in today's army is not easy it is a challenging but rewarding job.
11. I entered the office it was a very modern one with plants around the room.
12. We were once urged to buy and spend urgent messages to conserve are now coming at us from all directions.
13. This job was the most important thing in her life it was her chance to make it into the big time.

14. We fished in the stream until midnight it was illegal really to fish after dark.
15. She had just come out of the movie theater her face showed her satisfaction.

B. What kind of connective links the two clauses in each of the following sentences? What punctuation, if any, should there be in the blank space between the two clauses? After the number of the sentence, write C for comma, S for semicolon, or *No* for no punctuation.

1. My parents never pressured me about getting married _____ in fact, they wanted me to finish college first.
2. She wasn't a big-time photographer _____ but she had enough work to keep up her studio.
3. The furniture was all glass and steel _____ and the walls were painted a bright red.
4. Human beings could not survive on other planets _____ unless they created an artificial earthlike environment.
5. Before we knew it _____ the party was over.
6. Some store clerks had the disgusting habit of waiting on whites before blacks _____ no matter how long the blacks had been waiting for service.
7. Lawmakers must rid the country of crime _____ before it reaches epidemic proportions.
8. My father fought with Pancho Villa _____ he was, in fact, the only private in Villa's army.
9. My friends were the sons of captains or colonels _____ though a few fathers were admittedly mere sergeants and corporals.
10. Jobs were scarce and insecure _____ so my parents left town.
11. Many Spanish-speaking Americans call themselves Mexican-Americans _____ some parts of New Spain, however, were never a part of Mexico.
12. The whole crowd in the theater cheered _____ when the cavalry came to the rescue at the end of the movie.
13. When meteors hit the surface _____ they form craters like those made by volcanoes.
14. My parents never became thoroughly Americanized _____ but they had also become strangers in their native land.
15. Space exploration is incredibly expensive _____ therefore only a few of the richest nations take part.

C. Explain the use of punctuation marks in the following passage. Which adverbial clauses are *restrictive*? Which are *nonrestrictive*?

English and French were widely used in Africa until most African nations became independent. Now these countries are trying to assert their linguistic independence, although their people often speak several mutually incomprehensible native tongues. After the Belgians left the Congo, names like Leopoldville and Stanleyville disappeared. Swahili could become an official language in much of East Africa if linguistic minorities were willing to accept it. Similar developments accompanied the passing of colonialism in the Far East, where Batavia turned into Jakarta many years ago. A Malaysian city recently changed its name from Jesselton to Kinabalu, because Jesselton had been named for a British empire-builder.

P 3   PUNCTUATING MODIFIERS

p

Distinguish between modifiers set off by commas and those requiring no punctuation.

Often nouns and verbs carry along further material that develops or modifies their meaning. How we punctuate such modifiers depends on the role they play in the sentence.

P 3a   Unnecessary Commas

Unless other material intervenes, do not use punctuation between basic elements of a sentence.

Do not put a comma between a subject and its verb, between verb and complement, or between the two or three basic elements and various phrases added to describe circumstances, reasons, or conditions:

Andrea	studies	her textbooks	in bed.
Gaston	had been	a mess sergeant	during the war.
Jones	left	his job	to shoot elephants.

The rule against punctuation breaking up the basic sentence pattern applies even when the place of the subject or complement is taken by a *clause within a clause*. Such clauses, which appear in positions frequently occupied by nouns, are called **noun clauses**. They become *part* of another clause and should not be confused with clauses that are *joined* to another clause:

NOUN (SUBJECT):   *The writer* knew your name.

NOUN CLAUSE: *Whoever wrote it* knew your name.

NOUN (OBJECT):   John announced *his plans.*

NOUN CLAUSE: John announced *that he would retire.*

P 3b   Restrictive and Nonrestrictive

Do not set off restrictive modifiers; set off nonrestrictive modifiers by commas.

Different kinds of modifiers may follow a noun (or noun equivalent). Such modifiers become an essential part of the statement if *used for the purpose of identification.* In that case, they are **restrictive**.

They narrow down a general term like *student* to help the reader single out one particular student, or type of student. Restrictive modifiers are *not* set off:

> (*Which* student ordered the sandwich?)
> The student *wearing the red hunting cap* ordered the sandwich.
> (*Which* man took the money?)
> The man *dressed in the pink shirt* took it.
> (*What kind* of course appeals to you?)
> Courses *that require hard work* appeal to me.

Often a modifier merely gives *further information* about something already identified. It is **nonrestrictive**. Nonrestrictive material is set off from the rest of the sentence by a **comma.** Use a comma both before and after if it occurs in the middle of the sentence:

> The applicant requested an interview. (*What else* about her?)
> The applicant, *a recent graduate*, requested an interview.
> The applicant, *sounding eager*, requested an interview.
>
> She talked to her lawyer. (*What else* about this person?)
> She talked to her lawyer, *a well-known attorney*.
> She talked to her lawyer, *who is very impatient*.

Remember:

(1) *A proper name is usually adequate identification.* A modifier following the name is set off by commas:

> H. J. Heinz, *the Pittsburgh pickle packer*, keeps moving up in the food processing industry.
> In 1968, she joined the Actors' Theater, *a repertory company with strong political views*.

Note: Occasionally a *restrictive* modifier is needed to help the reader distinguish between several people of the same name:

> I find it hard to distinguish between Holmes *the author* and Holmes *the Supreme Court justice*.

(2) *The modifier after a noun may be a complete clause.* **Adjective clauses** modify a noun (or noun equivalent) and usually begin with *who, which,* or *that.* This kind of adjective clause, starting with a relative pronoun, is called a **relative clause.** Clauses beginning with *when, where,* and *why* are also adjective clauses if they are used to

modify a noun. Adjective clauses, like other modifiers, may be *either restrictive or nonrestrictive*:

RESTRICTIVE: According to my sister Irene, all boys *who carry briefcases* are "brains."

NONRESTRICTIVE: Teachers, *who have become more militant over the years,* are no longer satisfied with genteel poverty.

Two types of adjective clauses are *always* restrictive: those beginning with *that*, and those from which the pronoun or connective has been omitted:

NO COMMA: The book *that you sent me* was exciting reading.
NO COMMA: Most of the things [*that*] *I like to eat* are fattening.
NO COMMA: She wrote a long letter to the man [*whom*] *she loves.*

(3) *Occasionally a modifier already contains one or more commas.* Use **dashes** to set such a modifier off from the rest of the sentence:

My sister—*a tough, stubborn, hard-driving competitor*—won many prizes.

P 3c   Sentence Modifiers

Set sentence modifiers off by commas.

Modifiers may modify sentence elements other than nouns. They may also modify the sentence as a whole rather than any part of it. Look for the following:

(1) *Verbals and verbal phrases modifying a verb* may be either restrictive or nonrestrictive. Notice the **comma** showing the difference:

RESTRICTIVE: He always came into the office *carrying a shirt box full of letters under his arm.*

NONRESTRICTIVE: Deadline newspaper writing is rapid because it cheats, *depending heavily on clichés and stock phrases.*

(2) **Always** set off *verbal phrases modifying the sentence as a whole*:

To tell you the truth, I don't even recall his name.
The business outlook being rosy, he invested his savings in highly speculative stocks.
Our new manager has done rather well, *considering her lack of experience.*

(3) *If a sentence is introduced by a long modifying phrase,* use a **comma** to show where the main sentence starts. Use this comma after prepositional phrases of three words or more:

> *After an unusually solemn Sunday dinner,* Father called me into his study.
> *Like all newspapermen of good faith,* Mencken had long fumed at the low estate of the journalistic rank and file.—Philip M. Wagner, "Mencken Remembered," *The American Scholar*

Set off *introductory verbals and verbal phrases* even when they are short:

> *Smiling,* she dropped the match into the gas tank.
> *To start the motor,* turn the ignition key.

(4) If you wish, use the optional commas with *transitional expressions.* Expressions like *after all, of course, unfortunately, on the whole, as a rule,* and *certainly* often do not modify any one part of a sentence. Instead they help us go on from one sentence to another. Depending on the amount of emphasis you would give such a modifier when reading, make it stand out from the rest of the sentence by a *comma*:

> *After all,* we are in business primarily for profit.
> *On the other hand,* the records may never be found.
> You will submit the usual reports, *of course.*

Sentence modifiers that are set off require *two* commas if they do not come first or last in the sentence:

> We do not, *as a rule,* solicit applications.
> A great many things, *to be sure,* could be said for him.

EXERCISES

A. Check the following sentences for conventional punctuation of modifiers. After the number of each sentence, put *S* for satisfactory, *U* for unsatisfactory. Be prepared to explain how you would revise unsatisfactory sentences.

1. Faced with sympathy or kindness, we reply with reserve. (Octavio Paz)
2. A young woman in California failed to "come down" after ingesting STP, a powerful hallucinogen.
3. My father who taught in both high school and college gave me pointers on academic success.
4. Looking straight ahead you see a body of polluted water the Monongahela River.

5. Overdoses of the hardest drug, heroin, killed some 900 people in New York City alone.
6. Joe apparently not having any customers was sitting in his own barber chair and smoking a cigar.
7. For Chinese-speaking children in American schools, English used to be the only approved language of instruction.
8. A person who leases a car still has to pay for repairs and maintenance.
9. On the main island of Britain, the Welsh, whose own Gaelic tongue is radically different from English, are now mostly bilingual.
10. Having swallowed enough water to last me all summer I decided to leave water skiing alone.
11. A good example of our neglect of public health problems, is the lack of therapy for the mentally ill.
12. Spain, which once experienced a strong Arab influence, has a history of repressing its women.
13. People, who have grown up in Latin American countries, stand closer to each other in conversation than North Americans.
14. Owen Nielsen, my godfather, was a passionate man who would often shout at his family at the dinner table.
15. Everyone, who is physically able, should have some exercise each day.

B. What punctuation, if any, should appear at the blank space in each of the following sentences? After the number of the sentence, write C for comma, NC for no comma, or D for dash.

1. In spite of repeated promises _____ the shipment never arrived.
2. The agency collected debts _____ from delinquent customers.
3. Whipped by the wind _____ five-foot swells splash over the deck.
4. The book told the story of Amelia Earhart _____ who disappeared on a flight around the world.
5. A printed receipt will be sent to all students _____ who have paid their fees.
6. I looked with amazement at the crab pots _____ filled with large snapping Dungeness crabs.
7. Working on the pitching and rolling deck _____ we hauled up the heavy nets.
8. The owner, a large woman with mean eyes _____ watched us the whole time.
9. Back at the wharf _____ we sipped hot coffee, trying to get warm.
10. The city, on the other hand _____ has shown no interest in the project.
11. The mechanics working on a competitor's car _____ are racing against the clock.
12. The benches, which had been bolted to the planks _____ were torn loose by the waves.
13. My uncle—a jovial, fast-talking man _____ used to sell insurance.
14. Their performance has been unsatisfactory _____ to say the least.
15. The lawyer had promised _____ that all documents would be returned to us.

P 4   COORDINATION

p

Use the comma (and sometimes other marks) when several elements of the same kind appear together.

When we coordinate parts of a sentence, we make several similar or related elements work together.

P 4a   Series

Use commas to separate three or more items of the same kind in a series.

The most common pattern separates the elements in a series by **commas**. The last comma is followed by an *and* or *or* that ties the whole group together:

> After dinner, *we talked, laughed, and sang.*
>
> In the late spring, the hills are bright with *red, white, and brown* poppies.
>
> Only 18 percent of this country's 56 million families are conventionally "nuclear," with *breadwinning fathers, homemaking mothers, and resident children.*—Jane Howard, *Families*

This basic *A, B, and C* pattern can be expanded to four or more elements:

> The government tries to *stifle* the growth of the poppy at its source, *cut* the flow, *spread* a protective net around the land, and finally *seize* the shipments that have gotten through.

Notice the following variations:

(1) Occasionally, you will arrange in a series *groups of words that already contain commas.* To prevent misreading, use **semicolons** to show the major breaks:

> Three persons were mentioned in her will: *John, her brother; Martin, her nephew;* and *Helen, her faithful friend.*

(2) For variety or special effect, a writer may use *commas only,* leaving out the connective:

> The idea was to pool all the needs of all those who had in one way or another been bested by their environment—*the crippled, the sick, the hungry, the ragged.*—John Lear, "The Business of Giving," *Saturday Review*

Note: The *last comma* in a series is often left out, even in formal writing:

> Then amid the silence, he *took off* his hat, *laid it* on the table *and stood* up.—James Joyce, "Ivy Day in the Committee Room"

Most teachers, however, require the use of the last comma. Use it to be safe:

SAFE: I *took* out my license, *laid* it on the table, and *watched* the agent pick it up.

P 4b   Coordinate Adjectives

Separate coordinate adjectives by a comma.

Two adjectives describing different qualities of the same noun may be coordinated by a **comma** rather than by *and*. They are then called coordinate adjectives. Notice a characteristic break in speech:

a *black* and *shaggy* dog ⟶	a *black, shaggy* dog
a *starved* and *exhausted* stranger ⟶	a *starved, exhausted* stranger
a *grand* and *awe-inspiring* sunset ⟶	a *grand, awe-inspiring* sunset

Not every pair of adjectives falls into this pattern. Often an adjective combines with a noun to indicate a type of person or object (a *public* servant, a *short* story, a *black* market). An adjective preceding such a combination modifies the combination *as a whole*. Do not separate the adjectives by a comma. Use the comma only if you could use *and* instead:

NO COMMA: A *secretive* public servant (not "secretive *and* public")
A *long* short story (not "long *and* short")
A *lively* black market (not "lively *and* black")

P 4c   Dates and Addresses

Use commas with dates, addresses, measurements, and similar information that has three or four parts.

Dates, addresses, page references, and the like often come in several parts. The different items are kept separate from each other by a **comma**. The last item is followed by a comma unless it is at the same time the last word of the sentence:

DATE: The date was *Tuesday, December 3, 1976.*

ADDRESS: Please sent my mail to *483 Tulane Street, Jackson, Oklahoma,* starting the first of the month.

REFERENCE: The quotation is from *Chapter V, page 43, line 7,* of the second volume.

Commas are also used to keep separate the different parts of *measurements* employing more than one unit of measurement. Here the last item is usually *not* separated from the rest of the sentence:

> The boy is now *five feet, seven inches* tall.
> *Nine pounds, three ounces* is an unusual weight for this kind of fish.

P 4d   Repetition and Contrast

Use commas between repeated or contrasted elements.

Use commas between expressions that are *identical or give two different versions of the same meaning*. Use the **comma** after a word or phrase to be repeated or to be followed by a definition or paraphrase:

> *Produce, produce!* This is the law among artists.
> We were there in the nine days before Christmas, *the Navidad.*
> Undergraduate education must prepare the student *not to walk away from choices, not to leave them to the experts.*—Adele Simmons, "Harvard Flunks the Test," *Harper's*

Use commas also to separate words or groups of words that establish a *contrast*:

> *His wife, not his brother,* needs the money more.
> *The days were warm, the nights cool.*
> Many entering freshmen and their parents seek an education that leads to *job security, not critical and independent thinking.*—Adele Simmons, "Harvard Flunks the Test," *Harper's*

EXERCISES

A. Check the following sentences for punctuation of coordinate or closely related elements. After the number of each sentence, put *S* for satisfactory, *U* for unsatisfactory. Be prepared to explain how you would revise unsatisfactory sentences.

1. It was economics that altered the condition of slavery, not *Uncle Tom's Cabin.*
2. Mexicans have in them the placidity the gentleness and the patience of the Indian as well as the violence of the Spaniard.
3. He remembered the arenas with their intricate grillwork gates; the beautiful girls in festive gowns of red, purple, and every hue imaginable; and the excited crowds shouting "Bravo" to the fierce-eyed matador.
4. My cousin was always flying off to places like Chattanooga Tennessee or Missoula Montana.
5. The editorial offices of the magazine were located at 235 East 45th Street, New York, New York.

6. Aaron thought of himself as a noble, dedicated person persecuted by callous, materialistic teachers and employers.
7. Lee was known as a strategist not as a tactician.
8. The marooned astronauts came to know hunger, thirst, cold, and the continual throbbing headache of oxygen deprivation.
9. Ralph ran stumbling along the rocks, saved himself on the edge of the pink cliff, and screamed at the ship. (William Golding)
10. After a while the bagelman arrives with a large box full of breakfast: coffee, steaming hot; a triple order of bacon; two fried eggs; and bagels, split and buttered.
11. She had last been seen leaving church on Sunday, April 7, 1974, in Cleveland, Ohio.
12. The floor of the office was gritty with cigarette butts torn handbills and crushed cartons.
13. We had not expected to find such honest, public servants among such poor pessimistic people.
14. For them yoga was a way of life, a cause, and a religion.
15. One corner of the room is fitted with three worn turntables, a huge electric clock, and a cantilevered microphone that hangs over a console of switches, buttons, and dials.

  B. What should be the punctuation at the blank space in each of the following sentences? Put C for comma or NC for no comma after the number of the sentence.

1. Prosperity as we know it depends heavily on oil _____ coal, and natural gas.
2. The company had moved its offices to Atlanta _____ Georgia.
3. Young journalists dream of exposing corrupt _____ public officials.
4. Seven feet, two inches _____ was unusual even for a basketball player.
5. The information appears in chapter 3 _____ page 48.
6. They had started their shop as a hobby _____ not as a business.
7. Kidnappings _____ bombings, and armed attacks had become commonplace.
8. They had come to Jamestown, Virginia _____ from Liverpool, England.
9. We joined hands _____ and sang the old nostalgic songs.
10. The new mayor owed much to her loyal _____ confident supporters.

P 5 PARENTHETIC ELEMENTS

Use dashes, parentheses, or commas to set off parenthetic elements.

To some extent, conventions of punctuation follow the rhythms of speech. This is true of conventional ways of setting off parenthetic elements, which *interrupt* a sentence without becoming grammatically a part of it.

P 5a   Dashes   −/

Use the dash—sparingly—to signal a sharp break in a sentence.

A speaker may stop in the middle of a sentence to supply some preliminary detail or additional clarification. In writing, set such material off from the rest of a sentence by **dashes**. Use dashes for the following situations:

(1) A modifier that would normally be set off by commas in turn contains *internal commas*:

> The old-style family—*large, close-knit, firmly under the thumb of a patriarch or matriarch*—does still exist.—Anne Tyler, "The Resilient Institution," *Quest*

(2) *A complete sentence is inserted into another sentence*, without a connective or relative pronoun to join them:

> Lady Macbeth—*has this been noted?*—takes very little stock in the witches. —Mary McCarthy, "General Macbeth," *Harper's*

(3) A *list* interrupts rather than follows a clause:

> Women tolerate qualities in a lover—*moodiness, selfishness, unreliability, brutality*—that they would never countenance in a husband.—Susan Sontag, *Against Interpretation*

(4) After a list, a sentence starts anew with a summarizing *all*, *these*, or *those*:

> *The visual essay, the rhythmic album, the invitation to drop in on a casual conversation*—these are the traits by which television, as television, has come to be recognized.—Walter Kerr, "What Good Is Television?" *Horizon*

(5) A word or phrase is made to stand out for emphasis or for a *climactic effect*:

> After twenty-three years, he was leaving Newston jail—*a free man.*
> Every time you look at one of the marvels of modern technology, you find a by-product—*unintended, unpredictable, and often lethal.*

(6) A *humorous afterthought or ironic aside* follows after a pause:

> Traditionally, novels are read in the United States by 1.7 percent of the population—*which somewhat reduces their clout.*—Richard Condon, "That's Entertainment!" *Harper's*

P 5b   Parentheses ( )/

Use parentheses to enclose unimportant data (or mere asides).

Parentheses are most appropriate for facts or ideas mentioned in passing:

> The University of Mexico was founded in 1553 (*almost a century before Harvard*).
>
> Kazan directed the rest of his considerable steam into studying English (*he graduated with honors*), waiting on tables, and joining as many extracurricular campus clubs as he could.—Thomas B. Morgan, "Elia Kazan's Great Expectations," *Harper's*

Use parentheses around dates, addresses, page references, chemical formulas, and similar information if it might be of interest to some readers but is not an essential part of the text. Here are some typical examples: *(p. 34) (first published in 1910) (now called Market Street)*.

Note: When a sentence in parentheses begins *after* end punctuation, end punctuation is required inside the final parenthesis:

> Select your purchases with care. (*No refunds are permitted.*)

P 5c   Commas for Parenthetic Elements ,/

Use commas for parenthetic elements that blend into a sentence with only a slight break.

Sometimes we interrupt a sentence for clarification or comment, with only a minor break. Use **commas** to set off such "light interrupters":

> I do not believe that gifts, *whether of mind or character*, can be weighed like sugar and butter. (Virginia Woolf)

Note especially the following:

(1) Use commas when you interrupt a statement to *address the reader* or to *comment on* what you are saying:

DIRECT ADDRESS: Marriage, *dear boy*, is a serious business.

COMMENT: Politicians, *you will agree*, were never popular in this part of the country.
Our candidate, *it seems*, is not very well known.

(2) Use commas to set off *introductory greetings and exclamations*, as well as an introductory *yes* or *no*. Such introductory tags frequently precede a statement in conversation and in informal writing:

TAG OPENING: *Why,* I don't even know that man.
Yes, you can now buy Pinko napkins in different colors.
Well, you can't have everything.

(3) Use commas to set off the *"echo questions"* often added to a statement to ask for agreement or confirmation:

TAG QUESTION: You are my friend, *aren't you?*
So he says he is sick, *does he?*

(4) Use commas for slight breaks caused by *sentence elements that have changed their usual position in the sentence*:

Laws, *to be cheerfully obeyed,* must be both just and practicable.
The Spaniards, *at the height of their power,* were great builders of towns.

Note: Commas may take the place of dashes to set off a word for emphasis. They suggest a *thoughtful pause* rather than a dramatic break:

We should act, *and suffer,* in accordance with our principles.
People cannot, *or will not,* put down the facts.

EXERCISE

Check the following passages for conventional punctuation of parenthetic elements. After the number of each passage, write *S* for satisfactory, *U* for unsatisfactory. Explain why satisfactory passages were punctuated the way they were.

1. Well, you have made your point, Danny. The rest of us, you will agree, have the right to our own opinion.
2. Many discoveries though first made in wartime, were later put to peacetime uses.
3. Hard as it is for many of us to believe, women are not really superior to men in intelligence or humanity—they are only equal. (*Anne Roiphe*)
4. Most of the energy we use—whether from coal, oil, or water—ultimately derives from the sun.
5. Why if I were you I would return the whole shipment to the company.
6. Geothermal power in your backyard, unless you have a geyser on your property, just can't be achieved.

7. Most energy (as leaders of the ecology movement have told us for years) comes from fossil fuels.
8. Nuclear fuel would create an enormous waste problem (as indeed there is already with our existing uranium plants.
9. Many people would agree, offhand, that every creature lives its life and then dies. This might, indeed, be called a truism. But, like some other truisms, it is not true. The lowest forms of life, such as the amoebae, normally (that is, barring accidents) do not die. (Susanne K. Langer)
10. Fashions (especially adolescent fashions) do not, as a rule outlast their generation.

P 6   QUOTATION

Know how to punctuate different kinds of quoted material.

Often, you will need to show that you are reproducing information or ideas derived from a specific source. Show that you are quoting something first said or observed by someone else.

P 6a   Direct Quotation   "/

In repeating someone's exact words, distinguish them clearly from your own text.

Direct quotations are enclosed in **quotation marks**. They are usually separated by a **comma** from the credit tag (the statement identifying the source):

> She said, "Leave me alone."
> "I don't care," he said.
> I once asked her what she would like her epitaph to read. She replied, "She lived long enough to be of some use."—Jean Houston, "The Mind of Margaret Mead," *Quest*

The following variations are important:

(1) Often the *credit tag interrupts the quotation*. Use **commas** both before and after the credit tag if it splits one complete sentence:

> "Both marijuana and alcohol," *Dr. Jones reports*, "slow reaction times on a whole spectrum of tasks of varying complexities."

Use a comma before and a **period** (or semicolon) after the credit tag if it comes between two complete sentences:

"All men are curious," *Aristotle wrote.* "They naturally desire knowledge."
"Hurry back," *she said;* "we will wait for you."

(2) No comma is required with very *short quotations* or with *quotations worked into the pattern of a sentence* that is not a mere credit tag:

Your saying "I am sorry" was not enough to soothe his wounded pride.
The clatter of dishes and tableware, mingled with lusty shouts of "Seconds here!" and "Please pass the butter!", will resound across the country.—John Crawford, "A Plea for Physical Fatness," *Atlantic*

No comma is required when the credit tag follows a question or an exclamation:

"Is everybody all right?" he shouted at the top of his voice.

(3) *Long or formal quotations* are often introduced by a **colon** instead of a comma. Whether you use a comma or a colon, capitalize the first word of the quotation if it was capitalized in the original source (or if it would have been capitalized if written down):

Saarinen's definition of architecture's purposes describes his work: "To shelter and enhance man's life on earth and to fulfill his belief in the nobility of his existence."

(4) *Long quotations* (more than four or five typed lines) should be set off from the rest of a paper *not* by quotation marks but by indention and single-spacing. The same applies to quotations consisting of more than a full line of poetry. (See the sample research paper in Chapter 8 for examples of such **block quotations**.)

(5) Show when the person you are quoting is quoting someone else. In a quotation marked by the conventional set of double quotation marks, **single quotation marks** signal a *quotation within a quotation*:

He said, "Our congressman's constant cry of 'Cut that budget!' deceives no one."
"Many subjects," one researcher says, "only get through the rather scary effects of the drug by reassuring themselves with the knowledge that they will 'come down' in a few hours."

P 6b   Terminal Marks in Quotations   *p*

Observe conventional sequences when quotation marks coincide with other marks of punctuation.

Note the following guidelines:

(1) Commas conventionally *come before the final quotation mark*, whereas semicolons and colons conventionally follow it:

> As he said, "Don't worry about me," the ship pulled away from the quay.
> You said, "I don't need your sympathy"; therefore, I didn't offer any.

(2) End punctuation usually *comes before* the final quotation marks, as in all the examples given so far. Sometimes, however, you will have to use a question mark or an exclamation mark after the quotation has formally ended. This means that the quotation itself is not a question or an exclamation. Rather, you are asking a question or exclaiming *about the quotation*:

> Who said, "We are strangers here; the world is from of old"?
> Don't ever tell a girl, "There'll never be another woman like my mother"!

Note: A terminal mark is not duplicated at the end of a quotation, even when logic might seem to require its repetition. For instance, use only one question mark even when you are asking a question about a question:

> Were you the student who asked, "Could we hold the class on the lawn?"

P 6c   Insertions and Omissions   *p*

In direct quotation, indicate clearly any changes you make in the original text.

Use special marks as follows:

(1) If for any reason you insert *explanations or comments of your own*, set them off from the quoted material by **square brackets**:

> As Dr. Habenichts observes, "Again and again, they [the Indians] saw themselves deprived of lands of whose possession they had been assured with solemn oaths."
> The note read: "Left Camp B Wednesday, April 3 [actually April 4]. Are trying to reach Camp C before we run out of supplies."

(2) When you *omit unnecessary or irrelevant material* from a quotation, indicate the omission by three spaced periods (called an **ellipsis**). If the omission occurs after a period in the original text, retain the sentence period and then insert the ellipsis.

> The report concluded on an optimistic note: "All three of the patients . . . are making remarkable progress toward recovery."
>
> "To be a bird is to be alive more intensely than any other living creature, man included. . . . They live in a world that is always present, mostly full of joy." So wrote N. J. Berrill, Professor of Zoology at McGill University.—Joseph Wood Krutch, "If You Don't Mind My Saying So," *The American Scholar*

Note: To indicate *extensive omissions* (a line or more of poetry, a paragraph or more of prose), you may use a single typed line of spaced periods.

P 6d   Indirect Quotation   *p*

In indirect quotations, reproduce someone else's ideas or thoughts but translate them into your own words.

Indirectly quoted statements often take the form of noun clauses introduced by *that*. Indirectly quoted questions take the form of noun clauses introduced by words like *whether, why, how,* and *which*. Such clauses are *not* separated from the statement indicating the source by a comma or colon. They are *not* enclosed in quotation marks:

DIRECT: The mayor replied, "I doubt the wisdom of such a move."
INDIRECT: The mayor replied *that she doubted the wisdom of such a move.*

DIRECT: The artist asked, "Which of the drawings do you like best?"
INDIRECT: The artist asked *which of the drawings I liked best.*

Note two exceptions:

(1) We sometimes make *the source statement go with the indirect quotation as parenthetic material.* We may then need **commas**:

> *As Gandhi remarked,* the first consequence of nonviolent action is to harden the heart of those who are being assaulted by charity. But, *he continued,* all the while they are being driven to a frenzy of rage, they are haunted by the terrible knowledge of how wrong they are.—Michael Harrington, "Whence Comes Their Passion," *The Reporter*

(2) Even in an indirect quotation, you may want to keep *part of the original wording. Use* **quotation marks** to show you are repeating some words or phrases exactly as they were used:

> Like Thackeray's daughters, I read *Jane Eyre* in childhood, carried away "as by a whirlwind." (Adrienne Rich)

P 6e   Words Set Off from Context

Use quotation marks to indicate words and phrases that are not part of your normal vocabulary.

Mark expressions that are not your own, even though you may not be quoting them from any specific source:

(1) **Quotation marks** may identify words that you employ for *local color or ironic effect.* They enable you to hold an expression, as it were, at arm's length:

> It would seem that every modern child's pleasure must have its "constructive aspects."—Lois Phillips Hudson, "The Buggy on the Roof," *Atlantic*
>
> The argument that these taboos exist only because of "sexual hang-ups" ignores a much more likely explanation.—Barbara Lawrence, "Four-Letter Words Can Hurt You," *New York Times*

(2) Either quotation marks or italicized print (underlining in a typed manuscript) identifies *technical terms* probably new to the reader or *words discussed as words*, as in a discussion of grammar or meaning:

> She wore a "Mother Hubbard," a loose, full gown long since out of fashion.
> The word *mob* was attacked as slang by some eighteenth-century writers.

(3) **Italics** rather than quotation marks identify *words that have been borrowed from foreign languages* and have not become part of the general vocabulary of English.

> Young Latin American men are very touchy these days about *machismo*, best translated as "an emphasis on masculinity."—Linda Wolfe, "The Machismo Mystique," *New York*

Many legal and scientific terms borrowed from Latin belong in this category:

A writ of *certiorari* is used by a superior court to obtain judicial records from an inferior court or quasi-judicial agency.

The word "comet" comes from the Greek *aster kometes,* meaning long-haired star.

Note: We put quotation marks around the titles of poems, articles, songs, and the like that would normally be *part* of a larger publication. We italicize (underline in typing) the title of a complete publication:

The index to the *New York Times* devoted three column inches to the heading "Sex" in 1952.

For more on italics see **M 1d.**

EXERCISES

A. Check the following passages for conventional punctuation of quoted material. After the number of each passage, write *S* for satisfactory, *U* for unsatisfactory. Explain why the satisfactory passages were punctuated the way they were.

1. Tillie Olsen wrote about what she called "unprivileged lives."
2. "That was sweet of you," my cousin said.
3. The student's voice was loud and angry when she asked the dean, "What do you think we are, little kids."
4. "We've completely crossed the void," he told Ichor. "We are approaching the outer limits of a planetary system."
5. Stan Steiner has said, "the Chicano can rightly claim that he has been humiliated by the textbooks, tongue-tied by teachers, de-educated by the schools."
6. The man from Buffalo kept asking the guide "what he meant by primitive?"
7. This "ardent and avowed rebel," as she described herself to her friend Benjamin Franklin, had other schemes to keep her busy. (Miriam Troop)
8. The *Daily News,* in an editorial headed "We Beg to Differ," labeled the calling out of the National Guard "ill-advised and dangerous."
9. "Something is wrong here," she said, "people are not following their instructions."
10. When she came back from Mexico, she kept using words like *paseo* and *abrazo.*
11. She thought for a while and said, "All I remember is the announcement: 'Follow Code 305.'"
12. Would you have had the heart to tell him: "Time is up?"
13. The speaker charged "that the television audience resembled the ancient Romans, who liked to see the gladiators do battle to the death."
14. The speaker quoted Jefferson as saying that "our new circumstances" require "new words, new phrases, and the transfer of old words to new objects."
15. The constant war cry of my high school English teachers was give an example!

B. What punctuation, if any, is missing at the blank space in each of the following passages? Write it after the number of the passage. Write *No* if no punctuation is necessary. (Make no changes in capitalization.)

1. The chief psychologist said _____ the accidents will be simulated."
2. The lecturer was explaining what is meant by "total recall _____
3. Where does it say, "No minors are allowed _____
4. According to Rachel Carson, "Sir James Clark Ross set out from England in command of two ships 'bound for the utmost limits of the navigable globe _____
5. Restaurant owners were used to offering local police "something for their trouble _____
6. "The main problem," the commission said _____ is insufficient training of personnel."
7. "The main problem is not mechanical defects," the report said _____ it is human error."
8. "Where is the money going to come from _____ the governor asked.
9. He just mumbled _____ Excuse me" and walked on.
10. He carefully explained _____ why the regulations had not been followed.

Mechanics and Spelling

CHAPTER SIXTEEN

M 1 Manuscript Mechanics
    a Penmanship and Typing
    b Titles of Themes
    c Spacing and Syllabication
    d Italics

M 2 Abbreviations and Numbers
    a Abbreviations
    b Numbers

SP 1 Spelling Problems
    a Spelling and Pronunciation
    b Variant Forms
    c Confusing Pairs

SP 2 Spelling Rules
    a *I* Before *E*
    b Doubled Consonant
    c *Y* as a Vowel
    d Final *E*

SP 3 Words Often Misspelled

SP 4 The Apostrophe
    a Contractions
    b Possessives
    c Plurals of Letters and Symbols

SP 5 Capitals
    a Proper Names
    b Titles of Publications

SP 6 The Hyphen
    a Compound Words
    b Prefixes
    c Group Modifiers

Submit neat and competently prepared copy.

Whenever you hand in a theme or a report, the outward appearance of your manuscript is the first thing to strike your reader. A good first impression is likely to put the reader in a receptive mood.

M 1a   Penmanship and Typing

Make sure all copy, whether handwritten or typed, is neat and legible.

Remember the following guidelines:

(1) To produce legible *handwritten* copy, use composition paper of standard size, preferably ruled in *wide lines*, and a reliable pen. Prune your writing of flourishes; avoid excessive slanting or excessive crowding. Unconventional handwriting is much more likely to annoy than it is to impress the reader.

(2) To prepare *typewritten* copy, use unlined paper of standard size. Onionskin paper or semitransparent sheets are for carbon copies. *Double-space* all material except block quotations and footnotes. Leave two spaces after a period or other end punctuation. Use two hyphens—with no space on either side—to make a dash.

(3) Proofread all typewritten copy carefully. *Last-minute corrections* are permissible on the final copy, provided they look neat and are few in number:

• *To take out a word or phrase*, draw a line through it. Do not use parentheses or square brackets for this purpose:

> He started the complaints to which we had
> become accustomed ~~to~~.

• *To correct a word*, draw a line through it and insert the corrected word in the space immediately above. Do not cross out or insert individual letters:

> A person working in an office has to stay
>   collected
> calm, cool, and ~~collective~~.

• *To add a missing word*, insert a caret (∧) and write the word immediately above:

be

Discontent can∧and has been expressed in many ways.

• *To change the paragraphing of a paper*, insert the symbol ¶ to indicate an additional paragraph break. Insert *"no ¶"* in the margin to indicate that an existing paragraph break should be ignored.

M 1b   Titles of Themes

Use standard form for the titles of your themes.

Titles of themes follow the rules for the capitalization of words in titles of publications (see **SP 5b**). Do *not* underline or put in quotation marks the title that you assign to one of your own themes. Use a question mark or an exclamation mark after it where appropriate, but do *not* use a period even if your title is a complete sentence:

> Chivalry Is Dead
> Is Chivalry Dead?
> Chivalry Is Dead!

M 1c   Spacing and Syllabication   *div*

Observe conventional spacing and syllabication.

Whether your papers are handwritten or typed, leave adequate margins. An inch and a half on the left and at the top, and an inch on the right and at the bottom are about standard. Indent the first lines of paragraphs, about an inch in longhand or five spaces in typed copy.

Leaving a slightly uneven right margin is better than dividing words at the end of every second or third line. Dictionaries generally use centered dots to indicate where a word may conventionally be divided *(com·pli·ment)*. Remember:

(1) Setting off *single letters* saves little or no space and tends to confuse the reader. Do not divide words like *about*, *alone*, and *enough* or like *many* and *via*. Similarly, do not set off the ending *-ed* in words like *complained* or *renewed*.

(2) Hyphenated words become confusing when divided at any point *other* than at the original hyphen. Do not break up the *American* in "un-American" or the *sister* in "sister-in-law."

(3) Do not divide the *last word* on a page.

M 1d   Italics   *ital*

Use italics to set off special words and phrases from the rest of a sentence.

Italics (or slanted type) are indicated in the handwritten or typed manuscript by underlining.

(1) Italics identify *technical terms* and words borrowed from *foreign languages*. (See **P 6e**.)

(2) Italics *emphasize* or call special attention to part of a sentence:

> The judge told me to apologize *in person* to everyone who had sat down in the freshly painted pews.
> The company is not liable for accidents caused by the negligence of employees or *by mechanical defects*.

(3) Italics set off the *title of a publication* from the text in which it is cited. Italicize titles of periodicals and of works published as separate units. Use **quotation marks** to set off titles of articles, chapters, songs, or poems that are merely a part of a complete publication:

> In *El Laberinto de la Soledad*, Octavio Paz describes the Mexican character.
> The old songs like "The Jolly Ploughboy" and "The Green Glens of Antrim" gave way to "Galway Bay" and "I'll Take You Home Again, Kathleen."

M 2   ABBREVIATIONS AND NUMBERS

Avoid the overuse of abbreviations in ordinary prose.

Abbreviations save time and space. Here as in other matters, however, formal written English discourages excessive short cuts.

M 2a Abbreviations *ab*

Spell out inappropriate abbreviations.

The following abbreviations are *generally appropriate* in expository writing:

(1) Before or after names, the titles *Mr.*, *Mrs.*, *Dr.*, *St.* (*Saint*); the abbreviations *Jr.* and *Sr.*; degrees like *M.D.* and *Ph.D.* (Mr. John J. Smith, Jr.; Dr. Alfred Joyce or Alfred Joyce, M.D.). Use *Prof.* only before the *full* name: Prof. James F. Jones.

(2) Before or after numerals, the abbreviations *No.*, A.D. and B.C., A.M. and P.M., and the symbol $ (in 1066 A.D.; at 5:30 A.M.; $275).

(3) Initials standing for the names of agencies, organizations, business firms, technical processes, chemical compounds, and the like, when the full name is awkward or unfamiliar: *AFL-CIO*, *FBI*, *CIA*, *IBM*, *UNICEF*, *PTA*, *FM radio*.

(4) Some common Latin abbreviations: *e.g.* (for example), *etc.* (and so on), *i.e.* (that is). However, the modern tendency is to prefer the corresponding English expressions.

Other abbreviations are appropriate only in addresses, newspaper reports, technical reports, and other special contexts. Most of these have to be *written in full* in ordinary expository prose:

- With a a few exceptions, names of countries, states, streets, and the like are spelled out in ordinary writing: *United States; Schenectady, New York; Union Street.* (Exceptions: *USSR; Washington, D.C.)*

- The ampersand ("&") and abbreviations like *Inc.* and *Bros.* occur in ordinary writing only in references to organizations that employ those abbreviations in their official titles: *Smith & Company, Inc.* Spell out % and ¢.

- In ordinary expository prose, *lb.* (pound), *oz.* (ounce), *ft.* (foot), and *in.* (inch) are usually spelled out. Some units of measurement are more unwieldy and are abbreviated, provided they are used with figures: *45 mph, 1500 rpm.*

M 2b Numbers *ab*

Use figures in accordance with standard practice.

In ordinary expository prose, the use of figures is to some extent restricted. They are generally appropriate in references to the day of the month (*May 13*), the year (*1917*), street numbers (*1014 Union Avenue*), and page numbers (*Chapter 7, page 18*). For other uses of numbers, the following conventions are widely observed:

(1) Numbers from one to ten, and *round numbers* requiring no more than two words, are usually spelled out: *three dollars a seat, five hundred years later, ten thousand copies.*

(2) Figures are used for *exact sums, technical measurements, decimals, and percentages,* as well as for references to time using A.M. or P.M.: *$7.22; 500,673 inhabitants; 57 percent; 2:30* P.M.

(3) Figures are avoided at the beginning of a sentence: "Fifteen out of 28 replied . . ." or "When questioned, 15 out of 28 replied. . . ." Except in special situations like this one, changes from figures to words (and vice versa) in a series of numbers are generally avoided.

(4) When spelled out, *compound numbers* from 21 to 99 are hyphenated: *twenty-five, one hundred and forty-six.* (See also **SP 6a.**)

EXERCISE

Rewrite the following passage, using abbreviations and numerals in accordance with standard practice:

Mister Geo. Brown had resided at Eighteen N. Washington St. since Feb. nineteen-hundred and forty-four. Though he weighed only one hundred and twenty-six lbs. and measured little more than 5 ft., he was an ardent devotee of the rugged life. He did his exercises every A.M. and refused to send for the Dr. when he had a cold. 3 yrs. after he moved here from Chicago, Ill., the Boy Scouts of America made him an honorary member, & he soon became known in scout circles for the many $ he contributed to the Boy Scout movement. One Sat. afternoon B. forgot to spell out the amount on a check for one-hundred and twenty-five dollars intended for a bldg. drive and payable to the B.S. of A. The treasurer, Bernard Simpson of Arlington, Va., wrote in 2 additional figures, spelled out the changed amount, and left the U.S. after withdrawing B.'s life savings of twelve-thousand five-hundred and fifty dollars from the local bank. "Ah," said Geo. when he found 2$ and 36 cts. left in his account, "if I had only spelled out the No.'s and abbrev.!"

SP 1   SPELLING PROBLEMS   *sp*

Improve your spelling by developing good spelling habits.

Merely looking up misspelled words has little long-range effect. The following procedure has a good chance of producing results:

(1) *Master the true "unforgivables."* A handful of common words are misspelled again and again by poor spellers. No matter how intelligent or capable you are, misspelling one of these will make you look ignorant. Make absolutely sure that you master the words in the following list. Watch out for them in your writing. *Never* misspell one of these:

accept	definite	receive
all right	environment	similar
a lot	occurred	studying
basically	perform	surprise
believe	probably	writing

(2) *Start a record of your own personal spelling problems.* Whenever a piece of writing is returned to you, write down all the words that you misspelled. Work your way through a list of common spelling demons (such as the one printed under **SP 3**). List those that you have found troublesome in your own writing.

(3) *Put in twenty minutes three times a week over a period of time.* Unless you work on your spelling regularly, you will make little progress. You cannot unlearn in two or three hours the spelling habits that you developed over many years.

(4) *Fix each word firmly in your mind.* At each sitting, take up a group of perhaps ten or twenty spelling words. If you are a "visualizer," place your spelling words before you in clear, legible handwriting. Try putting them on a set of small note cards that you can carry around with you. Run your eyes over each word until you can see both the individual letters and the whole word at the same time. If you learn mainly by ear, read each word aloud. Then spell each letter individually: *Receive*—R-E-C-E-I-V-E. If you learn best when you can bring your nerves and muscles into play, try writing each word in large letters. Trace it over several times.

(5) *Make use of memory devices like the following:*

acquainted:	MAC got ACquainted.
all right:	ALL RIGHT means ALL is RIGHT.
beginning:	There's an INNING in begINNING.
believe:	Don't beLIEve LIEs.
criticism:	There's a CRITIC in CRITICism.
environment:	There's IRON in the envIRONment.
government:	People who GOVERN are a GOVERNment.
library:	The LiBRarians BRought BRicks for the LIBRARY.
performance:	He gave a PERfect PERformance.
recognition:	There's a COG in reCOGnition.

surprise: The SURfer had a SURPrise.
villain: There's a VILLA in VILLAin.

DIAGNOSTIC TEST

Look at the blank in each of the following sentences. Of the three choices that follow the sentences, which is the right one? Put the letter for the right choice after the number of the sentence.

1. We were _____ a trip to Wyoming.
   a. planing   b. planning   c. plannying
2. Everyone re _____ved a printed notice.
   a. cei   b. cie   c. cea
3. The two _____ houses had both been burglarized.
   a. family's   b. families   c. families'
4. I hesitate to say _____ to blame.
   a. who's   b. whose   c. whos
5. We usually took our vacation in Feb_____.
   a. uary   b. ruary   c. uerry
6. A political leader needs _____.
   a. self-confidance   b. self confidents   c. self-confidence
7. What happened to the old-fashioned _____?
   a. Forth Of July   b. fourth of july   c. Fourth of July
8. The ambulance _____ arrived sooner.
   a. should have   b. should of   c. shoudve
9. We were both taking a course in _____ literature.
   a. womans   b. women's   c. womens'
10. The rule _____ apply to people over sixty-five.
    a. doesnt   b. dosent   c. doesn't
11. The decision was _____ a mistake.
    a. definately   b. definitely   c. definitly
12. The organization included both teachers and _____.
    a. principles   b. principal's   c. principals
13. When the subsidy ran out, _____ was felt everywhere.
    a. its absence   b. it's absence   c. its absents
14. The design was bas_____ sound.
    a. ically   b. icly   c. icaly
15. The researchers were stud_____ yellowed documents.
    a. yng   b. ying   c. ing
16. My uncle just had his _____ birthday.
    a. fourty-fourth   b. forty fourth   c. forty-fourth
17. The _____ debts had doubled during the year.
    a. city's   b. cities   c. citys
18. They were reluctant to _____ handouts from the govern-ment.
    a. except   b. acept   c. accept
19. The neighborhood had many _____ families.
    a. polish american b. Polish-american   c. Polish-American

20. The mansion looked like something out of _____.
    a. *Gone With The Wind*   b. *Gone with the Wind*   c. *Gone with the wind*

SP 1a   Spelling and Pronunciation

Watch for differences between the spoken and the written word.

Some words become spelling problems because the gap between spelling and pronunciation is unusually wide.

(1) *Watch for sounds not clearly heard in much informal speech.* Be sure to include the italicized letters in the following words:

accidenta*l*ly	lib*r*ary
Feb*r*uary	proba*b*ly
cand*i*date	quant*i*ty
gove*rn*ment	

(2) *Watch for silent consonants.* Know how to spell the following:

condem*n*	de*b*t	mortgage
for*eig*n	dou*b*t	sover*eig*n

(3) *Watch for vowels in unstressed positions.* *A, e,* and *i* become indistinguishable in the endings *-ate* and *-ite, -able* and *-ible, -ance* and *-ence, -ant* and *-ent.* If you can, choose the right ending by associating the word with a closely related one: *definite* (finish, definition); *separate* (separation); *ultimate* (ultimatum); *indispensable* (dispensary). Watch out for the following:

- *a:* accept*a*ble, accept*a*nce, advis*a*ble, attend*a*nce, attend*a*nt, brilli*a*nt, performnce
- *e:* consist*e*nt, excell*e*nce, excell*e*nt, exist*e*nce, experi*e*nce, independ*e*nt, persist*e*nt, tend*e*ncy
- *i:* irresist*i*ble, plaus*i*ble, poss*i*ble, suscept*i*ble

(4) *Watch for* have *in combinations like* could have been, should have been, *and* might have been. Never substitute *of:*

WRONG:	could of been	should of known	might of failed
RIGHT:	could *have* been	should *have* known	might *have* failed

SP 1b Variant Forms

Watch for different forms of the same word.

Some words are confusing because they appear in different forms.

(1) Watch out for *different spellings of the same root*:

ti*ll*	*un*til
four, *four*teen	*fo*rty
nine, *nine*ty	*nin*th
*prec*ede	*proc*eed

(2) Watch out for spelling differences in pairs of words representing *different parts of speech*:

absor*b*—absor*p*tion	genero*us*—genero*s*ity
advi*se* (v.)—advi*ce* (n.)	geni*us*—ingeni*ous*
consci*ence*—consci*entious*	proc*eed*—proc*edure*
courte*ous*—courte*sy*	prono*unce*—pron*un*ciation
curi*ous*—curio*sity*	
disse*nt*—disse*ns*ion	

(3) Watch out when spelling changes because of *a change in the grammatical form* of the same word. For instance, we "choose" and "lead" in the present, but we "chose" and "led" in the past. Some plural forms cause spelling difficulties: one *man* but several *men*, one *woman* but several *women*. Remember these especially:

SINGULAR:	hero	Negro	potato	tomato	wife
PLURAL:	heroes	Negroes	potatoes	tomatoes	wives
SINGULAR:	freshman	postman	life	veto	calf
PLURAL:	freshmen	postmen	lives	vetoes	calves

Be sure to add the *-ed* for *past tense* or *past participle* in words like the following:

used to:	He *used* to live here.
supposed to:	She was *supposed* to write.
prejudiced:	They were *prejudiced* (biased) against me.

Note: Your dictionary lists the correct spelling of plural forms that are difficult or unusual. Sometimes it lists two acceptable forms: *buffalos* or *buffaloes*, *scarfs* or *scarves*.

SP 1c Confusing Pairs

Watch for words that sound similar or alike.

Some words need attention because they *sound* similar but differ in spelling or in meaning. Try to apply tests like the following:

WHOSE?   *their* car; they and *their* parents
WHERE?   here and *there*; it wasn't *there*

TAKE *ON*:   I *accepted* the job.
TAKE *OUT*:   The law *excepts* students.

Know the following pairs:

accept:	to *accept* a bribe; to find something *acceptable*; to make an *acceptance* speech
except:	everyone *except* Judy; to make an *exception*; to *except* (exempt, exclude) present company
capital:	unused *capital*; modern *capitalism*; the *capital* of France; *capital* letters
capitol:	the cupola of the *Capitol*; remodeling the façade of the *Capitol* (a building)
cite:	*cited* for bravery; to *cite* many different authorities; a *citation* for reckless driving
site:	the *site* of the new high school (where it is *situated* or located)
sight:	knew him by *sight* (vision)
council:	the members of the city *council*; *Councilor* Brown
counsel:	the *counseling* staff of the college; camp *counselors*
desert:	he lost his way in the *desert*; he *deserted* his family; he got his just *deserts*
dessert:	the dinner did not include a *dessert*
effect:	to *effect* (produce, bring about) a change; immediate *effects*; an *effective* speech
affect:	it *affected* (influenced) my grade; he spoke with an *affected* (artificial) British accent
loose:	*loose* and fast; *loosen* your grip
lose:	win or *lose*; a bad *loser*
personal:	a *personal* appeal; speak to her *personally* (in person)
personnel:	a *personnel* bureau; hire additional *personnel* (employees)
presents:	visitors bearing *presents* (gifts)
presence:	your *presence* is requested; *presence* of mind (being there)

| principal: | his principal (main) argument; the principal of the school; principal (main sum) and interest |
| principle: | principles (rules, standards) of conduct; the principles of economics |

| quiet: | be quiet; a quiet neighborhood |
| quite: | quite so; not quite (entirely) |

| than: | bigger than life; more trouble than it is worth (comparison) |
| then: | now and then; until then (time) |

| there: | here and there; there you are; no one was there |
| their: | they lost their appetite; mental ills and their cure |

| to: | go to bed, cut to pieces; easy to do, hard to deny |
| too: | too good to be true; bring your children, too (also) |

| whether: | whether good or bad |
| weather: | bad weather; to weather the storm |

EXERCISES

A. After the number of each sentence, write down the choice that fits the context.

1. Everyone *accepted/excepted* our invitation.
2. The injury *effected/affected* her hearing.
3. The *presence/presents* of heavily armed troops quieted the crowd.
4. The teachers shouted down the surprised *principle/principal*.
5. The new rules applied to all *personal/personnel*.
6. He loved the town, but staying *their/there* had become impossible.
7. She cherished the *quiet/quite* moments between visits.
8. The speaker had antagonized most of the *woman/women* in the audience.
9. Seymour was *too/to* short-tempered to work in public relations.
10. Anything was better *then/than* going back down the mountain.
11. Three members of the city *council/counsel* had resigned.
12. Most farms were *then/than* family-owned.
13. He always lectured us about sound business *principles/principals*.
14. The test was given to all incoming *freshman/freshmen*.
15. Her grandparents had been *prejudice/prejudiced* against poor immigrants.
16. Ever since he found the money, he has been bothered by his *conscious/conscience*.
17. Her mother *use/used* to run a store in a small Southern town.
18. Somebody should *of/have* called the police.
19. Several people had parked *their/there* motorcycles in the driveway.
20. No one knew *whether/weather* we could meet the deadline.

B. Insert the missing letter or letters in each of the following words: accept ___ nce, attend ___ nce, brilli ___ nt, consist ___ ncy, curi ___ sity, defin ___ te, excell ___ nt, exist ___ nce, experi ___ nce, independ ___ nt, indispens ___ ble, occurr ___ nce, irresist ___ ble, perform ___ nce, persist ___ nt, prec ___ ding, proc ___ dure pron ___ nciation, separ ___ te, tend ___ ncy.

C. Look up the plural of *cargo, Eskimo, hoof, mosquito, motto, piano, solo, soprano, wharf, zero.*

D. In available dictionaries, check the status of simplified spellings like *traveled, thru, anesthetic, tho, catalog,* or any others you have encountered.

SP 2   SPELLING RULES   *sp*

Let a few simple spelling rules help you with common errors.

The purpose of spelling rules is to help you memorize words that follow a common pattern. Spelling rules provide a key to a group of words that you would otherwise have to study individually.

SP 2a   *I* Before *E*

Put *i* before *e* except after *c*.

The same sound is often spelled differently in different words. For instance, *ie* and *ei* often stand for the same sound. If you sort out the words in question, you get the following:

ie:	achieve, believe, chief, grief, niece, piece (of pie), relieve
cei:	ceiling, conceited, conceive, perceive, receive, receipt

In the second group of words, the *ei* follows the letter *c*. In other words, it is *i* before *e* except after *c*. Exceptions:

ei:	either, leisure, neither, seize, weird
cie:	financier, species

SP 2b   Doubled Consonant

Double a single final consonant before an added vowel.

In many words, *a single final consonant* is doubled before an ending (or **suffix**) that begins with a vowel: *-ed, -er, -est, -ing.* Doubling occurs under the following conditions:

(1) *The vowel before the final consonant must be a single vowel.* It cannot be a "long" or double vowel (**diphthong**) indicated in writing by combinations like *oa, ea, ee,* and *ou* or by a silent final *e* (k*i*te, h*o*pe, h*a*te). Note the differences in pronunciation and in spelling in the following pairs:

DOUBLING	NO DOUBLING
bar—barred	bare—bared
bat—batted	boat—boating
hop—hopping	hope—hoping
plan—planned	plane—planed
red—redder	read—reading
scrap—scrapped	scrape—scraped
slip—slipped	sleep—sleeping
stop—stopped	stoop—stooped

(2) *The last syllable before the suffix must be the one stressed in pronunciation.* Sometimes a shift in stress will be reflected in a difference in the spelling of different forms of the same word. Compare the following groups:

DOUBLING	NO DOUBLING
admit, admitted, admittance	edit, edited, editing
forget, forgetting, forgettable	benefit, benefited
begin, beginning, beginner	harden, hardened
regret, regretted, regrettable	prohibit, prohibited, prohibitive
overlap, overlapping	develop, developing
prefer, preferred, preferring	preference, preferable
refer, referred, referring	reference

SP 2c   *Y* as a Vowel

Change *y* to *ie* before *s*.

Y is sometimes used *as a consonant* (*year*, *youth*), sometimes *as a vowel* (*my*, *dry*; *hurry*, *study*). As a single final vowel, the *y* changes to *ie* before *s*. It changes to *i* before all other endings except *-ing*.

ie: family—families, fly—flies, study—studies, try—tries, quantity—quantities

i: beauty—beautiful, bury—burial, busy—business, copy—copied, dry—drier, lively—livelihood, noisy—noisily

y: burying, copying, studying, trying, worrying

When it follows another vowel, *y* is usually preserved: *delays, joys, played, valleys.* A few common exceptions are *day—daily, gay—gaily, lay—laid, pay—paid, say—said.*

SP 2d   Final *E*

Drop the final silent *e* before an added vowel.

A silent *e* at the end of a word is dropped before an ending that *begins with a vowel.* It is preserved before an ending that begins with a consonant:

	DROPPED *e*	KEPT *e*
bore	boring	boredom
hate	hating	hateful
like	liking, likable	likely
love	loving, lovable	lovely

The following words are exceptions to this pattern: *argue—argument, due—duly, dye—dyeing* (as against *die—dying*), *mile—mileage, true—truly, whole—wholly.*

Note: A final *e* may signal the difference in pronunciation between the final consonants in *rag* and *rage*, or in *plastic* and *notice.* Such a final *e* is preserved not only before a consonant but also before *a* or *o*:

ge: advantage—advantageous, change—changeable, courage—courageous, outrage—outrageous

ce: notice—noticeable, peace—peaceable

EXERCISES

A. Insert *ei* or *ie*: ach ___ vement, bel ___ ver, dec ___ tful, f ___ ld, inconc ___ vable, misch ___ f, perc ___ ve, rec ___ ving, rel ___ f, s ___ ze, w ___ rd, y ___ ld.

B. Select the appropriate word in each of the numbered pairs: *(1) bared / (2) barred* from office; his *(3) bating / (4) batting* average; *(5) caned / (6) canned* meat; *(7) biding / (8) bidding* their time; *(9) hoping / (10) hopping* for the best; *(11) pined / (12) pinned* to the mat; a *(13) well-planed / (14) well-planned* outing; *(15) robed / (16) robbed* in white; a boy *(17) spiting / (18) spitting* his parents; *(19) taped / (20) tapped* him on the shoulder.

C. Combine the following words with the suggested endings: accompany ___ ed, advantage ___ ous, argue ___ ing, benefit ___ ed, carry ___ s, come ___ ing, confide ___ ing, differ ___ ing, excite ___ able, friendly ___ ness, lively ___ hood, occur ___ ing, prefer ___ ed, remit ___ ance, sad ___ er, satisfy ___ ed, shine ___ ing, sole ___ ly, study ___ ing, tragedy ___ s, try ___ s, use ___ ing, valley ___ s, whole ___ ly, write ___ ing.

D. For each blank space, what would be the right form of the word in parentheses? Put the right form after the number of the sentence.

1. (family) Several _____ were having a picnic.
2. (plan) The holdup had been _____ carefully.
3. (study) My friends were _____ in the library.

4. (regret)   I have always _____ this oversight.
5. (city)   We visited three _____ in one week.
6. (pay)   They had already _____ the bill.
7. (love)   They never stopped hating and _____ each other.
8. (quantity)   Great _____ of food had been consumed.
9. (beauty)   She always described her aunts as famous _____.
10. (occur)   The thought had _____ to us.
11. (begin)   My patience was _____ to wear thin.
12. (copy)   He had _____ the whole paragraph.
13. (refer)   Your doctor should have _____ you to a specialist.
14. (stop)   You should have _____ at the light.
15. (lay)   We had _____ the tile ourselves.

SP 3   WORDS OFTEN MISSPELLED   *sp*

Watch for words frequently misspelled.

The following are among the words most frequently misspelled in student writing. Take up a group of twenty or twenty-five at a time. Find the ones that would cause you trouble.

absence	aggressive	area
abundance	alleviate	argue
accessible	allotted	arguing
accidentally	allowed	argument
acclaim	all right	arising
accommodate	already	arrangement
accompanied	altar	article
accomplish	altogether	artistically
accumulate	always	ascend
accurately	amateur	assent
accuses	among	athlete
accustom	amount	athletic
achievement	analysis	attendance
acknowledgment	analyze	audience
acquaintance	annual	authority
acquire	anticipate	
acquitted	anxiety	balance
across	apologize	basically
actuality	apology	basis
address	apparatus	beauty
adequate	apparent	becoming
admit	appearance	before
adolescence	applies	beginning
advantageous	applying	belief
advertisement	appreciate	believe
afraid	approach	beneficial
against	appropriate	benefited
aggravate	approximately	boundaries

breath
brilliant
Britain
buses
business

calendar
candidate
career
careless
carrying
category
ceiling
cemetery
challenge
changeable
character
characteristic
chief
choose
chose
clothes
coarse
column
comfortable
comfortably
coming
commission
committed
committee
companies
competition
competitive
completely
comprehension
conceivable
conceive
concentrate
condemn
confident
confidential
conscience
conscientious
conscious
considerably
consistent
continually
continuous
control
controlled
convenience
convenient

coolly
courageous
course
courteous
criticism
criticize
cruelty
curiosity
curriculum

dealt
deceit
deceive
decision
definite
definitely
definition
dependent
describe
description
desirability
desirable
despair
desperate
destruction
devastate
develop
development
device
difference
different
difficult
dilemma
dining
disappear
disappearance
disappoint
disastrous
discipline
disease
disgusted
dissatisfaction
dissatisfied
doesn't
dominant
due
during

ecstasy
efficiency
efficient
eighth

eliminate
embarrass
embarrassment
eminent
emphasize
endeavor
enforce
enough
entertain
environment
equipped
especially
etc.
exaggerate
excellent
exceptionally
exercise
exhaust
exhilarate
existence
experience
explanation
extraordinary
extremely

familiar
families
fascinate
finally
financial
financier
foreign
forward
friend
fulfill
fundamentally
further

gaiety
generally
genius
government
governor
grammar
guaranteed
guidance

happily
happiness
height
heroes
heroine

Words often Misspelled

hindrance
hopeful
huge
humorous
hundred
hurriedly
hypocrisy
hypocrite

ignorant
imaginary
imagination
immediately
immensely
incidentally
indefinite
independent
indispensable
inevitable
influence
ingenious
insight
intellectual
intelligence
interest
interpret
interrupt
involve
irrelevant
irresistible
itself

jealous

knowledge

laboratory
laid
leisure
likelihood
literature
livelihood
loneliness
losing

magnificence
maintain
maintenance
manageable
manufacturer
marriage
mathematics
meant

medieval
merely
mileage
miniature
minute
mischievous
muscle
mysterious

naïve
necessarily
necessary
ninety
noticeable

obstacle
occasion
occasionally
occurred
occurrence
omit
operate
opinion
opponent
opportunity
optimism
original

paid
parallel
paralysis
paralyze
particularly
passed
past
peace
peculiar
perceive
perform
performance
permanent
persistent
persuade
pertain
phase
phenomenon
philosophy
physical
piece
pleasant
possess
possession
possible

practical
precede
prejudice
prepare
prevalent
privilege
probably
procedure
proceed
professor
prominent
propaganda
prophecy
psychology
pursue

quantity

really
recommend
regard
relief
relieve
religion
repetition
representative
resource
response
rhythm
ridiculous
roommate

safety
satisfactorily
schedule
seize
sense
separate
sergeant
shining
significance
similar
sincerely
sophomore
speech
sponsor
strength
stretch
strictly
studying
subtle
succeed

successful	together	using
summarize	tragedy	
surprise	transferred	various
	tries	vengeance
temperament		villain
tendency	undoubtedly	
therefore	unnecessary	weird
thorough	useful	writing

EXERCISE

Use the following to test your knowledge of words often misspelled. Have someone dictate these sentences to you. Make a list of the words that give you trouble.

1. *Amateurs benefited* more than other *athletes*.
2. The *committee* heard every *conceivable opinion*.
3. *Manufacturers developed* a new *device*.
4. We kept all *business decisions confidential*.
5. Her *appearance* was *definitely* a *surprise*.
6. She *accused* her *opponent* of *hypocrisy*.
7. The *absence* of *controls* proved *disastrous*.
8. We met a *prominent professor* of *psychology*.
9. Their *marriage succeeded exceptionally* well.
10. These *privileges* are *undoubtedly unnecessary*.
11. The *sponsor* was *dissatisfied* with the *performance*.
12. Their *approach* was *strictly practical*.
13. *Companies* can seldom just *eliminate* the *competition*.
14. A *repetition* of the *tragedy* is *inevitable*.
15. This *subtle difference* is *irrelevant*.

SP 4   THE APOSTROPHE   *ap*

Use the apostrophe for contractions and possessives.

The **apostrophe** has no exact equivalent in speech and is therefore easily omitted or misplaced.

SP 4a   Contractions

Use the apostrophe in informal contracted forms.

Use the apostrophe to show that one or more letters have been left out. Be sure to use it in contractions using a shortened form of *not*:

I'll go now.	It *can't* be true.
We're ready.	She *won't* say.
They're late.	He *isn't* here.
He's a friend.	They *wouldn't* answer.
You're welcome.	They *haven't* arrived.

Make sure not to misspell *don't* and *doesn't*, which are shortened forms of *do not* and *does not*:

DO NOT: We *don't* usually hire in the summer.

DOES NOT: The new converter *doesn't* work.

Remember:

It's means "it is" or "it has." *Its* means "of it," "belonging to it."
Who's means "who is" or "who has." *Whose* means "of whom" or "of which."
They're means "they are." It differs from *their* and *there:*

> *It's* time to give the cat *its* milk.
> *Who's* to say *whose* fault it is?
> If *their* lights are turned off, *they're* not *there.*

Note: Contractions are common in informal speech and writing. Avoid them in formal reports, research papers, and letters of application. Use them sparingly in ordinary prose.

SP 4b   Possessives

Use the apostrophe for the possessive of nouns.

The possessive is a special form of nouns that we use to show who owns something or where something belongs. We usually make up the possessive form by adding an apostrophe plus *s* to the plain form:

WHOSE?		
	my *sister's* car	Mr. *Smith's* garage
	her *aunt's* house	the *student's* name
	the *family's* debts	my *doctor's* address
	our *mayor's* office	one *person's* opinion

Besides ownership or possession, the possessive form shows various other relationships: the *girl's* friends, a *child's* innocence, the *general's* dismissal, *women's* rights, the *children's* activities. In addition, the possessive is frequently used in expressions dealing with time or value: *an hour's drive, the day's news, a moment's notice, a dollar's worth, tonight's paper.*

Note the following variations:

(1) *Use only the apostrophe if the plain form already has an -s.* This situation occurs with many plural forms—all those that use the plural *-s.* Contrast the members of the following pairs:

SINGULAR:	one *parent's* signature	a *week's* pay
PLURAL:	both *parents'* signatures	two *weeks'* pay

(2) *Follow your own preference when the name of an individual ends in -s.* You may or may not add a second *s,* depending on whether you would expect an extra syllable in pronunciation: *Mr. Jones' car—Mr. Jones's car; Dolores' hair—Dolores's hair; Charles Dickens' first novel— Charles Dickens's first novel.*

(3) *Do not use the apostrophe in the possessive forms of personal pronouns.* No apostrophe appears in *his, hers, its, ours, yours,* or *theirs.* It does appear, however, in the possessive forms of such indefinite pronouns as *one* (one's friends), *everyone* (to everyone's surprise), *someone* (at someone's suggestion; also, at someone else's house).

SP 4c   Plurals of Letters and Symbols

Use the apostrophe in special situations.

Use the apostrophe to separate the plural *s* from the name of a letter or a symbol or from a word named as a word (two large 7's; if's and but's):

> Those great big beautiful A's so avidly sought, those little miserly C's so often found, were meant for another time and another student body.—Oscar Handlin, "Are the Colleges Killing Education?" *Atlantic*

EXERCISES

A. Change each of the following to the possessive form. Examples: pay for a month—a *month's* pay; the wedding of my brother—my *brother's* wedding.

1. the playground for children
2. the budget of the President
3. wages for two weeks

4. the members of her family
5. the homes of many families
6. the pay of an officer
7. the future of America
8. the locker room for girls
9. a vacation of three months
10. the worth of a dollar
11. the employment record of a person
12. the fringe benefits of the employees
13. the vote for women
14. the retirement of the coach
15. the working hours of our custodians

B. Choose the right spelling in each of the following pairs.

1. When the mother and the father respect each *(1) other's / (2) others'* opinions, children learn to live harmoniously by following their *(3) elders / (4) elders'* example.
2. Since the *(5) treasurers / (6) treasurer's* resignation, the *(7) members / (8) member's* have been speculating about *(9) whose / (10) who's* going to succeed her.
3. *(11) Mrs. Beattys / (12) Mrs. Beatty's* husband still sends her *(13) flowers / (14) flower's* on *(15) Valentines / (16) Valentine's* Day.
4. We were all overjoyed when my *(17) brother's / (18) brothers'* baby took *(19) its / (20) it's* first faltering steps.
5. A *(21) student's / (22) students'* lack of interest is not always the *(23) teachers / (24) teacher's* fault.
6. *(25) Its / (26) It's* the *(27) parents / (28) parents'* responsibility to provide for their *(29) children's / (30) childrens'* religious education.
7. *(31) Lets / (32) Let's* borrow *(33) someones / (34) someone's* car and go for an *(35) hour's / (36) hours'* drive.
8. *(37) Charles / (38) Charles's* father murmured audibly that the assembled *(39) relatives / (40) relative's* had consumed at least ten *(41) dollars / (42) dollars'* worth of food.

SP 5 CAPITALS

cap

Capitalize proper names and words in titles.

We capitalize the first word of a sentence and the pronoun *I*. In addition, we use capitals for proper names and for words in titles.

SP 5a Proper Names

Capitalize proper names.

Proper names are always capitalized. Capitalize the names of persons, places, regions, countries, languages, historical periods, ships, days of the week, months (but not seasons), organizations, religions: *James, Brazil, Italian, the Middle Ages, S.S. Independence, Sunday, February, Buddhism.*

Remember the following:

(1) *Capitalize general words that become part of a proper name.* The general term for a title, family relationship, institution, or geographical feature is capitalized when it combines with a proper name: *Major Brown, Aunt Augusta, Sergeant Barnacle, Campbell High School, Indiana University, Tennessee Valley Authority, Medora Heights, Institute for the Blind, Lake Erie.* Some titles refer to only one person and can take the place of the person's name: *the Pope, the Queen* (of England), *the President* (of the United States).

(2) *Capitalize a general word that is put to special use as a proper name.* The same word may serve as a general term but also as a proper name for one person, institution, or place:

GENERAL WORD	PROPER NAME
democratic (many institutions)	Democratic (name of the party)
orthodox (many attitudes)	Orthodox (name of the church)
history (general subject)	History 31 (specific course)
west (general direction)	Middle West (specific area)
my mother (common relationship)	Mother (name of the person)

(3) *Capitalize words derived from proper names.* In particular, capitalize words that make use of the name of a country, nationality, place, or religion: *English grammar, French pastry, Mexican nationals, Spanish names, German beer, Parisian fashions, Christian charity, Marxist ideas.*

Note: In some words the proper name involved has been lost sight of, and a lower-case letter is used: *guinea pig, india rubber, pasteurized milk.*

SP 5b   Titles of Publications

Capitalize major words in titles.

A capital letter marks the first and all major words in the title of a book, other publication, or work of art. The only words not counting as major are articles (*a, an,* and *the*), prepositions (*at, in, on, of, from, with*), and connectives (*and, but, if, when*). Prepositions and connectives are usually capitalized when they have five or more letters. Observe these conventions in writing the titles of a theme:

```
Goalie Without a Mask
Travels with a Friend Through Suburbia
How to Lose Friends and Become a Public Enemy
```

The same conventions apply to titles of publications cited in a sentence:

> Several generations of Americans read *Sink or Swim*, *Phil the Fiddler*, *Mark the Match Boy*, and *From Canal Boy to President*, records of achievement which rewarded personal goodness with happiness and goods.—Saul Bellow, "The Writer as Moralist," *Atlantic*

EXERCISE

Which of the words in the following sentences should be capitalized? After the number of each sentence, write down and capitalize all such words.

1. A yale graduate, baird worked at chase manhattan and smith barney & co.
2. Pistol shots crackled in dearborn, the detroit suburb that is home to the ford motor company's sprawling river rouge plant.
3. Last october, a huge and very ugly statue of sir winston churchill was unveiled in parliament square, london.
4. As he was helped aboard, egyptian mohammed aly clutched a small blue-bound koran that had been given to him by the arab mayor of hebron.
5. The sprawling city of canton, 110 miles by rail from hong kong, has for centuries been china's principal gathering place for asian and european traders.
6. The american tourist cashing her traveler's check at tokyo's hotel okura got a bundle of good news.
7. Last week 3,500 delegates met in manhattan to celebrate the centennial of the union of american hebrew congregations, founded in cincinnati by rabbi isaac wise in 1873.
8. At columbia and barnard, at atlanta's morehouse college and the university of virginia, economics was suddenly the subject to take.
9. Seven novels by mickey spillane are among the thirty best-selling novels of all time, along with *gone with the wind*, *peyton place*, *lady chatterley's lover*, and *in his steps*, by charles monroe sheldon, 1897.
10. Like other newspapers, the *new york journal-american* had learned the art of catering to the irish catholics.

SP 6   THE HYPHEN   *hyp*

Use the hyphen where required by current practice.

Use of the **hyphen** is the least uniform and the least stable feature of English spelling. In doubtful cases, use the most recent edition of a good dictionary as your guide.

SP 6a   Compound Words

Know which compound words require a hyphen.

Treatment varies for words used together as a single expression. Some **compound words** are clearly distinguished from ordinary combinations by differences in both writing and pronunciation: *black bird* (black **BIRD**) but *blackbird* (**BLACK**bird), *dark room* (dark **ROOM**) but *darkroom* (**DARK**room). Such unmistakable compounds are *headache*, *highway*, and *stepmother*. In many similar compounds, however, the parts are kept separate: *high school*, *labor union*, *second cousin*. Still other compound words conventionally require a hyphen: *cave-in*, *great-grandfather*, *mother-in-law*.

ONE WORD:	*bellboy, bridesmaid, stepfather, checklist, highlight, headquarters, blackout, bittersweet*
TWO WORDS (OR MORE):	*commander in chief, goose flesh, vice versa, off year, high command*
HYPHEN:	*able-bodied, bull's-eye, drive-in, court-martial, merry-go-round, six-pack, in-laws, vice-president, Spanish-American, one-sided, off-season, in-group*

Remember:

(1) *Hyphenate compound numbers from twenty-one to ninety-nine.* Also hyphenate fractions used as modifiers:

There were *twenty-six* passengers.
The plane was *one-third* empty.
The tank was *three-quarters* full.

(2) Be sure to spell *today*, *tomorrow*, *nevertheless*, and *nowadays* as single words. Be sure *not* to spell as single words *all right*, *a lot* (a lot of time), *be able*, and *no one*.

SP 6b   Prefixes

Know which prefixes require a hyphen.

Many hyphenated compounds consist of a prefix and the word it precedes:

(1) *All-*, *ex-* (in the sense of "former"), *quasi-*, *self-*, and sometimes *co-* require a hyphen: *all-knowing*, *ex-husband*, *quasi-judicial*, *self-contained*, *co-author*.

(2) All prefixes require a hyphen before words beginning with a capital letter: *all-American*, *anti-American*, *pro-British*, *un-American*.

(3) Often a hyphen prevents the meeting of two identical vowels: *anti-intellectual, semi-independent*.

Note: Sometimes a hyphen distinguishes an unfamiliar use of a prefix from a familiar one: *recover—re-cover* (make a new cover), *recreation—re-creation* (creating again or anew).

SP 6c   Group Modifiers

Use the hyphen with group modifiers.

Several words may temporarily combine as a modifier preceding a noun. They are then usually joined to each other by hyphens: *a flying-saucer hat, a middle-of-the-road policy, a question-and-answer period, a step-by-step account, a devil-may-care attitude*. No hyphens are used when the same combinations serve some other function in a sentence: *tend toward the middle of the road; explain a process step by step*.

Note: No hyphen is used when a modifier preceding a noun is in turn modified by an adverb ending in *-ly: a fast-rising executive, a well-balanced account*; but *a rapidly growing city, a carefully documented study*.

EXERCISE

After the number of each sentence, write all combinations that should be hyphenated or written as one word.

1. She had won a hard fought grass roots campaign that toppled a well entrenched incumbent.
2. The room was only about two thirds full, with seventy five people in attendance.
3. Though at times her son in law seemed self conscious, he never the less had a well balanced personality.
4. He was the kind of law and order candidate who promises to crack down on ex convicts.
5. Several players from these Italian American families had gone on to become all Americans.
6. Those who denounced the parking privileges for out of town students were obviously not from out of town.
7. Both pro British and anti British Arabs were united in their contempt for ex king Farouk.
8. The anti intellectual local news paper had called our candidate an absent minded ex professor and a tool of the labor unions.
9. Now a days few self respecting candidates conduct old fashioned campaigns taking them into out of the way places.
10. Jane Andrews and her co author have written a well documented account of the un democratic procedures followed by quasi judicial agencies.

Glossary of Usage

CHAPTER SEVENTEEN

The following glossary reviews the status of words, word forms, and constructions that are frequently criticized as careless, illogical, too informal, or otherwise limited in appropriateness and effectiveness.

a, an The *a* should appear only before words that begin with a consonant when pronounced: *a desk, a chair, a house, a year, a* C, *a university*. The *an* should appear before words that begin with a vowel when pronounced (though in writing the first letter may be a consonant): *an eye, an essay question, an honest man, an* A, *an* M, *an uninformed reader*. In the latter position, *a* is nonstandard.

amount, number *Amount* is sometimes used loosely instead of *number* in reference to things counted individually and as separate units.

RIGHT: A large number [not *amount*] of people were waiting.

RIGHT: The *number* [not *amount*] of unsold cars on dealers' lots was growing steadily.

and and but at the beginning of a sentence When *and* and *but* are used at the beginning of a sentence, they partly cancel out the pause signaled by the period. They can therefore suggest a sudden or an important afterthought. But many modern writers start sentences with *and* or *but* merely to avoid heavier, more formal connectives like *moreover, furthermore, however,* and *nevertheless*.

and/or *And/or* is an awkward combination sometimes necessary in commercial or official documents. Avoid in ordinary writing.

angle, approach, slant *Angle, approach,* and *slant* are overused as synonyms for "attitude," "point of view," "position," or "procedure."

apt, liable, prone In informal English, *apt, liable,* and *prone* all appear in the sense of "likely." In formal usage, *apt* suggests that something is likely because of someone's aptitude ("She is apt to become a successful artist"). *Liable* suggests that what is likely is burdensome or undesirable ("He is liable to break his leg"). *Prone* suggests that something is almost inevitable because of strong habit or predisposition ("He is prone to suspect others").

as   *As* is nonstandard as a substitute for *that* or *whether* ("I don't know *as* I can come"). It is also nonstandard as a substitute for *who* ("Those *as* knew her avoided her"). As a substitute for *because* or *while*, *as* is often criticized as ambiguous, unemphatic, or overused:

> *As* [better: "because"] we had no money, we gave him a check.

attribute, contribute   *Contribute* means "to give one's share" or "to have a share" in something. *Attribute* means "to trace to a cause," or "credit to a source."

RIGHT: He *attributed* the crossing of the letters in the mail to the intervention of a supernatural power.

being as, being that   Nonstandard as substitutes for *because* or *since* ("*being that* I was ill").

between, among   *Between* is related to *twain*, which in turn is a form of *two*. As a result, grammarians have often restricted *between* to references to two of a kind (distinguish *between* right and wrong). They have required *among* in references to more than two (distinguish *among* different shades of color). *Between* is also appropriate when more than two things can be considered in pairs of two:

RIGHT: He had sand *between* his toes.
RIGHT: Bilateral trade agreements exist *between* many countries.

blame for, blame on   There are two idomatic uses of the word *blame*: "He blamed the passenger *for* the accident" and "He blamed the accident *on* the passenger." The first of these is preferred in formal English.

calculate, reckon, expect, guess   In formal written English, *calculate* and *reckon* imply computing or systematic reasoning. *Expect* implies expectation or anticipation; *guess* implies conjecture. In the sense of "think," "suppose," or "consider," these verbs are informal or dialectal.

can and may   Formal English uses *can* in the sense of "be able to."

It uses *may* to show permission. The use of *can* to indicate permission, common in speech and writing, is often considered informal:

FORMAL: You *may* (have my permission to) take as much as you *can* (are able to) eat.
INFORMAL: *Can* I speak to you for a minute?

cannot help but   Although occasionally found in writing, *cannot help but* is often criticized as illogical or confused:

RIGHT: I *cannot help* wishing that I had never met you.
RIGHT: I *cannot but* wish that I had never met you.

compare with, compare to   We compare two cities *with* each other to see what they have in common. We compare a city *to* an anthill to show what a city is like.

couple of   In formal writing, *couple* refers to two of a kind, a pair. Used in the sense of "several" or "a few," it is informal. Used before a plural noun without a connecting *of*, it is nonstandard.

INFORMAL: We had to wait a *couple of* minutes.
NONSTANDARD: We had only a *couple* dollars left.

credible, credulous, creditable   Stories may be credible or incredible. The people who read them may be credulous or incredulous. An act that does someone credit is a creditable act.

cute, great, lovely, wonderful   Words like *cute*, *great*, *lovely*, and *wonderful* often express thoughtless or insincere praise; their use in formal writing can suggest immaturity. *Cute* is colloquial.

different than   *Different from* used to be expected in formal English. Nevertheless, *different than*, widely used in speech, is becoming acceptable in writing ("Life in cadet school for Major Major was no *different than* life had been for him all along."—Joseph Heller, *Catch-22*). *Different than* is the more economical way of introducing a clause:

ECONOMICAL: We tried a different method *than* we had used last year.
LESS ECONOMICAL: We tried a different method *from the one* we had used last year.

disinterested, uninterested   In formal English, *disinterested* means "unswayed by personal, selfish interest" or "impartial." *Disin-*

terested used in the sense of "uninterested" or "indifferent" is objectionable to many readers:

RIGHT: We were sure she would be a *disinterested* judge.
RIGHT: He seemed *uninterested* in our problems.

double comparative, double superlative   Short adjectives usually form the comparative by adding the suffix *-er* (*cheaper*), the superlative by adding the suffix *-est* (*cheapest*). Long adjectives, and adverbs ending in *-ly*, usually employ the intensifiers *more* and *most* instead (*more expensive*, *most expensive*; *more carefully*, *most carefully*). Forms using both the suffix and the intensifier are nonstandard (*more cheaper*, *most cheapest*).

double negative   Double negatives say no twice. The use of additional negative words to reinforce a negation already expressed is nonstandard: "I *didn't* do *nothing*"; "*Nobody* comes to see me *no more*."

RIGHT: I *didn't* do *anything*.
RIGHT: *Nobody* comes to see me *anymore*.

***due to* as a preposition**   *Due to* is generally accepted as an adjective: "His absence was *due to* ill health." "His absence, *due to* ill health, upset our schedule." As a preposition meaning "because of," *due to* is often criticized:

OBJECTIONABLE: He canceled his lecture *due to* ill health.
SAFE: He canceled his lecture *because of* ill health.

each other, one another   Conservative writers distinguish between *each other* (referring to two persons or things) and *one another* (referring to more than two).

enthuse   *Enthuse* is a "back formation" from the noun *enthusiasm*. It is informal or slangy as a shortcut for "become enthusiastic" and "move to enthusiasm." (Similar back formations, like *reminisce* from *reminiscence*, have become generally acceptable. *Enthuse* still has a long way to go.)

etc.   *Etc.*, the Latin abbreviation for "and so on" or "and the like," often serves as a vague substitute for additional examples or illustrations. Furthermore, *ect.* is a common misspelling. "And etc." and "such as . . . etc." are redundant. To avoid trouble, do without *etc.* altogether.

farther, further; all the farther   A traditional rule required *farther* in references to space and distance ("We traveled *farther* than we had expected"), *further* in references to degree and quantity ("We discussed it *further* at our next meeting") and in the sense of "additional" ("without *further* delay"). *Further* is now widely accepted as appropriate in all three senses.

All the farther in the sense of "as far as" ("This is *all the farther* we go") is nonstandard or dialectal.

get, got, gotten   The verb *get* is used in many idiomatic expressions. Some of these are colloquial:

> *have got* (for "own," "possess," "have available")
> I *have got* ten dollars; she *has got* blue eyes; you *have got* ten minutes.
>
> *have got to* (for "have to," "must," "be obliged")
> I *have got to* leave now; we *have got to* think of our customers.
>
> *get to* (for "succeed")
> I finally *got to* see him.
>
> *get* (for "understand")
> *Get* it?
>
> *get* (for "arrest," "hit," "kill")
> The police finally *got* him.
>
> *get* (for "puzzle," "irritate," "annoy")
> What really *gets* me is that he never announces his tests.
>
> *got* (instead of *be, am, was, were* to form the passive)
> He *got hit* by a truck.

Note: In American English, *have gotten* is an acceptable alternative to *have got*, except when the latter means *have* or *have to*.

hadn't ought to   In formal English, *ought*, unlike some other auxiliaries, has no form for the past tense. *Hadn't ought* is informal, *had ought* is nonstandard.

INFORMAL: You *hadn't ought* to ask him.
FORMAL: You *ought not to have* asked him.

hopefully   When used instead of expressions like "I hope" or "let us hope," *hopefully* is considered illogical by conservative readers.

INFORMAL: *Hopefully,* the forms will be ready by Monday.
FORMAL: *I hope* the forms will be ready by Monday.

if, whether   Conservative readers object to *if* when used to express doubt or uncertainty after such verbs as *ask, don't know, wonder,* *doubt*. The more formal connective is *whether*: "I doubt *whether* his support would do much good."

in, into   Formal writing often requires *into* rather than *in* to indicate direction: "He came *into* [not *in*] the room."

in terms of   A vague all-purpose connective frequent in jargon: "What have you seen lately *in terms of* new plays?"

JARGON: *Virtue* originally meant "manliness" *in terms of* [better: "in the sense of"] warlike prowess or fortitude.

infer, imply   In formal English, *imply* means to "hint or suggest a conclusion." *Infer* means "to draw a conclusion on the basis of what has been hinted or suggested." A statement can have various implications, which may lead to inferences on the part of the reader.

irregardless   Used instead of *regardless*, *irregardless* is often heard in educated speech but is widely considered nonstandard.

it's me, it is I   Traditional grammarians required *it is I* on the grounds that the linking verb *is* equates the pronoun *I* with the subject *it* and thus makes necessary the use of the subject form. Modern grammarians accept *it is me* on the grounds that usual English word order (he hit *me*; she asked *me*) makes the object form natural. *It's me* is now freely used in informal speech. Other pronouns (*us, him, her*) are still occasionally criticized as uneducated usage.

INFORMAL: I thought it was *him*. It could have been *us*.
FORMAL: It was *she* who paid all the bills.

judicial, judicious   A "judicial" decision is a decision reached by a judge or by a court. A "judicious" decision shows sound judgment. Not every judicial decision is judicious.

later, latter   "Although both Alfred and Francis were supposed to arrive at eight, the former came earlier, the *latter later*."

learn, teach   In standard English, the teacher *teaches* (rather than *learns*) the learner. The learner is *taught* (rather than *learned*) by the teacher.

leave, let   In formal usage, *leave* does not mean "allow" or "permit." You do not "leave" somebody do something. Nor does *leave* take the place of *let* in suggestions like "Let us call a meeting."

less, fewer   *Less* is often used interchangeably with *fewer* before plural nouns. This use of *less* was once widely condemned. The safe practice is to use *less* in references to extent, amount, degree (*less* friction, *less* money, *less* heat). Do not use it in references to number (*fewer* people, *fewer* homes, *fewer* requirements).

like as a connective   In informal speech, *like* is widely used as a connective replacing *as* or *as if* at the beginning of a clause:

INFORMAL: Do *like* I tell you.
FORMAL: Do *as* I tell you.

INFORMAL: The patient felt *like* he had slept for days.
FORMAL: The patient felt *as if* [or *as though*] he had slept for days.

Note: Like is acceptable in formal usage as a preposition: "The girl looked *like* her mother."

moral, morale   We talk about the "moral" of a story but about the "morale" of troops. People with good morale are not necessarily very moral, and vice versa.

most, almost   *Most* is informal when used in the sense of "almost" or "nearly": "*Most* everybody was there." "Mrs. Jones considers herself an authority on *most* any subject."

on account of   Nonstandard as a substitute for *because*.

NONSTANDARD: Once they have been promoted, people may stop trying *on account of* [should be "because"] they have reached their goal.

plan on   In formal usage, substitute *plan to*.

INFORMAL: My parents had always *planned on* us taking over the farm.
FORMAL: My parents had always *planned to* have us take over the farm.

possessives with verbal nouns   A traditional rule requires that a verbal noun (gerund) be preceded by a possessive in sentences like the following:

FORMAL: He mentioned *John's winning* a scholarship.
FORMAL: I am looking forward to *your mother's staying* with us.

This rule is widely observed in formal writing. In informal speech and writing, the plain form is more common:

INFORMAL: Imagine *John winning* a scholarship!

A combination of a pronoun and a verbal with the *-ing* ending may express two different relationships. In the sentence "I saw *him returning* from the library," you actually saw *him*. In the sentence "I object to *his using* my toothbrush," you are not objecting to *him* but merely to one of *his* actions. Use the possessive pronoun (*my, our, his, their*) when the object of a verb or of a preposition is not the person himself but one of his or her actions, traits, or experiences:

RIGHT: We investigated the chances of *his* being elected.
RIGHT: There is no excuse for *their* not writing sooner.
RIGHT: I do not like *your* associating with the neighborhood children.

preposition at the end of a sentence   Teachers no longer tell students not to end a sentence with a preposition. The preposition that ends a sentence is idiomatic, natural English, though more frequent in informal than in formal use.

INFORMAL: I don't remember what we talked *about*.
INFORMAL: She found her in-laws hard to live *with*.

FORMAL: Let us not betray the ideals *for* which these men died.
FORMAL: Do not ask *for* whom the bell tolls.

prepositions often criticized   Look out for the following:

• *Inside of* (for *inside*), *outside of* (for *outside*), and *at about* (for *about*) are redundant.

• *Back of* for *behind* (*back of* the house), *inside of* for *within* (*inside of* three hours), *off of* for *off* (get *off of* the table), *outside of* for *besides* or *except* (no one *outside of* my friends), and *over with* for *over* (it's *over with*) are colloquial.

• *As to, as regards,* and *in regard to* can seem heavy-handed and bureaucratic when used as substitutes for briefer or more precise prepositions:

AWKWARD: I questioned him *as to* the nature of his injury.
PREFERABLE: I questioned him *about* his injury.

• *As to whether, in terms of,* and *on the basis of* flourish in all varieties of jargon.

• *Per* (a dollar *per* day), *as per* (*as per* your request), and *plus* (quality *plus* service) are common in business and newspaper English but inappropriate in a noncommercial context.

provided, provided that, providing   *Provided, provided that,* and *providing* are interchangeable in a sentence like "He will withdraw his complaint, *provided* you apologize." However, only *provided* has escaped criticism and is therefore the safest form to use.

reason is because   In informal speech, *the reason . . . is because* often takes the place of the more formal *the reason . . . is that.* The former construction is often criticized as redundant, since *because* repeats the idea of cause already expressed in the word *reason.* Either construction can make a sentence unnecessarily awkward.

INFORMAL: *The reason* that the majority rules *is because* it is strongest.
FORMAL: *The reason* that the majority rules *is that* it is strongest.
LESS AWKWARD: The majority rules *because* it is strongest.

shall, will   In current American usage, *will* usually indicates simply that something is going to happen:

I *will* ask him tomorrow.
You *will* find it on your desk.
Mr. Smith *will* inform you of our plans.

The more emphatic *shall* often indicates that something is going to happen as the result of strong determination, definite obligation, or authoritative command:

I *shall* return.
We *shall* do our best.
Wages of common laborers *shall* not exceed twenty dollars a day.

Shall is also common in questions that invite the listener's approval or consent:

Shall I wait for you?
Shall we dance?

Formal English used to require *shall* for simple future in the first person: "I *shall* see him tomorrow." Current handbooks of grammar have abandoned this rule.

so and **such**   In *formal English*, *so* and *such* show that something has reached a definite point, producing certain characteristic results:

> She was so frightened *that she was unable to speak.*
> There was such an uproar *that the chairman banged his gavel in vain.*

Informal English often omits the characteristic result. *So* and *such* then function as **intensifiers:** "I am *so* glad." "He is *such* a lovely boy." You can make such sentences generally acceptable in two different ways. Substitute an intensifier like *very* or *extremely:* "I am *very* glad." Or add a clause giving the characteristic result: "He is such a lovely boy *that all the girls adore him.*"

split infinitives   Occasionally a modifier breaks up an infinitive; that is, a verbal formed with *to* (*to come, to promise, to have written*). The resulting split infinitive has long been idiomatic English and occurs in the work of distinguished writers. The traditional rule against it has been widely abandoned. However, a split infinitive can be awkward if the modifier that splits the infinitive is more than one word:

AWKWARD: He ordered us *to* with all possible speed *return* to our stations.

BETTER: He ordered us *to return* to our stations with all possible speed.

subjunctive   *In formal usage,* we use subjunctive forms to point to possibilities rather than facts:

- After *if, as if,* and *as though,* use *were* instead of *was* if the possibility you have in mind is *contrary to fact or highly improbable:*

> The bird looked as if it *were* a plane.
> If I *were* you, I would try to improve my language habits.
> He acts as if his name *were* John D. Rockefeller.

Use *is* or *was* if you are considering a genuine possibility:

> If your brother *was* ill, he should have notified you.
> It looks as if the plane *is* going to be late.

- Use subjunctive forms in noun clauses *after verbs indicating that something is desirable or necessary* but has not yet come about. "I wish I *were* [not "I was"] a wise old man." Forms like *answer* instead of *answers, go* instead of *goes* or *went,* and *be* instead of *is* or *was* occur after verbs signaling a suggestion, a request, a command, or a resolution:

His supervisor insists that he *spend* more time in the office.
We demand that he *repay* all his debts.
I move that this question *be* referred to one of our committees.

superlative in reference to two   In informal speech and writing, the superlative rather than the comparative frequently occurs in comparisons between only two things. This use of the superlative used to be considered illogical:

INFORMAL: Which of the two candidates is the *best* speaker?
FORMAL: Which of the two candidates is the *better* speaker?

take and, try and, up and   *Take and* (in "I'd *take and* prune those roses") and *up and* (in "He *up and* died") are dialectal. *Try and* for *try to* ("I'd *try and* change his mind") is colloquial.

these kind   Agreement requires "*this kind* of car" or "*these kinds* of fish." "*These kind* of cars" and "*those kind* of cars" are informal.

titles: *Dr., Prof., Reverend*   In references to holders of academic degrees or titles, *Dr. Smith* and *Professor Brown* are courteous and correct. *Professor* is sometimes abbreviated when it precedes the full name: *Prof. Martha F. Brown*. In reference to clergy, *Reverend* is usually preceded by *the* and followed by the first name, by initials, or by *Mr. (the Reverend William Carper; the Reverend W. F. Carper; the Reverend Mr. Carper).*

type, type of, -type   Omitting the *of* in expressions like "this *type* of plane" is colloquial. *Type* is increasingly used as a suffix to turn nouns into adjectives: "an escape-type novel," "a drama-type program." Many readers object to such combinations. Often they turn simple ideas into fuzzy, wordy phrases: "A subsidy-type payment" says no more than "subsidy."

unique, perfect, equal   It used to be argued that one thing cannot be *more unique, more perfect,* or *more equal* than another. Either it is unique or it isn't. Formal English often substitutes *more nearly unique, more nearly perfect, more nearly equal.*

used to, didn't use to, used to could   *Used to* in questions or negative statements with *did* is informal and only occasionally seen in print ("the strident ... antipolice slogans which *didn't use to* be part of the hippie mode"—*National Review*).

INFORMAL   She *didn't use to* smoke.
FORMAL: She *used not to* smoke.

Used to could is nonstandard for *used to be able*.

where, where at, where to   In formal English, *where* takes the place of *where to* ("*Where* was it sent?") and *where at* ("*Where* is he?"). *Where* used instead of *that* ("I read in the paper *where* a boy was killed") is informal.

who, which, and that   *Who* and *whom* refer to persons ("the man *whom* I asked"). *Which* refers to ideas and things ("the car *which* I bought"). A *who, whom,* or *which* introducing a restrictive modifier may be replaced by *that* (but *need* not be):

The man *that* I asked liked the car *that* I bought.

A *whom* or a *which* that is the object in a restrictive modifier is often left out:

The man (*whom*) I asked liked the car (*which*) I bought.

Of which and *in which* can easily make a sentence awkward. *Whose* is therefore widely used and accepted in reference to ideas and things: "the Shank-Painter Swamp, *whose* expressive name . . . gave it importance in our eyes" (Thoreau).

-wise   People often change a noun into an adverb by tacking on *-wise*; this practice is common in business or advertising jargon:

JARGON: The delay was advantageous *tax-wise*.
BETTER: The delay was advantageous *for tax purposes*.

without   *Without* is nonstandard when used as a connective introducing a clause.

NONSTANDARD: The owner won't let me stay *without* I pay the rent.
STANDARD: The owner won't let me stay *unless* I pay the rent.

you with indefinite reference   Formal writing generally limits *you* to the meaning of "you, the reader." Much informal writing uses *you* with indefinite reference to refer to people in general; formal writing would substitute *one*:

INFORMAL: In ancient Rome, *you* had to be a patrician to be able to vote.
FORMAL: In ancient Rome, *one* had to be a patrician to be able to vote.

Practical Prose Forms

CHAPTER EIGHTEEN

X 1   Summaries

X 2   Letters
    a   Format and Style
    b   The Request
    c   The Letter of Application
    d   The Follow-Up Letter
    e   The Letter of Refusal

X 3   The Essay Examination

X 1 SUMMARIES

By writing summaries, train yourself to grasp the structure of written material and to concentrate on essentials.

Practice in writing summaries will benefit you in important ways as a student and as a writer:

- It will give you practice in *close, attentive reading*. Too many writers are ineffectual because they have not learned to listen first, to think second, and to formulate their own reactions third.

- It will strengthen your sense of *structure* in writing. It will make you pay close attention to how a writer organizes his material, how he develops a point, how he moves from one point to another.

- It will develop your sense of what is *important* in a piece of writing. It will make you distinguish between a key point, the material backing it up, and mere asides.

In writing a summary, concentrate on three closely related tasks:

(1) *Make sure you grasp the main trend of thought.* Above all, you need to see clearly the *organization* of what you are asked to summarize. Identify key sentences: the thesis that sums up the major point of an essay (or section of an essay); the topic sentence that is developed in the rest of a paragraph. Formulate in your own words major points that seem to be *implied* but not spelled out in a single sentence. Distinguish between the major steps in an argument and merely incidental comment.

(2) *Reduce explanation and illustration to the essential minimum.* Omit passages that are mere paraphrase, restating a point for clarity or emphasis. Drastically condense lengthy explanations. Preserve only the most important details, examples, statistics. Reduce or omit anecdotes, facetious asides, and the like.

(3) *Use the most economical wording possible.* Where the original uses a whole clause, try to sum up the same idea in a phrase. Where it uses a phrase, try to use a single word. Where several near-synonyms restate the same idea, choose the one that best gives the central common meaning. Cut out all grammatical deadwood.

Unless the original version is already severely condensed, a summary of about one-third or one-fourth the original length can usually preserve the essential points. The shorter the summary, however, the greater the danger of oversimplification or outright misrepresentation. Be careful to preserve essential conditions and distinctions: *if-* and *unless*-clauses; differences between *is, will,* and *might*; words like *only, almost,* and *on the whole.* Preserve the relative emphasis of the original, giving more prominence to a point treated at great length than to one mentioned in passing.

Study the following passage. The running commentary suggests points you would have to note in writing an adequate summary.

(1) *Key idea:* Emphasis will be on *form* rather than content of popular arts.

(2) *Essential qualification:* "Most often done" and "is said to be" show this view to be widely held, but not necessarily fully shared by *author.*

(3) *Synonyms:* "Simple," "uncomplicated," "artless," "flat," "straightforward," all reinforce same major point.

(4) *Added step:* Popular art is "standardized" as well as "simplified."

(5) *Another added step:* It is "mechanical" rather than "variable."

(6) *Major transition:* The "mechanical" element in the popular arts is what makes them popular.

(7) *Explanation:* Why is "deadly routine" easy to live with?

We might characterize popular art first, as is most often done, with respect to its *form.* Popular art is said to be simple and unsophisticated, aesthetically deficient because of its artlessness. It lacks quality because it makes no qualifications to its flat statement. Everything is straightforward, with no place for complications. And it is standardized as well as simplified: One product is much like another. It is lifeless, Bergson would say, because it is only a succession of mechanical repetitions, while what is vital in art is endlessly variable. But it is just the deadly routine that is so popular. Confronted with that, we know just where we are, know what we are being offered, and what is expected of us in return. It is less unsettling to deal with machines than with people, who have lives of their own to lead. For we can then respond with mechanical routines ourselves, and what could be simpler and more reliably satisfying?—Abraham Kaplan, "The Aesthetics of the Popular Arts," *Journal of Aesthetics and Art Criticism*

Here is the summary you might write after close study of the passage:

Summary   According to a widely held view, popular art is simple and uncomplicated in form, and therefore "artless." It is standardized, and it lacks life because of mechanical repetition. But it is just the mechanical quality that is popular, because it is simple to react to what we know, but unsettling to deal with something that has a life of its own.

(See also the section on summarizing quoted material in Chapter Nine, "The Research Paper.")

EXERCISES

A. Study the differences between the full text and the summary in each of the following pairs. Would you have noted the same major points and essential qualifications?

Original 1: The invention of the process of printing from movable type, which occurred in Germany about the middle of the fifteenth century, was destined to exercise a far-reaching influence on all the vernacular languages of Europe. Introduced into England about 1476 by William Caxton, who had learned the art on the continent, printing made such rapid progress that a scant century later it was observed that manuscript books were seldom to be met with and almost never used. Some idea of the rapidity with which the new process swept forward may be had from the fact that in Europe the number of books printed before the year 1500 reaches the surprising figure of 35,000. The majority of these, it is true, were in Latin, whereas it is in the modern languages that the effect of the printing press was chiefly to be felt. But in England over 20,000 titles in English had appeared by 1640, ranging all the way from mere pamphlets to massive folios. The result was to bring books, which had formerly been the expensive luxury of the few, within the reach of all. More important, however, was the fact, so obvious today, that it was possible to reproduce a book in a thousand copies or a hundred thousand, every one exactly like the other. A powerful force thus existed for promoting a standard uniform language, and the means were now available for spreading that language throughout the territory in which it was understood.—Albert C. Baugh, *A History of the English Language*

Summary: Printing from movable type, invented in Germany about 1450 and brought to England about 1476, had a far-reaching influence on all European languages. Within a hundred years, manuscript books had become rare. Though at first most printed books were in Latin, over 20,000 titles in English had appeared by 1640. Books were now within the reach of everyone and could exert a powerful standardizing influence upon language.

Original 2: The tendency to erect "systems"—which are then marketed as a whole—affects particularly the less mature sciences of medicine and psychology. In these subjects we have had a succession of intellectual edifices originally made available only in their entirety. It is as if one cannot rent a room or even a suite in a new building, but must lease the whole or not enter. Starting with a substantial contribution to medicine the authors of such systems expand their theories to include ambitious explanations of matters far beyond the original validated observations. And after the first pioneer, later and usually lesser contributors to the system add further accretions of mingled fact and theory. Consequently systems of this kind—like homeopathy, phrenology, psychoanalysis, and conditioned reflexology (the last dominant for years in Russia)—eventually contain almost inextricable mixtures of sense and nonsense. They capture fervid adherents, and it may take a generation or several for those who preserve some objectivity to succeed in salvaging the best in them while discarding the dross.—Dr. Ian Stevenson, "Scientists with Half-Closed Minds," *Harper's*

Summary: Medicine and psychology have produced a number of intellectual systems that one is asked to accept as a whole or not at all. The ambitious authors and adherents of such systems go beyond original valid findings to produce a mixture of truth and error that attracts enthusiastic supporters. Objective observers may not succeed in separating the valuable from the worthless till much later.

B. Select a passage of about 250 words from a history or science textbook. Prepare a summary running to about a third of the original length. Provide a copy of the original.

X 2 LETTERS

Make your business letters suggest the qualities prized by business people: competence and efficiency.

Correspondence creates special problems of manuscript form. In writing or answering a formal invitation, you will do well to follow forms suggested in a book of etiquette. In writing a personal letter, you may allow yourself considerable freedom, as long as you keep your handwriting legible and use presentable stationery. Between these extremes of formality and informality is the kind of letter that you may have to write to a teacher, to a college official, or to a future employer. In applying for a scholarship or for a job, follow a conventional letter form.

X 2a Format and Style

Make sure your business letters are neat, clear, consistent in format, and courteous in style. Study the samples of business correspondence on the following pages. Use them as models for spacing, indention, punctuation, and the like.

Notice the following possible variations:

(1) When you are not using the letterhead of a firm or institution, type in *your address* above the date, as follows:

```
                                      138 South Third Street
                                      San Jose, California  95126
                                      January 12, 1975



        Ms. Patricia Sobell
        Personnel Manager
        San Rafael Gazette
        2074 Washington Avenue
        San Rafael, California  94903

        Dear Ms. Sobell:
```

A standard business letter:

CALIFORNIA STATE COLLEGE, letterhead

109 East Victoria Street • *Dominguez Hills, California 90247*

heading ⟶ June 14, 19__

Institute for Better Business Writing, Inc.
1000 University Way
Los Angeles, California 90025 ⟵ inside address

Gentlemen: ⟵ salutation

I was happy to receive your request for information
regarding business letter formats.

The format of this letter is the one most frequently
used in business. It's called a modified block format. With the exception of the heading and the
signature block, all its elements begin at the left
hand margin, even the first word of each paragraph.
The body of the letter is single-spaced, with double
spacing between paragraphs.
body
Typists generally like the block format better than
the older indented formats. It has a clean and
precise appearance, and is quicker to type--no
fiddling around with indentations.

There are other formats in use, but the block format
seems to have the widest appeal. You won't go wrong
adopting it for all your official correspondence.

signature block

Sincerely yours,

complimentary close
signature
signature identification

Walter Wells

Walter Wells
Department of English

WW:mea ⟵ IEC block
cc: Dean Marion Carlota
        initials (of author and typist)
        enclosures
        carbon copies

A very short business letter, with a traditional *indented* format, and with its body double-spaced:

The Ironworks

2520 Eastern Avenue
Las Vegas, NE 89109

September 12, 1980

Mr. Perry Sneed, Manager
Green Thumb Nursery
3619 Kyrene Road
Tempe, Arizona 85282

Dear Mr. Sneed:

Your order for 3 dozen wrought iron potracks was shipped today.

We appreciate receiving Green Thumb Nursery as a new account. Thank you for your initial order, and we look forward to a pleasant business relationship.

Sincerely,

Lorraine Holloway

Lorraine Holloway
Sales Manager

fb

**postscript—
last-minute
addition to letter**

P.S. We have just learned that some of our shipments have been delayed briefly en route because of a handlers' strike. We apologize for any inconvenience.

Here are some examples of well-typed business envelopes. Remember: Accurate names and addresses are essential. Neatness counts.

Lawndale Pharmaceutical Company
5170 Medina Road
Akron, Ohio 44321

SPECIAL DELIVERY

Dr. William Carlson
10372 White Oak Avenue
Granada Hills, CA 91344

United Bank of Iowa
1640 Medina Road
Des Moines, Iowa 50313

Attention Ms. Sydney Corveau

Schrader Lock Company
624 South First Avenue
Sioux Falls, SD 57104

San Marcos Resort,
Country Club & Colony

Chandler, Arizona 85224

Confidential

Mr. Don Busche, President
Northridge Manufacturing Company
402 West Main Street
Northridge, Illinois 60162

A **memorandum**, or interoffice communication, is different from a business letter. It serves a different purpose—communication *within* an organization.

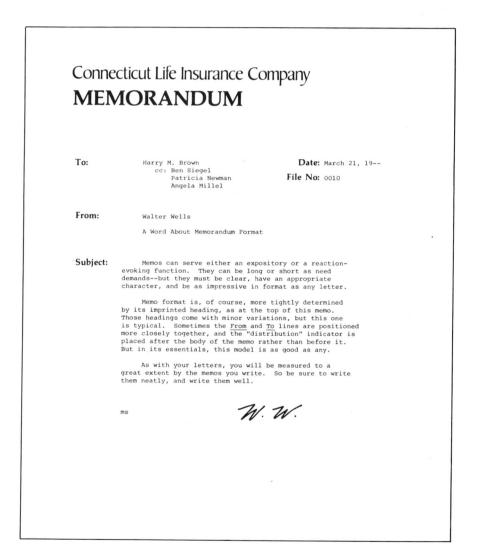

Connecticut Life Insurance Company
MEMORANDUM

To: Harry M. Brown
         cc: Ben Siegel
             Patricia Newman
             Angela Millel

Date: March 21, 19--
File No: 0010

From: Walter Wells

A Word About Memorandum Format

Subject: Memos can serve either an expository or a reaction-evoking function. They can be long or short as need demands--but they must be clear, have an appropriate character, and be as impressive in format as any letter.

Memo format is, of course, more tightly determined by its imprinted heading, as at the top of this memo. Those headings come with minor variations, but this one is typical. Sometimes the From and To lines are positioned more closely together, and the "distribution" indicator is placed after the body of the memo rather than before it. But in its essentials, this model is as good as any.

As with your letters, you will be measured to a great extent by the memos you write. So be sure to write them neatly, and write them well.

ms

W. W.

(2) A *married woman* may wish to put *(Mrs.)* in front of her typed name.

Try to write clearly and naturally. Do not use a special business jargon when you write a business letter. Avoid especially the following: a *stodgy*, old-fashioned businessese ("wish to advise that," "beg to acknowledge," "am in receipt of," "pursuant to," "the aforementioned"); a *breezy* "shirtsleeve" English ("give it the old college try," "fight tooth and nail," "give them a run for their money").

X 2b   The Request

State inquiries and requests clearly and positively, and aim them at the intended reader. Many of the business letters you write will ask someone else to *do* something for you: to provide information, to perform a service, to correct a mistake. Make such letters clear, businesslike, and persuasive.

(1) Make sure you state your request clearly and directly *early* in the letter. The basic question in your reader's mind is "What do you want?"

(2) If you are making *several* requests in the same letter, or if several points need attention, make sure *each* stands out clearly. Consider numbering them for emphasis. Too often, only the first major point gets attention; other matters, buried later in a letter, are forgotten.

(3) Whenever possible, relate your request directly to the *interests and responsibilities* of the person you are writing to. Avoid a "To-Whom-It-May-Concern" effect; avoid using form letters if at all possible.

(4) Even when you have a legitimate complaint, remain *courteous*. Emphasize the mutual satisfaction to be derived from a mistake corrected, rather than the mutual frustration occasioned when an error is first made.

The following sample letters attempt to put these principles into practice:[1]

---

[1] Most of the sample letters in this section are adapted from Walter Wells, *Communications in Business* (Belmont, California: Wadsworth, 1977).

Letter 1

Dear Mr. Bliss:

Largely because of the success of The Muse, your new
campus literary magazine, we at Colfax College feel
the time is right for a similar publication on this
campus. Your help on a few important questions would
get us moving in the right direction.

We would like to know

> 1. How you went about soliciting manuscripts
> for your first edition.
> 2. How you decided upon the proportions of
> space to devote to fiction, poetry, criticism,
> reviews, and advertising.
> 3. Whether you use university or commercial
> printing facilities.
> 4. What mailing list you used to solicit
> charter subscriptions.
> 5. Why you decided to price The Muse at $1.75.

Our enthusiasm runs high over the possibility of a
literary review at Colfax. Target date for the first
issue is October 1 of this year. We've got the administration's green light and the faculty is solidly
behind us. With your aid, we can be that much closer
to realizing our goal--a first-rate campus publication
capable of standing beside the best from the larger
schools, The Muse most certainly among them.

> Sincerely,
>
> *Martha Gronowsky*
>
> Martha Gronowsky
> Student Body Vice-President

Letter 2

Gentlemen:

I was surprised to receive your recent request for more transcripts to complete my application to the Graduate School. I will, of course, have them sent if absolutely necessary, but I do feel that your request penalizes me.

Upon coming to State as a transfer undergraduate in 1975, I paid two dollars, for transcripts in dupli-cate, to each of the three institutions I had pre-viously attended. At that time, you informed me that all my papers were in order, and you admitted me. Now you request the very same transcripts in support of my graduate application.

Would it not be possible for you to refer to the transcripts already in your possession? Or if copies must be sent to the graduate advisor, could you not duplicate my transcripts and send me the bill? In either case, you would save me the time of recon-tacting each institution, and perhaps preclude a delay in their responding.

I hope this request is in no way unjustified. It should be more expedient for both of us as you process my application.

Sincerely yours,

Kenneth Darwin

Kenneth Darwin

X 2c The Letter of Application

Make your letter of application suggest competence, confidence, and a genuine interest in the position for which you apply. Employers look for employees who will prove an asset to their organization and who are at the same time good to work with and good to know. They shy away from applicants who seem to promise problems, trouble, or an overinflated ego. Remember the following advice:

(1) *If possible, be specific about the position for which you apply.* Introduce the letter by mentioning the advertisement or the person that informed you of the vacancy (but do not mention leads that smack of the "grapevine").

(2) *Stress previous training.* Point out any practical experience that you can show to be relevant to the job. Give a factual tone to the account of your qualifications, while at the same time presenting them to advantage.

(3) *Give your letter character.* Establish your identity. Many job applications look very much the same. The anonymous, average applicant has little chance to be remembered—and to be preferred. If you have positive convictions about the work of the organization to which you apply, state them.

(4) *If you want to list references, first get permission from those whose names you want to use.* Quietly drop from your list the names of teachers or former employers who show little enthusiasm when you tell them about your plans.

(5) *Consider preparing a separate résumé.* If the account of your qualifications is extensive, put it on a separate "data sheet."

Study the following sample letters:

Letter 3

Dear Mr. Clark:

In answer to your advertisement, I wish to apply for a post as general reporter. My credentials are that I am a journalism major, and I have had some practical experience of working for a newspaper.

On February 1, I shall graduate from San Jose State University. While getting a degree, I have taken a broad range of courses, representing all areas of editing and reporting. Also, I have been a general reporter for the <u>Spartan Daily</u> for two years and a feature editor for one year. Last summer I worked for thirteen weeks on the <u>Santa Clara Journal</u>, as an "intern" sponsored by the Journalism Department of my college. I did general reporting and some photography.

The following people have agreed to supply references:

> Dr. Mary Jane Cahill
> Department of Journalism
> San Jose State University
> San Jose, California
>
> Mr. Thomas Bigelow
> General Manager
> Santa Clara Journal
> Santa Clara, California
>
> Mr. Richard H. James
> Editor
> Los Angeles Examiner
> Los Angeles, California

I am prepared to be interviewed when you find it convenient.

> Yours truly,
>
> *Pat C Romeros*
>
> Pat C. Romeros

Letter 4

Mr. Daniel Levin, Attorney at Law
Peale, Corman, Bishop, Levin & Dilworthy
80 Lomita Canyon Boulevard, Suite 7630
Beverly Hills, California 92025

Dear Mr. Levin:

Edith Winters informs me of an opening in your secretarial staff, a position for which I should very much like to become a candidate.

I understand that you need a legal secretary with a rapid stenographic skill and the ability to handle a large volume of correspondence. Along with my degree in legal stenography from Foothill Junior College, I have four years of secretarial experience in retail dry goods and in insurance. My shorthand speed is 145 words per minute. On my present job, I handle between forty and sixty letters every day. Both at Foothill and on the job, I have had training sufficient to prepare me to handle routine letters without supervision.

My present job at Southwestern Life & Indemnity has been quite satisfactory, but, having taken my degree recently, I seek the further challenges and rewards of a top-flight legal firm. Miss Winters assures me that I would like the job. I hope the enclosed résumé will help interest the firm in me.

I can be in Los Angeles for an interview any afternoon convenient for you. May I look forward to speaking with you about the position you have available?

Yours sincerely,

Pat Edmondson

Pat Edmondson

Sample Résumé

ADAM PIERCE

Demmler Hall   Age: 23
Valhalla University   Ht: 6-1 Wt: 170
Kent, Ohio 26780   Single
613 KE 8 7600   Willing to relocate

Education

B.S. in Industrial Engineering, Valhalla University, June 1979; top 10% of class, with special course work in statistics, motivational psychology, business law, and communications.

Won U.S. Paint Company Scholarship 1978
Member of Industrial Relations Club
Elected Secretary of the Student Council
On Dean's Honor Roll since 1976

Also attended Colfax College, Colfax, Indiana, 1974-75.

Experience

Staff Supervisor, Cleveland Boys' Club Camp, Kiowa, Ohio, summer 1978; responsible for housing, activities scheduling and occasional discipline of fourteen counselors and 110 campers.

Camp Counselor, Cleveland Boys' Club Camp, Kiowa, Ohio, summers of 1976 and 1977.

Personal Interests

Politics, world affairs, camping, chess, junior chamber of commerce member, and volunteer hospital worker.

References

Will gladly be provided upon request.

X 2d   The Follow-Up Letter

Keep interest alive, or reinforce a good first impression, by a timely follow-up letter. Though many business people pride themselves on being hard-headed calculators, in practice business is often 51 percent human relations. The follow-up letter serves important needs: It shows positive interest and thus reassures the recipient. It serves as a reminder, keeping alive an impression that is beginning to pale as other business calls for attention.

Study the following sample letter, written by an applicant *after* a job interview:

Letter 5

Dear Mr. Goodfellow:

Just a note of thanks for the many courtesies shown me during my interview on Monday. Seeing National Motors from the inside has, as I said then, made the Executive Training Program all the more attractive to me.

Incidentally, I located a copy of Michaelson's The Corporate Tempo and found his chapter on training programs as fascinating and as eye-opening as you did.

Needless to say, I am looking forward to hearing from you. After Monday's meeting, I am confident I can bring to the program the energy and ability for success at National Motors.

Sincerely,

Sandra Weinmetz

Sandra Weinmetz

X 2e   The Letter of Refusal

Write letters of refusal that create good will rather than antagonism. There are many ways of saying no. The basic difference is between "No, thank you" and "No—and good riddance." A refusal that at the same time shows an appreciation of the interest expressed generates good will and at the same time leaves the door open for future contacts.

Study the following sample letter:

Letter 6

Dear Mr. Tibbins:

I want to thank you for your letter of July 20 and for your generous offer of the post as market-research analyst at Continental.

With more qualms than I thought myself capable of, I
have decided to forsake that offer and accept one made
me by the Grollier Food Company of San Francisco.
While the salary they offer is slightly less than Continental's, their market-research department is small,
making possible, I feel, more rapid advancement. The
decision was made quite difficult by the obvious at-
tractiveness of your offer, not to mention the con-
geniality of your staff. Only time will prove if it's
a wise one.

Once again, let me express my genuine thanks for all
the consideration you and the Continental staff have
given my candidacy.

Very sincerely yours,

Michael Henriques

Michael Henriques

EXERCISES

A. In an effective business letter, as in all effective persuasion, the writer
shows his ability to imagine himself in the place of the reader. Compare and contrast the letters in each of the following pairs. Which letter in each pair is the more
successful in this respect?

1(a) Enclosed is our draft in the amount of $31.90,
which is the amount over your deductible for which
Smith Motors, the garage of your choice, agreed to
repair your automobile. You will also find enclosed a copy of the estimate on the basis of which
they agreed to repair.

1(b) I'm happy to send you our draft for $31.90. It rep-
resents the repair cost for your car in excess of
the deductible amount in your policy. The enclosed
repair estimate was, as you requested, made by
Smith Motors in Dalhart.

Smith will, I'm sure, get your car back into fine
running order. I know you will be glad to be back
on the road again.

2(a) Just what kind of outfit are you people running? We place a simple order, delivery takes forever, and when it finally gets here, half the pieces are broken. To top it all off, in the same day's mail we get your bill. Some joke!

We feel we can do without this kind of rotten service. There's no time left for us to place an order with a decent company (although we'd like to), so get on the ball and send us a replacement order right away.

2(b) On January 10, we placed an order with you for 500 pieces of glassware in various patterns. Yesterday the order arrived with only 234 pieces in salable condition. All the rest were chipped or broken.

You can understand our disappointment, I am sure. Customers have been requesting your glasses, and we have been promising them a prompt supply. Now some of them will probably go elsewhere--their faith in us destroyed, and our potential profit lost--unless you take immediate action.

We ask that you send us an immediate duplicate order, and allow us to adjust our payment to cover only the salable glassware. We are confident that you will be able to get this shipment to us as soon as possible.

    B. Find a project or recent development that merits publicity or support. Write a letter about it to the editors of a newspaper or magazine, to a legislator, or to a responsible official. Observe conventional letter form.

    C. Write a letter of inquiry or request in connection with some project in which you are currently interested. Observe conventional letter form.

    D. Write a letter of application for a position in which you have at one time or another taken an interest. State the qualifications that you might have by the time you are ready to apply for the position in earnest.

    E. Write a follow-up letter or a letter of refusal in connection with some business contact that you can imagine yourself being engaged in after your graduation from college. Observe conventional letter form.

X 3   THE ESSAY EXAMINATION

Learn to write a structured essay examination that makes the best possible use of what you know.

For many students, the most direct test of their writing ability is the essay examination. To improve your own performance on such examinations, remember the following points:

(1) *Study not for total recall but for a writing test.* In studying the material, identify the key terms that might provide the focal point for a paragraph or short essay: *alienation, irony, agrarianism.* Fix firmly in your mind the three or four points you would cover if asked to trace the major step in an argument, or the key stages in a process. Then, for each key term or major point, try to retain *supporting detail* that would help you define or illustrate it. Do not merely memorize material; ask yourself practice questions that make you *select and arrange* materials in different ways to prove a point, to trace a comparison.

(2) *Memorize verbatim at least some key phrases, definitions, or short passages.* These will give an authoritative, authentic air to your writing. Nothing more reliably identifies the student who aims at better than *C* than the sentence that follows a pattern like this:

The term _____, which Frederick Marcus defines as "_____
_____," has developed two important new applications: . . .
Michael Henchard, whom Thomas Hardy describes as "_____,"
was aware of his own capacity for impulsive action. . . .

(3) *Determine exactly what the instructions ask you to do.* Do not simply get a general notion of what the question is "about." Assume the question in a history course is "What do you consider the most important difference between the fall of Greece and the fall of Rome?" Do not simply put down everything you can remember about the fall of Greece and the fall of Rome. Focus on the key word in the instructions: *difference.* What *is* the difference? How can you line up material that will bring out this difference as clearly and convincingly as possible? Look also for specific writing instructions: Are you being asked to *summarize*, to *define*, to *compare*, to *evaluate*—or merely, more vaguely, to *discuss*?

(4) *No matter what the pressure of time, take time to structure your answer.* Come straight to the point. Especially in a one-paragraph answer, make your very first sentence sum up your key point, or

your answer to the question being asked. Then use the rest of a paragraph to explain, support, or argue your point. Select what is clearly relevant; try to avoid a mere rambling effect. Whenever you can, work from a brief *outline* jotted down on scratch paper before you begin to write.

In addition to these basic points, here are a few practical hints:

- Bring an extra pen.

- Budget your time, especially if there are several questions. If you gain five points by treating one question at great length, and then lose twenty-five points by slighting the next two questions, you are twenty points behind.

- Get a general picture of the examination before you start writing. If there are several questions or topics, work first on those that you feel best qualified to take up.

- Relax. You will need a cool head to read the instructions without missing an important point.

Study the following essay exam, rated as above average by the teacher. The comments that follow it point out some features likely to have made a favorable impression on the reader.

Exam question
: A common type of character in much contemporary literature is the individual who is trapped by a trick of fate, by the environment, or by his or her own nature. Choose such a character from a short story you have recently read. Define the trap in which the character is caught. Describe any struggle on the part of the character to become free.

Answer
: Miss Brill finds herself trapped by her spinsterhood and the advancement of age. She is old, as the story tells us; she's as old as her out-of-date fox fur. She is alone, with no friends, relatives, or close neighbors. This is her trap. Like a bird that will create its own prison in its own territory, Miss Brill makes hers. She does not socialize, nor does she try to make something useful out of her life but rather preys like a parasite on other people's more interesting, colorful lives. In her own way Miss Brill struggles to escape her prison. She daydreams. The world that she lives in is a fantasy world where all people are friendly and related. She "belongs" in this world whereas in the other world, the real world, she actually belongs to no one.

Quite successfully Miss Brill loses the real world for a time, but she cannot escape the real world entirely. The real world sticks its head in, in the form of a boy who says "Ah, go on with you now." So she goes home, more aware than ever of her prison's boundaries and helpless (by her own nature) to do anything else. She can only fly on home to the security and solitude of her cold dark nest.

Note the following points about this answer:

(1) It responds directly to the *key term or key idea* in the assignment. The assignment asks about a character who is *trapped*. Note how this word and its synonyms keep echoing *throughout* the student's answer: "trapped," "prison," "boundaries."

(2) The first sentence serves as a *topic sentence* for the answer as a whole. It gives the brief, clear definition of the "trap" that the question asks for.

(3) The point about the character's trying to escape through daydreaming responds to the *second* part of the question. But note that this point is worked *organically* into the first paragraph. The student has *planned* this answer; there are no afterthoughts, no "Oh-I-forgot" effect.

EXERCISES

A. Study the following assignment for an essay examination and the two answers that follow it. One of the answers was rated good, the other poor. Which is which? Defend your choice in detail.

Assignment: The following lines by Walt Whitman bear a close relationship to several ideas contained in essays you have read in this course. Explore, in an essay of 300 words, the connections you see.

> When I heard the learn'd astronomer,
> When the proofs, the figures, were ranged in columns before me,
> When I was shown the charts and diagrams, to add, divide, and measure them,
> When I sitting heard the astronomer where he lectured with much applause in
>   the lecture-room,
> How soon unaccountable I became tired and sick,
> Till rising and gliding out I wander'd off by myself,
> In the mystical moist night-air, and from time to time,
> Look'd up in perfect silence at the stars.

Answer 1: Several points in Walt Whitman's lines are important in exploring the connections between his ideas and the ideas pertaining to humanism in the essays we have read. First, we get the image of a man of letters attending a lecture of a man of science. Secondly, the lecture material consists of certainties—proofs and figures, charts, diagrams. Finally, we get a feeling of complete isolation and peacefulness as Whitman stands outside in the night air.

In C. P. Snow's essay on "The Two Cultures," the author states that our intellectual society is divided into two sections—scientific and literary. Each section believes the other is unaware of our human condition and shows no regard for its fellow human beings. Each section believes it has the "right" answer for society.

Each section is so intense in its feelings that no communication is possible between the two sections. C. P. Snow says that we must "rethink education" to achieve a broad outlook on life in contrast to the narrow outlook that is the result of specialization and technicalities in science and in literary studies. This is the thought that I get when Whitman attends the astronomer's lecture.

The lecture material contains figures, charts, diagrams to prove the astronomer's theories. I believe Whitman is putting across the same point as Saisselin in his essay on "Humanism, or the Eulogy of Error." Saisselin claims that there are no proofs or certainties for the humanist. Each of us is a single entity; we live alone and die alone. This is our fate. We must recognize this isolation and this potential for error. We must be flexible, but the astronomer suggests rigidity. Furthermore, we must not confine ourselves to one area in life but must be aware of the whole world about us. When Whitman steps outside into the night air and gazes at the stars, he feels the vastness of the universe. The astronomer looks at the universe to collect proofs and figures for his small world of lecture and research. He does not comprehend our common fate.

Answer 2: In the lines by Walt Whitman I am given the general impression that this person cannot comprehend the meaning of the lecture, the figures, or the charts and diagrams. It seems as though he is not scientifically inclined in his thinking and cannot grasp even a thread of the knowledge the lecturer is trying to communicate to him.

In his discussion of "The Two Cultures," C. P. Snow points out some of the reasons for the division between the literary and scientific scholars. One of these reasons is a lack of communication. The literary scholars feel that they are an elite intellectual group and that they should not talk to such illiterates as scientists. The scientists, on the other hand, have a much more exacting knowledge and think they are doing more for the world than reading or writing books.

Remy Saisselin said that humanism can't be defined. It is lived. I think this is true, and it shows in Walt Whitman's poem. The lines don't say anything about wanting to learn a little about philosophy or art or literature. Walt Whitman just wanted to look around. He had no real reason. He didn't want to become educated for a reward. He merely wanted to explore and become educated in something besides strict science for his own satisfaction and enjoyment.

Students today are made to specialize, and this cuts down on a general well-rounded education. If one lives in a small world of one type of life day after day, he cannot fully enjoy life. Diversity makes for more enjoyment. By learning a little in both science and the arts, a person becomes more happy with himself and those around him.

B. Do you have a copy of an essay examination you have written recently? Select one or more passages totaling 250–300 words. Rewrite the material in accordance with the suggestions in this section. If you can, submit the original assignment, the original answer, and the improved version.

Index

Alan, 466
Abbey, Edward, 181
Abbreviated forms, in informal language, 283
Abbreviations, 443–444
  in footnotes and bibliography, 223–225
Absolute constructions, 387
Abstraction
  in argument, 131
  and definition, 110–111
  and persuasion, 154–155.
  See also Concreteness
Accept/except, 450
Accuracy, and word choice, 289
Achebe, Chinua, 313
Active voice, 313–314
  tenses of, 369.
  See also Passive voice
Addresses
  numbers in, 444–445
  punctuation of, 427
Ad hominem arguments, 157
Adjective clauses, 366, 422–423. *See also*
  Clauses
Adjectives, 273, 352, 383–384
  comparative forms of, 392, 469
  coordinate, 427
  in predicate, 351
  superlative forms of, 157, 392–393, 469, 476.
  See also Modifiers
Adverbial clauses, in faulty equation, 390. *See*
  also Clauses
Adverbial connectives, 353, 416–417
Adverbs, 352, 384–385. *See also* Modifiers
Affect/effect, 450
Agreement
  blind, 365
  with collective nouns, 364
  with compound subjects, 364–365
  with confusing plurals, 363–364
  of indefinite antecedents, 377–378
  logical, 367
  of subject and verb, 362
  after *there* and *it*, 366
  after *who, which,* and *that*, 366
Albee, Edward, 187
Allen, Fred, 11
All-purpose nouns, 295
All the farther, 470
Allusions
  in formal writing, 178
  in informal writing, 180
  loaded, 163–164
Almost/most, 472
A lot, 283
Alternatives
  analysis of, 146
  and coherence, 40
  paragraph organization to express, 335–336
Alumnus, forms of, 363
Ambiguity
  of incomplete comparisons, 392–393
  of misplaced modifiers, 386–387
  of pronoun reference, 374–377
  and word choice, 108
American Heritage Dictionary, 271
Among/between, 467
Amount/number, 466
An/a, 466
Analogy, 20–21
  false, 140
And, 303
  at beginning of sentence, 466
  in compound subjects, 364–365
  parallelism with, 399–401.
  See also Connectives

And/or, 466
Anecdotes, 33, 34
Angelou, Maya, 188
Angle, 295, 466
Anglo-Saxon, 278
Antecedents
  ambiguity about, 374
  defined, 373
  implied, 376–377
  indefinite, 377–378
Antithesis, 144, 185, 319
Antonyms, 271–272
A number of, 363–364
Anywheres, 282
Apologies, 33
Apostrophe
  for contractions, 458–459
  for plurals, 460
  for possessives, 459–460
Application, letters of, 489–493
Appositives, 316, 355
  faulty, 391
Approach, 466
Apt/liable/prone, 466–467
Aptness, of figurative expressions, 291
Archaic words, 286–287
Argument
  ad hominem, 157
  circular, 137
  defined, 2
  examples in, 128–130
  fallacies in, 138–140
  reasoning in, 125, 126–128, 133–137
  statistics in, 137–138
  structure of, 142–146
Articles, 349, 462–463. *See also* Determiners
As, 467
  pronouns after, 381
As if, subjunctive after, 475
Asimov, Isaac, 28–29
Aspect, 295
As per, 474
As regards, 473
As though, subjunctive after, 475
As to, 473
As to whether, 473
As well as, 365
At about, 473
Attention, reader's, 70, 72–77
  and paragraph organization, 336–337
  and parallel structure, 318–319
Attribute/contribute, 467
Authenticity, 3, 74–75, 326
Author, omniscient, 252
Author card, in card catalog, 202
Authorities, as source of evidence, 95–97, 156
Autobiography
  authenticity in, 74–75
  defined, 2
  organization of, 77–80
  reader involvement in, 72–73
  uses of, 69–71
Auxiliaries, 350. *See also* Verbs
Awkwardness
  in repetition, 317–318
  in sentence construction, 312–317

Back formations, 469
Back of, 473
Bacteria, 363
Bad/badly, 385
Baldwin, James, 70–71, 99, 113, 172–173, 187,
  302, 414
Bandwagon effect, 156
Barrymore, Ethel, 319

Barzun, Jacques, 179
Be
　as auxiliary, 350, 371
　as linking verb, 384
Beardsley, Monroe C., 127
Because, 389
Being as/being that, 467
Bellow, Saul, 128, 393
Between/among, 467
Bible, references to, 221
Bibliographies, 197, 225–227
　cards for, 204–206
　as sources, 199
Bierce, Ambrose, 20
Biography, reference works for, 201. *See also* Autobiography
Biography Index, 201
Bird, Caroline, 133
Blame for/blame on, 467
Blind agreement, 365
Block quotations, 211, 215, 434
Bloom, Lynn Z., 110
Book Review Digest, 199
Books
　in bibliography, 225–226
　in footnotes, 219
Boulding, Kenneth E., 147
Bowen, Catherine Drinker, 9
Bowen, Elizabeth, 286
Brackets, 435
British usage, 286
Brontë, Charlotte, 320
Brooks, Paul, 55, 329
Broun, Heywood, 34
Brown, Harrison, 335–336
Brown, H. Rap, 185
Brustein, Robert, 35
Buckley, William F., Jr., 86
Burroughs, John, 60
Business letters. *See* Letters, business
But, 303, 328
　at beginning of sentence, 466
　parallelism with, 399–401.
　See also Connectives
Butler, Patrick, 176
By contrast, 328

Calculate, 467
Call numbers, 203–204
Cambridge Bibliography of English Literature, 201
Cambridge History of English Literature, 201
Can/may, 467–468
Cannot help but, 468
Cant, 74
Capital/capitol, 450
Capitalization
　of proper names, 461–462
　of quotations, 434
　of titles of works, 462–463
　of words derived from names, 462
Card catalogs, 202–204
Carson, Rachel, 333
Case, of pronouns, 379–383
Case histories, 326–327
　in essay of opinion, 100
　in persuasion, 169
Catchall words, 283
Catchwords, 97
Categories, as organization plan, 21–23
Caudill, Harry M., 165–166
Cause and effect
　analysis of, 145
　and paragraph organization, 335
Chapelle, Dickie, 301
Character study, 252–253
Choppiness, 308
Chronological order, 19–20, 260–261
Circular arguments, 137
Circular definitions, 115–116
Cite/site/sight, 450
Clarity, and repetition, 318. *See also* Ambiguity
Clark, Walter Van Tilburg, 64–65, 176
Classification, 21–23
　and definition, 115–116
　and induction, 127

Clauses
　adjective, 366, 422–423
　adverbial, 390
　independent, 353
　nonrestrictive, 418
　noun, 354, 421, 475–476
　punctuation of, 412–419
　relationship of, 303
　restrictive, 417.
　See also Dependent clauses
Clichés, 74–75, 291–292
Climax, 39
　dashes for, 430
　and paragraph organization, 337
　and parallel structure, 319–320
Coburn, Karen, 110
Coherence, 3, 38–40, 216
Collective nouns, 364
Collier's Encyclopedia, 199
Colloquialism, 180, 282–283
Colon
　with quotations, 434
　with sentence fragments, 410
Columbia Encyclopedia, 199
Comma
　in addresses, 427
　with adverbial connectives, 416–417
　in contrasts, 428
　with coordinate adjectives, 427
　with coordinators, 415
　in dates, 427
　with direct address, 431
　with indirect quotation, 436
　after introductory adverbial clause, 418
　after introductory phrase or verbal, 423–424
　in measurements, 427–428
　with modifiers, 421–424
　with nonrestrictive adverbial clauses, 418
　in page references, 427
　for parenthetic elements, 431–432
　with prepositional phrases, 424
　with quotation marks, 435
　with quotations, 433–434, 436
　in repetition, 428
　with sentence fragments, 409, 410
　with sentence modifiers, 423–424
　in series, 426–427
　with transitions, 424
　unnecessary, 421
Commager, Henry Steele, 45
Comma splice, 414, 416
Commitment, 175
Common cause, 167–168
Comparative
　double, 469
　forms of, 392
Compare with/compare to, 468
Comparison and contrast, 23–24
　in critical essays, 261–262
　in definitions, 116–117, 121–122
　in descriptive writing, 64
　paragraph organization for, 335
　and parallel structure, 319.
　See also Comparisons; Contrast
Comparisons
　and adjective forms, 352
　in formal writing, 178
　incomplete, 392–393
　parallel-order, 24
　in persuasion, 156
　point-by-point, 24, 261
　shortening of, 394
　three-cornered, 393.
　See also Comparison and contrast; Contrast
Complaints, 33
Complements, 310, 350
Completers, 310, 350
Compound subjects, 364–365
Compound words, hyphenation of, 464
Conclusions, 33–35
Concreteness, 54
　and definition, 110–112
　and style, 184
　and word choice, 58–59
Conditional, 397–398
Condon, Richard, 430

Conflict, in autobiography, 78
Conjunctions. *See* Connectives
Conjunctive adverbs, 353, 416–417
Connectives
  adverbial, 353, 416–417
  capitalization of, 462–463
  coordinating, 303, 353, 415
  omission of, 426
  paired, 400
  subordinating, 304–305, 353–354, 408–409,
    417–419
  unnecessary, 313
Connotation, 160–161, 272, 289
Conolly, Olga, 118
Consistency
  of figurative expressions, 291
  of passive, 399
  of pronoun reference, 398–399
  in tense, 396–398
Consonants, doubling of, 452–453
Context, 273
Continuity, and repetition, 318. *See also*
  Organization; Transitions
Contractions, 360, 458–459
Contrast
  in autobiography, 78
  in introductions, 32–33
  punctuation of, 414, 418, 428.
  See also Comparison and contrast;
    Comparisons
Contribute/attribute, 467
Cooke, Alistair, 411
Coombs, Orde, 154–155
Coordinate adjectives, punctuation with, 427
Coordinating connectives, 303, 353, 415
Coordination
  contraction in, 393–394
  effective, 303
  punctuation of, 425–429
Coordinators, 303, 353, 415
Corrections, in final copy, 441–442
Correlatives, 400
Coryell, Schofield, 332
Could of, 448
Council/counsel, 450
Couple of, 468
Crane, Stephen, 176, 318
Crawford, John, 434
Credible/credulous/creditable, 468
Critchfield, Richard, 4–5
Critical essays
  kinds of, 251–259
  organization of, 259–262
Critical terms, 256–257
Crosby, John, 152–153
Cross references, 224
Cunliffe, Marcus, 152
Current events, reference works for, 201–202
Cute, 468

Dangling modifiers, 386
Dashes, 429–430
  with modifiers, 423
  with sentence fragments, 409
  typing of, 441
Data, 363
Dates
  numbers in, 444–445
  punctuation of, 427
Davis, Kingsley, 329, 330
Deadwood, 312–313. *See also* Repetition
De Beauvoir, Simone, 86
Debs, Eugene, 320
Deduction, 133–142
Definition
  circular, 115–116
  defined, 2
  dictionary, 114
  extended, 119–123
  formal, 115–116
  methods of, 110–114, 116–117
  need for, 107–109
  operational, 117
  synonyms in, 116
Demonstrative pronouns, 349, 375
Denotation, 160–161, 272

Dependent clauses, 304–305, 353–354
  excessive use of, 315–316
  punctuation of, 417–419
  who/whom in, 382
Description
  defined, 1–2
  imaginative, 51
  incidental, 51–52
  organization of, 62–65
  sentence fragments in, 410–411
  uses of, 51–52
Desert/dessert, 450
Detail
  and paragraph structure, 325–328
  in process themes, 19–20
  relevant, 54–55
  sensory, 54
  for specificity, 53.
  See also Examples
"Detail-first" papers, 64–65
Determiners, 349, 375
Devoe, Alan, 51
Dewey decimal system, 204
Dialectic method, 144–145
Dialects, 286
Dickens, Charles, 10
Dickinson, Emily, 251
Diction. *See* Word choice; Words
Dictionaries
  American Heritage, 271
  definitions from, 114
  foreign words in, 280
  informal words in, 269, 271
  Oxford English, 277
  Random House College, 270, 271, 273, 282
  restrictive labels in, 281–288
  slang in, 269, 271
  Webster's New Collegiate, 269–270, 271, 277
  Webster's New World, 269, 272, 274
Dictionary of American Biography (DAB), 201
Dictionary of National Biography, 201
Didion, Joan, 70
Didn't use to, 476
Different from/different than, 468
Dillard, Annie, 60
Diphthongs, 452
Directions, 19
Directness, 294–299, 314–315
Direct objects, 350
Disinterested/uninterested, 468–469
Documentation, 197–198
  in footnotes, 217–224
  purpose of, 217
Double comparative, 469
Double negative, 469
Double superlative, 469
Drabble, Margaret, 175
Drama, and persuasion, 154–155
Drew, Elizabeth Brenner, 176
Drucker, Peter F., 187
Due to, 469
Duplication, in confused sentences, 388–389.
  See also Repetition

E, final, 453–454
Each, 363
Each other/one another, 469
Edition, in footnotes, 220
Editor, in footnotes, 220
Effect/affect, 450
Either, 363
Either . . . or, 365, 400
Element, 295
Ellipsis, 436
Elliptical constructions. *See* Omissions
Ellison, Ralph, 51–52
Emotions, and persuasion, 155, 157
Emotive language, 160–163
Emphasis
  italics for, 443
  punctuation for, 411, 430
  repetition for, 318
  and style, 184–186
Encyclopaedia Britannica, 199
Encyclopedia Americana, 199
Encyclopedias, 198–199, 221

Endings. *See* Inflections; Suffixes
End punctuation, 407–413
  with parentheses, 431
  with quotation marks, 435
English
  British, 286
  edited, 180
  formal and informal, 360–361 (*see also*
    Informal words)
  history of, 277–281
  Middle, 280
  Modern, 280
  Old, 278
  standard and nonstandard, 359–360.
    See also Language; Words
Enthuse, 469
Enumeration, for coherence, 39
Ephron, Nora, 319
Equal, 476
Essay examinations, 497–500
Etc., 469
Etymology, 119–120, 277–281
Euphemisms, 296
Evans, Bergen, 312
Everyone, 363
Evett, Robert, 192–193
Exaggeration, 157
Examples
  in definition, 112
  in essay of opinion, 100
  and generalization, 128–130
  and paragraph structure, 326–327
Examples-first paragraph, 327–328
Except/accept, 450
Exclamation mark, 411
Expect, 467
Expectations, and coherence, 39–40
Experience, 11
  authenticity of, 74–75
  as evidence, 69
  and reader involvement, 70
  and reality, 69
Experts, as source of evidence, 95–97, 156
Explication, in critical essays, 252
Expository prose, 1, 9
Expressive language, 289–294

Factor, 295
Facts, and inference, 87–89
Facts on File, 202
Fact that, 295
Fadiman, Clifton, 335
Fallacies, 138–140
False analogy, 140
False dilemma, 139
Farther/further, 470
Faulkner, William, 290
Faulty equation, 390
Faulty predication, 390
Fewer/less, 472
Figurative language, 59–60, 283, 290–291
Final *e*, 453–454
Final modifier, 310
First draft, 9
Fischer, John, 326
Fitzgerald, F. Scott, 109
Flowery diction, 297–298
Focus, 9, 12–18, 323
Follow-up letter, 493–494
Footnotes
  abbreviations in, 223–225
  explanatory, 217
  for first references, 218–222
  for later references, 222–224
  numbering of, 218
  position of, 218
  purpose of, 217–218
  typing of, 218
Foreign words
  in dictionaries, 280
  italics for, 437–438, 443
For example, 328, 410
For instance, 328, 410
Formal English, 360–361
Formal writing, 177–180

Fowler, H. W., 188
Fragments, sentence, 408–411
Franklin, Benjamin, 184, 357
French, as source of English words, 280
Freshness, 175, 186
Friedenberg, Edgar Z., 176, 187
Fromm, Erich, 186
Frost, Robert, 254
Frye, Northrop, 187, 310
Function words, 345, 348
Further/farther, 470
Furthermore, 328
Fused sentence, 414
Future tense, 369

Galbraith, John Kenneth, 92–93, 138–139, 191
G. & C. Merriam Company, 269
Gardner, Erle Stanley, 34
Gardner, John W., 40, 321
Generalization, 126–133, 135. *See also*
  Reasoning
Geographic labels, 285–286
Gerberding, William, 151–152
German, as source of English words, 278
Gerunds. *See* Verbal nouns
Get/got/gotten, 470
Gold, Herbert, 159
Golding, William, 429
Goodman, Paul, 116
Good/well, 385
Gordon, Mary, 37
Goring, C. A. I., 129
Got/get/gotten, 470
Gottlieb, Annie, 60, 166, 183, 187
Grammar, approaches to, 345–346
Graves, Robert, 201
Great, 468
Greek, as source of English words, 278–279
Greek Myths, The, 201
Greeley, Andrew M., 5–6
Greene, Graham, 60
Greer, Germaine, 71, 333–334
Griffin, Alice, 255–256
Group modifiers, hyphenation of, 465
Growing up, in autobiography, 79–80
Guess, 467
Guide to Reference Books, 201

Hadn't ought to, 470
Hamill, Pete, 338–339
Hamilton, Edith, 201
Handlin, Oscar, 460
Handwriting, 441
Hardin, Garrett, 142
Hardwick, Elizabeth, 191
Hardy, Thomas, 337
*Harper's Dictionary of Classical Literature and
  Antiquities*, 201
Harrington, Michael, 179, 436
Hart, Moss, 181
Have
  as auxiliary, 350
  in perfect tenses, 370, 371
  spelling problems with, 448
Hechinger, Fred M., 36, 153, 158
Heller, Joseph, 468
Hellman, Lillian, 187, 301, 338
Hemingway, Ernest, 59, 301, 303, 304, 305–306
Hidden premises, 137
Hinckle, Warren, 180, 293
Historical process, tracing of, 19
Hoagland, Edward, 79
Honesty, in autobiographical writing, 74–75
Honig, Louis, Jr., 331
Hopefully, 470
Horgan, Paul, 415
"House-that-Jack-built" sentences, 315
Houston, Jean, 433
Howard, Jane, 426
However, 328, 419
Hudson, Lois Phillips, 110, 437
Hufstedler, Shirley M., 44–45
Humanities Index, 200
Humor
  dashes in, 430

in slang, 284
uses of, 189
verbal, 189–190
Hutchins, Robert M., 185
Huxley, Aldous, 311
Huxley, Julian, 183, 188
Hyphen
  in compound words, 464
  with group modifiers, 465
  with prefixes, 464–465
Hypothesis, 127–128

I, capitalization of, 460
I before *e*, 452
Ibid., 223
-ics, as singular or plural, 364
Idioms, 269, 273–275, 289
If, subjunctive after, 475
If-because, 315
If/whether, 470–471
Images, and style, 184
Imaginative description, 51
Imperative, 351, 398–399
Impersonal constructions, 314–315
Implication, 163–164
Imply/infer, 471
In addition, 328
In addition to, 365
Incidental description, 51–52
Incomplete constructions, 392–395
Indefinite pronouns, 363, 375
  possessive of, 460
  as singular, 377–378
Independent clauses, 353. *See also* Clauses
Indexes, to periodicals, 199–200
Indirect objects, 350
Individuality, 175–176
Induction, 127–128, 134, 143
Inductive order, 336–337
Inference, 87–89
Infer/imply, 471
Infinitives, 355, 356
  punctuation with, 409
  split, 475
Inflections, 345, 347, 349
Informal English, 360–361
Informal words, 282–283
  dictionary treatment of, 269, 271
Informal writing, 180–181
Informed opinion, defined, 2
In/into, 471
Innuendo, 163
In regard to, 473
Insertions, in quotations, 435
Inside of, 473
Intensifiers, 361, 385, 475
Intensive pronouns, 375, 380
In terms of, 471, 473
Interrogative pronouns, 375
Into/in, 471
Intonation, 406
Intransitive verbs, 273
Introductions, 31–33
Introductory complement, 310
Introductory modifiers, 309
Introductory phrases, 295, 432
Inversion, 310
Ionesco, Eugene, 130
Irony, 190–191
  dashes in, 430
  quotation marks for, 437
  sentence fragments and, 411
Irregardless, 360, 471
Issues, identification of, 89–90
It
  agreement after, 366
  orphaned, 377
  pronouns after, 381
Italian, as source of English words, 280
Italics
  for emphasis, 443
  for foreign words, 437–438, 443
  for legal terms, 438
  for technical terms, 443
  for titles of works, 443

It-is sentences, 314, 315
It's/its, 459
It's me/it is I, 471

Jacobs, Jane, 69
James, Henry, 176
Jargon, 287, 296–297, 473, 477, 487
Johnson, Samuel, 291, 311
Johnson, Thomas, 97
Jones, Howard Mumford, 325–326
Jones, LeRoi, 184
Jong, Erica, 129
Jordan, Suzanne Britt, 321
Joyce, James, 411, 426
Judicial/judicious, 471

Kauffmann, Stanley, 132
Kazin, Alfred, 74, 318
Kerr, Walter, 430
Key idea, in descriptive themes, 63–64
Key questions, 13–14
Key terms, and theme, 255
Kind of, 283
King, Martin Luther, 155
Kraft, Joseph, 166
Krutch, Joseph Wood, 436
Kumlien, Gunnar D., 131

Labels
  cautious use of, 130–131
  in definition, 116
Lacy, Dan, 415
Lamott, Kenneth, 36–37
Langer, Susanne K., 131, 337, 433
Language
  emotive, 160–163
  expressive, 289–294
  figurative, 59–60, 283, 290–291
  flowery, 297–298.
  See also English; Words
Later/latter, 471
Latin
  abbreviations from, 223–225, 444
  as source of English words, 278–279
Latter/later, 471
Lawrence, Barbara, 437
Lay, forms of, 372
Laycock, George, 145
Lear, John, 426
Learn/teach, 471
Leave/let, 471
Legal terms, italics for, 438
Leonard, Jonathan Norton, 186
Lessard, Susannah, 122–123
Less/fewer, 472
Lessing, Doris, 303, 308
Let/leave, 471
Letters (alphabet), plurals of, 460
Letters, business
  of application, 489–493
  follow-up, 493–494
  format and style of, 482–487
  of refusal, 494–495
  of request, 487–489
Liable/apt/prone, 466–467
Library catalogs, 202–204
Library of Congress system, 203–204
Lie, forms of, 372
Like, 472
Limiting adjectives. *See* Articles; Pronouns
Line, 295
Linking verbs, 351
  adjectives after, 384
  in faulty equation, 390–391
  pronouns after, 381
Lippmann, Walter, 34, 139
Lists, punctuation of, 430
Literary History of the United States, 201
Literature
  reference works on, 201
  writing about, 249–263
Lloyd, Donald J., 39
Local color, quotation marks for, 437
Logic
  fallacies in, 138–140

Logic (continued)
  in organization, 260–261.
  See also Argument; Reasoning
Loose/lose, 450
Loose sentences, 310
Lopez, Enrique Hank, 330–331
Lose/loose, 450
Lots, 283
Lovely, 468

McCarthy, Mary, 69, 75, 96, 98–99, 176, 182,
    184, 190, 430
McLuhan, Marshall, 1
Macrorie, Ken, 309
McPherson, James Alan, 336–337, 338
Magazine articles, in footnotes, 219
Mailer, Norman, 61–62, 176
Mannes, Marya, 188–189
Margins, 442
Marquand, John P., 75
Martin, Kingsley, 313, 413
Matthews, T. S., 175
May, Rollo, 329
May/can, 467–468
Mead, Margaret, 117, 312
Measurements
  abbreviations for, 444
  punctuation of, 427–428
Medawar, Sir Peter, 114
Memorandums, 486
Memorizing, for essay exams, 497
Metaphors, 290–291
  defined, 59
  mixed, 291
Meyer, Peter, 24–25
Michener, James A., 319
Middle English, 280
Middle term, in syllogisms, 134
Might of, 448
Miller, Arthur, 254, 255, 256–257
Miller, Perry, 97
Misplaced modifiers, 386–387
Mixed construction, 389
Mixed metaphors, 291
Modals, as auxiliaries, 350
Modern English, 280
Modifiers, 352–353
  adjective and adverb forms of, 383–385
  awkward, 316
  dangling, 386
  dependent clauses as, 354
  effective, 305–306
  final, 310
  group, 465
  introductory, 309
  misplaced, 386
  nouns as, 316, 355, 391
  punctuation of, 421–425, 430
  restrictive and nonrestrictive, 421–423
  sentence, 423–424
  squinting, 387
  verbals as, 356
Momaday, N. Scott, 72
*Monthly Catalog of the United States
    Government Publications*, 202
Mood, establishment of, 63
Moral/morale, 472
Moreover, 328
Morgan, Lael, 193, 326, 327
Morgan, Thomas B., 431
Most/almost, 472
Multiple-example paragraph, 327
Munro, Alice, 305, 307
Mythology, 201

Namely, 410
Names
  capitalization of, 461–462
  possessives of, 460
  punctuation with, 422
  titles with, 444, 476
Narration, sentence fragments in, 411
Neill, A. S., 159
Neither, 363
Neither . . . nor, 365, 400

Neologisms, 287
Neruda, Pablo, 176
New English Dictionary on Historical Principles,
    276
Newspaper articles, in footnotes, 219
New York Times Index, 202
Nin, Anaïs, 119, 154
Nohow, 282
Nominative. *See* Subject form
None, agreement with, 378
Nonrestrictive clauses, punctuation of, 418
Nonrestrictive modifiers, 422–423
Nonstandard English, 282, 360
Nor, 365, 400, 415
Not, contractions of, 458–459
Notes
  organization of, 213–216
  taking of, 208–211
  use of, 211–213
Not only . . . but also, 400
Noun clauses, 354
  punctuation of, 421
  subjunctive in, 475–476
Noun markers. *See* Determiners
Nouns, 273, 348–349
  all-purpose, 295
  as appositives, 316, 355, 391
  collective, 364
  modifiers of, 352 (*see also* Adjectives)
  plural of, 349
  possessive forms of, 459–460
  in predicate, 350–351
Number, agreement in. *See* Agreement
Number/amount, 466
Number of, 363–364
Numbers, 444–445, 464

Object complements, 350
Object form, of pronouns, 379–381
Objective case. *See* Object form
Objects, direct and indirect, 350
Observation, 10
Obsolete words, 286–287
Of, as spelling error, 448
Off of, 360, 473
O'Flaherty, Terrence, 85
Old English, 278
Omissions
  in confused sentences, 388–389
  of connectives, 426
  of prepositions, 394
  from quotations, 436
On account of, 472
One, 314, 398, 477
One another/each other, 469
On the basis of, 473
On the contrary, 328
On the other hand, 328
Op. cit., 223–224
Open punctuation, 417
Operational definition, 117
Opinion, 11
  change in, 92–93, 101–102
  evaluation of, 95–96
  formation of, 85, 90–92
  organization of, 99–102
Or
  in compound subjects, 364–365
  parallelism with, 399–401
Organization, 9
  of arguments, 142–146
  of autobiographical themes, 77–80
  by classification, 21–23
  by comparison and contrast, 23–24
  of critical essay, 259–262
  of descriptive themes, 62–65
  in essay exams, 497–498
  of essay of opinion, 99–102
  of paragraphs, 332–339
  of process themes, 19–21
  in summarizing, 479
Orwell, George, 55, 184, 290
Outlines, 215–216
  for essay exams, 498
  purpose of, 41–42

sentence, 43–44
  suggestions for, 44
  topic, 43
  working, 42
Outside of, 473
Overlapping terms, 108
Oversimplification, 138–139
Over with, 473
Oxford English Dictionary (OED), 277

Packard, Vance, 309
Page numbers, 445
  in footnotes, 219, 220
  in text, 223
Pamphlets, in footnotes, 222
Panaceas, 35
Paper, for reports, 441
Paradox, 189–190
Paragraphs
  construction of, 323–332
  organization of, 332–339
Parallel-order comparison, 24, 261–262
Parallel structure, 318–320
  for emphasis, 185–186
  faulty, 399–401
  in outlines, 44
Paraphrase
  footnoting sources for, 217–224
  in note-taking, 210
  punctuation of, 214
Parentheses, 431
Parenthetic elements, punctuation of, 429–433
Parkinson, C. Northcote, 311
Parks, Gordon, 15
Parody, 192
Participles, 356. *See also* Verbals
Parts of speech, 345, 348. *See also* Nouns,
  Pronouns, etc.
Passive voice, 313, 351
  awkwardness of, 313–314
  shifts to, 399
  tenses in, 369
Past participles, 356
Past perfect tense, 396
Past tense, 370
Paz, Octavio, 110, 424
Pearlman, Joan, 110
Penmanship, 441
Per, 474
Perfect, 476
Perfect tenses, 370
Period
  with coordinators, 415
  at end of complete statement, 407–408
  with quotations, 433–434
Periodical indexes, 199–200
Periodicals, library catalogs of, 204
Periodic sentences, 310–311
Perrine, Laurence, 258–259
Personal/personnel, 450
Personal pronouns, 349, 375, 460
Personification, defined, 59
Persuasion
  defined, 2
  goals of, 151
  guidelines for, 151–153
  language of, 159–167
  limits of, 156–157
  and satire, 191–192
  strategies of, 167–172
  tools of, 153–159
Phrasal verbs, in informal language, 283
Phrases. *See* Prepositional phrases; Verbal
  phrases
Plagiarism, 197–198
Plan on, 472
Platitudes, 35
Plimpton, George, 129
Plurals
  anglicized, 363
  confusing, 363–364
  form of, 362, 460
  irregular, 363
  of nouns, 349

variant spellings of, 449.
  See also Agreement
Plus, 474
Podhoretz, Norman, 334
Poetry, quotation of, 215
Point-by-point comparisons, 24, 261
Pointing pronouns. *See* Demonstrative
  pronouns
Porter, Katherine Anne, 61
Possessive pronouns, 349, 375
Possessives
  apostrophe for, 459–460
  with verbal nouns, 472–473
Post hoc fallacy, 139
Precedents, in essay of opinion, 100
Predicate adjective, 351
Predicate noun, 350–351
Predicates, 302–303
  faulty, 390
  of sentences, 348, 349–351
  shifting of, 310–311
Predication
  effective, 302–303
  faulty, 390
Prefixes
  hyphenation with, 464–465
  Latin and Greek, 279
Prejudice, 97
Premises
  accuracy of, 136–137
  in deduction, 134–135
  hidden, 137
Prepositional phrases, 353
  in faulty equation, 390–391
  punctuation with, 409, 424
Prepositions, 352–353
  capitalization of, 462–463
  common mistakes with, 473–474
  at end of sentence, 473
  idiomatic uses of, 274–275
  object forms after, 380–381
  omission of, 394
  unnecessary, 313
Presence/presents, 450
Present participles, 356
Present perfect tense, 396
Present tense, 369
Prewriting, 9–11. *See also* Notes
Primary sources, 206. *See also* Sources
Principal/principle, 451
Pro-and-con paper, 143–145
Process themes, 19–21, 334
Progressive construction, 370
Prone/liable/apt, 466–467
Pronouns
  and antecedents, 373–375
  cases of, 379–383
  consistency in, 398
  demonstrative, 349, 375
  to eliminate deadwood, 313
  in formal writing, 179
  form of, 375
  indefinite, 363, 375, 377–378, 460
  in informal English, 181, 360–361
  intensive, 375, 380
  interrogative, 375
  and modifiers, 375–376
  personal, 349, 375, 460
  possessive, 349, 375
  and possessives, 376
  reflexive, 375, 380
  relative, 304, 354, 375, 409
  unnecessary, 313
Pronunciation, and spelling, 448, 453
Proofreading, 441
Proper names. *See* Names
Provided/provided that/providing, 474
Punctuation
  at end of sentence or fragment, 407–413
  linking, 413–420
  open, 417
  purpose of, 406
  of quotations, 214–215, 433–437.
    See also Comma, Dashes, etc.
Puns, 190

Qualifiers, in informal language, 283
Question mark, 411
Question pronouns, 375
Questions
  anticipation of, 336
  commas before, 432
  end punctuation for, 411
  rhetorical, 164
Question whether, 295
Quiet/quite, 451
Quotation marks, 433–438
  single, 434
  for titles, 443
Quotations
  block, 211, 215, 434
  capitalization of, 434
  in conclusion, 34
  direct, 214, 397
  footnoting sources of, 217–224
  incorporated into text, 212–213
  indirect, 397, 436–437
  in introduction, 32
  in note-taking, 210–211
  omissions from, 436
  punctuation of, 214–215, 433–437
  at second hand, 221–222
  tagging of, 211
  tenses in, 397
  in writing about literature, 249

Rachel, Phyllis, 5
Rainer, Peter, 290
Raise, forms of, 372
Random House College Dictionary, 270, 271,
  273, 282
Random House Dictionary, 114
Rationalization, 140
Rau, Santha Rama, 5
Reader involvement, 70, 72–77
Readers' Guide to Periodical Literature, 200
Reality, and experience, 69
Reasoning
  in argument, 125
  deductive, 133–142
  inductive, 127–128
Reason is because, 474
Reckon, 467
Recurrent terms, 329
Redundancy, 294–295
  in prepositions, 473.
  See also Repetition
Reference works
  general, 198–200
  specialized, 200–202
Reflexive pronouns, 375, 380
Refusal, letter of, 494–495
Regional words, 285–286
Relative clauses, punctuation of, 422–423
Relative pronouns, 304, 354, 375, 409
Relative words, 107
Relevance, 16, 54–55
Repetition, 33
  awkward, 317–318
  for emphasis, 185–186, 318
  for parallelism, 401
  punctuation of, 428
Request, letter of, 487–489
Research, 2–3, 11
  documentation of, 197–198
  guidelines for, 197
  sources for, 198–208.
  See also Footnotes; Notes
Restrictive clauses, punctuation of, 417
Restrictive labels, 281–288
Restrictive modifiers, 421–423
Résumés, 490, 492–493
Revision, 9, 216
Rexroth, Kenneth, 178
Rhetorical questions, 164
Rich, Adrienne, 258, 437
Rise, forms of, 372
Robinson, Lillian S., 162
Roche, John P., 41
Roiphe, Anne, 432
Roots, Latin and Greek, 278–279

Russell, Bertrand, 71, 189
Ryan, Joan, 193

Samples, representativeness of, 130
Sarcasm, 190
Satire, 191–192
Schlesinger, Arthur M., 38–39
Schmidt, Sarah, 36
Schneider, Anne, 55–56
Scientific process, explanation of, 19
Secondary sources, 206–207. *See also* Sources
Seesaw sentences, 316
Semantic change. *See* Etymology
Semicolons
  with adverbial connectives, 416
  between clauses, 413–414
  with coordinators, 415
  in series, 426
Sentence fragments, 408–411
Sentence modifiers, punctuation of, 423–424
Sentence outline, 43–44
Sentences
  awkwardness in, 312–317
  basic elements of, 348–351
  building of, 301–307
  clauses in, 353–354
  confused, 388–392
  in formal writing, 178
  fused, 414
  "House-that-Jack-built," 315
  importance of, 301
  in informal writing, 180
  length of, 308–309
  loose, 310
  modifiers in, 352–353
  patterns of, 345–346
  periodic, 310–311
  seesaw, 316
  source, 346
  special resources for, 355–356
  variety in, 307–312
Sentimentality, 74
Sequence of tenses, 396–397
Series
  parallelism in, 400–401
  punctuation of, 426–427
Set, forms of, 372
Sexton, Patricia Cayo, 52, 73, 175
Shakespeare, William, 255, 257
Shall/will, 474
Shaw, George Bernard, 162, 188, 189, 190, 308
Should of, 448
Sight/site/cite, 450
Silberman, Arlene, 152
Similarly, 328
Similes, 59, 290–291
Simmons, Adele, 93, 428
Simplistic arguments, 138–139
Single quotation marks, 434
Singular, form of, 349, 362. *See also* Agreement
Sit, forms of, 372
Site/cite/sight, 450
Situation, 295
Slang, 283–284
  dictionary treatment of, 269, 271
  in informal writing, 180
Slant, 466
Slogans, 98
Snow, C. P., 364
So, 415, 475
Social Sciences Index, 200
Sontag, Susan, 311, 414, 430
Sort of, 283
Sources
  citation of, 197–198 (*see also* Bibliographies;
    Footnotes)
  evaluation of, 206–207
  primary and secondary, 206–207
Source sentences, 346
Spacing, 442
Spanish, as source of English words, 280
Specialized terms, 108–109. *See also* Jargon
Specificity
  and definition, 111

and detail, 53
and word choice, 58, 290
Spelling
common errors in, 455–458
improvement of, 445–447
and pronunciation, 448
rules for, 452–455
of variant forms, 449
of words that sound alike, 450–451
Split infinitives, 475
Square brackets, 435
Squinting modifiers, 387
Standard College Dictionary, 287
Standard English, 359–360
Statistics, interpretation of, 137–138
Statistics, as singular or plural, 364
Stein, Edith M., 33
Steinbeck, John, 10, 60, 98, 176
Stereotypes, 96–97
Strickland, Anita, 290
Structural grammar, 345
Style
effectiveness of, 175–176
emphasis in, 184–186
and imagery, 184
and word choice, 183–184
Subject, of sentence, 348–349
agreement with, 362
compound, 364–365
postponed, 366
Subject cards, in card catalog, 203
Subject form, of pronouns, 379–381
Subjective case. *See* Subject form
Subjunctive, 475–476
Subordinate clauses. *See* Dependent clauses
Subordinating connectives. *See* Subordinators
Subordination
effective, 304
excessive, 315–316
upside-down, 304–305
Subordinators, 353–354
punctuation with, 417–419
in sentence fragments, 408–409
Subtitles, in footnotes, 219–220
Such, 475
Suffixes
adjective-forming, 352
doubled consonants before, 452–453
Latin and Greek, 279
noun-forming, 349
verb-forming, 350
Summaries, 209, 479–482
Superlatives, 157, 392–393, 469, 476
Sutton, Horace, 154
Swan, Jon, 250
Syllabication, 442–443
Syllogisms, 134–135
Symbols, in critical essays, 254
Symbols, plurals of, 460
Synonyms, 271–272, 329
for coherence, 38–39
in definitions, 116
Synthesis, 144

Tag statements, 302–303
Take and, 476
Teach/learn, 471
Technical terms, 58, 287–288
italics for, 438, 443
quotation marks with, 437
Tenses, 349, 369–370
consistency in, 396–398
spelling of, 449
Than, pronouns after, 381
Than/then, 451
That, 389
agreement after, 366
to introduce noun clause, 354
That-if, 315
That is, 410
That/which/who, 477
Their/there/they're, 451, 459
Theme, in critical essays, 255–256
Then/than, 451

There, 351
agreement after, 366
There are, 312
There-is sentences, 314, 315
There/their/they're, 451, 459
These kind, 476
Thesis
in descriptive themes, 63–64
in dialectic method, 144
in essay of opinion, 89, 100
in extended definition, 120
formulation of, 214
statement of, 14–15
support of, 15–16
Thesis-and-support paper, 100
They, orphaned, 377
They're/their/there, 459
This, vagueness of, 376
Thoreau, Henry David, 308
Though, 419
Time magazine, 194
Titles (of people), 444, 476
Titles (of works), 29–31
capitalization of, 462–463
form of, 442
italics for, 438, 443
quotation marks around, 438, 443
Tobias, Sheila, 93–94
Todd, Richard, 311
Toffler, Alvin, 311
Together with, 365
To illustrate, 328
Tone, 177
formal, 177–180
informal, 177, 180–181
Topic outline, 43
Topics, limitation of, 12–13
Topic sentences, 323–325, 333
To/too, 451
Toynbee, Arnold J., 366
Traditional grammar, 345
Transformational grammar, 346
Transformations, 346, 351
Transitions, 41, 216, 328–329
punctuation with, 424
roundabout, 295
with sentence fragments, 410
Transitive verbs, 273
Translators, in footnotes, 220
Troop, Miriam, 438
Try and, 476
Twain, Mark, 176, 184, 307, 311, 312, 411
Tyler, Anne, 430
Type/type of/-type, 476
Typing, 441–442
of bibliographies, 226
of footnotes, 218
of letters, 482

Understatement, 190–191
Uninterested/disinterested, 468–469
Unique, 476
Unity, and topic sentence, 324. *See also*
Organization
Unpublished material, in footnotes, 222
Up and, 476
Updike, John, 60, 176
Usage
defined, 359
standard and nonstandard, 359–360.
See also English; Language; Word choice;
Words
Used to, 476
Used to could, 476–477

Vagueness, in persuasion, 163
Vague words, 107–108. *See also* Ambiguity;
Concreteness
Validity, of deductions, 135–136
Van Druten, John, 309
Variety, in sentence style, 307–312
Verbal humor, 189–190
Verbal nouns, 355–356, 472–473

Verbal phrases, 316
  as absolute constructions, 387
  punctuation of, 423
Verbals, 355–356
  punctuation with, 423.
  See also Infinitives; Verbal nouns
Verbatim quotations, 210–211. *See also*
  Quotations
Verbs, 349–351
  active voice of, 313–314, 369
  consistency in tense of, 396–398
  imperative, 351, 398–399
  irregular, 370–372
  linking, 351, 381, 384, 390–391
  modifiers with, 384–385
  phrasal, 283
  shortening of, 394
  tenses of, 369–370
  transitive and intransitive, 273
Vidal, Gore, 338
Vocabulary, in formal writing, 177–178. *See*
  also Word choice; Words
Volume, pagination of, 206
Volume numbers, in footnotes, 220–221

Wagner, Philip M., 283, 331
Walker, Alice, 75
Warren, Robert Penn, 61
Weasel words, 296
Weather/whether, 451
Webster's New Collegiate Dictionary, 269–270,
  271, 277
Webster's New World Dictionary, 269, 272, 274
Webster's Third New International Dictionary,
  269
Wechsberg, Joseph, 335
Well/good, 385
Where/where at/where to, 477
Whether/if, 470–471
Whether . . . or, 400
Whether/weather, 451
Which
  agreement after, 366
  vagueness of, 376
Which-when, 315
Which/who/that, 477
Whipple, Fred L., 336
White, E. B., 288, 305
Whitehead, A. N., 397
Whitman, Walt, 64, 176
Who, agreement after, 366
"Who does what?" model, 301–302
Whose, with ideas and things, 477
Who's Who, 201
Who's Who in America, 201
Who's/whose, 459
Who were, 312

Who/which/that, 477
Who/whom, 381–382
Whyte, William H., 333
Wilde, Oscar, 190
Will, George W., 301
Will/shall, 474
Winchell, Constance M., 201
-wise, 477
Without, 477
Wolfe, Linda, 437
Wolfe, Tom, 192
Wolters, Richard A., 158
Wonderful, 468
Woolf, Virginia, 184, 250, 319, 431
Word choice
  and concreteness, 58–59
  and specificity, 58
  and style, 183–184
Word division, 442–443
Wordiness, 294–295
Word order, 345
  and meaning, 347
  varied, 309–311
Words
  abstract, 110–111
  accurate, 289
  ambiguous, 108
  and attitudes, 161, 162
  figurative, 290–291
  foreign sources of, 277–278
  fresh, 291–292
  functions of, 273
  history of, 119–120, 277–281
  newly coined, 287
  obsolete and archaic, 286–287
  overlapping, 108
  power of, 162–163
  regional, 285–286
  relative, 107
  specialized, 108–109
  specific, 290
  technical, 287–288
  vague, 107–108
  as words, 437, 460.
  See also Language; Vocabulary
Working outline, 42
Writing
  formal, 177–180
  importance of, 1
  informal, 180–181
  standards of, 3.
  See also Organization

Y, as a vowel, 453
"Yes, but" paper, 101
Yet, 415
You, with indefinite reference, 477

HANDBOOK KEY

WORDS

D 1 College Dictionaries 269
a Synonyms and Antonyms 271
b Denotation and
   Connotation 272
c Context 273
d Grammatical Labels 273
e Idiom 273

D 2 Word History 277
a Latin and Greek 278
b Borrowings from Other
   Sources 280

D 3 Varieties of Usage 281
a Nonstandard Words 282
b Informal Words 282
c Slang 283

D 4 Words in Limited Use 285
a Regional Labels 285
b Obsolete and Archaic 286
c Neologisms 287
d Subject Labels 287

D 5 Expressive Language 289
a Accurate Words 289
b Specific Words 290
c Figurative Words 290
d Fresh Words 291

D 6 Directness 294
a Redundancy 294
b Euphemisms 296
c Jargon 296
d Flowery Diction 297

SENTENCES

S 1 Sentence Building 301
a Effective Predication 302
b Effective Coordination 303
c Effective Subordination 304
d Effective Modifiers 305

S 2 Sentence Variety 307
a Sentence Length 308
b Varied Word Order 309

S 3 Awkward Construction 312
a Deadwood 312
b Awkward Passive 313
c Impersonal Constructions 314
d Excessive Subordination 315
e Awkward Modifiers 316

S 4 Repetition 317
a Awkward Repetition 317
b Emphatic Repetition 318
c Parallel Structure 318

PARAGRAPHS

**O 1 The Well-Made
       Paragraph 323**
a The Topic Sentence 323
b Relevant Detail 325
c Transition 328
d Recurrent Terms 329

**O 2 Organizing the
       Paragraph 332**
a The All-Purpose
   Paragraph 332
b Paragraphs with a Special
   Purpose 334
c Paragraphs with a Special
   Strategy 336

GRAMMAR AND USAGE

**G 1 A Bird's-Eye View of
       Grammar 346**
a Grammatical Devices 347
b Basic Sentence Elements 348
c Modifiers 352
d Joining Clauses 353
e Appositives and Verbals 355

G 2 Grammar and Usage 359
a Standard and
   Nonstandard 359
b Formal and Informal 360

G 3 Agreement 362
a Irregular Plurals 363
b Confusing Singulars and
   Plurals 363
c Compound Subjects 364
d Blind Agreement 365
e Agreement After *There* and
   It 366
f Agreement After *Who, Which,*
   and *That* 366
g Logical Agreement 367

G 4 Verb Forms 369
a Irregular Verbs 370
b *Lie, Sit,* and *Rise* 372